SOFT COMPUTING AND ITS APPLICATIONS

Volume II: Fuzzy Reasoning and Fuzzy Control

SOFT COMPUTING AND ITS APPLICATIONS

Volume II: Fuzzy Reasoning and Fuzzy Control

Kumar S. Ray, PhD

Apple Academic Press

TORONTO   NEW JERSEY

Apple Academic Press Inc. | Apple Academic Press Inc.
3333 Mistwell Crescent | 9 Spinnaker Way
Oakville, ON L6L 0A2 | Waretown, NJ 08758
Canada | USA

©2015 by Apple Academic Press, Inc.

First issued in paperback 2021

Exclusive worldwide distribution by CRC Press, a member of Taylor & Francis Group
No claim to original U.S. Government works

ISBN 13: 978-1-77463-087-7 (pbk)
ISBN 13: 978-1-77188-046-6 (hbk)

Library of Congress Control Number: 2014938388

Library and Archives Canada Cataloguing in Publication

Ray, Kumar S., author
Soft computing and its applications/Kumar S. Ray, PhD.

Includes bibliographical references and index.
Contents: Volume I. A unified engineering concept -- Volume II.
Fuzzy reasoning and fuzzy control.
ISBN 978-1-77188-047-3 (set).--ISBN 978-1-926895-38-3 (v. 1 :
bound).--ISBN 978-1-77188-046-6 (v. 2 : bound)
1. Soft computing. 2. Fuzzy logic. I. Title. II. Title: Unified engineering concept.. III. Title:
Fuzzy reasoning and fuzzy control

QA76.9.S63R37 2014   006.3   C2014-902599-8

Apple Academic Press also publishes its books in a variety of electronic formats. Some content that appears In print may not be available in electronic format. For information about Apple Academic Press products, visit our website at **www.appleacademicpress.com** and the CRC Press website at **www.crcpress.com**

ABOUT THE AUTHOR

Kumar S. Ray, PhD

Kumar S. Ray, PhD, is a Professor in the Electronics and Communication Science Unit at the Indian Statistical Institute, Kolkata, India. He is an alumnus of the University of Bradford, UK. He was a visiting faculty member under a fellowship program at the University of Texas, Austin, USA. Professor Ray was a member of the task force committee of the Government of India, Department of Electronics (DoE/MIT), for the application of AI in power plants. He is the founder and member of the Indian Society for Fuzzy Mathematics and Information Processing (ISFUMIP) and a member of the Indian Unit for Pattern Recognition and Artificial Intelligence (IUPRAI). In 1991, he was the recipient of the K. S. Krishnan memorial award for the best system-oriented paper in computer vision. He has written a number of research articles published in international journals and has presented at several professional meetings. He also serves as a reviewer of several International journals. His current research interests include artificial intelligence, computer vision, commonsense reasoning, soft computing, non-monotonic deductive database systems, and DNA computing.

He is the co-author of two edited volumes on approximate reasoning and fuzzy logic and fuzzy computing, and he is the co-author of *Case Studies in Intelligent Computing; Achievements and Trends*. He has is also the author of *Polygonal Approximation and Scale-Space Analysis of Closed Digital Curves*, published Apple Academic Press, Inc.

CONTENTS

List of Abbreviations .... *ix*

Preface .... *xiii*

1. **Fuzzy Reasoning** 01

2. **Fuzzy Reasoning Based on Concept of Similarity** 139

3. **Fuzzy Control** 233

4. **Concluding Remarks** 415

   References 435

   Index 449

LIST OF ABBREVIATIONS

AARS	Approximate analogical reasoning scheme
AI	Artificial intelligence
ANN	Artificial neural network
AR	Approximate reasoning
ART	Adaptive resonance theory
CBD	Case-based design
CBR	Case-based reasoning
CDR	Consequent dilation rule
CMI	Compatibility modification inference
CRI	Compositional rule of inference
DDC	Direct digital computer
DFI	Decomposed fuzzy implication
DID	Dynamic importance degree
DSM	Design structure matrices
EC	Evolutionary computation
FARMA	Fuzzy autoregressive moving average model
FSMC	Fuzzy sliding mode control
GMC	Generalized method-of-case
GMP	Generalized modus ponens
GPC	Generalized predictive control
LQR	Linear quadratic regular design
MEDI	Methodology for estimation of design intent
MFI	Multidimensional fuzzy implication
MFR	Multiple fuzzy reasoning
MIMO	Multi-input-multi-output
MIQ	Machine intelligence quotient
NARMA	Nonlinear autoregressive moving average
OSF	Output scaling factor
PGF	Pressure gradient force
PID	Proportional-integral-derivative
PTOS	Proximate time-optimal servomechanism
QFD	Quality function deployment
SBR	Similarity based reasoning
SCAD	Soft computing aided design
SIRMs	Single input rule modules
SOPSS	Self-organizing power system stabilizer
SPC	Smith predictor control
SSR	Solid state relay

Dedicated to:

Dhira Ray (wife)
Aratrika Ray (daughter)

PREFACE

At present the notion of soft computing is well established in various fields of science and engineering. The journey of soft computing started in the early 90s when Zadeh first coined the term 'soft computing'. Since then the topic soft computing has passed through growth and development through advanced features of fuzzy reasoning and its application to fuzzy control. Though the notion of vagueness was sensed from the period of Bertrand Russell and Max Black and continued through the multivalued concept of Lukasiewicz and till today, the formal notion of soft computing has been sensed by Zadeh, with his spirit and intuition about vagueness and its flexible representation to handle real life problem. Normally, science models real life; but to make the model accurate science crosses a certain threshold of precision for which the model itself becomes very complex or sometimes becomes impossible to represent. Under such circumstances the soft computing approach replaces the complexity of modelling and describes the real world in a more cost-effective manner using implicit model (fuzzy IF-THEN rules). Where our experience is concerned we understand that from car parking to moon landing, from life science to physical and earth science, from medical science to management science, there exists a high degree of complexity that can be easily represented by fuzzy IF-THEN models of soft computing. Hence the tool soft computing can be a landmark paradigm of computation with cognition which directly or indirectly tries to replicate rationality of a human being. Even though today we cannot quantify in a specific manner the term human intelligence for machine implementation, still there are several attempts to do so by some intelligent methods of computing which in our view is basically rational computing.

If we go by the fundamental slogan, 'Man is a rational animal' and if we consider human perception as a basic element of rationality, then our target of soft computing should be to mimic such cognitive process so that machine can also behave in a rational manner and it becomes indistinguishable from human rationality. At present it may appear that the above idea is over projected; still we should be optimistic about our promise on soft computing.

Keeping these ideas in mind, the present volume on soft computing essentially handles several advanced features of fuzzy reasoning and its application to fuzzy control which would be very attractive to the research communities and to the industries who are keen to make the technology more advanced to face the challenge of the real world. This book is very valuable for academic purposes and also for industry. It contains several real life applications to convince readers about the utility and potentiality of soft computing. The book is balanced between theory and practice.

— **Kumar S. Ray, PhD**

CHAPTER 1

FUZZY REASONING

1.1 INTRODUCTION

Human reasoning is basically a cognitive process. To mimic the cognitive process of human reasoning and its implementation through machine, we pass through a passage of a set of propositions, represented as premises, to a further proposition, taken as the conclusion (consequence) with some degree of confidence, which link the conclusion to the premises. Reasoning is approximate when some of the propositions are imprecise and the rules for derivation are inexact in nature.

Approximate reasoning is considered to be a powerful tool to study the remarkable human ability to understand real-world activities in terms of computational entities with immense confidence. As for instance, crossing the railway track safely even after seeing a train approaching with high speed or avoidance of a particular road and use of by-lanes to beat the office-hour rush are typical examples of approximate reasoning.

Approximate reasoning is defined as the process or processes by which an approximate conclusion may be deduced from a set of possibly imprecise information using some inexact rule for the derivation. It was first formally introduced by Zadeh. Since its inception in 1973, significant theoretical advances have established approximate reasoning as an important field of research. Different mechanisms of approximate reasoning with applications have been proposed and discussed in the literature. We have witnessed among many other things the birth of fuzzy logic controller, soft computing approach to pattern classification and object recognition, weather forecasting, and so on.

Zadeh's concept of approximate reasoning is based on the fuzzy logic and the theory of fuzzy sets.

In order to have an adequate understanding of the theory of approximate reasoning, some basic concepts are studied in the following:

1.2 MODEL OF APPROXIMATE REASONING

In 1979, Zadeh introduced a theory of approximate reasoning. It provides a powerful framework for reasoning in the face of imprecise and uncertain information. Central to this theory is the representation of crisp statements as statements assigning fuzzy sets as values to variables.

Suppose, we have two interactive variables $x \in X$ and $y \in Y$, and a causal relationship between x and y is completely known. Namely, we know that y is a function of x, that is $y = f(x)$.

Then, we can make inferences easily:

$$"y=f(x)"\text{and}"x=x_1" \rightarrow "y=f(x_1)" \tag{1.1}$$

This inference rule says that if we have $y = f(x)$, for all $x \in X$ and we observe that $x = x_1$ then y takes the value $f(x_1)$. More often than not, we do not know the complete causal link f between x and y, only we know the values of $f(x)$ for some particular values of x, that is:

$$R_1: \text{If } x = x_1 \text{ then } y = y_1$$

$$R_1: \text{If } x = x_2 \text{ then } y = y_2$$

$$\cdot$$
$$\cdot$$
$$\cdot$$
$$\cdot$$

$$R_n : \text{if } x = x_n \text{ then } y = y_n \tag{1.2}$$

If we are given an $x' \in X$ and want to find an $y' \in Y$ which corresponds to x' under the rule base $R = \{R_1,.....R_n\}$ then we have to solve an interpolation problem.

In this section, we present an analogy between approximate reasoning and the method interpolation for a large class of problems. We first describe the analogy and then illustrate it through several simple yet concrete examples. The results obtained through the method of interpolation are compared with those obtained by the application of the existing method of approximate reasoning. Thus, we show that approximate reasoning can also be realized effectively by the method of interpolation.

The celebrated concept of approximate reasoning has been tremendously used in different fields of science and engineering for solving problems having uncertain, imprecisem, and incomplete information. But, for performing approximate reasoning using compositional rule of inference, we have to approximate the linguistic vaguenesses by finite fuzzy sets. In most cases, it is also possible to represent the universe of those fuzzy sets by subsets of the real number systems. In Section 3.9 of Chapter 3 of volume 1 of this book, we have discussed the basic method of approximate reasoning with examples.

In this section, our aim is to pictorially visualize the method of approximate reasoning and to establish an analogy between the technique of approximate reasoning and the method of interpolation when the domain of definition of the fuzzy sets are approximated by some subsets of the real number system. Thus, we generate a deeper understanding with the tools and techniques of approximate reasoning.

We demonstrate that instead of inferring by performing approximate reasoning using a relation matrix R formed from a compound proposition:
p: if X is F then Y is G
and a simple proposition of the form
q: X is H
we can also infer, by constructing a simple conventional relation of the form

$$y = f(x) \qquad (1.3)$$

It is a value of Y for a particular value of X. The relation (1.3) can be constructed by fitting a curve through the points obtained by appropriately defuzzifying the compound proposition(s). And the particular value of the variable X can be obtained from the defuzzification of the fuzzy set H using any of the existing methods. Thus, in our proposed technique, we defuzzify all information before making any conclusion. Now, the working ranges of the variables x and y are known and hence, we can subdivide the entire range either into disjoint fuzzy sets or into overlapped fuzzy sets. Thus, if necessary, we can retranslate the exact inference y from the given relation (1.3) for a particular value of x, into some fuzzy sets.

Now, the method of approximate reasoning is based on fuzzy logic and the compositional rule of inference. The mechanism of the rule of inference is such that it does not take proper care in the change in truth values of generic elements in the fuzzy sets. This means that for a given rule, there exists a wide variety of fuzzy sets for which the outputs of the compositional rule of inference are the same, which is not at all desirable.

As for example consider the relational matrix:

$$R = \begin{array}{c} \\ 1 \\ 2 \\ 3 \\ 4 \\ 5 \end{array} \begin{pmatrix} 1 & 2 & 3 \\ 0.3 & 0.6 & 1.0 \\ 0.55 & 0.85 & 1.0 \\ 0.8 & 1.0 & 1.0 \\ 1.0 & 1.0 & 1.0 \\ 1.0 & 1.0 & 1.0 \end{pmatrix}$$

and the fuzzy set
$H = 0.5/1 + 0.75/2 + 1.0/3 + 0.75/4 + 0.50/5.$

By using the compositional rule of inference, we find:

H o R = 0.8/1 + 1.0/2 + 1.0/3.

Now, it is easy to verify that with all fuzzy sets of the form

H = p/1 + q/2 + 1.0/3 + r/4 + s/5

where p, q, r, and s are real numbers satisfying:

$$0 \leq p, q \leq 1.0 \text{ and } 0 \leq r, s \leq 0.8$$

The output of compositional rule of inference is same and is equal to the fuzzy set (0.8/1 + 1.0/2 + 1.0/3).

The above drawback of the compositional rule of inference motivates us to interpret approximate reasoning using finite fuzzy sets over real number system in the following way:

Let, there are two linguistic variables X and Y defined over the universe:

$U = \sum_{i=1}^{m} u_i$ and $V = \sum_{j=1}^{n} v_i$ respectively and let us consider the two proposition p and q as above.

The fuzzy sets F, G, and H are defined by:

$$F = \sum_{i_k} \mu_F(u_{i_k}) / u_{i_k}$$

$$G = \sum_{j_r} \mu_F(v_{j_r}) / u_{j_r}$$

$$H = \sum_{i'_1} \mu_H(v_{i'_1}) / u_{i'_1}$$

where $\{i_1, i_2, \ldots i_k\}$ and $\{i'_1, i'_2, \ldots i'_1\}$ are subsequences of the sequences $\{1, 2, \ldots, m\}$ and $\{j_1, j_2, \ldots j_r\}$ is a subsequence of the sequence $\{1, 2, \ldots, n\}$. Let us consider three mutually perpendicular axes in space. Out of these three, two axes represent the generic values of U and V and the third axis represents the membership values of those elements in the underlying fuzzy sets. Let us take this axis as vertical and the plane containing the other two as horizontal and also let us represent the corresponding membership values of generic elements by line segments. Now, translate the proposition p into a relational matrix R (say) using any translating rule. Then, plot the membership values against each pair (u_{i_k}, v_{j_r}) that are in the relational matrix R. We may view them as a forest in which trees are standing only at the junctions (u_{i_k}, v_{j_r}). and the height is equal to $\mu_R(u_{i_k}, v_{j_r})$. We call it a relational forest. Again if we plot the membership values against each u_{ij} that are in H we find a series of trees standing at different points on the axis of u and the height at u_{ij} is $\mu_H(u_{ij})$. By cylindrical extension of the fuzzy set H over V we mean a recta-ngular forest which we call a cylindrical forest in which trees are standing only at the junctions $(u_{ij}, v_{jr}$ and the height of the tree at this junction for a fixed value of l are the same and is equal to the height of the corresponding tree at u_{ij} in H.

The particularization of R by H is again a rectangular forest in which trees are standing only at the junctions (u_{i_k}, v_{j_r}) and the corresponding heights are:

$$\{\mu_R(u_{i_k}, v_{j_r}) \wedge \mu_H(u_{i_k})\}$$

where $\wedge$ denotes the well-known min operator. We call it the conjunctional forest. The projection of the conjunctional forest on the axis of V is a series of trees standing on the axis at the points v_{jr} and the height of which are:

$$\max_{u_{i_k}}\{\mu_R(u_{i_k}, v_{j_r}) \wedge \mu_H(u_{i_k})\}$$

To make the interpretation about approximate reasoning more clear we consider the following example:

Example 1.1 Let there be two proposition

$$p \Leftrightarrow \text{if X is "low" then Y is "high"}$$

and

$$q \Leftrightarrow \text{X is "medium"}$$

where $U = 1 + 2 + 3 + 4 + 5$ and $V = 1 + 2 + 3$ are the universe of discourses of the linguistic variables X and Y respectively. Again let there be three mutually perpendicular axis xyμ in space, as shown in the given set of figures (Figure 1–5), to represent the generic values of U, V, and the corresponding membership values.

The inexact concept "low", "medium", "high" are represented respectively by the following fuzzy sets over their domain of definition as:
  "low" = 1.0/1 + 0.75/2 + 0.50/3 + 0.25/4 + 0.0/5,
  "medium" = 0.50/1 + 0.75/2 + 1.0/3 + 0.75/4 + 0.50/5, and
  "high" = 0.3/1 + 0.6/2 + 1.0/3.

With these definitions a diagrammatic representation of the fuzzy set "medium" is shown in Figure 1.

Let the proposition p translate into the fuzzy relation:

R = 0.3/(1.1) + 0.55/(2,1) + 0.6/(1, 2) + 0.8/(3, 1) + 0.85/(2, 2) + 1.0/[(1, 3) + (2, 3) + (3, 2) + (3, 3) + (4, 1) + (4, 2) + (4, 3) + (5, 1) + (5, 2) + (5, 3)]

Where:

$$\mu_R(u, v) = \max[\{1 - \mu_{low}(u) + \mu_{high}(v)\}, 1]$$

A representation of this relational matrix is shown in Figure 2. Figure 3 represents the cylindrical extension of the fuzzy set "medium". Then a representation of the conjunction of the relational matrix R together with the cylindrical extension is shown in Figure 4. And the Figure 5 shows the representation of the projection of the conjunction on the axis of V which in this case is found to be fuzzy set (0.8/1 + 1.0/2 + 1.0/3).

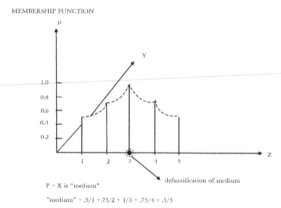

FIGURE 1   Representation of "medium."

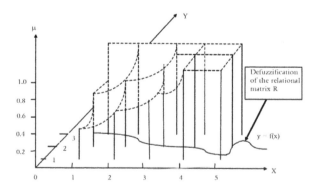

FIGURE 2   Relational forest.

Now, let us see the defuzzification of all the information as shown in these Figures. Let, U' and V' be defined over the entire real line. The defuzzified value of the

fuzzy set medium is the encircled point in Figure 1. This is the point in the domain U'
at which the membership value attains its maximum in the fuzzy set "medium". The
defuzzification of the relational matrix is as shown in Figure 2 with a hypothetical
curve through the points of defuzzification the line of which can be constructed using
any method of curve-fitting. The defuzzified version of the cylindrical extension of the
fuzzy set "medium" is shown in Figure 3. Again, a straight line is drawn to represent
the fitted curve through the points of defuzzification. The defuzzified representation of
the conjunction is shown in Figure 4. The projection of this defuzzified conjunction on
the axis of y is a point which, is shown in Figure 5 and which is close to the defuzzified
value of the fuzzy inference.

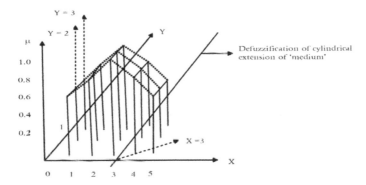

FIGURE 3 Cylindrical forest corresponding to "medium".

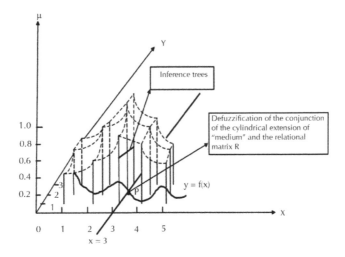

FIGURE 4 Conjunction forest.

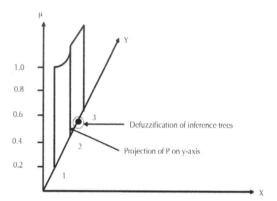

FIGURE 5   Projection of the conjunctional forest on the y-u plane and the rojection of the point p on Figure 4 on the y axis

FORMULATION OF THE PROBLEM

Let X and Y represent two linguistic variables taking values in U and V respectively.

Let

      $p \Leftrightarrow$ if X is F then Y is G

      $q \Leftrightarrow$ X is H

be two typical propositions expressed in natural language.

Also let the corresponding possibility assignment equations be:

$$p \to \Pi_{(X.Y)} = R(\text{say}),$$

$$q \to \Pi_x = H$$

where F and H are fuzzy subsets over U and G is a fuzzy subset over V and the relation R is a fuzzy subset of the Cartesian product U × V.

Using compositional rule of inference we obtain:

$$r \gets \Pi_Y = \Pi_X \circ \Pi_{(X,Y)} = H \circ R$$

where o denotes the well-known max-min composition operator and

$$\mu_{HoR}(v) = \max_u \{\mu_H(u) \wedge \mu_R(u,v)\}$$

Here, we consider the linguistic variables X and Y in the propositions p and q to range over finite sets or to be such that they can be approximated by variables ranging over such sets in order to represent F, G, H, and R by finite-dimensional relational matrices. Again, the relation R can be formed using any of the different translating rules. In this section, we consider only one such widely used translating rule, viz.

If X is F then Y is G:

$$\rightarrow \Pi_{(X,Y)} = \overline{F} \cap \overline{G} = F \times G$$

where $\prod(X,Y)$ denotes the possibility distribution of the binary variable (X, Y). $\overline{F}$ and $\overline{G}$ are the cylindrical extensions of F and G respectively, that is:

$$\overline{F} = F \times V \text{ and } \overline{G} = U \times G$$

F x G is the Cartesian product of F and G which is defined by:

$$\mu_{F \times G}(u, v) = \mu_F(u) \wedge \mu_G(v), u \in U, v \in V$$

where $\wedge$ denotes the min operator.

Now, every relation matrix R (of the form discussed so far), when defuzzified using the method stated below defines element wise relation between two distinct variables (say, current and rotational speed of a motor) and gives us information about variations of a single variable with a change in the independent variable. Thus, we can have a collection of pairs of observations of the two variables from the defuzzification of the above relation R. The relation R is defuzzified in the following way:

For a particular value of $X = u$, the corresponding value of $Y = v$ is that for which the pair (u, v) has maximum possibility in the relation R. If there is more than one such Y then we may take the mean value as a representation of that class. Thus, considering them as points in a two-dimensional plane we can always fit a polynomial that is defined over an extended domain containing $U \times V$. In the present discussion, let x and y be two classical variables which take on values in U' and V' respectively. Let $f = U' \rightarrow V'$ be a function generated from the relation R. This function can be formed using any standard method of curve-fitting. The problem of approximate reasoning then reduces to finding a value of y corresponding to a particular value of $x \in U'$. This is the well-known method of interpolation. The particular value of x is found from the defuzzification of the proposition

$$q \Leftrightarrow X \text{ is } H,$$

by using any method of defuzzification.

So far we consider only one fact and one rule. Let us consider a somewhat more practical model where there are a set of rules of the form:

$$p \Leftrightarrow \text{if } X \text{ is } F \text{ then } Y \text{ is } G,$$

viz.

$$p_1 \Leftrightarrow \text{if } X \text{ is } F_1 \text{ then } Y \text{ is } G_1$$

also

$$p_2 \Leftrightarrow \text{if } X \text{ is } F_2 \text{ then } Y \text{ is } G_2$$

.
.
.
.

also

$$p_n \Leftrightarrow \text{if } X \text{ is } F_n \text{ then } Y \text{ is } G_n$$

$$(n < \infty)$$

and a single fact of the form

$$q \Leftrightarrow X \text{ is } H$$

For this type of problem, we may find a unified relation matrix R and proceed as above. Let   …, , q be translated into the possibility assignment equations.

$$p_1 \rightarrow \Pi_{(X,Y)} = R$$
$$p_2 \rightarrow \Pi_{(X,Y)} = R$$

.
.
.
.
.

$$p_n \rightarrow \Pi_{(X,Y)} = R_n$$
and
$$q \rightarrow \Pi_X = H$$

Here, $R_1, R_2, \ldots\ldots R_n$ are fuzzy relations that are fuzzy subsets of $U \times V$.

Then, we construct a relation R by using union operation as:

$$R = R_1 \cup R_2 \cup \ldots\ldots R_n$$

where

$$\mu_R(u, v) = \max\{\mu_{R_1}(u, v), \mu_{R_2}(u, v)\ldots\ldots \mu_{R_n}(u, v)\}$$

Note that construction of R form R_i using standard $\cup$ or $\cap$ operation depends on the specific choice of the translating rule to translate a proposition p_i to R_i.

Now from q and R we can infer:

$$r \leftarrow \Pi_Y = \Pi \circ \Pi(X, Y) = H \circ R.$$

In the proposed method, we first defuzzify the unified relational matrix R according to the technique specified above and obtain a set of points in the plane which we use to construct the interpolating polynomial. Then, we defuzzify the fuzzy set H to obtain the particular value of x at which the functional value is desired. The inference then follows at once.

Again, if n > 1, we can construct the relation y = f(x) without constructing the relational matrix R. In such cases, we first defuzzify the fuzzy sets in the propositions and obtain the desired set of points for constructing the relation y = f(x).

We demonstrate, through several worked out examples, that for a wide variety of problems the technique of approximate reasoning can be effectively realized by the method of interpolation.

Example 1.2 Consider the following two proposition:

$p \Leftrightarrow X$ is "medium",

$q \Leftrightarrow$ is X is 'low' then Y is "high"
in which the linguistic variables range over the sets U and V respectively given by U = V = 1 + 2 + 3 + 4 and the inexact concepts "low", "medium', and "high" are defined by:
  "low" = 1.0/1 + 0.75/2 + 0.50/3 + 0.25/4 = F,
  "medium" = 0.5/1 + 0.75/2 + 0.75/3 + 0.50/4 = H, and
  "high" = 0.25/1 + 0.50/2 + 0.75/3 + 1.0/4 = G.
  In terms of these representations we have:

$p \Leftrightarrow X$ is "medium" $\Pi_X = H$

and

$q \Leftrightarrow$ if X is 'low' then Y is "high" $\rightarrow \prod_{(X,Y)} = R$

where R = 'low' x "high" and is given by:

$$
R = \begin{array}{c} \\ 1 \\ 2 \\ 3 \\ 4 \end{array}
\begin{array}{cccc}
1 & 2 & 3 & 4 \\
\left(\begin{array}{cccc}
0.25 & 0.50 & 0.75 & 1.0 \\
0.25 & 0.50 & 0.75 & 0.75 \\
0.25 & 0.50 & 0.50 & 0.50 \\
0.25 & 0.25 & 0.25 & 0.25
\end{array} \right)
\end{array}
$$

Let x and y represent two real variables to denote the defuzzy values of the linguistic variables X and Y respectively. The defuzzification of the relation matrix R, by the method stated earlier, gives the pairs (1, 4), (2, 3.5), (3, 3), and (4, 2.5).

The corresponding interpolating polynomial is:

y = 4.5 - 0.5x   (1.4)

which is defined over the entire real plane. Now, we defuzzify the fuzzy set "medium" by taking the arithmetic mean of the generic values of X for which the membership values are maximum in the fuzzy set.

This gives x = 2.5. From (1.4) for x = 2.5, we obtain:

y = 3.25   (1.5)

If we perform the compositional rule of inference then we get:

$$\prod_Y = \prod_X \circ \prod_{(X,Y)} = H \circ R$$

= 0.25/1 + 0.5/2 + 0.75/3 + 0.75/4

as the inference. The defuzzification of which by the same technique gives y = 3.5, which is close to (Equation 1.5) but not the same. This is due to the choice of translating rule and the method of defuzzification. But, the two results may belong to the same linguistic class and hence are equivalent.

Example 1.3 Assume that:

U = V = 1 + 2 + 3 + 4

and

A = 1.0/1 + 0.5/2 + 0.3/3 + 0.1/4,
B = 0.5/1 + 1.0/2 + 0.5/3 + 0.3/4,
C = 0.3/1 + 0.5/2 + 1.0/3 + 0.5/4,
D = 0.1/1 + 0.3/2 + 0.5/3 + 1.0/4, and
E = 0.8/1 + 0.8/2 + 0.5/3 + 0.3/4.

with the propositions

$$p \Leftrightarrow \text{ is } E$$

$$q_1 \Leftrightarrow \text{ if X is A then Y is C}$$

also $q_2 \Leftrightarrow$ if X is B then Y is D

also $q_3 \Leftrightarrow$ if X is C then Y is B

also $q_4 \Leftrightarrow$ if X is D then Y is A.

Let p translate to

$$p \rightarrow \Pi_X = E$$

TABLE 1 Relation matrices of Example 5.3

	1	2	3	4
$\bar{A} \cap \bar{C} = R_1$				
1	0.3	0.5	1.0	0.5
2	0.3	0.5	0.5	0.5
3	0.3	0.3	0.3	0.3
4	0.1	0.1	0.1	0.1
$\bar{B} \cap \bar{D} = R_2$				
1	0.1	0.3	0.5	0.5
2	0.1	0.3	0.5	1.0
3	0.1	0.3	0.5	0.5
4	0.1	0.3	0.3	0.3
$\bar{C} \cap \bar{D} = R_3$				
1	0.3	0.3	0.3	0.3
2	0.5	0.5	0.5	0.3
3	0.5	1.0	0.5	0.3
4	0.5	0.5	0.5	0.3
$\bar{D} \cap \bar{A} = R_4$				
1	0.1	0.1	0.1	0.1
2	0.3	0.3	0.3	0.1
3	0.5	0.5	0.3	0.1
4	1.0	0.5	0.3	0.1

The translation of the compound assertions into relation matrices gives the results of Table 1.

Now, we construct the rational matrix R as:

$$R = R_1 \cup R_2 \cup R_3 \cup R_4$$

$$= \begin{pmatrix} 0.3 & 0.5 & 1.0 & 0.5 \\ 0.5 & 0.5 & 0.5 & 1.0 \\ 0.5 & 1.0 & 0.5 & 0.5 \\ 1.0 & 0.5 & 0.5 & 0.3 \end{pmatrix}$$

The defuzzification of the relational matrix R gives the following set of points. Let x and y denote the defuzzified values of X and Y respectively.

Then we have[1]:

x =	1	2	3	4
y =	3	4	2	1

The interpolating polynomial through the above set of points are:

$$5y = 30 - 11x + 39x^2 - 13x^3, x \le 2,$$
$$15y = 20x^3 - 159x^2 + 385x - 234, 2 \le x \le 3, \text{ and}$$
$$15y = 495 - 344x + 84x^2 - 7x,^3 3 \le x.$$

The defuzzified value of the fuzzy set E is found to be x = 1.5. From the above relation, for x = 1.5, we find the corresponding value of y = 3.825. If, instead, we perform the compositional rule of inference using the relational matrix R with the fuzzy set E we would have obtained.

= 0.5/1 + 0.5/2 + 0.8/3 + 0.8/4

whose defuzzification yields y = 3.5. Here, also the two inferred values obtained from two different methods (viz. method of interpolation and method of approximate reasoning) are close to each other.

In this section, we establish an analogy between approximate reasoning and the method of interpolation for a given class of problems as stated earlier. There is no doubt that fuzzy logic is an important tool for modeling the intuition and experience of an expert. In most cases, it has been found that the output of approximate reasoning

---

[1]This observation was made in the year 1992 when a research experiment was conducted under the supervision of Prof. Kumar S. Ray at Electronics and Communication Sciences Unit of Indian Statistical Institute, Kolkata-700108. In the year 2001 G. Gerla made almost the same observation at the rule level (instead of Relational matrix level) in his paper [see section 2; 82].

system is defuzzified either conceptually (in case of medical consultancy, and so on) or physically (in case of process control, and so on). The result of this section establishes that instead of defuzzifying the output of an approximate reasoning system, we can de-fuzzify the vagueness of the linguistic statements at the structural level and construct a simple conventional relation that also captures the experience and intuition of an expert. Then, we can apply the method of interpolation for inference.

In the above treatment, we consider only one translating rule but certainly we can use any translating rules for the translation of the compound propositions and obtain results. Again, we use only one method of defuzzification of fuzzy sets but surely we can use other methods of defuzzification also. When defuzzified, the relation R gives us a class of pair of observations. It is well-known that the interpolating polynomials coincide with the given relation at least at these points. Hence, we can safely conclude that we are not losing any reasonable information due to defuzzification of the relation.

At least, we want to state that instead of creating any competition between the existing method of approximate reasoning and the method of interpolation, we can use them as neighbors of each other.

1.3   BASIC APPROACH TO ZADEH'S FUZZY REASONING

We consider the following form of inference:

$$\text{premise 1 : if } X \text{ is } A \text{ then } y \text{ is } B$$
$$\text{premise 2 : } X \text{ is } A' \tag{1.6}$$
$$\overline{\qquad\qquad\qquad\qquad\qquad\qquad}$$
$$\text{Consequence Y is B'}$$

where A, A' are fuzzy sets in U and B, B' are fuzzy sets in V. The consequence B' is deduced from premise 1 and premise 2 by taking the max-min composition o of the fuzzy set A' with the fuzzy relation $A \to B$ obtained from the fuzzy implication "if A then B". That means, we get:

$$B' = A' \circ (A \to B),$$

$$\mu_{B'}(\{v\}) = V_u \{\mu_{A'}(u) \wedge \mu_{A \to B}(u,v)\}$$

If the fuzzy set A' is a singleton , that is, $\mu_{A'}(\mu_0) = 1$ and $\mu_{A'}(u) = 0$ for $u \neq u_0$, the consequence B' is simplified as:

$$\left. \begin{array}{l} \mu_{B'}(v) = V_u \{\mu_{A'}(u) \wedge \mu_{A \to B}(u,v) \\ = V_{u(\neq u_0)} \{0 \wedge \mu_{A \to B}(u,v)\} \vee \{1 \wedge \mu_{A \to B}(u_0,v)\} \\ = \mu_{A \to B}(u_0,v) \end{array} \right\} \tag{1.7}$$

If the fuzzy implication $A \rightarrow B$ is represented by the direct product $A \times B$ of fuzzy sets A and B as in the case of Mamdani's method, B' is given as:

$$\mu_{B'}(v) = \mu_{A'}(u_0) \wedge \mu_B(v) \text{ at } A \rightarrow B = A \times B$$

TABLE 2   Some interpretations of fuzzy implications

$R_c : \mu_A(u_0) \wedge \mu_B(v)$	Mamdani
$R_p : \mu_A(u_0) \bullet \mu_B(v)$	Larsen
$R_{bp} : 0 V[\mu_A(u_0) + \mu_B(v) - 1]$	Bounded product
$R_{dp} = \begin{pmatrix} \mu_A(u_0), \mu_B(v) = 1 \\ \mu_B(v), \mu_A(u_0) = 1 \\ 0, \mu_A(u_0), \mu_B(v) < 1 \end{pmatrix}$	drastic product
$R_a : 1 \wedge [1 - \mu_A(u_0), \mu_B(v)]$	Zadeh's arithmetic rule
$R_m : [\mu_A(u_0) \wedge \mu_B(v)] \vee [1 - \mu_A(u_0)]$	Zadeh's maximum rule
$R_b : [1 - \mu_A(u_0)] \vee \mu_B(v)$	Boolean implication
$R_s : \begin{cases} 1, \mu_A(u_0) \leq \mu_B(v) \\ 0, \mu_A(u_0) > \mu_B(v) \end{cases}$	Standard sequence
$R_g : \begin{cases} 1, \mu_A(u_0) \leq \mu_B(v) \\ \mu_B(v), \mu_A(u_0) > \mu_B(v) \end{cases}$	Gödelian logic
$R_\Delta : \begin{cases} 1, \quad \mu_A(u_0) \leq \mu_B(v) \\ \mu_B / \mu_A(u_0), 1, \mu_A(u_0) > \mu_B(v) \end{cases}$	Gougen logic
$R^* : 1 - \mu_A(u_0) + \mu_A(v) \bullet \mu_B(v)$	Bandler logic
$R_\# : [1 - \mu_A(u_0) \vee \mu_B(v)] \wedge \mu_A(u_0) \vee$ $(1 - \mu_A(u_0)) \wedge [\mu_B(v)] \vee (1 - \mu_B(v))]$	Bandler logic

In Table 2, we list several fuzzy implications A which are used in the fuzzy reasoning approach to process control, pattern classification, weather forecasting, and so on.

It should be noted that the composition operator (for example, max-min) is uniquely related with the way in which the individual rules are combined. That means, the max-t composition is linked with the implications operator induced by the t-norm. In this sense, the list of interpretations of Table 2 should be infinite. But, our major objective is to establish the effectiveness of the method of fuzzy reasoning in the fields of science and engineering. Hence, we just suitably picked up few interpretations of fuzzy implications in Table 2.

Example 1.4 Let $U = \{u\} = \{1, 2, 3\}$ and $V = \{v\} = \{1, 2, 3, 4\}$. The fuzzy conditional statement expressing the dependence between two linguistic variables L and K is:

IF (L is "low") THEN (K is "high")

where

"low" = $\{1/1, 0.7/2, 0.3/3\}$ and "high" = $\{0.2/1, 0.5/2, 0.8/3, ¼\}$.

From the above conditional statement, we construct the fuzzy relation R using Mamdani's "min" operator (See Table 2):

$$R = \text{"low"} \wedge \text{"high"} = \begin{pmatrix} 1/1 \\ 0.7/2 \\ 0.3/3 \end{pmatrix} \wedge (0.2/1, \quad 0.5/2, \quad 0.8/3, \quad 1/4)$$

$$\begin{matrix} \Uparrow & & & \Uparrow \\ \text{low} & & & \text{high} \end{matrix}$$

$$\begin{matrix} & 1 & 2 & 3 & 4 \\ 1 & 1\wedge.2 & 1\wedge.5 & 1\wedge.8 & 1\wedge1 \\ 2 & .7\wedge.2 & .7\wedge.5 & .7\wedge.8 & .7\wedge1 \\ 3 & .3\wedge.2 & .7\wedge.5 & .3\wedge.8 & .3\wedge1 \end{matrix}$$

$$v$$

$$\mu_r(u, v) = u \begin{pmatrix} 0.2 & 0.5 & 0.8 & 1 \\ 0.2 & 0.5 & 0.7 & 0.7 \\ 0.2 & 0.3 & 0.3 & 0.3 \end{pmatrix}$$

If now L = "medium" $= \mu_m(u) = 0.5/1 + 1/2 + 0.5/3$, then the induced k is given by:

K = ("medium") ∘ R = $\max_{u \in \{1,2,3\}}(\mu_m(u) \wedge \mu_r(u,v))$ = 0.2/1 + 0.5/2 + 0.7/3 + 0.7/4, where ∘ is the max min composition operator.

The fuzzy conditional statement may be used to represent some simple relations between the linguistic variables. For more sophisticated relations, the fuzzy algorithms may be used. The linguistic variable and its related tools may be therefore used to model complex and "soft" situations.

Zadeh introduced a number of translation rules which allow us to represent some common linguistic statements in terms of propositions in our language.

In the following, we describe some of these translation rules:

Definition 1.1 Entailment rule:

x is A

A ⊂ B

----

x is B

Example 1.5

Dona is very young

very young ⊂ young

Dona is young.

Definition 1.2 Conjunction rule:

x is A

and x is B

----

x is A ∩ B.

Example 1.6

Temperature is not very high

and temperature is not very low

Temperature is not very high and not very low.

Definition 1.3 Disjunction rule:

x is A

or x is B

----

x is A ∪ B.

Example 1.7

temperature is not very high

or temperature is not very low

----

temperature is not very high or not very low.

Definition 1.4 Projection rule:

(x, y) have relation R

----

x is $\Pi_X(R)$

(x, y) have relation R

----

y is $\Pi_X(R)$.

Example 1.8

    (x, y) is close to (6, 5)   (x, y) is close to (6, 5)

    -----------------------------------   -----------------------------------

    x is close to 6   y is close to 5.

Definition 1.5 Negation rule:

    not (x is A)

    ----

    x is ~ A

Example 1.9

    not (x is high)

    ----

    x is not high .

In fuzzy logic based approximate reasoning, the most important fuzzy inference rule is the Generalized Modus Ponens (GMP).

The classical inference rule modus ponens (MP) says:

    premise: $p \rightarrow q$

    fact: p

    -----------------------------------   (1.8)

    consequence: q

This inference rule can be interpreted as:

If p is true and $p \rightarrow q$ is true then q is true.

If we have fuzzy sets, $A \in F(U)$ and $B \in F(V)$,, and a fuzzy implication in the premise, and the fact $A' \in F(U)$ is also a fuzzy set (usually, $A \neq A'$) then the consequence, $B' \in F(V)$, can be derived from the premise and the fact using generalized modus ponens.

This inference rule says:

    premise: if X is A then Y is B

    fact: X is A'

    -----------------------------------   (1.9)

    consequence: Y is B'

where the consequence B' is determined as a composition of the fact and the fuzzy implication:

$$B' = A' \text{ o } (A \rightarrow B),$$

that is:

$$B'(v) = {\sup_{u \in U}} \min\{A'(u), (A \to B)(u, v)\}, v \in V \qquad (1.10)$$

The consequence B' is nothing else but the shadow of $A \to B$, on A'. Instead of min operation, we can use any other t-norm as well. However, we must take care that the t-norm to be used belongs to the same DeMorgan triple of operations as the corresponding t-conorm, which is used to generate the implication. The generalized modus ponens, which reduces to classical modus ponens when A' = A and B' = B, is closely related to the forward data-driven inference, which is particularly useful in the fuzzy logic control.

In many practical cases, instead of sup-min composition, we use sup-T composition, where T is a t-norm. Thus, we define the rule of compositional inference in the general form.

Definition 1.6 Given a relation **R**, the scheme of the sup-T compositional rule of inference is given in the form:

      premise: if X is A then Y is B

      fact: X is A'

      --   (1.11)

      Consequence: Y is B'

where the consequence B is determined as composition of the fact and the premise:

B' = A' o (A **R** B)

That is:

$$B'(v) = \sup \{T (A' (u)), A\mathbf{R}B) (u, v) | u \in U\}, v \in V \qquad (1.12)$$

Compositional rule of inference is very general, in fact, GMP is a special case of it, where the relation R is implication operation.

Example 1.10 The GMP with Larsen's product implication, where the membership function of the consequence B' is defined by:

$$B' (v) = \sup \min \{A'(u), A(u) B(v)\} \qquad (1.13)$$

for all $y \in R$, where A, A', B, and B' are fuzzy subsets of R.

The classical Modus Tollens inference rule says:

If $p \to q$ is true and q is false then p is false.

Thus, the scheme for generalized Modus Tollens is:

      fact: if X is A then Y is B

      premise: Y is B'

      --   (1.14)

      Consequence: X is A'

which reduces to the classical modus tollens when B'$\equiv\sim$B and A'$\equiv\sim$A. This inference rule is related to the backward goal-driven inference, which is commonly used in expert systems, especially in the realm of medical diagnosis.

Suppose that A, B, and A' are fuzzy numbers. The GMP should satisfy some rational properties [73].

Property 1.1 Basic property (See Figure 6)

If x is A then y is B

    x is A

----

    y is B

Example 1.11

If pressure is big then volume is small

    pressure is big

----

volume is small

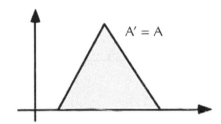 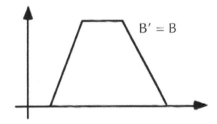

FIGURE 6   . Basic property.

Property 1.2 Total indeterinance (See Figure 7)

if x is A then y is B

    x is ~A

----

y is unknown

Example 1.12

If pressure is big then volume is small

    pressure is not big

----

volume is unknown

 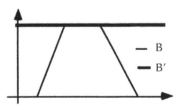

FIGURE 7   Total indeterminance.

Property 1.3 Subset (See Figure 8)
If x is A then y is B

x is $A' \subset A$

----

y is B

Example 1.13
If pressure is big then volume is small
    pressure is very big

----

volume is small

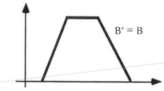

FIGURE 8   Subset property.

Property 2.4 Superset (See Figure 9)
If x is A then y is B
x is A'

----

y is $B' \supset B$

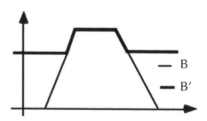

FIGURE 9   Superset property.

Suppose that A, B, and A' are fuzzy numbers.

We show that the Generalized Modus Ponens with Mamdani's implication operator does not satisfy all the four properties listed above.

The GMP with Mamdani implication inference rule says:
If x is A then y is B
    x is A'

----

    y is B'

where the membership function of the consequence B' is defined by (See Figure 10)

$$B'(y) = \sup \{A'(x) \wedge A(x) \wedge B(y) x \in R. \tag{1.15}$$

Basic property Let A' = A and let y ∈ R be arbitrarily fixed.
Then we have:

$$B'(y) = \sup_x \min \{A(x), \min \{A(x), B(y)\} = \sup_x \min \{A(x), B(y)\} = \min \{B(y),$$
$$\sup_x A(x)\} = \min \{B(y), 1\} = B(y).$$

So the basic property is satisfied.
Total indeterminance Let A' = ~A = 1 − A and let y ∈ R be arbitrarily fixed.
Then we have:
$$B'(y) = \sup_x \min \{1 - A(x), \min \{A(x), B(y)\} = \sup_x \min \{A(x), 1 - A(x), B(y)\} =$$
$$\min \{B(y), \sup_x \min \{A(x), 1 - A(x)\}\} = \min \{B(y), \tfrac{1}{2}\} = \tfrac{1}{2} B(y) < 1.$$
This means that the total indeterminance property is not satisfied.

Subset A' ⊂ A and R let y ∈ R be arbitrarily fixed.
Then we have:

$$B'(y) = \sup_x \min \{A'(x), \min \{A(x), B(y)\} = \sup_x \min \{A(x), A'(x), B(y)\} = \min \{B(y),$$
$$\sup_x A'(x)\} = \min \{B(y), 1\} = B(y).$$

So the subset property is satisfied.

Superset Let y ∈ R be arbitrarily fixed.
Then we have:
$$B'(y) = \sup_x \min \{A'(x), \min \{A(x), B(y)\} = \sup_x \min \{A(x), A'(x), B(y)\} \leq B(y).$$

So, the superset property of GMP is not satisfied by Mamdani's implication operator.

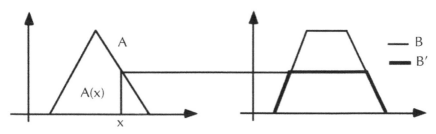

FIGURE 10   The GMP with Mamdani's implication operator.

The GMP with Larsen's product implication
If x is A then y is B
　　x is A'

　　-----------------------------------

　　y is B'
where the membership function of the consequence B' is defined by (See Figure 11)

$$B'(y) = \sup \min \{A'(x), A(x)B(y) \mid x \in R\}, \ y \in R. \qquad (1.16)$$

Basic Property Let A' = A and let y ∈ R be arbitrarily fixed.
Then we have:

$$B'(y) = \text{Sup}_x \min \{A(x), A(x)B(y)\} = B(y).$$

So the basic property is satisfied.

Total indeterminance Let A' = ~A = 1 - A and let y ∈ R be arbitrarily fixed.
Then we have:

$$B'(y) = \text{Sup}_x \min \{1 - A(x), A(x)B(y)\} = \frac{B(y)}{1+B(y)} < 1.$$

This means that the total indeterminance property is not satisfied.

Subset Let A' ⊂ A and let y ∈ R be arbitrarily fixed.

Then we have:

$$B'(y) = \text{Sup}_x \min \{A'(x), \min A(x)B(y)\} = \text{Sup}_x \min \{A(x), A'(x), B(y)\} = B(y)$$

So the subset property is satisfied.
Superset Let R be arbitrarily fixed.
Then we have:

$$B'(y) = \text{Sup}_x \min \{A'(x), A(x), B(y)\} \leq B(y).$$

So the superset property is not satisfied.

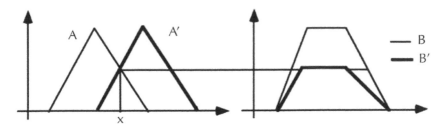

FIGURE 11   The GMP with Larsen's implication operator.

Note that the GMP with Gödel implication does satisfy all the four properties listed above.

1.4   EXTENDED FUZZY REASONING

Now, we consider the following form of inference proposed by Mizumoto, in which a fuzzy conditional proposition "if ..." contains two fuzzy propositions "X is A" and "Y is B" combined using the connective "and"

$$\left.\begin{array}{l} \text{premise} 1 : X \text{ is } A \text{ then } Y \text{ is } B \text{ then } Z \text{ is } C \\ \text{premise} 2 : X \text{ is } A' \text{and } Y \text{ is } B' \end{array}\right\} \qquad (1.17)$$

Consequence Z is B'

where A, A' are fuzzy sets in U; B, B' are fuzzy sets in V and C, C' are fuzzy sets in W.

The consequence C' can be deduced from Premise 1 and Premise 2 by taking the max-min composition o of a fuzzy set (A' and B') in Y x V and a fuzzy relation (A and B) $\rightarrow$ C in U x V x W.

That means, we get:

$$\left.\begin{array}{l} C' = (A' and B')0(A and B) \rightarrow C] \\ \mu_{c'}(w) = \vee_{u,v}\left\{\left[\mu_A'(u) \wedge \mu_{B'}(v)\right] \wedge \left[\mu_A(u) \wedge \mu_B(v)\right) \rightarrow \mu_c(w)\right]\right\} \end{array}\right\} \quad (1.18)$$

In the case of Mamdani's method R_c in Table 2, the fuzzy implication [(A and B) $\rightarrow$ C] is translated into $\mu_A(u) \wedge \mu_B(v) \wedge \mu_c(w)$ by virtue of a $\rightarrow$ b=a $\wedge$ b. Thus, the consequence C' is given as,

$$\mu_{c'}(w) = V_{u,v}\left\{\left[\mu_{A'}(u) \wedge \mu_{B'}(V)\right] \wedge \left[(\mu_A(u) \wedge \mu_B(V)) \rightarrow \mu_c(w)\right]\right\} \qquad (1.19)$$

Let $R_c(A, B; C) = (A and B) \rightarrow C, R_c(A; C) = A \rightarrow C$ and $R_c(B; C) = B \rightarrow C$

be fuzzy implications by Mamdani's method R_c Then, the consequence C' of equation (1.19) is reduced to,

$$\mu_{c'}(w) = \vee_u \left\{ \mu_{A'}(u) \wedge \mu_A(u) \wedge \mu_c(w) \wedge \vee_v \left[\mu_{B'}(v) \wedge \mu_B(v) \wedge \mu_c(w) \right] \right\}$$

$$= V_u \left\{ \mu_{A'}(u) \wedge \mu_A(u) \wedge \mu_C(w) \wedge \mu_{B' \, oR_C(B;C)}(w) \right\}$$

$$= \mu_{A' \, oRc(B;C)}(w) \wedge \mu_{B' oR_c(B;C)}(w)$$

Therefore, the consequence C'= (A' and B') o Rc (A, B; C) can be obtained as the intersection of A' o R_c (A;C) and B' o R_c (B;C) for Mamdani's implication R_c. That means, we get,

$$C' = (A' \text{ and } B') \text{ o } A' \text{ o } R_c (A, B; C)$$

$$= [A' \text{ o } R_c (A;C)] \cap [B' \text{ o } R_c (B;C)]$$

Similarly, we can have,

$$(A' \text{ and } B') \text{ o } [(A \text{ and } B) \to C] = \left[A'o(A' \to C) \right] \cap \left[B'o(B \to C) \right] \quad (1.20)$$

for the fuzzy implications R_p, R_{pp}, and R_{dp} Table 2.

Note that, $R_a, R_b, R^*, R_s, R_g,$ and R_Δ in Table 2 for which equality $(a \wedge b) \to c = (a \to c) \wedge (b \to c)$ holds, satisfy the following:

$$\left(A' \text{and } B' \right) \circ \left[\left(A \text{and } B \right) \to C \right] = [A' \circ (A \to C)] \cup [B' \circ (B \to C)] \quad (1.21)$$

If the fuzzy sets A' and B' are singletons in (1.7), that is, $A' = \mu_0$ and $B' = v_0$, the consequence C' of (1.17) is represented as:

$$= \hat{e}_{\substack{u(\neq u_0) \\ or \, v(\neq v_0)}} \{0\} \, [(\mu_A(u) \i \quad \mu_B(v) \to \mu_C(w)]\}$$

$$\hat{e}\ \{1\ì\ [(\ \mu_A(u_o)\ì\ \ \mu_B(v_o) \to \mu_C(w)]\} \tag{1.22}$$

$$= [\ \mu_A(u_o)\ì\ \ \mu_B(v_o)] \to \mu_C(w)$$

For example, in the case of R_c and R_a we have consequences C' at A' = u_o and B' = v_o as follows,

$$R_c : [\mu_A(u_o) \wedge \mu_B(v_o)] \to \mu_c(w), \tag{1.23}$$

$$R_a : 1 \wedge [1 - (\mu_A(u_o) \wedge \mu_B(v_o)) \to \mu_c(w)]. \tag{1.24}$$

Similar results can be obtained from other fuzzy implications in Table 2.

In the above discussion, the operation $\wedge$ (= min) is used as the meaning of "and". It is possible to introduce other operations, say, algebraic product • and more generally t-norms as "and".

Example 1.11 X = {x} = {1, 2, 3}, Y = {y} = {1, 2, 3, 4}, and Z = { z } = {1, 2, 3}.

The fuzzy conditional statement expressing the dependence among the linguistic variables L, K, and M is:

If (L is "low") and (K is "high") THEN (M is "medium")

Where "low" = 1/1 + 0.6/2 + 0.2/3 (considering X as universe of discourse of L)
"high" = 0.1/1 + 0.4/2 + 0.7/3 + ¼ (considering Y as universe of discourse of K)
And "medium" = .5/1 + ½ + .5/3 (considering Z as universe of discourse of M).

Now, if we interpret the connective "and" of the said conditional statement as "min" operator (we may attach any other interpretation to the connective "and"; for example, the Algebraic product), then we may translate, using Mamdani's law of implication, the conditional statement as follows:

The antecedent clause of the conditional statement can be represented by the following relation:

Relation formed by antecedent clauses (RAC) $\equiv$

$$\left\{ \frac{.1}{(1,1)}, \frac{.4}{(1,2)}, \frac{.7}{(1,3)}, \frac{1}{(1,4)}, \frac{.1}{(2,1)}, \frac{.4}{(2,2)}, \frac{.6}{(2,3)}, \frac{.6}{(2,4)}, \frac{.1}{(3,1)}, \frac{2}{(3,2)}, \frac{.2}{(3,3)}, \frac{.2}{(3,4)} \right\}$$

Finally, the conditional statement can be represented by the following relation:

$$\left\{ \frac{.1}{(1,1,1)}, \frac{.1}{(1,1,2)}, \frac{.1}{(1,1,3)}, \frac{.4}{(1,2,1)}, \frac{.4}{(1,2,2)}, \frac{.4}{(1,2,3)}, \frac{.5}{(1,3,1)}, \frac{.7}{(13,2)}, \frac{.5}{(1,3,3)}, \frac{.5}{(1,4,1)} \right\},$$

$$\frac{1}{(1,4,2)}, \frac{.5}{(1,4,3)}, \frac{.1}{(2,1,1)}, \frac{.1}{2,1,2}, \frac{.1}{(2,1,3)}, \frac{.4}{(2,2,1)}, \frac{.4}{(2,2,2)}, \frac{.4}{(2,2,3)}, \frac{.5}{(2,3,1)}, \frac{.6}{(2,3,2)},$$

$$\frac{.5}{(2,3,3)}, \frac{.5}{(2,4,1)}, \frac{.6}{(2,4,2)}, \frac{.5}{(2,4,3)}, \frac{.1}{(3,1,1)}, \frac{.1}{(3,1,2)}, \frac{.1}{(3,1,3)}, \frac{.2}{(3,2,1)}, \frac{.2}{(3,2,2)}, \frac{.2}{(,3,2,3,)},$$

$$\frac{.2}{3,3,1}, \frac{.2}{(3,3,2)}, \frac{2}{(3,3,3)}, \frac{.2}{(3,4,1)}, \frac{.2}{(3,4,2)}, \frac{.2}{(3,4,3)} \}.$$

Now, if L is "medium" = $4/1 + \frac{1}{2} + 4/3$
And K is "low" = $1/1 + 7/2 + 4/3 + 1/4$,
We get the following relation:

$$\left\{ \frac{.4}{1,1}, \frac{.4}{(1,2)}, \frac{.4}{(1,3)}, \frac{.1}{(1,4)}, \frac{1}{(2,1)}, \frac{.7}{(2,2)}, \frac{.4}{(2,3)}, \frac{.1}{(2,4)}, \frac{.4}{(3.1)}, \frac{.4}{(3,2)}, \frac{.4}{(3,3)}, \frac{.1}{3.4} \right\}$$

Corresponding to the above relation, the induced M, using max-min composition, is given by:

(4/1 + 4/2 + 4/3)

1.5   FURTHER EXTENSION OF FUZZY REASONING

Since the first formal description of fuzzy reasoning by Zadeh (See Section 1.3), many researchers have discussed different forms of fuzzy reasoning. Mizumoto presented a possible extention of fuzzy reasoning (See Section 1.4).

In ordinary fuzzy reasoning as suggested by Zadeh, we make inferences of the form:

P : if X is A then Y is B
q :   X is A'

(concl.) r ← Y is B

where the variables X,Y take values in universes of discourse U,V respectively and A, A', B, B'are (possibly inexact) description of the linguistic variables X and Y, which are approximated by fuzzy sets over U,U,V,V respectively.

In extended fuzzy reasoning as suggested by Mizumoto, we make inferences of the form

P : if X_1 is A_1 and X_2 is A_2 and ... X_n is A_n then Y is B
q: if X_1 is A'_1 and X_2 is A'_2 and ... X_n is A'_n then Y is B

(concl.) r ← Y is B'

where X_i' s are variables taking values in universes of discourse U_i, $i = 1,2,...,n$, and Y is a variable taking values in V. A_i and A_i' are fuzzy subsets U_i, $i = 1,2,...,n$. B and B' are fuzzy subsets of V.

This second form of reasoning is tremendously used in fuzzy control problems. Here, the conclusion is simple and possibly an imprecise statement that actually reveals the possible truth values of different states of a single variable Y. Thus, in order to obtain a conclusion, we require prior information about all variables that appear in the body of the rule. But in controlling a real plant/system, it has often been found that all the information regarding the firing of a complex rule of the form p is not explicitly available. For instance, we may consider a rule based output feedback design of a plant/system of which not all state parameters are field measurable (observable).

Hence, in this section, we propose a method that is applicable in deducing resolvent (conclusion) when the expert does not have adequate information regarding one or more parameters appearing in the body of the rule.

As in this case also the existence of the information in the set of fact(s) and rule induces a possibility distribution which is implied by the dependence between the variables expressed, we are considering the derivation of a resolvent (conclusion), possibly a relation from the above set.

For this, Raha and Ray [193] consider the derivation of a resolvent from a rule of the form p consisting of a number of simple but possibly imprecise propositions in the body of the rule combined using the connective "and" together with a simple premise at the head of the rule. The body and the head are connected by an implication connective, and a compound proposition q consists of a finite number of possibly imprecise simple propositions combined using the connective "and".

Finally, a procedure to deduce a rule from the above relations is presented, in which the body of the rule consists of the variables about which no prior information is found.

Thus, in the proposed technique of Raha and Ray [193], we are going to make inference from the induced relational matrix a rule of the form r as given in the following scheme:

p: if X_1 is A_1 and X_2 is A_2 and ... X_n is A_n then Y is B
q: if X_1 is A'_1 and X_2 is A'_2 and ... A_m is A'_m (1.25)

(concl.) r ← if X_{m+1} is A'_{m+1} and X_{m+2} is A'_{m+2} and ...X_n is A'_n then Y is B'.
Here the case m + n corresponds to Mizumoto's extended fuzzy reasoning.

MATHEMATICAL FORMULATION OF THE PROBLEM

For some $n < \infty$, let

$$X_1, X_2, \cdots, X_n, X_{n+1}$$

be n+1 linguistic variables taking values in universes of discourse

$$U_1, U_2, \cdots, U_n, U_{n+1}$$

respectively and let there be two typical premises expressed as

p: if X_1 is A_1 and X_2 is A_2 and ... X_n is A_n then X_{n+1} is A_{n+1}

q: if X_1 is A'_1 and X_2 is A'_2 and ... X_m is A'_m.

Here A_i $(i = 1, 2, \cdots, n+1)$, A'_i $(i = 1, 2, \cdots, m)$ are inexact concepts that when approximated by fuzzy sets over their respective universes takes the form

$$A_i = \Sigma_{j=1}^{ji} \left(\mu_A \left(u_i^j \right) / u_i^j \right) \subset U_i = \Sigma_{j=1}^{ji} u_i^j, i = 1, 2, \cdots n+1, \qquad (1.26)$$

$$A'_i = \Sigma_{j=1}^{ji} \left(\mu_{A'_i} \left(u_i^j \right) / u_i^j \right) \subset U_i, \quad i = 1, 2, \cdots, m. \qquad (1.27)$$

In the case where the variables appearing in q are not in the said order, we can rearrange the appearance of the variables in both premises p and q and then rename them to obtain the same result.

The translation of the logical relation between sentences appearing in premises p and q (depends on the possible interpretations of the connecting operators) into mathematical relations R and S will be given by

$$p \rightarrow \prod_{(X_1, X_2 \cdots X_n, X_{n+1})} = R \subset U_1 \times U_2 \times \cdots U_n \times U_{n+1} \qquad (1.28)$$

and

$$q \rightarrow \prod_{(X_1, X_2 \cdots X_m)} = S \subset U_1 \times U_2 \times \cdots U_n \times U_m. \qquad (1.29)$$

These two relational matrices R and S can be constructed using any existing rule for translation of compound fuzzy propositions in fuzzy logic. In the following we use the most frequently used rule of translation due to Mamdani. Certainly one can safely use other rules for this purpose.

In case, we have two relational matrices R and S induced by the proposition p and q. Te particularization of R by S can be obtained according to the following

$$\prod_{(X_1, X_2 \cdots X_n, X_{n+1})} \left[\prod_{(X_1, X_2 \cdots X_m)} = S \right] = R \cap \bar{S}, \qquad (1.30)$$

the corresponding relational matrix from which the inference follows where $\bar{S} = S \times U_{m1} \times U_{m2} \times U_{m+1}$ is the cylindrical extension of S. Projecting $R \cap \bar{S}$ on $U_{m+1} \times U_{m+2} \times \cdots U_{n+1} \times U_{n+1}$ we have the required inference, a possible relation.

Thus from premises p and q we can have a conclusion r that is an (n-m_1) the-order relational matrix corresponding to n-m+1 linguistic variables, viz $X_{m+1}, X_{m+2}, \cdots X_n, X_{n+1}$. To convert it to a rule with X_{n+1} at the head we first find the induced possibility distributions of each variables independently, using the projection principle, and obtain

$$r_i \leftarrow X_i \text{ is } A_i' \quad i = m+1, m+2, ..., n, n+1$$

where A'_I are fuzzy sets defined over U_i (I = m+1,...,n, n+1) respectively and are given by

$$A_i' = \text{Proj}_{Ui} \left[\prod_{(X_{m+1,} X_{m+2,} ... X_n, X_{n+1})} \right], \quad i = m+1, ..., n, n+1. \tag{1.31}$$

Hence from propositions p and q we obtain a resolvent r, possibly a rule of the form

if X_{m+1} is A'_{m+1} and X_{m+2} is A'_{m+2} ... and X_n is A'_n then X_{n+1} is A'_{n+1}

in the above formulation if we use Mamdani's min rule for the translation of the compound propositions such as p and Zadch's well-known compositional rule of inference we will find that

$$\mu_R(u_1, u_2, \cdots u_{n+1}) = \min\{\mu A_1(u_1), \mu_{A_2}(u_2), \cdots \mu A_{n+1}(u_{n+1})\},$$

$$\mu_S(u_1, u_2, ... u_m) = \min\{\mu A_1'(u_1), \mu_{A_2}'(u_2), \cdots \mu_{A_m}'(u_m)\},$$

and

$$\mu R \cap \overline{S}(u_{m+1}, \cdots, u_n, u_{n+1}) = \text{Sup}_{(u_1, u_2, \cdots u_m)}\{\mu_R \wedge \mu_S\}. \tag{1.32}$$

Now the obvious demand that the resolvent be

if X_{m+1} is A_{m+1} and X_{m+2} is A_{m+2} ... and X_n is A_n then X_{n+1} is A_{n+1}

whenever $A'_i = A_i$, I = 1,2,...1,2,...,m, can be met if we choose all the underlying fuzzy sets as normal and the translating rule as stated. It has been found that as the number of variables appearing in the body of the rule becomes large the dimensionality of the relational matrix becomes very large and this causes lot of problems in handling. To avoid this we use a somewhat simplified formula for the said resolvent.

$$\mu_{A_i'}(u_i) = Sup_{u_1 \in U_1} Sup_{u_2 \in U_2} \tag{1.33}$$

$$\cdots Sup_{u_{i-1} \in U_{i-1}} \ Sup_{u_{i+1} \in U_{i+1}} \ Sup_{u_{n+1} \in U_{n+1}} \left[\mu_{A_1}(u_1) \wedge \mu_{A_2}(u_2) \wedge \ldots \wedge \mu_{A_{n+1}}(u_{n+1}) \wedge \right.$$
$$\left. \mu_{A_1'}(u_1) \wedge \ldots \wedge \mu A_{m'}(u_m) \right].$$

It can be easily verified that if $A_i' = A_i$, $i = 1, 2, m$, $A_i' = A_i$, $i = m+1, m+2, \cdots, n+1$.

Example 1.12. We consider a simple but concrete example to demonstrate effectiveness of the proposed technique for obtaining a resolvent. For that let there be a rule of the form

p1 : if X is A and Y is B then Z is C

and a premise of the form

p2 : X is A'.

Let U, V, W respectively denote the universes of discourse of the three linguistic variables X, Y, Z, A, A', B, C are fuzzy subsets over the universes of U, U, V, and W respectively. Also let them be

$$A = 0.50/u_1 + 0.75/u_2 + 1.0/u_3 + 0.75/u_4$$

$$A' = 0.75/u_1 + 1.0u_2 + 0.75/u_3 + 0.50/u_4,$$

$$B = 2.0/v_1 + 0.75/v_2 + 0.50/v_3 + 0.25/v_4,$$

$$C = 0.25/w_1 + 0.50/w_2 + 0.75/w_3 + 1.0/w_4$$

From this model we can infer at once that:

r← if Y is B' then Z is C'

where

$$\mu_{B'}(v) = Sup_u \ Sup_w \ \{ \mu_A(u) \wedge \mu_B(v) \wedge \mu_C(w) \wedge \mu_{A'}(u) \}$$

And

$$\mu_{C'}(w) = Sup_u \ Sup_v \ \{ \mu_A(u) \wedge \mu_B(v) \wedge \mu_C(w) \wedge \mu_{A'}(u) \}$$

Using the simplest method of comparison.

In the above example, we find after comparison that:

$$B' = 0.75/v_1 + 0.75/v_2 + 0.50/v_3 + 0.25/v_4 \ ,$$

$$C = 0.25 / w_1 + 0.50 / w_2 + 0.75 / w_3 \, 0.75 / w_4$$

If instead

$$A' = (0.5625, 1.0, 0.5625, 0.25)$$

then

$$B' = (1.0, 0.75, 0.50, 0.25) = B \text{ and } C' = (0.25, 0.50, 0.75, 1.0) = C.$$

Also if we choose A' = A then B' = B and C' = C. Now let A' = (1.0, 1.0, 0.75, 0.50) ≠ A. Then we find after necessary comparisons that B' = B and C' = C.

Again if:

A = (0.75, 1.0, 1.0, 0.75) and A' = (0.25, 0.65, 1.0, 0.5625) with B and C unaltered then we find after necessary comparisons that B' = B and C' = C.

Thus we can safely conclude that in case of normal fuzzy sets A_i (i = 1, 2, ..., n+1

so long as the membership of an element $u_i^j \in A_i \subseteq U_i$ for which $\mu_A(u_i^j)$ is a maximum in A_i remains unaltered in $A_i' \subseteq U_i$ we find that $A_i' = A_i, i = m+1, m+2, \cdots, n+1$.

The above idea of Raha and Ray [193] further generalizes the existing concept of extended fuzzy reasoning proposed by Mizumoto, which is considered to be a potential tool for designing a controller of a real plant/system. Also it follows from the above discussion that the proposed technique sequentially generates the result of extended fuzzy reasoning as given by Mizumoto. Throughout the discussion, we use only one rule for the translation of compound fuzzy propositions into relational matrices but we can safely use other rules as well to obtain a resolvent.

1.6   GENERALIZED FORM OF FUZZY REASONING

As a generalized form of fuzzy reason, we shall consider fuzzy reasoning with several fuzzy conditional propositions combined with "else".

$$\left. \begin{array}{l} \textit{Premise} 1: \textit{If } X \textit{ is } A_1 \textit{ and } Y \textit{ is } B_1 \textit{ then } Z \textit{ is } C_1 \textit{ else} \\ \textit{Premise} 2: X \textit{ is } A_2 \textit{ and } Y \textit{ is } B_2 \textit{ then } Z \textit{ is } C_2 \textit{ else} \\ \qquad \qquad \vdots \\ \textit{Premise} n: \textit{If } X \textit{ is } A_n \textit{ and } Y \textit{ is } B_n \textit{ then } Z \textit{ is } C_n \\ \textit{Premise} n+1: \quad \textit{If } X \textit{ is } A' \textit{ and } Y \textit{ is } B' \end{array} \right\} \tag{1.34}$$

Consequence Z is C'

If we interpret "else" as union (U) which is valid for the fuzzy implications ,R_e, R_p, R_{bp} and R_{dp} in Table 2, we can deduce the consequences C' (refer Equation (1.20)) as:

$$C' = (A' and\ b')o\left[((A_1\ and\ B_1) \to C_1) \cup ...((A_n and\ B_n) \to C_n)\right]$$
$$= \left[(A'oA_1 \to C_1) \cap (B'oB_1 \to C_1)\right] \cup ...\cup \left[(A'oA_n \to C_n) \cap (B'oB_n \to C_n)\right] \quad (1.35)$$
$$= \quad C'_1 \cup \to C'_2 \cup ...\cup C'n$$

whereas, for the fuzzy implications ,R_a, R_m, R_b R^*, $R_\#$, and R_Δ in Table 2, "else" in (1.35) is interpreted as intersection ($\cap$).

Thus, the consequences C' for these fuzzy implications are defined as:

$$C' = (A'\ and\ B')\ o\ \left[((A_1\ and\ B_1) \to C_1) \cap ... \cap ((A_n\ and\ B_n) \to C_n)\right]$$

$$\subseteq \cdot[(A'oA_1 \to C_1) \cup (B'oB_1 \to C_1)] \cap ... \cap [(A'oA_n \to C_n) \cup (B'oB_n \to C_n)]..$$

It is noted that the consequence C' is not equal to! but contained in the intersection of fuzzy inference results $[(A'oA_i \to C_i) \cup (B'oB_i \to C_i)]$ $\forall_i$. However, for simplicity of calculation C' is represented as:

$$C' = C'\cdot = \cdot C'_1 \cap C'_2 \cap ...\cap C'_n \qquad (1.36)$$

1.7 APPLICATION OF FUZZY REASONING FOR PREDICTION OF RADIATION FOG

Model based approach for prediction of radiation fog essentially deals with thermo-dynamics and dynamics of meteorological parameters. In model based approach, the prediction of radiation fog is represented in terms of visibility. But such mathematical model is site specific. And very often educated guesses are needed to supplement actual result of model based prediction simply because the physical processes are not always well understood and sometimes beyond the resolution of existing model. Hence, we switch over to fuzzy rule based approach to predict the occurrence of radiation fog. Most experience forecaster suggests that experience is the best tool for forecasting such events which are inherently vague and imprecise. As most of the expert knowledge is full of imprecision and uncertainty, we model such knowledge by fuzzy rule based approach and utilize it for prediction of radiation fog. In course of doing this, we compare the performance of our fuzzy rule based approach for prediction of radiation fog to that of model based approach with an aim to utilize one approach as an complement of other.

Radiation fog forecasting is one application domain where the knowledge of experts is needed. Radiation fog is formed by the cooling of land after sunset by thermal radiation in calm conditions with clear sky. The cool ground produces condensation in the nearby air by heat conduction. In perfect calm condition, the fog layer can be less than a meter deep but turbulence can promote a thicker layer. Radiation fog occurs at night, and usually does not last long after sunrise. A brief description on the physical mathematical model of radiation fog is given in the appendix. Radiation fog can reduce visibility to less than 1 km. Since it reduces the visibility, it may cause car accident on high way and may cause severe difficulty for safe landing of planes. So, there is a specific need for radiation fog prediction system to avoid such accidents to maintain the safe traveling schedules.

Radiation fog has always been difficult to forecast. Although, there has been a lot of improvement in the numerical modeling techniques, still there exist difficulties in giving accurate predictions. This is due to fact that physical processes behind these are not yet well understood and are beyond the resolution of the existing models. Hence, the need for alternative methods for analysis and subsequent prognosis. Most experienced forecasters suggest that experience is the best tool for forecasting such events.

Most of the expert knowledge is pervaded with imprecision (that is, using linguistic instead of numerical values for the variables involved) and uncertainty (that is, using specifications such as possible, probable, more-or-less, very, and so on) One way of representing the knowledge of experts in building a particular expert system is by using IF-THEN rule. For instance, in case of radiation fog expert may say something like this.

If "Dew-point is DRY" AND "Dew-point spread is VERY SATURATED" AND "Rate of change of dew-point spread is DRYING" AND "Wind speed is TOO LIGHT" AND "Sky condition is CLEAR" THEN "Visibility is HIGH."

Expert system models the rule in such a way that, from the set of IF-THEN rules and a fact (real-time situation), we can predict the phenomenon like time of occurrence of radiation fog, depth of radiation fog, and visibility.

1.7.1   GOVERNING EQUATIONS FOR RADIATION FOG MODEL

$$\frac{\partial u}{\partial t} = f(v - v_g) - \frac{\overline{\partial w' u'}}{\partial z}$$

$$\frac{\partial v}{\partial t} = -f(u - u_g) - \frac{\overline{\partial w' v'}}{\partial z}$$

$$\frac{\partial \theta q}{\partial t} = -\frac{\overline{\partial w' \theta q'}}{\partial z} - \frac{\theta}{\rho cp T0} \frac{\partial F}{\partial z}$$

$$\frac{\partial q}{\partial z} = -\frac{\overline{\partial w' q'}}{\partial z} - C$$

where f is coriolis parameter, u and v are the orthogonal components of the horizontal wind, θ is the potential temperature, T is the temperature of air, and q is the humidity mixing ratio in air, $\overline{w'\alpha'}$ represents the turbulent flux of quantity α(where α = u,v, θ,q), F is the net radiative flux, C is the condensation rate by air mass unit , c_p is the specific heat of air, L is the latent heat of evaporation, ρ is the air density and z is the height from the surface.

The orthogonal components of geostropic winds (u_g and v_g) are external forcing terms.

The unknown turbulent fluxes will be parameterized with the gradient approach as:

$$\overline{w'a'} = -K_a \frac{\partial a}{\partial z}, \; for \, a = u,v,\theta q.$$

The turbulent kinetic diffusion coefficients K_α are given in terms of stability dependent mixing length $l_á$ and the turbulent kinetic energy : E_k

$$K_\alpha = C_\alpha l_\alpha E_k$$

where $C_á$ is a constant value taken equal to 0.4.

The following equation allows us to calculate the time evolution of turbulent kinetic energy:

$$\frac{\partial Ek}{\partial t} = -\frac{\overline{\partial \omega' Ek'}}{\partial z} - \overline{u'w'}\frac{\partial u}{\partial z} - \overline{v'w'}\frac{\partial u}{\partial z} + \frac{g}{T}\overline{w'\theta'} - \varepsilon$$

where g is the gravity acceleration and ε the kinetic energy dissipation.

Various parameterization of the mixing length has been used for boundary modeling.

We have used the following relation:

$$l_n = \begin{cases} l_n(1-5Ri) & Ri \leq 0.16 \\ l_n(1+41Ri) & Ri > 0.16 \end{cases}$$

where Ri is the Richardson number and l_n is the neutral mixing length, expressed as:

$$l_n = \frac{kz}{1+(kz \, / \, Gn)}$$

where k is the von Karman constant and G_n = 4 X 10^{-4} $u_g f^{1}$.

The equation for time evolution of the liquid water content is:

$$\frac{\partial q_l}{\partial t} = \frac{\partial}{\partial z}\left(Kz \frac{\partial q_l}{\partial z} \right) + \frac{\partial G}{\partial z} + C$$

The main difficulty lies in determining gravitational settling flux G. G can be expressed as follows:

$$G = v_i q_l$$

where v_i is settling velocity and $v_i = 62.5 \times 10^2 q_L$
The horizontal visibility is computed from the liquid water content by the relation

$$vis = \frac{3.9}{144.7(\rho\rho_l)^{0.88}}.$$

VISIBILITY

The greatest distance in a given direction at which it is just possible to see and identify with the unaided eye:
1) In the daytime, a prominent dark object against the sky at the horizon
2) At night, a known, preferably unfocused, and moderately intense light source.
The international definition of fog is a visibility of less than 1 kilometre (3,300ft); mist is a visibility of between 1 kilometre (0.62 mi) and 2 kilometres (1.2 mi) and haze from 2 kilometres (1.2 mi) to 5 kilometres (3.1 mi).

DESCRIPTION OF SOME PARAMETERS USED IN ABOVE EQUATIONS

Potential Temperature
The potential temperature of a parcel of fluid at pressure P is the temperature that the parcel would acquire if adiabatically brought to a standard reference pressure P_0, usually 1000 millibars.
The potential temperature is denoted by θ and, for air, is often given by:

$$\theta = T\left(\frac{p_0}{p} \right)^{\frac{R}{c_p}}$$

where T is the current absolute temperature (in K) of the parcel, R is the gas constant of air, and cp is the specific heat capacity at a constant pressure.

CORIOLIS PARAMETER

The Coriolis Parameter is defined as twice the vertical component of the earth's angular velocity w about the local vertical, and is given by $f = 2\ w\ \sin\Phi$, where Φ is the latitude.

GEOSTROPIC WIND

An air parcel initially at rest will move from high pressure to low pressure because of the pressure gradient force (PGF). However, as that air parcel begins to move, it is deflected by the Coriolis force to the right in the northern hemisphere (to the left on the southern hemisphere). As the wind gains speed, the deflection increases until the Coriolis force equals the pressure gradient force. At this point, the wind will be blowing parallel to the isobars. When this happens, the wind is referred to as geostrophic.

Initial conditions for simulating the model are given below:

where $z \equiv$ height(m), $u \equiv$ wind speed in x-direction(km/hr), $v \equiv$ wind speed in y-direction(km/hr), $F \equiv$ net radiative flux(W/m²), $\theta \equiv$ potential temperature(°C), $q \equiv$ mixing ratio(gm/gm), LWC ≡ l iquid water content(gm/gm), and TKE ≡ Turbulent kinetic energy.

The corresponding numerical values are as follows (See Table 3):

TABLE 3   Initial conditions for simulating the model

z	u	v	F	θ	mixing ratio	LWC	TKE
1	0.68	1.04	-70.00	14.43	10.12	0.0296	0.0001
2	0713	1.08	-70.03	14.46	10.122	0.0298	00028
3	074	1.129	-70.06	14.49	10.1227	0.0300	0.0055

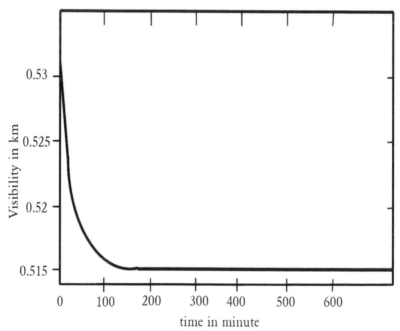

FIGURE 12   Visibility *vs.* time plot.

1.7.2 OBJECTIVE OF THE FUZZY RULE BASED APPROACH TO PREDICTION OF RADIATION FOG

The basic aim of this section is to achieve the following three objectives for prediction of radiation fog by fuzzy rule based approach:
- Forecast the time of occurrence of radiation fog,
- Depth of the radiation fog, and
- Visibility at that time.

We consider the generalized form of fuzzy reasoning of Section 1.6 to build up an expert system approach for prediction of radiation fog.

1.7.3 MODIFICATION OF THE GENERALIZED FORM OF FUZZY REASONING

The reasoning approach stated in Section 1.6 claims that when a fact occurs which would be fired (after fuzzyfication) with each and every rule of the database and the final consequents would be other of the form of Equation (1.35) or of the form of Equation (1.36) as shown in Section 1.6. But such an exhaustive firing of all rules by the observed fact of a particular instant most of the time, produce unacceptable result. To overcome this problem, we only fire a limited number of rules from the set of rules stored in the database with the observed fact (after fuzzyfication) depending upon the degree of similarity between the antecedent part of each rule and the observed fact (after fuzzification).

To measure the degree of similarity we consider few standard similarity measures as given below:

Let A and B are two fuzzy sets.

Measure based on maximum difference:

$$L_{A,B} = 1 - \max_i (|a_i - b_i|) \tag{1.37}$$

Measure based on the difference and the sum:

$$S_{A,B} = 1 - \frac{\sum_{i=1}^{n} |a_i - b_i|}{\sum_{i=1}^{n} |a_i + b_i|} \tag{1.38}$$

Measure based on the Union and Intersection:

$$M_{A,B} = 1 - \frac{|A \cap B|}{|A \cup B|} \tag{1.39}$$

Measure based on Geometric distance:

$$W_{A,B} = 1 - \frac{\sum_{i=1}^{n} |a_i - b_i|}{n} \tag{1.40}$$

Measure based on set theory:

$$T_{A,B} = \max_{x \in U} \left((A \cap B)(x) \right)$$

(1.41)

Measure based on matching:

$$P_{A,B} = \frac{\sum_{i=1}^{n} a_i \cdot b_i}{\max(\sum_{i=1}^{n} a_i \cdot a_i, \sum_{i=1}^{n} b_i \cdot b_i)}$$

(1.42)

Now, we are in position to measure similarity between fuzzified version of the sensor data and the corresponding antecedent part of the rule by any of the similarity measure expression as stated above. The similarities between each antecedent clause of the each rule with the corresponding fuzzified version of sensor data is collected together and algebraically added to establish the overall similarity of the antecedent part of the rules with the sensor data. At this point to select the number of rules to be fired with the fuzzified version of the sensor data is determined either by the degree of similarity or by selecting the rules having maximum similarity. To measure the degree of similarity, we may put a threshold on the overall similarity between the sensor data and the antecedent parts of each rule. The basic philosophy behind this modification of the above stated form of fuzzy reasoning is to consider only those rules whose antecedents parts are close to the sensor data. Thus, instead of firing all the rules generated by the expert, we prune a large set of rules due to their dissimilarities with the sensor data.

Therefore, the generalized form of fuzzy reasoning is modified with the concept of similarity measure.

1.7.4 FUZZY RULE BASED APPROACH FOR RADIATION FOG PREDICTION

Our objective is to develop an expert system to predict the occurrence of radiation fog. For this purpose, we write a C program. We take sensor data as input parameter and we predict the visibility for the given data after a certain time. To predict the occurrence of radiation fog, we take five input parameters from sensor. These input parameters are fuzzified. We used these fuzzified data to measure the similarity between the antecedent parts of the rules of the rule base. By doing this, we chose the appropriate rule from the rule base. Then we use the compositional rule of inference (Zadeh's approximate reasoning) to predict the fuzzified value of visibility. We defuzzy the value of visibility to predict the occurrence of radiation fog.

In this section, we model the phenomenon of radiation fog by rules. Usual parameters responsible for radiation fog are dew point, dew point spread, the rate of the change of spread per day, wind speed, and sky coverage. Other parameters may be considered to forecast radiation fog, for example, wind direction, and so on. Given these parameters, our primary task is to predict possibility of visibility to predict radiation fog. The occurrence of different parameters responsible for radiation fog will be represented by appropriate fuzzy sets defined over the different dynamic ranges as discussed below one by one.

Parameters of the Radiation Fog

- **Dew Point:** The temperature to which humid air can be cooled at constant pressure without causing condensation is called the dew point temperature or dew point. It is represented by Td and measured in (°C). Here, domain of dew point is $T_d = -30°C$ to $30°C$, which is quantized as, $\{-30 \leq T_d < -25, -25 \leq T_d < -20, \ldots\ldots,$ $20 \leq T_d < 25, 25 \leq T_d \leq 30\}$ Primary fuzzy sets defined over the said domain are dry,

moderate, moist, and very moist.

The fuzzy sets and their membership functions are given as follows:

Dewpoint dry $\equiv$

$$\left\{ \frac{1}{(-30 \leq T_d < -25)}, \frac{0.9}{(-25 \leq T_d < -20)}, \ldots\ldots\ldots, \frac{0}{(20 \leq T_d < 25)}, \frac{0}{(25 \leq T_d \leq 30)} \right\}$$

Dew Point Spread: The difference between the air temperature (T) and dew point (T_d) is termed as dew point spread. It is represented by ΔT and measured in (°C). Here, domain of dew point spread is $\Delta T = -12°C$ to $12°C$, which is quantized as, $\{-12 \leq \Delta T < -10, -10 \leq \Delta T < -8, \ldots\ldots, 8 \leq \Delta T < 10, 10 \leq \Delta T \leq 12\}$. Primary fuzzy sets defined over the said domain are very saturated, saturated, and unsaturated.

The fuzzy sets and their membership functions are given as follows:
Dew point spread very saturated $\equiv$

$$\left\{ \frac{1}{(-12 \leq \Delta T < -10)}, \frac{0.9}{(-10 \leq \Delta T < -8)}, \ldots\ldots\ldots, \frac{0}{(8 \leq \Delta T < 10)}, \frac{0}{(10 \leq \Delta T \leq 12)} \right\}$$

The Rate of change of Dew Point Spread: The difference between the dew point spreads of two consecutive days is defined as the rate of the change of spread per day. It is represented by $\Delta T'$ and measured in (°C). Here, domain of $\Delta T'' = \{-5°C$ to $6°C\}$, which is quantized as, $\{-5 \leq \Delta T' < -4, \ldots\ldots, 4 \leq \Delta T' < 5, 5 \leq \Delta T' \leq 6\}$. Primary fuzzy sets defined over the said domain are drying and saturating.

- The fuzzy sets and their membership functions are given as follows:

- Dew point spread saturating $\equiv \left\{ \frac{1}{(-5 \leq \Delta T' < -4)}, \frac{0.9}{(-4 \leq \Delta T' < -3)}, \right.$

$$\ldots\ldots\ldots, \frac{0}{(4 \leq \Delta T' < 5)}, \frac{0}{(5 \leq \Delta T' \leq 6)} \left.\right\}$$

Wind Speed: Wind speed is the speed of wind in Knts/hr. W represents it. Here domain of wind speed is $W = -5$ Knts/hr to 25 Knts/hr , which is quantized as, $\{-5 \leq W <-$

2.5,-2.5≤W<0,......................., 20≤W<22.5, 22.5≤W≤25}. Primary fuzzy sets defined over the said domain are too light, excellent, and too strong.

The fuzzy sets and their membership functions are given as follows:
* Wind Speed Too light ≡

$$\left\{ \frac{1}{(-5 \leq W < -2.5)}, \frac{0.9}{(-2.5 \leq W < 0)}, ..., \frac{0}{20 \leq W < 22.5}, \frac{0}{(22.5 \leq W \leq 25)} \right\}$$

Sky Condition: Sky coverage is in terms of percentage of cloud coverage perceptually judged by inspection. It is represented by S and measured in (%). Here, domain of S = {0% to 100%}, which is quantized as {0≤ S< 10, 10≤ S< 20, ...,80≤ S< 90, 90 ≤ S ≤ 100}. Primary fuzzy sets defined over the said domain are clear sky, partially cloudy and cloudy.

The fuzzy sets and their membership functions are as follows:
Sky coverage Clear ≡

$$\left\{ \frac{1}{(0 \leq S < 10)}, \frac{0.9}{(10 \leq S < 20)}, ..., \frac{0.1}{80 \leq S < 90}, \frac{0}{(90 \leq S \leq 100)} \right\}$$

* **Possibility of visibility:** As no standard or well established visibility *versus* fog (haze) classification exists we consider the following ranges of visibility from international defination of fog (V< 1 km.). Depending upon the different ranges of visibility, we consider five primary fuzzy sets as shown below, where very low ≡ dense fog, low ≡ light fog, medium ≡ dense haze, high ≡ light haze, and very high ≡ clear (see Table 4).

TABLE 4 Primary fuzzy sets and their membership functions (visibility)

Visibility V(km)	Very low	Low	Medium	High	Very high
V<1	1.0	0.7	0.5	0.3	0.1
1≤V<5	0.7	1.0	0.7	0.5	0.3
5≤V<10	0.5	0.7	1.0	0.7	0.5
10≤V<16	0.3	0.5	0.7	1.0	0.7
V≤16	0.1	0.3	0.5	0.7	1.0

NUMBER OF RULES GENERATED FOR PREDICTION OF RADIATION FOG

Here, the number of possible rules is $C_1^4 \times C_1^3 \times C_1^2 \times C_1^3 \times C_1^3 = 216$. The general formula of determining the number of possible rules is the product of combinations of the number of primary sets taking one at a time from each of them.

The antecedents of some applicable rules along with their corresponding consequents are given as follows:

- IF "Dewpoint is DRY" AND "Dewpoint spread is VERY SATURATED" AND "Rate of change of dewpoint spread is DRYING" AND "Wind speed is TOO LIGHT" AND "Sky condition is CLEAR" THEN "Visibility is HIGH."
- IF "Dewpoint is DRY" AND "Dewpoint spread is VERY SATURATED" AND "Rate of change of dewpoint spread is DRYING" AND "Wind speed is TOO-LIGHT" AND "Sky condition is PARTIALLY CLOUDY" THEN "Visibility is HIGH."

THE ALGORITHM

Our objective is to develop an expert system to predict the occurrence of radiation fog. For this purpose, we write a Java program. We take sensor data as input parameter and we predict the visibility for the given data after a certain time. To predict the occurrence of radiation fog, we take five input parameters from sensor. These input parameters are fuzzified. We used these fuzzified data to measure the similarity between the antecedent parts of the rules of the rule base. By doing this, we chose the appropriate rule from the rule base. Then we use the compositional rule of inference to predict the fuzzified value of visibility. The final consequence will be either guided by Equation (1.35) or Equation (1.36) depending upon the choice of appropriate implication operator as stated in Table 1. We defuzzy the value of visibility to predict the occurrence of radiation fog.

Algorithm (*rules; fuzzy values; sensor input*)

input: rules, fuzzy values, sensor input(five parameters)

output: conclusion

begin

Step 1: Read the rules and corresponding fuzzy values.

Step 2: Read the input sensor values and fuzzify the input data (using triangulation).

Step 3: Let the five parameters after fuzzification A0, B0, C0, D0, and E0:

Step 4: For each rule i

Step 5: do

Let the primary fuzzy sets of five parameters antecedents of a rule i are A_i, B_i, C_i, D_i, E_i, and consequent F_i.

Find the similarity between A_i and A_0, let it be SA_i (by using some similarity measure)

Similarly, find similarity between corresponding input data and primary fuzzy sets, let those are SBi, SCi, SDi, and SEi.

Over all similarity of rule i is Si = SAi + SBi + SCi + SDi + SEi

Step 6: Select a rule "X" at which Si is maximum (if more than one rules are selected then go to step 9).

Step 7: Apply compositional rule of inference to the selected rule for the given input data to calculate the visibility.

Step 8: Defuzzy the visibility value.

Step 9: Apply compositional rule of inference to all selected rules for the given input data to calculate the visibility.

Step 10: Perform max operation between the fuzzified visibility values to get the ultimate value of visibility.

Step 11: Defuzzy the visibility value.

end

1.7.5   RESULT AND DISCUSSION

Now we are testing the effectiveness of the expert rules for prediction of radiation fog based on the following sensor data. Let us consider the input (Link: http://www.ncdc. noaa.gov/pub) as Td = 25.00C, ΔT = - 4.00C, ΔT' = - 2.00C, W = 7.0 Knts/hr, and S = 10.1%. According to Zadeh's arithmetic rule, Ra: 1[1 - μA(uo) + μB(v)] and "Max-Min" composition over relations(R), we get the results for visibility:

The fuzzified versions of sensor data (by using method of triangulation) are as follows:

Dew point temperature (25.00°C): 0 0 0 0 0 0 0 0 0 0 0 0.5 1.0,

Dew point spread (-4.00°C): 0 0 0 0.5 1.0 0.5 0 0 0 0 0 0,

Rate of change of dew point spread (-2.00°C): 0 0 0.5 1.0 0.5 0 0 0 0 0 0,

Wind speed (7.0 Knts/hr): 0 0 0 0.5 1.0 0.5 0 0 0 0 0 0,

Sky Condition (10.1%): 0.5 1.0 0.5 0 0 0 0 0 0 0.

The threshold_similarity is selected as 2.37.

Thus, visibility for rule 171:

$$\frac{0.8}{(V<1)}, \frac{1.0}{(1 \le V < 5)}, \frac{0.8}{(5 \le V < 10)}, \frac{0.6}{(10 \le V < 16)}, \frac{0.4}{(16 \le V)} \qquad (1.43)$$

The defuzzy interpretation of the above fuzzy consequences (See Equation 1.43) shows that visibility is low, that means possibility of fog is high.

Normally, the fuzzy consequence of approximate reasoning is defuzzified by taking the element of the universe of consequence having highest membership value. In case of "tie" situation, we can break the tie by taking arbitrary decision or we can take the average of all tie values or we can consider the entire range of tie values. There are many other approaches to defuzzify a fuzzy consequence. The choice of particular process of defuzzification depends on the need of the problem.

Now, if we compare the computational result with the input value and the corresponding experience (obtained from an expert), it clearly indicates that computational result totally supports the experience of an expert based on the input data.

Now, instead of Zadeh's arithmetic rule, we may choose any other suitable rule from Table 1 and can infer the consequence for prediction of radiation fog interms of visibility.

Now, if we consider the sensor data stated above and apply them, along with other data, on the mathematical model, we get almost similar result (See Figure 12) which further establishes the validity of the proposed fuzzy rule based expert system for prediction of radiation fog. Fuzzy rule based expert system always need less number of data compare to model based system. Further, any change in environment can easily be incorporated in fuzzy rule based system. Whereas in model system such a change can be adapted by putting huge effort to manipulate the parameters of section. Thus, fuzzy rule based method is more adaptive to any change in environment. However, we can always use model based approach for prediction as a complement of rule based approach for the same.

We have successfully developed an expert system for prediction of radiation fog using fuzzy rules. It has several advantages over the model based approach for the same and very much adaptive to any changes in the environment. It can easily handle the vagueness of the sensed data due to environment noise and measurement errors. It requires less number of parameters compare to model based approach for prediction of radiation fog. We can predict the visibility in term of membership function as well as defuzzy value of visibility which indirectly implies the possibility of occurrence of radiation fog.

1.8   AGGREGATION IN FUZZY SYSTEM MODELING

Many applications of fuzzy set theory involve the use of a fuzzy rule base to model complex and perhaps ill-defined systems. These applications include fuzzy logic control, fuzzy expert systems and fuzzy systems modeling, and so on.

Typical of these situations are set of n rules of the form:

R_1: if x is A_1 then y = C_1,
R_2: if x is A_2 then y = C_2,

.

.

.

.

.

R_n: if x is A_n then y is C_n (1.44)

A fuzzy inference process consists of the following four step algorithm:

- *Step 1:* Determination of the relevance or matching of each rule to the current input value.
- *Step 2:* Determination of the output of each rule as fuzzy subset of the output space. We shall denote these individual rule output as
- *Step 3:* Aggregation of the individual rule outputs to obtain the overall fuzzy system output as fuzzy subset of the output space. We shall denote this overall output as R.
- *Step 4:* Selection of some action based upon the output set.

Our purpose is to investigate the requirements for the operations that can be used to implement this reasoning process. We are particularly connected with the third step, the rule output aggregation [73]. Note that in chapter 2 of volume 1 of this book, we have thoroughly discussed about aggregation operator.

1.8.1   MULTIPLE FUZZY REASONING WHEN RULES ARE HAVING ONE ANTECEDENT CLAUSE

Suppose we are given one block of fuzzy rules of the form:

R_1: if x is A_1 then z is C_1

R_2: if x is A_2 then z is C_2

.

.

.

.

.

R_n: if x is A_n then z is C_n
fact: x is A

--   (1.45)

consequence: z is C

where the rules are connected with the (hidden) sentence connective also. The i-th fuzzy rule from this rule-base, $R = \{R_1, ..., R_n\}$, is implemented by a fuzzy implication and is defined as:

$$R_i(u, w) = A_i(u) \rightarrow C_i(w)$$

There are two main approaches to determine the consequence C:

- Combine the Rules First

   In this approach, we first combine all the rules by an aggregation operator **Agg** into one rule, that is:

   $R = $ **Agg** $(R_1, R_2, ..., R_n)$ which is used to obtain C from A.

   If the implicit sentence connective "also" is interpreted as and then we get:

$$R(u,w) = \bigcap_{i=1}^{n} R_i(u,w) = \min (A_i(u) \rightarrow C_i(w)),$$

or by using a t-norm T for modeling the connective 'and' we get,

$$R(u,w) = T(R_1(u,w), ..., R_n(u,w)).$$

If the implicit sentence connective 'also' is interpreted as 'or' then we get

$$R(u,w) = \bigcup_{i=1}^{1} R_i(u,v,w) = \max \left(A_i(u) \rightarrow C_i(w) \right),$$

or by using a t-conorm T^* for modeling the connective 'or' we get,

$$R(u,w) = T^*(R_1(u,w), ..., R_n(u,w)).$$

Then we compute C from A by the compositional rule of inference as

$$C = A \circ R = A \circ \mathbf{Agg}\ (R_1, R_2 \ldots, R_n).$$

- Fire the rules first

Fire the rules individually, given A, and then combine their results into C. First compose A with each R_i producing intermediate result

$$C'_i \ldots = A \circ R_i$$

for $i - 1, \ldots,$ n and then combine C'_i component wise into C' by some aggregation operator **Agg**,

$$C' = \mathbf{Agg}\ (C'_1, \ldots, C'_n) = \mathbf{Agg}\ (A \circ R_1, \ldots, A \circ R_n).$$

We show that the sup- min compositional operator and the connective 'also' interpreted as the union operator are commutative. Thus the consequence, C, inferred from the complete set of rules is equivalent to the aggregated result, C', derived from individual rules [73].

Lemma 1.1. Let,

$$C = A \circ \bigcup\nolimits_{i=1}^{n} R_i$$

be defined by standard sup-min composition as

$$C(w) = \sup_u \min \{ A(u), \max \{R_1(u, w), \ldots, R_n(u, w)\} \}$$

and let

$$C' = \bigcup\nolimits_{i=1}^{n} A \circ R_i$$

defined by the sup-min composition as

$$C'(w) = \max_{i=1,\ldots,n} \{\sup_u A(u) \wedge R_i(u, w)\}.$$

Then C(w)= C'(w) for all w from the universe of discourse W.

Proof. Using the distributivity of $\wedge$ over $\vee$ we get

$C(w) = \sup_u \{A(u) \wedge (R_1(u,w) \vee \ldots \vee R_n(u,w))\} = \sup_u \{ (A(u) \wedge R_1(u,w)) \vee \ldots \vee (A(u) \wedge R_n(u,w))\} = \max \{\sup_u A(u) \wedge R_1(u,w), \ldots, \sup_u A(u) \wedge R_n(u,w)\} = C'(w).$

Similar statement hold for the sup-product compositional rule of inference, i.e the sup-product compositional operator and the connective also as the union operator are commutative [73]:

Lemma 1.2. Let,

$$C = A \text{ o } \bigcup_{i=1}^{n} R_i$$

be defined by sup-product composition as

$$C(w) = \sup_{u} A(u) \max \{R_1(u,w) \dots, R_n(u,w)\}$$

and let $C' = A \text{ o } \bigcup_{i=1}^{n} R_i$
defined by the sup- product composition as $C'(w) = \max \{\sup_u A(u) Ri(u, w), \dots$
supu A (u) Rn (u, w)}.

Then C (w) = C'(w) holds for each w from the universe of discourse W.

However, the sup-min compositional operator and the connective "also" inter-preted as the "intersection" operator are not usually commutative. In this case, the consequence, C, inferred from the complete set of rules is included in the aggregated result, C', derived from individual rules.

Lemma 1.3 Let

$$C = A \text{ o } \bigcap_{i=1}^{n} A \text{ o } Ri$$

be defined by standard sup-min composition as:

$$C(w) = \sup_{u} \min \{A(u), \min \{R_1(u,w), \dots R_n(u,w)\}\}$$

and let

$$C' = A \text{ o } \bigcap_{i=1}^{n} A \text{ o } Ri$$

defined by standard sup-min composition as:

$$C'(w) = \min \{\sup_{u} \{A(u) \wedge R_i(u,w)\}, \dots, \sup_{u} \{A(u) \wedge R_n(u,w)\}\}.$$

Then $C \subset C'$, that is $C(w) \leq C'(w)$ holds for all w from the universe of discourse W.

Proof. From the relationship

$$A \circ \bigcap_{i=1}^{n} R_i \subset A \circ R_i$$

for each $i = 1, ..., n$, we get

$$A \circ \bigcap_{i=1}^{n} R_i \subset \bigcap_{i=1}^{n} A \circ R_i .$$

Similar statement holds for the sup-t-norm compositional rule of inference, i.e the sup-product compositional operator and the connective 'also' interpreted as the 'intersection' operator are not commutative. In this case the consequence, C, inferred from the complete set of rules is included in the aggregated result, C', derived from individual rules.

Lemma 1.4. Let,

$$C = A \circ \bigcap_{i=1}^{n} R_i$$

be defined by sup- T composition as

$$C(w) = \sup_{u} T(A(u), \min \{R_1(u,w), ..., R_n(u,w)\})$$

and let

$$C' = \bigcap_{i=1}^{n} A \circ R_i$$

defined by the sup-T composition. Then $C \subset C'$, i.e $(w) \leq C'(w)$ holds for all w from the universe of discourse W.

If $U = \{u_1, ..., u_n\}$ is a finite set and A is a fuzzy set in U then we often use the notation

$$A = \mu_1 / \mu_1 + ... + \mu_n / \mu_n$$

where the term μ_i / u_i, $i = 1, ..., n$ signifies that μ_i is the grade of membership of u_i in A and the plus sign represents the union.

Example 1.13. We illustrate Lemma 1.3 by a simple example. Assume we have two fuzzy rules of the form

$$R_1: \text{if x is } A_1 \text{ then z is } C_1$$

$$R_2: \text{if x is } A_2 \text{ then z is } C_2$$

where A_1, A_2 and C_1, C_2 are discrete fuzzy numbers of the universe of discourses $\{x_1, x_2\}$ and $\{z_1, z_2\}$, respectively. Suppose that we input a fuzzy set $A = a_1/x_1 + a_2/x_2$ to the system and let

$$R_1 = \begin{array}{c} \\ x_1 \\ x_2 \end{array}\begin{pmatrix} z_1 & z_2 \\ 0 & 1 \\ 1 & 0 \end{pmatrix}, \quad R_2 = \begin{array}{c} \\ x_1 \\ x_2 \end{array}\begin{pmatrix} z_1 & z_2 \\ 1 & 0 \\ 0 & 1 \end{pmatrix}$$

represent the fuzzy rules. We first compute the consequence C by

$$C = A \, o \, (R_1 \cap R_2).$$

Using the definition of intersection of fuzzy relations we get

$$C = (a_1/x_1 + a_2/x_2) \, o \, \left[\begin{array}{c} \\ x_1 \\ x_2 \end{array}\begin{array}{c} z_1 \ z_2 \\ \begin{pmatrix} 0 & 1 \\ 1 & 0 \end{pmatrix} \end{array} \cap \begin{array}{c} \\ x_1 \\ x_2 \end{array}\begin{array}{c} z_1 \ z_2 \\ \begin{pmatrix} 1 & 0 \\ 0 & 1 \end{pmatrix}\end{array} \right]$$

$$= (a_1/x_1 + a_2/x_2) \, o \, \left[\begin{array}{c} \\ x_1 \\ x_2 \end{array}\begin{array}{c} z_1 \ z_2 \\ \begin{pmatrix} 0 & 0 \\ 0 & 0 \end{pmatrix}\end{array} \right] = \emptyset.$$

Let us compute now the membership function of the consequence C' by

$$C' = (A \, o \, R_1) \cap (A \, o \, R_2).$$

Using the definition of sup-min composition we get

$$A \, o \, R_1 = (a_1/x_1 + a_2/x_2) \, o \, \left[\begin{array}{c} \\ x_1 \\ x_2 \end{array}\begin{array}{c} z_1 \ z_2 \\ \begin{pmatrix} 0 & 1 \\ 1 & 0 \end{pmatrix}\end{array} \right].$$

Considering the numerical values we get,
$(A \, o \, R_1)(z_1) = \max \{a_1 \wedge 0, a_2 \wedge 1\} = a_2, (A \, 0 \, R_1)(z_2) = \max \{a_1 \wedge 1, a_2 \wedge 0\} = a_1.$
Therefore,

$$A \, o \, R_1 = \{a_2/z_1 + a_1/z_2\}.$$

Similarly we get,

$$A \circ R_2 = (a_1/x_1 + a_2/x_2) \circ \begin{bmatrix} & z_1 & z_2 \\ x_1 & \begin{pmatrix} 0 & 0 \\ 0 & 0 \end{pmatrix} \\ x_2 \end{bmatrix}$$

$$= A \circ R_2 = \{a_1/z_1 + a_2/z_2\} .$$

Finally,

$$C' = \{a_2/z_1 + a_1/z_2\} \cap \{a_1/z_1 + a_2/z_2\} = \{(a_1 \wedge a_2)/z_1 + (a_1 \wedge a_2)/z_2\},$$

Which means that C is a proper subset of C' whenever min $\{a_1, a_2\} \neq 0$.

Suppose now that the fact of GMP is given by a fuzzy singleton, $\bar{x}_0, x_0 \in R$ (see Fig. 13). Then the process of computation of the membership function of the consequence becomes very simple. For example, if we use Mamdani's implication operator in the GMP then

rule 1:   if x is A_1 then z is C_1

fact: x is $\bar{x}_0$

---

consequence: z is c

where the membership function of the consequence C is computed as

$$C(w) = \sup_u \min \{ \bar{x}_0 (u), (A_1 \to C_1)(u,w) \} = \sup_u \min \{ \bar{x}_0 (u), \min\{A_1 (u), C_1 (w)\} \},$$

for all $w \in W$. Observing that $\bar{x}_0 (u) = 0, \forall u \neq x_0$ the supremum turns into a simple minimum

$$C(w) = \min \bar{x}_0 (x_0) \wedge A_1 (x_0) \wedge C_1 (w)\} = \min \{1 \wedge A_1 (x_0) \wedge C_1 (w)\} = \min \{A_1 (x_0), C_1 (w)\}$$

for all $w \in W$. (see Fig. 14).

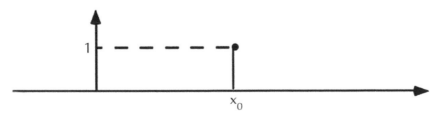

FIGURE 13   Fuzzy singleton.

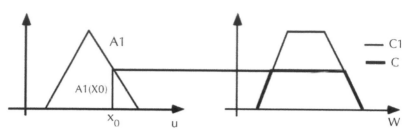

FIGURE 14   Inference with Mamdani's implication operator.

If we use Gödel implication operator in the GMP then:

$$C(w) = \sup_u \min \{ \overline{xo}\,(u), (A_1 \rightarrow C_1)\,(u,w)\} = A_1\,(x_0) \rightarrow C_1\,(w).$$

That is (See Figure 15):

$$C(w)\cdot = \cdot \begin{cases} 1 & \text{if } A_1(x_0) \leq C_1(w) \\ C_1(w) & \text{otherwise}. \end{cases}$$

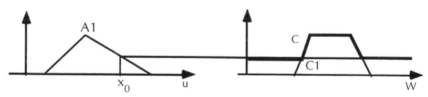

FIGURE 15   Inference with Gödel implication operator.

Lemma 1.5 Consider one block of fuzzy rules of the form

$$R_i: \text{if x is } A_i \text{ then z is } C_i, 1 \leq i \leq n$$

and suppose that the input to the system is a fuzzy singleton. Then the consequence, C, inferred from the complete set of rules is equal to the aggregated result, C', derived from individual rules. This statements holds for any kind of aggregation operators used to combine the rules [73].

Proof Suppose that the input of the system $A = \overline{xo}$ is a fuzzy singleton. On the one hand, we have:

$$C(w) = (A \circ \text{Agg}(R_1, \ldots, R_n)\,(w) = \text{Agg}\,(R_1\,(x_0, w), \ldots R_n\,(x_0, w)).$$

On the other hand

$$C'(w) = Agg(A \circ R_1, \ldots, A \circ R_n) (w) = Agg (R_1(x_0, w), \ldots R_n (x_0, w)) = C(w).$$

Consider one block of fuzzy rules of the form

$$R = \{ A_1 \rightarrow C_i, 1 \leq i \leq n \}$$

where A_i and C_i are fuzzy numbers.

Lemma 1.6. Suppose that in R the supports of A_i are pairwise disjunctive:

$supp\ A_i \cap supp\ A_j = \varnothing$, for $i \neq j$.

If the Gödel implication operator is used in R then we get

$$\bigcap_{i=1}^{n} A_i \circ (A_i \rightarrow C_i) = C_i$$

holds for $i = 1, \ldots, n$.

Proof. Since the GMP with Gödel implication satisfies basic property we get

$$A_i \circ (A_j \rightarrow C_i) = A_i.$$

From $supp\ (A_i) \cap supp\ (A_j) = \varnothing$, for $i \neq j$ it follows that

$$A_i \circ (A_j \rightarrow C_i) = 1, i \neq j$$

where 1 is the universal fuzzy set. So,

$$\bigcap_{i=1}^{n} A_i \circ (A_i \rightarrow C_i) = C_i \cap 1 = C_i$$

This property means that deleting any of the rules from R leaves a point $\hat{x}$ to which no rule applies. It means that every rule is useful.

Definition 1.7. The rule-base R is said to be separated if the core of A_i, defined by

$$Core\ (A_i) = \{x \mid A_i (x) = 1\},$$

is not contained in

$$\bigcap_{j \neq i} Supp\ A_j$$

for $i = 1, \ldots, n$.

Fig. 16 shows the separated rule base.

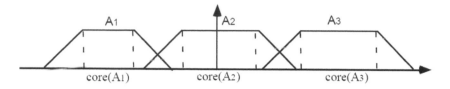

FIGURE 16   Separated rule-base.

The following theorem show that Lemma 1.6 remains valid for separated rule bases.

Theorem 1.1. Let R be separated. If the implication is modeled by the Gödel implication operator then

$$\bigcap_{i=l}^{n} A_i\, o\left(A_i \rightarrow C_i \right) = C_i \qquad \forall I = 1,,\ldots\ldots, n.$$

Proof. Since the Gödel implication satisfies the basic property of GMP we get

$$A_i\, o\, (A_i \rightarrow C_i) = A_i.$$

Since core $(A_i)\, \cap\, \text{SUPP}\,(A_i) \neq ,\varnothing$ for $i \neq j$ there exists an element $\hat{x}$ such that $\hat{x} \in$ core (A_i) and $\hat{x} \notin$ Supp(A_j), $i \neq j$. That is $A_i\,(\hat{x}) = 1$ and $A_j\,(\hat{x})=0$, $i \neq j$. Applying the compositional rule of inference with Gödel implication operator we get

$(A_i\, o\, A_j \rightarrow C_j\,(z) = \sup_x \min\{A_i\,(x), A_j\,(x) \rightarrow C_j\,(x))\} \leq \min\,\{A_i\,(\hat{x}), A_j\,(\hat{x}) \rightarrow C_j\,(\hat{x})\} = 1, i \neq j$
for any z. Therefore,

$$\bigcap_{i=1}^{n} A_i\, o\left(A_i \rightarrow C_i \right) = \rightarrow C_i \cap 1 = C_i.$$

1.8.2   SIMPLIFIED FUZZY REASONING WHEN RULES ARE HAVING ONE ANTECEDENT CLAUSE

Consider a block of fuzzy IF-THEN rules

R_1: if x is A_1 then z is C_1
also
R_2: if x is A_2 then z is C_2
also

. . . .

also

R_n: if x is A_n then z is C_n

fact: x is $\overline{xo}$

_____

consequence: z is C

The i-th fuzzy rule from this rule-base

R_i: if x is A_i then z is C_i

is implemented by a *fuzzy implication Ri* and is defined as:

$$R_i(u,w) = (A_i \rightarrow C_i)(u,w) = A_i(u) \rightarrow C_i(w)$$

for $i = 1, \ldots, n$.

Find C from the input x_0 and from the rule base:

$$R = \{R_1, \ldots, R_n\}.$$

We first compose $\overline{xo}$ with each R_i producing intermediate result

$$C'i = \overline{xo} \ \ R_i$$

for $i = 1, \ldots, n$.

C'_i is called the output of the i-th rule

$C'_i(w) = A_i(x_0) \rightarrow C_i(w)$,

for each w.

Then combine the C'_i component wise into C' by some aggregation operator:

$$C = \bigcup_{i=1}^{n} C'_i = \overline{x}_0 \ o \ R_1 \cup \cdots \cup \overline{x}_0 \ o \ R_n$$

$$C(w) = A_1(x0) \rightarrow C_1(w) \ v \ldots \ldots v \ A_n(x_0) \rightarrow C_n(w).$$

So, the inference process is the following:

- Input to the system is x_0
- Fuzzified input is $\overline{x}_0$
- Firing strength of the i-th rule is $A_i(x_0)$
- The i-th individual rule output is

$$C'_i(w): = A_i(x_0) \rightarrow C_i(w)$$

- Overall system output (action) is

$$C = C'_1 \bigcup \ldots \ldots \bigcup C'_n$$

Overall system output = union of the individual rule outputs.
Example 1.14

Mamdani $(a \rightarrow b = a \wedge b)$

- Input to the system is x_0
- Fuzzified input is $\overline{xo}$
- Firing strength of the i-th rule is $A_i(x_0)$
- The i-th individual rule output is:

$$C'i(w) = A_i(x_0) \rightarrow C_i(w)$$

- Overall system output (action) is:

$$C(w) = V_{i=1}^n A_i(x_0) \wedge C_i(w).$$

For $i = 2$, the result of deduction of the consequence C using Mamdani's implication operator is shown in Figure 17.

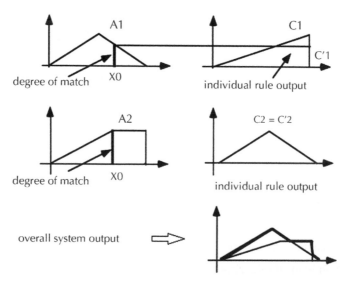

FIGURE 17   Deduction of consequence C using Mamdani's implication operator.

Larsen $(a \rightarrow b = ab)$
- input to the system is x_0
- fuzzified input is $\overline{xo}$
- firing strength of the i-th rule is $A_i(x_0)$
- the i-th individual rule output is

$$C'_i(w) = A_i(x_0) \, C_i(w)$$

- overall system output (action) is

$$C(w) = V_{i=1}^n \, A_i(x_0)C_i(w).$$

For $i = 2$, the result of deduction of the consequence C using Larsen's implication operator is shown in Figure 18.

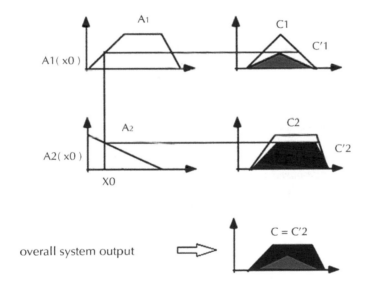

FIGURE 18 Deduction of consequence C using Larsen's implication operator.

The output of the inference process so far is a fuzzy set, specifying a possibility distribution of the consequence. If a nonfuzzy (crisp) decision is required. We must defuzzify the fuzzy consequence inferred from the fuzzy reasoning algorithm, that is:

$$z_0 = defuzzifier(C),$$

where z_0 is the crisp action and *defuzzifier* is the defuzzification operator.

To illustrate the concept of simplified fuzzy reasoning with one antecedent clause, we consider the following example which converts a deterministic rule base system to simplified fuzzy reasoning system.

Example 1.15 A deterministic rule base can be formed as follows (See Figure 19)

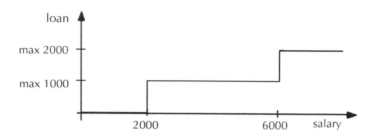

FIGURE 19   Discrete causal link between "salary and loan".

R_1: if $2000 \leq s \leq 6000$ then   loan is max 1000
R_2: if $s \geq 6000$ then   loan is max 2000
R_3: if $s \leq 2000$ then   no loan at all .

The data base describes the maximum loan capacity of individual applicant with respect to his/her salary.

Now, we convert the above deterministic rule base system to simplified fuzzy reasoning system as follows:

• *In fuzzy logic everything is a matter of degree*

If x is the amount of the salary then x belongs to fuzzy set (see Fig 20)

• • $A_1 = small$ with degree of membership $0 \leq A_1(x) \leq 1$
• • $A_2 = big$ with degree of membership $0 \leq A_2(x) \leq 1$

• *In fuzzy rule-based systems each rule fires*

The degree of match of the input to a rule (which is the firing strength) is the membership degree of the input in the fuzzy set characterizing the antecedent part of the rule.

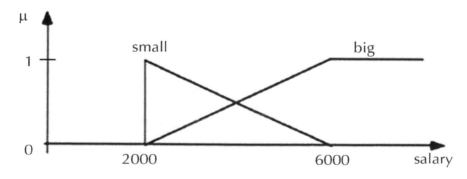

FIGURE 20   Membership functions for "small" and "big".

The overall system output is the weighted average of the individual rule outputs, where the weight of a rule is its firing strength with respect to the input.

The simplified fuzzy rule based system for the above problem is represented as follows;

R_1:   if   salary is *small* then   loan is C_1

also

R_2:   if   salary is *big* then   loan is C_2

fact: salary is $\bar{x}_0$

---

action: loan is C

Then our reasoning system is the following

- input to the system is x_0

- fuzzified input is $\bar{x}_0$
- the firing level of the first rule is $\alpha_1 = A_1(x_0)$
- the firing level of the second rule is $\alpha_2 = A_2(x_0)$
- the overall system output is computed as the weighted average of the individual rule outputs

$$Z_0 = \frac{\alpha_1 z_1 + \alpha_2 z_2}{\alpha_1 + \alpha_2}$$

That is

$$Z_0 = \frac{A_1(x_0)z_1 + A_2(x_0)z_2}{A_1(x_0) + A_2(x_0)}, \text{ where}$$

$$A_1(x_0) = \begin{cases} 1-(x_0-2000)/4000 & \text{if } 2000 \le x_0 \le 6000 \\ 0 & \text{Otherwise} \end{cases}$$

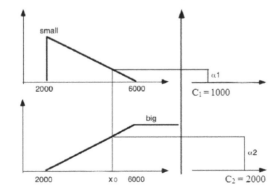

FIGURE 21   Example of simplified fuzzy reasoning

$$A_2(x_0) \begin{cases} 1 & \text{if } x_0 \geq 6000 \\ 1(6000 - x_0)/4000 & \text{if } 2000 \leq x_0 \leq 6000 \\ 0 & \text{otherwise} \end{cases}$$

It is easy to see that the relationship:

$$A_1(x_0) + A_2(x_0) = 1$$

holds for all $x_0 \geq 2000$.

Thus, the system output can be written in the form. (See Figure 21)

$$C_0 = \alpha_1 C_1 + \alpha_2 C_2 = A_1(x_0)C_1 + A_2(x_0)C_2$$

Therefore we get:

- if $\overline{xo} \leq 2000$ then loan C = 0
- if $\overline{xo} \geq 6000$ then loan C = 2000
- if $2000 \leq \overline{xo} \leq 6000$ then loan

$$C = \left(1 = \frac{x_0 - 2000}{40000}\right)c_1 + \left(1\frac{60000x_0}{4000}\right)c_2$$

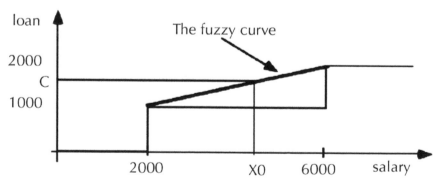

FIGURE 22   Input/output function derived from fuzzy rules.

The (linear) input/output relationship is illustrated in Figure 22.

1.8.3 MULTIPLE FUZZY REASONING WHEN RULES ARE HAVING MORE THAN ONE ANTECEDENT CLAUSES

If several linguistic variables are involved in the antecedents and the consequents of the rules then the system will be referred to as a multi-input-multi-output fuzzy system. For example, the case of two-input-single-output (MISO) fuzzy systems is of the form [73].

$$R_i: \text{ if x is } A_i \text{ and y is } B_i, \text{ then z is } C_i$$

where x and y are the process state variables, z is the control variable, A_i, B_i, and C_i, are linguistic values of the linguistic variables x, y, and z in the universes of discourse U, V, and W, respectively, and an implicit sentence connective also links the rules into a rule set or, equivalently, a rule-base.

The procedure for obtaining the fuzzy output of such a knowledge base consists of the following three steps:
- Find the firing level of each of the rules.
- Find the output of each of the rules.
- Aggregate the individual rule outputs to obtain the overall system outputs.

To infer the output z from the given process states x,y and fuzzy relations , we apply the compositional rule of inference:

$$R_1: \text{ if x is } A_1 \text{ and y is } B_1 \text{ then z is } C_1$$
$$R_2: \text{ if x is } A^2 \text{ and y is } B_2 \text{ then z is } C_2$$

$$R_n: \text{ if x is } A_n \text{ and y is } B_n \text{ then z is } C_n$$

$$\text{fact: x is } \overline{xo} \text{ and y is } \overline{y_0}$$

--- (1.46)

consequence: z is C

where the consequence is computed by:

consequence = **Agg** (fact o R_1, ..., fact o R_n). (1.47)

That is:

$$C = \text{Agg} (\overline{xo} \times \overline{y_0} \text{ o } R_1, ..., \overline{xo} \times \overline{y_0} \text{ o } R_n)$$

taking into consideration that $\overline{xo} (u) = 0$, $u \neq x_0$ and $\overline{y_0} (v) = 0$, $v \neq y_0$, the computational of the membership function of C is very simple:

$$C(w) - \text{Agg} \{ A_1 (x_0) \times B_1 (y_0) \rightarrow C_1 (w), ..., A_n(x_0) \times B_n (y_0) \rightarrow C_n (w) \}$$

for all $w \in$ W.

The procedure for obtaining the fuzzy output of such a knowledge base can be formulated as:

- The firing level of the i-th rule is determined by:

$$A_i(x_0) \times B_i(y_0).$$

- The output of the i-th rule is calculated by:

$$C_i'(w) = A_i(x_0) \times B_i(y_0) \to C_i(w)$$

for all w ∈ W.

- The overall system output, C, is obtained from the individual rule outputs C_i' (by

$$C(w) = \text{Agg} \{ C_i', ..., C_n' \} \tag{1.48}$$

for all w∈ W.

Example 1.16 If the sentence connective also is interpreted as adding the rules by using minimum-norm then the membership function of the consequence is computed as:

$$C = \left(\overline{x_0} \times \overline{y_0} \circ R_1 \right) \cap \cdots \cap \left(\overline{x_0} \times \overline{y_0} \circ R_n \right).$$

That is:

$$C(w) - \min \{A_1(x_0) \times B_1(Y_0) \to C_1(w), ... A_n(x_0) \times B_n(y_0) \to C_n(w)\},$$

for all w ∈ W.

Example 1.17 If the sentence connective also is interpreted as oring the rules by using minimum-norm then the membership function of the consequence is computed as:

$$C = (\overline{xo} \times \overline{y_0} \circ R_1) \cup ... \cup (\overline{xo} \times \overline{y_0} \circ R_n).$$

That is:

$$C(w) - \min \{ A_1(x_0) \times B_1(y_0) \to C_1(w), ... A_n(x_0) \times B_n(y_0) \to C_n(w)\},$$

for all w ∈ W.

Example 1.18 Suppose that the Cartesian product and implication operation are implemented by the t-norm $T(u, v) = uv$. If the sentence connective also is interpreted as oring, the rules by using maximum-norm then the membership function of the consequence is computed as:

$$C = \left(\overline{x_0} \times \overline{y_0} \circ R_1 \right) \cup \cdots \cup \left(\overline{x_0} \times \overline{y_0} \circ R_n \right).$$

That is,

$$C(w) = \max \{ A_1(x_0) \times B_1(y_0) \xrightarrow{} C_1(w), \ldots A_n(x_0) \times B_n(y_0) \, C_n(w) \},$$

for all $w \in W$.

We present five well-known inference mechanisms in MISO fuzzy systems [73]. For simplicity, we assume that we have two fuzzy rules of the form

R_1 :   if x is A_1 and y is B_1 then z_1 is C_1
R_2 :   if x is A_2 and y is B_2 then z_2 is C_2

fact :   x is $\overline{x_0}$ and y is $\overline{y_0}$

----

consequence: z is C

Mamdani: The fuzzy implication is modeled by Mamdani's minimum operator and the sentence connective also is interpreted as oring the propositions and defined by max operator:

The firing levels of the rules, denoted by a_i, $I = 1, 2$, are computed by:

$$\alpha_1 = A_1(x_0) \wedge B_1(y_0),$$

$$\alpha_2 = A_2(x_0) \wedge B_2(y_0)$$

The individual rule outputs are obtained by:

$$C_1'(w) = (\alpha_1 \wedge C_1(w)),$$

$$C_2'(w) = (\alpha_2 \wedge C_2(w))$$

Then the overall system output is computed by oring the individual rule outputs (See Figure 23)

$$C(w) = C_1'(w) \vee C_2'(w) = (\alpha_1 \wedge C_1(w)) \vee (\alpha_2 \wedge C_2(w)). \tag{1.49}$$

Finally, to obtain a deterministic control action, we employ any defuzzification strategy.

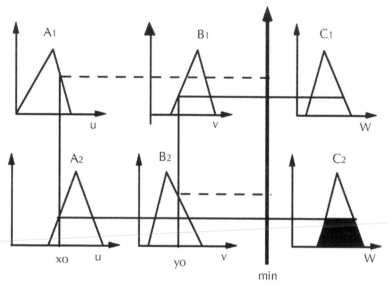

FIGURE 23   Inference with Mamdani's implication operator.

- **Tsukamato**: All linguistic terms are supposed to have monotonic membership functions.

The firing levels of the rules are computed by:

$$\alpha_1 = A_1(x_0) \wedge B_1(y_0), \ \alpha_2 = A_2(x_0) \wedge B_2(y_0).$$

In this mode of reasoning, the individual crisp control actions z_1 and z_2 are computed from the equations $\alpha_1 = c_1(z_1)$ and $\alpha_2 = C_2(z_2)$, and the overall crisp control action is expressed as:

$$z_0 = \frac{\alpha_1 z_1 + \alpha_2 z_2}{\alpha_1 + \alpha_2} = \frac{\alpha_1 C_1^{-1}(\alpha_1) + \alpha_2 C_2^{-1}(\alpha_{12})}{\alpha_1 + \alpha_2} \tag{1.50}$$

i.e., z_0 is computed by the discrete Cemnter-of-Gravity method.

If we have n rules in our rule-base then the crisp control action is computed as

$$z_0 = \frac{\sum_{i=1}^{n} a_i z_i}{\sum_{i=1}^{n} a_i},$$

where is the firing level and z_i is the (crisp) output of the i-th rule, i = 1, ..., n

Example 1.19. We illustrate Tsukamoto's reasoning method by the following simple example(See Figure 24)

R_1: if x is A_1 and y is B_1 then z is C_1

also

R_2: if x is A_2 and y is B_2 then z is C_2

fact: x is $\overline{xo}$ and y is $\overline{y_0}$

Consequence: z is C

Then according to the figure, we see that:

$$A_1\,(x_0) = 0.7, \qquad B_1\,(y_0) = 0.3$$

Therefore, the firing level of the first rule is:

$$\alpha_1 = \min\,\{A_1\,(x_0), B_1\,(y_0)\} = \min\,\{\,0.7, 0.3\,\} = 0.3,$$

And from

$$A_2\,(x_0) = 0.6$$

$$B_2(y_0) = 0.83$$

It follows that the firing level of the second rule is:

$$\alpha_2 = \min\,\{A_2\,(x_0), \quad B_2\,(y_0)\} = \min\,\{0.6, 0.8\,\} = 0.6$$

The individual rule outputs $z_1 = 8$ and $z_2 = 4$ are derived from the equations:

$$C_1\,(z_1) = 0.3, \qquad C_2\,(z_2) = 0.6$$

and the crisp control action is:

$$z_0 = (8 \times 0.3 + 4 \times 0.6)/(0.3 + 0.6) = 6.$$

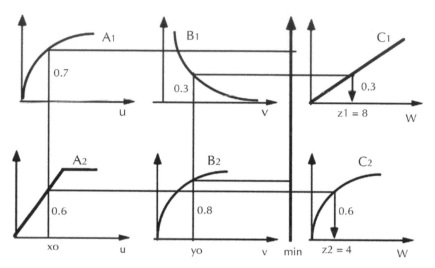

FIGURE 24 Tsukamoto's inference mechanism.

- Sugeno and Takagi use the following architecture:

R_1: if x is A_1 and y is B_1 then $z_1 = a_1 x + b_1 y$

R_2: if x is A_2 and y is B_2 then $z_2 = a_2 x + b_2 y$

fact: x is $\overline{xo}$ and y is $\overline{y_0}$

----

consequence: z_0

The firing levels of the rules are computed by:

$$\alpha_1 = A_1(x_0) \wedge B_1(y_0), \quad \alpha_2 = A_2(x_0) \wedge B_2(y_0) \qquad (1.51)$$

Then, the individual rule of outputs is derived from the relationship:

$$z_1^* = a_1 x_0 + b_1 x_0, \quad z_2^* = a_2 x_2 + b_2 y_0,$$

and the crisp control action is expressed as

$$z_0 = \frac{a_1 z_1^* + a_2 z_2^*}{a_1 + a_2}.$$

If we have m rules in our rule-base then the crisp control action is computed as

$$Z_0 = \frac{\alpha_1 z_1^* + \ldots + \alpha_m z_m^*}{\alpha_1 + \ldots + \alpha_m}, \tag{1.52}$$

where a_i denotes the firing level of the i-th rule, i = 1, ..., m.

Example 1.20 We illustrate Sugeno and Takagi's reasoning method by the following simple example (See Figure 25)

R_1: if x is BIG and y is small then $z_1 = x + y$

also

R_2: if x is MEDIUM and y is BIG then $z_2 = 2x - y$

fact: x_0 is and y_0 is 2

----

consequence: z_0

Then according to the figure we see that:

$$\mu_{BIG}(x_0) = \mu_{BIG}(3) = 0.8,$$

$$\mu_{SMALL}(y_0) = \mu_{SMALL}(2) = 0.2$$

Therefore, the firing level of the first rule is

$$a_1 = \min\{\mu_{BIG}(x_0), \mu_{SMALL}(y_0)\} = \min\{0.8, 0.2\} = 0.2$$

and from

$$\mu_{MEDIUM}(x_0) = \mu_{MEDIUM}(3) = 0.6,$$

$$\mu_{BIG}(y_0) = \mu_{BIG}(2) = 0.9$$

it follows that the firing level of the second rule is

$$a_2 = \min\{\mu_{MEDIUM}(x_0), \mu_{BIG}(y_0)\} = \min\{0.6, 0.9\} = 0.6.$$

The individual rule outputs are computed as:

$$z_1^* = x_0 + y_0 = 3 + 2 = 5, \quad z_2^* = 2x_0 - y_0 = 2 \times 3 - 2 = 4$$

So the crisp control action is:

$$Z_0 = (5 \times 0.2 + 4 \times 0.6)/(0.2 + 0.6) = 4.25.$$

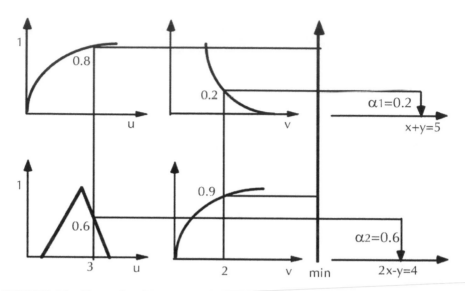

FIGURE 25 Example of Sugeno and Takagi's inference mechanism.

- **Larsen** The fuzzy implication is modeled by Larsen's product operator and the sentence connective also is interpreted as oring the propositions and defined by max operator.

Let us denote α_1, the firing level of the i-th rule, i = 1,2

$$\alpha_1 = A_1(x_0) \wedge B_1(y_0),$$

$$\alpha_2 = A_2(x_0) \wedge B_2(y_0).$$

Then membership function of the inferred consequence C is point wise given by (See Figure 26):

$$C(w) = (\alpha_1 C_1(w)) \vee (\alpha_2 C_2(w)).$$

To obtain a deterministic control action, we employ any defuzzification strategy. If we have n rules in our rule-base then the consequence C is computed as:

$$C(w) = \vee_{i=1}^{n} (\alpha_i C_1(w))(\alpha_i C_1(w))$$

where α_i denotes the firing level of the i-th rule, i = 1, ..., n

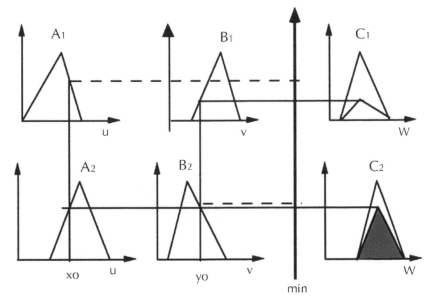

FIGURE 26   Inference with Larsen's product operation rule.

- **Simplified fuzzy reasoning with multiple antecedent clauses** In the context, the word simplified means that the individual rule outputs are given by crisp numbers, and therefore, we can use their weighted sum (where the weights are the firing strengths of the corresponding rules) to obtain the overall system output:

R_1: if x is A_1 and y is B_1 then C_1
R_2: if x is A_2 and y is B_2 then C_2
fact: x is u_1 and y is u_2

----

consequence: C

where A_1, A_2, B_1, and B_2 are values of the linguistic variables x and y, respectively. We derive from the initial content of the database, $\{ u_1, u_2\}$ and from the fuzzy rule base $\{R_1, R_2\}$ by the simplified fuzzy reasoning scheme as:

$$z_0 = \frac{\alpha_1 C_1 + \alpha_2 C_2}{\alpha_1 + \alpha_2}$$

(1.53)

where denotes the firing level of the i-th rule.

If we have n rules in our rule-base then the crisp control action is computed as:

$$z_0 = \frac{\sum_{i=1}^{n} \alpha_i c_i}{\sum_{i=1}^{n} \alpha_i},$$

Where α_1 denotes the firing level of the i-th rule, i = 1, ..., n (See Figure 27)

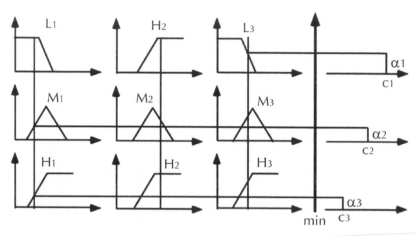

FIGURE 27 Simplified fuzzy reasoning.

1.9   SINGLE INPUT RULE MODULES (SIRMS) CONNECTED FUZZY REASONING METHOD

In if-then form fuzzy reasoning method, such as simplified fuzzy reasoning, all the input items of a system are set to antecedent clauses and all the output items are set to consequent clauses of the rules. As a result, the number of rules becomes huge and to tune the rules becomes very time-consuming. Whereas, single input rule modules (SIRMs) connected type fuzzy reasoning method, which unifies the reasoning output from fuzzy rule modules of one type if-then form, can reduce number of fuzzy rules sharply. In this section, a relation between SIRMs method and simplified fuzzy reasoning method has been established and the conversion procedure from SIRMs method to simplified fuzzy reasoning method is discussed but not (in general) vice versa [210].

We briefly review SIRMs connected type fuzzy reasoning method. The SIRMs method has n rule modules, and final inference result by SIRMs method is obtained by the weighted sum of n inference results from rule modules and n weights.

Rule modules of SIRMs method are given as:

Rules-1: $\left\{x_1 = A_j^1 \rightarrow y_1 = y_j^1\right\}_{j=1}^{m_1}$

Rules-i: $x_i = A_j^i ? y_i = y_{j(j=1)}^{i\,(m_i)}$　　　　　　　　　　　　　　　　　　(1.54)

Rules-n: $\left\{x_n = A_j^n \rightarrow y_n = y_j^n\right\}_{j=1}^{m_n}$

where Rules-i stands for the i-th single input rule module, the i-th input item is the sole variable of the antecedent part of the Rules-i, and stands for the variable of its

consequent part. A^i_j means the fuzzy set of the j-th rule of the Rules-i, y^i_j is real value of consequent part, and i=1, 2, ..., n. j=1, 2, ...m_i.
  ,The degree of the antecedent part in j-th rule of Rules-i is obtained by (1.55) for

input , and the inference result y^0_i from Rules-i is given as (1.56):

$$h^i_j = A^i_j(x^0_i))$$ (1.55)

$$y^0_i = \frac{\sum_{k=1}^{m_i} h^i_k \, y^i_k}{\sum_{k=1}^{m_i} h^i_k}$$ (1.56)

Final inference result of SIRMs method is given by (1.57), where importance degree of cach input x_i (i=1,2,..,n) is set as w_i.
  That is:

$$y^0 = \sum_{i=1}^{n} w_i \, y^0_i$$ (1.57)

Example 1.21 We consider the following rule modules:

$$\text{Rules-1} = \begin{cases} x_1 = A^1_1 \to y_1 - 1 \\ x_1 = A^1_2 \to y_1 = 2 \\ x_1 = A^1_3 \to v_1 = 1 \end{cases}$$ (1.58)

$$\text{Rules-1} = \begin{cases} x_2 = A^2_1 \to y_2 = 1 \\ x_2 = A^2_2 \to y_2 = 3 \\ x_2 = A^2_3 \to y_2 = 5 \end{cases}$$

where fuzzy sets in Figure 28 are used.

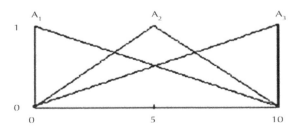

FIGURE 28   Fuzzy sets.

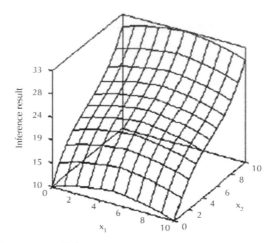

FIGURE 29   Inference result by SIRM method.

From (1.56) and (1.57), inference result of (1.58) is obtained as Figure 29.

1.9.1   RELATIONSHIP BETWEEN SIRMS REASONING METHOD AND SIMPLIFIED FUZZY REASONING METHOD

This section describes the relationship between SIRMs reasoning method and simplified fuzzy reasoning method [210].
- Conversion from SIRMs reasoning method to simplified fuzzy reasoning method

This section describes the conversion method from SIRMs reasoning method to simplified fuzzy reasoning method.

In order to distinguish subscript j of Rules-i in (1.54), is used, and (1.54) is rewritten as:

$$\text{Rules-i: } \left\{ x_i = A^i_{j_i} \rightarrow y_i = y^i_{j_i} \right\}^{m_i}_{j_i=1} \tag{1.59}$$

We can obtain the following rules of simplified fuzzy reasoning method which corresponds to (1.59) of rules of SIRMs method by:

$$x_1 = A^1_{j_1} \ , \quad x_2 = A^2_{j_2} \ , \ \dots, \ x_n = A^n_{j_n} \ \rightarrow$$

$$y = w_1 \, y^1_{j_1} + w_2 \, y^2_{j_2} + \dots + w_n \, y^n_{j_n} \tag{1.60}$$

where $j_i=1,2,\dots,m_i$.

We have the following theorem:

Theorem 1.2 In SIRMs method, if the rule modules of (1.59) are transformed to simplified fuzzy reasoning method by (1.60), the inference results by both methods are equal

TABLE 5   Rules of Simplified Fuzzy Reasoning Method obtained from (1.58)

		x_2		
		A_1^2	A_2^2	A_3^2
x_1	A_1^1	1	2	3
	A_2^1	1.5	2.5	3.5
	A_3^1	1	2	3

Example 1.22 Considering two inputs and , suppose that rule modules of SIRMs method is given as:

$$Rule-1 = \begin{cases} x_1 = A_1^1 \rightarrow y_1 = y_1^1 \\ x_1 = A_2^1 \rightarrow y_1 = y_2^1 \\ x_1 = A_3^1 \rightarrow y_1 = y_3^1 \end{cases} \text{(1.61)}$$

$$Rule-2 = \begin{cases} x_2 = A_1^2 \rightarrow y_2 = y_1^2 \\ x_2 = A_2^2 \rightarrow y_2 = y_2^2 \\ x_2 = A_3^2 \rightarrow y_2 = y_3^2 \end{cases}$$

Then, the fuzzy rule of simplified fuzzy reasoning method is given as:

$$x_1 = A_{j_1}^1, x_2 = A_{j_2}^2 \rightarrow y = w_1 y_{j_1}^1 + w_2 y_{j_2}^2 \tag{1.62}$$

where $j_1, j_2 = 1, 2, 3$.

For example, given the rule modules of (1.58), the rules of simplified fuzzy reasoning method can be obtained as in Table 5 and fuzzy sets of antecedent part A_1^i, A_2^i, A_3^i , and are given in Figure 28, $w_1 = w_2 = 1/2$.

Namely, the rules of simplified fuzzy reasoning method are obtained as follows.

$$x_1 = A_1^1, x_2 = A_1^2 \rightarrow y = 1\left(=\frac{1+1}{2}\right)$$

$$x_1 = A_1^1, x_2 = A_1^2 \rightarrow y = 2\left(=\frac{1+3}{2}\right).$$

Inference result of simplified fuzzy reasoning method in Table 5 obtains Figure 30.

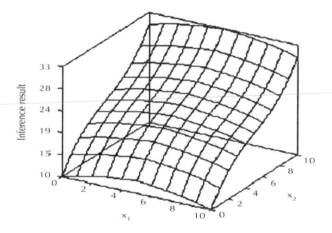

FIGURE 30   Inference result by the simplified fuzzy reasoning method in Table 5.

From the above discussion, inference result of simplified fuzzy reasoning method in Table 5 is the same as the inference result in Figure 29.
   • Conversion from simplified fuzzy reasoning method to SIRMs reasoning method

In previous section, we have described the conversion to simplified fuzzy reasoning method from SIRMs method. Although, the vice versa is impossible in general, this subsection shows that when the conditions shown in this subsection are satisfied, rules of simplified fuzzy reasoning methods are convertible to those of SIRMS method [210].

Generally, rules of simplified fuzzy reasoning method are expressed as:

$$x_1 = A_{j1}^1, x_2 = A_{j2}^2, \cdots, x_n = A_{jn}^n \rightarrow y = y(j_1, \cdots, j_n) \qquad (1.63)$$

where $y(j_1, \dots, j_n)$ is consequent part and the subscript $(j_1, \dots, j_n)$ corresponds to that of fuzzy sets $A_{j1}^1, \dots, A_{jn}^n$, ...,

Now, for convenience, suppose that the rules of simplified fuzzy reasoning method are given as in Table 6. Then Table 6 and (Equation 1.63) of the rules of simplified fuzzy reasoning method become (1.64).

$$x_1 = A_1^1, x_2 = A_1^2 \rightarrow y = y(y_{(1,1)}) = a$$

$$x_1 = A_1^1, x_2 = A_2^2 \rightarrow y = y(y_{(1,2)}) = b \qquad (1.64)$$

$$x_1 = A_2^1, x_2 = A_1^2 \rightarrow y = y(y_{(2,1)}) = c$$

$$x_1 = A_2^1, x_2 = A_2^2 \rightarrow y = y(y_{(2,2)}) = d$$

Suppose that the rules of SIRMS method corresponding to (1.64) are given as follows:

$$\text{Rules 1} = \begin{cases} x_1 = A_1^1 \rightarrow y_1 = y_1^1 \\ x_1 = A_2^1 \rightarrow y_1 = y_2^1 \end{cases} \qquad (1.65)$$

$$\text{Rules 2} = \begin{cases} x_2 = A_1^2 \rightarrow y_2 = y_1^2 \\ x_2 = A_2^2 \rightarrow y_2 = y_2^2 \end{cases}$$

Then, according to (1.59) and (1.60), the following can be deduced from (1.65):

$$x_1 = A_1^1, x_2 = A_1^2 \rightarrow y = w_1 y_1^1 + w_2 y_1^2$$

$$x_1 = A_1^1, x_2 = A_2^2 \rightarrow y = w_1 y_1^1 + w_2 y_2^2 \qquad (1.66)$$

$$x_1 = A_2^1, x_2 = A_1^2 \rightarrow y = w_1 y_2^1 + w_2 y_1^2$$

$$x_1 = A_1^1, x_2 = A_2^2 \rightarrow y = w_1 y_2^1 + w_2 y_2^2$$

TABLE 6   Rules of simplified fuzzy reasoning method

	A_1^2	A_2^2
A_1^1	a	b
A_2^1	c	d

TABLE 7   Rules of simplified fuzzy reasoning method

	x_2		
	A_1^2	A_2^2	A_3^2
A_1^1	y(1,1)	y(1,2)	y(1,3)
A_2^1	y(2,1)	y(2,2)	y(2,3)
A_3^1	y(3,1)	y(3,2)	y(3,3)

From the correspondence of (1.64) and (1.66), we have:

$$w_1 y_1^1 + w_2 y_1^2 = a$$

$$w_1 y_1^1 + w_2 y_2^2 = b \qquad\qquad (1.67)$$

$$w_1 y_2^1 + w_2 y_1^2 = c$$

$$w_1 y_2^1 + w_2 y_2^2 = d$$

From (1.67), the relation (1.68) is obtained:

$$a + d = b + c \qquad\qquad (1.68)$$

This shows that two diagonal sums in Table 6 are equal.

Under the conditions of (1.68), the rules of SIRMs method of (1.65) can be obtained if w_1, w_2, $y_1^1, y_2^1, y_1^2, y_2^2$ and of (1.67) are fixed.

Moreover, when the rules of simplified fuzzy reasoning method are given in Table 7, the corresponding relations between the rules of simplified fuzzy reasoning method and those of SIRMs method become (1.69) from (1.59) and (1.60).

$$x_1 = A_1^1, x_2 = A_1^2 \rightarrow y = w_1 y_1^1 + w_2 y_1^2 = y_{(1,1)}$$

$$x_1 = A_1^1, x_2 = A_2^2 \rightarrow y = w_1 y_1^1 + w_2 y_2^2 = y_{(1,2)}$$

$$x_1 = A_2^1, x_2 = A_3^2 \rightarrow y = w_1 y_1^1 + w_2 y_3^2 = y_{(1,3)}$$

$$x_1 = A_2^1, x_2 = A_1^2 \rightarrow y = w_1 y_2^1 + w_2 y_1^2 = y_{(2,1)} \tag{1.69}$$

$$x_1 = A_2^1, x_2 = A_2^2 \rightarrow y = w_1 y_2^1 + w_2 y_2^2 = y_{(2,2)}$$

$$x_1 = A_2^1, x_2 = A_3^2 \rightarrow y = w_1 y_2^1 + w_2 y_3^2 = y_{(2,3)}$$

$$x_1 = A_3^1, x_2 = A_1^2 \rightarrow y = w_1 y_3^1 + w_2 y_1^2 = y_{(3,1)}$$

$$x_1 = A_3^1, x_2 = A_2^2 \rightarrow y = w_1 y_3^1 + w_2 y_2^2 = y_{(3,2)}$$

$$x_1 = A_3^1, x_2 = A_3^2 \rightarrow y = w_1 y_3^1 + w_2 y_3^2 = y_{(3,3)}$$

From the above conditions of (1.69), the following relation is obtained by solving (1.69).

$$y_{(1,1)} + y_{(2,2)} = y_{(1,2)} + y_{(2,1)}$$

$$y_{(1,2)} + y_{(2,3)} = y_{(1,3)} + y_{(2,2)}$$

$$y_{(2,1)} + y_{(3,2)} = y_{(2,2)} + y_{(3,1)} \tag{1.70}$$

$$y_{(2,2)} + y_{(3,3)} = y_{(2,3)} + y_{(3,2)}$$

Therefore, the rules of SIRMs method is obtained by each w_i and y_j^i, fixed under the conditions of (1.70).

Example 1.23 The fuzzy rules in Table 5 satisfy the conditions of (1.70) and are expressed in table form. Thus the conversion is fulfilled.

Therefore, we get:

$$x_1 = A_1^1, x_2 = A_1^2 \rightarrow y = w_1 y_1^1 + w_2 y_1^2 = 1$$

$$x_1 = A_1^1, x_2 = A_2^2 \rightarrow y = w_1 y_1^1 + w_2 y_2^2 = 2$$

$$x_1 = A_1^1, x_2 = A_3^2 \rightarrow y = w_1 y_1^1 + w_2 y_3^2 = .3$$

$$x_1 = A_2^1, x_2 = A_1^2 \rightarrow y = w_1 y_2^1 + w_2 y_1^2 = 1.5$$ (1.71)

$$x_1 = A_2^1, x_2 = A_2^2 \rightarrow y = w_1 y_2^1 + w_2 y_2^2 = 2.5$$

$$x_1 = A_2^1, x_2 = A_3^2 \rightarrow y = w_1 y_2^1 + w_2 y_3^2 = \cdot 3.5$$

$$x_1 = A_3^1, x_2 = A_1^2 \rightarrow y = w_1 y_3^1 + w_2 y_1^2 = \cdot 1$$

$$x_1 = A_3^1, x_2 = A_2^2 \rightarrow y = w_1 y_3^1 + w_2 y_2^2 = \cdot 2$$

$$x_1 = A_3^1, \cdots x_2 = A_3^2 \rightarrow y = w_1 y_3^1 + w_2 y_3^2 = \cdot 3$$

Given each w_i each y_j^i, is determined from the equations of the right-hand side of (1.71).

For example, let $w_1 = w_2 = 0.5$, then $y_1^1 = 1, y_2^1 = 2, y_3^1 = 1, y_1^2 = 1, y_2^2 = 3, y_3^2 = 5$ in (1.71) are realized and thus the rule modules of SIRMs method of (1.58) are obtained.

Furthermore, for different w_i different y_j^i which satisfy (1.71) exist. For example, given $w_1 = 0.1$ and $w_2 = 0.5$, we have $y_1^1 = 2, y_2^1 = 7, y_3^1 = 2, y_1^2 = 1.6, y_2^2 = 3.6, y_3^2 = 5.6$. Thus, Equation 1.71 is realized and the following rule modules of SIRMs method are obtained.

$$\text{Rules-1} = \begin{cases} x_1 = A_1^1 \rightarrow y_1 = 2 \\ x_1 = A_2^1 \rightarrow y_1 = 7 \\ x_1 = A_3^1 \rightarrow y_1 = 2 \end{cases} \tag{1.72}$$

$$\text{Rules-2} = \begin{cases} x_2 = A_1^2 \rightarrow y_2 = 1.6 \\ x_2 = A_2^2 \rightarrow y_2 = 3.6 \\ x_2 = A_3^2 \rightarrow y_2 = 5.6 \end{cases}$$

Note that, w_1, w_2 $y_1^1, \dots, y_3^2$ satisfy (1.71) and exist innumerably under the conditions of (1.70) as shown in this examples. Therefore, it turns out that corresponding rule modules of SIRMs method exist innumerably.

Generally, for the reasons mentioned above, in the case that the rules of simplified fuzzy reasoning presuppose that they are given as in Table 8 and have primary formula as:

$$x_1 = A_{j1}^1, x_2 = A_{j2}^2 \rightarrow y = y_{(i.j)} \tag{1.73}$$

Thus, we have the equivalent SIRMs method.

From the above results, we obtain the following theorem:

Theorem 1.3 In simplified fuzzy reasoning method, when the rules of simplified fuzzy reasoning method are given in table form and following condition is satisfied, the inference result is equal to that of SIRMs method.

$$y_j^i + y_{j+1}^{i+1} = y_{j+1}^i + y_j^{i+1} \tag{1.74}$$

TABLE 8 Rules of simplified reasoning method

		x_2			
		A_1^2	A_2^2		A_n^2
x_1	A_1^1	$y_{(1,1)}$	$y_{(1,2)}$	...	$y_{(1,n)}$
	A_2^1	$y_{(2,1)}$	$y_{(2,2)}$	...	$y_{(2,n)}$
	$\vdots$	$\vdots$	$\vdots$		$\vdots$
	A_m^1	$y_{(m,1)}$	$y_{(m,2)}$	...	$y_{(m,n)}$

From the reasons mentioned above, all these things make it clear that SRIMs method is a special case of simplified fuzzy reasoning method. However, it follows from (1.59) that although, the number of rules of SIRMs method is $\sum_{i=1}^{n} m_i$ to realize the result of SIRMs method, the number of the rules of simplified fuzzy reasoning method of (1.60) is $M = \prod_{i=1}^{n} m_i$ and thus, too many rules are required in simplified fuzzy reasoning method.

- Conversion to SIRMs method from simplified fuzzy reasoning method in general case

As is shown in the previous section, when rules of simplified fuzzy reasoning method fulfill the condition of Theorem 1.3, simplified fuzzy reasoning method can be transformed into SIRMs method. However, generally, simplified fuzzy reasoning method cannot be transformed into SIRMs method. Therefore, we consider the rules of SIRMs method which realizes supremum and infimum of the reasoning results of simplified fuzzy reasoning method.

We describe the rules of SIRMs method which realizes supremum and infimum of the reasoning method rules of simplified fuzzy reasoning method are given in table form, and, generally, conversion to SIRMs method is impossible. However, the rules of SIRMs method which realize the minimum and maximum results of simplified fuzzy reasoning method can be generated.

Now, when the rules of simplified fuzzy reasoning method are given in table form of Table 8, rule modules of SIRMs method which realize the minimum and maximum of the reasoning results by simplified fuzzy reasoning method can be given as follows [210].

The setting method obtains rule modules rules- 1, 2 of SIRMs reasoning method by taking min $(= \wedge)$ to each row and each column of Table 8.

$$\text{Rules 1} = \begin{cases} x_1 = A_1^1 \rightarrow y_1 = \bigwedge_{i=1}^{n} y_{(1,i)} \\ \vdots \\ x_1 = A_m^1 \rightarrow y_1 = \bigwedge_{i=1}^{n} y_{(m,i)} \end{cases} \tag{1.75}$$

$$\text{Rules 2} = \begin{cases} x_2 = A_1^2 \rightarrow y_2 = \wedge_{i=1}^{m} y_{(i,1)} \\ \vdots \\ x_2 = A_n^2 \rightarrow y_2 = \wedge_{i=1}^{m} y_{(i,n)}. \end{cases}$$

Similarly, the following rule modules are obtained by taking max$(= V)$ to each row and each column of Table 8.

$$
\text{Rules } 1 = \begin{cases} x_1 = A_1^1 \rightarrow y_1 = \vee_{i=1}^n y_{(1,i)} \\ \quad \vdots \\ x_1 = A_m^1 \rightarrow y_1 = \vee_{i=1}^n y_{(m,i)} \end{cases} \tag{1.76}
$$

$$
\text{Rules } 2 = \begin{cases} x_2 = A_1^2 \rightarrow y_2 = \vee_{i=1}^m y_{(i,1)} \\ \quad \vdots \\ x_2 = A_n^2 \rightarrow y_2 = \vee_{i=1}^m y_{(i,n)}. \end{cases}
$$

Thus, it turns out that the inference result of two kinds of rule modules (1.75) and (1.76) of SIRMs method taking min and max is equal to, respectively, the minimum and maximum of inference results of simplified fuzzy reasoning method of Tale 8.

When the rules of simplified fuzzy reasoning method are given in Table 9, the rule modules Rules-1, 2 of SIRMs method which realizes minimum of inference results of simplified fuzzy reasoning method of Table 9 can be obtained by taking min($= \wedge$) to each row and each column of Table 9 according to the input items and

$$
\text{Rules } 1 = \begin{cases} x_1 = A_1^1 \rightarrow y_1 = 1\grave{\imath}\ 2\grave{\imath}\ 3 = 1 \\ x_1 = A_2^1 \rightarrow y_1 = 1.5\grave{\imath}\ 2.5\grave{\imath}\ 3.5 = 1.5 \\ x_1 = A_3^1 \rightarrow y_1 = 1\grave{\imath}\ 2\grave{\imath}\ 3 = 1 \end{cases} \tag{1.77}
$$

$$
\text{Rules } 2 = \begin{cases} x_2 = A_1^2 \rightarrow y_2 = 1\grave{\imath}\ 1.5\grave{\imath}\ 1 = 1 \\ x_2 = A_2^2 \rightarrow y_2 = 2\grave{\imath}\ 2.5\grave{\imath}\ 2 = 2 \cdot . \\ x_2 = A_3^2 \rightarrow y_2 = 3\grave{\imath}\ 3.5\grave{\imath}\ 3 = 3 \end{cases}
$$

Similarly, by taking max ($=$ V) to each row and each column, rule modules of (1.78) are obtained and maximum of inference results of Table 9 is realized.

$$
\text{Rules } 1 = \begin{cases} x_1 = A_1^1 \rightarrow y_1 = 1\hat{e}\ 2\hat{e}\ 3 = 3 \\ x_1 = A_2^1 \rightarrow y_1 = 1.5\hat{e}\ 2.5\hat{e}\ 3.5 = 3.5 \\ x_1 = A_3^1 \rightarrow y_1 = 1\hat{e}\ 2\hat{e}\ 3 = 3 \end{cases} \tag{1.78}
$$

$$\text{Rules } 2 = \begin{cases} x_2 = A_1^2 \to y_2 = 1 \hat{e} \ 1.5 \hat{e} \ 1 = 1.5 \\ x_2 = A_2^2 \to y_2 = 2 \hat{e} \ 2.5 \hat{e} \ 2 = 2.5 \\ x_2 = A_3^2 \to y_2 = 3 \hat{e} \ 3.5 \hat{e} \ 3 = 3.5 \end{cases}$$

TABLE 9   Examples of rules of simplified fuzzy reasoning method

		x_2		
		A_1^2	A_2^2	A_3^2
x_1	A_1^1	1	2	3
	A_2^1	1.5	2.5	3.5
	A_3^1	1	2	3

Therefore, we have the following theorem:

Theorem 1.4 [210] The inference result of SIRMS method, whose rule modules are obtained by taking min or max to each row for each column of the rules of simplified fuzzy reasoning method, are equal to the inference result of simplified fuzzy reasoning method using spremum or infimum, respectively.

Simplified fuzzy reasoning method, which is a special case of T-S reasoning method, is currently mostly used. Therefore, although, SIRMs method is also the special case of simplified fuzzy reasoning method, SIRMs method can be expected that the method can be also used.

1.10   SOME PROPERTIES OF COMPOSITIONAL RULE OF INFERENCE

In sections 1.3–1.8, we have extensively used the method of compositional rule of inference. In this section, following Fullr and Zimmermann and Fullr and Werners [74], we show two very important features of the compositional rule of inference under triangular norms.

We prove that:

(i)   If a t-norm defining a composition and a membership function of an observation are continuous, then the conclusion depends continuously on the observation.

(ii)   If a t-norm and a membership function of the relation are continuous, then the observation has a continuous membership function. We consider the compositional rule of inference with different observations P and P':

Observation:	X has property P
Relation:	X and Y are in relation R
Conclusion:	Y has property Q

Observation   X has property P'
Relation   X and Y are in relation R

Conclusion: Y has property Q'.

According to Zadeh's compositional rule of inference.

Q and Q' are computed as:

$$Q = P \circ R, \ Q' = P' \circ R,$$

That is:

$$\mu_Q(y) = \sup_{x \in R} T\left(\mu_p(x), \mu_R(x,y)\right) \quad \mu_{Q'}(y) = \sup_{x \in R} T\left(\mu_{p'}(x), \mu_R(x,y)\right).$$

The following theorem shows that when the observations are close to each other in the metric D, then there can be only small deviation in the membership functions of the conclusion.

Theorem 1.5 Let $\delta \geq 0$ and T be a continuous triangular norm, and let P, P' be fuzzy intervals. If D(P, P') $< \ \delta$ then:

$$\sup_{x \in R} \ \mu_Q(y) - \mu_{Q'}(y) \leq \omega_T \ (\max \{ \ \omega_p(\delta), \ \omega_{p'}(\delta) \}).$$

where $\omega_p(\delta)$ and $\omega_{p'}(\delta)$ denotes the modulus of continuity of P and P' at δ.

It should be noted that the stability property of the conclusion Q with respect to small changes in the membership function of the observation P in the compositional rule of inference scheme is independent from the relation R (its membership function can be discontinuous). Since, the membership function of the conclusion in the compositional rule of inference can have unbounded support, it is possible that the maximal distance between the α - level sets of Q and Q' is infinite but their membership grades are arbitrarily close to each other.

The following theorem establishes the continuity property of the conclusion in the compositional rule of inference scheme:

Theorem 1.6 Let R be continuous fuzzy relation and let T be a continuous T-norm. Then Q is continuous and

$$\omega_Q\left(\delta \leq \omega_T\left(\omega_R(\delta)\right)\right)$$

for each $\delta > 0$.

From Theorem 1.6, it follows that the continuity property of the membership function of the conclusion Q in the compositional rule of inference scheme is independent from the observation P (its membership function can be discontinuous). The next theorem shows that the stability property of the conclusion under small changes in the membership function of the observation holds in the discrete case, too.

Theorem 1.7 Let T be a continuous t-norm. If the observation P and the relation matrix R are finite, then:

$$H(Q, Q') \leq \omega_T (H (P, P')),$$

where H denotes the Hamming distance and the conclusions Q and Q' are computed as

$$\mu_Q(y_i) = \max_{i=1,\cdots,m} T(\mu_P(x_i), \mu_R(x_i, y_i)),$$

$$\mu_{Q'}(y_i) = \max_{i=1,\cdots,m} T(\mu_{P'}(x_i), \mu_R(x_i, y_i)),$$

for i = 1,..., n, supp (μ_Q)= supp $(\mu_{Q'})$= { $y_1,...,y_n$} and supp (μ_P)= supp $(\mu_{P'})$= $\{x_1,...,x_m\}$.

It should be noted that in case of T(u, v) = min {u,v} yields:

$$H(Q, Q') \leq H(P, P').$$

Theorems 1.5 and 1.6 can be easily extended to the compositional rule of inference with several relations:

Observation: X has property P
Relation 1: X and Y are in relation

.
.
.
.
.

Relation m: X and Y are relation W_m

Conclusion: Y has property Q

Observation: X has property P'
Relation 1: X and Y are in relation W_l

t
.
.
.
.

Relation m: X and Y are relation W_m

Conclusion: Y has property Q'.

According to Zadeh's compositiona rule of inference, Q and Q' are computed by sup-T composition as follows:

$$Q = \bigcap_{i=1}^{m} P \circ W_i \quad \text{and} \, Q' \, \bigcap_{i=1}^{m} P' \circ W_i \,. \tag{1.79}$$

Generalizing Theorems 1.5 and 1.6 about the case of single relation, we show that when the observations are close to each other in the metric D, then there can be only a small deviation in the membership functions of the conclusion even if we have several relations.

Theorem 1.8 Let $\delta \geq 0$ and T be a continuous triangular norm and let P, P' be continuous fuzzy intervals. If:

$$D(P, P') \leq \delta$$

then

$$sup_{y \in R} | \mu_Q(y) - \mu_Q(y)| \leq (\omega_T (\max \{ \omega_P (\delta), \omega_P (\delta)\})$$

where Q and Q' are computed by (1.79).

In the following theorem, we establish the continuity property of the conclusion under continuous fuzzy relation and continuous t-norm T.

Theorem 1.9 Let W_i be continuous fuzzy relation, $i = 1, \ldots, m$, and let T be a continuous t-norm. Then Q is continuous and

$$\omega_Q (\delta) \leq (\omega_T (\omega(\delta)) \text{ for each } \delta > 0,$$

where $\omega (\delta) = \max \{ \omega_{W_1} (\delta), \ldots, \omega_{W_m} (\omega(\delta))\}$.

The above theorem are also valid for multiple Fuzzy Reasoning (MFR) schemes:

Observation : P P'
Implication 1 : $P_1 \rightarrow Q_1$ $P'_1 \rightarrow Q'_1$

  ⋮   ⋮   ⋮

Implication m: $P_m \rightarrow Q_m$ $P'_m \rightarrow Q'_m$

Conclusion :   Q   Q'

where Q and Q' are computed by sup-T composition as follows:

$$Q = P \circ \bigcap_{i=1}^{m} P_i \rightarrow Q_i \quad Q' = P \circ \bigcap_{i=1}^{m} P'_i \rightarrow Q'_i$$

i.e.

$$\mu_Q (y) = \sup_{x \in R} T\big(\mu_P (x)\big) \quad \underset{i=1,...,m}{\min} \quad \mu P_i (x) \rightarrow \mu_{Qi} (y)$$

$$\mu_{Q'} (y) = \sup_{x \in R} T\big(\mu_{P'} (x)\big) \quad \underset{i=1,...,m}{\min} \quad \mu P_i' (x) \rightarrow \mu_{Q'i} (y)$$

Then the following theorems hold.

Theorem 1.10. Let $\delta \geq 0$, let T be a continuous triangular norm, let $P, P', P_i, P_i', Q_i, Q_i' = 1,...,m$, be fuzzy intervals and let $\rightarrow$ be a continous fuzzy implication operator. If
Then

$$\max \{D(P, P'), \ \max_{i=1,...1m} D(P_i, P_i'), \qquad \max_{i=1,...1m} D(Q_i, Q_i')\} \leq \delta$$

then

$$sup_{x \in R} \mid \mu_Q (y) - \mu_{Q'} (y) \mid \leq \mid \omega_T (\max \{ \omega (\delta), \omega \rightarrow (\omega(\delta))\}),$$

where

$$\omega(\delta) = \max\big\{\omega P_i (\delta), \omega P_i' (\delta), \omega Q_i (\delta), \omega Q_i' (\delta)\big\}$$

and $\omega \rightarrow$ denotes the modulas of continuity of the fuzzy implication operation.

Theorem 1.11. Let ' $\rightarrow$ ' be a continuous fuzzy implication, let $P, P', P_i, P_i', Q_i, Q_i'$, $i = 1,...,m$ be fuzzy intervals and let T be a continous t-norm. Then Q is continuous and

$$\omega_Q (\delta) \leq \omega_T (\omega \rightarrow (\omega(\delta))) \text{ for each } \delta \geq 0$$

where

$$\omega_Q (\delta) = \max\big\{\omega_{P_i} (\delta), \omega_{P_i'} (\delta), \omega_{Q_i} (\delta)\ \omega_{Q_i'} (\delta)\big\},$$

and $\omega \rightarrow$ denotes the modulas of continuity of the fuzzy implication operation.

From $\lim_{\delta \to \omega}(\delta) = 0$ and Theorem 1.10 it follows that

$$\big\|\mu_Q - \mu_{Q'}\big\|_\infty = \sup_y \big|\mu_Q (y) - \mu_{Q'} (y)\big| \rightarrow 0$$

Whenever $D(P, P') \to 0, D(P_i, P_i') \to 0$, and $D(Q_i, Q_i') \to 0, i = 1,..., m$, which means the stability of the conclusion under small changes of the membership function of the observation and rules guarantees that small rounding errors of digital computation and small errors of measurement of the input data can cause only a small deviation in the conclusion, i.e. every successive approximation method can be applied to the computation of the linguistic approximation of the exact conclusion.

1.11 COMPUTATION OF COMPOSITIONAL RULE OF INFERENCE UNDER T-NORMS

In approximate reasoning, there are several kinds of inference rules, which deal with the problem of deduction of conclusion in an imprecise setting. An important problem is the (approximate) computation of the membership function of the conclusion in these schemes. Throughout this Section, we shall use $\phi-$ functions for the representation of linguistic terms in the compositional rule of inference [76].

Definition 1.8 A $\phi-$ function is defined by:

$$
\phi \ (x, a, b, c, d) = \begin{cases} 1 & \textit{if } b \ x \leq c, \\ \phi_1 \left(\frac{x-a}{b-c} \right) & \textit{if } a \leq x \leq b, a < b, \\ \phi_2 \left(\frac{x-a}{b-c} \right) & \textit{if } c \leq x \leq d, c < d, \\ 0 & \textit{otherwise.} \end{cases} \tag{1.80}
$$

where : [0,1] [0,1] is continuous, monotonically increasing function and ϕ_1 (0) = 0, $\phi_1 (1) = 1$; ϕ_2 : [0,1] [0,1] is continuous, monotonically decreasing function and ϕ_2 (0) = 1, ϕ_2 (1) = 0. So ϕ is a function which is 0 to the left of a, increases to 1 in]a, b[, is 1 in [b, c], decreases to 0 in]c, d[, and is 0 to the right of d (for the sake of simplicity, we do not consider the cases a = b or c = d).

It should be noted that ϕ can be considered as the membership function of the fuzzy interval $= (b, c, b - a, d - c)_{LR}$, with R(x) = ϕ_2 (x) and L(x) = ϕ_1 (1 - x).

Hellendoorn showed the closure property of the compositional rule of inference under supmin composition and presented exact calculation formulas for the membership function of the conclusion when both the observation and relation parts are given by S-, $\pi-$, or -function.

He proved the following theorem:

Theorem 1.12 In the compositional rule of inference under minimum norm:
Observation: X has property P
Relation: X and Y are in relation W

\--

Conclusion: Y has property Q

is true that, when $(x) = \phi(x;, a_1, a_2, a_3, a_4)$ and $\mu_W(x,y) = \phi(y - x; , b_1, b_2, b_3, b_4)$ then

$$\mu_Q(y) = \phi(y; a_1 + b_1, a_2 + b_2, a_3 + b_3, a_4 + b_4),$$

where the function ϕ is defined by (1.80).

In this section, following Fullér and Werners, and Fullér and Zimmermann, generalizing Hellendoorn's results, we derive exact calculation formulas for the compositional rule of inferce under triangular norms when both the observation and the part of the relation (rule) are given by concave $\phi-$-function, and the t-norm is Archimedean with a strictly convex additive generator function. The efficiency of this method stems from the fact that the distributions, involved in the relation and observation, are represented by a parameterized $\phi-$ function. The deduction process then consists of some simple computations performed on the parameters.

We consider the compositional rule of inference, where, the membership functions of P and W are defined by mean of a particular $\phi-$ function, and the membership function of the conclusion Q is defined by sup-T comcosition of P and W.

$$Q(y) = (P \circ W)(y) = \sup{}_x T(P(x), W(x, y)), y \in R.$$

The following theorem presents an efficient method for the exact computation of the membership function of the conclusion.

Theorem 1.13 [76] Let T be an Archimedean t-norm with additive generator f and let $P(x) = \phi(x; a, b, c, d)$ and $W(x, y) = \phi(y - x; a + u, b + u, c + v, d + v)$. If ϕ_1 and ϕ_2 are twice differentiable concave functions, and f is a twice differentiable strictly convex function, then:

$$Q(y) = \begin{cases} 1 & \text{if } 2b + u \leq y \leq 2c + v \\ f^{[-1]}\left(2f\left(\phi_1\left[\dfrac{y - 2a - u}{2(b - a)}\right]\right)\right) & \text{if } 2a + u \leq y \leq 2c + u \\ f^{[-1]}\left(2f\left(\phi_1\left[\dfrac{y - 2a - u}{2(b - a)}\right]\right)\right) & \text{if } 2c + v \leq y \leq 2d + v \\ 0 & \text{otherwise}. \end{cases}$$

It should be noted that we have calculated the membership function of Q under the assumption that the left and right spreads of P, do not differ from the left and right spreads of W (the lengths of their tops can be different). To determine the exact membership function of Q in the general case: $P(x) = \phi(x; a_1, a_2, a_3, a_4,)$ and $W(x, y) = \phi(y - x; b_1, b_2, b_3, b_4,)$ can be very different to represent.

Using Theorem 1.13, we compute the exact membership function of the conclusion Q in the case of Yager's, Dombi's, and Hamacher's parametrized t-norm.

Let us consider the following scheme:

$P(x) = \phi \ (x; a, b, c, d)$

$W(y, x) = \phi \ (y - x; a + u, b + u, c + v, d + v)$

$Q(y) = (P \ o \ W) \ (y)$

Denoting

$$\sigma := \frac{y - 2a - u}{2(b - a)} \qquad \theta: \frac{y - 2c - v}{2(d - c)} \quad ,$$

We get the following formulas for the membership function of the conclusion Q.

- Yager's t-norm with $p > 1$. Here

$$T(x, y) = 1 - \min \{1, \ \sqrt[p]{(1 = x)^p + (1 = y)^p} \ \}$$

with generator $f(t) = (1-t)^p$, and

$$Q(y) = \begin{cases} 1 - \sqrt[p]{2}\left(1 - \phi_1(\sigma)\right) & \text{if } 0 < \sigma < \phi_1^{-1}\left(2^{-\frac{1}{p}}\right) \\ 1 & \text{if } 2b + u \le y \le 2c + v \\ 1 - \sqrt[p]{2}\left(1 - \phi_2(\theta)\right) & \text{if } 0 < \theta < \phi_2^{-1}\left(1 - 2^{\frac{1}{p}}\right) \end{cases} \qquad (1.81)$$

- Hamacher's t-norm with $p \le 2$ Here

$$T(x, y) = \frac{xy}{p + (1 - p)(x + y - xy)}$$

with generator

$$f(t) = \ln \frac{p + (1 - p)t}{t}$$

and

$$Q(y) = \begin{cases} \dfrac{p}{\tau_1^2 - 1 + p} & \text{if } 0 < \sigma < 1, \\[2mm] 1 & \text{if } 2b + u \leq y \leq 2c + v \\[2mm] \dfrac{p}{\tau_2^2 - 1 + p} & \text{if } 0 < \theta < 1, \end{cases}$$

where

$$\tau_1 = \frac{p + (1-p)\phi_1(\sigma)}{\phi_1(\sigma)}, \quad \tau_2 = \frac{p + (1-p)\phi_2(\sigma)}{\phi_2(\sigma)}$$

•   Domb's t-norm with $p > 1$.
Here:

$$T(x,y) = \frac{1}{1 + \sqrt[p]{(\frac{1}{x} - 1)^p + (\frac{1}{y} - 1)^p}}$$

With additive generator

$$f(t) = ((1/t - 1)^p ,$$

and

$$Q(y) = \begin{cases} \dfrac{1}{1 + 2^{1/p_{\tau_3}}} & \text{if } 0 < \sigma < 1, \\[2mm] 1 & \text{if } 2b + u \leq y \leq 2c + v, \\[2mm] \dfrac{1}{1 + 2^{1/p_{\tau_4}}} & \text{if } 0 < \theta < 1, \end{cases}$$

where

$$\tau_3 = \frac{1}{\phi_1(\sigma)} - 1, \quad \tau_4 = \frac{1}{\phi_2(\sigma)} - 1.$$

Example 1.24 We illustrate the above result by the following example [76]:

x is close to 3 φ(x; 1, 3, 4, 7)

x and y are approximately equal φ(y - x; -2, 0, 0, 3)

---

y is more or less close to [3, 4] Q(y)

where

$$
Q(y) = \begin{cases}
1 & \text{if } 2b+ u\leq\ y\leq\ 2c+ v \\
f^{[-1]}\left(2f(\varphi_1[\dfrac{y-2a-u}{2(b-a)}])\right) & \text{if } 2a+ u\leq\ y\leq\ 2b+ v \\
f^{[-1]}\left(2f(\varphi_2[\dfrac{y-2c-v}{2(d-c)}])\right) & \text{if } 2c+ u\leq\ y\leq\ 2d+ v \\
0 & \text{otherwise .}
\end{cases}
$$

We use the membership function ϕ (y - x; -2, 0, 0, 3) to describe "x and y are approximately equal". This means that the membership degree is one, if x and y are equal in the classical sense. If y - x > 2 or x - y > 3, then the degree of membership is 0. The conclusion Q has been called "y is more of less close to [3, 4]", because P(t) = Q(t) = 1, when t ∈ [3,4] and P(t) < Q(t) otherwise. Figure 31, 32, and 33 show results at different situations.

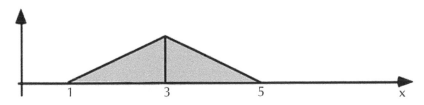

FIGURE 31 "x is close to [3, 4]."

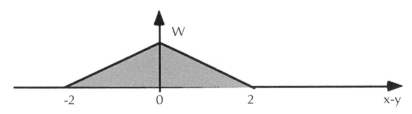

FIGURE 32 "x and y are approximately equal."

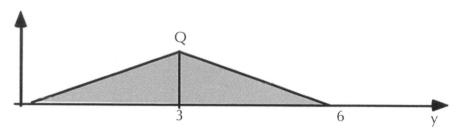

FIGURE 33   "y is more or less close to [3, 4]", Yager's t-norm.

1.12   INVERSE APPROXIMATE REASONING

In this section, we consider the problem as given the conclusion of a fuzzy rule, determine the "best" data (input), that would produce the given conclusion. To solve this problem, we consider an approach based on generalized Modus Tollens [69].

Let us consider the following rule:

$$\text{If } x = A \text{ then } y = A \tag{1.82}$$

where A(B) is a fuzzy subset of a universe of discourse U (V). Given data on X, say X = A' also a fuzzy subset of U, and employing some method of approximating reasoning, we conclude that Y = B' a fuzzy subset of V. Now given B', let $\Omega(B')$ be the set of all fuzzy subsets of A' of U so that given X = A', the rule in Equation (1.82), and some specific method of approximating reasoning, we always conclude that Y = B'. Our problem is to choose, in some sense a "best" member (or "best" members) of This defines an inverse mapping, which we call inverse approximate reasoning from fuzzy subsets of V into fuzzy subsets of U (assuming $\Omega(B')$ is nonempty). We make this more precise in the next section where we use the generalized modus ponens in the forward approximate reasoning (mapping A' to B') and investigate the generalized modus tollens for inverse approximating reasoning.

We consider using the generalized modus tollens to pick out a "best" element $\Omega(Be)$ in given Y = B' [69].

1.12.1   STATEMENT OF THE PROBLEM AND THE BASIC APPROACH TO SOLVE THE PROBLEM

We assume that all fuzzy sets are discrete because this is necessary for machine implication of the method.

Let $U = \{u_1, u_2, ..., u_m\}$, $V = \{v_1, v_2, ..., v_n\}$ and   let   the   membership   value   of   A(B)   at $u_i(v_j)$ be a_i for $1 \le i \le m$ $(b_j \text{ for } 1 \le j \le n)$. Also   let   the   membership   value   of   A'(B')   be a_i' for $1 \le i \le m$ $(b_j' \text{ for } 1 \le j \le n)$. Set

$$a = \{(a_1, a_2, ..., a_m), \quad a' = (a_1', a_2', ..., a_m'), \quad b = (b_1, b_2, ...b_n) \; b' = (b_1', b_2', ..., b_n')\}$$

We model the implication of the rule in Equation (1.82) with an implication operator .

Let

$r_{ij} = I_1(a_i , b_j)$ for all i,j and define mn matrix M_1 to be $[r_{ij}]$.

We obtain b' from a' using the generalized modus ponens as follows:

$$b' = a' o M_1 .$$ (1.83)

where "o" is a max = (t-norm) composition.

Therefore:

$$b'_j = \max_{1 \le i \le m} (T_1(a'_i, r_{ij})),$$ (1.84)

for all j, where T_1 is a t-norm.

Computing b' from a' is called forward approximate reasoning. Let $F(U)$ and $F(V)$ denote all fuzzy subsets of U and V, respectively. Forward approximate reasoning is a mapping from $F(U)$ into $F(V)$. Denote this mapping by ϕ (defined by I_1 and T_1).

Then:

$\phi : F(U) \rightarrow F(V)$ is specified by Equation (1.84)

We write:

$$\phi(a') = b', or \ \phi(A') = B'$$

Let us consider the generalized modus tollens. Using the rule given in Equation (1.82) and given the data Y = B* (a fuzzy subset of V) we conclude X = A* (a fuzzy subset of U).

Equivalently, we can state as follows:

If Y = not (B), then X = not (A) (1.85)

with data Y = B* and conclusion X = A*. The membership values of not(B) (not(A)) are $1-b_j(1-a_j)$ at $v_j(u_i)$ To evaluate the rule in Equation (1.85), we model the implication using some implication operator I_2. Let $s_{ij} = I_2(1-b_j, 1-a_j)$ for $1 \le i \le n$ $1 \le j \le m$ and let matrix M_2 be $[s_{ij}]$. Consider the membership values of A^* (B^* as $a_i^*(b_j^*)$ and,

$$a^* = (a_1^*, a_2^*, ..., a_m^*), b^* = (b_1^*, b_2^*, ..., b_n^*).$$

We obtain   from   as follows:

$$a^* = b^* \text{ o } M_2 \qquad\qquad (1.86)$$

for "o" a max-(t-norm) composition.

Therefore:

$$a_j^* = \max_{1 \le i \le m} (T_2(b_i^*, s_{ij})) \qquad\qquad (1.87)$$

for $1 \le j \le m$ and $t - \text{norm } T_2$

Computing a^* from b^* is called inverse approximate reasoning. It is a mapping from $F(V)$ into $F(U)$. Denote this mapping by j (defined by I_2, T_2). Then $j: F(V) \to F(U)$ and we write

$$j(b^*) = a^* \text{ or } j(B^*) = A^*.$$

We want to know if ϕ and j can be inverses of each other. Since neither ϕ nor j is usually one-to-one, these cannot have inverse in the usual sense. So we say that j is a pseudo-inverse (p-inverse) of ϕ;

$$\text{if } (\phi \text{ o } j \text{ o } \phi)(a') = b' \text{ whenever } \phi(a') = b' \text{ and } \phi \qquad\qquad (1.88)$$

is a pseudo-inverse (p-inverse) of j,

$$\text{if } (j \text{ o } \phi \text{ o } j)(b') = a', \text{ whenever } j(b') = a' \qquad\qquad (1.89)$$

In other words, j is a p-inverse of ϕ

$$\text{if } (J o \varnothing)(a') \in \varnothing^{-1}(a'), \qquad\qquad (1.90)$$

and $\varnothing$ is a p-inverse of J;

$$\text{if} \left(\phi \circ j\right)\left(b'\right) \in j^{-1}\left(b'\right) \qquad (1.91)$$

So, given A, B, I_1, T_1, I_2, T_2 if Eq. (1.90) holds for a given A', then j(B') would be a candidate for a "best" member of $\Omega(B')$. The following theorem and corollaries are concerned with when Eq. (1.90) will hold and when Eq. (1.90) is not true.

We have to consider some reasonable conditions on I_1 and I_2 because just any mapping from $[0, 1]^2$ into $[0, 1]$ would not be an acceptable implication operator. For example, if $I_k(a, b) = 1$ for all a, b in $[0, 1]$ for k=1, 2, then j is a p-inverse of ϕ but we would not employ such an I.

For the rest of this section we consider that $T_1 = T_2 = T$ and $I_1 = I_2 = I$ and I is generated by a t-norm or a t-conorm. I is a S-implication if $I(a, b) = S(1-a, b)$ for a t-conorm S.

I is a R-implication if $I(a, b) = \sup\left\{c \in [0,1] : T(a, c) \le b\right\}$. For the rest of this section I either a S-implication or a R-implication.

We may assume that $a_1 \le a_2 \le .. \le a_m$ and $b_1 \le b_2 \le .. \le b_n$ for otherwise we can renumber the elements in U and/or V so that these inequalities are true. Also, by associativity we can extend all t-norms to 3 and 4 arguments. That is, T (a, b, c, d) = T (a, T (b, c, d)) = T (T (a, b, c, d)) etc.

Theorem 1.14. [69] j is a p-inverse of ϕ if and only if

$$\max_k T\left(a'_k, r_{kn}, s_{n1}, r_{1j}\right) = \max_k T\left(a'_k, r_{kj}\right), \qquad (1.92)$$

for all j.

Corollary 1.1. If A, B, and A' are all normalized, then j is a p-inverse of ϕ if and only if

$$r_{1j} = \max_k T\left(a'_k, r_{kj}\right) \qquad (1.93)$$

for all j.

For the rest of this section we assume that A, B, and A' are normalized.

Corollary 1.2. If for some j we have $T(a'_1, r_{1j}) < r_{1j}$ and $r_{2j} < r_{1j}$ then j is not a p-inverse of ϕ

We expect that there is some j for $r_{2j} < r_{1j}$. If $a'_1 < r_{1j}$ for a j for which $r_{2j} < r_{1j}$, then $T(a'_1 < r_{1j}) \le a'_1 < r_{1j}$ and j is not a p-inverse of ϕ. For example, $a'_1 = 0$ always give $T(a'_1, r_{1j}) = 0 < r_{1j}$ if $r_{1j} > 0$

Corollary 1.3.

a. If $r_{2j} < r_{1j}$ for some j, then for this j $b'_j = r_{1j}$ if and only if $T(a'_1, r_{1j}) = r_{1j}$.

b. If $r_{2j} = r_{1j} > r_{3j}$ for some j then for this j, $b'_j = r_{1j}$ if and only if $T(a'_i, r_{1j}) = r_{1j}$ for $i = 1$ or 2.

Corollary 1.3 can be expanded to: if $r_{1j} = r_{2j} = r_{3j} > r_{4j}$ for some j, then $b'_j = r_{1j}$ if and only if $T(a'_k, r_{kj}) = r_{kj}$ for k = 1, 2, or 3 etc.

Corollary 1.3 may be used to verify that j is a p-inverse of ϕ . For example, if $a'_1 = 1$, then $T(a'_1, r_{1j}) = r_{1j}$ and from Corollary 1.3 we have that j is a p-inverse of ϕ . Also, if T = min and (i) $a'_1 \geq r_{1j}$ whenever $r_{2j} < r_{1j}$ (iii) $a'_1 \geq r_{1j}$ or $a'_2 \geq r_{2j}$ whenever $r_{2j} = r_{1j} \geq r_{3j}$ etc. guarantees that j is a p-inverse of ϕ .

In this section we investigate the use of the generalized modus tollens for inverse approximate reasoning. That is, we consider the generalized modus tollens (GMT) as a pseudo-inverse of the generalized modus ponens (GMP). We give a necessary and sufficient condition for the GMT to be a pseudo-inverse of the GMP for arbitrary discrete fuzzy sets and when the discrete fuzzy sets are normalized. We also present sufficient conditions for the GMT to be, and not to be, a pseudo-inverse of GMP for normalized discrete fuzzy sets.

Considering the rule: If X = A, then Y = B, X = A' given, with conclusion Y = B', we might think that the closer A' is to A the more likely the GMT, given Y = B', can be used to produce something near X = A'. However, the opposite is true as shown by Corollaries 1.2 and 1.3. For example, we assumed that $a_1 \leq a_2 \leq, ..., \leq a_m$ where the $a'_j s$ are the membership values of discrete A and let $a'_i, 1 \leq i \leq m$ be the membership values of A'. Usually we would expect a_1 to be zero, so assume that $a_1 = 0$· Corollaries 1.2 and 1.3 show that: (1) if $a'_1 < 1$, then the GMT is not a pseudo-inverse of the GMP; and (2) if $a'_1 = 1$ the GMT is a pseudo-inverse of the GMP. So, with $a_1 = 0$ we need the complete opposite in the data $(a'_1 = 1)$ to obtain the GMT a pseudo-inverse of the GMP.

1.13   INTERPOLATIVE FUZZY REASONING

In this section, we consider an approximate fuzzy reasoning method based on interpolation in the vague environment of the fuzzy rule base. The major advantage of the propoesed method is its simplicity. It can be implemented in a simple and quick manner in practical situations [124].

The interpolative fuzzy reasoning essential deals with vague environment. The vague environment is described by the linguistic terms and the fuzzy partitions of the primary fuzzy set can be implemented by scaling functions. The fuzzy reasoning is replaced by classical interpolation (also See Section 1.2). The concept of vague environment is handled using the similarity or indistinguishability of the elements. Two values in the vague environment are ε-distinguishable if their distance is greater than ε. The distances in vague environment are weighted distances.

The weighting factor or function is called scaling function (factor).

Two values in the vague environment X are ε-distinguishable if:

$$\varepsilon > \delta, (x_1, x_2) = |\int_{x_2}^{x_1} s(x)\,dx| \qquad (1.94)$$

where $\delta_x (x_1, x_2)$ is the vague distance of the values x_1, x_2 and $s(x)$ is the scaling function on X. For finding connections between fuzzy sets and a vague environment, the membership $\mu_A(x)$ can be introduced as a level of similarity a to x, as the degree to which x is distinguishable to a. The -cuts of the fuzzy set $\mu_A(x)$ are the sets which contain the elements those arc (1 - α indistinguishable from a (See Figure 34):

$$\delta_s(a, b) \le 1 - \alpha, \mu_A(x) = 1 - \min\{\delta_s(a, b), 1\} = 1 - \min\left\{\left|\int_a^b s(x)\,dx\right|, 1\right\} \quad (1.95)$$

As shown in Figure 34, the vague distance of points a and b $\delta_s(a, b)$ is the Disconsistency Measure (S_D) of the fuzzy sets A and B (where B is a singleton):

$$S_D = 1 - \sup_{x \in X} \mu_{A \cap B} (x) = \delta_s(a, b) \text{ if } \delta_s(a, b) \in [0, 1] \qquad (1.96)$$

where

is the min t-norm $\mu_{A \cap B} (x) = \min\left[\mu_A(x), \mu_B(x) \right] \forall x \in X$

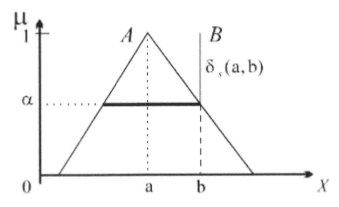

FIGURE 34   The α-cut of $_A$(x) contains the elements that are (1-α)-indistinguishable from a

From the viewpoint of fuzzy reasoning and fuzzy rule bases, where an observation fuzzy set is needed to be compared to rule antecedents built up member fuzzy sets (linguistic terms) of the antecedent fuzzy partitions (1.95) and (1.96) means that the disconsistency measures between member fuzzy sets of a fuzzy partition and a singleton, can be calculated as vague distances of points in the vague environment of the fuzzy partition. The main difference between the disconsistency measure and the vague distance is, that the vague distance is a value in the range of , while the disconsistency measure is limited to [0, 1].

The vague environment is described by its scaling function. For generating a vague environment of a fuzzy partition, an appropriate scaling function is needed to be find, which describes the shapes of all the terms in the fuzzy partition.

A fuzzy partition can be characterized by a single vague environment if and only if the membership function of the terms fulfill the following requirement:

$$sx = |\mu'(x)| = |\frac{d\mu}{dx}| \text{ exists iff min } \{\mu_i(x), \mu_j(x)\} > 0 \Rightarrow |\mu'_i(x)| = |\mu'_j(x)|, \quad (1.97)$$

$\forall i, j \in I$, where $s(x)$ is the vague environment (for example, See Figure 35 and Figure 36).

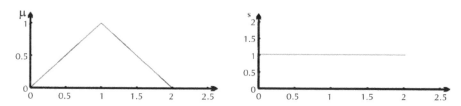

FIGURE 35   A fuzzy set and its scaling function.

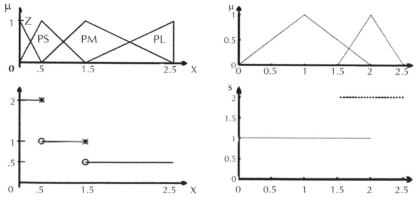

FIGURE 36   A fuzzy partition and its scaling function.

In general condition, Equation 1.97 is not fulfilled. We need to describe all fuzzy sets of the fuzzy partition with one "universal" scaling function. For this task, the concept of approximate scaling function is proposed. An approximation of the scaling functions describes the terms of the fuzzy partition separately. A partition built-up triangular fuzzy set is shown in Figure 37. The corresponding approximate scaling functions are shown in Figure 38 (linear interpolation) and in Figure 39 (non-linear interpolation).

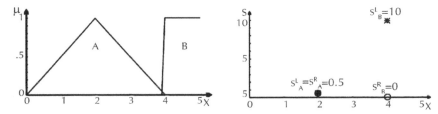

FIGURE 37 Fuzzy partitions built up triangular fuzzy sets can be characterized by triples, by the values of the left S^L and the right S^R scaling factors and the cores.

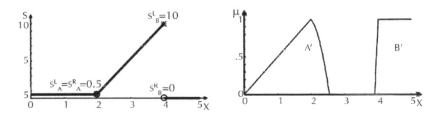

FIGURE 38 Linearly interpolated scaling function of the fuzzy partition shown on Figure 37 and the partition as the approximate scaling function describes it (A', B')

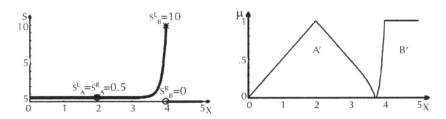

FIGURE 39 Approximate scaling function generated by non-linear interpolation of the fuzzy partition shown on Figure 37, and the partition as the approximate scaling function describes it (A',B').

If the vague environment of a fuzzy partition (the scaling function or the approximate scaling function) exists, the member sets of the fuzzy partition can be characterized by points in the vague environment. These points are characterizing the cores of the fuzzy terms, while the membership functions are described by the scaling function itself. If all the vague environments of the antecedent and consequent universes of the fuzzy rule base are exist, all the primary fuzzy sets (linguistic terms) built-up the fuzzy rule base can be characterized by points in their vague environment. Therefore the fuzzy rules (built-up from the primary fuzzy sets) can be characterized by points in the vague environment of the fuzzy rule base too. This case the approximate fuzzy reasoning can be handled as a classical interpolation task. Applying the concept of vague environment (the distances of points are weighted distances), any interpolation, extrapolation, or regression methods can be adapted very simply for approximate fuzzy reasoning (also See Section 1.2).

Because of its simple multidimensional applicability, for interpolation-based fuzzy reasoning in this section, the adaptation of the Shepard operator based interpolation is suggested. Beside the existing deep application oriented investigation of the Shepard operator, it is also successfully applied in the Koczy–Hirota fuzzy interpolation.

The Shepard interpolation method for arbitrarily placed bivariate data was introduced as follows:

$$
S_0(f, x, y) = \begin{cases} f_k & if\,(x, y) = (x_k, y_k) \quad for\,some\,k, \\ \left(\sum_{k=0}^{n} f(x_k, y_k)/d_k^{\lambda}\right) \bigg/ \left(\sum_{k=0}^{n} 1/d_k^{\lambda}\right) & otherwise, \end{cases} \tag{1.98}
$$

where measurement points x_k, $y_k\,(k \in [0, n])$ are irregularly spaced on the domain of $f \in R^2 \rightarrow R$, $\lambda > 0$, and $d_k = [(x - x_k)^2\,(y - y_k)^2]^{1/2}$. This function can be typically used when a surface model is required to interpolate scattered spatial measurements.

The adaptation of the Shepard interpolation method for interpolation-based fuzzy reasoning in the vague environment of the fuzzy rule base is straightforward by substituting the Euclidian distances with vague distances $\delta_{s,k}$:

$$
\delta_{s,k} = \delta_s(a_k, x) = \left[\sum_{i=1}^{m} \left(\int_{a_{k,j}}^{x_1} S_{x_i}(x_i)\,dx_i \right)^2 \right]^{1/2}, \tag{1.99}
$$

Where S_{x_i} is the ith scaling function of the m dimensional antecedent universe, x is the m dimensional crisp observation, and a_k are the cores of the m dimensional fuzzy rule antecedents A_k .

Thus, in case of singleton rule, consequents fuzzy rules :

$$\text{If } x_1 = A_{k,1} \text{ and } x_2 = A_{k,2} \text{ And } x_m = A_{k,m} \text{ Then } y = c_k \qquad (1.100)$$

By substituting (1.99) to (1.98) the conclusion of the interpolative fuzzy reasoning can be obtained as:

$$y(x) = \begin{cases} c_k & \text{if } x = a_k \quad \text{for some } k, \\ \left(\sum_{k=1}^{r} c_k \ / \ \delta_{s,k}^{\lambda} \right) \Big/ \left(\sum_{k=1}^{r} 1 / \delta_{s,k}^{\lambda} \right) & \text{otherwise.} \end{cases} \qquad (1.101)$$

The interpolative fuzzy reasoning (1.101) is extended to handle fuzzy conclusion by introducing the vague environment (scaling function) of the consequence universe. In this case, the fuzzy rules has the following form:

$$\text{If } x_1 = A_{k,1}, \ x_2 = A_{k,2} \text{ , and } x_m = A_{k,m} \text{ Then } y = B_k \qquad (1.102)$$

By introducing vague distances on the consequence universe:

$$\delta_s(b_k, y) = \left[\left(\int_{b_k}^{y} S_Y(y) \, dy \right)^2 \right]^{1/2}, \qquad (1.103)$$

where S_Y is the ith scaling function of the one dimensional consequent universe, b_k are the cores of the one dimensional fuzzy rule consequents B_k .

Introducing the first element of the one dimensional consequence universe b_0 ($Y: b_0 \leq y \quad \forall \ y \in Y$), based on (1.101) and (1.103) the desired one dimensional conclusion $y(x)$ is obtained as follows:

$$\delta_s\big(y(x), \ b_0\big) = \begin{cases} \delta_s(b_k, b_0) & \text{if } x = a_k \quad \text{for some } k, \\ \left(\sum_{k=1}^{r} \delta_s(b_k, b_0) / \delta_{s,k}^{\lambda} \right) \Big/ \left(\sum_{k=1}^{r} 1 / \delta_{s,k}^{\lambda} \right) & \text{otherwise.} \end{cases} \qquad (1.104)$$

A simple one-dimensional example for the approximate scaling function and the Shepard operator based interpolation (1.104) is introduced in Figure 40–43 [124].

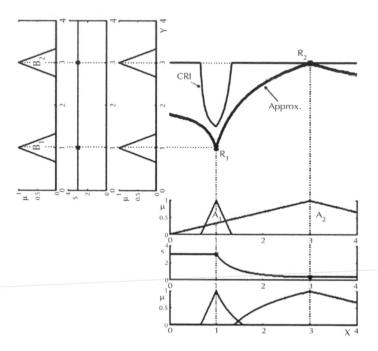

FIGURE 40   Interpolation of two fuzzy rules ($R_i: A_i \rightarrow B_i$) (See Figure 43 for notation).

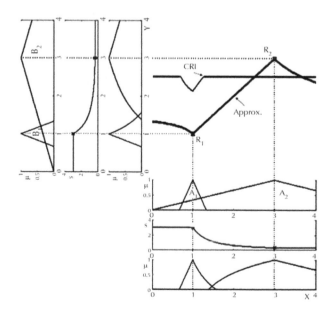

FIGURE 41   Interpolation of two fuzzy rules ($R_i: A_i \rightarrow B_i$) (See Figure 43 for notation).

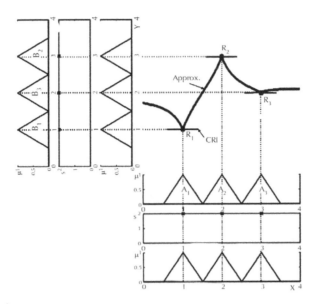

FIGURE 42 Interpolation of three fuzzy rules (R_i: $A_i \rightarrow B_i$) (See Figure 43 for notation).

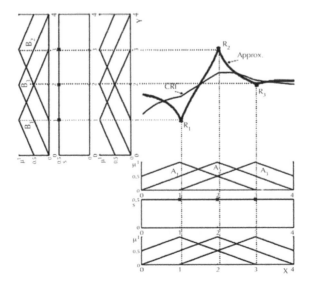

FIGURE 43 Interpolation of three fuzzy rules (R_i: $A_i \rightarrow B_i$) in the approximated vague environment of the fuzzy rule base, using the Shepard operator based interpolation 1.104 ($\lambda = 1$) (*Approx.*), and the min-max. The CRI with the centre of gravity defuzzification (CRI), where μ is the membership grade, and s is the scaling function.

For comparing the crisp conclusion of the interpolation-based fuzzy reasoning and the classical methods, the conclusion generated by the max-min compositional rule of inference (CRI) and the center of gravity defuzzification for the same rule base is also demonstrated on the example Figures (Figure 40–43).

Example 1.25 For demonstrating the simplicity of interpolation-based fuzzy reasoning, we consider a user adaptive information retrieval system [124].

In user adaptive information retrieval system, the user adaptivity is handled by combination of existing (off-line collected) human opinions (user models) in the function of their approximated similarity to the actual user opinions. The goal of the state-transition control is to estimate the "current state", the actual suitability of the existing user models. Based on the observations (inputs), the conclusion of the user feedback (the similarity of the user feedback to the existing user models SS_i for all the possible models $\forall i \in [1,N]$) and the previsous state S_i (estimation), the state transition rule base has to estimate the new state values, and the next approximation of the vector of the suitability of the existing user models.

The heuristic, we consider is very simple. If we already find a suitable model (S_i) and the user feedback is still supporting it (SS_i), we have to keep it even if the user feedback begins to support some other models too. If there are no suitable models but the user feedback begins to support one, we have to pick it at once. In case of interpolation-based fuzzy reasoning, the above heuristic can be simply implemented by the following state transition rule base.

For the ith state variable S_i, i $\in$ [1,N] of the state vector S:

If S_i = One	and SS_i = One	Then S_i = One	(a)
If S_i = Zero	and SS_i = Zero	Then S_i = Zero	(b)
If S_i = One	and SS_i = Zero		(c)

and SS_k = Zero Then S_i = One, $\forall k \in [1,N], k \neq i$

If S_i = Zero	and SS_i = One	(d)

and S_k = Zero and SS_k = Zero   Then S_i = One $\forall k \in [1,N], k \neq i$

If S_i= Zero	and SS_i = One	(e)

And S_k = One   and SS_k = One   Then S_i = Zero $\exists k \in [1,N], k \neq i$ (1.105)

where SS_i is the similarity of the user feedback to the ith existing user model $\forall i \in [1,N]$ and N is the number of known user models (state variables). The structure of the state-transition rules is similar for all the state variables. Zero and One are linguistic labels of fuzzy sets (linguistic terms) representing high and low similarity. The interpretations of the Zero and One fuzzy sets can be different in each S_i, SS_i universes. Note that rule base (1.105) is sparse.

It contains the main rules for the following straightforward goals only:

Rule (a) simply keeps the previously chosen state values, if the symptom evaluation also agrees. The rule (b) has the opposite meaning, if the state values are not chosen, and moreover the symptom evaluation also disagrees the state value should be suppressed. The rule (c) keeps the already selected state values (previous approximation), if it has no better idea even if the symptom evaluation disagrees. Rules (d) and (e) have the task of ensuring the relatively quick convergence of the system to the sometimes unstable (changeable) situations, as new state variables which seem to be fit, can be chosen in one step, if there is no previously chosen state, which is still accepted by the symptom evaluation (d). Rule (e) has the task to suppress this selection in the case if there exists a still acceptable state which has already chosen. The goal of this heuristic is to gain a relatively quick convergence for the system to fit the opinions of the actual user, if there is no state value high enough to be previously accepted. This quick convergence could be very important in many application areas for example, in case of an on-line user adaptive selection system, where the user feed-back information needed for the state changes are very limited.

Some state changes of the state-transition control in the function of the user feed-back (SS_1, SS_2) for the two states case (applying the state transition rule base (1.105)) are visualized on Figure 44 and Figure 45.

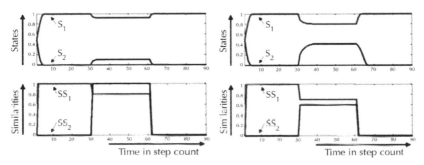

FIGURE 44   Do not "pick up" a new state if the previous approximation is still adequate.

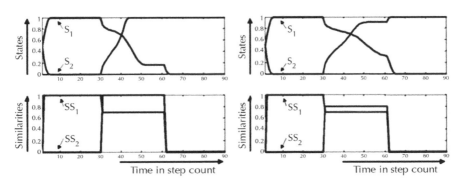

FIGURE 45   But "pick it up" if it seems better.

Counting the rules of the classical (for example, compositional) fuzzy reasoning for the same strategy we find, that in the two state case the complete rule base needs 16 rules (as we have four observation universes $(S_1, SS_1, S_2,$ and $SS_2)$ each with two terms fuzzy partitions (Zero, One) – 2^4 rules), while the sparse rule base (1.105) contains 5 rules only (See Table 10 for the state-transition rule base of state S_1). Taking into account that in the proposed behavior-based control structure, a separate rule base is needed for each state variables, the behavior coordination needs 32 rules, while 10 is enough in case of applying the proposed interpolation-based fuzzy reasoning method. Increasing the number of the state variables, the situation became even worse. In case of three state variables (S_1, S_2, and S_3), the rate become 3.2^6 ($n.2^{2n}$, where n is the number of the states) and 3.6 ($n.(n + 3)$) up to the interpolation based method (See Table 11).

TABLE 10   State-transition rule base of state S1 in case of two state variables (S1, S2) according to rule base (1.105).

R_{S1}	S_1	SS_1	S_2	SS_2	S_1	
1.	One	One			One	(according to (a))
2.	Zero	Zero			Zero	(according to (b))
3.	One	Zero		Zero	One	(according to (c))
4.	Zero	One	Zero	Zero	One	(according to (d))
5.	Zero	One	One	One	Zero	(according to (e))

TABLE 11   State-transition rule base of state S_1 in case of three state variables (S_1, S_2, S_3) according to rule base (1.105)

R_{S1}	S_1	SS_1	S_2	SS_2	S_3	SS_3	S_1	
1.	One	One					One	(a)
2.	Zero	Zero					Zero	(b)
3.	One	Zero		Zero		Zero	One	(c)
4.	Zero	One	Zero	Zero	Zero	Zero	One	(d)
5.	Zero	One	One	One			Zero	(e)
6.	Zero	One			One	One	Zero	(e)

In case of increasing number of the input variables, the exponential rule number "explosion" makes many heuristic ideas unimplementable. In case the behavior coordination module applied for user adaptive information retrieval system has 4 state variables (one for each emotional models), our simple rule base (1.105) practically becomes unimplementable as a complete rule base ($4.2^8 = 1024$ rules). While our working demonstrational example has only 28 rules. This is the advantage of the interpolation-based fuzzy reasoning method.

1.14   ON GENERALIZED METHOD-OF-CASE INFERENCE RULE

In this Section, we deal with the generalized method-of-case (GMC) inference scheme with fuzzy antecedents, which has been introduced by Da [52]. We show that when fuzzy numbers involved in the observation part of the scheme have continuous membership function and a t-norm, t-conorm used in the definition of the membership function of the conclusion are continuous, then the conclusion defined by the compositional rule of inference depends continuously on the observation.

When predicates are crisp then the method of cases reads:

Observation: A or B

Antecedent 1: if A then C

Antecedent 2: if B then C

Conclusion: C

This is equivalent to saying that the formula is a tautology in binary logic where A, B, and C are propositional variables. The proof of many theorems in conventional mathematics is based on this scheme, for example, theorems involving the absolute value of a real variable are usually proved by considering separately positive and non-positive values of the variable, and the conclusion is derived in each of these cases.

We investigate the effect of small changes of the observation to the conclusion of similar deduction schemes when the antecedents involve fuzzy concepts.

Let X, Y, and Z be variables taking values in universes U, V, and W, respectively and let A, A' $\in$ F(U), B, B' $\in$ F (V), and C $\in$ F (W), then the generalized method of cases reads:

Observation: X is A' OR Y is B'

Antecedent 1: IF X is A THEN Z is C

Antecedent 2: IF Y is B THEN Z is C

Conclusion: Z is C'

The conclusion C' is given by applying the general composition rule of inference:

$$C'(w) = sup_{(u,v) \in U \times V} \ T(S(A'(u), B'(v)), I(A(u), C(w)), I(B(v), C(w))) \quad (1.106)$$

where T is an arbitrary triangular norm, S is an arbitrary conorm, and I represents an arbitrary fuzzy implication.

For instance:

Observation: This bunch of grapes is fairly sweet OR this brunch of grapes is more less yellow.

Antecedent 1: IF a bunch of grapes is yellow THEN the bunch of grapes is ripe.
Antecedent 2: IF a bunch of grapes is sweet THEN the bunch of grapes is ripe.

Conclusion: This bunch of grapes is more or less ripe.

Consider now the generalized method-of-case scheme with different fuzzy observations A', A'', B', and B''.

X is A' OR Y is B'	X is A'' OR Y is B''
IF X is A THEN Z is C	IF X is A THEN Z is C
IF Y is B THEN Z is C	IF Y is B THEN Z is C
------------------------------	------------------------------
Z is C'	Z is C''

where C' and C'' are defined by the compositional rue of inference, in the sense of (1.106), that is:

$$C'(w) = sup_{(u,v) \in U \times V} \ T(S(A'(u), B'(v)), I(A(u), C(w)), I(B(v), C(w))), \quad (1.107)$$

$$C''(w) = sup_{(u,v) \in U \times V} \ T(S(A''(u), B''(v)), I(A(u), C(w)), I(B(v), C(w))). \quad (1.108)$$

The following theorem gives an upper estimation for the distance between the conclusions C' and C'' obtained from GMC schemes above.

Theorem 1.15 Let T and S be continuous functions and let A', A'', B', and B'' be continuous fuzzy numbers. Then with the notation:

$$\Delta = max\{\omega_{A'}(D(A', A'')), \omega_{A''}(D(A', A'')), \omega_{B'}(D(B', B'')), \omega_{B''}(D(B', B''))\}$$

We have:

$$sup_{w \in W} \left| C'(w) - C''(w) \right| \le \omega_T(\omega_S(\Delta)), \quad (1.109)$$

where the conclusion C', C'' are defined by (1.107) and (1.108), respectively.

It should be note that:

(i)   From (1.109), it follows that C' → C'' uniformly as Δ → 0, which means the stability (in classical sense) of the conclusion under small changes of the fuzzy terms,

(ii)   The stability or instability of the conclusion does not depend on the implication operation I.

Example 1.26 For illustration consider the following schemes with arbitrary continuous fuzzy numbers A, B, and C:

X is A OR Y is B	X is A OR Y is more or less B
IF X is A THEN Z is C	IF X is A THEN Z is C
IF X is B THEN Z is C	IF X is B THEN Z is C

--------------------------------   --------------------------------------

Z is C'   Z is C"

where

(more of less B) (y): $== \sqrt{B(y)}$,
for y ∈ R,

   T(u, v) = min {u, v} (minimum norm);

   S(x,y) = max (u,v) (maximum conorm);

$$I(x,y) = \begin{cases} 1 \; if \; x \le y \\ y \; otherwise \end{cases}$$ (Gödel's implication operation).

Following D, we get C' = C and C" = more or less C' that is:

$$C"(w) = \sqrt{C(w)} \, , \, w \in R$$

So

$$sup_{w \in R} |C'(w) - C"(w)| = sup_{w \in R} |C'(w) - \sqrt{C(w)}| = \frac{1}{4} \, ;$$

$$D(A,A) = 0, \quad D(B, \text{more or less } B) \le \frac{1}{4} ; \; \omega_S(\Delta) = \Delta, \omega_I(\Delta) = \Delta, \Delta > 0; \; ;$$

Theorem 1.15 gives:

$$sup_{w \in R} |C'(w) - C"(w)| \le \max \omega_B (1/4), \omega_{\text{more or less } B}(1/4) \le \frac{1}{4}$$

which means that our estimation (1.109) is sharp, that is there exist C' and C", such that:

$$sup_{w \in R} |C'(w) - C"(w)| = \omega_I(\omega_S(\Delta)).$$

1.15   GENERALIZED DISJUNCTIVE SYLLOGISM

In this section, we discuss a deductive process "Generalized Disjunctive Syllogism" through mathematical formulation and illustration only. The approach deals with inexact proposition is which attached with an inexact truth value like "Arnab is tall is quite true". This is essentially developed by Raha and Ray [193].

1.15.1 MATHEMATICAL PRELIMINARIES

In this section, we first present some definitions and basic concepts related to fuzzy logic. The mostly used rules in fuzzy logic are the conjunction principle, the projection principle, and the entailment principle.

CONJUNCTION PRINCIPLE

Let p and q be two propositions whose translations are expressed as:

$$q \to \Pi_{(X_1, X_2, ..., X_n)} = S \quad q \to \Pi_{(X_1, X_2, ..., X_n, Y_1, Y_2, ..., Y_k)} = T \ \left(m \leq n; m, n, k < \infty\right)$$

S and T are fuzzy relations. $X_1, X_2, ..., X_m$ are the variable which appear in both premises p and q. U_i (i=1, 2,...,n), V_j (j = 1, 2,...,n) are the universes of discourse associated respectively with the variables X_i and Y_j. Let

$$X = \left(X_1, X_2, ..., X_n\right) \quad X' = \left(X_1, X_2, ..., X_m\right) \text{ and } Y = \left(Y_1, Y_2, ..., Y_k\right)$$

$\overline{S}, \overline{T}$ respectively denote the cylindrical extension of S and T in D, the Cartesian product $U_1 \times U_2 \times ... \times U_n \times V_1 \times V_2 \times ... \times V_k$ Then the conjunction priniciple asserts that r may be inferred from p and q according to the following scheme:

$$p \to \Pi_x = S$$
$$\frac{q \to \Pi_{(X', Y)} = T}{r \leftarrow \Pi_{(X, Y)} = \overline{S} \cap \overline{T}}$$

PROJECTION PRINCIPLE

Let p be a fuzzy proposition whose translation is expressed as $p \to \Pi_{(X_1, X_2, ..., X_n)} = F$ a fuzzy relation and let $X' = (X_1, X_2, ..., X_m)$ denote a sub-variable ($m \leq n$; to preserve the order of appearance it may require renaming and then rearranging of linguistic variables $X_1, X_2, ..., X_n$). Then the projection of F on $U_1 \times U_2 \times ... \times U_m$ is defined as the fuzzy relation given by the possibility distribution function

$$\pi_{X'}\left(u_{m+1}, u_{m+2}, ..., u_n\right) = \sup_{u_1, u_2, ..., u_m} \mu_F\left(u_1, ... u_{m-1}, u_m, u_{m+1}, ..., u_n\right)$$

u_i is a generic element of U_i.

Let q be the retranslation of the above possibility assignment equation. Then the projection principle asserts that q may be inferred from p according to the following scheme:

$$p \rightarrow \Pi_{(X_1, X_2, \ldots, X_n)} = F$$

$$q \rightarrow \Pi_{(X_{m+1}, \ldots, X_n)} = \text{Proj}_{(U_1 \times U_2 \times \ldots \times U_m)} F$$

where the right hand side of the latter equation is a fuzzy relation defined by the induced possibility distribution function.

It should be mentioned here that a proper combination of the application of the conjunction principle followed by an application of projection principle results in the well-known conpositional rule of inference due to Zadeh.

ENTAILMENT PRINCIPLE

The entailment principle asserts that from any fuzzy proposition another fuzzy proposition can be inferred if the possibility distribution induced by the inferred fuzzy proposition contains the possibility distribution function of the former (from which it is inferred) one.

FORMULAS IN FUZZY LOGIC

We consider a simple fuzzy formula as follows:

X is F; T is C.

X and T are two linguistic variables of which T explicitly denotes the truth value. F and C are fuzzy subsets of respective universes. Thus if $(X_1, X_2, \ldots, X_n)$ are n-linguistic variables and $X = (X_1, X_2, \ldots, X_n)$ then we consider a fuzzy formula in fuzzy logic as $F(X)$; $C(T)$ where F is a fuzzy relation defined over $U_1 \times U_2 \times \ldots \times U_n$; U_i being universes of discourse of the linguistic variables X_i $(i=1, 2, \ldots, n)$. This formula actually determines a possibility assignment equation

$$\Pi_{(X:T)} = R \qquad (\text{say})$$

where R is a fuzzy relation defined over $U_1 \times U_2 \times \ldots \times U_n \times V$; V being the universe of discourse of T.

Consider a fuzzy proposition (fuzzy) X is G on the assumption X is F; T is C is given by C' where $C' = \text{Proj}_U R$; R being the universe of discourse of X. R is a fuzzy relation defined by $R = \overline{G} \cap (F \times C)$; $\overline{G}$ is the cylindrical extension of G over $U \times V$, V being the universe of discourse of T. Thus,

$$\mu_{C'}(v) = \sup_{u}\{\mu_G(u) \wedge \mu_{F \times C}(u, v)\}$$

$$= \sup_{u}\{\mu_G(u) \wedge \mu_F(u) \wedge \mu_C(v)\}$$

$$= \sup_{u}\{\mu_F(u) \wedge \mu_C(v)\} \, [\text{since } F \subseteq G]$$

$$= \mu_C(v) \qquad \text{if } (\exists u)_v \, \mu_F(u) \geq \sup_{v}\{\mu_C(v)\}$$

Thus C' = C if we choose F to be a normal fuzzy set.

DISJUNCTIVE SYLLOGISM

In two-valued logic, the law of disjunctive syllogism can be stated as "Given a disjunction and a negation of any of the disjuncts, the other can be inferred".
   Symbolically:

   prem1: $p \vee q$

   prem 2: $\sim p$

   Concl: q

   In using this rule, the user must be sure that the disjunct as appears in prem 2 is exactly the negation of the one that appears in prem1 that is, they must be contradictory pairs. No doubt, such condition is a restriction so long as the real-life problems are concerned. Here, we often find certain pairs of information which are not completely contradictory but certainly close to the same. In this case, the above framework is not admissible. For this, let us remove this restriction on exactness and generalize this concept to the case where the disjuncts are inexact/imprecise in nature and hence, the "degree of contradiction" is not absolutely specified. But as the first premise is a restriction of the disjuncts, and the user may have some possibly inexact knowledge about any of the disjuncts, whatever the level of contradiction may be, it is always possible to infer the induced possibility distribution of the other disjunct.
   Thus we get:

   prem1: $p \vee q$

   prem 2: p'

   Concl: q'

and q' is close to q as p' is close to $\sim p$.

1.15.2 MATHEMATICAL FORMULATION OF GENERALIZED DISJUNCTIVE SYLLOGISM

Let X, Y, and T be three linguistic variables that take values from the domains U, V, and W, respectively of which T explicitly denotes the truth values. We consider the derivation of an inexact conclusion r from two typical knowledge (premises) p and q according to the following scheme:

$$p : X \text{ is A or Y is B; T is C}$$
$$q: X \text{ is A'; T is C'}$$

$$r \leftarrow Y \text{ is B'; T is C''}$$

where the A's, B's, and C's are approximations of possibly inexact concepts by fuzzy sets over U, V, and W respectively.

The deduction of r follows the following basic steps:

Let

$$U = \sum_{i=1}^{m} u_i, \quad V = \sum_{i=1}^{n} v_i, \quad W = \sum_{i=1}^{p} w_i.$$

Then a possible translation of p and q can be given by the following possibility assignment equations:

$$p \rightarrow \prod_{(X,Y;T)} = R = \sum_i \sum_j \sum_k \mu_R(u_i, v_j; w_k) / (u_i, v_j; w_k)$$

and

$$q \rightarrow \prod_{(X;T)} = S = \sum_i \sum_k \mu_S(u_i \ ; w_k) / (u_i \ ; w_k)$$

where

$$\mu_R(u, v, w) = \min\{1 - \mu_A(u), \mu_B(v), \mu_C(w)\} \text{ and } \mu_S(u;w) = \min\{\mu_{A'}(u), \mu_{C'}(w)\}$$

It should be noted that other meaningful interpretations of R and S are possible as well.

The conjunction of R and S, to be denoted by $R \cap \bar{S}$, is given by

$$R \cap \bar{S} = \prod_{(X,Y;T)} [\prod_{(X;T)} = S]$$

$$= \sum_i \sum_j \sum_k \mu_{R \cap \bar{S}}(u_i, v_j; w_k) / (u_i, v_j; w_k)$$

where $\mu_{R \cap \bar{S}}(u_i, v_j; w_k) = \inf \mu_R(u_i, v_j; w_k), \mu_S(u_i \ ; w_k)]$.

Projecting $R \cap \bar{S}$ on $V \times W$ we obtain the relational matrix for conclusion as (induced)

$$\prod_{(Y;T)} = \operatorname{Proj}_{V \times W} [R \cap \bar{S}]$$

such that $\pi(v; w) = \sup_{u} \{ \mu_{R \cap \bar{S}} (u, v; w)]$

In order to obtain the above conclusion in the form of r project $\prod_{(Y;T)}$ separately on V and W. Thus:

$$B' = \operatorname{Proj}_{V} \prod_{(Y;T)} = \sup_{w} \sup_{u} [\mu_{R \cap \bar{S}} (u, v; w)] \text{ and}$$

$$C'' = \operatorname{Proj}_{w} \prod_{(Y;T)} = \sup_{v} \sup_{u} [\mu_{R \cap \bar{S}} (u, v; w)].$$

Now, since

$$\prod_{(X,Y;T)} \left[\prod_{(X;T)} = Q \right] = R \cap \bar{Q},$$

$$Q = \sum_{i} \sum_{k} \mu_{Q}(u_i \; ; \; w_k) \text{ where } \mu_{Q}(u_i \; ; \; w_k) = \inf \{ \mu_{A'}(u), \mu_{C'}(w) \}$$

as the possible translation of an inexact premise $q : X$ is A' ; T is C' into a possibility assignment equation. Hence, if we choose $A' = $ not A and C' = C then:

$$\prod_{(Y;T)} = \operatorname{Proj}_{V \times W} \left(\prod_{(X,Y;T)} \left[\prod_{(X;T)} = Q \right] \right)$$

$$= \sup_{u} \{ \mu_{R} (u, v; w) \wedge \mu_{Q}(u; w) \}$$

$$= \sup_{u} \{ \inf (1 - \mu_{A}(u), \mu_{B}(v), \mu_{C}(w)) \wedge \inf (1 - \mu_{A}(w), \mu_{C}(w)) \}$$

$$= \sup_{u} \{ \inf (1 - \mu_{A}(u), \mu_{B}(v), \mu_{C}(w)) \}$$

$$= \sup_{u} \{ (1 - \mu_{A}(u)) \wedge \mu_{B}(v) \wedge \mu_{C}(w) \}$$

$$= \{ \mu_{B}(v), \mu_{C}(w) \} \text{ if } \sup_{u} (1 - \mu_{A}(u)) \geq \{ \mu_{B}(v), \mu_{C}(w) \}$$

Then projecting $\Pi_{(Y;T)}$ on V and W respectively we obtain after retranslation (Y is B; T is C).

Next let X_i (i = 1, 2, ..,n) be n such variable and V_i (I = 1, 2, ...,n) be the respective universes of discourse.

Let

$$U_i = \sum_{j=1}^{j_i} u_j^i , \quad i = 1,2,\ldots,n.$$

Consider a second model where from premises p and q we derive a conclusion r of the form

$p : X_1$ is A_1 or X_2 is A_2 or ... or X_n is A_n; T is C

$q : X_1$ is A_1' ; T is C'

$r \leftarrow X_2$ is A'$_2$ or X$_3$ is A'$_3$ or ... or X$_n$ is A'$_n$ T is C".

Here, $A_i, A_i' (i=1,2,....,n)$ are possibly approximate representations of inexact concepts by fuzzy sets over U_i $(i = 1,2, ..., n)$.

The translation of the logical relation between sentences appearing in the premise P into a fuzzy relation gives:

$$p \rightarrow \Pi_{(X_1, X_2, X_n :T)} = R \subseteq U_1 \times U_2 \times \ldots \times TU_n \times W$$

where

$$\mu_R (u_1, u_2, \ldots, u_n; w) = \inf \{1 - \mu_{A1} (u_1), \mu A_2 (u_2, \ldots, \mu_{An}), \mu_c (w)\},$$

and translation of q gives:

$$q \rightarrow \Pi_{(X:T)} = S \text{ where } \mu_S (u; w) = \inf \{\mu_{A_1'} (u), \mu_{C'} (w)\}.$$

The conjunction of R and S, denoted by $R \cap \bar{S}$, is given as follows:

$$R \cap \bar{S} = \Pi_{(x_1, x_2, \ldots, x_n :T)} \left[\Pi_{(x:T)} = S \right]$$

such that

$$\mu_{R\cap\bar{S}}\left(u_1, u_2, \ u_n \ ; w\right) = \mu_R\left(u_1, u_2, \ ,u_n \ ; w\right) \wedge \mu_S\left(u_1 \ ; w\right)\}.$$

Then projecting $R \cap \bar{S}$ on $U_2 \times U_3 \times ... \times U_n \times W$ we obtain, for conclusion, a relational matrix:

$$\Pi_{\left(X_2, X_3, \ ...,X_n:T\right)} = \operatorname{Proj}_{U_2 \times U_3 \times .. \times U_n \times w}\left[R \cap \bar{S}\right] = M \quad (\text{say})$$

where

$$\mu_M\left(u_2, u_3, ..., u_n; w\right) = \sup_{u_i}\left\{\mu_{R\cap\bar{S}}\left(u_1, u_2, ...u_n; w\right)\right\}$$

For a more meaningful inference we project M over u_i (i = 2, 3, ...,n) and then W separately to obtain

$$r \leftarrow X_2 \text{ is } A_2' \text{ or } X_3 \text{ is } A_3' \text{ or ... or } X_n \text{ is } A_n' \ ; \text{ T is C''}$$

where

$$A_i' = \operatorname{Proj}_{U_i} \ M; \quad i = 2,3, \ n \text{ and } C'' = \operatorname{Proj}_w \ M.$$

Let us now consider a third model:

$$p : X_1 \text{ is } A_1 \text{ or } X_2 \text{ is } A_2 \text{ or ... or } X_m \text{ is } A_m; \text{ T is C} \quad (m \le n)$$

$$q : X_1 \text{ is } A_1' \text{ or } X_{S_1} \text{ is } A_{S_1}' \text{ or ..., or } X_{S_k} \text{ is } A_{S_k}' \text{ or } X_{m+1} \text{ is } A_{m+1} \text{ or ... or } X_n \text{ is}$$
$$A_n \ ; \text{ T is C'}$$

$$r \leftarrow X_2 \text{ is } A_2'' \text{ or... or } X_m \text{ is } A_m'' \text{ or ... or } X_{m+1} \text{ is } A_{m+1}' \text{ or ... or } X_n \text{ is } A_n'' ; \text{ T}$$
is C''
where the sequence $\{S_1, S_2, ...,S_k\}$ is a subsequence of $\{2, 3, ..., m\}$ In this case, as before, the translation of p into a possibility assignment equation is given by

$$p \to \Pi_{\left(X_1, X_2, ...X_m:T\right)} = R$$

where

$$\mu_R\left(u_1, u_2, ..., u_m; w\right) = \inf\left\{1 - \mu_{A_1}\left(u_1\right), \mu_{A_2}\left(u_2\right), ..., \mu_{A_m}\left(u_m\right), \mu_C\left(w\right)\right\}$$

and the translation of q into a possibility assignment equation is given by

$$q \to \Pi_{\left(X_1, X_{S_1} X_{S_2}, ... X_{S_k}, X_{m+1}, X_{m+2}, ... X_n : T\right)} = S$$

where

$$\mu_S\left(u_1, u_{S_1}, u_{S_2}, ..., u_{S_k}, u_{m+1}, ..., u_n; w\right)$$

$$= \inf\left\{\mu_{A_1'}\left(u_1\right), \mu_{S_1'}\left(u_{S_1}\right), ..., \mu_{A_{s_k}'}\left(\mu_{S_k}\right), \mu_{A_{m+1}}\left(u_{m+1}\right), ..., \mu_{A_m}\left(u_m\right), \mu_c'\left(w\right)\right\}.$$

Now let $\overline{R}$ and $\overline{S}$ respectively denote the cylindrical extension of R and S over the domain

$$U_1 \times U_2 \times ... \times U_n \times W.$$

Then the conjunction of R and S, denoted by $\overline{R} \bigcap \overline{S}$ is given as

$$\Pi_{(X_1, X_2, ..., X_m : T)}\left[\Pi_{(X_1, X_{S_1}, ..., X_{S_k}, X_{m+1}, ..., X_n : T)} = S\right] = \overline{R} \bigcap \overline{S} = M\left(Say\right)$$

where

$$\mu_M\left(u_1, u_2, ..., u_n; w\right) = \inf\left\{\mu_R\left(u_1, u_2, u_2, ... u_m; w\right), \mu_S\left(u_1, u_{S_1}, ..., u_{S_k}, u_{m+1}, ..., u_n; w\right)\right\}.$$

Projecting M over $U_2 \times U_3 \times ... \times U_n \times w$ we obtain, for conclusion,

$$\Pi_{(X_2, X_3, ..., X_n : T)} = \text{Proj}_{U_2 \times U_3 \times ... \times U_n \times W.}$$

For a meaningful inference of the form r project $\text{Proj}_{U_2 \times U_3 \times ... \times U_n \times W}$ M over U_i and W (i = 2, 3, ..., n) one by one to obtain,

$r \leftarrow X_2$ is A_2'' or... or X_m is A_2'' or X_{m+1} is A_{m+1}' or ... or X_n is A_n' ; T is C"

where

$$A_i'' = \text{Proj}_{U_i} \left[\text{Proj}_{U_2 x...xUnxw} W \right], \quad i = 2,3,...,m,$$

$$A_i' = \text{Proj}_{U_i} \left[\text{Proj}_{U_2 \times ... \times U_n \times W} W \right], \quad i = m+1,...,n,$$

$$C_i'' = \text{Proj}_W \left[\text{Proj}_{U_2 \times ... \times U_n \times w} M \right].$$

Now, we consider examples to illustrate the models presented above. We consider variables that range over finite sets or can be approximated by variables ranging over such sets.

Example 1.27 Consider the premises:

P: X is large or Y is small, T is true

q: X is not very large, T is very true

in which X, Y, T range over U, V, W, and large, small, and so on are defined (approximately) by:

large = $0.1/\mu_1 + 0.45/\mu_2 + 0.95/\mu_3 + 0.9/\mu_4$,

not very large = $1/u_1 + 0.8/u_2 + 0.1/u_3 + 0.2/u_4$,

small = $0.9/v_1 + 0.95/v_2 + 0.45/v_3 + 0.1/v_4$,

true = $0.1/w_1 + 0.45/w_2 + 1/w_3 + 1/w_4$, and

very true = $0.01/w_1 + 0.2/w_2 + 0.75/w_3 + 1/w_4$.

In terms of these definitions, the translations of p and q may be expressed as:

$$p \rightarrow \prod_{(X,Y;T)} = R \text{ (say)} \quad \text{and} \quad q \rightarrow \prod_{(X;T)} = S \quad \text{(say)}.$$

Then, for conclusion, we have $\prod_{(Y;T)} = \text{Proj}_{V \times W} \left(R \cap \bar{S} \right)$. Hence, $B = \text{Proj}_V [\prod_{(Y;T)}]$ such that

$$\mu_B(v) = \sup_w \sup_u \left[\mu_{R \cap \bar{S}}(u,v;w) \right] = \sup_w \sup_u \left[\inf\{\mu_R(u,v;w), \mu_S(u;w)\} \right]$$

and $C = \text{Proj}_w [\prod_{(Y;T)}]$ such that:

$$\mu_C(w) = \sup_v \sup_u \left[\inf \mu_R(u,v;w), \mu_S(u;w) \right].$$

After simple comparisons, we find:

$$B = 0.9 / v_1 + 0.9 / v_2 + 0.45 / v_3 + 0.1 / v_4$$

and $\qquad C = 0.01 / w_1 + 0.2 / w_2 + 0.7 / 5 w_3 + 0.9 / w_4.$

Thus, from premises p and q, we infer r as given by:

$$r \leftarrow Y \text{ is } B; T \text{ is } C.$$

Example 1.28 Consider the premises
$P : X_1$ is A_1 or X_2 is A_2; T is C

$q : X_1$ is A_1' or X_3 is A_3; T is C'
where

$$A_1 = 0.1 / u_1^1 + 0.5 / u_2^1 + 0.75 / u_3^1 + 1 / u_4^1 \, ,$$
$$A_1' = 0.68 / u_1^1 + 0.29 / u_2^1 + 0.13 / u_3^1 + 0 / u_4^1 \, ,$$
$$A_2 = 0.7 / u_1^2 + 0.95 / u_2^2 + 1 / u_3^2 + 0.82 / u_4^2 \, ,$$
$$A_3 = 0.86 / u_1^3 + 0.97 / u_2^3 + 0.75 / u_3^3 + 1 / u_4^3 \, ,$$
$$C = 0.01 / w_1 + 0.2 / w_2 + 0.75 / w_3 + 1 / w_4 \, ,$$

and

$$C' = 0.1 / w_1 + 0.45 / w_2 + 1 / w_3 + 1 / w_4.$$

With these definitions the translations of p and q may be expressed as:

$$p \rightarrow \prod_{(X_1, X_2; T)} = R \text{ (say) and } q \rightarrow \prod_{(X_1, X_2; T)} = S \text{ (say)}.$$

Then, for conclusion, as given in the third model $\prod_{(X_2, X_3; T)} = \text{Proj}_{U_2 \times U_3 \times W} (\bar{R} \cap \bar{S})$
and conclude:

$$X_2 \text{ is } A_2' \text{ or } X_3 \text{ is } A_3' ; \text{T is C"}$$

where

$$A_2' = \text{Proj}_{U_2}[\text{Proj}_{U_2 \times U_3 \times W}(\overline{R} \cap \overline{S})],$$

$$A_3' = \text{Proj}_{U_3}[\text{Proj}_{U_3 \times U_3 \times W}(\overline{R} \cap \overline{S})], \text{ and}$$

and

$$C" = \text{Proj}_W[\text{Proj}_{U_2 \times U_3 \times W}(\overline{R} \cap \overline{S})].$$

Ray and Raha develop [193] a new direction in approximate reasoning based on fuzzy logic. As it is based on extended concept of the law of disjunctive syllogism, therefore, it may help to derive a resolution principle in fuzzy logic.

1.16   RAY'S BOTTOM-UP INFERENCES

Ray has extended [198] the concept of resolution principle, based on refutation, from binary logic to fuzzy logic. The extension depends on the concept of linguistic variable, compositional rules of inference, approximate reasoning, and plausible reasoning. Ray considers the fuzzy resolution principle for the propositional logic and then extends it to first order logic. The completeness of the fuzzy resolution principle is discussed. The present fuzzy resolution principle provides a powerful tool for logic programming in uncertain environment.

1.16.1   FUZZY LOGIC AND FORMULAS

Fuzzy logic is an algebraic system $< [0, 1]$, $\wedge, \vee, \sim$, where the closed interval [0,1] is a set of truth values. The logical truth values are derived from the concept of multiple-valued logic. This concept can be extended to the linguistic truth values for the fuzzy linguistic variables.

The logical operations AND ($\wedge$), OR (V), and NOT ($\sim$) are defined as follows:

$A \wedge B = \min(A, B)$

$A \vee B = \max(A, B)$

$\sim A = 1 - A, A, B \in [0,1]$.

We assume that a fuzzy function is a function of variables/linguistic variables

$x_1, x_2, \ldots, x_n$, each of which assume values in the closed interval [0,1].

Definition 1.9 Fuzzy formulas are defined recursively as follows:

1.   A variable x_i is fuzzy formula

2. If F is a fuzzy formula then ~ F is also a fuzzy formula
3. If F and G are fuzzy formulas then F ∧ G and F∨G are fuzzy formulas,
4. The above are the only fuzzy formulas.

Definition 1.10 A variable x_i $(i = 1,\ldots, n)$ of its negation ~ x_i is said to be a literal

and x_i and ~ x_i are said to be complements of each other or a pair of complementary variable.

Definition 1.11 A clause is a disjunction of literals or is a formula consisting or OR (V) of some literals.

Definition 1.12 When a clause contains no literal, we call it the empty clause.

Given an interpretation I, the truth value of a clause C is determined uniquely by substituting a value of the closed interval [0, 1] determined by the interpretation I for each variable of the clause.

Denoting the truth value assigned to x_i by $T(x_i)$, the truth value of a fuzzy formulas is T(F) and the truthvalue of a fuzzy formulas is T(F) and the truth value of a fuzzy clause C is T(C).

If binary logic is used in a theorem proving or problem solving system, we store a statement A instead of ~ A, if the truth value of A is 1. In case the truth value of a statement A is 0, we simply store ~ A. In fuzzy logic, we should store a statement A instead of ~ A, if the truth value of A is greater than or equal to that of ~ A. That is we store A if T(A) ≥ 1 − T(A). In this case T(A) ≥ .5.

We can use this concept to define satisfiability in fuzzy logic as follows:

Definition 1.13 An interpretation I is said to satisfy a formula F if T(F) ≥ 0.5. An interpretation I is said to falsify F if T(F) ≤ 0.5. If T(F) = 0.5 under I, then I both satisfies and falsifies F. So, the truth value 0.5 is said to be a meaningless point in fuzzy inference system.

Definition 1.14 A formula is said to be unsatisfiable if and only if it is falsified by all its interpretations.

1.16.2 BOTTOM UP INFERENCE WITH FUZZY REASONING

A bottom up refutation begins with assertions in the input set of clauses. It uses implications to derive new assertions from old ones, and ends with the derivation of assertions, which explicitly contradict the denial of the goal. Bottom-up inference is a generalization of instrantiation combined with the classical rule of modus ponens. Instantiation is restricted to the minimum needed to match assertions with conditions, so that modus ponens can be applied. A more precise definition of bottom up inference is given in [118]. Bottom up inference is a special case of the hyper resolution rule defined and proved by Robinson [119].

The classical bottom-up inference deals with precise facts and rules. For further clarity interested readers are referred to [118].

Example 1.29 In this case, facts and rules are represented by fuzzy linguistic variables. But the left hand sides of the rules perfectly match with the given facts.

F1: K is big => big (K) ≡ {k} = $\{\frac{.7}{8},\frac{.8}{9},\frac{1}{10}\}$

F2: L is small => small (L) ≡ {1} = $\{\frac{1}{1},\frac{.5}{2},\frac{.3}{3}\}$

R1: big (K) – >medium (M), where

medium (M) ≡ {m} = $\{\frac{.5}{5},\frac{1}{6},\frac{.5}{7}\}$

R2: medium (M) and small (L) – >big (X), where

big (X) ≡ {x} = $\{\frac{.7}{7},\frac{.8}{8},\frac{.9}{9},\frac{10}{1}\}$

Goal: X is big ≡ big (X)

F*: Denial of the goal: ~ big (X)
The Figure 46 illustrates the bottom-up inference.

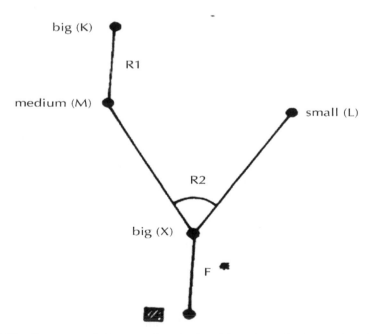

FIGURE 46   Bottom-up inference when body of the rule perfectly matches the given fact.

In this case, we have applied Mamdani's translating rule R_c. It is seen that the deduction starts with the given assertions and derives (using the compositional rules of inference) the goal state"big (X)", which fuzzily contradicts the negation of the goal state, that is, "~ big (X)". The fuzzy contradiction is achieved by taking the intersection between "big (X)" and "~ big (X)". At the end of fuzzy contradiction, we do not end up with the empty clause ☐. Instead we achieve one formula represented by ▨ having some truth values. In this particular example we get, ▨ ≡ (.3, .2, .1, 0). To give an interpretation 1 to the formula ▨ we pick up the maximum membership value/values of the formula ▨.

If the maximum membership value/values is/are less than .5, then (according to the Definition 1.13), the formula is falsified. If the formula is falsified for the maximum membership value then it would be falsified for all other membership values. Thus, the statement is unsatisfiable (according to the Definition 1.14). Hence, the denial of the goal is inconsistent with the given facts and rules which are fuzzily stated.

Example 1.30 In this case, facts and rules are represented by fuzzy linguistic variables but the left hand sides of the rules do not perfectly match with given facts.

$$Fl: \text{K' is more or less big} \Rightarrow \text{more or less big } (K') = \{k'\} = \{\frac{7.5}{0.6}, \frac{8}{0.7}, \frac{9.5}{0.9}\}$$

$$F2: \text{L is small} \Rightarrow \text{small } (L) \equiv \{l\} = \left\{\frac{1}{1}, \frac{5}{.2}, \frac{.3}{.3}\right\}$$

$$R1: \text{big (K)} -> \text{Medium (m), where Medium } (M) \equiv \{m\} = \left\{\frac{5}{.5}, \frac{6}{1}, \frac{7}{5}\right\}$$

R2: Medium (M) and small (L) -> big (x). where

Goal: x is big ≡ big(x)

F*: Denial of the goal: ~ big (x)

The Figure 47 illustrates the bottom–up inference:

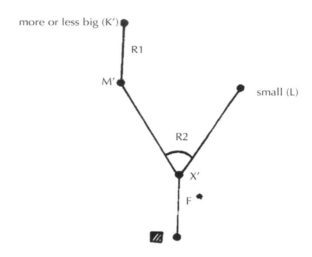

FIGURE 47 Bottom-up inference when body of the rule does not perfectly matches the given fact.

Here, M' = K'o R (K; m) = (.5, .9, .5) and either X'(according to Zadeh' s arithmetic rule)

$$\equiv \{x'\} = (M'oR(M;X)) \vee (LOR (L; X))$$
$$= (.7, .8, .9, 1)$$

or X' (according to the Mamdani's translating rule)

$$\equiv \{x'\} = (M' oR (M; X)) (LoR(L; X))$$

$$= (.7, .8, .9, .9).$$

In this particular example, we have to apply generalized modus ponens instead of modus pones. Hence, we may either use Zedeh's arithmetic rule R_a or Mamdani's translating rule R_c. Here, the extended Hausedorff distance measures between the fuzzy sets of (K, K') and (x, X') are within the reasonable limit. Ultimately, we derive Z', which is either having the truth values (.7, .8, 1) or (.7, .8, .9, .9). When X' fuzzily contradicts F*, we derive X', which is either having the truth values (.7,.8,.9, 1) or (.7, .8, .9 ,.9). When X' fuzzily contradicts F* we end up with the formula 🔳 having truthvalues (.3, .2, .1, 0). Hence, as per Example 1.29, we can say that the denial of the goal is inconsistent with the given facts and rules which are fuzzily stated.

If the extended Hausdorff with distance between any two matchable fuzzy sets is beyond the reasonable limit, we cannot say anything specifically about our inference mechanism.

In order to change a predicate into a proposition, each individual variable of change a predicate must be bound. This may be achieved in two ways. One way is to bind an individual variable by assigning a value to it. The other method of binding individual variable is by quantification of the variable. The most common forms of quantification are universal and existential. By the approaches of substitution and unification of binary logic we can easily extend the fuzzy resolution principle into first order logic.

Example 1.31.

F1 : Mr. A is tall $=>$ tall (Mr.A) $\equiv \{h\} = \left\{\dfrac{.7}{5'9''}, \dfrac{.8}{6'3''}, \dfrac{1}{6'5''}\right\}$

F2 : Mr. A has average weight $=>$ average weitht (Mr.A) $\equiv \{w\} = \left\{\dfrac{.7}{60\,kg}, \dfrac{.75}{65\,kg}, \dfrac{1}{70\,kg}\right\}$

R1 : tall (Mr. X) and average weight (Mr.X) $->$ healthy (X).

where healthy (X) $\equiv \{x\} = \left\{\dfrac{.8}{5'9'';65\,kg}, \dfrac{.9}{6'3'';70\,kg}, \dfrac{1}{6'5'';75\,kg}\right\}$

Goal: Mr. A is healthy (x) $\equiv$ healthy (Mr. A).

F* : Denial of the goal : ~healthy (Mr. A).

The Figure 48 below illustrates the bottom up inference.

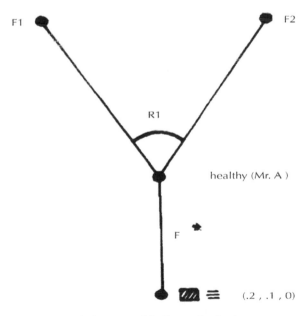

FIGURE 48 Bottom-up inference with first order logic.

Now we stipulate the following result.

Theorem 1.16 (completeness of the resolution principle) A set S of fuzzy formulas is unsatisfiable if and only if there is a deduction of the formulas in ▨ having maximum membership function below .5.

Proof: Deduction starts with the input assertions and derives (using the compositional rules of inference) the goal state which fuzzily contradicts the negation of the goal state.

Let all the possible membership functions of the goal state is either above of below the meaningless point 5, then the fuzzy contradiction which is the intersections between goal state and its negation will always yield the formula having maximum membership function below .5. Hence, according to the definitions 1.13 and 1.14, S is unsatisfiable.

Conversely, let all the possible membership functions of the goal state is distributed on and /or around the meaningless point .5, then the fuzzy contradictions may always yield the formula having maximum membership function .5. If the maximum membership function is .5, it becomes a meaningless point for refutational inference.

By theorem 1.16, we understand that if the linguistic variable of the goal state is not very much fuzzy in nature (that is, the meaningless point.5) then the fuzzy resolution principle is complete. For the distribution of the membership function, we may consider the S or π - function as proposed by several researchers.

By the fuzzy resolution principle, we can perform inference in fuzzy propositional and first order logic as effectively as in binary logic. We have proved the completeness of the fuzzy resolution principle. The present approach is based on linguistic variable and compositional rules of inference. Based on the present fuzzy resolution principle, we can have a more flexible logic programming system for uncertain environment.

1.17   MULTIDIMENSIONAL FUZZY REASONING BASED ON MULTIDIMENSIONAL FUZZY IMPLICATION

For simplicity of discussion and/or demonstration, let us restrict ourselves on R^2. Without lack of any generality, all the discussions and/or demonstrations are valid for

the problem on R^c, $c > 2$.

Let us consider the following multidimensional fuzzy implication (MFI)

$$\text{If } \begin{bmatrix} X \text{ is } A \\ Y \text{ is } B \end{bmatrix} \text{ then Z is C} \qquad\qquad (1.110)$$

where A,B, and C are fuzzy sets.

A conventional interpretation of equation (1.110) is as follows:

　　　　If x is A and y is B then z is C (a)

　　　　If x is A then y is B then z is C (b)   .   (1.111)

From the antecedent part of a MFI, we first try to establish the notion of "fuzzy state variable" of physical objects as a vector of linguistic variable instead of numerical variables. In classical physics, the state of a system or an object is represented by a set of observables. For example, in Newtonian mechanics, the state of an object (a particle with mass m) is given by the pair of values of the object's position vector x and its momentum vector p. These two values implicate all other properties of the object that are relevant in the Newtonian theory of mechanics. Thus, the representation of the state of a classical object is related either to the measure process or to the perception process of the observer. Due to the possible errors of measurement and the systematic errors occurring in every experiment, we can attribute their probability of this being the real value to all measured values of observables. Thus, the state of an object in Newtonian mechanics is given by the pair of the values of position x and momentum p and their probability distribution.

As our aim is to establish the notion of "fuzzy state variable" for all practical reasons, we replace the probability representation of the state of a classical object by possibilistic approach. For assignment of probability to an observable needs some experiment to measure the frequency of occurrence of the said observable, whereas assignment of possibility is an instantaneous reflection of human perception about the said observable and does not depend on any experiment. The possibilistic approach yields to the interpretation of the "fuzzy state" of a classical physical object as a pair $S = (LV_x, LV_p)$ of the two linguistic variables, viz. position LV_x and momentum LV_p. Both the linguistic variables operate on fuzzy sets with appropriate membership functions and described by the primary fuzzy term set, for example, {very small, small, big, very big,....., and so on}.

With this impression in mind about the fuzzy state of classical object, we represent Ray's fuzzy vector as shown in Figure 49 which is constructed from the antecedent part of a MFI (See Equation 1.110).

Before we give the formal definition of Ray's fuzzy vector (See Figure 49), we consider the following remarks:

Remark 1.1 We quantize the universe of individual features axis by a small line segments as shown in figure 49. Thus, we make the universe of each feature axis finite.

Remark 1.2 Over the quantized universe of the individual feature axis we define the primary fuzzy terms Z_i, S_i, M_i, B_i, $\forall_i$; where $Z_i \equiv$ zero, $S_i \equiv$ small, $M_i \equiv$ medium and $B_i \equiv$ big (See Figure 49).

Remark 1.3 Primary fuzzy terms Z_i and S_i are completely overlapped as shown in Figure 49. Also Z_i and S_i may be partially overlapped without any lack of generality.

Remark 1.4 For the present treatment, we assume the primary fuzzy term Z_i $\forall_i$ as fuzzy singleton. It may not be a fuzzy singleton in general.

Remark 1.5 As we have quantized the space on R^2 by small square grids (See Figure 49), a fuzzy point on the quantized pattern space is represented by an area ABCD, which contains a fuzzy relation which is a fuzzy set in the quantized product space $U_1 \times U_2$. Each element of the said fuzzy set is a small square grid with appropriate membership value (See Figure 49) which indicates the degree of belongingness of the element to the set.

Remark 1.6 The fuzzy point as stated in Remark 1.5, is linguistically described as (M_1, M_2) on the quantized product space and it represents a "fuzzy state" of classical object as stated earlier.

Remark 1.7 In Figure 49, the tuple $(F_1$ is $Z_1,\ F_2$ is $Z_2)$ is the initial point in the quantized product space. This initial point is a fuzzy point which is a fuzzy singleton in the quantized product space. This is basically a single point fuzzy relation having membership values 1 in the quantized product space.

Remark 1.8 In the present text, we use the term quantized product space $(U_1 \times U_2)$. But, it can be called as quantized fuzzy state space. They are the one and same thing.

Now, we consider the formal definition of Ray's fuzzy vector (See Figure 49) between the initial point and a fuzzy point on the quantized product space.

Definition 1.15 (Ray's fuzzy vector) Let $\vec{F}_f$ be a fuzzy vector having "c" components each of which is a fuzzy set defined over the universe U_i of the state axis F_i . The fuzzy vector $\vec{F}_f$ is a fuzzy set in the quantized product space $U_1 \times U_2 \times \ldots \times U_c$. Each element of the fuzzy set is a vector having the same initial point but different terminal points which are the elements of the fuzzy point which is a fuzzy set (see remark 1.5). Each terminal point of each vector in the set carries one membership value indicating its (vector's) degree of belongingness to the set $\vec{F}_f$. A fuzzy vector $\vec{F}_f$ is represented as:

$$\vec{F}_f = \{(\mu_{\vec{F}_f}(\vec{V}), \vec{V}) \ \forall \ \vec{V} \in U_1 \times U_2 \times \ldots \times U_c\}$$

where $\mu_{\vec{F}_f} : U_1 \times U_2 \times \ldots \times U_c \rightarrow [0,1]$ is the membership function of $\vec{F}_f$ and $\mu_{\vec{F}_f}(\vec{V})$ is the grade of membership of $\vec{V}$ in $\vec{F}_f$.

Remark 1.9 In the quantized product space $U_1 \times U_2 \times \ldots \times U_n$ we have two types of fuzzy sets. The one fuzzy set is related to the fuzzy point as mentioned in Remark 1.5. The other fuzzy set is related to Ray's fuzzy vector as stated in Definition 1.15. The two fuzzy sets are highly related to each other. The fuzzy set, which is a fuzzy point, is located by the fuzzy set, which is a fuzzy vector. The degree of belongingness of an element (that is a small square grid) to the fuzzy set (that is the fuzzy point) is same as the degree of belongingness of an element (that is a vector between the initial point and the said small square grid) to the fuzzy set which is a fuzzy vector. That is why both the said two fuzzy sets are having the same membership function interpreted in two different ways.

Remark 1.10 Without lack of generality, we may extend the Definition 1.15 of Ray's fuzzy vector between two fuzzy points. But such generality is not needed for the present discussion.

The process of defuzzification of Ray's fuzzy vector $\vec{F}_f$ is performed based on selecting the elements of the fuzzy vector $\vec{F}_f$, which is a fuzzy set, having the highest membership values. The defuzzified version of the fuzzy vector $\vec{F}_f$ is a fuzzy vector, which is a fuzzy set. In case defuzzified version of the fuzzy vector $\vec{F}_f$ represents a fuzzy set which is a fuzzy singleton then the defuzzified version of $\vec{F}_f$ becomes the crisp vector as stated in this section (See Example 1.32). The fuzzy set D^i as mentioned in the Definition 1.15 is an element of the term set as discussed in Remark 1.2. The universe of the components of $\vec{F}_f$ that is the fuzzy set D^i, may be continuous/ discrete and the universe of $\vec{F}_f$ may be continuous/discrete. In case universes are discrete, we should follow the numerical definition of membership functions, otherwise, we should follow the functional definition. In case, the defuzzified version of $\vec{F}_f$ reduces to the crisp vector as stated earlier the membership value at the terminal point of the vector $\vec{V}$ of $\vec{F}_f$ can alternatively be interpreted as the highest possibility of $\vec{V}$ to hold the property of the fuzzy vector $\vec{F}_f$. By the term "property", we want to mean a particular combination of the elements of different term sets. For instance, with respect to Figure 49 the property assumed by Ray's fuzzy vector $\vec{F}_f$ is $\left(M_1, \ M_2 \right)^T$. Like this we can have property $\left(M_1, \ S_2 \right)^T$, $\left(M_1, B_2 \right)^T$, and so on.

Thus, we introduce the notion of Ray's fuzzy vector (that is $\vec{F}_f$) which is essentially formed by the antecedent clauses of a fuzzy if-then rule and which is an analogous representation of $\vec{F}_c$ on R^2 (see Figure 49). When we write fuzzy if-then rules to grossly represent the information of the space on R^2 the fuzzy vector as stated above represents a fuzzy macro granule represented by the area ABCD (see Figure 49). Thus, the tip of the fuzzy vector no longer represents a single attribute on R^2, rather it represents a population of attributes which consists of fuzzy micro granules (small square grids of the region ABCD of Figure 49). At this juncture interested readers are referred to Kumar's conjecture as stated in [page 157, 197].

Example 1.32 Let us consider the following fuzzy vector (See Figure 49):

$$\begin{bmatrix} F_1 \text{ is } M_1 \\ F_2 \text{ is } M_2 \end{bmatrix} = \vec{F}_f = \mu_{\vec{F}_f}(\vec{V})/\vec{F}\} = \sum_{i=1}^{17}\sum_{j=1}^{13} = 1\mu_{\vec{F}_f}(\vec{V}_{i,j})/\vec{V}_{i,j} = 0.1/\vec{V}_{5,4} + \ \ldots \ 1.0/\vec{V}_{9,7} + \ldots + 0.1/\vec{V}_{13,10} + \ldots, \ 0.1/\vec{V}_{13,10} + \ldots,$$

where "+" and "$\sum$" are in the set theoretic sense and M_1 is a fuzzy set $\{0.1/u_5, 0.3/$

$u_6, 0.5/u_7, 0.7/u_8, 1.0/u_9, 0.7/u_{10}, 0.5/u_{11}, 0.3/u_{12},$ and $0.1/u_{13}\}$ on the universe

U_1, M_2 is a fuzzy set $\{0.1/v_4, 0.4/v_5, 0.7/v_6, 1.0/v_7, 0.7/v_8, 0.4/v_9,$ and $0.1/v_{10}\}$

on the universe U_2 and each vector $\vec{V}_{i,j}$ which is a generic element of the fuzzy set

$\vec{F}_f$ locates one small quantized zone (that is a small square grid) on the space R^2.

Thus, instead of single attribute, a population of attributes is represented by $\vec{F}_f$. Here,

the fuzzy set $\vec{F}_f$ is defined over the universe $U_1 \times U_2$, that is the quantized product

space. In this case, also note that the defuzzified version of the fuzzy vector $\vec{F}_f$ is a

fuzzy singleton represented by the vector $\vec{V}_{9,7}$.

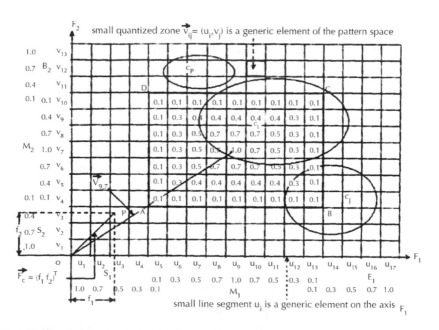

FIGURE 49   Representation of fuzzy pattern vector.

Key: The area ABCD represents the tip of Ray's fuzzy vector $\vec{F}_f = (M_1, M_2)^T$,

where M_1 and M_2 are the fuzzy sets on F_1 and F_2 axes. The membership values of small quantized zones are determined by the relation $\mu_{\bar{F}_f}(\bar{V}_{i,j}) = \min(\mu_{M_1}(u_i), \mu_{M_2}(v_j))$, where $\bar{V}_{i,j} = (u_i, v_j) \forall_i = 1, 2, \ldots, 17; j = 1, 2, \ldots, 13$. Instead of "min" operator we may use algebraic product, and so on depending upon the way we want to write the relation formed by the antecedent clauses of an one dimensional fuzzy implication.

In the quantized product $U_1 \times U_2$ (if $c = 2$), we define three types of fuzzy sets; the first two fuzzy sets are stated in Remark 1.9 and the third fuzzy set is the consequent part of MFI. The consequent part of a MFI, which is a fuzzy set, simply indicates the relative position of a fuzzy vector with respect to different classes of information in the quantized pattern space. Once the antecedent part and the consequent part of a MFI are represented by two different fuzzy sets as stated above, our next job is to attach a meaningful interpretation to the said representations.

Example 1.33 Let us consider the fuzzy pattern vector $\vec{F}_f$ of Figure 49. The position of $\vec{F}_f$ on the space R^2 means the area ABCD. The position ABCD of $\vec{F}_f$ is obtained when:

$$\vec{F}_f = \begin{bmatrix} F_1 \ is \ M_1 \\ F_2 \ is \ M_2 \end{bmatrix}$$

And the position of $\vec{F}_f$ is changed when:

$$\vec{F}_f = \begin{bmatrix} F_1 \ is \ M_1 \\ F_2 \ is \ S_2 \end{bmatrix} \ etc$$

Now if we try to compute the fuzzy set C which is the consequent part of the following MFI:

$$if = \begin{pmatrix} F_1 \ is \ M_1 \\ F_2 \ is \ M_2 \end{pmatrix} \rightarrow C,$$

We have to consider the relative position of $\vec{F}_f$, that is the area ABCD with respect to the defined cover c_i, c_j and c_p. For simplicity of demonstration we consider partial cover.

From Figure 49, it is obvious that the area of class represented by the property c_i is substantially occupied by the tip ABCD. Loouing at the membership values of the small quantized zones of c_i occupied by the tip ABCD, we can have the following four types of estimate of the class membership for the property c_i.

For class c_i, which is a particular property of an object:
- *Optimistic Estimate*: The highest membership value of the small quantized zones of the area of class c_i occupied by the tip ABCD. For instance, 1.0 indicated by $\vec{V}_{9,7}$ of Figure 49 (also See Example 1.32).
- *Pessimistic Estimate*: The lowest membership value of the small quantized zones of the area of class c_i occupied by the tip ABCD. For instance, 0.1 (See Figure 49).
- *Expected Estimate*: Average of the membership values of all the small quantized zones of the area of class c_i occupied by the tip ABCD. For instance, 0.381 (See Figure 49).
- *Most likely Estimate*: It comes from the subjective quantification of human perception. Here, in this example the subjective quantification of belongingness of a population of objects to a particular class (say property c_i) is achieved looking at the area of the said class occupied by the tip of Ray's fuzzy vector. For instance, 0.7 (See Figure 49), which is the subjective quantification of human perception as stated above and which may vary like 0.6 or 0.8 as perception from one person to another varies within certain limit but cannot be changed abruptly like 0.1 or 0.2 , and so on which is an indication of wrong perception. For further verification of the subjective quantification of our perception, we may consider the following simple calculation.

Let the area of the class c_i of Figure 49 be approximated by the total number of small quantized zones covered up (partly or fully) by the contour of the class c_i. The area of the class c_i occupied by the tip ABCD of the fuzzy vector is 32 zones. Now, if we take the ratio $(32 \div 46) = 0.696$ which is the computed value of the degree of belongingness of a population of objects/attributes to class c_i with respect to Ray's fuzzy vector $\vec{F}_f$ of Figure 49, then, we see that the subjective quantification of the degree of belongingness of a population of objects that is 0.7 of 0.6 or 0.8 lies close to that of the computed value.

Similarly we can have the estimates of the class-membership for the classes c_j and c_p .

For class c_j
- Optimistic estimate = 0.3.
- Pessimistic estimate = 0.1.
- Expected estimate = $(0.3 + 0.3 + 0.1 + 0.1 + 0.1 + 0.1)/6 = 1.0/6 = 0.167$.

- Most likely estimate = 0.3. Note that here the computed value of the degree of belongingness is $(6 \div 23) = 0.26$.

For class c_p
All estimates are zero.
Thus, we get four fuzzy sets for the consequent part of a MFI (that is the fuzzy set C)

$$C_{opt} = \{1.0/c_i,\ 0.3/c_j,\ 0.0/c_p\}$$
$$C_{pess} = \{0.1/c_i,\ 0.1/c_j,\ 0.0/c_p\}$$
$$C_{expt} = \{0.381/c_i,\ 0.167/c_j,\ 0.0/c_p\}$$
$$C_{most} = \{0.7/c_i,\ 0.3/c_j,\ 0.0/c_p\}.$$

According to Tsukamoto [225], a multidimensional fuzzy implication (MFI) can alternatively be interpreted as,

If x is A   then z is C
and   if y is B   then z is C   (1.112)

The intersection $C' \cap C''$, where C' is the inferred value from the first implication and C" is that from the second implication, is taken for the consequence of reasoning.

To tackle the problem of fuzzy reasoning, we provide the following new interpretation of the multidimensional fuzzy implication (MFI):

If x is A   then z is C^1

and   if y is B   then z is C^2 .   (1.113)

The intersection $C^{1'} \cap C^{2'}$, where $C^{1'}$ is the inferred value from the first implication and $C^{2'}$ is that from the second implication, is taken for the consequence of

reasoning. Note that the fuzzy set $\hat{C} = C^1 \cap C^2$ is a logical estimate of the fuzzy set C of Equation (1.110). As the estimate of the fuzzy set C of Equation (1.110) is done through the logical operation $\cap$, so we introduce the term logical estimate. Such logical estimate has a desirable property that $\hat{C}$ and C of Equation (1.110) carry the same defuzzy information. For defuzzification of the fuzzy set C and $\hat{C}$, we go by selecting the element having highest membership value. In case of the tie situation, we go by taking multiple choices.

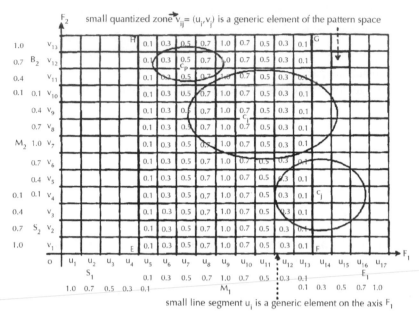

FIGURE 50 Representation of Ray's fuzzy vector induced by the cylindrical extension of fuzzy set M_1.

Key: The area EFGH represents the tip of Ray's fuzzy vector induced by the cylindrical extension of the fuzzy set M_1 on the feature axis F_2. The vectors $\vec{V}_{9,j}$, $j=1, 2, ..., 13$, are the elements of the fuzzy set, which are obtained by defuzzification of the fuzzy vector $\vec{F}_f$ as mentioned in Example 1.33.

To deal with the individual Decomposed Fuzzy Implication (DFI) of Equation (1.113) means to deal with a single antecedent clause along with its cylindrical extension over the appropriate universe of the axis and the consequence C^i, where i vary from 1 to 2 (in case we consider R^2). The necessity of considering the cylindrical extension of the fuzzy set which represents the antecedent clause of a DFI is to induce a relation in the product space. The induced relation due to the cylindrical extension of the said fuzzy set is itself a fuzzy set (See Figure 50) which according to Definition 1.15 is Ray's fuzzy vector. Thus, we can locate objects on the space R^2 by Ray's fuzzy vector $\vec{F}_f$ induced by the cylindrical extension of the fuzzy set of the antecedent clause of a DFI. The consequence is C^i, i vary from 1 to 2.

The essential difference between Tsukamoto model (that is Equation (1.112)) and the newly proposed models (that is Equation (1.113)), proposed by Ray, occurs at the interpretation of the consequent part of each of the (DFI) of the (MFI). According to Tsukamoto, the consequent parts of the DFIs (See Equation (1.112)) of a MFI are same as the consequent part of the said MFI. Whereas, according to the newly proposed model of Ray, the consequent parts of the DFIs (See Equation (1.113)) are different from the consequent part of the MFI. The linguistic connective 'and' of Equations (1.112) and (1.113) has logical interpretation "$\cap$".

Example 1.34 Let us consider Figures 49, 50, and 51. For simplicity of demonstration, we do not consider the total cover on space R^2.

From Figure 49:

$$\text{If} \begin{pmatrix} F_1 \ is \ M_1 \\ F_2 \ is \ M_2 \end{pmatrix} \rightarrow C = \{1.0/c_i, \ 1.0/c_j, \ 1.0/c_p\}$$

where the fuzzy set C is obtained optimistically from the position of the fuzzy sets M_1 and M_2 on the universes of the feature axes F_1 and F_2 respectively, that means from the relative position of Ray's fuzzy vector $\vec{F}_f$ (that is the relative position of the area ABCD) with respect to the defined cover of space R^2.

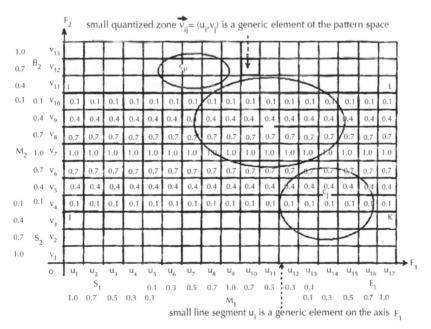

FIGURE 51 Representation of Ray's fuzzy vector induced by the cylindrical extension of fuzzy set M_2.

Key: The area IJKL represents the tip of Ray's fuzzy vector induced by the cylindrical extension of the fuzzy set M_2 on the feature axis F_1.

Whereas

$$\text{If } F_1 \text{ is } F_1 \rightarrow C^1 = \{1.0\,/c_i, 0.3\,/c_j, 1.0\,/c_p\}.$$

where the fuzzy set C^1 is obtained optimistically from the cylindrical extension of M_1 over the universe U_2 of the feature axis F_2 (that is, from the position of the area EFGH on the space R^2 of Figure 50) and well defined cover of the space.

and if F_2 is $M_2 \rightarrow C^2 = 1.0\,/c_i, 0.7\,/c_j, 0.0\,/c_p\}$,

where the fuzzy set C^2 is obtained optimistically from the cylindrical extension of M_2 over the universe U_1 of the feature axis F_1 (that is, from the position of the area IJKL on the space R^2 of Figure 51) and the well-defined cover of the space, then we get the logical estimate of C as:

$$\hat{C} = C_1 \cap C^2 = \{1.0\,/c_i, 0.3\,/c_j, 0.0\,/c_p\},$$

which is accidently not different from C and defuzzy information provided by $\hat{C}$ and C are same, that is the class c_i (we go by selecting the class having highest membership value, in case of the tie situation, we take the multiple choice).

Now instead of considering the optimistic estimates of the fuzzy sets C, C^1 and C^2 if we go by most likely estimates of C, C^1 and C^2 then we get:

$$\hat{C} = C_1 \cap C^2 = \{0.8\,/c_i, 0.4\,/c_j, 0.0\,/c_p\},$$

which is different from $C = \{0.7\,/c_i,\ 0.3\,/c_j,\ 0.0\,/c_p\}$ but the defuzzy information provided by $\hat{C}$ and C are same as before, that is the class c_i.

Similarly, if we go by pessimistic estimates or expected estimates of C, C^1 and C^2 we will get ingeneral two different fuzzy sets $\hat{C} = C_1 \cap C^2$ and C but their defuzzy information are desired to be the same. In case the defuzzy information obtained from $\hat{C}$ and C are different but closely related (in terms of any suitable measure) we may go ahead with the estimate $\hat{C}$, otherwise we have to recheck the entire newly proposed model, by further tuning the membership functions of the associated fuzzy sets.

Now for fuzzy reasoning based on multidimensional fuzzy implication (MFI), we may either go by the conventional interpretation MFI, that is the equation (1.111) or go by the new interpretation of MFI, that is the equation (1.113). Depending upon any particular need of a design study, once we select a particular interpretation of MFI, we can consider a suitable reasoning method as stated in the previous sections on fuzzy reasoning of this chapter.

KEYWORDS

- **Defuzzification**
- **Modus ponens**
- **Fuzzy logic**

CHAPTER 2

FUZZY REASONING BASED ON CONCEPT OF SIMILARITY

2.1 INTRODUCTION

The concept of similarity is a fundamental notion of human cognition. Similarity plays an essential role in fuzzy reasoning (approximate reasoning), recognition, case-based reasoning, taxonomy, and many other fields. There are many aspects of similarity that need formalization. According to Zadeh, "*Formulation of a valid, general-purpose definition of similarity is a challenging problem*". Though, there does not exist a valid, general-purpose definition of similarity but several special-purpose definitions of similarity exist, which have been employed with success in pattern classification, object recognition, cluster analysis, image retrieval from large image database, diagnostics, and so on. There are several similarity measures that are proposed and used for approximate reasoning (AR) for various purposes.

The similarity measures are classified into three categories:
1. Metric based measures,
2. Set-theoretic based measures, and
3. Implicators based measures.

While dealing with distance based similarity measures, examples have been constructed for perceptual similarity where, every distance axiom is clearly violated by dissimilarity measures viz. the triangle inequality. As a result the corresponding similarity measure disobeys transitivity. In these cases, a distinction is made between perceived dissimilarity d and the judged dissimilarity δ. If A and B are two points in the universe X then there exists a suitable non-decreasing function g such that, $\delta((A, B)) = g[d(a, B)]$. This model postulates that the perceptual distance satisfies the metric axioms, the empirical validity of which has been experimentally challenged by several researchers, particularly the triangle inequality. Similarly in case of set theoretic similarity measures, it is observed that crisp transitivity is a much stronger condition to be put upon similarity measure.

Set theoretic similarity measures are further subdivided in two groups:
a. Measures based on crisp set and
b. Measures based on fuzzy set.

In most of the applications such as in image databases, measures based on fuzzy set appear to be more effective than their crisp counterparts. Even in case of fuzzy set theoretic measures the perceived similarities do not follow T-transitivity. There are other models containing a list of axioms that a reasonable similarity measure must satisfy. One such set of axioms constructed for interval valued measures of similarity is available. The notion of similarity initiates the intuitive feeling about approximate equality between any two entities. Based on such feeling about approximate equality the basic notion of AR is developed.

But, the notion AR bears two different meanings in two different communities. Often, the notion is associated with uncertainty reasoning, for example, in the sense of fuzzy or probabilistic approaches. The notion of AR we use in section refers to AR algorithms for fuzzy propositional and fuzzy first-order logic.

Now, we give some examples of fuzzy similarity measure from different aspects of similarity.

Example 2.1 From the aspect of distance function, the fuzzy similarity measure between two fuzzy sets A and B can be defined as:

$$FS_1(A,B)(X) \triangleq 1 - |A(X) - B(X)|$$

Example 2.2 From the aspect of logic function, such as "max" or "min", the fuzzy similarity measure between two fuzzy sets A and B can be defined as:

$$FS_2(A,B)(X) \triangleq \begin{cases} \dfrac{2(A(X) \wedge B(X))}{A(X) + B(X)}, & A(x) + B(X) \neq 0; \\ 1, & A(X) + B(X) = 0. \end{cases}$$

Example 2.3 From the aspect of match function, the fuzzy similarity measure between two fuzzy sets A and B can be defined as:

$$FS_3(A,B)(X) \triangleq \begin{cases} \dfrac{(A(X) \cdot (X))}{max\{A(X) \cdot A(X), .B(x).B\}}, & A(X) + B(X) \neq 0, \\ 1, & A(X) + B(X) = 0. \end{cases}$$

Wang revises the Kleene's implication operator and proposes R_0 implication operator, which can be utilized for similarity measure between two different entities. As pointed out that R_0 is, in setting logic foundations for diverse fuzzy reasoning's better than other implication operators such as Kleenes operator R_K, Lukasiewiczs operator R_L, Godels operator R_G, Gaines Reschers operator R_{GR}, and Zadehs operator R_Z.

Example 2.4 Fuzzy similarity measure can be defined from the aspect of logic operation as:

$$FS_4 (A, B)\ (X) \triangleq . (A(X) \rightarrow B(X)\ \wedge\ (B(X) \rightarrow A(X)).$$

Where the operator "$\rightarrow$"can select R_O-implication:

$$a \rightarrow b = \begin{cases} 1, a \le b; \\ \sim a \vee b, a > b. \end{cases}, \sim a = 1 - a.$$

2.2 FUZZY REASONING USING SIMILARITY

In chapter 1, we have already discussed very much in detail about compositional rule of inferences (CRIs) and their variants, which are essentially pivoted on Zadeh's approach to AR. In this chapter, we essentially concentrate on AR (fuzzy reasoning) using the concept of similarity of all the various approaches taken in such schemes in AR, two of them have been prevalent in the literature, viz., reasoning methods based on the following:"

i.   Zadeh's CRI (See Chapter 3 of volume 1 of this book and chapter 1).
ii. Similarity between inputs and antecedents and the subsequent modification of the consequent, usually called Similarity Based Reasoning (SBR) or plausible reasoning. Compatibility Modification Inference (CMI) and Approximate Analogical Reasoning Scheme (AARS) are some representative samples of such approach.

There are many other approaches that do not strictly fall under the above two categories, for example, Raha et al. proposes an inference that is a combination of both the above approaches, Baldwin's Fuzzy Truth Value Modification inference, the scheme proposed by Ughetto et al. for implication based rules, and so on. Some earlier papers of Mizumoto, Roger, and so on also deal with fuzzy reasoning.

Any inference scheme proposed under the AR is essentially judged based on the reasonableness of inference and the complexity of the algorithm. Given a fuzzy if-then rule of the type $A \rightarrow B$ and a fuzzy input A', Generalized Modus Ponens (GMP) allows us to infer the output fuzzy set B' even if $A' \ne A$. Hence, the different schemes under the AR are evaluated based on their approximation abilities as well as based on the "goodness" of inference as given by how well they satisfy the "axioms" of GMP.

We know that the inferencing schemes in AR are generally resource consuming (both memory and time), since, these schemes often consist of discretisation of the input and output spaces followed by computations in each point. Also an increase in the number of rules only exacerbates the problem. As the number on input variables and/or input/output fuzzy sets increases, there is a combinatorial explosion of rules in multiple fuzzy rule based systems. Hence, several attempts have been developed to reduce the complexity of the inference procedure. For reducing complexity, rule reduction methods are proposed for fuzzy systems, where the main aim is to approximate the behavior of a system under consideration, which is a function of its inputs.

One important feature of the rule reduction techniques is that it should be lossless with respect to inference, that is, the inference obtained from the original rule base and that obtained from the reduced rule base should be identical. There are several attempts for rule reduction in fuzzy reasoning, where, there is a tradeoff between approximation accuracy and complexity of inference algorithm.

In the following sections, we consider only inference schemes in AR that can be grouped under the SBR. According to inferences in SBR, given a fuzzy if-them rule of the type $A \to B$ and a fuzzy input A', the input is matched to the antecedent A to obtain a measure of similarity s = M(A, A'). The output fuzzy set B' is obtained by modifying the consequent B using this similarity measures and a modification function. In this work, we consider an efficient inferencing approach through rule reduction. The rule reduction technique is a simple technique of combining the antecedents of rules with same consequents. We propose some sufficient conditions on the different operators employed in SBR inferencing that insure that the inference obtained from the original rule bade is identical to that obtained from the reduced rule base.

2.3   SIMILARITY BASED FUZZY REASONING METHOD

Let us consider, ifis A then is B, be a given fuzzy if-then rule and the given input be is A'.

According to Similarity Based Fuzzy Reasoning (SBR) schemes in the inferred value is obtained by modifying the consequent B using a modification junction J, which depend on the similarity (compatibility) measure M(A, A') between the input A' and antecedent A of the rule.

Some of the well-known examples of SBR are Compatibility Modification Inference (CMI) "Approximate Analogical Reasoning Scheme" (AARS) and "Consequent Dilation Rule" (CDR), Smets and Magrez, Chen, and so on. For a comparative study of many SBR inference schemes are available. In this section, we detail the typical inferencing mechanism in SBR, both in the case of SISO and MISO fuzzy rule bases [7].

SIMILARITY (COMPATIBILITY) MEASURE M

Given two fuzzy sets, say A, A', on the same domain a similarity (compatibility) measure M compares them to get a degree of similarity, which is expressed as a real in the [0, 1] interval. We refer to M as the Matching Function and define it as follows:
Definition 2.1 A matching function M:

$$\mathcal{F}(X) \times \mathcal{F}(X) \to [0,1],$$

where(X) is the fuzzy power set of a non-empty set X, that is:

$$\mathcal{F}(X) = \{A \mid A : X \to [0,1]\}.$$

Example 2.5 Let X be a non-empty set and $A, A' \in \mathcal{F}(X)$. Below we list a few of the matching functions employed in the literature.

- Zadeh's max-min: $M_Z(A, A') = \max_x \min (A(x), A'(x))$.

- Magrez – Smets' Measure: $M_M(A, A') = \max_x \min \left(\overline{A(x)} \right), A'(x))$, where $\overline{A(x)}$ is the negation of $A(x)$.

- Measure of Subsethood: $M_S(A, A') = \min_x I(A'(x), A(x))$, where I is a fuzzy implication.

- Scalar Product: $M_C (A, A') = \dfrac{A.A'}{\max(A.A, A'.A')}$, where the domain X is discretized into n points, that is, $X = \{x_1, x_2, \ldots, x_n\}$ and hence $A' \in [0, 1]^n$ with '.' is the scalar product of the "vectors" A, A'.

- Disconsistency Measure: $M_{TK}(A, A') - \left[\dfrac{\sum (A(x_1) - A'(x_1))^2}{n} \right]^{1/2}$, once again the domain X is discretized into n points.

REMARK 2.1

i.   Zwich et al. have compared 19 such similarity measures based on a few parameters.
ii. Note that a matching function M is not required to be symmetric. For example, since, a fuzzy implication I is not commutative, the subsethood measure M_S of A' in A is different from than that of A in A'.

2.3.1 SBR INFERENCE FOR SISO FUZZY RULE BASE

Let us again consider, if x is A then y is B to be the given SISO fuzzy if then rule and

x is A' the observed fuzzy input. Let $s = M(A, A') \in [0, 1]$ be a measure of the similarity (compatibility) of A' to A.

MODIFICATION FUNCTION J

Let Y be a non-empty set and $B \in \mathcal{F}(Y)$. The modification function J is a function from [0, 1] to [0, 1] and produces a modification $B' \in \mathcal{F}(Y)$ based on s and B. Then the consequence in SBR, using the modification function J, is given by:

$$B'(y) = J(s, B(y)) = J(M(A, A'), B(y)), \quad y \in Y. \qquad (2.1)$$

In AARS the following modification operators have been proposed, for any y Y:

i.   More or less: $J_{ML}(s, B) = B'(y) = \min\{1, B(y)/s\}$,

ii. Membership value reduction: $J_{MVR}(s, B) = B'(y) = B(y)\ s$.

AGGREGATION FUNCTION G

In the case of multiple rules:

$$R_i: \text{if } \tilde{x} \text{ is } A_i \text{ then } \tilde{y} \text{ is } B_i, i = 1, 2, ..., m.$$

We infer the final output by aggregating over the rules, using an associative aggregation operator G: $[0, 1]^2 \to [0, 1]$: 05-07-13

$$B'(y) = G_{i=1}^m (J(M(Ai, A'), B_i(y))), y \in Y. \qquad (2.2)$$

Usually, G is either a t-norm, t-conorm, or a uninorm, that is, $G \in \mathcal{J} \cup \partial \cup \mathsf{V}$.

2.3.2   SBR INFERENCE FOR MISO FUZZY RULE BASE

On the other hand, if we consider a Multi Input Single Output (MISO) fuzzy if-then rule of the form:

If x_1 is A_1 and ... and x_n is A_n Then y is C,

Then given the input that $(x_n$ is $A'_1, ..., x_1$ is $A'_n)$, the consequence $c'(y)$ in SBR is given as follows:

COMBINER FUNCTION K

$$C'(y) = (J\left(K\left(M\left(A_1, A'_1\right)........., M\left(A_n, A'_n\right)\right), C(y)\right), = J\left(K_{i=1}^n\left(M\left(A_i, A'_i\right)\right), C(y)\right), y \in Y \qquad (2.3)$$

where K: $[0, 1]^2 \to [0, 1]$, referred to as "Combiner" in the sequel, is an associative and commutative function that combines the matching degrees of $A_i A'_i$, for all $i = 1, 2, ..., n$. Once again typically, $K \in \mathcal{J} \cup \mathcal{L} \cup \mathsf{V}$.

In the case of MISO multiple rules:

$$R_j \text{ if } x_1 \text{ is } A_{1j} \text{ and ... and } x_n \text{ is } A_{nj} \text{ then } y \text{ is } C, j = 1, 2, ..., m,$$

given the input that x_1 is $A_1 ... x_n$ is A_n, we infer the final output by aggregating over the rules,

$$C'(y) = G_{j=1}^{m}(J\left(K_{i=1}^{n}\left(M\left(A_{ij}, A_i\right)\right), C(y)\right)); y \in Y \qquad (2.4)$$

TABLE 2 Lists some SBR inference schemes along with their inference operators

SBR scheme	G	J	K	M
CMI	T	I	T	M_Z
AARS	S_M	$J_{MVR} \, ' J_{ML}$	$A_{vg'}$	M_{Tk}, M_l
CDR	T_M		-	Ms'

Table 1 Some SBR inference schemes along with their inference operators, where T is any t-norm l is any fuzzy implication and $Avg.$ is the averaging operator.

J_{MVR} '.' can be generalized to any t-norm T, In CMI and CDR J is taken to be a fuzzy implication operator. Note that J need not be either commutative or associative.

2.4 RULE REDUCTION IS SBR

In this section, we propose a simple rule reduction technique of combining the antecedents of rules with identical consequents. Such a procedure of combining antecedents in fuzzy rules with identical consequents was considered by Dubois and Prade. The focus of their study was the conditions on the underlying possibility distributions that enabled meaningful combination, whereas our agenda here is to study the conditions on the operators used in the SBR inference mechanisms that allows combining antecedents without losing the obtained inference.

In SBR the steps involved are the following:

- Selection of a matching function M to match the antecedent A of the rule to the current input/observation A'.
- Selection of the modification function J to modify the consequent B according to the degree of compatibility between A and A' to obtain B'.
- In the case of MISO fuzzy rule bases, an additional step employing a commutative and associative operator K is required for combining the matching degree of the antecedents A_i to the given inputs A_i'.
- When there is more than one rule, an associative aggregation operator g is employed over the rules and the inference is obtained by Equation 2.2 or Equation 2.4, using J, M, and K. à.

We denote the SBR inference scheme employed in the case of SISO fuzzy rule base by the quadruple (R, G, J, M), where R denotes the SISO fuzzy rule base given and the inference is given by Equation 2.1. Similarly, we denote the SBR inference scheme employed in the case of MISO fuzzy rulebase by the quintuple (R, G, J, K, M), where R denotes the MISO fuzzy rule base given and the inference is given by Equation 2.3.

Theorem 2.1 [7] Let aMISO fuzzyrule base R be given with the non-empty input universes of discourses X_i for $i = 1, 2, ..., n$ andan output universe of discourse Y. Let the inference be drawn using the SBR inference scheme ($\mathcal{R}$, G, J, K, M), viz. Equation 2.4 If the operators K, J, G, M are such that the following distributive equations hold:

$$G(J(x,z), J(y,z)) = J(K(x,y),z), \qquad (2.5)$$

$$M(K(A_1 < A_2), A') = K(M(A_1, A'), M(A_2, A')), \qquad (2.6)$$

where A_1, A_2, $A \in \mathcal{F}(X)$ and x, y, z, $\in [0, 1]$, then inference invariant rule reduction is possible by combining antecedents of those rules in , whose consequents are identical.

Proof: For the sake of clarity, we consider a 2-input-1-output MISO rule base with just three rules as given in ($\mathcal{R}_0$), where $\widetilde{x}_1$, $\widetilde{x}_2$, $\widetilde{y}$ are linguistic variables assuming the linguistic values $A_1, A_2, A_3 \in \mathcal{F}(X_1)$, B_1, B_2, $B_3 \in \mathcal{F}(X_2)$ and $C, D \in \mathcal{F}(Y)$,

Respectively, and X_1, X_2 are the non-empty input domains, while Y is the non-empty output domain:

$$\text{If } \tilde{x}_1 \text{ is } A_1 \text{ and } \tilde{x}_2 \text{ is } B_1 \text{ then } \tilde{y} \text{ is } C ,$$

$$\text{If } \tilde{x}_1 \text{ is } A_2 \text{ and } \tilde{x}_2 \text{ is } B_2 \text{ then } \tilde{y} \text{ is } C, \qquad (2.7)$$

$$\text{If } \tilde{x}_1 \text{ is } A_3 \text{ and } \tilde{x}_2 \text{ is } B_3 \text{ then } \tilde{y} \text{ is } C$$

In the presence of an input $(\tilde{x}_1 \text{ is } A', \tilde{x}_2 \text{ is } B')$, where $A \in \mathcal{F}(X_1)$ and $B' \in \mathcal{F}(X_2)$, the inference is given by (8). For every $y \in Y$, as follows:

$$C'(y) = G_{i=1}^{3}(J[M(A_i, A') M(B_i, B')], C_i(y))).$$
$$= G(J(K(M(A_1, A') M(B_1, B')), C(y) \ J(K(M(A_2, A') < M(B_2, B')), C(y)), J(K(M(A_3, A') M(B_3, B')), D(y)))). \quad (2.8)$$

Let the operators K, J, G, M be such that Equation 2.5 and Equation 2.6 hold. We claim that the above rule ($\mathcal{R}_0$) can be reduced to the following rule base ($\mathcal{R}_R$) with two rules:

$$\text{If } \tilde{x}_1 \text{ is } K(A_1, A_2) \text{ and } \tilde{x}_2 \text{ is } K(B_1, B_2) \text{ then } \tilde{y} \text{ is } C, \qquad (2.9)$$

$$\text{If } \tilde{x}_1 \text{ is } A_3 \text{ and } \tilde{x}_2 \text{ is } B_3 \text{ then } \tilde{y} \text{ is } D,$$

Such that the inference obtained from the reduced rule base ($\mathcal{R}_R$) for the identical input ($\tilde{x}_1$ is A', $\tilde{x}_2$ is B') is equivalent to Equation 2.8. Indeed, the inference obtained in this case, as given by Equation 2.4 is, for every y $\in$ Y:

$$C'(y)=G(J(K(M(K(K(A_1,A_2),A'),M(K(B_1,B_2),B')),C_i(y)),J(K(M(A_3,A'),M(B_3,B')),D(y))).$$
$$= G(J(K(M(K(M(A_1,A'),M(A_2,A')),K(M(B_1,B'),M(B_2,B'))),C(y)),$$
$$J(K(M(A_3,A'),M(B_3,B')),D(y))) \qquad \text{[By (2.6)]}$$
$$= G(J(K(M(K(M(A_1,A'),M(A_2,A'),M(B_1,B'),M(B_2,B')),C(y)),$$
$$J(K(M(A_3,A'),M(B_3,B')),D(y))) \qquad \text{[By } associativity\ of\ \ K\text{]}$$
$$= G(J(K(K(K(M(A_1,A'),M(B_1,B')),K(M(A_2,A'),M(B_2,B'))),C(y)),$$
$$J(K(M(A_3,A'),M(B_3,B')),D(y)))$$
$$= G(J(K(M(A_1,A'),M(B_1,B')),C(y)),J(K(M(A_2,A'),M(B_2,B')),C(y)),$$
$$J(K(M(A_3,A'),M(B_3,B')),D(y)) \qquad \text{[By (2.5)]}$$
$$= ((2.8)).$$

Thus, when K, J, G, M are such that Equation 2.5 and Equation 2.6 hold, inference invariant rule reduction as proposed above is possible in the SBR inference scheme ($\mathcal{R}, G, J, K, M$).

Notice that in the case of SISO rules, the combiner operator K, though does not play a role in inferencing does play a role in rule reduction, as can be seen from the following result, which follows immediately from Theorem 2.1 above.

Theorem 2.2 [7] Let a SISO fuzzy rule base $\mathcal{R}$ be given with the input and output universes of discourses being non-empty sets X, Y, respectively. Let the inference be drawn using the SBR inference scheme ($\mathcal{R}, G, J, M$), viz., Equation 2.2. If there exists an associative and commutative operator k: $[0, 1]^2 \rightarrow [0, 1]$ such that Equation 2.5 and Equation 2.6 hold, then inference invariant rule reduction is possible by combining antecedents of those rules in $\mathcal{R}$, whose consequents are identical.

Summarizing the above results, Table 2 gives examples of sets of operators G, J, K, M that satisfy the conditions Equation 2.5 and Equation 2.6 of Theorem 2.1.

Example 2.6 [7] In this section, we present a numerical example to show the efficiency and invariance in the inference obtained, when the above rule reduction procedure is employed. Consider a rule base consisting of the following three rules:

$$\textit{If } \tilde{x}_1 \textit{ is } A_1 \textit{ and } \tilde{x}_2 \textit{ is } B_1 \textit{ then } \tilde{y} \textit{ is } C,$$

$$\textit{If } \tilde{x}_1 \textit{ is } A_2 \textit{ and } \tilde{x}_2 \textit{ is } B_2 \textit{ then } \tilde{y} \textit{ is } C, \qquad (2.10)$$

$$\textit{If } \tilde{x}_1 \textit{ is } A_3 \textit{ and } \tilde{x}_2 \textit{ is } B_3 \textit{ then } \tilde{y} \textit{ is } D$$

TABLE 2   Some classes of operators obeying Equations 2.5 and 2.6

G	J	K	M
S_M	J_{MVR}	S_M	M_Z
S_M	$I\tau$	T_M	M_S
T_M	I_s/I_τ	S_M	$M_{S_M.T}$
S_M	I_s/I_τ	T_M	
U_c	I_s	U_d	$M_{T_M.S'}$
U_d	I_s	U_c	$M_{U_d.U}$
U_c	$I\tau$	U_d	$M_{U_c.U}$
U_d	$I\tau$	U_c	$M_{U_d.U}$
T	I_U	S	
S	I_U	T	$M_{U_c.U}$
U_c	I_U	U_d	$M_{S.U}$
U_d	I_U	U_c	$M_{T.U}$
			$M_{U_d.U}$
			$M_{U_c.U}$

Where A_i, B_i for $I = 1, 2, 3$, and C, D are fuzzy sets defined on $X = \{x_1, x_2, x_3, x_4\}$, $Y = \{y_1, y_2, y_3\}$ and $Z = \{z_1, z_2, z_3\}$, respectively, and are given as follows:

$$A1 = [.3, .5, 0\ 1],\ B1 = [.3 .4 .9]\ C = [1 .8 .4 .7]$$
$$A_2 = [.36 .25 .3 .8],\ B_2 = [.12 .67 .99]\ D = [.8 .7 .0\ 1]$$
$$A_3 = [.9\ 0 .8 .5],\ B_3 = [.2 .7 .6]$$

We employ the AARS Inference scheme of Turksen et al. with $G = S_M$, $J=J_{MVR}$, K
$= S_M$, $M = M_Z$ (See Table 2). Let the given input be ($\tilde{x}_1$ is A', is B') where:

$$A' = [.4 \; .7 \; .8 \; 0] \text{ and } B' = [.2 \; 0 \; 1].$$

In the following, we infer both with the original rule base ($\mathcal{R}_0$) and the reduced rule
base ($\mathcal{R}_R$) and show that the inferred output is identical in both the cases.

INFERENCE WITH THE ORIGINAL RULE BASE (R_0)

Calculating the matching degrees:
   $M_Z(A_2, A') = max(36, .25, .3, 0) = 0.36$, $M_Z(B_2, B') = max(.12, 0, .99) = 0.99$
   $M_Z(A_3, A') = max(.4, 0, .8, 0) = 0.8$, $M_Z(B_3, B') = max(.2, 0, .6) = 0.6$.
   Combining the matching degrees to obtain similarity values S_i:
   $S_1 = K(M_Z(A_1, A'), MZ(B_1, B')) = max(0.5, 0.9) = 0.9$
   $S_2 = max(0.36, 0.99) = 0.99$
   $S_3 = max(0.8, 0.6) = 0.8$.
   Modifying the consequents based on the similarity values S_i:

$$J(S_1, C) = J_{MVR}(S_1, C) = (0.9). [1 \; .8 \; .4 \; .7] = [.9 \; .72 \; .36 \; .63] = c_1'$$

$$J(S_2, C) - J_{MVR}(S_2, C) - (0.99). [1 \; .8 \; .4 \; .7] = [.99 \; .79 \; .396 \; .69] - c_2'$$

$$J(S_3, D) = J_{MVR}(S_3, D) = (0.8). [.8 \; .7 \; 0 \; 1] - [64 \; .56 \; 0 \; .8] = c_3'$$
   Combining the obtained consequents for a conclusion:

$$C' = G(C_1', C_2', C_3') = S_M(C_1', C_2', C_3') = [.99 \; .79 \; .396 \; .8]. \tag{2.11}$$

INFERENCE WITH THE REDUCED RULE BASE (R_R)

As can be seen, the first two rules in the original rule base ($\mathcal{R}_0$) have the same
consequent fuzzy set C and hence can be reduced to the rule base consisting of the
following two rules:

$$\text{If } \tilde{x}_1 \text{ is } A^* \text{ and } \tilde{x}_2 \text{ is } B^* \text{ Then } \tilde{Y} \text{ is } C, \tag{2.12}$$

$$\text{If } \tilde{x}_1 \text{ is } A_3 \text{ and } \tilde{x}_2 \text{ is } B_3 \text{ Then } \tilde{Y} \text{ is } D$$

Where:

$$A^* = K(A_1, A_2) = S_M(A_1, A_2) \quad = \quad [.36 \; .5 \quad .3 \quad 1]$$

$$B^* = K(B_1, B_2) = S_M(B_1, B_2) \quad = \quad [.3 \; .67 \quad .99].$$

Once again, calculating tn matching degrees with respect to the same input pair (A'; B') we obtain:

$M_Z(A^*, A') = M_Z(S_M(A_1, A_2)A') = \max(.36, .5, .3, 0) = 0.5,$
$M_Z(B^*, B') = M_Z(S_M(B_1, B_2)B') = \max(.2, 0, .99) = 0.99.$

Hence, the similarity value of the input to the new rule is $s_1^* = \max(0.5, 0.99) = 0.99$, which modifies the consequent C as:

$$C_1^* = J(s_1^*, C) = J_{MVR}(s_1^*, C) = (0.99). \quad [1 \, .8 \, .4 \, .7] \quad = \quad [.99 \, .79 \, .396 \, .69].$$

Combining the obtained consequents for conclusion we obtain:

$$C'' = G(C_1^*, C_3') = S_M(C_1^*, C_3') = \quad [.99 \, .79 \, .396 \, .8].$$

That is, C" = C' in (16). Equivalently, we have shown that the inference obtained for the same inputs from the original and reduced rule bases are identical.

Remark 2.2 In the example above, the operators G, K turned out to be the same because of the choice of the operator J. It should be noted that if $J = 1$, a fuzzy implication, then G, K are usually different as can be seen from Table 2.

In the following section, we propose some new similarity measures and subsequently develop a modified fuzzy reasoning, which is a combination of similarity measure and compositional rules of inference (Section 2.5, 2.6, and 2.7)[1].

2.5 PROPOSED SIMILARITY MEASURE

In order to provide a definition for similarity index, a number of factors must be considered. A primary consideration is that, whatever way we choose to define such an index, it must satisfy the properties as already mentioned. Similarity measures, when expressed through pure numbers are found to be non-transitive.

Keeping all these in mind, we expect that, a similarity measure S(A, B) should satisfy the following properties.

For all fuzzy sets A, B:

P1 S(B, A) = S(A, B)

---

1   This work is basically developed from 1994–1999 as a part of a Ph.D. thesis [193] under the supervision of Prof. K. S. Ray at Electronics and Communication Sciences Unit of Indian Statistical Institute, Kolkata-108.

P2 $S(A^C, B^C) = S(A, B)$, A^C being some negation of A.
P3 $0 \leq S \leq (A, B) \leq 1$.
P4 $A = B$ if $S(A, B) = 1$.

P5 If $S(A, B) = 0$ then either $A \cap B = \phi$ (null), or $A^C \cap B^C = \phi$; or $B = 1 - A$.

For $0 \leq \epsilon \leq 1$ 1, if $S(A, B) \geq \epsilon$, we way that the two fuzzy sets A and B are ϵ-similar. Thus, the case for $\epsilon = 1$ correspond to equality of fuzzy sets. There may be many functions satisfying properties **P1** through **P5**. One such measure of similarity satisfying properties **P1** through **P5** is given in Definition 2.2.

Definition 2.2 Let A and B be two fuzzy sets defined over the universe of discourse U. The similarity index of the pair {A, B} is defined by:

$$S(A, B) = min\{\alpha(A, B), \alpha(A^c, B^c)\} \qquad (2.13)$$

Where,

$$\alpha(A, B) = \left\{ \frac{\sum_{u \in U} \{\mu_A(u), \mu_{AB}(u)\}}{\sum_{u \in U} [max\{\mu_A(u) \cdot \mu_{AB}(u)\}]^2} \right\}^{1/2} \qquad (2.14)$$

and,

$$\mu A^C(u_{ij}) = 1 - \mu_A(u_{ij}).$$

It is easy to see that properties **P1** and **P2** are satisfied by definition 2.2. The other properties may be verified as follows:

VERIFICATION OF P3

Let A and B be two fuzzy sets defined on the same universe of discourse U. It is known that:

$$0 \leq \mu_A(u), \mu_B(u).$$

If:

$$\sum_{u \in U} [max\{\mu_A(u), \mu_B(u)\}]^2 = 0.$$

Then $\forall u \in U, \mu_A(u) = \mu_B(u) = 0$ and hence $\alpha(A, B) = 1$. Also, in this case, $1 - \mu_A(u) = 1 - \mu_B(u) = 1$. So that $\alpha(A^c, B^c) = 1$. Therefore, $S(A, B) = 1$.

Otherwise, $\exists u \in U$,   such   that $max\{\mu_A(u), \mu_B(u)\} > 0$, making $\alpha(A, B) \geq 0$.   Similarly,

$\alpha(A^C, B^C) \geq 0$. Therefore,

$$S(A, B) \geq 0.$$

   Again,

$$\forall u \in U$$

$$\mu_A(u) \leq max\{\mu_A(u), \mu_B(u)\}$$

and,

$$\mu_B(u) \leq max\{\mu_A(u), \mu_B(u)\}$$

will imply at once that:

$$\sum_{u \in U}\{\mu_A(u).\mu_B(u)\} \leq \sum_{u \in U}\left[max\{\mu_A(u), \mu_B(u)\}^2\right],$$

that is, $\alpha(A, B) \leq 1$. Similarly $(A^C, B^C) \leq 1$ and hence, S(A,B) ≤ 1.. Thus, the proposition:

$$0 \leq S(A, B) \leq 1$$

is valid.

VERIFICATION OF P4

Let us suppose that S(A, B) = 1 that is:

$$min\{\alpha(A, B), \alpha(A^C, B^C)\} = 1 \qquad (2.15)$$

   By P3, since,

$$\alpha(A, B) \leq 1 \, and \, \alpha(A^C, B^C) \leq 1,$$

it follows from Equation 2.15 that:

$$\alpha(A,B),\alpha(A^c,B^c)=1.$$

Now, (A, B) = 1 will apply that:

$$\sum_{u\in U}\{\mu_A(u).\mu_B(u)\}=\sum_{u\in U}\left[max\{\mu_A(u).\mu_B(u)\}\right]^{1/2} \tag{2.16}$$

Again,

$$\mu_A(u)\leq max\{\mu_A(u),\mu_B(u)\}$$

and,

$$\mu_B(u)\leq max\{\mu_A(u),\mu_B(u)\}$$

that is,

$$\mu_A(u).\mu_B(u)\leq\left[max\{\mu_A(u),\mu_B(u)\}\right]^{1/2},\forall u\in U \tag{2.17}$$

Each termon either side of the inequality Equation 2.17 is non-negative. For in Equation 2.17 to be true, we must have:

$$\mu_A(u).\mu_B(u)=\left[max\{\mu_A(u),\mu_B(u)\}\right]^{1/2} \tag{2.18}$$

Otherwise, if for a particular u ∈U:

$$\mu_A(u).\mu_B(u)<\left[max\{\mu_A(u),\mu_B(u)\}\right]^{1/2}.$$

Thenα(A, B) would become less than unity, which is not true. Hence:

$$\mu_A(u).\mu_B(u)=\left[max\{\mu_A(u),\mu_B(u)\}\right]^{1/2},\forall u\in U \tag{2.19}$$

If now $\mu_A(u)\geq\mu_B(u)$ then we find that:

$$\mu_A(u).\mu_B(u)=\{\mu_A(u)\}^2. \tag{2.20}$$

If $\mu_A(u)=0$ then from the given condition, we find that $\mu_B(u)=\mu_A(u)=0, \forall u \in U$.

Otherwise, cancelling $\mu_A(u)$ from both sides of Equation2.20, we find that:

$$\mu_B(u)=\mu_A(u)$$

$$\Rightarrow \mu_B(u)=\mu_A(u) \neq 0$$

or,

$$\mu_B(u)=\mu_A(u)=0.$$

So that, in any case, it is true that B = A.

If, on the other hand, $\mu_B(u) \geq \mu_A(u)$ then from Equation 2.19 we find that:

$$\mu_A(u).\mu_B(u)=\{\mu_B(u)\}^2. \tag{2.21}$$

In this case also:
either,

$$\mu_A(u)=\mu_A(u) \neq 0$$

or,

$$\mu_A(u)=\mu_B(u)=0.$$

Hence, the proposition B = A is valid.

If, we suppose that two fuzzy sets A and B are such that A = B then from the Definition 2.2, it follows at once that S(A, B) = 1.

VERIFICATION OF P5

Here, it is given that S(A, B) = 0. By Definition 2.2, it follows that:

$$min\{\alpha(A,B),\alpha(A^C,B^C)\}=0,$$

that is, either or both of α(A, B) = 0 or α (A^c, B^c) = 0 or both. Let us suppose:

$$\alpha(A, B) = 0$$

that is,

$$\sum_{u \in U} \mu_A(u).\mu_B(u) = 0 \tag{2.22}$$

Since,

$$\mu_A(u).\mu_B(u) \geq 0, \forall u \in U$$

therefore,

$$\text{Equation } 2.22 \Rightarrow \mu_A(u).\mu_B(u) \geq 0, \forall u \in U,$$

that is,

$$\min\{\mu_A(u).\mu_B(u) \geq 0\}, \forall u \in U,$$

that is,

$$A \cap B = \phi.$$

On the other hand, if $\alpha(A^C, B^C) = 0$, then:

$$\sum_{u \in U}\{(1 - \mu_A(u)).(1 - \mu_B(\mu_B))\} = 0 \tag{2.23}$$

Since, each term underthe summation is non-negative:

$$\text{Equation } 2.23 \Rightarrow (1 - \mu_A(u)).1(1 - \mu_B(\mu_B)) = 0, \forall u \in U,$$

that is,

$$min(1 - \mu_A(u)).(1 - \mu_B(u)) = 0, \forall u \in U,$$

that is,

$$A^C \cap B^C = \phi,$$

the NULL set.
and, when both are zero then:

$$\mu_A(u).\mu_B(u) \geq 0, \forall u \in U,$$

as well as,

$$1 - \left\{ \mu_A(u).\left(1 - \mu_B(u)\right) \right\} = 0; \forall u \in U.$$

Now if:

$$\mu_A(u) = 0 \, then \, \mu_B(u) = 1$$

else if,

$$\mu_B(u) = 0 \, then \, \mu_A(u) = 1,$$

that is,

$$B = 1 - A.$$

Hence, the above proposition is valid.
Example 2.7 Let:

$$U = \left\{ u_1, u_2, u_3, u_4, u_5 \right\}$$

and,

$$A = .1/u_1 + .3/u_2 + .5/u_3 + .75/u_4 + 1/u_5,$$

$$B = .01/u_1 + .09/u_2 + .25/u_3 + .5625/u_4 + 1/u_5,$$

$$C = .31/u_1 + .55/u_2 + .707/u_3 + .866/u_4 + 1/u_5.$$

Be defined as above. Then:

$$\alpha(A, B) = 0.82346405 \, (approximately).$$

Similarly,

$$\alpha\left(A^{C}, \, B^{C}\right) = \alpha\left(1 \, - \, A, \, 1 \, - \, B\right) \, = \, 0.78543776 \, \left(approximately\right).$$

Therefore,

$$S(A, \, B) \; = \; 0.78543776 \; \left(approximately\right).$$

Again if C is considered, instead of B, then:

$$\alpha(A, \, C) \; = \; 0.82936142 \; \left(approximately\right).$$

Similarly,

$$\alpha(A^{c}, B^{c}) = \alpha(1 - A, 1 - C) = 0.68874419 \, (approximately).$$

Therefore,

$$S(A, \, C) \; = \; 0.688744119 \; \left(approximately\right).$$

Although, the last property **P5** is a plausible and an intuitively appealing one, it is possible to argue in favor of a stricter condition for which S(A, B) should be zero. Two crisp sets A and B are completely dissimilar only, when A∩ B =ϕ. If A∩ B≠ϕ then they have some similarity as A and B have some elements in common, in terms of grade. The similarity between the two increases as the number of elements by which the two sets differ decreases. The similarity becomes maximum (the maximum value may be thought of as 1), when the two sets are identical, that is:

$$| A \cap B | = | A | = | B |. \tag{2.24}$$

Here, we consider a direct extension of this concept (3.40) in defining the similarity between fuzzy sets. For two fuzzy sets, it is reasonable to assume, that the similarity should be zero if and only if A∩ B = ϕ. Property **P5** may now be reformulated as**P5'**. For all fuzzy sets A, B, S(A, B) = 0 if A ∩ B = ϕ.

The need, thus, arises to find measures of similarity satisfying properties **P1** through **P4** and **P5'**. There could be several such measures a family of such simple measures may be given by the following Definition 2.3.

Definition 2.3 Let:

$$A = \sum_{u \in U} \mu_A(u)/u$$

and,

$$B = \sum_{u \in U} \mu_B(u)/u$$

betwo fuzzy sets defined over the same universe of discourse U. The similarity index of the pair {A, B} is denoted by S(A, B) and is defined by:

$$S(A,B) = 1 - \left(\frac{\sum_u |\mu_A(u) - \mu_B(u)|^q}{n} \right)^{1/2}$$

$$(2.25)$$

Wherenis the cardinality of the universe of discourse andqis the family parameter.
From the above Definition 2.3 it is clear that **P1**, that is, S(A, B) = S(B, A), is satisfied.

Next,

$$S(A,B) = 1 - \left(\frac{\sum_u |\mu_A(u) - \mu_B(u)|^q}{n} \right)^{1/2}$$

$$= 1 - \left(\frac{\sum_u |(1 - \mu_A(u)) - (1\mu_B(u))|^q}{n} \right)^{1/2}$$

$$= S(A^c, B^c).$$

hence, property **P2**.
In order to verify property **P3** we proceed as follows:

$$0 \leq \left| \mu_A(u) - \mu_B(u) \right| \leq 1$$

$$\text{i.e } 0 \leq \left| \mu_A(u) - \mu_B(u) \right|^q \leq 1$$

$$\text{i.e } 0 \leq \Sigma_{u=1}^{n} \left| \mu_A(u) - \mu_B(u) \right|^q \leq n$$

$$\text{i.e } 0 \leq \left(\frac{\Sigma_{u=1}^{n} \left| \mu_A(u) - \mu_B(u) \right|^q}{n} \right) \leq 1$$

$$\text{i.e } 0 \leq \left(\frac{\Sigma_{u=1}^{n} \left| \mu_A(u) - \mu_B(u) \right|^q}{n} \right) \frac{1}{q} \leq 1$$

Therefore, $0 \leq S(A, B) \leq 1$ which is property **P3**.
For P4, it is easy to see that

$$S(A, B) = 1 \Leftrightarrow \left(\frac{\sum_u \left| \mu_A(u) - \mu_B(u) \right|^q}{n} \right) \frac{1}{q} = 0$$

that is,

$$\Leftrightarrow \mu_A(u) - \mu_B(u) = 0 \, \forall u$$

that is,

$$\Leftrightarrow \mu_A(u) = \mu_B(u) = \forall u$$

that is,

$$\Leftrightarrow A = B.$$

Hence, property **P4** is established.
Note that this also ensures S(ϕ, ϕ) = 1. Next, property **P5'** is verified. For that, let us suppose:

$$S(A, B) = 1 - \left(\frac{\sum_u \left| \mu_A(u) - \mu_B(u) \right|^q}{n} \right) \frac{1}{q} = 0.$$

$$\Leftrightarrow \left(\frac{\sum_u |\mu_A(u) - \mu_B(u)|^q}{n} \right) \frac{1}{q} = 1.$$

$$\Leftrightarrow \sum_n |\mu_A(u) - \mu_B(u)|^q = n$$

$$\Leftrightarrow |\mu_A(u) - \mu_B(u)|^q = \forall u$$

$$\Leftrightarrow |\mu_A(u) - \mu_B(u)| = 1 \forall u.$$

If $\mu_A(u) \geq \mu_B(u)$ then $\mu_A(u) = 1$ and $\mu_B(u)| = 0$, while if $\mu_A(u) \leq 1\mu_B(u)$ then $\mu_A(u) = 0, \mu_B(u) = 1$ and this is true for all u. Thus, S(A, B) = 1 if A ∩ B = ϕ, that is, when A and B are crisp and $A = B^C$.

Example 2.8 Let:

$$U = \{u_1, u_2, u_3, u_4, u_5\}.$$

and,

$$A = .1/u_1 + .3/u_2 + .5/u_3 + .75/u_4 + 1/u_5,$$

$$B = .01/u_1 + .09/u_2 + .25/u_3 + .5625/u_4 + 1/u_5,$$

$$C = .316/u_1 + .55/u_2 + .707/u_3 + .866/u_4 + 1/u_5.$$

With q=2 it is found that:

$$S(A, B) = 0.92257746 \ (approximately).$$

Similarly, if C is considered in place of B then:

$$S(A, C) = 0.91864620 \ (approximately).$$

S(A, B)≥S(A, C) will imply that "B is at least as close to A as C is close to A". S(A, B), as given in Definition 2.3, is quite sensitive every change in A or B will be reflected in S(A, B). Next some more property of S is discussed in the following:

Theorem 2.3 If S(A, B) = 1 and S(B, C) = 1 then S(A, C) = 1.

Proof:

$$S(A, B) = 1 \Rightarrow A = B, \ S(B, C) = 1 \Rightarrow B = C \Rightarrow A = B = C \Rightarrow S(A, C) = 1.$$

Of course, in general, for all fuzzy sets A, B and C the numbers S(A, B) and S(B, C) cannot always determine S(A, C). If some structural arrangement between them may be prescribed then, we may find an estimate for the same as in Theorem 2.4.

Theorem 2.4 For all fuzzy sets A, B, C

if either,

$$A \subseteq B \subseteq C \text{ or } A \supseteq B \supseteq C$$

Then,

$$S(A, C) \leq \min\{S(A, B), S(B, C)\}.$$

Proof: Suppose,

$$A \subseteq B \subseteq C,$$

that is,

$$\mu_A(u) \leq \mu_B(u) \leq \mu_C(u), \forall u \in U$$

that is,

$$\mu_B(u) \leq \mu_A(u) \leq \mu_C(u) - \mu_A(u), \forall u \in U$$

that is,

$$\mu_B(u) \leq \mu_A(u)| \leq |\mu_C(u) - \mu_A(u)|, \forall u \in U$$

that is,

$$\frac{1}{n}\sum_{u \in U} |\mu_B(u) - \mu_A(u)|^q \leq \frac{1}{n}\sum_{u \in U} |\mu_C(u) - \mu_A(u)|^q,$$

that is,

$$\left(\frac{1}{n}\sum_{u\in U}|\mu_B(u)-\mu_A(u)|^q\right)^{\frac{1}{q}}\leq\left(\frac{1}{n}\sum_{u\in U}|\mu_C(u)-\mu_A(u)|^q\right)^{\frac{1}{q}},$$

that is,

$$1-\left(\frac{1}{n}\sum_{u\in U}|\mu_B(u)-\mu_A(u)|^q\right)^{\frac{1}{q}}\geq1-\left(\frac{1}{n}\sum_{u\in U}|\mu_C(u)-\mu_A(u)|^q\right)^{\frac{1}{q}},$$

that is,

$$S(A, B)\geq S(A, C).$$

Similarly,

$$S(B, C)\geq S(A, C).$$

Hence,

$$S(A, C)\leq\min\{S(A, B), S(B, C)\}.$$

On the other hand, suppose that:

$$A\supseteq B\supseteq C$$

that is,

$$\mu_A(u)\leq\mu_B(u)\leq\mu_C(u), \forall u\in U$$

that is,

$$\mu_B(u)\leq\mu_C(u)\leq\mu_A(u)-\mu_C(u), \forall u\in U$$

that is,

$$|\mu_B(u)|\leq|\mu_C(u)\leq\mu_A(u)-\mu_C(u)|, \forall u\in U$$

that is,

$$\frac{1}{n}\sum_{u\in U}|\mu_B(u)-\mu_C(u)|^q \le \frac{1}{n}\sum_{u\in U}|\mu_A(u)-\mu_C(u)|^q,$$

that is,

$$\text{i.e}\left(\frac{1}{n}\sum_{u\in U}|\mu_B(u)-\mu_C(u)|^q\right)^{\frac{1}{q}} \le \left(\frac{1}{n}\sum_{u\in U}|\mu_{BA}(u)-\mu_C(u)|^q\right)^{\frac{1}{q}}$$

$$\text{i.e } 1-\left(\frac{1}{n}\sum_{u\in U}|\mu_B(u)-\mu_C(u)|^q\right)^{\frac{1}{q}} \ge \left(\frac{1}{n}\sum_{u\in U}|\mu_{BA}(u)-\mu_C(u)|^q\right)^{\frac{1}{q}}$$

that is,

$$S(B,\ C)\ge S(A,\ C).$$

Similarly,

$$S(A,\ B)\ge S(A,\ C).$$

Hence,

$$S(A,\ C)\le \min\{S(A,\ B),\ S(B,\ C)\}.$$

Hence, the theorem.

Theorem 2.4 motivates us to consider the property of monotonicity of similarity between fuzzy sets to satisfy another axiom for some kind of monotonicity. So, we are now in a position to state the axioms for similarity measure as follows:

For all fuzzy sets A, B

A1 S(B, A) = S(A, B).

A2 $S(A^C, B^C) = S(A, B)$, A^C being some negation of A.

A3 $0 \le S(A,\ B) \le 1$.

A4 A = B if S(A, B) = 1.

A5 S(A, B) = 0 if and only if A ∩ B φ.

A6 If $A \supseteq B \supseteq C$, then $S(A, B) \geq S(A, C)$.

Here, we note that, A^c, the complement of a fuzzy set A is to be defined first. Throughout, the thesis we used the ideal of '1-' as the complementation. A general characterization of similarity index satisfying the set of axioms is not in the present scope of the thesis. On the basis of the above axioms, it is easy to see that the family of similarity measures defined in Definition 2.3 is a valid choice.

2.5.1   MORE ON SIMILARITY MEASURE

Our interest is on machine-oriented measures for solving practical problems. For that, so far we have considered similarity measures for fuzzy sets having finite support set. In this section, we study some measures of similarity between fuzzy sets having arbitrary support set. Already we have listed some of them in the review section. For example, the measures defined in (3.14) and (3.22) may be directly extended to infinite sets.

Let U be any arbitrary set and let $F(U)$ be the collection of all fuzzy subsets of U. To specify a degree of similarity between elements of $F(U)$, we first define a distance function:

$$D(A, B) = \sup_{u \in U} |\mu_A(u) - \mu_B(u)|, A, B \in F(U) \tag{2.26}$$

The corresponding similarity index S(A, B) may be obtained as:

$$S(A, B) = 1 - d(A, B \tag{2.27}$$

Thus, given any $\varepsilon \in [0,1]$, two members of $F(U)$ are said to be ε-similar, if and only if $S(A, B) \geq \varepsilon$.

If we go back to the axioms of the previous section we find that (3.43) satisfies all except axiom **A5**. Nevertheless, it is a reasonable definition. Let us now propose a family of similarity indices for countably infinite fuzzy sets as follows:

$$D(A, B) = \left[\sum_{n=1}^{\infty} \frac{|\mu_A(u_n) - \mu_B(u_n)|^q}{2^n} \right]^{\frac{1}{q}}, A, B \in F(U); q \geq 1 \tag{2.28}$$

The corresponding similarity index S (A, B) may be obtained as

$$S(A, B) = 1 - d(A, B). \tag{2.29}$$

Now, since

$$0 \leq |\mu_A(u_n) - \mu_B(u_n)| \leq 1 \tag{2.30}$$

It is clear that, the infinite series is convergent and converges to 1.

In the above case, we see that the similarity index depends not only on the corresponding membership values but also on the order of their appearance because of the presence of the weight factor. This may be avoided, if we consider the supreme over all possible combinations. The above concept is soul for mathematical theory construction but found to be inappropriate in terms of computational aspect.

Thus, we see that similarity or indistinguishability between fuzzy sets may be captured by aggregating the dissimilarity or distinguishability between membership values of elements in the corresponding fuzzy sets. Such an index, being a pure number, does not give any information about the ordering. This is why these measures are not transitive. Similarity matching is inherent in reasoning with imprecise concepts. In this section, we show how similarity measure may be made to work in reasoning with vague concepts.

2.6 FUZZY REASONING USING SIMILARITY MEASURES AND COMPUTATIONAL RULE OF INFERENCE

In the previous section, we developed the concept of similarity index for measuring the likeness of fuzzy sets over a given universe of discourse and proposed two new measures for the same. We discussed some basic properties and results in connection with these measures. Here, we restrict ourselves to the said two similarity measures for fuzzy sets having finite support (Definition 2.2, Definition 2.3). We will consider the introduction of the concept of similarity in AR methodology.

To begin with, in this section, we take a close look at the different methods of inference based on a similarity measure. It has been shown that the method is applicable to both point-valued and interval valued-fuzzy sets. Two other methods based on different modification procedures have been proposed.

In all these works, the authors considered that similarity based fuzzy reasoning methods do not require the construction of a fuzzy relation. According, they are based on the computation of the degree of similarity between the fact and the antecedent of a rule, in a rule-based system. Then, based on the similarity value between the membership values of the elements of the fuzzy set representation of the fact and the corresponding fuzzy set in the antecedent of the rule, the membership value of each element of the consequent fuzzy set of the rule is modified to obtain a conclusion. This is the same for all existing SBR schema. The modification procedure is different schema.

We propose two new similarity based AR methods. In the process, we consider both similarity based models and resolution based models, for similarity based AR. With different results we show that the proposed similarity based AR methods are reasonable. In the proposed methods, for inference in a rule-based system, the conditional rule and for inference in a resolution-based system, the disjunction is first expressed as a fuzzy binary relation. In translation, we prefer to use triangular norms in the first case and triangular conforms in the other case, for a better understanding. Other interpretations are also possible. Then, new facts are used to compute the similarity between the fact and the antecedent of the rule, in a rule-based system and one of the disjunct defined over the same universe in a resolution-based system, to modify the above fuzzy binary relation and not the consequence of the rule as done in the existing SBR mechanisms. The modification is based on a measure of similarity following some scheme to be presented. The result is interpreted as the induced fuzzy binary relation. Then the inference is computed from the induced fuzzy binary relation using the well known sup-operation, in a rule-based system and in-operation in a resolution-based system.

In the following, we present a brief review on the existing similarity based fuzzy reasoning mechanisms. Then, we formulate two new schema of reasoning based on similarity measures. The above schema is used in formulating different models (rule-based and resolution-based). We provide some simple examples for a better understanding of the proposed schema.

p: X is A then YisB

q: X is A'

----

r: Y is B'.

A BRIEF REVIEW

Many fuzzy systems are based on Zadeh's CRI. Despite their success in various systems, researchers have indicated certain drawbacks in the mechanism. This motivates the introduction of SBR mechanisms as proposed here.

In such SBR schema, we see that, from a given fact, the desired conclusion is derived using only a measure of similarity between the fact and the antecedent, in a rule-based system. In some cases, a threshold value π is associated with a rule. If the degree of similarity, between the antecedent of the rule and the given fact, exceeds the real value ofπ, associated with the rule under consideration, then only that rule is assumed to be fired. The conclusion is derived using some modification procedure.

As an illustration, let us consider the two premises. Here, A and A' are fuzzy sets defined over the same universe of discourse $U = \{u_1, u_2, ..., u_m\}$ and B, B' are defined over the universe of discourse $V = \{v_1, v_2, ..., v_n\}$. Let S(A, B) denote some measure of similarity between two fuzzy sets A, B. As per Euclidean distance:

$$D_2(A, A') = \left[\frac{\sum_{i=1}^{m}\left[\mu_{A'}(u_i) - \mu_A(u_i)\right]^2}{m}\right]^{\frac{1}{2}}. \qquad (2.31)$$

The similarity is then defined as:

$$S(A, B) = \left[1 + D_2(A, A')\right]^{-1} \qquad (2.32)$$

In the existing mechanisms, if S(A, A') >π then the rule will be fired and the consequent of the rule is modified to produce the desired conclusion. Based on the change of membership grade of the consequent, two types of modification procedures are as follows:

Expansion type inference and reduction type inference.

Let:

$$B' = \sum_{i=1}^{n} \left\{ \mu_{B'}(v_i) / v_i \right\} \text{ and } s = s\left(S(A,B), \pi \right)$$

Expansion form:

$$\mu_{B'}(v_i) = min\left(1, \mu_B(v_i)/s\right) \tag{2.33}$$

Reduction form:

$$\mu_{B'}(v_i) = \left(\mu_B(v_i)\right).s \tag{2.34}$$

The authors have also extended this method to handle interval-valued fuzzy sets. Both the methods proposed use the threshold value, a confidence factor and the reduction form of inference without providing any argument as to the choice of modification procedure. In one of them, each fuzzy set is first conceived as an m-component vector and then use the concept of vector dot product for finding the similarity, called the matching function as:

$$S(A,B) = \frac{|A| A' cos(\theta)}{\left(max\left(|A|^2 |A'|^2\right)\right)} \tag{2.35}$$

Where |A| is the length of the vector A and $cos(\theta)$ is the cosine of the angle between the two vectors. If S(A, B) ≥ π, the predefined threshold value, then the rule will be fired and strength of confirmation is calculated by S(A, B) *μ, , where μ is the confidence factor associated with the rule. In the other method, the author used weights with each propositions for the calculation of similarity. In this case, the similarity between fuzzy sets is computed as:

$$S(A,B) = \sum_{i=1}^{m} \left[T\left(\mu_{A'}(u_i), \mu_A(u_i)\right) . \frac{w_i}{\sum_{k=1}^{m} w_k} \right] \tag{2.36}$$

Where,

$$T\left(\mu_{A'}\left(u_i\right),\mu_A\left(u_i\right)\right)=1-|\left(\mu_{A'}\left(u_i\right),\mu_A\left(u_i\right)\right)|.$$

The procedure for the computation of the conclusion remains the same.

In another approach the authors used the value of certainty factor associated with the rules in the modification procedure. The inference is based on the number of propositions in the antecedent of the rule(s) as well as the operator(s) connecting them. In each case, the inference is one of expansion type. There are also two more modification procedures and claimed two new fuzzy reasoning methods. One modification is based on Zadeh's inclusion and cardinality measure and the other one is based on equality and cardinality measure. Other operations remain almost identical.

2.6.1 PROPOSED METHOD

In this section, we show how conclusions may be obtained from given premises with the help of such a similarity measure. In the process, we consider both rule-based and resolution-based models. Let X, Y be two linguistic variables and let U, V respectively denote the universes of discourse. Two typical propositions p and q are given and we derive a conclusion according to similarity based inference. The scheme may be best described in Table 3.

Let:

$$U=\left\{u_1,u_2,...,u_l\right\},$$

$$V=\left\{v_1,v_2,...,u_m\right\},$$

Denote the respective universe of discourse of the linguistic variables X and Y. Let fuzzy sets A, A' and B in Table 3 be defined as:

$$A=\sum_{i=1}^{l}\left\{\mu_A\left(u_i\right)/u_i\right\}, \tag{2.37}$$

$$A'=\sum_{i=1}^{l}\left\{\mu_{A'}\left(u_i\right)/u_i\right\}, \tag{2.38}$$

$$B=\sum_{i=1}^{m}\left\{\mu_B\left(v_i\right)/v_i\right\}, \tag{2.39}$$

$$B' = \sum_{i=1}^{m} \left\{ \mu_{B'}(v_i) / v_i \right\}. \qquad (2.40)$$

OUTLINE

It is easy to see that all the existing methods use the similarity measure for a direct computation of inference without considering the induced relation, that is, how the underlyingrelation(a condition) is modified in presence of the given fact.

TABLE 3   Ordinary approximate reasoning

> p: X is A then Y is B
>
> q: X is A'
>
> ----------------------------------
>
> r: Y is B'.

This is important in deriving a consequence of the fact from the rule. Consequently, those methods provide the same conclusion, ifA and A'are interchanged in the propositions concerned. Thus, ifp, q, and p', q' be defined as in the following:
  i.   P; if X isA then Y is B, π and q: X is A'
  ii. P: if X is A' then Y is B, π and q: X is A
then both (i) and (ii) will produce the same conclusion. This is not appealing. This happens because the conclusion is derived just by a modification of the consequent of the rule. It should be noted here that, this is not the case with Zadeh's compositionalrule of inference. Another notable fact is that we need to consider the threshold or certainty factor in order to tackle the problem of the rule misfiring.

The first drawback may at once be eliminated if we consider the interpretation of the relational operator present in the conditional premise, as is done in executing CRI. It is easy to verify that for a class of nested fuzzy sets, each different from the other, the consequence of a rule using CRI, becomes the same. We seek a reasoning system, where every change in the concept(s) as appear in the conditional statement and that in the fact, be incorporated in the induced relation between the variables defining the condition, in this case, X and Y. Only then the inference will be influenced by the change.

In order to avoid the use of certainty factor for rule-misfiring, we modify the inference scheme in such a way that significant change will make the conclusion less specific. This is done if an expansion type of inference scheme be chosen. Here, the "UNKNOWN" case, that is, the fuzzy set B' = V, may be taken as the limit. Explicitly, when the similarity value becomes low, that is, when A and A' differ significantly, the reasoning process should be such that the onlyinference be B' = V. As A' = A, we expect that B' = B. This, in turn, implies that nothing better than what the rule says should be allowed as a valid conclusion.

SCHEMA

In view of the above observations, we propose a similarity based inference method for deriving the consequence r. We first generate the fuzzy relation between the antecedent variables(s) and the consequent variable as done in executing CRI. Then we compute the absolute change in linguistic labels, represented as fuzzy sets, and systematically propagate the same into the conditional relation in order obtain the induced modified conditional relation. From this induced modified relation, a possible conclusion may be drawn using the sup-operation. The scheme for computation may be presented in the following algorithm.

ALGORITHM SAR

Similarly based ordinary AR:
- **Step 1** Translate premisepand computeR(A, B) using any suitable translating rule possibly, A T-norm operator.
- **Step 2** Compute S(A, A') according to either Definition 2.2 or Definition 2.3 or by some other similar definitions.
- **Step 3** Modify R(A, B) with S(A, A') to obtain the modified conditional relation R(A | A', B) according to some scheme C.
- **Step 4** Use sup-projection operation on R(A | A' B) to obtain B' as:

$$\mu_{B'}(v) = \overset{sup}{\underset{u}{}} \mu_{R(A'|A,B)}(u, v) \tag{2.41}$$

Now, for a given fact q: X is A' and from the condition p:if X is A then Y is B, we propose two schema C1 and C2 for computation of the modified conditional relation R(A | A', B) as given in Step 3.

SCHEME C1

We may recall here that, the authors computed the conclusion B' = min(1, B/s), where-sis the measure of similarity between fuzzy set's A and A' without considering the information suggested by the conditional rule. Here, we propose to modify the conditional relation according to the Equation 2.42.

$$R(A|A',B) = [r'_{u,v}] \, l \times m \begin{bmatrix} r'_{u,v} & = min(1, r_{u,v}/s) if \ s > 0 \\ = 1 & otherwise \end{bmatrix} \tag{2.42}$$

It is clear that, the proposed scheme, does not produce the same conclusion, when A and A'are interchanged. It is not difficult to see that in Equation 2.42, if $S \le r_{u,v}$ for some v $\in$ v then $r'u$, becomes equal to one. Thus, making the membership of that v in the resultant fuzzy set equal to one.

Example 2.9 Let us consider aproblem as posed schematically in Table 3, where

$U = \{u_1, u_2, u_3, u_4\}$ and $\{v_1, v_2, v_3, v_4\}$. Also let:

$$A = 1.00/u_1 + 0.75/u_2 + 0.50/u_3 + 0.25/u_4,$$
$$A' = 1.00/u_1 + 0.80/u_2 + 0.40/u_3 + 0.15/u_4,$$
$$B = 0.25/v_1 + 0.50/v_2 + 0.75/v_3 + 1.00/v_4.$$

Using Mamdani's min-rule for translation we first construct the fuzzy binary relation on U x V as:

$$
R(A,B) = \begin{array}{c} \\ u_1 \\ u_2 \\ u_3 \\ u_4 \end{array}
\begin{array}{cccc}
v_1 & v_2 & v_3 & v_4 \\
\left[\begin{array}{cccc}
0.25 & 0.50 & 0.75 & 1.00 \\
0.25 & 0.50 & 0.75 & 0.75 \\
0.25 & 0.50 & 0.50 & 0.50 \\
0.25 & 0.25 & 0.25 & 0.25
\end{array}\right]
\end{array} \tag{2.43}
$$

Thus, using Definition 2.3, we compute S(A, a') = 0.95322928 (approx). The modified relation, R(A, B) that is R(A| A'B) using scheme C 1 may be found to be:

$$
R(A'|A,B) = \begin{array}{c} \\ u_1 \\ u_2 \\ u_3 \\ u_4 \end{array}
\begin{array}{cccc}
v_1 & v_2 & v_3 & v_4 \\
\left[\begin{array}{cccc}
0.2623 & 0.5245 & 0.7868 & 1.00 \\
0.2623 & 0.5245 & 0.7868 & 0.7868 \\
0.2623 & 0.5245 & 0.5245 & 0.5245 \\
0.2623 & 0.2623 & 0.2623 & 0.2623
\end{array}\right]
\end{array} \tag{2.44}
$$

Therefore, using Equation 2.41, we find the consequence as:

$$B' = sup_{u \in U}\left[R(A'|A,B)\right] = 0.2623/v_1 + 0.5245/v_2 + 0.7868/v_3 + 1/v_4. \tag{2.45}$$

Instead of using Madmani's min operator if we use max (0, a+b-1) for the translation of the conditional statement then we find the conditional relation as:

$$
R(A,B) = \begin{array}{c} \\ u_1 \\ u_2 \\ u_3 \\ u_4 \end{array}
\begin{array}{cccc}
v_1 & v_2 & v_3 & v_4 \\
\left[\begin{array}{cccc}
0.2500 & 0.5000 & 0.7500 & 1.0 \\
0.2623 & 0.5245 & 0.7868 & 1.0 \\
0.2751 & 0.5503 & 0.8254 & 1.0 \\
0.2886 & 0.5775 & 0.8569 & 1.0
\end{array}\right]
\end{array} \tag{2.46}
$$

The modified relation R(A, B) that is R(A'| A, B) will be given by:

$$R(A'|A,B) \begin{array}{cccc} & v_1 & v_2 & v_3 & v_4 \\ u_1 & \begin{bmatrix} 0.2623 & 0.5245 & 0.7868 & 1.0 \\ u_2 & 0.2751 & 0.5503 & 0.8254 & 1.0 \\ u_3 & 0.2886 & 0.5773 & 0.8569 & 1.0 \\ u_4 & 0.3028 & 0.6056 & 0.9084 & 1.0 \end{bmatrix} \end{array} \qquad (2.47)$$

Therefore, using Equation 2.41, the consequence become:

$$B' = sup_{u \in U} \left[R(A'|A,B) \right] = 0.3028/v_1 + 0.6056/v_2 + 0.9084/v_3 + 1/v_4. \quad (2.48)$$

This scheme, although a heuristic one, is intuitively a plausible scheme. Our next scheme C 2 for computation of R(A'| a, B) is based on a set of axioms.

SCHEME C 2

We believe that in a SBR methodology, a scheme for computation of the induced relation, when a fact and a conditional statement is given, should satisfy the following axioms:

A4.1. If S(A, a') = 1, i.e., if A' = A, then

$$\mu_{R(A'|A,B)} = \mu_{R(A,B)}(u, v); \left(\forall (u, v) \right) \in U \times V \qquad (2.49)$$

A4.2. If S(A, A') = 0, i.e., if $A' \cap A = \phi$ then

$$\mu_{R(A'|A,B)} = 1 \forall (u, v) \in U \times V \qquad (2.50)$$

A.4.3. As S(A, A') increase from 0 to 1 $\mu_{R(A'|A,B)} = (u, v)$ decreases uniformly

from 0 to 1 $\mu_{R(A,B)}(u, v); \left(\forall (u, v) \right) \in U \times V$

Axiom A1 Assets that we should not modify the conditional relation as and when A' and A remain equal.

Axiom A2 Asserts that when A' is completely dissimilar to A, that is, A' and a have disjoint support, we should not conclude specifically. In such a situation, anything is possible. **A3** says that as the fact A' changes from the most dissimilar case (similarity value zero) to the most similar one (similarity value one), the inferred conclusion should change from the most non-specific case that is, the UNKNOWN case (B' V) to the most specific case, that is, B' = B. This, in turn, means that whatever A' be, R(A'| A, B) ⊇ R(A, B), that is, the induced relation should not be more specific than what is

given as a condition. For notational simplicity, let us denote S(A, A') by and $R_{A'|A,B}$ by r'. Now, axiom **A3** uniquely suggests a function of the form:

$$\frac{dr'}{ds} = k\,(cons\tan t)$$

$$\Rightarrow r' = k\,s + c,\ c \text{ is a constant.}$$

These two constants may be determined from the conditions already prescribed in axiom **A1** and axiom **A2**. More explicitly, when s = 1 we know that r' = r (from axiom **A1**) and when s = 0 we know that r' = 1 (from axiom **A2**). This gives:

$$R' = 1 - (1 - r)s \qquad (2.51).$$

asour new scheme for the modification of the conditional relational.

Therefore, axiom **A1** through axiom **A3** uniquely suggest the scheme C2 as:

$$\mu_{R(A'|A,B)}(u,v) = 1 - \left(1 - \mu_{R(A,B)}(u,v)\right).S(A,A') \qquad (2.52)$$

From the Equation 2.41 and Equation 2.52, it is easy to see that when S(A, A') = 0 we have B' = V, in other words, it is impossible to conclude anything, when {A, A'} are completely dissimilar. It is also easy to see when S(A, A') is close to unity, then R(A', | A, B) is close to R(A, B) and hence the inferred fuzzy set B' will be close to B, that is, S(B, B') is close to unity. Axiom **A3** also ensures that a small change in the input produces a small change in the output and hence, in this sense the above mechanism of inference is stable. As in the previous case, it is easy to see that in Equation

2.52, if either $S(A, a') = 0$ or $\mu_r(A, B) = then\, r'_{u,v}$ becomes equal to one.

Let us now show that the above scheme may be modified to handle the concept of threshold associated with a rule in a natural manner. Let τ be the threshold associated with the rule. For that, we are to modify axiom **A2** according to the following:

A 4 If $S(A, A') \le \tau < 1$ then:

$$\mu_{R(A'|A,B)} = 1 \forall (u,\ v) \in U \times V.$$

$$(2.53)$$

Accordingly, simple calculations, as before, resulted in the following:

$$\mu_{R(A'|A,B)} = min\left[1, \left(1 - \mu_{R(A,B)}\right) = \frac{s - \tau}{1 - \tau}\right] \qquad (2.54)$$

as the general scheme for relation membership modification. It is easy to see that the case $\tau = 0$ correspond to the scheme presented by Equation 2.48. This scheme ensures that with all fuzzy sets A' having similarity value S(A, A') less or equal to the threshold value , τ, the inference B' Equation 2.41 will be "UKNOWN".

Example 2.10 Let us consider the problem as posed in Table 3. For simplicity, let

$U = \{u_1, u_2, u_3, u_4\}$ and $V = \{v_1, v_2, v_3, v_4\}$. Also let the fuzzy sets be given as follows:

$$A = 1.00 / u_1 + 0.75 / u_2 + 0.50 / u_3 + 0.25 / u_4,$$

$$A' = 1.00 / u_1 + 0.805 / u_2 + 0.40 / u_3 + 0.10 / u_4,$$

$$B = 0.25 / v_1 + 0.50 / v_2 + 0.75 / v_3 + 1.00 / v_4.$$

It is required to find a fuzzy set B' using the mechanism described in algorithm SAR. Using min-rule for translation, we first compute the conditional relation R(A, B) as follows:

$$R(A,B) \begin{array}{c} \\ u_1 \\ u_2 \\ u_3 \\ u_4 \end{array} \begin{array}{cccc} v_1 & v_2 & v_3 & v_4 \\ \begin{bmatrix} 0.25 & 0.50 & 0.75 & 1.00 \\ 0.25 & 0.50 & 0.75 & 1.75 \\ 0.25 & 0.50 & 0.50 & 0.50 \\ 0.25 & 0.25 & 0.25 & 0.25 \end{bmatrix} \end{array} \qquad (2.55)$$

Then, using Definition 2.3, we compute the similarity between A and A' as S(A, A') = 0.95322928 (approx.). Next, using Equation 2.52, the modified relation R(A'| A, B) may be computed as:

$$R(A'|A,B) = \begin{array}{c} \\ u_1 \\ u_2 \\ u_3 \\ u_4 \end{array} \begin{array}{cccc} v_1 & v_2 & v_3 & v_4 \\ \begin{bmatrix} 0.2851 & 0.5234 & 0.7617 & 1.00 \\ 0.2851 & 0.5234 & 0.7617 & 1.7617 \\ 0.2851 & 0.5234 & 0.5234 & 0.5234 \\ 0.2851 & 0.2851 & 0.2851 & 0.2851 \end{bmatrix} \end{array} \qquad (2.56)$$

Therefore, using Equation 2.41, we find the consequence as:

$$B' = sup_{u \in U}\left[R(A'|A,B)\right]=0.2851/v_1 + 0.5234/v_2 + 0.7671/v_3 + 1/v_4. \quad (2.57)$$

Instead of using similarity based AR methodology in deriving a consequence, if we consider the existing max-min CRI then the result would be:

$$B'_1 = 0.25/v_1 + 0.5/v_2 + 0.75/v_3 + 1/v_4. \quad (2.58)$$

From Equation 2.58, it is easy to see that, there is no change in output although the inputs differ significantly. Also, it may be shown that the same happens for a large class of fuzzy sets each different from the other. This is supposed to be a drawback in executing max-min CRI in its present form. In order to generate some "feeling" about the proposed inference mechanism, in the following, we present a pictorial description. For that, let us consider the two propositions pandqas in the following, where A, B and A' are normalized fuzzy sets defined as follows:

$$\mu_A(x) = \begin{cases} 1 - \dfrac{1}{4}|x-4|, & \text{if } 0 \le |x-4| \le 4 \\ 0 & \text{otherwise} \end{cases} \quad (2.59)$$

$$\mu_{B(y)}(x) = \begin{cases} 1 - \dfrac{1}{5}|y-5|, & \text{if } 0 \le |y-5| \le 5 \\ 0 & \text{otherwise} \end{cases} \quad (2.60)$$

$$\mu_{A'}(x) = \begin{cases} 1 - \dfrac{1}{16}(x-4)^2, & \text{if } 0 \le |x-4| \le 4 \\ 0 & \text{otherwise} \end{cases} \quad (2.61)$$

From p and q, we would like to conclude a proposition r: Y is B' using algorithm SAR. The support of each fuzzy set is uniformly quantized into 50 levels. The Figure 1 depicts the simultaneous representation of the fuzzy sets A and A'. The Figure 2 corresponds to the representation of the fuzzy set B, the consequent part of the conditional statement p. The Figure 3 gives a pictorial representation of the relational matrix R(A, B) using the min-rule for the translation of the conditional statement. Using Scheme C 2, the modified relational matrix R(A'| A, B) has been shown in Figure 4. In Figure 5, a pictorial representation of the conclusion B', has been shown. For comparison, the conclusion using Zadeh's CRI has been presented in Figure 6. It is interesting to see that the concluded B' as shown in Figure 6 and the fuzzy set B as shown in Figure 2 are the same, although:

p: X is A then Y is B

q: X is A'

A and A' are significantly different. Another important feature of the proposed similarity based approach that B is more specific B', may be seen after the comparison of Figure 2 and Figure 5. Thus, the conclusion is not better than B, the consequent of the rule.

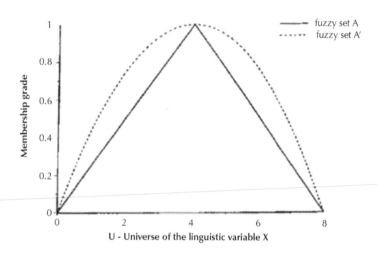

FIGURE 1   Simultaneous representation of the fuzzy sets A and A'.

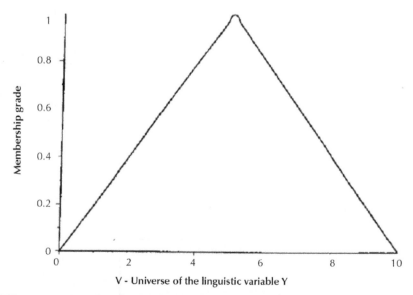

FIGURE 2   Representation of the fuzzy set B.

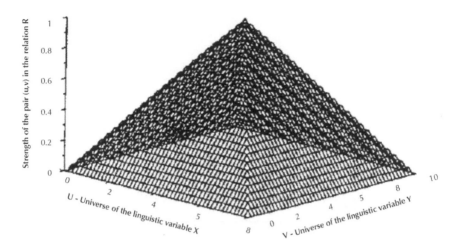

FIGURE 3   Representation of the conditional relation.

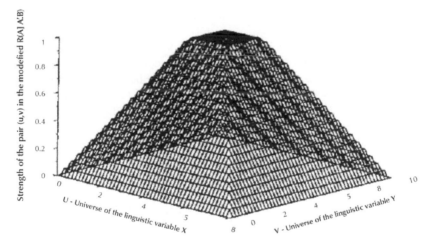

FIGURE 4   Representation of the induced relation.

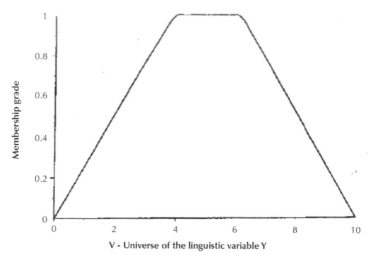

FIGURE 5   The inferred fuzzy set B.

Remark 2.3 If Mamdani's min-rule is used for the translation of the implication statement and only normal fuzzy sets are considered in the manipulation then A' = A will imply that B' = B. This is simply because, in this case, S(A, a') = 1 and hence R(A' | A, B) will be equal R(A, B).

Let A be a normal fuzzy set. If we assume that the translating rule used in generating the conditional relation is one of T-norm type then, as is already proposed, a basic and desirable result of the inferred proposition, nothing better than what the rule says may be concluded may be established as in the following. For that, let us consider the model as in Table 3. For all A, A', the following result is valid.

Theorem 2.5 B' $\supseteq$ B.

Proof: Let us consider Scheme C 2. From Equation 2.41 and the result of application of Scheme C 2, we have:

$$\mu_{B'}(v) = \sup_{u \in U} \mu_{R(A'|A,B)}(u, v)$$

$$= \sup_{u \in U} \{1 - (1 - \mu_{R(A,B)}(u, v).S(A, A')\}$$

$$\geq \sup_{u \in U} \mu_{R(A,B)}(u, v)\}, (\text{since, } 0 \leq S(A, A') \leq 1)$$

that is,

$$\mu_{B'}(v) = \frac{sup}{u \in U} \{\mu_A(u) o \mu_B(v)\}$$

where o is any T-norm operator.

Therefore, $(\forall v \varepsilon V), \mu_{B'}(v) \geq \mu_B(v)$ since, A is normal.

Let us now consider Scheme C1. From equation 2.47 and using the result of application of Scheme C1, we have:

$$\mu_{B'}(v) = \frac{sup}{u \in U} \mu_{R(A'|A,B)} (u, v)$$

$$= \frac{sup}{u \in U} \{1 - (1 - \mu_{R(A,B)}(u, v) / S(A, A')\}$$

$$\geq \frac{sup}{u \in U} \{\mu_{R(A,B)}(u, v) / S(A, A')\},$$

$$\geq \frac{sup}{u \in U} \mu_{R(A,B)}(u, v)\}, \quad (\text{since, } 0 \leq S(A, A') \leq 1)$$

that is,

$$\mu_{B'}(v) = \frac{sup}{u \in U} \{\mu_A(u) o \mu_B(v)\}$$

where o is any T-norm operator.

Therefore, $(\forall v \varepsilon V), \mu_{B'}(v) \geq \mu_B(v)$ since, A is normal.

With the above understanding of SBR methodology, let us now propose different models for reasoning.

2.7 APPLICATIONS TO DIFFERENT MODELS

In this section, we consider the application of the proposed similarity based AR mechanism to different models of AR rule-based and resolution-based.

RULE-BASED MODELS

Let $X_1, X_2, ..., X_k$, Y be k + 1 − linguistic variables defined respectively over universes of discourse $U_1, U_2, ..., U_k$, V and let U_i $\{u_i^j\}$: j = 1, 2, ..., j_i . Let us consider a pattern for AR with vague knowledge, as presented in the following: A consequence r may be derived according to the following basic steps.

Let the representation of the imprecise concepts in the propositions through fuzzy sets be given by:

$$A_i = \Sigma_{j=1}^{ji} \mu_A \frac{(u_i^j)}{u_i^j} ; i = 1, 2..., k$$

$$A_i' = \Sigma_{j=1}^{ji} \mu_{A'} \frac{(u_i^j)}{u_i^j} ; i = 1, 2..., k;$$

$$B = \Sigma_{i=1}^{m} \mu_B \frac{(v_i)}{v_i}$$

Here the conditional propositions p is first translated into a fuzzy relation R on the product space $U_1, U_2, ..., U_k$ x V. Now R may be computed using any suitable translating rule, possibly a T-norm operator. Then, we compute $S(A_i, A'_i)$ for i = 1, 2, ..., k and set:

$$S = \min \{S(A_1, A'_1), S(A_2, A'_2) ..., (A_k, A'_k)\}.$$

TABLE 4   Extended approximate reasoning

p: if X_1 is A_1 and X_2 is A_2 and... X_k is A_k then Y is B
q: X_1 is A'_1 and X_2 is A'_2 and... X_k is A'_k

---

r←

If now s = 0 then at least one pair (A_i, A'_i) are complementary (disjoint support/ dissimilar) and we find it impossible to conclude anything in particular, until further information is available. This may be represented by the fact that anything follows as conclusion. Hence, we set B' = V(UNKNOWN).

Otherwise, the conditional relation is modified using one of the two Schemes: Scheme C1 and Scheme C2. If Scheme C1 is used then we have,

R' = $R(A'_1 | A_1, A'_2 | (A_2, ..., (A'_k | (A_k, B)$ according to:

$$\mu_{R'}(u_1, u_2, ..., u_k, v) = \min\left\{1, \frac{1}{s}\mu_R(u_1, u_2, ..., u_k, v\right\}.$$

If, instead Scheme C2 is used then we find:

$$\mu_{R'}(u_1, u_2, ..., u_k, v) = 1 - \mu_R(u_1, u_2, ..., u_k, v))\ s.$$

In both cases, the conclusion B' will be given by:

$$\mu_{B'}(V) = \sup_{u_1, u_2, ..., u_k} \mu_{R\left(A'_1|A_1, A_2|A_2, ..., A'_k|A_k, B\right)}\left(u_1, u_2, ..., u_k, v\right) \qquad (2.62)$$

ALGORITHM A 1

Step 1 Compute S (A_i), i= for I = 1, 2, ..., k and set:

$$S = \min\{S(A_1, A'_1), S(A_2, A'_2), ..., S((A_k, A'_k)\}.$$

Step 2 Translate premisepand compute R $(A_1, A_2, ..., A_k, B)$ using any suitable translating rule possibly, a T-norm operator.

Step 3 Modify R(A, B) with s to obtain the modified conditional relation R' = R $(A'_1 | A'_2 | A_2, ..., A'_k | A_k, B)$ according to either Equation 2.42 or 2.52.

Step 4 Use sup-projection operation of R' to obtain B' as given in Equation 2.62.
Example 2.11 Let us consider the model presented in Table 4. Let k=2 and

$$U_1 = \{u_1^1, u_1^2, u_1^3, u_1^4, u_1^5\},$$
$$U_2 = \{u_2^1, u_2^2, u_2^3, u_2^4, u_2^5\},$$
$$V = \{v_1, v_2, v_3, v_4, v_5\},$$

$$A_1 = 0.3/u_1^1 + 0.55/u_1^2 + 0.7/u_1^3 + 0.85/u_1^4 + 1.0/u_1^5,$$

TABLE 5 Applicable form of approximate reasoning

if	X_1 is A_{11} and X_2 is A_{12} ...X_n is A_{1n} then Y is B_1
else if	X_1 is A_{21} and X_2 is A_{22} ...X_n is A_{2n} then Y is B_2
else if	X_1 is A_{m1} and X_2 is A_{m2} ...X_n is A_{mn} then Y is B_m
	X_1 is A_1 and X_2 is A_2 ... X_n is A_n

Conclusion	Y is B

$$A'_1 = 0.9/u_1^1 + 0.3025/u_1^2 + 0.49/u_1^3 + 0.7225/u_1^4 + 1.0/u_1^5;$$
$$A_2 = 0.9/u_2^1 + 1.0/u_2^2 + 0.85/u_2^3 + 0.7/u_2^4 + 0.55/u_2^5;$$
$$A'_2 = 0.9486/u_2^1 + 1.0/u_2^2 + 0.992/u_2^3 + 0.8367/u_2^4 + 0.7416/u_2^5;$$
$$B = 1.0/v_1 + 0.75/v_2 + 0.5/v_3 + 0.05/v_4 + 0.05/v_5.$$

Using Definition 2.3 with q = 2 it is found that $S(A_1, A'_1) = 0.81794918$ (approx.) and $S(A_2, A'_2) = 0.887007$ (approx.) So, we set s = 0.81794918 (approx.) Let us use min-rule for translation of premises p and q. On the basis of scheme C2, and Equation 2.62, it is found that:

$$B' = 1.0/v_1 + 0.795513/v_2 + 0.591025/v_3 + 0.386538/v_4 + 0.222948/v_5.$$

If instead, scheme C1 is used, then the inference would become:

$$B' = 1.0/v_1 + 0.916927/v_2 + 0.611285/v_3 + 0.305642/v_4 + 0.061128/v_5.$$

The difference in the last two results show that the change of membership values in the second case is more than the other one. In the first case (using Scheme C2), the expansion in fuzzy set membership is gradual. In the second case (using Scheme C1), the set membership becomes all one, that is, the inference becomes "UNKNOWN" even for non-zero and sometimes high similarity value.

Next, let us consider a generalized mode as presented in Table 5. This form of reasoning is used in many rule-based fuzzy systems. In particular, it is used in pattern classification and fuzzy control. Let there be n-linguistic variables associated with another linguistic variable Y according to the following m-fuzzy rules. The problem is to find the linguistic value of the variable Y as suggested by the rules, when the values of the n-variables are given. Under the conventional mechanism, for each rule, the consequent fuzzy set is calculated according to existing method of inference s already described and then the union of all consequent fuzzy sets is taken as the conclusion, which is then defuzzified, if necessary, using some defuzzification scheme. In the present case of SBR we cannot do this, as the3 membership values computed from the modified induced relation becomes less and less specific as the similarity between the facts and antecedent of a rule decreases. In conventional paradigm also, the membership values of various elements becomes equal to the maximum, making it an ambiguous one (more alternatives with similar membership values at the positive level) with the reduction of the firing strength (used in deriving a conclusion) but the membership values at which the ambiguity occurs becomes less than one. For example, in case of Mamdani-type of reasoning, if the firing strength of a rule is, say 0.3, then all alternatives, which have membership values greater than or equal to 0.3 take membership values of 0.3. On the other hand, in the present case, if the similarity value is 0.3, then the membership values of elements in the inferred fuzzy set will be at least 0.3. Moreover, the elements having membership value greater than or equal to 0.3 in the consequent of the rule will be equal to '1' in the consequent fuzzy set. This means that, with decrease in similarity the computed membership values increase and ultimately moves close to the least specific case (with membership values of 1 for all alternatives). The above discussion is illustrated with the help of a diagram. In Figure 2.7, let us suppose, the symmetric triangular fuzzy set represents the consequent of a rule. When the firing strength of the rule is 0.3, the derived conclusion from the rule is given by the trapezoid with height 0.3. Clearly, every value of [a, b] in Figure 7 has the same membership grade 0.3 that is, the possibility of becoming the solution. On the other hand, if the similarity between the fact and the antecedent of the rule is 0.3 then the conclusion derived using similarity based mechanisms is given by the trapezoidal fuzzy set with height$\alpha \geq 0.3$ (shown in dotted line in the same Figure 2.7). In this case, every alternative of [c, d] in Figure 7 could be a solution with membership value of α. Here, not only more alternatives have been offered (since [a, b] $\subseteq$ [c, d]) with the same membership value than the previous case but also the conclusion becomes more close to the least specific case. For this reason, we propose a new scheme, for computing the final conclusion, based on a measure of similarity. A detailed discussion on the same is presented in the next section. Our method is based on rule-selection and then rule-execution. In both cases, we use the concept of similarity between fuzzy sets as a basis of the task. For that, first of all we compute $S(A_{ij}, A_j)$;, I = 1,2, ..., m. Then we perform the same operation for different j = 1,2, ..., n. Let S_{ij} denote the different similarity values. Next, we compute the overall rule matching index from the above data as:

$$S^i = \overset{\min}{\underset{j}{}} S_{ij} \tag{2.63}$$

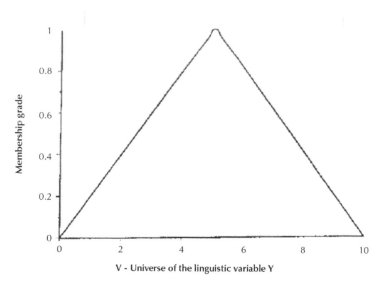

FIGURE 6   The inferred fuzzy set B using Zadeh's CRI.

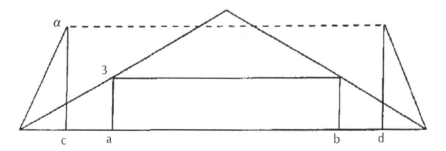

FIGURE 7   Comparison of firing strength based and similarity based reasoning.

From among the m distinct rules we choose those rules for which $S^i > \epsilon$. This may be interpreted as a threshold in our case. Then we apply algorithm A1 to generate a conclusion from each rule conformal for firing. The output may be generated using the intersection of fuzzy sets. It is important to note that the intersection operation is chosen in order to justify the rule-selection procedure. Here, fewer rules are fired and the output of each rule is significant.

ALGORITHM A2

- **Step 1** Compute S_{ij} for i = 1,2, ..., m, j = 1,2, ..., n and then s^i according to Equation 2.63.
- **Step 2** Define ϵ and find the rules conformal for firing.
- **Step 3** Translate the ith rule, provided $s^i > \epsilon$ and compute the relation R_i using any suitable translating rule possibly, a T-norm operator.

- **Step 4** Modify R_i with s^i toobtain the modified conditional relation R'_i according to either Equation 2.42 or 2.52.
- **Step 5** Use sup-projection operation on R'_i to obtain B'_i

$$\mu_{B'}(v) = \sup_{u_1,\ u_2,\ \dots\ u_k} \mu_{R(A_1 \mid A_{i1}, A_2 \mid A_{i\dots}, 2,\ A'_k \mid A_k,\ B)}(u_1, u_2,\ \dots,\ u_k,\ v) \quad (2.64)$$

- **Step 6** Compute the output $B = \bigcap_i B'_i$.

RESOLUTION-BASED MODELS

Now, let us consider resolution-based models for reasoning with vague concepts. Let there be two typical premises p and q and we derive a conclusion r using SBR mechanisms.

TABLE 6   Resolution-based approximate reasoning

P: X is A or Y is B
q: X is'

_____

r←   Y is B'.

$$U = \{u_1, u_2,\ \dots,\ u_l\},\ V = v_1, v_2,\ \dots,\ v_m\}$$

The entire scheme may be put in a Table 6. Let denote the respective universe of discourse of the linguistic variables X and Y. First we translate the imprecise concepts in the premises p and q into appropriate fuzzy sets and obtain:

$$A = \sum_{i=1}^{l} \mu_A(u_i)/u_i,$$

$$A' = \sum_{i=1}^{l} \mu_{A'}(u_i)/u_i,$$

$$B = \sum_{i=1}^{l} \mu_B(v_i)/v_i,$$

Next, we translate the conditional premise p into some binary fuzzy relation R on$U$ x V using an appropriate operator for the fuzzy connector "or". We use some T-conorm operator for the translation. Thus, we have:

$$\mu_R (u, v) = \mu_A (u) \circ \mu_B (v), \circ \text{ is some T-conorm operator.} \qquad (2.65)$$

Then using the fuzzy set A', we modify the fuzzy binaryrelation R(A, B) with S(A, A'). Here, in modification, we use the fact that for a resolution-based model the dissimilarity between the fact and the anteccdent of the rule is considered for a meaningful resolvent. Then we generate a modified fuzzy binary relation R(A'| A, B) on $U \times V$. Here, we use either:

$$\mu'_R (u, v) = 1 - (1 - \mu_R (u, v)) * d \qquad (2.66)$$

Or,

$$\mu'_R (u, v) = \mu_R (u, v)) / d, \text{ d is the dissimilarity index} \qquad (2.67)$$

for modification of the conditional relation. Since, we use a T-conorm function in translation, and we choose expansion type modification procedure, therefore, for the best solution from among a class of solutions we perform inf-operation on R' in order to obtain the desired fuzzy value for the linguistic variable Y.

Here, d is taken as a measure of dissimilarity between the two fuzzy sets A and A'. In order to formulate the disjunctive syllogism in fuzzy logic, we need to introduce d in the inference procedure. When d = 0, we find that B' = V. So that, anything, in particular, may be concluded about Y. Again when d = 1 that isS(A, A') = 0 that is, A and A' are disjoint sets, we need not modify the relation and see that B' = B may be obtained. This is, in accordance with, the law of generalized disjunctive syllogism.

ALGORITHM A3

- *Step 1* Compute S(S, A') according to either Definition 2.2 or Definition 2.3 or by some other similar definitions. Set d = 1 -S(A, A').
- *Step 2* Translate premise p and compute R(A, B) using any suitable translating rule possibly, a T-conorm operator.
- *Step 3* Modify R(A, B) with S(A, A') to obtain the modified conditional relation R(A|A', B) according to either Equation 2.66 or 2.67.
- *Step 4* Use inf-operation on R(A|A', B) to obtain B' as:

$$\mu_{B'} (v) = \inf_{u \in U} \mu_{R(A'|A, B)}(u, v) \qquad (2.68)$$

*Example 2.12*Let us consider the model presented in Table 6. Let:

$$U = \{u_1, u_2, u_3, u_4, u_5\}$$
$$V = \{v_1, v_2, v_3, v_4,\}$$
$$A = 1.0 / u_1 + 0.5625 / u_2 + 0.25 / u_3 + 0.0625 / u_4,$$
$$A' = 0.4375 / u_2 + 0.75 / u_3 + 0.9375 / u_4 + 1.0 / u_5,$$
$$B = 0.25 / v_1 + 0.5 / v_2 + 0.75 / v_3 + 1.0 / v_4.$$

For a conclusion of the form r, let us first compute S(A, A') according to Definition 2.3. Here, we find that S(A, A') = 0.3475. Wesetd = 1 -S(A, A') = 0.6525. Now Let us translate premisepas a relation R(A, B) using max operator, where:

$$\mu_{R(A,B)}(u, v) = max[\mu_A(u), \mu_B(v)]. \tag{2.69}$$

More explicitly, we have,

TABLE 7 Resolution-based generalized approx. reasoning

P: X_1 is A_1 or X_2 is A_1 or...X_k is A_k
q: X_1 is A'_1

r: or X_2 is A'_2 or...X_k is A'_k

$$R(A,B) \begin{array}{c} \\ u_1 \\ u_2 \\ u_3 \\ u_4 \end{array} \begin{array}{cccc} v_1 & v_2 & v_3 & v_3 \\ \begin{bmatrix} 1.0 & 1.0 & 1.0 & 1.0 \\ 0.5625 & 0.5625 & 0.775 & 1.0 \\ 0.25 & 0.50 & 0.75 & 1.0 \\ 0.25 & 0.50 & 0.75 & 1.0 \end{bmatrix} \end{array} \tag{2.70}$$

Next, using equation 2.66 with d, the modified relation R(A'|A, B) may be given by:

$$R(A,B) \begin{array}{c} \\ u_1 \\ u_2 \\ u_3 \\ u_4 \end{array} \begin{array}{cccc} v_1 & v_2 & v_3 & v_3 \\ \begin{bmatrix} 1.0 & 1.0 & 1.0 & 1.0 \\ 0.7145 & 0.7145 & 0.8368 & 1.0 \\ 0.5106 & 0.6737 & 0.8368 & 1.0 \\ 0.5106 & 0.6737 & 0.8368 & 1.0 \end{bmatrix} \end{array} \tag{2.71}$$

Therefore,

$$B' = 0.5106 /v_1 + .6737 /v_2 + .8368 /v_3 + 1.0 /v_4.$$

On simple calculation it is found that S(B, B') = 0.9157. This imply because A, A' are almost complementary pair, having S(A, A') = 0.3475.

In the end, let us consider a generalized resolution-based model as presented in Table 7. Let $X_1, X_2, ..., X_k$ be k-linguistic variables defined respectively over universe of discourses $U_1, U_2, ..., U_k$ and let $U_i = \{u_i^j\}, j = 1, 2, j_i$. We consider a generalized model, m where from premises pand qwe derive a conclusionr. As usual, we first compute $S(A_1, A_1')$. Then with d we follow the following steps:

ALGORITHM A4

- **Step 1**. Translate premise p into a fuzzy relation and compute R(A$_1$, A$_2$, ..., A$_k$) using any suitable translating operator for the 'or' in the rule possibly, a T-conorm operator.

- **Step 2**. Compute $S(A_1, A_1')$ and set $d = 1 - S(A_1, A_1')$.
- **Step 3**. Modify R(A$_1$, A$_2$, ..., A$_k$) with d to obtain the modified conditional relation $R' = R(A_1' | A_1, A_1' | A_2, ..., A_k' | A_k)$ according to either (2.66) or (2.67).

- *Step 4* Perform inf-operation separately to obtain

$$\mu A'_i (u_i^j) = \inf_{j : j \neq i} \mu_{r'}(u_1, ..., u_k); j = 1, j_i; I = 2, ..., k. \qquad (2.72)$$

In the process, we find a conceptual change in similarity based inference mechanism. A closer look at the connection between the proposed schema and the existing schema allow us to conclude that our schema may be thought of as an integration of Zadeh's CRI and similarity based inference schema. Such a scheme is expected to produce efficiency in inference mechanisms. The above procedure is applied in the design of important rule-based fuzzy systems.

2.8   REASONING BASED ON TOTAL FUZZY SIMILARITY

It is observed that fuzzy inference is based on similarity. Kosko writes "*Fuzzymembership ... represents similarities of objects to imprecisely defined prope*rties". Dubois and Prade consider the same problem by writing "*... The evaluation of similarity between two multi feature descriptions of objects may be specially of interest in analogical reasoning. If we assume that each feature is associated with an attribute domain equipped with similarity relation modeling approximate equality on this domain, the problem is then toaggregate the degrees of similarity between the objects pertaining to each feature into a global similarity index. This means that the resulting index should still have properties like reflexivity, symmetry, and max -$\odot$-transitivity .... Moreover, we may think of a weighted aggregation if we consider that we are dealing with a fuzzy set of features having different levels of importance.*"

Ultimately it turns out that, based on the concept of Lukasiewicz-Pavelka well-definedmany-valued logic, we can perform fuzzy reasoning for inference, which essentiallyrely on experts knowledge.

Infact, similarities based on the injective MV-algebra can be combined to a fuzzy relation, which turns out to a fuzzy similarity suchinduced fuzzy relation is called total fuzzy similarity.

Fuzzy IF-THEN inference systems are, in fact, problems of choice: Compare each IF-part of the rule base with an actual input value, find the most similar case and fire the corresponding THEN-part, if it is not unique, use a criteria given by an expert to proceed [156].

MATHEMATICAL PRELIMINARIES

A Wajsberg algebra is a non-void set L containing a fixed element 1. A binary operation →and a unary operation * such that, for each x, y, z ∈ L:

$$1 \to x = 1 \qquad\qquad (2.73)$$

$$(x \to y) \to [(y \to z) \to (x \to z)] = 1 \qquad\qquad (2.74)$$

$$(x \to y) \to y = (y \to x) \to x \qquad\qquad (2.75)$$

$$(x^* \to y^*) \to (y \to x) = 1. \qquad\qquad (2.76)$$

There is a one-to-one correspondence between Wajsberg algebra and MV-algebras. The MV-operations can be obtained by stipulations $x \odot y = (x \to y^*)^*$, $x \oplus y = ^* \to y$ and $0 = 1^*$. A Wajsberg algebragenerates a lattice. If this lattice is complete, then the corresponding Wajsberg algebra is called complete. An element b of an MV-algebra L is called an n-divisor of an element $a \in L$ If $(a^* \oplus (n-1)b)^* = b$ and $nb = a$, where $nb = b \oplus ... \oplus b$ (n times). If all elements a of a Wajsberg algebra L have n-divisors for each natural n, then L is called divisible. A Wajsberg-algebra L is called injective if:

L is complete, and (2.77)
L is divisible (2.78)

We will see that the axioms Equation 2.73–2.78 are sufficient to construct fuzzy IF THEN inference systems. A canonical example of an injective Wajsberg algebra is the Lukasiewicz algebradefined on the real unit interval: $1 = 1$, $x^* = 1 - x$ and $x \to y = \min\{1, 1 - x + y\}$.

Di Nola and Sessa prove that L is an injective MV-algebra if, and only if L is isomorphic to $F(L)$, where $F(L)$ is the MV-algebra of continuous [0, 1]-valued functions on the set of all maximal ideals of L, and $1(\text{M}) = 1$, $(f \to g)(\text{M}) = \min\{1,1 -f(\text{M}) + g(f(\text{M}))\}$, $f^*(\text{M}) = 1- f(\text{M})$ for any maximal ideal M of L.

Theorem 2.6 [156] In an injective MV-algebra, any n-divisor is unique.

Proof: It is enough to show that the statement holds in any injective *MV*-Algebra *F(L)*.

Let $f \in F(L)$, n a natural number and g, h two n-divisors of f. Let M of be a maximal ideal of L. If $f(M) = a < 1$, then $ng(M) = (ng) (M) = a = (nh)(M) = (nh)(M)$, which implies $g(M) = h(M)$. Now assume $f(M) = 1$. Then $1 - g(M) = g^*(M) = f^*(M) \oplus (n-1)g(M)(n-1)$ $g(M)$. If $(n-1) g(M)$ would be equal to 1, then $g(M)$ should be equal to 0, which is clearly not the case. Therefore $(n-1) g(M) < 1$. Similarly $(n-1)h(M) = 1- h(M) < 1$. Let a counter assumption $g(M) < h(M)$ hold. Then $(n-1)h(M) = h^*(M) < g^*(M) = (n-1) g(M)$, which implies $h(M) < g(M)$, a contradiction. An assumption $h(M) < g(M)$ leads to a similar contradiction. We conclude $h(M) = g(M)$ for any maximal ideal M of L. Therefore $g = h$.

By the above Theorem, we may denote the unique n-divisor of an element by $\dfrac{a}{n}$.

For any maximal ideal M of an injective MV-algebra L it holds that $n\dfrac{f(M)}{n} = f(M)$

Moreover, $\left[f^*(M) \oplus (n-1)\dfrac{f(M)}{n} \right]^* = [1 - f(M) + \dfrac{(n-1)f(M)}{n}]^* = \dfrac{f(M)}{n}$. We

therefore conclude $\dfrac{f}{n}(M) = \dfrac{f(M)}{n}$.

We state, the following proposition.

Proposition 2.1 In the Lukasiewicz structure:

$$if \ a_i \ominus b_i \leq c_i \ for \ i = 1,\ldots, n \ then \ \frac{1}{n}\sum_{i=1}^{n} a_i \ominus \frac{1}{n} \sum_{i=1}^{n} b_i \leq \frac{1}{n}.\sum_{i=1}^{n} c_i.$$

Clearly, in the Łukasiewicz structure we have:

$$\frac{a_1}{n} \oplus \ldots \oplus \frac{a_n}{n} = \sum_{i=1}^{n} \frac{a_i}{n} = \frac{1}{n} \sum_{i=1}^{n} a_i.$$

Thus, in $F(L)$ if $f_i \ominus g_i \leq h_i$ for I = 1,…, n then, for any maximal ideal M it holds that:

$$((\frac{f_1}{n} \oplus ... \oplus \frac{f_n}{n}) \ominus (\frac{g_1}{n} \oplus ... \oplus \frac{g_n}{n}))(M) = (\sum_{i=1}^{n} \frac{f_i(M)}{n}) \ominus (\sum_{i=1}^{n} \frac{g_i(M)}{n})$$

$$\leq (\sum_{i=1}^{n} \frac{h_i(M)}{n})$$

$$= (\frac{h_1}{n} \oplus ... \oplus \frac{h_n}{n})(M).$$

Proposition 2.2 In an injective MV-algebra L:

if $a_i \odot b_i \leq c_i$ for all $I = 1, ..., n$ then

$$\left(\frac{a_1}{n} \oplus ... \oplus \frac{a_n}{n}\right) \ominus \left(\frac{b_1}{n} \oplus ... \oplus \frac{b_n}{n}\right) \leq \left(\frac{c_1}{n} \oplus ... \oplus \frac{c_n}{n.}\right).$$

Castro and Klawonn among others set the following important.

Definition 2.4 Let A be a non-void set and $\odot$ a continuous t-norm. Then a fuzzy similarity S on A is such a binary fuzzy relation that, for each x, y, z $\in$ A,

i.   S<x, x > − 1 (everything is similar to itself),

ii.   S < x, y > = S < y, x > (fuzzy similarity is symmetric),

iii. S < x, y > $\odot$ S < y, z > $\leq$ S < x, z > (fuzzy similarity is weakly transitive).

Trivially, fuzzy similarity is a generalization of classical equivalence relation, thus, called many-valued equivalence, too.

This definition can be generalized to any residuatedlattice L. Moreover, an L-valued fuzzy set $X$is an ordered couple (A, μ x), where the reference set A is a non-void set andthe membership functionm x: $A \searrow L$ tells the degree to which an element $a \in A$ belongs to the fuzzy set X.

Theorem 2.7 [156]Any fuzzy set (A, μ X) on a reference set A generates a fuzzy similarity S on A, defined by:

$$S(x, y) = \mu_X(x) \leftrightarrow \mu_X(x),$$

where x, y are elements of A. Moreover,

$$\text{If} \mu_X(y) = 1 \text{ then } S(x, y) = \mu_X(x).$$

Moreover, it is worth noting that, inLukasiewicz algebra, "the negation of equivalenceis distance". Indeed, for all a, b $\in$ [0, 1],

$$(a \leftrightarrow b)^* = 1[1 - \max\{a, b\} + \min\{a, b\}] = |a - b|.$$

Theorem 2.8 [156] Consider n injective MV-algebra based fuzzy similarities S_i, i = 1,..., n on a set X. Then:

$$S\langle x,y \rangle = \frac{S_1\langle x,y \rangle}{n} \oplus ... \oplus \frac{S_n\langle x,y \rangle}{n}$$

Is an injective MV-algebra valued fuzzy similarity on X. More generally, the weighted mean

$$S\langle x,y \rangle = \frac{m_1 S_1\langle x,y \rangle}{M} \oplus ... \oplus \frac{m_n S_n\langle x,y \rangle}{M},$$

Where $M = \sum_{i=1}^{n} m_i$ and m_i are natural numbers, is again an injective MV-algebra based fuzzy similarity on X.

Proof:Since, all S_i, $I = 1,...,$ n are reflexive and symmetric so is S. The weak transitivity of S can be seen in the following way. Let $A = S <s, y> \odot S <y, z>$. If $A = 0$, then trivially $A \leq S<x, z>$, therefore assume $A > 0$. Then by Proposition 2.2:

$$A = (\frac{S_1\langle x,y \rangle}{n} \oplus ... \oplus \frac{S_n\langle x,y \rangle}{n}) \ominus (\frac{S_1\langle y,z \rangle}{n} \oplus ... \oplus \frac{S_n\langle y,z \rangle}{n})$$

$$\leq \frac{S_1\langle x,z \rangle}{n} \oplus ... \oplus \frac{S_n\langle x,z \rangle}{n}$$

$$= S\langle x,z \rangle.$$

Thus, S is weakly transitive and therefore an injective MV-algebra based fuzzy similarity on X. The other part is now an easy generalization of this result.

If two objects A and B agree on k attributes and disagree on m attributes, then the number:

$$si\, m(A, B) = \frac{k}{k+m}$$

canbe taken to measure the degree of similarity or partial identity between A and B.

Proposition 2.3 "sim" is a fuzzy similarity relation with respect to Lukasicwicz algebra.

Proof: sim(A, B) is a reflexiveand symmetric fuzzy relation. It is weakly transitive with respect to Lukasicwicz product too. Let N be the number of all attributes and, moreover, let m be the number of attributes only A has, p be the number of attributes only B has, q be the number of attributes only C has, k be the number of attributes only A and B have, s be the number of attributes only A and C have, r be the number of attributes only B and C have, and t be the number of attributes A, B and C have.

Then:

$$k + t + r \leq N, N = m + k + s + t,$$

thus,

$$0 \leq s \leq N - k - t, \text{ and } N = q + s + t + r,$$

thus,

$$0 \leq r \leq N - s - t.$$

Now sim $(A, B) \odot$ sim $(B, C) \leq$ sim (A, C) if $\dfrac{k \mid t}{N} + \dfrac{t+r}{N} - 1 \leq \dfrac{s+t}{N}$ if $k + t + t +$

$r - N \leq s + t$ iff $k + t + r - s \leq N$, which holds true us $k + t + r < N$.

The Proposition 2.3 does not hold for Godel or Product algebras. Indeed, consider $A = \{a, b\}$, $B = \{b, 1\}$, $C = \{1, 2\}$. Then sim$(A, B) =$ sim$(B, C) = 0.5$, while sim$(A, C) = 0$.

2.8.1 AN ALGORITHM TO CONSTRUCT FUZZY IF-THEN INFERENCE SYSTEMS.

The dynamics of a system S are characterized by a finite collection of IF-THEN-rules, for example:

Rule 1 IF x is A_1 and y is B_1 and z isC_1 THENw is D_1
Rule 2 IF x is A_2 and y is $B_2$and z isC_2 THENw is D_2

$$\vdots$$

Rule k IF x is A_k and y is B_k and z isC_k THENw is D_k

Where $A_1, ..., D_k$are fuzzy sets of height 1, that is, in each fuzzy set there is atleast one element that obtains the membership degree 1. Generally, the output fuzzy sets $D_1, ..., D_k$ should obtain all the same values $\in L$ the input fuzzy sets $A_1, ..., C_k$ do. However, the outputs can be crisp actions, too. We avoid disjunction between the rules by allowing some of the output fuzzy sets D_i and D_j, $i \neq j$, be possibly equal. Thus, a fixed THEN-part can be followed by various IF-parts. Some of the input fuzzy sets may be equal, too (for example, $B_i = B_j$ for some $i \neq j$). However, the rule base should be consistent, a fixed IF-part precedes a fixed THEN-part. Moreover, the rule base can be incomplete, if an expert is not able to define the THEN-part of some combination "IF x is A_i and y is B_i and z is C_i" then the rule should be skipped.

Now we can construct a total fuzzy similarity based inference system.

- **Step 1** Create the dynamics of S, that is define the IF-THEN rules, where of the input fuzzy sets (for example, $A_1 \ldots, C_k$) and the output fuzzy sets (for example, $D_1 \ldots, D_k$), are appropriately defined.

- **Step 2** Give weights to various parts of the input fuzzy sets(for example, to A_i. s B_i. s, and C_i. s) to emphasize the mutual importance of the corresponding, input variables.

- **Step 3** List the IF-THEN-rules in order from best to worst with respect to their mutual importance, or give some criteria on how this can be done when necessary, that is give a criteria on how to distinguish inputs causing equal degree of total fuzzy similarity in different IF-parts.

- **Step 4** For each THEN-part i, give a criteria on how to distinguish outputs with equal degree on membership (for example, w_0 and v_0 such that $\mu D_i(w_0) = \mu D_i(v_0)$, $(w_0 \neq v v_0)$.

- A general framework for the inference system is now ready. Assume then that we have actual input values, for example, (x_0, y_0, z_0). The corresponding output value w_0 is found in the following way.

- **Step 5** Consider each IF-part of the rule base as a crisp case, and compare the actual input values separately with each IF-part, in other words, count total fuzzy similarities between the actual inputs and each IF-part of the rule base, by the above Theorems, this is equivalent to counting weighted means, for example:

$$\frac{m_1\mu A_1(x_0)}{m_1+m_2+m_1} \oplus \frac{m_2\mu B_1(y_0)}{m_1+m_2+m_1} \oplus \frac{m_3\mu C_1(z_0)}{m_1+m_2+m_1} = Similarity(actual, Rule\ 1)$$

$$\frac{m_1\mu A_2(x_0)}{m_1+m_2+m_1} \oplus \frac{m_2\mu B_2(y_0)}{m_1+m_2+m_1} \oplus \frac{m_3\mu C_2(z_0)}{m_1+m_2+m_1} = Similarity(actual, Rule\ 2)$$

$$\vdots$$

$$\frac{m_1\mu A_k(x_0)}{m_1+m_2+m_1} \oplus \frac{m_2\mu B_k(y_0)}{m_1+m_2+m_1} \oplus \frac{m_3\mu C_k(z_0)}{m_1+m_2+m_1} = Similarity(actual, Rule\ k)$$

werem$_1$, m$_2$, and m$_3$ are the weights given inStep 2.

- **Step 6** Fire an output value w_0 such that:

$$\mu D_i(w_0) = Similarity\ (actual, Rule\ i)$$

Corresponding to the maximal total fuzzy similarity–similarity (actual, Rule i), if such Rule I is not unique, use the order of quality given in Step 3 and, if there are several such output values w_0, utilize the criteria given in Step 4.

Notice that Step 6 can be view as an instance of GMP in the sense of Pavelka's well-defined fuzzy logic, that is:

$$R_{GMP} \quad : \quad \frac{\alpha, (\alpha \ im \ p \ \beta)}{\beta}, \frac{a, b}{a \ominus b}$$

Where a corresponds to the IF-part, b corresponds to the THEN-part, a is the degree of maximal total fuzzy similarity and b = 1. In general, this gives a many-valued logic based theoretical justification to Step 6. In case, the outputs are concrete actions that can either be taken or not we define "take the action only in case $\alpha \in [c,1]$, where c is a suitable value".

2.8.2 SOME FEATURES OF THE ALGORITHM

We have introduced an axiomatic approach to construct fuzzy IF-THEN inference systems. This approach considers fuzzy inference as a problem of choice: Each IF-part of the rule base is compared with an actual input value, the most similar case is searched and the corresponding THEN-part is fires, if it is not unique, a criteria given by an expert is used.

Of course, we can specify our algorithm by putting extra demands, for example, in some cases the degree of total fuzzy similarity of the best alternative should be greater than some fixed value $\alpha \in L$, sometimes all the alternatives possessing the highest fuzzy similarity should be indicated, of the difference between the best candidate and second one should be larger than a fixed value $\beta \in L$. All this depends on an actual control problem.

The algorithm does not guarantee that the performance of control would always be smooth in a sense that small change in input causes small change in output. Indeed, the smoothness depends on the shapes of fuzzy sets and the number of rules in the system. This feature is typical of all fuzzy control systems. A measure for the smoothness of performance of a general fuzzy inference system is also available. This measure utilizes many-valued similarity and can be easily generalized to concern all injective MV-algebra based inference systems.

Example 2.13 [156] We consider a problem of traffic signal control. Consider a T-junction (Figure 8), where traffic flow on the main street (phase A) is assumed to be two to ten times more intensive than traffic flow from the other direction. Normally, the green traffic signal phase order is A-B-C-A. If there is low request that is very few or no vehicles in the next phase B or C, then this phase can be skipped. Thus, the order can be for example, A-C-A-B-C or A-B-A-B-C. The task is to determine the right phase order, fuzzy selector - imitating traffic policeman's action - decides the next signal group.

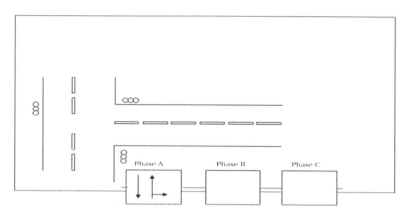

FIGURE 8   Layout and three phases of a T-junction.

The basic principle is that phase B can be skipped if there is no request or of total waiting time if vehicles V(B) in phase B is low, and similarly, phase C can be skipped if there is no request or of total waiting time of vehicles V(C) in phase C is low. Therefore, after phase B the next phase is C or A, and after phase C the next phase is A. In details, the dynamics of the inference is the following:

After phase A,

IF V (B) is high	AND V(C) is any	THEN phase is B
IF V (B) is medium	AND V(C) is over saturated	THEN phase is C
IF V (B) is Low	AND V(C) is more than medium	THEN phase is C
IF V (B) is less than low	AND V (C) is more than medium	THEN phase is C

The corresponding fuzzy sets are defined by the following membership functions given in Table 8 and Table 9.

TABLE 8 Membership function of V(B)

Total wait time V(B) [10 sec]

	0	1	2	3	4	5	6	7	8	9	10	11	12	13	14	15
less than low	1.0	0.1	0.0	0.0	0.0	0.0	0.0	0.0	0.0	0.0	0.0	0.0	0.0	0.0	0.0	0.0
low	0.0	0.3	0.7	1.0	0.7	0.3	0.0	0.0	0.0	0.0	0.0	0.0	0.0	0.0	0.0	0.0
medium	0.0	0.0	0.0	0.0	0.5	1.0	1.0	1.0	1.0	1.0	0.5	0.0	0.0	0.0	0.0	0.0
high	0.0	0.0	0.0	0.0	0.0	0.0	0.0	0.2	0.3	0.5	0.7	0.8	1.0	1.0	1.0	1.0

TABLE 9 Membership function of V(C)

Total wait time V(C) [10 sec]

	0	1	2	3	4	5	6	7	8	9	10	11	12	13	14	15
over saturated	0.0	0.0	0.0	0.0	0.0	0.0	0.0	0.0	0.0	0.0	0.0	0.5	1.0	1.0	1.0	1.0
more than medi	0.0	0.0	0.0	0.0	0.0	0.0	0.0	0.0	0.0	0.5	1.0	1.0	1.0	1.0	1.0	1.0
any	1.0	1.0	1.0	1.0	1.0	1.0	1.0	1.0	1.0	1.0	1.0	1.0	1.0	1.0	1.0	1.0

Corresponding to Step 3 of the Algorithm, if the maximal total similarity is not unique, the phase with the longest waiting time is fired, or in the worst case, the next phase is not skipped. The performance of the fuzzy phase control is now straight forward, for example, after phase A, if there are 7 vehicles in phase B and 3 vehicles in phase C, then the next phase will be B.

HUTSIM traffic simulator simulated the performance of this control system, constructed at Helsinki University of Technology, and the results where compared to those determined by a fuzzy phase control based on a Mamdani-style fuzzy controller and a non-fuzzy phase control algorithm. The average waiting time per vehicle turned out to be the shortest in fuzzy similarity based control as can be seen in Table 10, Table 11, and Table 12.

TABLE 10   Average waiting time/vehicle, Vehicle flow ratio 10:1

Tot. sim	12.2	12.2	12.6	13.1	12.9	13.8	14.6	15.5
Mamdani	12.1	13.0	12.7	14.9	14.4	15.7	17.2	17.6
Non-fuz	12.1	12.9	13.5	13.9	14.6	16.1	17.2	17.5
Veh/hour	200	400	600	800	1000	1200	1400	1600

TABLE 11   Average waiting time/vehicle, Vehicle flow ratio 10:2

Tot. sim	12.9	12.7	13.2	12.7	12.8	13.9	15.8	17.2
Mamdani	12.7	13.0	13.7	14.0	14.2	15.3	16.8	21.5
Non-fuz	13.7	12.8	13.3	13.1	14.3	15.3	17.8	19.9
Veh/hour	200	400	600	800	1000	1200	1400	1600

TABLE 12.   Average waiting time/vehicle, Vehicle flow ratio 10:5

Tot. sim	11.2	11.9	12.4	13.4	14.1	18.0	17.4	20.5
Mamdani	11.7	13.2	13.5	13.9	14.0	18.1	18.1	22.0
Non-fuz	12.4	11.9	13.4	14.1	14.2	17.6	18.3	77.6
Veh/hour	200	400	600	800	1000	1200	1400	1600

2.9   SIMILARITY-BASED BIDIRECTIONAL APPROXIMATE REASONING

The theory of fuzzy sets has been used as useful framework for the formal analysis and modeling of human activities. It is often the case that while real-world decision making problems can be handled easily by humans, they are often too difficult to be handled by machines. Hence, there is an increasing demand to improve the machnes' capability to handle fuzzy decision-making problems.

One of the approaches to solve this problem is a method based on fuzzy relational equations. Here, human knowledge is viewed as a collection of facts and rules, each of which may be represented as a fuzzy relation. From this fact, several forms of fuzzy relational equations and their analyticalmethods have been presented. However, the analytical approach is usually based on the impractical assumption that there exists a fuzzy relation matrix exactly satisfying all pairs of input and output fuzzy data simultaneously. Moreover, the fuzzy relational equations often do not render a solution for the inverse problem and so it is difficult to implement a backward AR, which is usually required to model deicion-making problems.

To overcome these problems, a new approach the so-called similarity-based fuzzy reasoning method has been studied. This approach is advantageous in that it does not require the construction of a fuzzy relation between input and output fuzzy data. Also, it is possible to implement a backward reasoning scheme more simply. On the other hand, in this similarity-based approach, as the name implies, the adopted similarity measure plays a key role in performing the AR. Recently, various similarity measures, which are usually based on the geometric model, the set-theoretic approach, and the matching function have been proposed in the previous scetion of the chapter. However, almost all suggested similarity measures render only a fixed value and thus reasoning methods based on these cannot express a disposition, which a decision maker has and a situation on which a decision making problem is given. As Zimmermann and Zysno have already mentioned, if the theory of fuzzy sets is used to model decision-making problems, then the operators used most commonly so far-minimum, maximum, and product- will have to be modified and adapted to this area of applications. In particular, they pointed out that the aggregation of subjective categories in the framework of human decision almost always shows some degree of compensation, which usually belongs between the non-compensatory logical connectives "and" and the fully-compensatory "or". Therefore, a new reasoning method is required to reflect an aggregation process like that of human reasoning from pessimistic to optimistic behavior.

In this section, we extend the works to develop a new type of similarity measure to express the disposition of a decision maker and specifications, which may be given with the decision-making problems. And also, we derive a simple and flexible type of bidirectional AR method based on the proposed similarity measure, which can support the making of a decision under more complex situations such as industrial inspection systems.

2.9.1 OWA OPERATORS AND A NEW SIMILARITY MEASURE

In this section, we will briefly describe the properties of the ordered weighted aggregation (OWA) operator, which was proposed by Yagerfor aggregations lying between the logical "or" and "and", and then we will propose a similarity measure using the OWA operator (See Section 2.11.5 of chapter 2 of volume 1 of this book) [36].

OWA OPERATORS AND THEIR PROPERTIES

Definition 2.5 An OWA operator of n dimension is a mapping OWA: $R^n \rightarrow R$ that has an associated weighting vector $W = [w_1, w_2, ..., w_n]^T$ such that (1) $w_i \in [0,1]$, (2) $\sum_i w_i = 1$. Furthermore, OWA $(a_1, a_2, ..., a_n) \sum_j w_j b_j$ where b_j is the jth largest among the a_i.

The OWA operator is characterizd by its weighting vector. If we choose $W = W_{max} = [1 \, 0 \, 0 ... 0]$ and $W = W_{min} = [0 \; 0 \; 0 .. \; 1]$, then $OWA_1(a_1, a_2, ..., a_n) = Min_i(a_i)$ and $OWA_1(a_1, a_2, ..., a_n) = Min_i(a_i)$, respectively. When $W = W_{avg} = [1/n \; 1/n ... 1/n]$, the OWA operator performs the averaging operation such as OWA $_a(a_1, a_2, ..., a_n) = (1/n) \sum_i a_i$. From the definition of the OWA operator, we can show:

$$OWA_1(a_1, a_2, ..., a_n) \leq OWA(a_1, a_2, ..., a_n) \leq OWA_u(a_1, a_2, ..., a_n). \quad (2.79)$$

Here, we will describe an important measure related to an OWA operator. The orness measure is defined as:

$$\text{orness}(W) = \frac{1}{(n-1)} \sum_{i-1}^{n} ((n-i) w_i). \quad (2.80)$$

It can be easily shown that: orness $(W_{max}) = 1$ (i) orness$(W_{avg}) = 0.5$ (iii) orness $(W_{min}) = 0$

On the other hand, the measure of "andness" is defined as:

$$\text{andness}(W) = 1 - \text{orness}(W) \quad (2.81)$$

It is noted that the OWA operator enables us to move continuously from the logic "and" to logic "or" by appropriate choice of the weighting vector. Furthermore, we can measure how near W is to logic "or", that is, the orlike by using Equation 2.80.

Similarily, we can also measure how near W is to logic "and", that is, the andlike by using Equation 2.81.

In fact, the most important procedure on using the OWA operator is to choose a suitable weighting vector for a given problem. Related to this, we shall adopt the S-OWA operator in this work due to its flexibility is defined by a family of OWA weights with $\alpha \in [0,1]$ such that:

$$w_i = \begin{cases} \dfrac{1}{n}(1-\alpha)+\alpha & \text{for } i=1, \\[3mm] \dfrac{1}{n}(1-\alpha) & \text{for } i=2,...,n. \end{cases} \qquad (2.82)$$

$$OWA_{so}(a_1,a_2,...,a_n) = \alpha \, Max_i(a_i) + \frac{1}{n}(1-\alpha)\sum_i a_i. \qquad (2.83)$$

The orness measure of this aggregation orness (w_{so}) becomes $((\alpha+1)/2)$. Since $\alpha \in [0,1]$, the orness (W_{so}) $[0.5,1]$. It is noted that when $\alpha = 1$ we get $OWA_{SO} = Max_i(a_i)$ and orness $(W_{so}) = 1$, that is $OWA_{so} \, OWA_u$, and when $\alpha = 0$ we get $OWA_{SO} = (1/n)\sum_i a_i$ and orness $(W_{SO}) = 0.5$, that is, $OWA_{SO} = OWA_a$.

The andlike S-OWA operator, denoted OWA_{SA} with weighting vector $W_{SA} = [w_1,w_2,...,w_n]$, is defined by a family of OWA weights with $\beta \in [0,1]$ such that

$$w_i = \begin{cases} \dfrac{1}{n}(1-\beta) & \text{for } i=1,\ 2,...,\ n-1 \\[3mm] \dfrac{1}{n}(1-\beta)+\beta & \text{for } i=n. \end{cases} \qquad (2.84)$$

From these weights, we can obtain OWA_{SA} as

$$OWA_{SA}(a_1,a_2,...,a_n) = \beta \, Min_i(a_i) + \frac{1}{n}(1-\beta)\sum_i a_i \qquad (2.85)$$

The orness measure of this aggregation orness (OWA_{SA}) becomes $((1-\beta))/2$. Since $\phi \in [0,1]$, the orness $(OWA_{SA}) \in [0,0.5]$. When $\beta = 1$ we get $OWA_{SA} = Min_i(a_i)$ and orness $(W_{SA}) = 0$, that is, OWA_{SA} OWA_1, and when $\beta = 0$ we get $OWA_{SA} = (1/n)\sum_i a_i$ and orness $(W_{SA}) = 0.5$, that is, $OWA_{SA} = OWA_a$.

One of the advantages of using these $S-OWA$ operators is that the weighting vector can be easily obtained by using a unique value of orness, λ as follows:

1.   If $\lambda \geq 0.5$, then use an orlike S-OWA, OWA_{SO} with $\alpha = 2\lambda - 1$.

2.   If $\lambda < 0.5$, then use an andlike S-OWA, OWA_{SA} with $\beta = 1 - 2\lambda$.

In the sequel, we shall denote the aggregation of the S-OWA operators, OWA_λ, as

$$OWA_\lambda \begin{cases} OWA_{so} \text{ with } \alpha = 2\lambda\text{-1} & \text{if } \lambda \geq 0.5, \\ OWA_{SA} \text{ with } \beta = 1\text{-}2\lambda & \text{if } \lambda < 0.5. \end{cases} \qquad (2.86)$$

A NEW SIMILARITY MEASURE

Now, let us consider a similarity measure between two fuzzy vectors $x \in [0,1]^n$ and $y \in [0,1]^n$. Pedrycz proposes a similarity index $q = (x \equiv y)$ for two fuzzy values $x \in [0,1]$ and $y \in [0,1]$ having a logical background expressed as [36]:

$$q = (x \equiv y) = \frac{1}{2}\left[(x \to y) \wedge (y \to x) + (\bar{x} \to \bar{y}) \wedge (\bar{y} \to \bar{x})\right] \qquad (2.87)$$

Where " $\to$ " denotes an implication and $\bar{x} = 1 - x$ is the complement of x. In Equation 2.87, the term $(x \to y) \wedge (y \to x)$ describe a degree of similarity between each component x and y, or a minimum of degrees to which x implies y and vice versa. Similarly, $(\bar{x} \to \bar{y}) \wedge (\bar{y} \to \bar{x})$ denotes the degree of similarity between complements of the values observed at x and y. Also, it is remarked that in Equation 2.87, the implication and $\wedge$ can be replaced by other forms with a corresponding t-norm. In the sequel, we shall simply adopt the Lukasiewicz implication:

$$x \to y = \min(1, 1 + y - x) \qquad (2.88)$$

Inserting Figure 10 in Figure 9, we obtain the following similarity index between two components:

$$q = (x \equiv y) = 1 - |x - y|. \tag{2.89}$$

On the other hand, Bien and Chun defined a similarity measure $S_B \in [0,1]$ between twon-dimentional fuzzy vectors $X = [x_1, x_2, ..., x_n]$ and $Y = [y_1, y_2, ..., y_n]$ as

$$S_B = 1/n \sum_{i=1}^{n} \frac{1}{2}[(x_i \rightarrow y_i) \wedge (y_i \rightarrow x_i) + (\bar{x}_i \rightarrow \bar{y}_i) \wedge (\bar{y}_i \rightarrow \bar{x}_i)] \tag{2.90}$$

$$= 1/n \sum_{i=1}^{n} q_i, \tag{2.91}$$

Where q_i is the similarity index between x_i and y_i given by Equation 2.88. The above similarity measure, however, renders only a fixed value from the arithmetic average for all similarity indices given by Equation 2.87. So, we propose a new similarity measure based on the OWA operator, which can express a disposition, which a decision makers has, and a situation on which a decision making problem is given.

Definition 2.6 For two fuzzy vectors $X = (x_1, x_2, ... x_n)$ and $Y = [y_1, y_2, ..., y_n]$, a new similarity measure, S_1, which can reflect its circumstance is defined as:

$$S_\lambda = (X \equiv Y) = OWA_\lambda(q_1, q_2, ..., q_n), \tag{2.92}$$

Where q_i is the similarity index between x_i and y_i given by Equation 2.88.
We can see some properties of the measure as follows:

1. If we select $\lambda = 1$, that is, $w = [1\,0...0]^T$, then $S_{1.0} = Max_i(q_i) = OWA_u$. Similarlyif we select $\lambda = 0$, that is, $w = [0\,0...1]^T$, then $S_{0.0} = Min_i(q_i) = OWA_l$. Therefore, $OWA_l \leq S_\lambda \leq OWA_u$ for $0 \leq \lambda \leq 1$.

2. If we take $\lambda = 0.5$, that is, $w = [1/n\,1/n\,...1/n]^T$, then $S_{0.5} = 1/n \sum_i (q_i) = OWA_a$. This shows that the similarity measure S_B is a special case of S_λ with $\lambda = 0.5$.

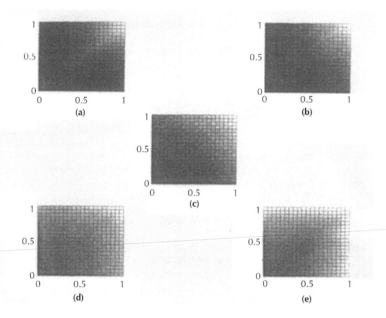

FIGURE 9 similarity measures (a) λ=0.0 (b) λ=0.25 (c) λ=0.5 (d) λ=0.75 and (e) λ=1.0.

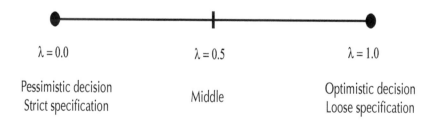

λ = 0.0	λ = 0.5	λ = 1.0
Pessimistic decision Strict specification	Middle	Optimistic decision Loose specification

FIGURE 10 Selection guide for the factor λ.

To show the qualitative aspect of the proposed similarity measure, we denote the similarity measure $S_\lambda(q_1, q_2)$ in Figure 1 between $X = [x_1, x_2]$ and $Y = [y_1, y_2]$ for each similarity index $q_1 = (x_1 \equiv y_1) \in [0, 1]$ and $q_2 = (x_2 \equiv y_2) \in [0.1]$. Figure 9(a)–(e) show $S_{0.0}, S_{0.25}, S_{0.5}, S_{0.75},$ and $S_{1.0}$, respectively. In the figure, a brighter part means

higher similarity value. From the qualitative point of view, we can consider $S_{1.0}$ as an

optimistic aggregator because it takes the maximum value among similarity indices.

Similarity, nwe can take $S_{0.0}$ as a pessimistic aggregator. On the other hand, $S_{0.5}$ lies

between these two aggregates.

The above interpretation can also be applied to the case of $n-$ dimensional fuzzy
vectors. In such a manner, we can express the disposition of a decision maker and a
specification, which may be given with the decision making problems by using an appropriate value of λ. Figure 10 shows a selection guide for the parameter (ornss) λ.

2.9.2 A SIMILARITY-BASED BIDIRECTIONAL APPROXIMATE REASONING

BIDIRECTIONAL APPROXIMATE REASONING AND DECISION MAKING
SYSTEMS

Let us consider a general fuzzy production system, which consists of a set T of l pairs
of fuzzy input and output data with two parameters:

$$\left\{\left(X_j, Y_j, c_j, 0_j\right) \middle| X_j \in [0,1]^n, Y_j \in [0,1]^m, c_j \in [0,1], 0_j \in [0,1] \, j=1, 2 \dots, 1\right\}$$

which can be considered as a fuzzy production rule $R_j \, (1 \le j \le l)$. Here, the parameter

c_j is the certainty factor of the rule, R_j, representing the belief of the rule. The other

parameter θ_j is the threshold value, that is, the rule R_j is executed if the degree of

matching is not less than the value of θ_j. It is to be noted that the parameters θ_j and

c_j are usually assigned at the phase of knowledge acquisition when the fuzzy production rules are extracted [36]:

$$\text{Let } X' = \left\{X_j, j=1, 2, \dots, l\right\} \text{ and } Y' = \left\{Y_j, j=1, 2, \dots, l\right\}.$$

Then, our problem is to give a bidirectional AR method, which performs a fuzzy

relational mapping from $[0,1]^n$ to $[0,1]^m$ in such a way that if $X \left(\notin X'\right)$ is similar to

X_j, then the output Y of the reasoning method is to be similar to Y_j. Similarly, the reasoning method can perform a fuzzy relational mapping from $[0,1]^m$ to $[0,1]^n$ so that if $Y(\notin Y')$ is similar to Y_j, then the output x is similar to x_j. Here, when one establishes a bidirectional AR method for a fuzzy decision making problem, the method can deal with a real situation requirng to express a decision maker's disposition and to reflect a given specification. As noted, the aggregation of subjective categories in the framework of human decision almost always shows some degree of compensation, which usually lies between the non-compensatory logical connectives "and(min)" and

the fully-compensatory "or (max)". Therefore, we adopt λ to denote the degree of compensation for the minimally and maximally aggregate value for the similarity indices and finally to render a fuzzy decision value according to a given situation.

Now, consider the realization of the bidirectional AR method for the decision making system. First, define two matrices $W \in [0,1]^{l \times n}$ and $R \in [0,1]^{l \times m}$ whose $j$throw vectors are:

$$W_j = \left[w_{j1}, w_{j2}, ..., w_{jn} \right] (j=1,2,...,l) \text{ and } R_j = \left[r_{j1}, r_{j2}, ..., r_{jm} \right] (j=1,2,...,l),$$

respectively. Also denote the fuzzy input and output data as:

$$X_j = \left[x_1^j, x_2^j, ..., x_n^j \right] \text{ and } Y_j = \left[y_1^j, y_2^j, ..., y_m^j \right], \ j=1,2,...,l$$

And then assign the values of the matrices as follows:

$$W_j = X_j \text{ and } R_j = Y_j, j=1,2,...,l. \tag{2.93}$$

Now, we shall derive a forward AR algorithm [36].

- **Step 1** For a given fuzzy input vector $X = [x_1, x_2, ..., x_n] \in [0,1]^n$, compute the similarity index vector $Q_j^f = \left(q_{j1}^f, q_{j2}^f, ..., q_{jn}^f \right), \ j=1,2,...,l$. Here, a similarity index $q_{ji} \ (i=1, 2,..., n)$ is given as $l - |x_i - w_{ji}|$ from Figure 9 with Lukasiewicz implication.

- **Step 2** For the obtained $Q_j^f = \left(q_{j1}^f, q_{j2}^f, ..., q_{jn}^f \right), \ (j=1,2,...,l)$, compute the similarity measure vector $S_\lambda^f = \left[s_\lambda^1, s_\lambda^2, ..., s_\lambda^l \right]$ where $s_\lambda^j \ (j=1,2,...,l)$ is computed as follows:

$$s_\lambda^j = OWA_\lambda\left(q_{j1}^f, q_{j2}^f, ..., q_{jn}^f\right).$$ (2.94)

- **Step 3** Obtain a modified similarity measure vector $\widetilde{S}_\lambda^f = \left[\widetilde{s}_\lambda^1, \widetilde{s}_\lambda^2, ..., \widetilde{s}_\lambda^l\right]$ by re-

flecting the certainty factor $c_i\ (1 \le i \le l) \in [0,1]$ as:

$$\widetilde{s}_\lambda^j = c_j \cdot s_\lambda^j, \quad (j = 1, 2, ...1).$$ (2.95)

- As you can see, if a certainty factor c_j is 1 for the fuzzy production rule R_i

, then the similarity measure is not affected by it. Otherwise, the value of the

similarity measure becomes smaller.

- **Step 4** For the computed $\widetilde{S}_\lambda^f = \left[\widetilde{s}_\lambda^1, \widetilde{s}_\lambda^2, ..., \widetilde{s}_\lambda^l\right]$ find $Z_\lambda^f = \left[z_\lambda^1, z_\lambda^2, ..., z_\lambda^l\right]$ after

reflecting the threshold values as:

$$z_\lambda^f = \begin{cases} \widetilde{s}_\lambda^j & \text{if } \widetilde{s}_\lambda^f \ge \theta_j \\ 0 & \text{otherwise} \end{cases}$$ (2.96)

- **Step 5** Finally, a fuzzy output vector $\widetilde{Y}_\lambda = \left[\widetilde{y}_\lambda^1, \widetilde{y}_\lambda^2, ..., \widetilde{y}_\lambda^m\right] \in [0\ 1]^m$ is obtained
from the max-min composition as a fuzzy decision value as follows:

$$\widetilde{Y}_\lambda = Z_\lambda^f \circ R$$ (2.97)

That is,

$$\widetilde{y}_\lambda^j = \max_{1 \le i \le l}\left(\min\left(z_\lambda^j, r_{ij}^f\right)\right), \quad 1 \le j \le m.$$

The backward reasoning algorithm can also be described similarly as follows:

- **Step 1** For a given fuzzy output vector $Y = [y_1, y_2, ..., y_m] \in [0,1]^m$, compute the

similarity index vector $Q_j^b = \left(q_{j1}^b, q_{j2}^b, ..., q_{jm}^b\right), j = 1, 2, ..., l$. Here, a similarity index q_j^b $(i=1,2,...,n)$ is given as $1-|y_i - r_{ji}|$ from (9) with Łukasiewicz implica-

tion.

- **Step 2** For the obtained $Q_j^b = (q_{j1}^b, q_{j2}^b, ..., q_{jm}^b)$ $(j=1,2,...,l)$, compute the similarity mea-

sure vector $S_\lambda^b = [s_\lambda^1, s_\lambda^2, ..., s_\lambda^l]$, where s_λ^j $(j=1,2,...,1)$ is computed as follows:

$$s_\lambda^j = OWA_\lambda \left(q_{j1}^b, q_{j2}^b, ..., q_{jm}^b \right) \tag{2.98}$$

- **Step 3**: Obtain a modified similarity measure vector $\widetilde{S}_\lambda^b = (\widetilde{s}_\lambda^1, \widetilde{s}_\lambda^2, ..., \widetilde{s}_\lambda^l)$ by

reflecting the certainty factor c_i $(1 \le i \le l)$ $\in [0,1]$ as:

$$\widetilde{s}_\lambda^j = c_i \cdot s_\lambda^j \quad (j=1,2,...,1) \tag{2.99}$$

- **Step 4** : For the computed $\widetilde{S}_\lambda^b = (\widetilde{s}_\lambda^1, \widetilde{s}_\lambda^2, ..., \widetilde{s}_\lambda^l)$ find $Z_\lambda^b = [z_\lambda^1, z_\lambda^2, ..., z_\lambda^l]$ by applying the threshold values as

$$z_\lambda^b = \begin{cases} \widetilde{s}_\lambda^j & \text{if } \widetilde{s}_\lambda^b \ge \theta_j, \\ 0 & \text{otherwise} \end{cases} \tag{2.100}$$

- **Step 5** : Finally, a corresponding fuzzy input vector $\check{X}_\lambda = [\check{x}_\lambda^1, \check{x}_\lambda^2, ..., \check{x}_\lambda^n] \in [0,1]^n$ is
obtained as a final decision value as follows :

$$\widetilde{X}_\lambda = Z_\lambda^b \circ W \tag{2.101}$$

Example 2.14. [36] Now, consider an industrial inspection process as one of the decision making systems. Here, the industrial inspection process uses six feature points, f_i $(i=1,2,...,6) \in [0,1]$ which come from a vision system and other instruments to measue five quality indices, q_i $(i=1,2,...,5) \in [0,1]$ for each product.

Suppose that the fuzzy production rules are extracted from an experienced inspector as follows :

R_1 :   If $\{(f_1, 0.32), (f_2, 1.00), (f_3, 0.52), (f_4, 0.25), (f_5, 0.12), (f_6, 0.95)\}$

than $\{(q_1, 1.00),(q_2, 0.82),(q_3, 0.53),(q_4, 0.34),\ (q_5, 0.72)\}$, $c_1 = 0.92, 0_1 = 0.30$.

R_2 : If $\{(f_1, 0.19),(f_2, 0.92),(f_3, 1.00),(f_4, 0.51),(f_5, 0.43),(f_6, 0.37)\}$

than $\{(q_1, 0.42),(q_2, 1.00),(q_3, 0.62),(q_4, 0.56),\ (q_5, 0.51)\}$, $c_2 = 0.98, \theta_2 = 0.25$.

R_3 : If $\{(f_1, 0.53),(f_2, 0.74),(f_3, 0.21),(f_4, 1.00),(f_5, 0.12),(f_6, 0.64)\}$

than $\{(q_1, 0.73),(q_2, 0.30),(q_3, 0.93),(q_4, 0.17),(q_5, 0.37)\}$, $c_3 = 0.95, \theta_3 = 0.21$.

R_4 : If $\{(f_1, 1.00),(f_2, 0.73),(f_3, 0.52),(f_4, 0.33),(f_5, 1.00),(f_6, 0.72)\}$

than $\{(q_1, 0.15),(q_2, 0.40),(q_3, 0.34),(q_4, 0.94),(q_5, 0.48)\}$, $c_4 = 0.88, \theta_4 = 0.33$

R_5 : If $\{(f_1, 0.32),(f_2, 0.62),(f_3, 0.83),(f_4, 0.71),(f_5, 0.12),(f_6, 1.00)\}$

than $\{(q_1, 0.32),(q_2, 0.62),(q_3, 0.46),(q_4, 0.62),(q_5, 1.00)\}$, $c_5 = 0.92, \theta_5 = 0.22$

The above fuzzy production system can be expressed by a form of fuzzy input and output data with two parameters.

$$X_1 = \begin{bmatrix} 0.32 & 1.00 & 0.52 & 0.25 & 0.12 & 0.95 \end{bmatrix}, \quad Y_1 = \begin{bmatrix} 1.00 & 0.82 & 0.53 & 0.34 & 0.72 \end{bmatrix},$$
$$c_1 = 0.92 \quad \theta_1 = 0.30, \quad X_2 = \begin{bmatrix} 0.19 & 0.92 & 1.00 & 0.51 & 0.43 & 0.37 \end{bmatrix},$$
$$Y_2 = \begin{bmatrix} 0.42 & 1.00 & 0.62 & 0.56 & 0.51 \end{bmatrix}, \quad c_2 = 0.98 \quad \theta_2 = 0.25$$

$$X_3 = \begin{bmatrix} 0.52 & 0.74 & 0.21 & 1.00 & 0.12 & 0.64 \end{bmatrix},$$
$$Y_3 = \begin{bmatrix} 0.73 & 0.30 & 0.93 & 0.17 & 0.37 \end{bmatrix} \quad c_3 = 0.95 \quad \theta_3 = 0.21$$

$$X_4 = \begin{bmatrix} 1.00 & 0.73 & 0.52 & 0.33 & 1.00 & 0.72 \end{bmatrix} \quad Y_4 = \begin{bmatrix} 0.15 & 0.40 & 0.34 & 0.94 & 0.48 \end{bmatrix},$$
$$c_4 = 0.88 \quad \theta_4 = 0.33 \quad X_5 = \begin{bmatrix} 0.32 & 0.62 & 0.83 & 0.71 & 0.12 & 1.00 \end{bmatrix},$$
$$Y_5 = \begin{bmatrix} 0.32 & 0.62 & 0.46 & 0.62 & 1.00 \end{bmatrix}, \quad c_5 = 0.92 \quad \theta_5 = 0.22$$

And then, W and R are composed as follows :

$$W = \begin{bmatrix} 0.32 & 1.00 & 0.52 & 0.25 & 0.12 & 0.95 \\ 0.19 & 0.92 & 1.00 & 0.51 & 0.43 & 0.37 \\ 0.53 & 0.74 & 0.21 & 1.00 & 0.12 & 0.64 \\ 1.00 & 0.73 & 0.52 & 0.33 & 1.00 & 0.72 \\ 0.32 & 0.62 & 0.83 & 0.71 & 0.12 & 1.00 \end{bmatrix},$$

$$R = \begin{bmatrix} 1.00 & 0.83 & 0.53 & 0.34 & 0.72 \\ 0.42 & 1.00 & 0.62 & 0.56 & 0.51 \\ 0.73 & 0.30 & 0.93 & 0.17 & 0.37 \\ 0.15 & 0.40 & 0.34 & 0.94 & 0.48 \\ 0.32 & 0.62 & 0.46 & 0.62 & 1.00 \end{bmatrix},$$

For an obtained feature vector $x = \begin{bmatrix} 1.00 & 0.45 & 0.32 & 0.67 & 0.75 & 0.53 \end{bmatrix}$, the similarity measure for $\lambda = 0.0, 0.25, 0.50, 0.75,$ and 1.00 are computed as

$$s^f_{0.00} = \begin{bmatrix} 0.32 & 0.19 & 0.37 & 0.66 & 0.32 \end{bmatrix},$$

$$s^f_{0.25} = \begin{bmatrix} 0.41 & 0.37 & 0.53 & 0.71 & 0.44 \end{bmatrix},$$

$$s^f_{0.50} = \begin{bmatrix} 0.50 & 0.55 & 0.69 & 0.78 & 0.57 \end{bmatrix},$$

$$S^f_{0.75} = [0.60 \quad 0.70 \quad 0.84 \quad 0.89 \quad 0.76],$$

$$S^f_{1.00} = [0.71 \quad 0.84 \quad 0.98 \quad 1.00 \quad 0.96],$$

And finally, after reflecting the certainty factors and threshold values, the reasoning results are given as follows :

$$\tilde{Y}_{0.00} = [0.35 \quad 0.40 \quad 0.35 \quad 0.58 \quad 0.48],$$

$$\tilde{Y}_{0.25} = [0.50 \quad 0.40 \quad 0.50 \quad 0.63 \quad 0.48],$$

$$\tilde{Y}_{0.75} = [0.73 \quad 0.68 \quad 0.79 \quad 0.78 \quad 0.70],$$

$$\tilde{Y}_{1.00} = [0.73 \quad 0.82 \quad 0.93 \quad 0.88 \quad 0.88],$$

Figure 11. shows the reasoning results.

The qualitative meaning of $\tilde{Y}_{0.00}$, $\tilde{Y}_{0.50}$, and $\tilde{Y}_{1.00}$ in the inspection process can be interpreted as follows: $\tilde{Y}_{0.00}$ is the value given by applying the inspection rule most tightly and $\tilde{Y}_{1.00}$ is the value given by applying the inspection rule most loosely. On the other hand $\tilde{Y}_{0.50}$ is the avaraged value.

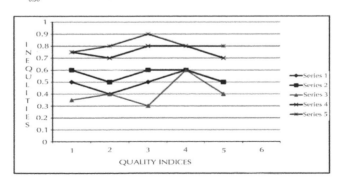

FIGURE 11   Approximate reasoning results according to λ.

Now, let us consider that a specification for an inspection process is given as "All quality indices $q_i(i=1,2,...,5)$ of a product of should be greater than 0.3 at least for the decision of classifying it as a good quality product". For the above example, we can see from the least value of $\tilde{Y}_{0.00}$ that all $q_i(i=1,2,...,5)$ are greater than 0.3. Thus, the product can be classified as a good quality product. Now consider another case wherein a specification is given as "If the quality indices satisfy $q_1 < 0.95$, $q_2 < 0.95$, $q_3 < 0.95$, $q_4 < 0.80$, and $q_5 < 0.9$ for any case, then the product has a good quality", one can see from the upper value of $\tilde{Y}_{1.00}$ that $q_4 < 0.88$. Therefore, we can conclude that the product cannot satisfy the specification. In fact, the criteria of decision for a good or bad product are usually given strictly or loosely in the industrial inspection system under various situations. Thus, an AR method is required to reflect these situations. Since, the proposed reasoning method can render the interval valued results, it can be applied to this kind of decision-making systems.

On the other hand, the backward reasoning method can be applied to the case wherein the X vectors denote the fuzzy propositions related to disorders and the Y vectors represent the fuzzy propositions related to symptoms such as the medical diagnostic system. In that case, if a set of symptoms with fuzzy values is given for the decision-making system as a fuzzy input, then it will produce a set of possible disorders with fuzzy values as a fuzzy decision value. Here, we will not give a detailed example of a backward reasoning method, since, it can be similarly described and applied as that of the forward reasoning case.

2.10   LOGICAL APPROACHES TO FUZZY SIMILARITY-BASED REASONING

Due to the essential vagueness and approximation of human thinking, the logical treatment of uncertainty is of increasing importance in artificial intelligence and related research. Nowadays, a considerable number of logical systems have been carried out as formalizations of vague concepts and AR (for example, seeGarrgov, Gerla, Goguen, Hajek, Lano, Marquis, Novak, Pavelka, Takeuti, and Titani). However, reasoning in these logics is still exact, that is in order to apply an inference rule, the antecedent clauses of this rule must be equal either to some premises or to logical axioms or previously proven formulas. Recently, Using proposed a new approach, in which we can really make ARs, that is, it is possible to allow the antecedent clauses of a rule to match its premises (or logical axioms of previously proven formulas) only approximately. The starting point is a similarity R defined in the set of propositional variables and its "natural" extension $\overline{R}$ to the whole set of propositional formulas. Subsequently, Biacino and Gerla generalized the definition of an approximate consequence operator given and clarified its connection with Pavelka's logic.

2.10.1   APPROXIMATE APPROACH TO THEOREM PROVING USING FUZZY SIMILARITY [19]

We consider inferences that may be approximated by allowing the antecedent clauses of a rule to match its premises only approximately. In particular, the classical SLD Resolution is modified in order to overcome failure situations in the unification process if the entities involved in the matching have a non-zero similarity degree. Such a procedure allows us to compute numeric values belonging to the interval [0,1], named approximation degrees, which provide an approximation measure of the obtained solutions. This framework, which we call Similarity Propositional Logic Programming (SPLP), is the propositional version of the one proposal by Sessa, which is based on first order language. We find the first proposal to introduce similarity in the frame of the declarative paradigm of Logic Programming. Logic programs on function-free languages are considered and approximate and imprecise information are represented by introducing a similarity relation between constant and predicate symbols. Two transformation techniques of logic programs are defined. In the underlying logic, the inference rule (Resolution rule)as well as the usual crisprepresentation of the considered universe is not modified. It allows to avoid both the introduction of weights on the clauses and the use of fuzzy sets as elements of the language. The semantic equivalence between the two inference processes associated with two kinds of transformed programs has been proved by using an abstract interpretation technique. Moreover, the notion of fuzzy least Herbrand modelhas been introduced. The generalization of this approach to the case of programs with function symbols is provided by introducing the general notion of structural translation of languages. The operational counterpart of this extension is faced by introducing a modified SLD resolution procedure, which allows us to perform these kinds of extended computations exploiting the original logic program, without any preprocessingsteps in order to transform the given program. Some relations, which allow to state the computational equivalence between these different approaches, has been proved. For completeness sake, we considera different-generalized unification algorithm based on similarity.

We consider a similarityrelation S (reflexive, symmetric, and min-transitive relation) defined on the set Var of propositional variables. The first problem is to extend the similarity S over Varto a similarity over a propositional language **L** built from Var. In Ying and Gerla'spapers the extension is done as follows:

- First S is extended to $\overline{S}$ on L by the following recursive definition:

$$\overline{S}(p, q) = \begin{cases} S(p, q), & \text{if } p, q \in \text{Var} \\ S(s, s') \wedge S(t, t') & \text{if } p = s \rightarrow t \text{ and } q = s' \rightarrow t' \\ 0 & \text{otherwise} \end{cases}$$

Notice that $\overline{S}$ is not compatible with the logical equivalence. Take, for example, for every and a simple computation shows that $\overline{S}(F \rightarrow p, p \rightarrow p) = 0$.

- Second they consider the minimal similarity relation S_e over $\mathcal{L}$ compatible with logical equivalence and containing $\overline{S}$, as:

$$S_e(p, q) = \sup\{ \overline{S}(p_1, p_2) \wedge \ldots \wedge \overline{S}(p_{2n-1}, p_{2n}) \mid p_1 = p, p_{2n} = q \text{ and } p_{2k} \equiv p_{2k+1} \\ \text{for } k = 1, n - 1\}.$$

To compute the relation S_e is the main problem of this approach. Now we state the results:

i.   There does not exist a functional extension of S compatible with logical equivalence.

ii.   Any similarity relation preserving logical equivalence defines a similarity relation between classes of logical equivalent formulas and thus a similarity relation between subsets of interpretations that is subsets of Ω. Take into account that, in the finite case, there exists an isomorphism between proposition and subsets of interpretations. Moreover, any similarity relation over the set of subsets of Ω defines a similarity relation over L compatible with logical equivalence.

iii. Relations S_e obtained from a similarity relation S over the set Var by Ying-Gerla' smethod do not over all similarity relations compatible with logical equivalence. For example, if $S_e(p, q) = \alpha \neq 0$, then $S_e(p, q \wedge q) \geq \min(\overline{s}(p, q),$ $\overline{s}(p \wedge p, q \wedge q)) = a$ and this is not necessarily true in a similarity relation compatible with logical equivalence.

Based on Se we define a consequence operator, Cone: $F(L) \times L \rightarrow [0,1]$, $F(L)$ being the set of fuzzy subsets of L, by:

$$Con_e (\Gamma, q) = \wedge \{\overline{S}_e \ (Taut \ U \ \Gamma, \ B) \mid B \vdash q\}$$

Where Taut denotes the set of classical tautologies and $\overline{S}_e$ is defined as:

$$\overline{S}_e (\Gamma, B) = \wedge_{q \in B} \vee_{p \in L} \Gamma(p) \wedge S_e(p, q)$$

For all $\Gamma \in F(L), B \subseteq L$ and p, q $\in$L. The relation $\overline{S}_e$ is not symmetrical. It may be interpreted as the degree in which B can be considered included in Γ. If Γ is a crisp set of formulas, then $\overline{S}_e (\Gamma, B) = 1$ whenever $B \subseteq \Gamma$. An easy computation shows that a form of generalized Modus ponens is preserved by this consequence operator, since the inequality

$$Con_e \left(\{p \rightarrow q, p'\}, p'\right) \geq \overline{S}_e (p, p')$$

holds for any propositions p, q and p'

We consider an application of these ideas in the framework of logic programming. For simplicity, we only consider below the propositional version. We start by recalling that a logic program P on L is a conjunction of definite clauses of L, denoted as $q \leftarrow p_1, ..., p_n, n \geq 0$ and a goal is a negative clause, denoted with $\leftarrow q_1, ..., q_n, n \geq 1$ where the symbol ", " that separates the propositional variables has to be interpreted as conjunction, where $p_1, ..., p_n, q, q_1, ..., q_n \in Var$. A SPLP- program is a pair (P, S), where P is a logic program defined on L and S is a similarity on Var. Given P, the least herbrand model of P is given by $M_p = \{p \in Var \mid P \Vdash p\}$, where $\Vdash$ denotes classical logical entailment. M_p is equivalent to the corresponding procedural semantics of p, defined by considering the SLD resolution. In the classical case, a mismatch between tow propositional constant names causes a failure of the unification process. Then it is rather natural to admit a more flexible unification, in which the syntactical identity is substituted by a similarity S defined on Var. The modified version of the SLD resolution, which we call similarity-based SLD resolution, exploits this simple variation in the unification process. The basic idea of this procedure for first order languages has also been outlined. The following definitions formalize these ideas in the case of propositional languages.

Definition 2.7 Let S: Var $\times$ Var $\to [0,1]$ be a similarity and p, q $\in$ Var be two propositional constants in apropositional language $\mathcal{L}$. We define the unification-degree of p and q with respect to S the value S(p, q). p and q areλ – unifiable if S(p, q) = λ with $\lambda >$ 0, otherwise we say that they are not unifiable.

Definition 2.8. Given a similarity $S :$ Var$\times$Var $\to [0,1]$ a program P and a goal G_0 a similarity-based SLD derivation of $P \cup \{G_0\}$, denoted by $G_0 \Rightarrow_{C_1 \alpha_1,} G_1 \Rightarrow_{C_k \alpha_k} G_k$, consists of a sequence $G_0, G_1, \ldots G_k$ of negative clauses, together with a sequence $C_1, C_2, \ldots, C_k$ of clauses, P and a sequence $\alpha_1, \alpha_2, \ldots, \alpha_k$ of values in [0, 1], such that for all $i \in \{1, \ldots, k\}, G_i$ is a resolvent of G_{i-1} and C_i with unification degree α_1. The approximation degree of the derivation is $\alpha \inf\{\alpha_1, \ldots, \alpha_k\}$. if G_k is the empty clause $\perp$, for some finite k, the derivation is called a Similarity-based SLD refutation, otherwise it is called failed.

In case, the similarity S is the identity, the previous definition provides theclassical notion of SLD refutation. The values α_1 can be consider as constraints that allow the success of the unification processes. Then it is natural to consider the best unification degree that allows us to satisfy all these constraints. In general, as answer can be obtained with different SLDrefutations and different approximation degrees, then the maximum α of these values characterizes the best refutations of the goal. In particular, a refutation with approximation-degree I provides an exact solution. Let us stress that α belongs to the set $\lambda_1, \lambda_2 \ldots$ of the possible similarity values in S.

Whenever we consider Similarity-based SLD resolution we assume left most selection rule. However, all the results can be analogously stated for any selection rule that does not depend on the propositional constant names and on the history of the derivation. Similarity-based SLD resolution provides a characterization of the fuzzy least herbrand model $M_{p, S}$ for (P, S).

Proposition 2.4 Let α similarity S and α logic program P (on a propositional language L) be given. For any q $\in$ Var, $M_{p, S}$ (q) = $\alpha > 0$ if α is the maximum value in [0,1] for which there exists αsimilarity-based SLD refutation for P $\cup$ {$\neg$ P} with approximation degree α.

The degree of membership $M_{p, S}$ (q) of an atom q is given by the best "tolerance" level $\alpha \in [0,1]$, which allows us to prove q exploiting the similarity-based SLD resolution of $P \cup \{\neg P\}$. Moreover, if S is strict and $M_p$denotes the classical least herbrand model of the program P, then $q \in M_p$ if $M_{p, S}$ (q) = 1.

2.11   FUZZY RESOLUTION BASED ON SIMILARITY BASED UNIFICATION [85]

In the field of deductive data bases and information retrieval system an ever demanding approach is to deal with flexible queries and answers. Deductive data bases, try to answer flexible queries with the help of AR mechanism. Researches in such a direction were based on a threshold-based resolution process within the semantic framework of a many-valued logic, later, Mukaidono replaced the threshold-based inference with graded resolution based on possibility distribution over clauses. A quite different extension of resolution has been considered, where an evidential distribution has been used in the unification process and classical first order terms have been replaced by fuzzy sets, in a more general framework, Virtanen has proposed a similar approach. Despite, its fallouts and motivations are to be found mainly in the extensions of logic program, the extension of unification theory is a subject of its own.

In this section, classical unification is modified to a "relaxed" unification when, the classical process fails. In the declarative paradigm of Logic Programming the unification plays a central role. Moreover, such a technique could be usefully exploited in the context of deductive databases. We will consider languages where no function symbol occurs.

Classical unification fails because of a "mismatch" among constants. Therefore, it is necessary to dilute the concept of "mismatch" by weakening of the classical identity, similarities seem to be a promising candidates to do this. In this section, a basic concept is to consider the "extended constant", replacing the usual constant. Extended constants, which we call clouds, areobtained by dissolving the notion of singleton into the set of pairwise "similar" elements. The concept of cloud, based on the notion of similarity, coincides neither with fuzzy set nor with classical set. Clouds have a strong connection with the "conceptual spaces" which gives structural analogies among objects. We introduce a similarity in a first-order language, in our case, constants are clouds. The notion of identity between constants is replaced with the notion of "equivalence" between clouds. Thus we obtain an extended version of most general unifier (e-mgu) and generate an algorithm to compute the e-mgu of a set of equations. Such an algorithm of fuzzy unification provides both an e-mgu of the set of atomic formulae and an associated numerical value, called unification degree, which is the "cost" paid to strike a success in an unification that, classically, would result into a failure.

2.11.1   SIMILARITY RELATIONS AND CLOUDS

Our approach is based on the notion of similarity on which is based our approach is a many valued extension of the classical notion of equality. We consider two binary operations $\wedge$ and $\vee$ in $[0,1]$by setting $x \wedge y = min\{x, y\}$, $x \vee y = max\{x, y\}$ for any $x, y \in [0, 1]$. We denote by $\vee$ and $\wedge$ the lowest upper bound and the greatest lower bound operators, respectively.

Definition 2.9 A similarity on a domain $\mathcal{U}$ is a fuzzy subsetR: $\mathcal{U} \times \mathcal{U} \longrightarrow [0, 1]$ of $\mathcal{U} \times \mathcal{U}$ having the following properties:

  i. $\mathcal{R} \{x, x) = 1$ for any$x \in \mathcal{U}$(reflexivity)
  ii. $\mathcal{R} \{x, y) = \mathcal{R} \{y, x) =$for any$xy \in \mathcal{U}$(symmetry)

iii. $\mathcal{R}\{x, z\} \geq \mathcal{R}\{x, y\} \wedge \mathcal{R}\{y, z\}$ for any x y $z \in \mathcal{U}$(transitivity).
For any $\lambda \in [0,1]$, the closed λ-cut of $\mathcal{R}$ is the classical relation:

$$\mathcal{R}_\lambda = \{(x, y) \in \mathcal{U} \times \mathcal{U} \mid \mathcal{R}\{x, y\} \geq \lambda\}.$$

If $(x, y) \in \mathcal{R}_\lambda$, we say that x is λ-similar to y. Such a notion identifies the similarities with suitable families of equivalence relations.

Proposition 2.5 [85] Let $\mathcal{R}$ be a similarity on a domain $\mathcal{U}$ and, for any $\lambda \in [0, 1]$, denote by $\mathcal{R}_\lambda$ the closed λ-cut $\{(x, y) \in \mathcal{U} \times \mathcal{U} \mid \mathcal{R}\{x, y\} \geq \lambda\}$. Then $(\mathcal{R}_\lambda)_{\lambda \in [0, 1]}$ is a family of equivalence relations such that:

i. $\lambda \leq \mu \Rightarrow \mathcal{R}_\lambda \supseteq \mathcal{R}_\mu$ for any μ and λ in $[0,1]$

ii. $\bigcap_{\lambda \leq \mu} \mathcal{R}_\lambda = \mathcal{R}_\mu$ for any μ in $[0,1]$

Conversely, let $(\mathcal{R}_\lambda)_{\lambda \in [0, 1]}$ be a family of equivalence relations satisfying i) and ii). Then the fuzzy relation defined by setting:

$$\mathcal{R}\{x, y\} = \vee \{\lambda \in [0,1] \mid x \mathcal{R}_\lambda y\}$$

is a similarity, whose λ-cuts are the relations $\mathcal{R}_\lambda$.

Example 2.15 [85] Let $\mathcal{U} = \{$circle, square, polygon, rectangle, ellipse$\}$ and consider the following family of partitions $(\prod_\lambda)_{\lambda \in [0, 1]}$ of $\mathcal{U}$:

$\prod_\lambda = \{\{$square, circle, polygon, rectangle, ellipse$\}\}$ for $\lambda \in [0, 0.1]$
$\prod_\lambda = \{\{$square, polygon, rectangle$\}, \{$circle, ellipse$\}\}$ for $\lambda \in [0.1, 0.5]$
$\prod_\lambda = \{\{$square, rectangle$\}, \{$polygon$\}, \{$circle, ellipse$\}\}$ for $\lambda \in [0.5, 0.8]$
$\prod_\lambda = \{\{$square$\}, \{$circle$\}, \{$polygon$\}, \{$rectangle$\}, \{$ellipse$\}\}$ for $\lambda \in [0.8, 1]$.

We obtain a similarity $\mathcal{R}$ on the domain $\mathcal{U}$ by considering the family of equivalence relations $(\mathcal{R}_\lambda)_{\lambda \in [0, 1]}$ associated with $(\prod_\lambda)_{\lambda \in [0, 1]}$. For instance:
$\mathcal{R}($square, rectangle$) = 0.8$, $\mathcal{R}$ (square, polygon) $= 0.5$, $\mathcal{R}$ (square, circle) $= 0.1$.

We can associate to every subset X of $\mathcal{U}$ a number $\mu(X)$ to represent the "worst" value of similarity between pairs of elements in X:

$$\mu(X) = \wedge_{x, \acute{x} \in X} \mathcal{R}(x, \acute{x}).$$

Note that, since, $\wedge_{x, \acute{x} \in x} \mathcal{R}(x, \acute{x}) = \wedge \emptyset = 1$, it is $\mu(\emptyset) = 1$. For instance, in Example we have μ ($\{$square, polygon, rectangle$\}$) $= 0.5$ and $\mu(\mathcal{U}) = 0.1$. We call $\mu(X)$ co-diameter of X since the function $\mathcal{R}'(x, y) = 1 - \mathcal{R}(x, y)$ behaves like a distance, whose related diameter is the function $\mu'(X) = \vee_{x, y \in X} \mathcal{R}'(x, y) = 1 - \mu(X)$. Clouds are the subsets of a domain $\mathcal{U}$, where a similarity $\mathcal{R}$ is defined, thus, we say that $\mu(X)$ is the co-diameter of the cloud X. A cloud is not a fuzzy subset since no membership function is defined on the elements. We consider a non-empty cloud X as a point and the number $\mu(X)$ as a many valued evaluation of the claim that X is a point. If $\lambda \in [0,1]$, and X is an non-empty cloud such that $\mu(X) \geq \lambda$, we say also that X is a λ-point. Then a λ-point is a part of a complete class of equivalence modulo the λ-similarity. The following proposition shows that $\mu(X)$ is the largest level for which the elements of X can be considered pairwise λ-similar, that is, for which X is λ-point.

Proposition 2.6 [85] Let X be a subset of $\mathcal{U}$. Then:

$$\mu(X) = \vee\{\lambda \in [0,1] \mid X \text{ is a } \lambda\text{-point}\}.$$

Proof: Indeed:

$$\mu(X) = \vee\{\lambda \in [0,1] \mid \lambda \leq \mu(X)\}$$

$$= \vee\{\lambda \in [0,1] \mid \lambda \leq \mathcal{R}(x, y)\forall x, y \in X\}.$$

The following is a simple characterization of the co-diameter of a non-empty cloud.
Proposition 2.7 [85] Assume that $c \in X$, then:

$$\mu(X) = \vee_{x \in X}\mathcal{R}(x, c).$$

Consequently, given a finite sequence $X1,\ldots,n$ of clouds such that $\bigcap_{i=1} X_i \neq \phi,$

$$\mu\left(\bigcup_{i=1}^{n} X_i\right) = \bigwedge_{i=1}^{n} \mu(X_i).$$

Proof: Clearly, $\bigwedge_{x \in X} \mathcal{R}(x, c) \geq \mu(X)$. Moreover, for any $x, y \in X$:

$$\mathcal{R}(x, y) \geq \mathcal{R}(x, c) \wedge \mathcal{R}(c, y) \geq \bigwedge_{x \in X} \mathcal{R}(x, c).$$

Therefore $\mu(X) \geq \vee_{x \in X} \mathcal{R}(x, c)$.

A system of clouds is a finite set of clouds. Given a system of clouds $Z = \{X_1 \ldots, X_n\}$ we call crispness degree of Z the number:

$$\xi(Z) = \bigwedge_{i=1}^{n} \mu(X_i).$$

As usual we have that $\xi(\emptyset) = 1$. $\xi(Z)$ is a many-valued evaluation of the claim that each element in Z is a point. It is immediate that if Z' is obtained from Z by deleting the empty cloud and all the singletons, then $\xi(Z) = \xi(Z')$.

2.11.2 COMPACTNESS OF SYSTEMS OF CLOUDS

We say that two clouds X and Y overlap if $X \cap Y \neq \emptyset$. A system of clouds Z is compact provided that no pair of clouds in Z overlaps. To establish a procedure for compactness of a system of clouds, we consider the following definition.

Definition 2.10 [85] Given a system of clouds Z we set, for $M \in Z$:

$$T_Z(M) = \cup \{M' \in Z \mid M \cap M' \neq \emptyset\}.$$

We define an operator T as:

$$T(Z) = T_Z(M) \mid M \in Z .0$$

The following example clarify the previous notion

Example 2.16 Let us consider the domain $U = \{a, b, c, d, e, f, p, q\}$. Given the system of clouds:

$$Z = \{\{a, c\}, \{d\}, \{c, d\}\}$$

we have that,

$$T_Z(\{a, c\}) = \{a, c, d\}, T_Z(\{d\}) = \{c, d\}, T_Z\{c, d\}) = \{a, c, d\}$$

Then,

$$T(Z) = \{\{a, c, d\}, \{c, d\}\}.$$

Z is a compact system of clouds if and only if Z is a fixed point for T. We consider the following proposition to show that T does not change the crispness degree of a system of clouds.

Proposition 2.8 Let Z be a system of clouds. Then:

$$\Xi(Z) = \xi(T(Z)).$$

Proof: By Proposition 2.7:

$$\Xi(T(Z)) = \underset{M \in Z}{\wedge} \left(\underset{Y \cap M \neq \phi, Y \in Z}{\wedge} \mu(Y) \right)$$

Since, for any $M \in Z$, $\underset{Y \cap M \neq \phi, Y \in Z}{\wedge} \mu(Y) \geq \Xi(Z)$, it follows that:

$$\xi(T(Z)) \geq \xi(Z).$$

Conversely, since, $M \cap M \neq \emptyset$, for any $M \in Z$, $\bigwedge_{Y \cap M \neq \emptyset, Y \in Z} \mu(Y) \leq \mu(M)$ Therefore:

$$\xi(T(Z)) \leq \xi(Z).$$

By the following definition we obtain the least compact system of clouds "containing" a given system. We set $T^0(Z) = Z$ and $T^{n+1}(Z) = T(T^n(Z))$.

Definition 2.11 [85] Let Z be a system *of clouds*. The $T-$ degree of Z the number is defined as:

$$\Phi(Z) = \min\{n \mid T^n(Z) = T^{n+1}(Z)\}.$$

The operator *Compact* is defined as:

$$Compact\ (Z) = T^{\Phi(Z)}(Z).$$

Since, Z is a finite system of finite clouds, the T-degree of Z is a finite non-negative integer By the above definitions, Z is a compact system of clouds if and only if $\Phi(Z) = 0$. Since $T^{\Phi(Z)}(Z)$ is a fixed point for T, we have that Compact (Z) is compact. So Compact transforms a system of clouds into a compact system. The following results summarize the main features of Compact.

Proposition 2.9 [85] Let Z be a system of clouds, then:

i. $\xi(Z) = \xi\ (Compact(Z))$
ii. Compact (Compact (Z)) =Compact (Z)
iii. Z is compact if and only if Z is a fixed point for compact
iv. Compact (Z) is Compact.

Proof: The proof of ii), iii), and iv) are immediate. Property i) is a consequence if the fact that

$$\xi(Z) = \xi(T^n(Z)).$$

That, in turn, is a consequence of Proposition 3.1.

2.11.3 EXTENDING UNIFICATION THROUGH A SIMILARITY RELATION

Let $\mathcal{L}$ be a function-free first-order language and:
- v its set of variables,
- C its set of constants, and
- P itsset of predicate symbols.

We assume that V is ordered in a sequence $x_1, x_2, \ldots$ also, denote by L' is the language with the same variables and predicate symbols as L but whose set of constants is the set C' ofnon-empty clouds of constants in L. L' is an extension of L, indeed we can identify any constant c in C with the singleton {c} in C'. We call extended-type (briefly e-type), with type $\in$ {constant, term, formula} a type of L'. $\tau_{V,C}$ is the set of w-terms, that is, the set $V \cup C'$. An extended substitution(denoted by e-substitution) is a map $\emptyset: V \to \tau_{V,C}$. Θ is the set of e-substitution.

We assume as primitive a similarity relation equation on $P \cup C \cup V$ such that equation $(t, t') = 0$ whenever:

- t and t' are not both in V or C or P
- t and t' are in V and $t \neq t'$
- t and t' are are predicates with different arities.

Alternatively, we can state that, equation is union of a similarity in C, the identity in V and similarity among symbols of predicates with the same arities. Given two e-terms t, t', we get:

$$t \,\dot\cup\, t' = \begin{cases} t \cup t' & if \ t \ and \ t' \in C' \\ \{t\} \cup t' & if \ t \in V, t' \in C' \\ \{t'\} \cup t & if \ t \in C' \ t' \in V \\ \{t, t'\} & if \ t, t' \in V. \end{cases}$$

We define a relation $\overline{eq}$ on the set of atomic e-formulae as:

$$\overline{eq}\big(p(t_1, ..., t_n), q(t_1', ..., t_m')\big) = \begin{cases} eq(p, q) \wedge \left(\bigwedge_{i=1}^{n} \mu\big(t_i \,\dot\cup\, t_i'\big) \right) & if \ n = m \\ 0 & otherwise \end{cases}$$

Such a relation is not a similarity since it may be not reflexive. Indeed, if t is not a singleton, $\mu(t \,\dot\cup\, t) = \mu(t) \neq 1$, in general.

Definition 2.12 An extended equation (e-equation) is an equation between two atomic e-formulas with the same arity.

Given a system of e-equations S, and an e-substitution θ, we define the unification degree $v(S, \theta)$ of S with respect to θ as follows:

$$v(S, \theta) = \bigwedge_{e=e' \in S} \overline{eq}\big(\theta(e), \theta(e')\big)$$

Therefore, the unification degree U(S) of a system of e-equations S is defined as:

$$U(S) = \bigvee_{\theta \in \Theta} v(S, \theta)$$

The following example illustrates the above concept.

Example 2.17 Let us consider the domain U = {a, b, c, d, e, f, p, q} and a similarity $\mathcal{R}$ such that $\mathcal{R}(a, b) = \mathcal{R}(d, e) = \mathcal{R}(e, f) = \mathcal{R}(f, d) = .7$, $\mathcal{R}(p, q) = .5$, $\mathcal{R}(a, c) = \mathcal{R}(c, b) = .4$. If we consider the substitution $\theta = \{x/\{a\}, y/\{b\}\}$ and the set of e-equations:

S = {p(x, {e, d}) = q ({a}, {f}), p({a}, {y}) = p({a, b}, {b})},
Since, it is:

$$\overline{eq}\big(\theta\big(p(x,\{e,d\})\big)\big)=\theta\big(q(\{a\},\{f\})\big)\big)=eq(p,q)\wedge\mu(\{a\})\wedge\mu(\{e,d,f\})=0.5\wedge1\wedge0.7=0.5$$

$$\overline{eq}\big(\theta\big(p(\{a\},\{y\})\big)\big)=\theta\big(p(\{a,b\},\{b\})\big)\big)=eq(p,p)\wedge\mu(\{a,b\})\wedge\mu(\{b\})=1\wedge0.7\wedge1=0.7$$

It follows that

$$v(S,\theta)=\overline{eq}\big(\theta\big(p(x,\{e,d\})\big)\big)=\theta\big(p(\{a\},\{f\})\big)\big)=\overline{eq}\big(\theta(p)(\{a\},\{y\})\big)\big)=\theta\big(p\{a,b\},\{b\}\big)=0.5\wedge0.7=0.5$$

It is easy to verify that .5 is the maximum possible unification degree, then U(S) = v (S< θ) = .5

Notice that, differently from the classical case, the fact that the left and the right sides of the equations in S coincide, does not entails that U(S)= 1. As an example, let r be an unary predicate and a and b two constants such that eq(a, b) ≠ 1. Then, by setting S = {r({a, b}). =r({a, b})}, we obtain that:

$$U(S) = eq(r, r)\wedge\mu(\{a, b\})= eq(a, b)\neq1$$

Definition 2.13 Given system of e-equations S such that U(S) ≠ 0, an e-substitution θ is defined as extended unifier (e-unifier) for S provided that v(S, θ) = U(S).

The notion of e-unifier coincides with the usual one of unifier, when S is a system of equations and equation is the identity relation.

2.11.4 E-UNIFIERS OF SYSTEMS OF CLOUDS

We consider clouds that are either subsets of $C \sqcup V$ or subsets of p. If M is a cloud in $C \sqcup V$, we write $M = X \sqcup D$ to denote that X is the set of variables and D the set of constants occurring in M. The systems of clouds are used to compute e-unifiers for systems of e-equations. We define a function associating to any compact system of clouds $Z = \{X_1 \sqcup D_1, ..., X_n \sqcup D_n\}$ as an e-substitution θ_Z = Assoc-sub (Z) where, for any $x \in V$:

$$\Theta_Z(x) = x \text{ if } x \notin X_1 \cup ... \cup X_n$$

$$\Theta_Z(x) = D_i \text{ if } x \in X_i \text{ and } D_i \neq \emptyset$$

$$\Theta_Z(x) = x_j \text{ if } x \in X_i, D_i = \emptyset \text{ and } X_j \text{ is the first variable occurring in } X_i.$$

We consider two functions *Trans_t* and *Trans_p* by transforming a system of e-equations into two systems' of clouds in $C \sqcup V$ and p, respectively. Thus, we obtain two systems of clouds as:

Split_p (p $(t_1, ..., t_m) = q (t'_1, ..., t'_m)) = \{\{p, q\}\}$

Split_t (p $(t_1, ..., t_m) = q (t'_1, ..., t'_m)) = \{t_1 \overset{\circ}{U} t'_1, ..., t_m \overset{\circ}{U} t'_m\}$.

If $S = \bigcup_{i=1}^{n} \{e_i = e'_i\}$, we get:

$$Trans\_p(S) = \bigcup_{i=1...n} Split\_p(e_i = e'_i)$$

$$Trans\_t(S) = \bigcup_{i=1...n} Split\_t(e_i = e'_i).$$

We consider both *Trans_p(S)* and *Trans_t(S)* as systems of clouds.

Example 2.18 Let S = {p(x,{a, c}, y) = q(a, b, b), r(x, x, y) = s(a, {b, c}, c)}. Then:

$$Trans\_p(S) = \{p\{p, q\}, \{r, s\}\}$$

$$Trans\_t(S) = \{\{x, a\}, \{a, b, c\}, \{y, b\}, \{x, b, c\}, \{y, c\}\}$$

An e-unifier of a system of e-equations S is computed through the associated system of clouds *Compact(Trans_t(S))*. More precisely, we show that the function *Assoc_sub(Compact(Trans_t(S)))* provides an e-unifier of S.

Given a cloud M in $V \cup C$ and a e-substitution θ, we denote by $\theta(M)$ the cloud obtained by substituting each variable x in M with:

-$\Theta(x)$ if $\theta(x)$ is a variable

-the elements in $\Theta(x)$ if $\Theta(x)$ is a cloud of constants,

Since, θ operates only on the variables, if $M = X \cup D$ then $\theta(X \cup D) = \theta(X) \cup D$. Given a system $Z = \{M_1, ..., M_n\}$ where $M_1, ..., M_n$ are clouds in $C \cup V$, we denote with $\theta(Z)$ the system $\{\theta(M_1), ..., \theta(M_n)\}$.

Proposition 2.10 [85] Let Z be a compact system of clouds such that $U(Z) \neq 0$. Then *Assoc_sub(Z)* is an e-unifier of Z and:

$$U(Z) = \xi(Ground (Z)).$$

Given a system S of e-equation, we get:

Cond(S) = Ground(Compact(Trans_t(S))) $\cup$ Compact(Trans_p(S)).

We state that *Cond(S)* is the system of conditions for the unification of *S*. If every cloud in *Cond(S)* is a singleton then *S* admits a classical unifier. Otherwise, the degree of crispness of *Cond(S)* gives the degree of unification of *S*. In other words, $\xi(Con(S))$ is the "cost" we have to pay to allow the unification process.

Theorem 2.9 [85] Let S be a system of e-equations, then:

$$U(S) = \xi(Cond\ (S)).$$

If $U(S) \neq o$ then:

$$\Theta_s = Assoc\text{-}sun(Compact(Trans\_T(S)))$$

is an e-unifier of S.

Proof: It is an immediate consequence of Theorem 7.1 and Proposition 2.1.

Thus, we get an effective procedure to compute the unification degree of a system of e-equations *S*, and, at the same time, an e-unifier of *S*.

Corollary 2.1 Let S be a system of e-equations, then θ is an e-unifier of S if and only if either

-θ is an unifier of *Compact(Trans_t(S))*

Or

$$-\xi(\theta(Compact(Trans\_t(S)))) \geq \xi(Compact(Trans\_p(S))).$$

We can further characterize the class of e-unifiers of a system of e-equations by the following proposition.

Proposition 2.11 [85] Let S be a system of e-equations such that $U(S) \neq 0$. An e-substitution θ is an e-unifier of S if and only if:

$$\xi(\theta(Compact(Trans\_t(S)))) \geq U(S).$$

Proof:
$\Rightarrow$Since, θ is an e-unifier, $v(S,\ \theta) = U(S)$. Then, by theorem 7.1, $U(S) = v(Compact(Trans\_t(S)),\ \theta) \wedge \xi(Compact(Trans\_p(S)))$.

As a consequence, $v(\theta(Compact(Trans\_t(S)))\ ) \geq U(S)$.

$\Leftarrow$Since, $\xi(\theta(Compact(Trans\_t(S)))) \geq U(S)$, by Theorem 7.1, $v(S,\ \theta) \geq U(S)$. The thesis follows immediately.

Example 2.19 [85] Consider the system of e-equations:

$$S=\{P(c,\ w,\ c\} =q(x,\ x,\ y),\ p(x,\ z,\ x) = r(d,\{a,\ e\},\ b)\}.$$

Then,

$$Trans\_p(S) = \{\{p,\ q\},\ \{p,\ r\}\},$$

$$Trans\_t(S) = \{\{x,\ c\},\ \{w,\ x\}\},\ \{\{c,\ y\},\ \{x,\ d\},\ \{z,\ a,\ e\},\ \{x,\ b\}$$

and therefore,

Compact $(Trans\_p(S)) = \{\{p, q, r\}\}$, Compact $(Trans\_t(S)) = \{\{x, y, w, c, b, d\}, \{z, a, e\}\}$,

This entails that,

$$Cond(S) = \{\{p, q, r\}, \{c, b, d\}, \{a, e\}\}$$

And therefore,

$$U(S) = \mu(\{p, q, r\}), \wedge\mu (\{c, b, d\}) \wedge\mu(\{a, e\}).$$

Finally, if $U(S) \neq 0$, the e-substitution:

$$\Theta_S = \{x/c, b, d\}, y/\{c, b, d\}, w/\{c, b, d\}, z/\{a, e\}\}$$

is an e-unifier of S.

2.11.5 THE MOST GENERAL UNIFIER

To prove that the unifier θ_S as stated above is the best one (in a sense, it represents the whole class of unifiers for S) we have to extend the classical concept of most general unifier (mgu). Recall that, given two substitutions θ and θ', we say that θ' is more general than θ, and write $\theta' \leqslant \theta$, if there exists a substitution m such that, for any variable x, $\theta(x) - m(\theta'(x))$. In order to extend such a notion, we replace the identity with the relation $\equiv_\lambda$. As usual, if m and θ are two e-substitutions, we define θ_m as the e-substitution which sets $\theta_m(x) = \theta(x)$, if $\theta(x)$ is a ground e-term, and $\theta_m(x) = m(\theta(x))$ otherwise

Definition 2.14 Let $\lambda \in (0,1]$, θ is a λ-substitutions if and only if $\theta(x)$ is a λ-point for any variable x.

Obviously, if both m and θ are λ-substitutions then θ m is a λ-substitution, too. Also, we extend $\cong_\lambda$ to λ-substitution sin a point wise manner by setting $\theta \cong_\lambda \theta$', whenever $\theta(x) \cong_\lambda \theta'(x)$ for any $x \in V$.

Definition 2.15 Let $\lambda \in (0, 1]$ and let θ and θ' be two λ-substitution. Then we get $\theta \leqslant_\lambda \theta$' if a λ-substitution τ exists such that, $\theta' \cong_\lambda \theta_\tau$. Hence, θ is more general than θ'(w r t the level λ).

Proposition 2.12 For any $\lambda \in (0, 1]$ the relation $\leqslant_\lambda$ is a pre-order over the set of λ-substitutions.

Proof: Since $\equiv_\lambda$ is reflexive, it is immediate that $\leqslant_\lambda$ is reflexive. Let θ, θ' and θ" be λ-substitutions such that $\theta \leqslant_\lambda \theta'$ and $\theta' \leqslant_\lambda \theta$". By definition, there exist two λ-substitutions τ and τ' such that, for any variable x in V, $\theta'(x) \equiv_\lambda \tau(\theta(x))$ and $\theta''(x) \tau'(\theta'(x))$. We claim that $\theta''(x) \equiv_\lambda \tau'(\tau(\theta(x)))$ and therefore that $\theta \leqslant_\lambda \theta$". Indeed, if $\theta'(x)$ is ground then:

$$\theta''(x) \equiv_\lambda \tau'(\theta'(x)) = \theta'(x)\theta'(x) \equiv_\lambda \tau(\theta(x)).$$

If $\theta'(x) \in V$ then, since, $\lambda \neq 0$, $\tau(\theta(x))$ is a variable, too, and $\theta'(x) = \tau(\theta(x))$. By substituting in $\theta''(x) \equiv_\lambda \tau'(\theta'(x))$ we obtain $\theta''(x) \equiv_\lambda \tau'(\tau(\theta(x)))$.

The following is a characterization of $\leqslant_\lambda$ that does not use e-substitutions.

Proposition 2.13 [85] Let θ and θ' be two λ-*substitutions. Then* $\theta \leqslant_\lambda \theta'$ *if and only if the following conditions hold:*

i. $\theta(x)$ ground $\Rightarrow \theta'(x) \cong_\lambda \theta(x)$

ii. $\theta(x)$ variable $\Rightarrow [\theta(x) = \theta(y) \Rightarrow \theta'(x) \cong_\lambda \theta'(y)]$.

Proof: Suppose that, $\theta \leqslant_\lambda \theta'$ and therefore that an e-substitution τ exists such that $\theta'(x) \cong_\lambda \tau(\theta(x))$. Then if $\theta(x)$ is ground, $\theta'(x) \cong_\lambda \tau(\theta(x)) = \theta(x)$. Assume that $\theta(x) \in V$ and that $\theta(x) = \theta(y)$. Then:

$$\theta'(x) \cong_\lambda \tau(\theta(x)) = \tau(\theta(x)) \cong_\lambda \theta'(y).$$

Conversely, suppose that conditions i) and ii) hold. Then, the substitution τ, defined as follows:

$$\tau(z) = \begin{cases} \theta'(y) \; if \; y \; is \; the \; first \; variable \; such \; that \quad z = \theta(y) \\ z \; \; if \; no \; variabl \; \; y \; \; exists \; such \; that \quad z = \theta(y) \end{cases}$$

is well defined. Moreover, for any x in V, $\theta'(x) \cong_\lambda \tau(\theta(x))$. In fact, if $\theta(x)$ is a variable, then there exists the first variable y such that $\theta(x) = \theta(y)$. By construction, $\tau(\theta(x)) = \theta'(y)$ and by property ii) $\tau(\theta(x)) \cong_\lambda \theta'(x)$. if $\theta(x)$ is ground, it is immediate that $\tau(\theta(x)) = \theta(x)$ and, by property i), $\tau(\theta(x)) \cong_\lambda \theta'(x)$.

Give a system of e-equations S, we consider the relation $\leqslant U(S)$.

Definition 2.16[85] Let S be a system of e-equations with $U(S) \neq 0$ and θ an e-substitution. Then θ is an extended most general unifier (e-mgu) for S if:

- θ is an e-unifier of S
- for any e-unifier γ for S, $\theta \leqslant_{U(S)} \gamma$.

It is easy to see that the e-unifier in the Example 5.1 is an e-mgu.

We can conclude this section by showing that the unifier furnished in the previous section is the best one.

Theorem 2.10 Let S be a system of e-equations such that $U(S) \neq 0$ and:

$$\Theta_S = Assoc\_sub(Compact(Trans\_t(S))).$$

ThenΘ_S is a most general e-unifier of S.

Based on the above definition and results we state as follows:

Theorem 2.11 Let S be a system of e-equations and θ an e-mgu S. Then θ' is an e-unifier of S if and only if, $\theta \leqslant_{U(S)} \theta'$.

We conclude by observing that the unifier θ_S furnished by the proposed algorithm is still unsatisfactory.

Example 2.20 Consider the previous Example and assume that:

$$eq(a, e) = eq(c, b) = eq(d, c) = 0.6, \; eq(f, d) = 0.9, \; eq(p, q) = eq(q, r) = 1.$$

Then,

$$U(S) = v(S, \theta_s) = \xi(\{\{c, b, d\}, \{a, e\}\}) = 0.6$$

Since,

$$eq(f, d) = 0.9 \geq 0.6,$$

we have also that,

$$\mu(\{f, b, c, d\}) = \mu(\{c, b, d\}).$$

This means that the e-unifier,

$$\theta' = \{x/\{f, c, b, d\}, y/\{f, c, b, d\}, z/\{a, c\}, w/\{f, c, b, d\}\}$$

solves the unification problem at the same "cost" of θ. Moreover, θ' is more significative than θ from the point of view of the information conveyed. Indeed, if we admit the threshold of validity 0.6, then no reason exists in distinguishing from the elements in *{c, b, d}*. Hence, we present a manner of expanding the clouds in an unifier without altering the cost played for the unification.

2.11.6 EXTENDED RESOLUTION AS A SET OF CONSTRAINTS

We start from a definition of extended resolution, which is a straightforward extension of the classical resolution for definite programs. A definite (logic) e-program P is defined according to its classical counterpart that is it is a finite set of e-clauses, namely e-formulas of the kind $A \leftarrow B_p, ..., B_n$, where C and $B_{i, I = 1, ..., n}$ are atomic e-formulas. *A negative e-clause* is an e-formula of the king $\neg A_1 V ... V \neg A_k$, where A_i are atomic e-formulas.

We introduce the concept of "e-resolvent". As usual, a variant of an e-clause C in a definite e-program P will be a renaming of the free variables occurring in C.

Definition 2.17[85]Let P be a definite e-program, let $N = \neg A_1 V ... V \neg A_k$ be a negative e-clause and let $C = A \leftarrow B_1, ..., B_n$ be a variant of an e-clause in P. The negative e-clause:

$$N' = \leftarrow \theta(A_1 ..., A_{i-1}, B_1, ..., B_n, A_{i+1}, ..., A_m)$$

Is called an e-resolvent of N and C with e-mgu θ, and set of constraint Cond provided that e-formula Ai unifies with the atomic e-formula in the head of C according to the similarity-based unification algorithm described in section 2.11, yielding an e-mhu θ and set of constraints, Cond = Ground(Compact(Trand_t(S))∪ Compact(Trans_p(S), where S = { A = Head (c)}.

We are now ready to give the following definition of extended SLD derivation.

Definition 2.18 [85] Let P a definite e-program and let N be a negative e-clause. An extended SLD-derivation if $PU\{N\}$, briefly e-SLD derivation is a maximal sequence of negative e-clauses N_i, a sequence of variants of an e-clause C_i, a sequence of e-substitutions θ_i, a sequence of systems of e-equations S_i and a sequence of systems of clouds C_i such that, for any i:

$$-N_0 = N$$

$-N_{i+1}$ is an e-resolvent of N_i and C_i with θ_i as e-mgu and C_i is a set of constraints.
- $S_i = \{A_i = B_i\}$, where A_i is an atomic e-formula in N_i and B_i is the atomic e-formula in the head of the clause C_i.
- C_i – Ground (Compact(Trans _ t(S$_i$)) U Compact(Trans_p(S$_i$))
- Θ_i is an e-mhu of the system of e-equations D_i, in particular, $\theta i = \theta_{Si}$
- C_i has no variable in common with $N_0, C_0, ..., C_{i-1}$.

If, for some integer $\bar{n}$, $N_{\bar{n}}$ is empty, then the e-SLD derivation halts and it is

called e-SLDrefutation. In this case the set $\bigcup_{i=1,...,\bar{n}} C_i$ is called the constraint set of the

e-SLD refutation. Still, the restriction of e-substitution $\theta_{\bar{n}} \circ \theta_{\bar{n}-1} \circ ...\theta_1$ to the variable in N will be called e-computed answer substitution for $\{N\} \, U \, P$.

If an e-SLD derivation is finite and it is not an e-refutation, it is called a failed derivation. The e-clauses C_i are called input e-clauses.

Given an e-refutation $\gamma_{P,N}$ of $P \, U \, \{N\}$, halting after $\bar{n}+1$ steps, we call degree of

the e-refutation $\{N\} \, U \, P$, and we denote it $h(\gamma_{P,N})$, the number $\xi(Compact(\bigcup_{i=0,...,\bar{n}} C_i))$.
In the following we give an example of e-SLD refutation.

Example 2.21 Let P be the following program:

$$p(x, y) \leftarrow q(x), r(y).$$
$$r(x) \leftarrow s(x, y), s(y, z).$$
$$q'(a).$$
$$s'(a, c)$$
$$s''(e, f).$$

Let $N_0 = p(x, y)$
We have the following e-SLD derivation of $P \, U \, \{N\}$:

$$N_0 = p(x, y),$$
$$C_0 = p(x_1, y_1) \leftarrow q(x_1), r(y_1)$$
$$\Theta_0 = \{x \rightarrow x_1, y \rightarrow y_1\}$$
$$S_0 = \{p(x, y) = p(x_1, y_1)\}$$
$$C_0 = \{\{p\}\}$$
$$N_1 = p(x_1), r(y_1)$$

$$C_1 = q'(a).$$
$$\Theta_1 = \{x \to a\}$$
$$S_1 = \{q'(x_1) = q(a)\}$$
$$C_1 = \theta$$
$$N_2 = r(y_1)$$
$$C_2 = r(x_2) \leftarrow s(x_2, y_2), s(y_2, z_2)$$
$$S_2 = \{r(y_1) = r(x_2)\}$$
$$\theta_2 = \{y_1 \to x_2\}$$
$$C_2 = \theta$$
$$N_3 = s(x_2, y_2), s(y_2, z_2)$$
$$C_3 = s'(a, c).$$
$$\Theta_3 = \{x_2 \to a, y_2 \to c\}$$
$$S_3 = \{s(x_2, y_2) = s'(a, c)\}$$
$$C_3 = \{\{a\}, \{c\}, \{s, s'\}\}$$
$$N_4 = s(c_2, z_2)$$
$$C_4 = s''(e, f)\theta_4 = \{z_2 \to f\}$$
$$S_4 = \{s(c_2, z_2) - s''(e, f)\}$$
$$\Theta_4 = \{\{e, c\}, \{s, s''\}\}$$
$$R_4 = s(c, z_2)$$

$$C_4 = s''(e, f)$$

In this case, the e-SLD resolution chain is an e-refutation and the e-computed answer substitution of the e-refutation is $\theta = \{x \to a, y \to a\}$. The degree of the e-refutation is:

$$\xi\left(Compact\left(\bigcup_{i=0,\dots,4} C_i\right)\right) = \xi\left(\{\{e, c\}, \{s, s', s''\}, \{q, p'\}, \{j\}, \{c\}, \{a\}\}\right)$$

This is the turn to pay to flatten into a set of singletons the set of constraints and make a classical refutation out of an e-refutation.

A negative e-clause N may have several e-refutation with respect to a given definite e-program P.

Definition 2.19 Let $\mathcal{R}(P, N)$ be the set of e-refutation of $\{N\} \sqcup \{P\}$. We say that a negative e-clause N is derivable from P with degree λ if:

$$\lambda = \bigvee_{r \in R(p, N)} h(r)$$

2.11.7 INTRODUCING SIMILARITY IN A DEDUCTIVE DATA BASE

Deductive data base can be viewed as information retrieval systems, where knowledge is stored both explicitly, through a record-based data structure, both implicitly, through a set of rules that specify data in an intentional manner. Data are extracted through a "query evaluation" method. The introduction of a similarity in a database gives certain flexibility, both in terms of data and query.

The extended resolution described in the previous section is a flexible evaluation method or answering queries that cannot be satisfied in the classical case,

Example 2.20 Consider the following classical database of books of different kinds with some associated rules:

Adventurous (Isle _ of _ treasure).

Adventurous (murder _ on _ orient _ express).

Adventurous (james _ bond).

horror (drakula).

good (X): -interesting (X), cheap (X).

cheap (X): -cost $(X, L)L = < 10$.

The goal good (X) has no classical solution, since, no fact in the database unifies with the atom interesting (X). Nevertheless, it seems reasonable to consider the constants interesting and adventurous as "similar" to a certain degree.

More precisely, consider the following similarity relation $\mathcal{R}$, evaluated using any continuous t-norm for the following conjunctions:

-R (adventurous, interesting) = 0.9

-R (adventurous, horror) = 0.7

-R (horror, interesting) = 0.9

-R $(a, b) = 0$ for any $a, b \in$ {murder _ on _ orient _ express,

Isle _ of _ treasure, james _ bond, drakula}

The query good (X) can be evaluated with an e-SLD derivation, giving as a result the following pairs of computed e-substitution answers and constraint sets: $< \{X \rightarrow$ James _ Bond\}, {adventurous, interesting} $>$,

$< \{X \rightarrow$ isle _of_treasure\},

{adventurous, interesting} $>$,

$< \{X \rightarrow$ murder _ on _ orient _ express\},

{adventurous, interesting} $>$,

$< \{X \rightarrow$ drakula\}, {horror, interesting} $>$.

This means that the query good (X) yields, for example, the answer isle _ of _ treasure under the condition that the genre horror is similar to interesting, in other words, the co-diameter ξ ({horror, interesting}) of the cloud{horror, interesting} represents the cost one must pay to have a classical refutation of good (X) with $X - >$ isle _ of _ treasure as computed answer substitution.

KEYWORDS

- **Deductive data base**
- **Fuzzy reasoning**
- **Generalized modus ponens**
- **Measures**
- **Rule reduction technique**

CHAPTER 3

FUZZY CONTROL

3.1 INTRODUCTION

The birth of control theory goes back to the period of World War II when the analysis and design of servo mechanisms play a key role in the development of feedback control. The evolution of control theory starts from simple frequency domain approach to linear control systems to mathematically enriched theory of linear/nonlinear systems based on the theory of differential equations for dynamical systems. Essentially, the advent of the space age in 1957 changes the basic spirit of control theory. The competition in space and the challenges posed by the complexity of control problems related to the guidance of space vehicles, attract a number of prominent mathematics, most notably L.S. Pontryagin in the USSR and R.E. Bellman in the United States towards control theory. As a result, the level of mathematical sophistication of the theory begins to grow very rapidly, swinging the pendulum all the way from the low-brow approaches of the forties and fifties to the high-brow mathematical formalism of the seventies, eighties, and nineties and till to date.Conventional controllers based on existing control theory techniques are designed either from the frequency domain model, that is the transfer function model, or from the time domain model, that is the state space model of the open loop system (process). The objective of the feedback controller is to guarantee a desired response of the output y.The process of keeping the output y close to the setpoint (reference input) y*, despite the presence of disturbances of the system parameters and noisy measurements, is called regulation. The output of the controller (which is the input of the system) is the control action u.

The general form of the discrete-time control law is:

$$u(k) = f(e(k), e(k - 1), ..., e(k - \tau), u(k - 1), ..., u(k - \tau)) \qquad (3.1)$$

providing a control action that describes the relationship between the input and the output of the controller, where:

- The e represents the error between the desired setpoint y* and the output of the system y,
- Parameter τ defines the order of the controller, and
- The f is in general a nonlinear function.

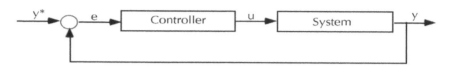

FIGURE 1   Represents a basic feedback control system.

The achievements of model based (Transfer function model/ State space model) control theory are already established through several applications in real life problems on earth. The successful launching of manned and/or unmanned vehicles from the surface of the earth to the surface of the moon and/or mars represents the amazing achievements of control theory. Still, there are situations which are imprecise, unknown, and highly chaotic and which cannot be properly handled by a model based analysis, synthesis and design technique. Under such circumstances some attempts have been made to cope up with above said problems by qualitativeapproaches. Fuzzy control is one among them.

The seminal work by L.A. Zadeh (1973) on fuzzy algorithms introduced the idea of formulating the control laws using fuzzy if then rules and compositional rules of inferences as stated in chapter 3of volume 1 of this book and chapter 1 of volume 2.

In contrast to conventional control, fuzzy control is initially introduced as a model-freedesign method to construct a controller of a system (process) based on a representation of the knowledge and the reasoning process of a human operator who is, by virtue of experience, already well aware and exposed to the qualitative dynamic behavior of the system (process). Fuzzy logic can capture the continuous nature of human decision processes and as such is a definite improvement over methods based on binary logic (which are widely used in industrial controllers). Hence, it is not surprising that practical applications of fuzzy control start to appear very quickly after the method has been introduced in publications. A drawback of knowledge-based, model-free fuzzy control is that it does not allow for any kind of stability or robustness analysis, unless a model of the process is available. However, if that is the case, we can of course use the model for design, as in standard control. The possibility to analyze stability, performance, and robustness give rise to the recent interest in model-based fuzzy control design and in identification for obtaining fuzzy models from process data. It has been recognized that fuzzy systems are universal function approximators and hence can be used to model a wide class of processes.

At the present situation fuzzy control is characterized by a certain mismatch between the main motivation of readability (using understandable rules, computing with words) and the use of mathematically involved and rather non-transparent techniques to ensure robust performance in direct analogy with mainstream (nonlinear) control.

From a research point of view, in the low-level control loop the knowledge-based approach seems to have been superseded by the model-based one. The knowledge-based approach mainly remains an option in higher control levels (supervision, diagnosis).

Although, fuzzy control is initially introduced as a model-free controller design method based on the knowledge of human operator, current research is almost exclusively devoted to model-based fuzzy control methods that can guarantee stability and robustness of the closed-loop system. State-of-the-art technique for identifying fuzzy models and designing model-based controllers are considered in this chapter. Attention is also paid to the role of fuzzy system in higher levels of the control hierarchy, such as expert control, supervision, and diagnostic systems. Open issues are highlighted and an attempt is made to give some directions for future research.

3.2 FUZZY CONTROLLER

Using a fuzzy controller, the dynamic behavior of a system is controlled by a set of linguistic rules based on expert knowledge. The expert knowledge is usually of the form.

IF (a set of conditions are satisfied) THEN (a set of consequences can be inferred).

Since the antecedents and the consequents of these IF-THEN rules are associated with fuzzy concepts (linguistic terms), they are often called fuzzy conditional statements (see chapter 4 of volume 1 of this book).

In our terminology, a model-free fuzzy controller is a collection of fuzzy conditional statements. In each fuzzy conditional statement the antecedent is a condition in its application domain and the consequent is a control action for the system under control.

Basically, fuzzy control rules provide a convenient way for expressing control policy and domain knowledge.Furthermore, several linguistic variables might be involved in the antecedents and the consequents of theserules.When this is the case, the system is referred to as a multi-input-multi-output (MIMO) fuzzy system. For example, in the case of two-input-single-output (MISO) fuzzy systems, fuzzy control rules are as follows:

R_1: if x isA_1 and y isB_1 then z is C_1
also
R_2: if x isA_2 and y is B_2 then z is C_2
also

...

also
R_n:if x is A_n and y is B_n then z isC_n
where x and y are the process state variables, z is the control variable,$A_i, B_i,$ andC_i are linguistic values of the linguistic variables x,y, and z in the universes of discourse U, V, and W, respectively, "and"is an implicit sentence connectiveand"also"links the rules intoa set of rules or equivalently a rule-base.

We can represent the fuzzy control in a form similar to the conventional control law:

$$u(k) = F(e(k), e(k - 1), ..., e(k-\tau), u(k - 1), ..., u(k - \tau)) \qquad (3.2)$$

where the function F is described by a fuzzy rule-base. However, it does not mean that the model-free fuzzy control depends on any kind of transfer function or state space equation of the system.

The knowledge-based nature of fuzzy control dictates a limited usage of the past values of the error e and control u because it is rather unreasonable to expect meaningful linguistic statements for $e(k-3)$, $e(k-4)$, ..., $e(k-\tau)$.

A typical fuzzy control describes the relationship between the changes of the control:

$$\Delta u(k) = u(k) - u(k-1)$$

on the one hand, the error $e(k)$ and its change are:

$$\Delta e(k) = e(k) - e(k-1).$$

on the other hand, such control law can be formalized as:

$$\Delta u(k) = F(e(k), \Delta(e(k))) \qquad\qquad (3.3)$$

and is a manifestation of the general fuzzy control expression with: $\tau = 1$

The actual output of the controller $u(k)$ is obtained from the previous value of control $u(k-1)$ that is updated by $\Delta u(k)$, that is:

$$u(k) = u(k-1) + \Delta u(k)$$

This type of controller is suggested originally by Mamdani and Assilian in 1975 and is called the Mamdani-type fuzzy control. This is basically a model free approach to design fuzzy control.

A prototypical rule-base of a simple fuzzy control realizing the control law above is listed in the following:

R_1: If e is "positive" and Δe is "nearzero" then Δu is "positive"
R_2: If e is "negative" and Δe is "near zero" then Δu is "negative"
R_3: Ifeis "near zero" and Δe is "near zero" then Δu is "near zero"
R_4: Ifeis "near zero" and Δe is "positive" then Δu is "positive"
R_5: If e is "near zero" and Δe is "negative" then Δu is "negative".

So, our task is to find a crisp control action from the fuzzy rule-base and from the actual crisp inputs $\overline{x_0}$ and $\overline{y_0}$:

R_1: if x is A_1 and y is B_1 then z is C_1.
also
R_2: if x is A_2 and y isB_2 then z is C_2.
also
...
also

R_n:if x isA$_n$and y isB$_n$then z is C$_n$

Input x is $\overline{x}_0$ and y is $\overline{y}_0$

Output: $\overline{z}_0$

Of course, the inputs of fuzzy rule-based systems should be given by fuzzy sets, and therefore, we have to fuzzify the crisp inputs. Furthermore, the output of a fuzzy system is always a fuzzy set, and therefore to get crisp value we have to defuzzify it.

Fuzzy control systems usually consist of four major parts:

- Fuzzification interface,
- Fuzzy rule-base,
- Fuzzy inference machine and
- defuzzificationinterface.

A fuzzification operator has the effect of transforming crisp data into fuzzy sets. There are generally three types of fuzzifiers, viz.:

- Singleton fuzzifier,
- Gaussian fuzzifier, and
- Trapezoidal or triangular fuzzifier.

In most of the cases, we use fuzzy singleton as fuzzifier, that is:

Fuzzifier $(x_0):= \overline{x}_0$

where $\overline{x}_0$ is a crisp input value from a process.

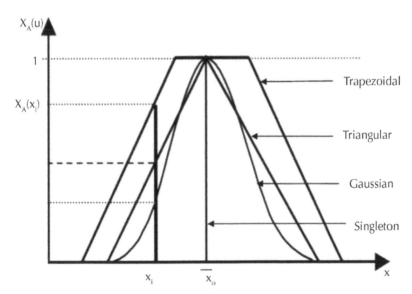

FIGURE 2   Shows different fuzzification processes.

i.   x is a fuzzy singleton, such that:

$$\mu_x\left(\overline{x_0}\right)=\begin{cases}1 & \text{if } x=\overline{x_0} \\ 0 & \text{otherwise.}\end{cases} \tag{3.4}$$

ii. x is a fuzzy set, such that:

$$\mu_x\left(\overline{x_0}\right)=\begin{cases}1 & \text{if } x=\overline{x_0} \\ \text{decreases from 1 as } x \text{ moves from } x_i\end{cases} \tag{3.5}$$

Singleton fuzzification is generally used in implementation where there is no noise. Figure3 shows a schematic representation of a fuzzy feedback controller.

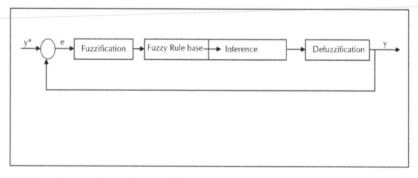

FIGURE 3   Fuzzy feedback controller.

Suppose that we have two input variables x and y. A fuzzy control rule:

$$R_1: \text{if } (x \text{ is} A_i \text{ a and } y \text{ is } B_i) \text{then } (z \text{ is} C_i)$$

is implemented by a fuzzy implication$R_i$and is defind as:

$$R_i(u,\ v,\ w)\ =\ \left[A_i(u)\text{ and } B_i(v)\right] \rightarrow C_i(w)$$

where the logical connective "and"is implemented by the minimum operator, that is:

$$\left[A_i(u)\text{ and } B_i(v)\right] \rightarrow C_i(w) = \left[A_i(u) \times B_i(v)\right] \rightarrow C_i(w) = \min\left\{A_i(u), B_i(v)\right\} \rightarrow C_i(w)$$

Of course, we can use any t-norm to model the logical connective "and".Fuzzy control rules are combined by using the sentence connective "also".

Since each fuzzy control rule is represented by a fuzzy relation, the overall behavior of a fuzzy system is characterized by these fuzzy relations. In other words, a fuzzy system can be characterized by a single fuzzy relation obtained from a set of rules which are combined by the sentence connective "also".

Symbolically, if we have a collection of rules:

R_1 : if x is A_1 and y is B_1 then z is C_1

also

R_2 : if x is A_2 and y is B_2 then z is C_2

also

...

also

R_n : if x is A_n and y is B_n then z is C_n

Then, the procedure for obtaining the fuzzy output from such a knowledge base consists of the following three steps:
- Find the firing level of each of the rules.
- Find the output of each of the rules.
- Aggregate the individual rule outputs to obtain the overall system output.

To infer the output z from the given process states x, y, and fuzzy relations R_i, we usually apply the compositional rule of inference:

R_1: if x is A_1 and y is B_1 then z is C_1
R_2: if x is A_2 and y is B_2 then z is C_2
....
R_n: if x is A_n and y is B_n then z is C_n

Fact: x is $\overline{x}_0$ and y is $\overline{y}_0$

Consequence: z is C

where the consequence is computed by:

Consequence $=$ Agg (fact oR_1, ..., fact oR_n).

That is:

$$C = \text{Agg}\left(\overline{x}_0 \times \overline{y}_0 \ oR_1, ..., \overline{x}_0 \times \overline{y}_0 \ oR_n\right)$$

Taking into consideration that:

$$\overline{x}_0(u) = 0, \ u \neq x_0$$

and

$$\bar{y}_0(v) = 0, \ v \neq y_0,$$

The computation of the consequence C is:

$$C(w) = \text{Agg}\{A_1(x_0) \times B_1(y_0) \to C_1(w), ..., (x_0), B_n(y_0) \to C_n(w)\}, \forall w \in W.$$

The procedure for obtaining the fuzzy output of such a knowledge base can be formulated as (See Section 1.3, 1.4, and 1.6 of Chapter1).
- The firing level of the ith rule is determined by:

$$A_i(x_0) \times B_i(y_0)$$

- The output of of the i-th rule is calculated by

$$C_i'(w) := A_i(x_0) \times B_i(y_0) \to C_i(w) \ \forall \ w \in W$$

- The overall system output, C, is obtained from the individual rule outputs C_i' by

$$C(w) = \text{Agg}\{C_i', ... C_n'\} \forall \ w \in W$$

In Section 3.4.1 of this chapter, we describe this type of fuzzy controller based on fuzzy IF-THEN rules of Type I.

Example 3.1 If the sentence connective also is interpreted as "oring"the rules then by using minimum-norm the membership function of the consequence is computed as:

$$C = \left(\bar{x}_0 \times \bar{y}_0 \circ R_1\right) \cup ... \cup \left(\bar{x}_0 \times \bar{y}_0 \circ R_n\right).$$

That is:

$$C(w) = A_1(\bar{x}_0) \times B_1(\bar{y}_0) \to (C_1)(w) \vee ... \vee A_n(x_0) \times B_n(y_0) \to (C_n)(w), \forall w \in W.$$

3.2.1   DEFUZZIFICATION METHODS

The output of the inference process is a fuzzy set, specifying a possibility distribution of control action. For implementation of control action a nonfuzzy (crisp) control action is usually required.Hence, we have to defuzzify the fuzzy control action (out-put) inferred from the fuzzy control algorithm, namely:

$$\overline{z_0} = \text{defuzzifier (C)}$$

where $\overline{z_0}$ is the nonfuzzy control output and defuzzifier is the defuzzification operator.

Definition 3.1Defuzzification is a process to select a representative element from the fuzzy output C inferred from the fuzzy control algorithm.

The most often used defuzzification operators are given below:

Max-membership Method: The max-membership method is both simple and quick method. It is also known as the height method. This method takes the peak value of each fuzzy set and builds the weighted sum of these peak values.

This method is given by the algebraic expression as:

$$\mu_c(x^*) \geq \mu_c(x) \text{ for all } x \in X \tag{3.6}$$

This is shown in Figure 4(a).

Centre of Gravity Method: It is also known ascenter of area and centroid method. This is the most used and prevalent and physically appealing of all the defuzzification methods. The center of area method divides the first moment of area under membership function into half, and the x value marking the dividing line is the defuzzified value of X.

In the continuous case, it is given by the expression as:

$$x^* = \frac{\int \mu_c(x), x \, dx}{\int \mu_c(x) \, dx} \tag{3.7}$$

or for a discrete universe with m quantization levels in the output

$$x^* = \frac{\sum_{j=1}^{m} \mu_c(x_i), x_i}{\sum_{j=1}^{m} \mu_c(x_i)} \tag{3.8}$$

This method determines the center of the area below the combined membership function.

Figure 4(b) shows this operation in a graphical way:

Weighted Average Method: This method is only valid for symmetrical output membership functions.

It is given by the algebraic expression as:

$$x* = \frac{\sum \mu_c(x), x}{\sum \mu_c(x)} \qquad (3.9)$$

where $\sum$ denotes an algebraic sum. It is shown in Figure 4(c).

The two functions shown in Figure 4(c) would result in the following defuzzified value:

$$x* = \frac{\{a(1)+b(0.5)\}}{(1+0.5)}$$

Mean-max Membership: It is also called middle of maxima. If the mean or average of all local maxima in X is taken, a single defuzzified output is generated by this mean of maximum approach through

$$x* = \frac{\sum_{i=1}^{N}\mu_{max}(x_i)}{N} \qquad (3.10)$$

where $= \max(x)$ and N is the number of times the membership function reaches the maximum support value. It is shown in Figure 4 (d).

The defuzzified output is then:

$$x* = \frac{(a+b)}{2} \qquad (3.11)$$

Centre of Sums: This is faster than many defuzzification methods that are presently in use. This process involves the algebraic sum of individual output fuzzy sets say and, C_1 and C_2 instead of their union. One drawback of this method is that the intersecting areas are added twice.

The defuzzified value x* is given in discrete case by the following expression:

$$x* = \frac{\sum_{i=1}^{m} x_i \cdot \sum_{k=1}^{n} \mu_k(\mu_i)}{\sum_{i=1}^{m} \cdot \sum_{k=1}^{n} \mu_k(x_i)} \qquad (3.12)$$

Centre of sums method is shown in Figure 4(e).

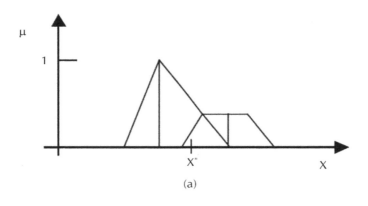

(a)

(a)

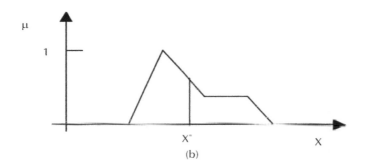

(b)

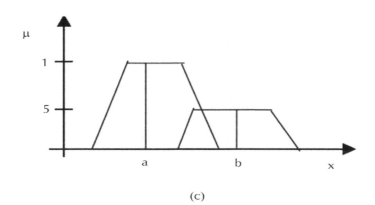

(c)

FIGURE 4   *(continued)*

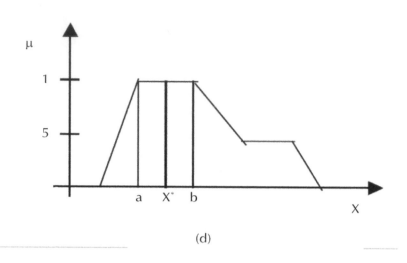

(d)

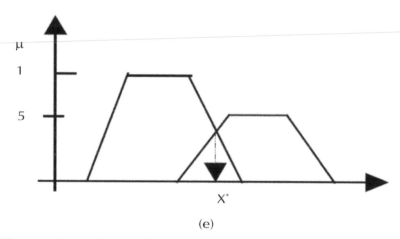

(e)

FIGURE 4   Methods of defuzzification.

Example 3.2 Consider a fuzzy controller steering a car in the way to avoid obstacles. If an obstacle occurs right ahead, the plausible control action depicted in Figure 5 could be interpreted as:

- "Turn right or left".
- Both Center-of-Area and Middle-of-Maxima defuzzification methods results in a control action "drive ahead straightforward" which causes an accident.
- A suitable defuzzification method would have to choose between different control actions (choose one of two triangles in the Figure) and then transform the fuzzy set into a crisp value.

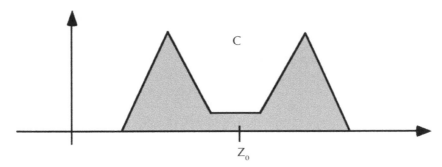

FIGURE 5 Undesired result by Center-of-Area and Middle-of-Maxima defuzzification methods.

3.2.2 EFFECTIVITY OF FUZZY CONTROL SYSTEMS

Using the Stone–Weierstrass theorem Wang (1992) shows that fuzzy logic control systems of the form: if x is and y is then z is, i = 1,..., n

R_i :if x is A_i and y is B_i then z is, C_i, i $= 1,...,n$ with

- Gaussian membership function

$$A_i(u) = \exp\left[-\frac{1}{2}(\frac{u - \alpha_{i1}}{\beta_{i1}})^2\right],$$

$$B_i(v) = \exp\left[-\frac{1}{2}\left(\frac{v - \alpha_{i1}}{\beta_{i3}}\right)^2\right],$$

$$C_i(w) = \exp\left[-\frac{1}{2}\left(\frac{w - \alpha_{i3}}{\beta_{i3}}\right)^2\right],$$

- Singleton fuzzifier

  fuzzifier (x): $= \overline{x}$,fuzzifier (y): $= \overline{y}$,
- Product fuzzy conjunction

$$\left[A_i(u) \text{ and } B_i(v)\right] = A_i(u) B_i(v),$$

- Product fuzzy implication (Larsen implication)

$$\left[A_i(u) \text{ and } B_i(v)\right] \rightarrow C_i(w) = A_i(u) B_i(v) C_i(w),$$

- Centroid defuzzification method

$$z = \frac{\sum_{i=1}^{n} \alpha_{i3} \Lambda_i(x) B_i(y)}{\sum_{i=1}^{n} A_i(x) B_i(y)}$$

where α_{i3} is the center of, C_i, are universal approximators, that is they can approximate any continuous function on a compact set to arbitrary accuracy.

Wang proves the following theorem:

Theorem 3.1 For a given real-valued continuous function g on the compact set X and arbitrary $\in > 0$, there exists a fuzzy control system with output function f such that:

$$\sup_{x \in X} \left\| g(x) - f(x) \right\| \leq \in .$$

In 1995, Castro showsthatMamdani's fuzzy controllers

$$R_i : \text{if } x \text{ is } A_i \text{ and } y \text{ is } B_i \text{ then } z \text{ is } C_i, \ i = 1,\dots, n$$

with
- Symmetric triangular membership functions

$$A_i(u) = \begin{cases} 1 - |a_1 - u| \big/ \alpha_i & \text{if } |a_1 - u| \leq \alpha_i \\ 0 & \text{otherwise} \end{cases}$$

$$B_i(v) = \begin{cases} 1 - |b_i - v| \big/ \beta_i & \text{if } |b_i - u| \leq \beta_i \\ 0 & \text{otherwise} \end{cases}$$

$$C_i(u) = \begin{cases} 1 - |c_i - u| \big/ \gamma_i & \text{if } |c_i - u| \leq \gamma_i \\ 0 & \text{otherwise} \end{cases}$$

- Singleton fuzzifier

$$\text{fuzzifier}(x_0) : =, \overline{x} ,$$

- Minimum norm fuzzy conjunction

$$\left[A_i\left(\mathrm{u}\right) \text{ and } B_i\left(\mathrm{v}\right)\right] = \min\left\{A_i\left(\mathrm{u}\right) B_i\left(\mathrm{v}\right)\right\},$$

• Minimum norm fuzzy implication

$$\left[A_i\left(\mathrm{u}\right) \text{ and } B_i\left(\mathrm{v}\right)\right] \rightarrow C_i\left(w\right) = \min\left\{A_i\left(\mathrm{u}\right) B_i\left(\mathrm{v}\right) C_i\left(w\right)\right\},$$

• Maximum t-conorm rule aggregation

$$\mathrm{Agg}\left(R_1, R_2, ..., R_n\right) = \max\left(R_1, R_2, ..., R_n\right)$$

• Centroid defuzzification method

$$z = \frac{\sum_{i=1}^{n} c_i \min\{A_i\left(x\right),\ B_i\left(y\right)\}}{\sum_{i=1}^{n} \min\{A_i\left(x\right),\ B_i\left(y\right)\}}$$

where c_i is the center of C_i, are also universal approximators.

3.3 ILLUSTRATION ON BASIC APPROACHES TO FUZZY CONTROL

To illustrate the basic approaches to design fuzzy IF-THEN controller of Type I, we consider the following examples. Note that, design of such controller does not depend on state-space or transfer function model of the system (process). Such approach to design controller is called model free approach. It essentially depends on the experience, intuition, and domain specific knowledge of an expert.

*Example3.3*We consider a simple system which represents how the heating power of a gas burner depends on the oxygen supply(assuming a constant gas supply).We represent the oxygen (O_2) flow rate by x and the heating power (joule) by y. The set of primary fuzzy terms over x is A = {Low, Medium, and High}, and Y is B= {Low, High}.

The qualitative description of the system in terms of the system input and output is expressed by the following rules:

R_1: **If** 0_2 flow rate **is** Low **then** heating power **is** Low.
R_2: **If** 0_2 flow rate **is** Medium **then** heating power **is**High.
R_3: **If** 0_2 flow rate **is** High **then** heating power **is** Low.

The primary fuzzy terms of the set A and B are represented by the corresponding membership functions as depicted in Figure 6. The numerical values along the base variables are selected somewhat arbitrarily. The qualitative relationship expressed by the rules is assumed to be valid.

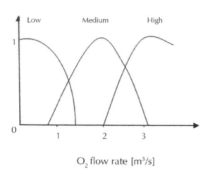
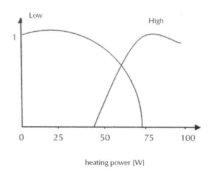

O₂ flow rate [m³/s]   heating power [W]

FIGURE 6   Membership functions.

The fuzzy rule based model of the above system can be used to compute the output value, given some input value. The algorithm is called the fuzzy inference algorithm (or mechanism). The fuzzy inference of the output value can be derived by compositional rules of inference as stated in Section 1.3 of Chapter 1. For simplicity of demonstration, we consider the Mamdani's interpretation of the implication operator, that is the mean operator as stated in Table 2 of chapter 1.

Ifwe use Min operator, A ∧ B, the interpretation of the if-then rules is "it is true that A and B are simultaneously hold". In this example, we restrict ourselves to the Mamdani's Min operator method.

The fuzzy relation R is computed by the minimum (∧) operator:

$$R_i = A_i \times B_i \text{ that is, } \mu_{R_i}(x, y) = \mu_{A_i}(X) \wedge \mu_{B_i}(y) \qquad (3.13)$$

Note that the minimum is computed on the Cartesian product space of X and Y, i.e. for all possible pairs of x and y. The fuzzy relation R representing the entire model is given by the disjunction (union) of the n individual rule's R_i:

$$R = \bigcup_{i=1}^{n} R_i \text{ that is, } \mu_R(x, y) = \max_{1 \leq i \leq 1}\left[\mu_{A_i}(x) \wedge \mu_{B_i}(y)\right] \qquad (3.14)$$

Now, entire rule base is encoded in the fuzzy relation R. Given an input ($\overline{x}$) that is the flow rate of O_2, the fuzzy output ($\overline{y}$) of the linguistic model can be computed by the max-min composition (o):

$$\overline{y} = \overline{x} \circ R \qquad (3.15)$$

Example 3.4 Let us compute the fuzzy relation for the linguistic model of Example 3.3. First, we discretize the input and output domains by small line segments as shown in the leftmost column of Table 1 and 2. The (discrete) membership functions are given in Table1 for the antecedent linguistic terms and in Table 2 for the consequent terms.

TABLE 1 Membership function for antecedent clauses over the discrete universe X

X	Low	Medium	high
$0 \le O_2 < .5$	1	0	0
$.5 \le O_2 < 1$	.8	.3	0
$1 \le O_2 < 1.5$	.6	.5	0
$1.5 \le O_2 < 2$	.4	1	.3
$2 \le O_2 < 2.5$	.2	.5	.5
$2.5 \le O_2 \le 3$	0	.3	1

TABLE 2 Membership function for consequent clauses over the discrete universe Y

Y	Low	High
$0 \le J < 10$	1	0
$10 \le J < 20$	.9	0
$20 \le J < 30$	.8	0
$30 \le J < 40$	.6	0
$40 \le J < 50$	.4	.1
$50 \le J < 60$	.2	.3
$60 \le J < 70$	0	.5
$70 \le J < 80$	0	.8
$80 \le J < 90$	0	.9
$90 \le J \le 100$	0	1

The fuzzy relations R_i corresponding to the individual rule can now be computed by using equation (3.13). For rule R_1, we have R_1 = Low × Low, for rule R_2, we obtain R_2 = Medium × High, and finally for rule R_3, R_3 = High × Low. The fuzzy relation R, which represents the entire rule base, is the union (element-wise maximum) of the relations R_i:

$$R = \begin{pmatrix} 1 \\ .8 \\ .6 \\ .4 \\ .2 \\ 0 \end{pmatrix} (1 \quad .9 \quad .8 \quad .6 \quad .4 \quad .2 \quad 0 \quad 0 \quad 0 \quad 0).$$

$$= \begin{pmatrix} 1 & .9 & .8 & .6 & .4 & .2 & 0 & 0 & 0 & 0 \\ .8 & .8 & .8 & .6 & .4 & .2 & 0 & 0 & 0 & 0 \\ .6 & .6 & .6 & .6 & .4 & .2 & 0 & 0 & 0 & 0 \\ .4 & .4 & .4 & .4 & .4 & .2 & 0 & 0 & 0 & 0 \\ .2 & .2 & .2 & .2 & .2 & .2 & 0 & 0 & 0 & 0 \\ 0 & 0 & 0 & 0 & 0 & 0 & 0 & 0 & 0 & 0 \end{pmatrix}$$

$$R_2 = \begin{pmatrix} 0 \\ .3 \\ .5 \\ 1 \\ .5 \\ .3 \end{pmatrix} (0 \quad 0 \quad 0 \quad 0 \quad .1 \quad .3 \quad .5 \quad .8 \quad .9 \quad 1)$$

$$= \begin{pmatrix} 0 & 0 & 0 & 0 & 0 & 0 & 0 & 0 & 0 & 0 \\ 0 & 0 & 0 & 0 & .1 & .3 & .3 & .3 & .3 & .3 \\ 0 & 0 & 0 & 0 & .1 & .3 & .5 & .5 & .5 & .5 \\ 0 & 0 & 0 & 0 & .1 & .3 & .5 & .8 & .9 & 1 \\ 0 & 0 & 0 & 0 & .1 & .3 & .5 & .5 & .5 & .5 \\ 0 & 0 & 0 & 0 & .1 & .3 & .3 & .3 & .3 & .3 \end{pmatrix}.$$

$$R_1 = \begin{pmatrix} 0 \\ 0 \\ 0 \\ .3 \\ .5 \\ 1 \end{pmatrix} (1 \quad .9 \quad .8 \quad .6 \quad .4 \quad .2 \quad 0 \quad 0 \quad 0 \quad 0)$$

$$
= \begin{pmatrix}
0 & 0 & 0 & 0 & 0 & 0 & 0 & 0 & 0 & 0 \\
0 & 0 & 0 & 0 & 0 & 0 & 0 & 0 & 0 & 0 \\
0 & 0 & 0 & 0 & 0 & 0 & 0 & 0 & 0 & 0 \\
.3 & .3 & .3 & .3 & .3 & .2 & 0 & 0 & 0 & 0 \\
.5 & .5 & .5 & .5 & .4 & .2 & 0 & 0 & 0 & 0 \\
1 & .9 & .8 & .6 & .4 & .2 & 0 & 0 & 0 & 0
\end{pmatrix}.
$$

Therefore:

$$
R = \begin{pmatrix}
1 & .9 & .8 & .6 & .4 & .2 & 0 & 0 & 0 & 0 \\
.8 & .8 & .8 & .6 & .4 & .3 & .3 & .3 & .3 & .3 \\
.6 & .6 & .6 & .6 & .4 & .3 & .5 & .5 & .5 & .5 \\
.4 & .4 & .4 & .4 & .4 & .3 & .5 & .8 & .9 & 1 \\
.5 & .5 & .5 & .5 & .4 & .3 & .5 & .5 & .5 & .5 \\
1 & .9 & .8 & .6 & .4 & .3 & .3 & .3 & .3 & .3
\end{pmatrix}.
$$

Given input:

$A' = \begin{pmatrix} 1 & 1 & .8 & .5 & .2 & 0 \end{pmatrix}$, which is linguistically very low in comparison with the distribution low of Table 1.

We get:

$B' = \begin{pmatrix} 1 & .9 & .8 & .6 & .4 & .3 & .5 & .5 & .5 & .5 \end{pmatrix}$, which is linguistically low in comparison with the distribution low of Table 2.

Similarly, given input:

$A' = \begin{pmatrix} 0 & 0 & .3 & .5 & .8 & 1 \end{pmatrix}$, which is linguistically very high.

We get:

$B' = \begin{pmatrix} 1 & .9 & .8 & .6 & .4 & .3 & .5 & .5 & .5 & .5 \end{pmatrix}$, which is linguistically low.

And given input:

$A' = \begin{pmatrix} 0 & 0 & .3 & 1 & .3 & 0 \end{pmatrix}$, which is linguistically medium.

We get:

$B' = \begin{pmatrix} .4 & .4 & .4 & .4 & .4 & .3 & .5 & .8 & .9 & 1 \end{pmatrix}$, which is linguistically high.

Thus, according to Equation (3.15), we get reasonable results by compositional rules of inference. Note that the processes of fuzzification and defuzzification have not been discussed here.

Example 3.5 Letus consider a fuzzy system with two inputs x_1 *and* x_2 (antecedents) and a single output y (consequent). Inputs x_1 *and* x_2 have three linguistic variables small, medium,and big with triangular membership function. Output y has two linguistic variables small and big with triangular memberships function.

The rule-base consists of the two following rules:

IF X_1 is *small* AND X_2 is *medium* THEN y is *big*
IF X_1 is *medium* AND X_2 is *big*THENy is *small* .

Inputs x_1 *and* x_2 are crisp values and the membership values of inputs x_1 *and* x_2 are calculated for triangular memberships functions.

The aggregated output for *r* rules is given by:

$$\mu(y) = \max{}^i \left[\min \left[\mu\left(x_1^i\right), \mu\left(x_2^i\right) \right] \right]$$

where

$$i = 1, 2, 3, \ldots, r.$$

In this example r equals to 2. The minimum membership value for the antecedents propagates through to the consequent and truncates the membership function for the consequent of each rule. The truncated membership functions for each rule are aggregated using the graphical equivalent of either for conjunctive or disjunctive rules.

The aggregation operation max results in an aggregated membership function comprised of the outer envelope of the individual truncated membership forms from each rule. Figure 7 illustrates the rule-base and aggregation process using max-min method of inference.

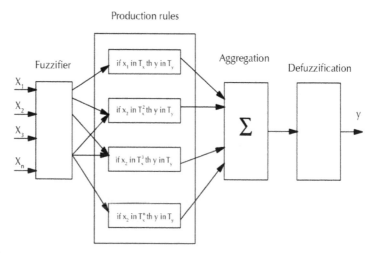

FIGURE 7   Representation of rule base and aggregation process for fuzzy inference.

3.3.1 FUZZY ASSOCIATIVE MEMORY

For a fuzzy controller, the collection of all of its fuzzy rules is called the fuzzy associative memory. For every control cycle, each of the fuzzy rules is evaluated. This can be done by massively parallel processing. The output of each fuzzy rule is a fuzzy variable.

The output of the fuzzy associative memory is equal to the (vector) sum of all these fuzzy variables:

In the case of a scalar control signal $u(t)$, the signal space is the real line, $U=R$.

Summing the fuzzy variables involves calculating the sum $g_u = \Sigma_j g_j$ of their modulated function g_j. Notice that the fuzzy variable v_u at the output of the fuzzy associative memory is represented exclusively by the ("modulated") function g_u (that is, this fuzzy variable has no directly underlying fuzzy set which is modulated by some degree d_u to yield the function g_u).

In the case of a vector control signal $u(t) \in R^m$, typically, the signal space of each of the components $u_i(t)$ is the real line, that is, $U_i = R \ for \ I = 1,...,m$. Summing the fuzzy variables involves calculating the$m$ sums $g_{u_i} = \Sigma_j g_{ij}$ of the modulated functions g_{ij} for each index $i, i = 1, ..., m$.

The summing operator Σ takes the pointwise sum of its argument functions.The sum $g(u)$ may exceed 1 for some values of the argument u. This poses no problem. (Clipping $g(u)$ to the maximal value 1 would be counterproductive because the centroid of g would be shifted.)

Example 3.6 For further illustration of the intuitive concept of rule-based fuzzy control (model-free approach), we consider an example wherea dog is chasing a cat. Like most dogs, this dog is not smart enough to use proportional navigation. Rather, he always tries to run in the direction where he sees the cat.

The dog probably explains his scheme of navigation by the following qualitative rules for choosing the direction of his next leap [81]:

- If the cat is straight ahead, then take the next leap in the same direction,
- If the cat is a little bit to the left (right), then turn a little bit to the left (right) for the next leap, and
- If the cat is very much to the left (right), then turn quite a bit to the left (right) for the next leap.

Obviously, for this scheme of navigation a fuzzy one-input one-output feedback controller can be formulated with five fuzzy sets for the line of sight angle $\alpha(t_k)$, five fuzzy sets for the change of the dog's heading angle $\Delta\gamma(t_k)$ for the next leap, and five fuzzy SISO-rules.

Figure 8 shows the fuzzy sets covering the signal space A = [- 180°, 180°] where the line of sight angle $\alpha(t_k)$ occurs. Figure 9 shows the fuzzy sets covering the signal space $U = R$ where the change of the dog's heading angle $\Delta\gamma(t_k)$ occurs.

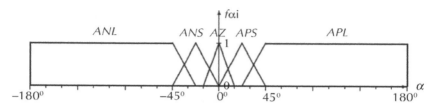

FIGURE 8   Fuzzy sets covering the signal space of line of sight.

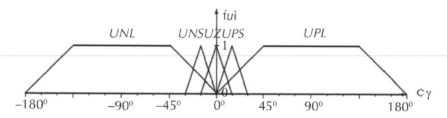

FIGURE 9   Fuzzy sets covering the signal space of dog's heading angle.

The five fuzzy rules of the fuzzy associative memory of the fuzzy feedback controller can be written as follows:

$$ANL \rightarrow UNL, ANS \rightarrow UNS, AZ \rightarrow UZ, APS \rightarrow UPS, and\ APL \rightarrow UPL.$$

This should be read as follows:

If $\alpha T(t_k)$ belongs to the fuzzy set ANL to degree d, then the fuzzy set UNL for the change of heading angle should be fired to degree d, and so on.

Since, it is not quite clear what the dog means by "turning a little bit" or "turning pretty much", a multiplicative doggy gain K is introduced. Furthermore, it is assumed that the dog cannot change his heading angle by more than 90° in either direction from one step to the next.

This leads to the final control law:

$$uT(t_k) = \Delta\gamma(t_k) = KD\{v_u(t_k)\},$$

where K is doggy gain, D is defuzzification and $v_u(t_k)$ is the fuzzy variable at the output of the fuzzy associative memory at time t_k. In order to evaluate the effectiveness of the dog's fuzzy feedback control, a "dog chases cat" scenario is simulated.

In Figures 10 and 11, the cat runs along a rectangular course at constant speed, starting in the northwest corner. The dog starts running at a position close to the center of the rectangle. The dog's speed exceeds the cat's speed by 32.5%. A blood stain is left on the ground whenever the dog intercepts the cat with very high precision but the chase continues immediately.

A natural value for the doggy gain is K=0.5,since, there is no reason why the dog should turn by more than 45° when the cat is off by 45°. The simulation for this value of the doggy gain is shown in Figure 10. Obviously, the dog performs reasonably well. Of course, whenever the dog overshoots the cat, he has to manoeuvre with a high turning rate until the cat is again "in front" of him.

In Figure 11, the simulation is done with K=1. Now, the dog is zig-zagging most of the time, changing his direction by + 90° from step to step. He only catches the cat because he luckily happens to cut the southeast corner in an efficient way. Essentially, the dog fails his mission with this high value of the doggy gain. Note however, that the critical value for the doggy gain depends on how much the dog's speed exceeds the cat's speed.

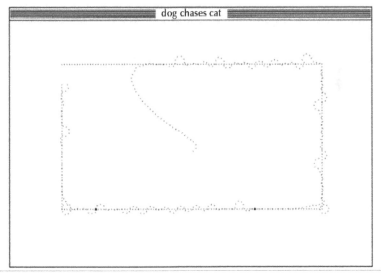

FIGURE 10   Chasing of dog with gain k=0.5.

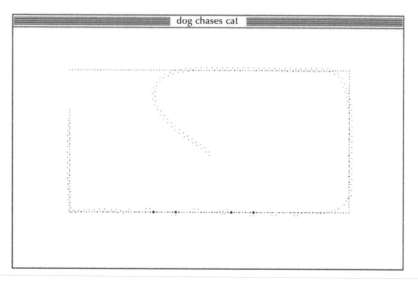

Figure 11   Chasing of dog with gain k=1.

Fuzzy control can be classified into static fuzzy control and adaptive fuzzy control. In static fuzzy control, the structure and parameters of the fuzzy controller are fixed and do not change during real-time operation. On the other hand, in adaptive fuzzy control, the structure and/or parameters of the fuzzy controller change during real-time operation. Static fuzzy control is simpler than adaptive fuzzy control but requires more knowledge of the process model or heuristic rules. Adaptive fuzzy control, other hand, is more expensive to implement but requires less information and may perform better.

3.4   FUZZY CONTROLLER DESIGN

Fuzzy controls and conventional control have similarities and differences. They are similar in sense that they must address the same issues that are common to any problem, such as stability and performance. However, there is a fundamental difference between fuzzy control and conventional control. Conventional control starts with a mathematical model of the process, and controllers are designed based on the model. On the other hand, fuzzycontrolstarts with heuristics and human expertise (in terms of fuzzy IF-THEN rules) and controllers are designed by synthesizing these rules. That is, the information used to construct the two types of controllers is different. Advanced fuzzy controllers, however, can make use of both heuristics and mathematical models.

For many practical problems, it is difficult to obtain an accurate yet simple mathematical model, but there are human experts who can provide heuristics and rule-of-thumb that are very useful for controlling the process. Fuzzy control is most useful for these kinds of problems. If the mathematical model of the process is unknown, we can design fuzzy controllers in a systematic manner that guarantees certain key performance criteria.

The design techniques for fuzzy controllers can be classified into the trial-and-error approach and the theoretical approach. In the trial-and-error approach, a set of fuzzy IF-THEN rules are collected from human experts or documented knowledge base, and the fuzzy controllers are constructed from these fuzzy IF-THEN rules. The fuzzy controllers are tested in the real system and if the performance is not satisfactory, the rules are fine-tuned or redesigned in a number of trial-and-error cycles until the performance is satisfactory. In theoretical approach, the structure and parameters of the fuzzy controller are designed in such a way that certain performance criteria are guaranteed. Both approaches, of course, can be combined to give the best fuzzy controllers.

3.4.1   TRIAL-AND-ERROR APPROACH

The trial-and-error approach to fuzzy controller design can be summarized in the following steps:
- Select state and control variables. The state variables should characterize the key features of the system and the control variables should be able to influence the states of the states of the system. The state variables are the inputs to the fuzzy controller and the control variables are the output of the fuzzy controller.
- Construct IF-THEN rules between the state and control variables. The formulation of these rules can be achieved in two different heuristic approaches. The most common approach is the linguistic verbalization of human experts. Another approach is to interrogate experienced experts of operators using a carefully organized questionnaire.
- Test the fuzzy IF-THEN rules in the system. The closed-loop system with the fuzzy controller is run and if the performance is not satisfactory, fine tune or redesign the fuzzy controller and repeat the procedure until the performance is satisfactory.

The resulting fuzzy IF-THEN rule can be in the following two types:

$$Type I : IF\ x_1\ is\ A_1^i\ AND ... AND\ x_n\ is\ A_n^i,$$

THEN u is B^j

$$Type II : IF\ x_1\ is\ A_1^i\ AND ... AND\ x_n\ is\ A_n^i,$$

$$THEN\ u\ is\ c_0^i + c_1^i\ x_1 + ... + c_n^i\ x_n.$$

In Type I, both the antecedent and consequent have linguistic variables, $A_k^i, k = 1, 2, ..., n$ and B^j, respectively. On the other hand in Type II, the consequent is a parameterized function of the input to the fuzzy controller, or the state variables. Comparing the two types, the THEN part of the rule is changed from a linguistic description to a simple mathematical formula. This change makes it easier to combine the rules. In fact, Type II, the Takagi–Sugeno system, is a weighted average of the rules in the THEN parts of the rules. This framework is useful in tuning the rules mathematically.

Type II, on the other hand has drawbacks:

(i) Its THEN part is a mathematical formula and therefore may not provide a natural framework to represent human knowledge and

(ii) There is not much freedom left to apply different principles in fuzzy logic, so that the versatility of fuzzy systems is not fully represented in this framework. The major tools and techniques for trial-and-error approach to fuzzy control are already discussed in Chapter 3 of Volume1 of this book and Chapter 1 of Volume2. In the following, we consider a fuzzy controller of Type I for a dynamical system.

Let the dynamics of the ball and beam systems as shown in Figure 12 are given by [223]:

$$\left(m+\frac{I_b}{r^2}\right)\ddot{x}=x\alpha^2-\sin\alpha$$

$$\left(\phi+mx^2\right)\ddot{\alpha}=2m\dot{x}\dot{x}\alpha-mgx\cos\alpha+u$$

where the parameters are g = 9.81, m = 0.01679

g = 9.81: Gravitational force

m = 0.01679: Mass (kg)

$r=\dfrac{2.54}{1000}$: Levelradius = 2.54 cm.

$x=\dfrac{50}{100}=0.5\text{m},\ |x|<\dfrac{50}{100}$

$I_b=\left(\dfrac{2}{5}\right)mR^2=8.645\,X\,10^{-6}$: Ball inertia

$\phi=0.0079$: Rotational inertia of the bream ($kg\,m^2$).

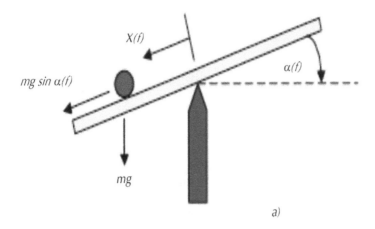

FIGURE 12 Ball beam system.

Now, we can write in the state-space model as follow:

$$
\left.
\begin{aligned}
\dot{x}_1 &= x_2 \\
\dot{x}_2 &= \frac{x\dot{\alpha}^2\, g\sin\alpha}{\left(m + \dfrac{I_b}{r^2}\right)} \\
\dot{x}_3 &= x_4 \\
\dot{x}_4 &= \frac{\left(-2m\,x_1\,x_2\,x_4 - mg\,x_1\cos x_{3+u}\right)}{\left(\Phi + m x_1^2\right)}
\end{aligned}
\right\}
\tag{3.16}
$$

which can be written as:

$$
\dot{x}(t) =
\begin{bmatrix}
0 & 1 & 0 & 0 \\[2mm]
0 & 0 & \dfrac{-g}{\left(m + \dfrac{I_b}{r^2}\right)} & 0 \\[4mm]
0 & 0 & 0 & 1 \\[2mm]
\dfrac{-2m}{\Phi} & 0 & 0 & 0
\end{bmatrix}
x(t) +
\begin{bmatrix}
0 \\ 0 \\ 0 \\ \dfrac{1}{\Phi}
\end{bmatrix}
u.
$$

Finally, we get:

$$\dot{x}(t)\begin{bmatrix} 0 & 1 & 0 & 0 \\ 0 & 0 & -7.223 & 0 \\ 0 & 0 & 0 & 0 \\ -20828 & 0 & 0 & 0 \end{bmatrix} x(t) + \begin{bmatrix} 0 \\ 0 \\ 0 \\ 126.58 \end{bmatrix} u \qquad (3.17)$$

y(t)=x(t).

The system has four state variables. We know that the system needs torque to control the angle of the beam. The control system is designed as multi-input and single-output fuzzy system. The inputs of the controller are $x_1, x_2, x_3, and\ x_4$. The output of the controller is u [223].

FUZZY CONTROL RULES

Step 1: Construct the membership function for inputs $x_1, x_2, x_3, and\ x_4$. Consider the put x_1, which has three membership functions. In this case, we define the membership functions as the following values: positive (P), zero (Z), and negative (N). The inputs $x_1, x_2, x_3, and\ x_4$ are also defined the same as the inputs $x_1, x_2, x_3, and\ x_4$ are shown as follows:

Inputs x_1 has P, Z, and N

Inputs x_2 has P, Z, and N

Inputs x_3 has P, Z, and N

Inputs x_4 has P, Z, and N

Step 2: Construct the membership function for the output. Start with nine membership functions for output u, which can be defined as positive-max, positive-big, positive, positive-small, zero, negative-small, negative, negative-big, and negative-max.

Step 3: The fuzzy controller has four inputs and one output. In this step, the truth table is used to analyze the output. The results of a truth table are the control actions. These results are used as the rules of fuzzy controller. The number of fuzzy rules is equal to 3 x 3 x 3 x 3 = 81. All rules involve the inputs $x_1, x_2, x_3, and\ x_4$.

Step 4: From the physical system shows in Figure 12, set the regions of the inputs and output as follows:

- Inputs x_1 is the position of the ball, x, then we have, $-\frac{1}{2} < x < \frac{1}{2}, (m)$ wherel is the range of the beam (m)

- Inputs x_2 is the derivative of distance, x, then we have, $-\frac{1}{2}<\dot{x}<\frac{1}{2},\left(\frac{m}{\sec}\right)$.

- Inputs x_3 is the angle of the beam shaft, α, then we have, $-\alpha_{max}<\alpha<\alpha_{max}$ (red).

- Inputs x_4 is the derivatie of the angle, α, then we have, $-\dot{\alpha}_{max}<\dot{\alpha}<\dot{\alpha}_{max}$ (red/sec).

All inputs can be adjusted by using $g_1, g_2, g_3, and\ g_4$ can be found by using Nonlinear Control Design or using Linear Quadratic Regular design (LQR). For LQR, the gains $g_1, g_2, g_3, and\ g_4$ are based on the linerized model.

Output u is the input of ball and beam system, which generated torque. Let us assume that the system needs input $-10<u<10,\left(\frac{Nm}{Amp}\frac{V}{red/sec}\right)$. The fuzzy inference system for this method is shown in Figure13.

Step 5:Replace all parameters in the ball and beam system and simulate the control system to obtain the results.

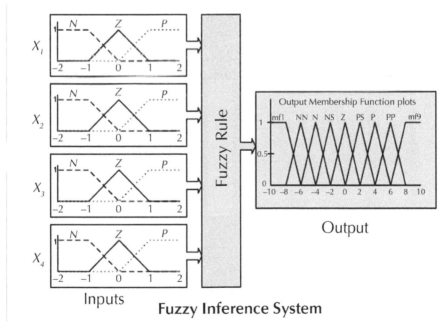

FIGURE 13   Fuzzy inference system.

SIMULATION OF FUZZY CONTROL

The gains $g_1, g_2, g_3, and\ g_4$ can be found by using nonlinear control and linear quadratic regulator (LQR) design technique.

The results can be shown as Table 3:

TABLE 3   Using nonlinear control and LQR technique to find gains $g_1, g_2, g_3, and\ g_4$

Gains	Nonlinear Control	LQR
g_1	-1.2731	-1.1780
g_2	-1.5576	-1.5407
g_3	5.4775	4.8957
g_4	0.9064	1.0380

The outputs of the system are the ball position (x) and the beam angle (α). The simulation results are shown in Figure 14 and 15. The results are somewhat similar.

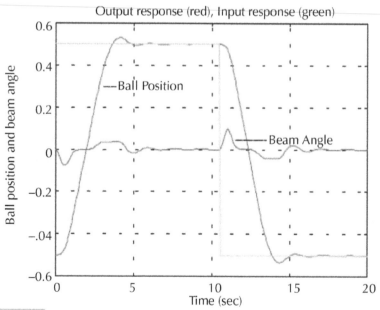

FIGURE 14   The output responses of direct fuzzy control system with nonlinear control design.

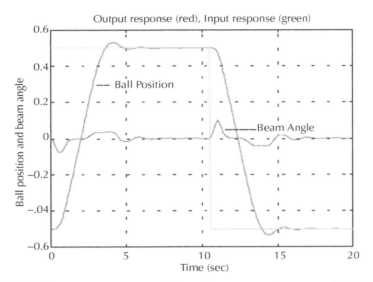

FIGURE 15 The output responses of direct fuzzy control system with LQR design the gains g_1, g_2, g_3, and g_4 are based on the linearized model.

3.4.2 THEORETICAL APPROACH

Mathematical model of a system is not a necessary condition for designing fuzzy controllers. However, in order to analyze the performance of the closedloop fuzzy control system theoretically, we need to have some knowledge on the model of the system. This approach assumes a mathematical model for the system, so that mathematical analysis can be performed to establish the properties of the designed system.

In real life,almostall physical dynamical systems have a nonlinear nature. Linear control methods rely on the key assumption of small range of operation for the linear model, acquired from linearizing the nonlinear system. When required operation range is large, a linear controller is prone to be unstable, because the nonlinearities in the plant cannot be properly dealt with. However, the highly nonlinear and discontinuous nature of many mechanical and electrical systems does not allow linear approximation. Nevertheless, for many nonlinear plants that are chemical process, building a mathematical model is very difficult and only the input-output data yielded from running the process is accessible for estimation. Many control problems involve uncertainties in the model parameters. A controller based on inaccurate or obsolete values of the model parameters may show significant performance degradation or even instability. There are some complicated approaches like auto-regressive model based on the input-output data to compensate model uncertainties, which usually use to design a process control. However, due to the high nonlinearity of the process, the order of the model often becomes very high so that past effects are taken into account, even if that is physically unrealistic.

One way to cope with such difficulty is to develop a nonlinear model composing of a number of sub-models which are simple, understandable, and responsible for respective sub-domains. The idea of multi-model approach is not new but the idea of fuzzy modeling using the concept of the fuzzy sets theory offers a new technique to build multi-models of the process based on the input-output data or the original mathematical model of the system. Facing complex and nonlinear systems, we have to recognize that modeling is an art and it is important to realize system modeling is generally an act to understand things directly rather than by computer. At most, a linear combination like a fuzzy model is clearly understandable.

The fuzzy model proposed by Takagi and Sugeno is described by fuzzy IF-THEN rules,which represents local input-output relations of a nonlinear system. The main feature of a Takagi–Sugeno fuzzy model is to express the local dynamics of each fuzzy implication (rule) by a linear system model. The overall fuzzy model of the system is achieved by fuzzy "blending" of the linear system models. In this section, we first provide an example to motivate readers with our notion of model based fuzzy controller design. We demonstrate that almost all nonlinear dynamical systems can be represented by Takagi–Sugeno fuzzy models to high degree of precision. In fact, it is proved that Takagi–Sugeno fuzzy models are universal approximators of any smooth nonlinear system.

A fuzzy controller uses fuzzy rules, which are linguistic if-then statements involving fuzzy sets, fuzzy logic, and fuzzy inference. Fuzzy rules play a key role in representing expert control/modeling knowledge and experience and in linking the input variables of fuzzy controllers/models to output variable (or variables). Two major types of fuzzy rules exist, namely, Mamdani fuzzy rules and Takagi–Sugeno (*TS*, for short) fuzzy rules(see discussions of chapter 1).

Let us consider the familiar Mamdani fuzzy systems. A simple but representative Mamdani fuzzy rule describing the movement of a car is:

IF *Speed is High* AND *Acceleration* is *Small* THEN *Braking* is (should be) *Modest*, where*Speed* and *Acceleration* are input variables and *Braking* is an output variable. "High," "Small", and "Modest" are fuzzy sets, and the first two are called input fuzzy sets while the last one is named the output fuzzy set.

The variables as well as linguistic terms, such as "High", can be represented by mathematical symbols. Thus, a Mamdani fuzzy rule for a fuzzy controller involving three input variables and two output variables can be described as follows:

$$\text{IF } x_1 \text{ is } M_1 \text{ and } x_2 \text{ is } M_2 \text{ and } x_3 \text{ is } M_3 \text{ then} u_1 \text{ is } M_4, u_2 \text{ is } M_5, \quad (3.18)$$

where $x_1, x_2, and\, x_3$ are input variables (for example, error, its first derivative and its second derivative), and $u_1\, and\, u_2$ are output variables (for example, valve openness). In theory, these variables can be either continuous or discrete; practically speaking, however, they should be discrete because virtually all fuzzy controllers and models are implemented using digital computers. $M_1, M_2, M_3, M_4, and\, M_5$ are fuzzy sets, and AND are fuzzy logic AND operators. " *IF x_1 is M_1 and, x_2 is M_2, and x_3 is M_3* " is called the rule antecedent, whereas the remaining part is named the rule consequent.

The structure of Mamdani fuzzy rules for fuzzy modeling is the same. The variables involved, however, are different.

An example of a Mamdani fuzzy rule for fuzzy modeling is:

$$IF\ y(n)\ is\ M_1\ and\ y(n-1)\ is\ M_2\ and\ y(n-2)\ is\ M_3\ and\ u(n)\ is\ M_4, u(n-1)\ is\ M_5\ then\ y(n+1)\ is\ M_6$$
$$(3.19)$$

where $M_1, M_2, M_3, M_4, M_5,\ and\ M_6$ are fuzzy sets, $y(n), y(n-1)$, and $y(n-2)$ are the output of the system to be modeled at sampling time $n, n-1$ and n-2, respectively. And, u(n) and u(n-1) are system input at time n and n-1, respectively; y(n+1) is system output at the next sampling time, n+1.

Now, let us look at the so-called TS fuzzy rules. Unlike Mamdani fuzzy rules, TS rules use functions of input variables as the rule consequent.

For fuzzy control, a TS rule corresponding to the Mamdani rule (3.18) is:

IF x_1 is M_1 AND x_2 is M_2 AND x_3 is M_3 THEN $u_1 = f(x_1, x_2, x_3)$, $u_2 = g(x_1, x_2, x_3)$ where f() and g() are two real functions of any type. Similarly, for fuzzy modeling, a TS rule analogous to the Mamdani rule (3.19) is in the following form:

$$IF\ y(n)\ is\ M_1\ and\ y(n-1)\ is\ M_2\ and\ y(n-2)\ is\ M_3\ and\ u(n)\ is\ M_4, u(n-1)\ is$$
$$M_5\ then\ y(n+1) = F\big(y(n), y(n-1), y(n-2), (u(n), u(n-1))\big),$$

where F() is an arbitrary function.

Figure 16 utilizes a two-rule two-input fuzzy inference system to show different types of fuzzy system mentioned above. Type I is the widely-used Mamdani type fuzzy system which the output function is determined based on overall fuzzy output, some of them are centroid of area, min of maxima, maximum of maxima, and so on. Type II is the Takage–Sugeno type fuzzy system.

In this section, we focus only on fuzzy models that use the *T-S* rule consequent [139].

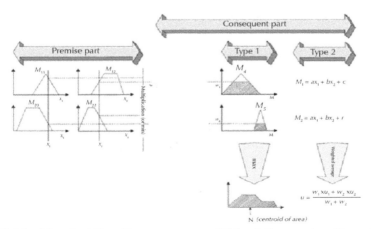

FIGURE 16   Mamdani Type Fuzzy system and Takagi–Sugeno type Fuzzy System.

SECTOR BOUND NONLINEARITY

The idea of using nonlinearity in fuzzy model construction appeared in [139]. Sector bound nonlinearity is based on the following idea. Consider a simple nonlinear system $\dot{x} = f(x(t))$, where $f(0)=0$. The aim is to find the global sector such that $\dot{x} = f(x) \in [a_1 a_2] x(t)$. Figure 17 illustrates the sector nonlinearity approach. This approach guarantees an exact fuzzy model construction. However, it is sometimes difficult to find global sector for general nonlinear systems. In this case, we consider local sector nonlinearity. This is reasonable as variables of physical systems are always bounded. Figure 17 shows the local sector nonlinearity, where two lines become the local sectors under $-d < x(t) < d$. The fuzzy model exactly represents the *local* region, that is, $-d < x(t) < d$. The following two examples illustrate the concrete steps to construct fuzzy model.

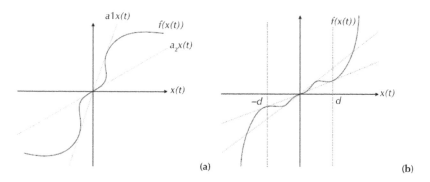

(a)   (b)

FIGURE 17   Representation of sector bound non linearity.

FUZZY MATHEMATICS FOR MODELING

Let us consider the following nonlinear system:

$$\left.\begin{array}{l} \dot{x}_1 = x_2 \\ \dot{x}_1 = x_1^2 + x_2^2 + u \end{array}\right\} \tag{3.20}$$

Our aim is to derive a *T-S* fuzzy model from the above given nonlinear system equations by the sector bound nonlinearity approach so that the response of the *T-S* fuzzy model in the specified domain exactly match with the response of the original system with the same input u.

The following steps are taken to derive the *T-S* fuzzy model of (3.20). For simplicity, we assume that $x_1 \in [0.5, 3.5]$ and $x_2 \in [-1, 4]$. In the last expression of Equation 3.20, x_1 *and* x_2 are nonlinear terms. We consider them as fuzzy variables. Generally, they are denoted as z_1, *and* z_2, are known as premise variables that may be functions of state variables, input variables, external disturbances, and/or time.

Therefore $z_1 = x_1$ *and* $z_2 = x_2$.
Equation (3.20) can be written as:

$$\dot{x}(t) = \begin{bmatrix} 0 & 1 \\ x_1 & x_2 \end{bmatrix} x(t) + \begin{bmatrix} 0 \\ 1 \end{bmatrix} u.$$

where $x(t) = [x_1(t) x_2(t)]^T$. The first step for any kind of fuzzy modeling is to determine the fuzzy variables and fuzzy sets or so-called membership functions. Although, there is no general procedure for this step and it can be done by various methods predominantly trial and error, in exact fuzzy modeling using sector nonlinearity, it is quite routine. It is assumed that the premise variables are just functions of the state variables for the sake of simplicity. This assumption is needed to avoid a complicated defuzzification process of the fuzzy controllers [139].

To acquire membership functions, we should calculate the minimum and maximum values of $z_1(t)$ *and* $z_2(t)$ which under $x_1 \in [0.5, 3.5]$ *and* $x_2 \in [-1, 4]$, which are presented as:

$$\max z_1(t) = 3.5, \quad \min z_1(t) = 0.5,$$
$$\max z_2(t) = 4 \quad \quad \min z_2(t) = -1.$$

Therefore x_1 and x_2 can be represented by for membership functions M_1, M_2, N_1 and N_2 as follows:

$$z_1(t) = x_1(t) = M_1(z_1(t)) \cdot 3.5 + M_2(z_1(t)) \cdot 0.5,$$

$$z_2(t) = x_2(t) = N_1(z_2(t)) \cdot 4 + N_2(z_2(t)) \cdot (-1),$$

and because M_1, M_2, N_1 and N_2 are actually fuzzy sets according to fuzzy mathematics:

$$M_1\left(z_1(t)\right) + M_2\left(z_1(t)\right) = 1,$$

$$N_1\left(z_2(t)\right) + N_2\left(z_2(t)\right) = 1.$$

We name the membership functions "Positive", "Negative", "Big", and "Small", respectively. Figure 18 shows these membership functions.

Here, we can generalize that the ith rule of the continuous *T-S* fuzzy models are of the following forms:

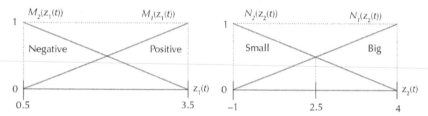

FIGURE 18   Membership functions $M_1(z_1(t))$, $M_2(z_2(t))$, $N_1(z_2(t))$ and $N_2(z_2(t))$.

MODEL RULE I

$$\text{IF } z_1(t) \text{ is } M_{i1} \text{ and } \dots \text{ and } z_p(t) \text{ is } M_{ip},$$

$$THEN \begin{cases} \dot{x} = A_i\, x(t) + B_i\, u(t), & i = 1, 2, \dots, r; \\ y(t) = C_i\, x(t), & i = 1, 2, \dots, r. \end{cases} \qquad (3.21)$$

Here, M_{ij} is the fuzzy set and r is the number of model rules; x(t) is the state vector, u(t) is the input vector, y(t) is the output vector, A_i is the square matrix with real elements and $z_1(t), \dots, z_p(t)$ are known premise variables as mentioned before. Each linear consequent equation represented by $A_i x(t) + B_i u(t)$ is called a subsystem.

Therefore, the nonlinear system (3.20) is modeled by the following fuzzy rules (we donot consider input u(t) in this stage):

Model Rule 1:IF $z_1(t)$ is "Positive" and $z_2(t)$ is "Big" THEN $\dot{x}(t) = A_1\, x(t)$.

Model Rule 2: IF $z_1(t)$ is "Positive" and $z_2(t)$ is "Small" THEN $\dot{x}(t) = A_2\, x(t)$.

Model Rule 3:IF $z_1(t)$ is "Negative" and $z_2(t)$ is "Big" THEN $\dot{x}(t) = A_3\, x(t)$.

Model Rule 4:IF $z_1(t)$ is "Negative" and $z_2(t)$ is "Small" THEN $\dot{x}(t) = A_4 x(t)$.
where the subsystems are determined as:

$$A_1 = \begin{bmatrix} 0 & 1 \\ \underset{z_1 \in \text{Positive}}{max} z_1 & \underset{z_2 \in \text{Big}}{max} z_2 \end{bmatrix}, \quad A_2 = \begin{bmatrix} 0 & 1 \\ \underset{z_1 \in \text{Positive}}{max} z_1 & \underset{z_2 \in \text{Small}}{max} z_2 \end{bmatrix},$$

$$A_3 = \begin{bmatrix} 0 & 1 \\ \underset{z_1 \in \text{Negative}}{max} z_1 & \underset{z_2 \in \text{Big}}{max} z_2 \end{bmatrix}, \quad A_4 = \begin{bmatrix} 0 & 1 \\ \underset{z_1 \in \text{Negative}}{max} z_1 & \underset{z_2 \in \text{Small}}{max} z_2 \end{bmatrix},$$

which are

$$A_1 = \begin{bmatrix} 0 & 1 \\ 3.5 & 4 \end{bmatrix}, \quad A_2 = \begin{bmatrix} 0 & 1 \\ 3.5 & -1 \end{bmatrix}, and$$

$$A_3 = \begin{bmatrix} 0 & 1 \\ 0.5 & 4 \end{bmatrix}, \quad A_4 = \begin{bmatrix} 0 & 1 \\ 0.5 & -1 \end{bmatrix},$$

Now, $\dot{x}$ can be derived out of defuzzification process as:

$$\dot{x}(t) = h_1\left(z(t)\right) A_1 x(t) + h_2\left(z(t)\right) A_2 x(t) + h_3\left(z(t)\right) A_3 x(t) + h_4\left(z(t)\right) A_4 x(t)$$

where

$$h_1\left(z(t)\right) = M_1\left(z_1(t)\right) \times N_1\left(z_2(t)\right),$$

$$h_2\left(z(t)\right) = M_1\left(z_1(t)\right) \times N_2\left(z_2(t)\right),$$

$$h_3\left(z(t)\right) = M_2\left(z_1(t)\right) \times N_1\left(z_2(t)\right),$$

$$h_4\left(z(t)\right) = M_2\left(z_1(t)\right) \times N_2\left(z_2(t)\right).$$

This T-S fuzzy model can exactly represent the nonlinear system in the region $[0.5, 3.5] \times [-1, 4]$ on the $x_1 - x_2$ space. To have a clear picture of the fuzzy modeling procedure above, we calculate the final output of for the specific given values of and .

Model Rule 1: IF $z_1(t)$ is "Positive" and $z_2(t)$ is "Big" THEN $\begin{cases} \dot{x}_1 = x_2 \\ \dot{x}_2 = 3.5 x_1 + 4 x_2 \end{cases}$.

Model Rule 2: IF $z_1(t)$ is "Positive" and $z_2(t)$ is "Small" THEN $\begin{cases} \dot{x}_1 = x_2 \\ \dot{x}_2 = 3.5 x_1 - x_2 \end{cases}$.

Model Rule 3: IF $z_1(t)$ is "Negative" and $z_2(t)$ is "Big" THEN $\begin{cases} \dot{x}_1 = x_2 \\ \dot{x}_2 = 0.5 x_1 + 4 x_2 \end{cases}$.

Model Rule 4: IF $z_1(t)$ is "Negative" and $z_2(t)$ is "Small" THEN $\begin{cases} \dot{x}_1 = x_2 \\ \dot{x}_2 = 0.5 x_1 - x_2 \end{cases}$.

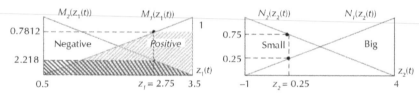

FIGURE 19   Given the value of z_1=2.75 and z_2=0.25 to the membership functions.

Therefore, according to Figure 19, if $z_1 = x_1 = 2.75 \, and \, z_2 = x_2 = 0.25$, the T-S fuzzy modeling implication can be derived as shown in Table 4:

TABLE 4   The TS fuzzy modeling

Implication	Premise	Consequence	Truth value
Rule 1	$M_1(z_1) = 0.7812,$ $N_1(z_2) = 0.25$	$\begin{cases} \dot{x}_1 = 0.25 \\ \dot{x}_2 = 3.5 \times 2.75 + 4 \times 0.25 \end{cases}$	$0.7812 \wedge 0.25 = 0.25$
Rule 2	$M_1(z_1) = 0.7812,$ $N_2(z_2) = 0.75$	$\begin{cases} \dot{x}_1 = 0.25 \\ \dot{x}_2 = 3.5 \times 2.75 - 0.25 \end{cases}$	$0.7812 \wedge 0.75 = 0.75$
Rule 3	$M_2(z_1) = 0.218,$ $N_1(z_2) = 0.25$	$\begin{cases} \dot{x}_1 = 0.25 \\ \dot{x}_2 = 0.5 \times 2.75 + 4 \times 0.25 \end{cases}$	$0.218 \wedge 0.25 = 0.218$
Rule 4	$M_2(z_1) = 0.218,$ $N_2(z_2) = 0.75$	$\begin{cases} \dot{x}_1 = 0.25 \\ \dot{x}_2 = 0.5 \times 2.75 - 0.25 \end{cases}$	$0.218 \wedge 0.75 = 0.218$

The final values for and $\dot{x}_1\ and\ \dot{x}_2$, in T-S fuzzy defuzzification process, can be calculated as:

$$
\begin{cases}
\dot{x}_1 = \dfrac{0.25\times0.25+0.25\times0.75+0.25\times0.218+0.25\times0.218}{0.25+0.75+0.218+0.218}=0.25 \\[4mm]
\dot{x}_2 = \dfrac{10.625\times0.25+9.375\times0.75+2.375\times0.218+1.125\times0.218}{0.25+0.75+0.218+0.218}=7.2775 \ .
\end{cases}
\tag{3.22}
$$

Comparing,the values of $\dot{x}_1 =0.25\ and\ \dot{x}_2 =7.6225$, we can see that the T-S fuzzy approximation does the good job and small value difference of $\dot{x}_2$ actually comes from rounding error of the premise fuzzy variables.

Given a pair of (x(t), u(t)) for the model rule, the final outputs of the fuzzy model for the Continuous Fuzzy System are inferred as follows:

$$
\dot{x}=\frac{\sum_{i=1}^{r} w_i\big(z(t)\big)\{A_i\, x(t)+B_i\, u(t)\}}{\sum_{i=1}^{r} w_i\big(z(t)\big)}
$$

$$
=\sum_{i=1}^{r} h_i\big(z(t)\big)\{A_i\, x(t)+B_i\, u(t)\}
\tag{3.23}
$$

$$
y(t)=\frac{\sum_{i=1}^{r} w_i\big(z(t)\big)C_i\, x(t)}{\sum_{i=1}^{r} w_i\big(z(t)\big)}
$$

$$
=\sum_{i=1}^{r} h_i\big(z(t)\big)C_i\, x(t).
\tag{3.24}
$$

where

$$
z(t)=[z_1(t)...z_p(t)],
$$

$$w_i\big(z(t)\big)=\prod_{j=1}^{p}M_{ij}\big(z_j(t)\big),$$

and weighting functions w_i should be normalized as:

$$h_i\big(z(t)\big)=\frac{w_i\big(z(t)\big)}{\sum_{i=1}^{r}w_i\big(z(t)\big)}$$

for all t. The term $M_{ij}\big(z_j(t)\big)$ is the grade of membership of $z_j(t)$ in M_{ij}. Since,

$$\left\{\begin{array}{l}\displaystyle\sum_{i=1}^{r}w_i\big(z(t)\big)>0,\\[2mm]w_i\big(z(t)\big)\geq 0,\end{array}\right. \qquad i=1,2,\ldots,r, \tag{3.25}$$

we have:

$$\left\{\begin{array}{l}\displaystyle\sum_{i=1}^{r}h_i\big(z(t)\big)=1,\\[2mm]h_i\big(z(t)\big)\geq 0,\end{array}\right. \qquad i=1,2,\ldots,r, \tag{3.26}$$

for all t.

LOCAL APPROXIMATION IN FUZZY PARTITION SPACES

Another approach to obtain *T-S* fuzzy models is the so-called local approximation in Fuzzy Partition Spaces. The spirit of the approach is to approximate nonlinear terms by judiciously chosen linear terms. This procedure leads to reduction of the number of model rules. For instance, if we try to exactly represent the inverted pendulum by *T-S* fuzzy model as the way in the previous section, it ends up with 16 rules. In comparison, using local approximation, a *T-S* model with 4 or 2 rules can be constructed. The number of model rules is directly related to the complexity of the design study for generating the *T-S* fuzzy controller. This is because the number of model rules for the overall *T-S* fuzzy control system is basically the combination of the model rules and control rules [139].

Example 3.8 The equations of motion for the inverted pendulum are:

$$\begin{cases} \dot{x}_1(t) = x_2(t), \\ \dot{x}_2(t) = \dfrac{g\sin(x_1(t)) - aml\, x_2^2(t)\sin(2x_1(t))/2 - a\cos(x_1(t))u(t)}{\dfrac{4l}{3} - aml\cos^2(x_1(t))}, \end{cases} \quad (3.27)$$

where $x_1(t)$ denotes the angle (in radians) of the pendulum from the vertical and $x_2(t)$ is the angular velocity, g=9.8 m/s2is the gravity constant, m is the mass of the pendulum, M is the mass of the cart, 2l is the length of the pendulum, and u is the force applied to the cart (in newtons), $a = 1/(m+M)$.

When $x_1(t)$ is near zero, the nonlinear equations can be simplified as:

$$\dot{x}_1(t) = x_2(t), \quad (3.28)$$

$$\dot{x}_2(t) = \frac{g x_1(t) - au(t)}{4l/3 - aml} \quad (3.29)$$

When $x_1(t)$ is near $\pm \pi/2$, the nonlinear equations can be simplified as:

$$\dot{x}_1(t) = x_2(t) \quad (3.30)$$

$$\dot{x}_2(t) = \frac{2g x_1(t)/\pi - a\beta u(t)}{4l/3 - aml\beta^2} \quad (3.31)$$

where $\beta = \cos(88°)\cos()$Note that (3.28)–(3.31) are now linear systems.

We arrive at the following fuzzy model based on linear subsystems:

Model Rule 1: IF $x_1(t)$ is about 0 THEN $\dot{x}(t) = A_1 x(t) + B_1 u(t)$.

Model Rule 2: IF $x_1(t)$ is about $\pm \pi/2(2|x_1|<\pi/2)$ THEN $\dot{x}(t) = A_2 x(t) + B_2 u(t)$.

Here,

$$A_1 = \begin{bmatrix} 0 & 1 \\ \dfrac{g}{4l/3 - aml} & 0 \end{bmatrix}, \qquad B_1 = \begin{bmatrix} 0 \\ -\dfrac{a}{4l/3 - aml} \end{bmatrix},$$

$$A_2 = \begin{bmatrix} 0 & 1 \\ \dfrac{2g}{\pi(\dfrac{4l}{3} - aml\,\beta^2)} & 0 \end{bmatrix}, \quad B_2 = \begin{bmatrix} 0 \\ -\dfrac{\alpha\beta}{4l/3 - aml\,\beta^2} \end{bmatrix},$$

and $\beta = \cos(88°)$. Membership functions for *Rule 1* and *Rule 2* can be simply defined as shown in Figure 20.

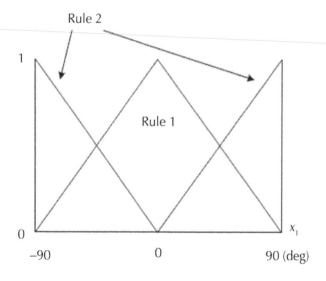

FIGURE 20   Membership functions of two-rule model.

Now, suppose the pendulum on the cart system is built in such a way that the work space of the pendulum is the full circle $[-\pi, \pi]$. We consider the result to the range of $x_1 \in [-\pi, \pi]$ except for a thin strip near $\pm\pi/2$. Balancing the pendulum for the angle range of $\pi/2 < |x_1| \le \pi$ is referred to as a swing-up control of the pendulum. Recall that for $x_1 = \pm\pi/2$, the system is uncontrollable. We add two more rules (Rules 3 and 4) to the fuzzy model.

Model Rule 1: IF $x_1(t)$ is about 0 THEN $\dot{x}(t) = A_1 x(t) + B_1 u(t)$.

Model Rule 2: IF $x_1(t)$ is about $\pm\pi/2(2\,|\,x_1\,|>\pi/2)$ THEN $\dot{x}(t)=A_2\,x(t)+B_2\,u(t)$.

Model Rule 3: IF $x_1(t)$ is about $\pm\pi/2(2\,|\,x_1\,|>\pi/2)$ THEN $\dot{x}(t)=A_3\,x(t)+B_3\,u(t)$.

Model Rule 4: IF $x_1(t)$ is about π THEN $\dot{x}(t)=A_4\,x(t)+B_4\,u(t)$.

Here A_1, B_1, A_2 and B_2 are the same as above and

$$A_3 = \begin{bmatrix} 0 & 1 \\ \dfrac{2g}{\pi(4l/3-aml\,\beta^2)} & 0 \end{bmatrix}, \quad B_3 = \begin{bmatrix} 0 \\ -\dfrac{a\beta}{4l/3-aml\,\beta^2} \end{bmatrix},$$

$$A_4 = \begin{bmatrix} 0 & 1 \\ 0 & 0 \end{bmatrix}, \quad B_4 = \begin{bmatrix} 0 \\ -\dfrac{a}{4l/3-aml\,\beta^2} \end{bmatrix}.$$

The membership functions of this four-rule fuzzy model are shown in Figure 21.

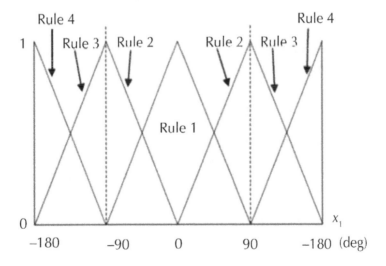

FIGURE 21   Membership functions of four rule model.

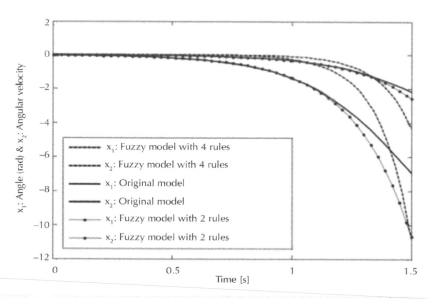

FIGURE 22   Time responses of original inverted pendulum system and their fuzzy approximations.

3.4.3   *TRANSFORMATION OF TAKAGI–SUGENO FUZZY MODEL INTO PIECEWISE AFFINE MODEL*

As fuzzy modeling can approximate any process with prescribed accuracy, it can be classified as universal approximation. In this section, we focus our attention on application of fuzzy models for prediction pattern sin Model Predictive Control (MPC). The MPC is an optimization-based control policy and is widely used in industry because of its capacity to provide optimal performance together with constraint satisfaction. According to the MPC approach, the prior knowledge of the process behavior, represented by the prediction model, isused to design as equence of control inputs such that certain performance criterion is optimized. Contrary to classical proportional-integral-derivative (PID) controllers, the decisions are taken based on the process properties and constraints.

Depending on the model used, slightly different approaches are developed. An excellent comparative study provides a deeper view into four recently developed predictive strategies. Each strategy uses the Generalized Predictive Control (GPC) approach but the control action is calculated differently.Either a linear combination of all locally designed controllers is considered or a global controller based on linear time- varying models (LTM) isused. A hierarchical structure of multipleTakagi–Sugeno models deploys the GPC approach where the controller is obtained by weighted aggregation over governing local rules. But all the approaches, as mentioned above, do not address the issues of closed-loop stability. Stability concerns are partially resolved using Linear Matrix Inequalities (LMI). These techniques are, however, overly conservative, since they assume that all possible local dynamical models are all active at the same time.

Motivated by the lack of rigorous results in the field of synthesis of stabilizing MPC controllers based on fuzzy Takagi–Sugeno (*TS*) models we consider a different way of assuring closed-loop stability and feasibility. Considering the recent advances in the field of hybridsys tems, we convert a given Takagi–Sugeno fuzzy model into a PWA model, so that efficient control strategies along with closed-loop stability and infinite-time feasibility are ensured. Unlike TS fuzzy models, the PWA description requires that the regions, over which individual dynamical modes are defined, to be non-overlapping. Therefore,we propose to over-approximate the overlaps naturally present in *TS* models by means of an unknown but bounded additive uncertainty [100].

DISCRETE FUZZY SYSTEMS

The class of Takagi–Sugeno (TS) models can be generally described by fuzzy "IF... THEN" rules where the fuzzy sets stay on the antecedent side while the consequence is given by a linear dynamics.

Generally, the ith TS rule can be expressed as:

$$\text{IF } x_{1,k} \text{ is } M_{i1} \text{ and } ...x_{n,k} \text{ is } M_{in} \text{ THEN } x_{k+1} = A_i x_k + B_i u_k \quad (3.32)$$

Where $x_k \in R^{n \times 1}$ is the state vector, $u_k \in R^{m \times 1}$ denotes the vector of manipulated variables, M_{ij} are input fuzzy sets for $i = 1, ..., r$ rules. $A_i \in R^{n \times n}$, $B_i \in R^{n \times m}$ are matrices representing the system dynamics. The process dynamics is assumed to be discretized with k denoting one sampling instant.

The aggregated system output is modeled using the max-product inference, that is:

$$x_{k+1} = \frac{\sum_{i=1}^{r} w_i(x_k)(A_i x_k + B_i u_k)}{\sum_{i=1}^{r} w_i(x_k)} \quad (3.33)$$

$$w_i(x_k) \prod_{j=1}^{n} M_{ij}(x_{j,k}) \quad (3.34)$$

where the membership function M_{ij} measures the activation of the fuzzy set **j** in the rule i. Using the notation

$$\alpha_i(x_k) = \frac{w_i(x_k)}{\sum_{i=1}^{r} w_i(x_k)}, \alpha_i(x_k) > 0, \qquad \sum_{i=1}^{r} \alpha_i(x_k) = 1 \quad (3.35)$$

$$x_{k+1} = \sum_{i=1}^{r} \alpha_i(x_k)(A_i x_k + B_i u_k) \tag{3.36}$$

We consider a simple *TS* model using three rules with linear fuzzy membership functions as shown in Figure 23. It can be seen that each dynamics contributes to the over all model with its corresponding membership function. If the state belongs to a region where more than one dynamic become active, then the weighted contribution of over lapping nodes is considered.

THE TRANSFORMATION PROCEDURE

Consider the TS model (3.32) with linear fuzzy membership functions.

The fuzzy input sets **Mij** can be decomposed in the following manner:

$$\text{IF } x_k \in P_i \text{ THEN } x_{k+1} = A_i x_k + B_i u_k \tag{3.37}$$

where the region P_i, in which the corresponding rule is active, can be described by a polyhedral set:

$$P_i := \{H_i x_k \leq K_i\}. \tag{3.38}$$

Our aim is to transform the TS model into a Piece wise Affine (PWA) model of the following form:

$$x_{k+1} = f \, PWA(xk, uk, wk) \tag{3.39}$$

$$= A_i x_k + B_i u_k + f_i + w_k \text{ if } x_k \in D_i$$

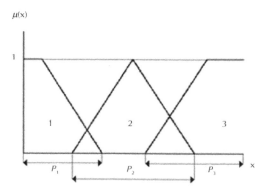

FIGURE 23 Linear membership functions for three rules of the Takagi–Sugeno model.

With $A_i \in R^{nXn}$, $B_i \in R^{mXn}$, and $f_i \in R^{nX1}$. Here, $\{D_i\}_{i=1}^{n_d} \in R^n$ denotes a

polyhedral partition satisfying $D = \bigcup_{i=1}^{n_d} D_i$. The measured state is denoted by x_k, manipulated inputs correspond to u_k, and w_k denotes an unknown additive disturbance. The system states x, control inputs u as well as the disturbance w of the system (3.39) are subject to the constraints.

$$X_k \in X \subseteq R^n, u_k \in U \subseteq R^m, w_k \in W \subseteq R^n, \forall k \in \{0, ..., N\} \quad (3.40)$$

where X, U, and W are polyhedral sets containing the origin in the irrespective interiors.

To obtain the strictly separated regions D_i, the overlaps in the membership functions of the TS model have to be removed first.

This can be done in a straight forward manner by defining new regions for each intersection of the neighboring fuzzy sets, that is:

$$D_j = P_i \cap P_{i+1} \, j = 1, ..., n_i \quad (3.41)$$

which is also a polyhedral set. If the set D_j is a subset of the next set (for example, when more than 2 fuzzy sets intersect) then the statement:

$$D_j \subset D_{j+1} \Rightarrow D_j = \emptyset \quad (3.42)$$

implies that the redundant sets are removed. Figure 24 depicts the decomposition of the fuzzy sets to a crisp sets by introducing additional regions D_2 and D_4, respectively. Because the regions, Pi are represented by convex polytopes as in (3.38), the overall calculation of intersections can be performed using standard algebraic manipulation techniques.

The remaining regions can be obtained by:

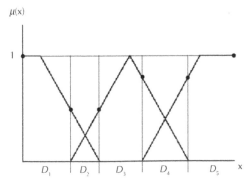

FIGURE 24   Fuzzy sets are replaced by new regions with crisp boundaries.

Set –difference operation

$$D_j = \bigcup_i P_i \setminus \bigcup_{i=1}^{n_i} D_i := \left\{ x_k \in R^n \mid x_k \in \bigcup_i P_i, x_k \notin \bigcup_{i=1}^{n_i} D_i \right\} j = n_i \ldots \ldots n_d \ (3.43)$$

It is important to determine the mean PWA description for each region with bounded additive uncertainty that is to express the transition from (3.33) to (3.39). To do so, the worst case perturbations of the mean model have to be considered. Obviously, these values are located at the boundary of each region, as indicated by black dots in Figure24. Thus, the mean model for region D_j is given by arithmetic mean of neighboring models corresponding to the boundary of a given region, that is:

$$\hat{A}_j = \frac{1}{n_n} \sum_i A_i, \hat{B}_j = \frac{1}{n_n} \sum_i B_i,$$

$$(3.44)$$

With $i \in I_j$ where I_j stands for the index set of dynamics active in the region D_j and n_n denotes the number of overlapping models.

The next step is to determine the affine term f_j and the maximal allowed uncertainty w_j in each region D_j. For this purpose the maximum allowed reachable set of the uncertain system is explored. Let A_j, B_j denote the families of possible realizations of matrices $\hat{A}_j, \hat{B}_j$.

An over-approximation of the maximum reachable set for the region Dj is given by:

$$T_j = \{ x_{k+1} \mid x_{k+1} \le x_{k+1} \le x_{k+1} \}$$

$$(3.45)$$

where the update x_{k+1} of the state is driven by the *TS* model(3.36) and x_{k+1} and x_{k+1} denote, respectively, the lower and upper limit so fall possible realizations of x_{k+1}.

The key idea is to use an approximation of the form:

$$x_{k+1} \cong \hat{x}_{k+1}$$

$$\sum_{i=1}^{r} \alpha(x_k) (A_i x_k + B_i u_k) \cong \hat{A}_j x_k + \hat{B}_j u_k \ \textit{if } x_k \in D_j \subset X \qquad (3.46)$$

$$\text{s.t } u_k \in U, \hat{A}_j \in A_j, \hat{B}_j \in B_j, j = 1 \ldots n_d$$

and to transform the model (3.46) into a PWA system with bounded additive disturbances (3.39). Note that the PWA model (3.39) actually over-approximates the behavior of the original problem (3.46) because even if the linearization for the particular regions Dj is determined, the conservatism appears in the unknown signal w where the maximum allowed disturbance is considered. Obviously, the transformation will be applied to regions where multiple membership functions overlap. In the remaining regions only a single dynamical model will be active.

Obtaining the maximum reachable set Tj for the sector Dj via solving (3.46) can be viewed as a collection of polytope operations. Define the partial reachable set for the model i in the region Dj by

$$Q_{ji} = \{x_{k+1} | x_{k+1} = A_i \, x_k + B_i \, u_k, \, x_k \in D_j, \, u_k \in U\} \tag{3.47}$$

Consequently, the maximum reachable set for the region D_j can be found as the bounding box of the union of the partial sets, that is:

$$T_j = B\,box\left(\bigcup_{i=1}^{n_n} Q_{ji}\right) \tag{3.48}$$

Where the operator B box is defined as follows:

Definition 3.2A bounding box B box (P) of a set P is the smallest hyper- rectangle which contains the set P. If P is defined as a (possibly) non-convex union of convex polytopes Pi that is $P = \bigcup_i P_i$ then the bounding box can be computed by solving 2nd linear programs per each element of the set P. Here, n denotes the dimension of P.

The maximum estimated reachable set $\hat{T}j$ can be computed similarly as a bounding box of the reachable sets for the mean model (3.39):

$$\hat{T}_j = B\,box\left(\hat{Q}_j\right) \tag{3.49}$$

With

$$\hat{Q}_j = \left\{x_{k+1} \mid x_{k+1} = \hat{A}_j \, x_k + \hat{B}_j \, u_k, \, x_k \in D_j, u_k \in U\right\} \tag{3.50}$$

The affine terms fj of (3.39) can now be computed as a difference between the analytic centers of the reachable sets for the "true" and for the "approximated" system:

$$f_j = ce(T_j) - ce(\hat{T}_j) \tag{3.51}$$

where the operator *ce* is given by:

$$ce(T) = \overline{x} - \frac{\overline{x} - x}{2} \tag{3.52}$$

These sets are depicted in Figure25 (a). It can be seen in Figure25 (b) that the transformation procedure shifts these sets to one common analytic center. The allowable disturbance is then selected as the maximum distance over the edges of the sets in the sector D_j, that is:

$$w_j = \begin{cases} \max\left(T_j - \left(\hat{T}_j + f_j\right)\right) & \text{if } T_j \geq \hat{T}_j + f_j \\ 0 & \text{otherwise.} \end{cases} \tag{3.53}$$

In other words, if the approximated reachable set $\hat{T}_j$ shifted by the offset f, is smaller than the original reachable set T_j, then the difference is modeled by an unknown but bounded disturbance w_j, whose element-wise bounds are given by (3.53). By applying the same procedure to each sector Dj the original fuzzy.

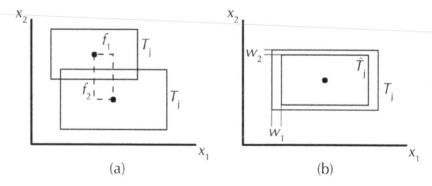

FIGURE 25   The transformation procedure shifts the reachable sets to one common center.

model (3.33) can be converted to a PWA description (3.39). In the next section, the pattern are demonstrated on an illustrative example [100].

Example 3.9 [100] Consider a *TS* model (3.32) described by two linear dynamics

$$A_1 = \begin{pmatrix} 0.3216 & 0.0114 \\ 0.0864 & -0.8143 \end{pmatrix}, B_1 = \begin{pmatrix} -0.5867 \\ 0.5451 \end{pmatrix}$$

$$A_2 = \begin{pmatrix} 0.5331 & -0.7570 \\ -0.0404 & -0.2694 \end{pmatrix}, B_2 = \begin{pmatrix} -0.2836 \\ 0.6453 \end{pmatrix}$$

Associated with the following membership functions:

$$M_1(x_1) = \begin{cases} M_1(x_1) = 0 & \text{if } |x_1| \geq 1.5 \\ M_1(x_1) = 1 - \dfrac{2}{3}|x_1| & \text{otherwise} \end{cases}$$

$$M_2(x_1) = \begin{cases} M_2(x_1) = 0 & \text{if } |x_1| \leq 1.0 \\ M_2(x_1) = -\dfrac{1}{2} + \dfrac{1}{2}|x_1| & \text{otherwise.} \end{cases}$$

The functions are depicted in Figure 26. Constraints imposed for this example are the closed intervals.

$$u \in [5, -5], \quad x \in [-3, 3] \times [-2, 2] \tag{3.54}$$

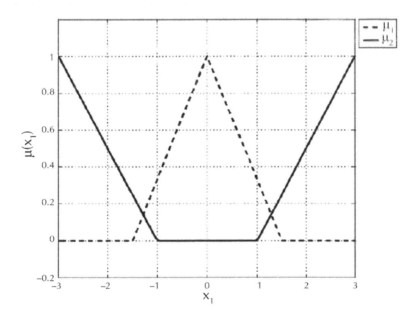

FIGURE 26 Membership functions.

To convert a given TS model into the PWA form (3.39),the feasible region (3.54) is first decomposed into 5 intervals given by following polytopes:

$$D_1 \geq = \begin{pmatrix} -1 & 0 \\ 1 & 0 \end{pmatrix} x \leq \begin{pmatrix} 3 \\ -1.5 \end{pmatrix}, \; D_2 := \begin{pmatrix} -1 & 0 \\ 1 & 0 \end{pmatrix} x \leq \begin{pmatrix} 1.5 \\ -1 \end{pmatrix}, \; D_3 := \begin{pmatrix} -1 & 0 \\ 1 & 0 \end{pmatrix} x \leq \begin{pmatrix} 1 \\ 1 \end{pmatrix}$$

$$D_4 := \begin{pmatrix} -1 & 0 \\ 1 & 0 \end{pmatrix} x \leq \begin{pmatrix} -1 \\ 1.5 \end{pmatrix}, \; D_5 := \begin{pmatrix} -1 & 0 \\ 1 & 0 \end{pmatrix} x \leq \begin{pmatrix} -1.5 \\ 3 \end{pmatrix}$$

The polytopes (3.55) have been selected following the procedure illustrated in Figure 24.

The PWA model takes the affine form:

$$x_{k+1} = \begin{cases} A_2 x_k + B_2 u_k + w & \text{if } x \in D_1 \\ (0.5A_2 + 0.5A_1) x_k + (0.5B_2 + 0.5B_1) u_k + f_2 + w & \text{if } x \in D_2 \\ A_2 x_k + B_1 u_k + w & \text{if } x \in D_3 \\ (0.5A_1 + 0.5A_2) x_k + (0.5B_1 + 0.5B_2) u_k + f_4 + w & \text{if } x \in D_4 \\ A_2 x_k + B_2 u_k + w & \text{if } x \in D_5 \end{cases} \qquad (3.56)$$

Note that modes 2 and 4 (which are active in sectors D_2 and D_4) are averaged due to overlapping membership functions.

Using reachability analysis and computing T_j as per (3.48), we get:

$$T_1 = \begin{bmatrix} -3.7317, & 2.6347 \\ -4.4838, & 4.2677 \end{bmatrix}, \; T_4 = \begin{bmatrix} -2.6347, & 3.7317 \\ -4.2677, & 4.4838 \end{bmatrix} \qquad (3.57)$$

The maximum approximated reachable sets $\hat{T}_j$ can be computed using (3.49) and are given by following axis-aligned intervals:

$$\hat{T}_2 = \begin{bmatrix} -3.5624, & 2.4940 \\ -4.0942, & 4.0367 \end{bmatrix}, \hat{T}_4 \begin{bmatrix} -2.4949, & 3.5624 \\ -4.0367, & 4.0942 \end{bmatrix} \qquad (3.58)$$

The affine terms f_j in (3.56), and the range for the maximum allowable disturbance w have been computed according to (3.51) and (3.53), respectively, as:

$$f_2 = \begin{pmatrix} -0.0142 \\ -0.0792 \end{pmatrix}, \; f_4 = \begin{pmatrix} 0.0142 \\ 0.0792 \end{pmatrix}, \begin{pmatrix} -0.1551 \\ -0.3102 \end{pmatrix} \leq w \leq \begin{pmatrix} 0.1551 \\ 0.3102 \end{pmatrix} \qquad (3.59)$$

The final PWA model of the form (3.39) is then composed of (3.56) and (3.59), where the region D_i over which each dynamics is active is given by (3.55).

We consider a methodology of transforming fuzzy Takagi–Sugeno models into a Piece wise Affine representation has been presented. The approximation is based on deinterlacing the regions in which several membership functions overlap and subsequently approximating the effect of such overlaps by an unknown but bounded disturbance. Computation of the bounds of the unknown disturbance is performed using reachability analysis. The resulting PWA model can then be used as aprediction model to derive MPC feedback laws with stability and feasibility guarantees. Since, the PWA representation over-approximates the behavior of a given fuzzy Takagi–Sugeno model, the stability guarantees naturally extend to this class of models as well.

Theoretical approaches to fuzzy controller design and stability studies are discussed as follows:

i.   Stable controller design
ii. Input-output stability study
iii. Optimal controller design
iv. Sliding mode controller design
v.   Fuzzy Bang–Bang control
vi. Supervisory controller design
vii. Fuzzy system model-based controller design

i.   *Stable Controller Design:* For control systems, stability is the most important requirement.

Conceptually, there are two classes of stability:

• Lyapunov stability and
• Input-output stability.

We assume that the system is represented as a linear system and the fuzzy controller is connected in the feedback path as shown in Figure 27.

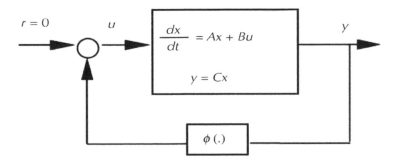

FIGURE 27   Fuzzy feedback control.

The overall system is described by the following equations:

$$\frac{dx(t)}{dt} = Ax(t) + Bu(t), \qquad (3.60)$$

$$y(t) = Cx(t), \tag{3.61}$$

$$u(t) = -\Phi\big[y(t)\big], \tag{3.62}$$

where x(t), u(t), $Y(t)\in \mathfrak{N}$, and ϕ ia a fuzzy system.

Then we have the following exponential stability theorem:

Theorem 3.2 Consider the system (5.60)–(5.61), and suppose that (a) all eigenvalues of A lie in the open left half of the complex plane, (b) the system is controllable and observable, and (c) the transfer function of the system is strictly positive real. If the nonlinear function Φ satisfies $\Phi(0) = 0$ and

$$y\phi(y) \geq 0, \forall y \in R \tag{3.63}$$

then the equilibrium point x = 0 of the closed-loop system (3.60)–(3.62) is globally exponentially stable.

Conditions (a)–(c) in the theorem are imposed on the system under control, not on the controller. They are simply requiring that the open-loop system is stable and well-behaved. Conceptually, these systems are not difficult to control, and the conditions on the fuzzy controller are not very strong. The theorem guarantees that if we design a fuzzy controller $\phi(y)$ that satisfies $\phi(0) = 0$ and (3.63), then the closed-loop system is globally exponentially stable, provided that the system under control is linear and satisfies conditions (a)–(c). This leads to the design of a stable fuzzy logic controller:

DESIGN PROCEDURE

Step 1. Define 2N + 1 fuzzy sets A'on the output space [-1, 1] that are normal, consistent, and complete with the triangular membership functions as shown in Figure 28, where the first N fuzzy sets cover the negative interval [-1, 0], the last N fuzzy sets cover the positive interval [0, 1], and the center of the middle fuzzy set for $l = N + 1$ is at zero.

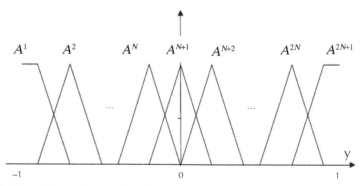

FIGURE 28   Triangular membership function.

Step 2. Define the following 2N + 1 fuzzy IF-THEN rules:

$$\text{IF } y \text{ is } A^l_, \text{ THEN } u \text{ is } B^l \qquad (3.64)$$

where $l = 1,2, \ldots , 2N + 1$, and the centers of fuzzy setsare chosen such that:

$$u^{-i} \begin{cases} \le i \ \text{ for } l = 1,\ldots, N \\ = 0 \ \text{ for } l = N+1 \\ \ge 0 \ \ l = N + 2,\ldots, 2n + 1 \end{cases} \qquad (3.65)$$

Step 3. Design the fuzzy controller from the IF-THEN rules (3.64) using the product inference engine, singleton fuzzifier, and center average defuzzyfier,that is, the designed fuzzy controller is

$$u = -\phi(y) = -\frac{\sum_{i=1}^{(2N+1)^{-1}} u \mu_{A'}(y)}{\sum_{i=1}^{(2N+1)^{-1}} \mu_{A'}(y)} \qquad (3.66)$$

Where $\mu_{A'}(y)$ are shown in Fig. 28 and u^{-1} satisfy (3.65).

The above design steps imply that in designing the fuzzy controller, we do not need to know the system model. Also, there is much freedom in choosing the parameters of the fuzzy controller.

When a nonzero input is applied to the fuzzy controlled system shown in Figure 27, the input-output stability can be established the following theorem:

Theorem 3.3 Consider the system in Figure 27 and suppose that the nonlinear controller (y) is globallyLipschitz continuous, that is:

$$|(y_1) - \phi(y_2)| \le K |y_1 - y_2|, \forall y_1, y_2 \in R \qquad (3.67)$$

for some constant K. If the eigenvalues of A lie in the open left-half complex plane,

then the closed-loop system in Figure 27 is L_p-stable for all $p \in [1, \infty]$.

It can be shown that the fuzzy controller $\phi(y)$ is continuous, bounded, and piecewise linear, and hence satisfies the Lipschitz condition. Thus, the closed-loop fuzzy control system in Figure27 is -stable for all $p \in [1, \infty]$.

The stable fuzzy controller design can be easily extended to multi-unit multi-output variables. The IF-THEN rule (3.64) is generalized for the jth group (j = 1, 2, ..., m) to the set of $\Pi_{i=1}^{m}(2N_i + 1)$ rules

$$\text{IF } y_1 \text{ is } A_1^{l_1} \text{ and } \ldots \text{ and } y_m \text{ is } A_m^{l_m} \text{ THEN } u_j \text{ is } B_j^{l_1 \ldots l_m} \qquad (3.68)$$

where $l_i = 1, 2, \ldots, 2N_i + 1$, $I = 1, 2, \ldots, m$ and the centers of fuzzy sets $B_j^{l_1 \ldots l_m}$ are chosen such that

$$
u^{-i \ldots l_m} \begin{cases} \leq 0 & \text{for } I_j = 1, \ldots 1, N \\ = 0 & \text{for } I_j = N_j + 1 \\ \geq 1 & I_j = N_j + 2, \ldots, N_j + 1 \end{cases}
\tag{3.69}
$$

where l_i for $I = 1, 2, \ldots, m$ can take any values from $\{1, 2, \ldots, 2N_i + 1\}$.
The resulting fuzzy controller is:

$$
u_j = -\Phi_j(y) = -\frac{\sum_{l_1=1}^{2N+1} \ldots \sum_{m, l=1}^{2N+1} - I_1 \ldots I_m \left(\Pi_{i=1}^m \mu_{l_i}(y_i) \right)}{\sum_{l_1=1}^{2N+1} \ldots \sum_{l_1=1}^{2N+1} \left(\Pi_{i=1}^m \mu_{l_i}(y_i) \right)}
\tag{3.70} \qquad \text{(3.70)}
$$

where $j = 1, 2, \ldots, m$.

ii. *Input-Output stability study:* Flexibility and simplicity of the fuzzy controller make it popular not only in test cases but also in real industrial applications. Sometimes, it has been observed that fuzzy controllers applied to the nonfuzzy industrial processes, such as warm water plant, heat exchanger system, sinter plant, and so on. Work much better than those of classical nonfuzzy controllers, for example, Direct Digital Computer (DDC) algorithm or propositional, Integral and Derivative (PID) controller. Theattempt of Pappis and Mamdani- for designing a traffic function system indicates that other problems can also be successfully treated in the same method.Kickert and Mamdani have shown that under certain restrictive assumptions the fuzzy controllers can be viewed as a multidimensional (multiple inputs and single-output) multilevel relay. In this framework, a frequency domain stability analysis has been carried out on systems having a fuzzy controller and nonfuzzy modeled process. It has also been shown by them that the fuzzycontroller is virtually reduced to a conventional nonlinear relay type control element. But their methods cannot be generalized to the multivariable system.

The aim of this section is to give generalized Nyquist type stability criteria for single-input single-output (SISO) and multi-input multi-output (MIMO) systems associated with fuzzy logic controllers using the concept of sector bound nonlinearity. Thus, we can overcome the restriction of low-pass linear system which was necessary for stability analysis made by Kickert and Mamdani. As we consider the concept of sector bound nonlinearity of the fuzzy logic controller, it is quite meaningful even in multidimensional case (that is more than one-input and single-output) which was not so meaningfully represented through describing-function method. The present method can also tackle the multivariable problem which Kickert and Mamdani did not consider.

THE FUZZY CONTROLLER AND MULITLEVEL RELAY ANALOGY

The fuzzy sets defined on the positive input range E induce a partition of that input E into regions as shown in Figure29.

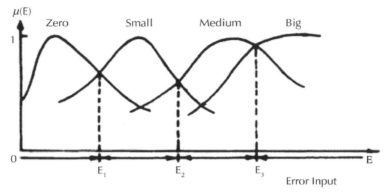

FIGURE 29   Regions corresponding to fuzzy error input set.

The output action corresponding to a particular range of positive input fuzzy sets is shown in Figure30.

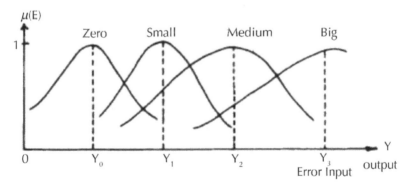

FIGURE 30   Action corresponding to fuzzy output.

The input-output function of this fuzzy control algorithm is shown in Figure31. From Figure31, it is obvious that the fuzzy logic controller can be visualized as a multilevel relay.

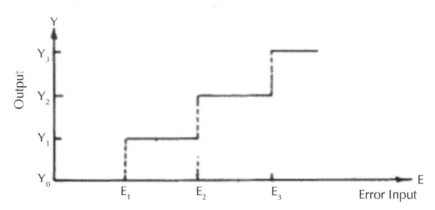

FIGURE 31   Input-output function.

Now, for negative input range E, we get a similar type of output but symmetrically opposite in nature. Hence, the fuzzy logic controller defined over the entire positive and negative range of operation can be

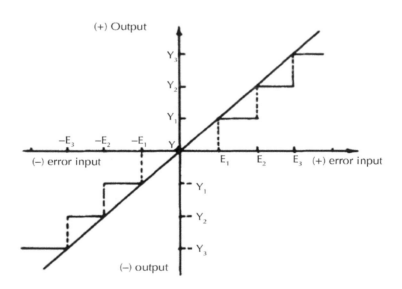

FIGURE 32   Input-output function over positive and negative range of operation.

visualized as multilevel relay which is symmetrical with respect to zero. The total input-output function of the fuzzy logic controller is depicted in Figure32.

In case of feedback control system, the aforesaid positive or negative range of inputs represents the positive or negative range of error inputs to the fuzzy logic controller of a system. A schematic representation of the closed-loop system is given in Figure33. Normally, feedback systems are considered in real application because there

are many disadvantages to the implementation of open-loop control, though apparently it is not impossible to apply, if it is desired to regulate the process in real time.
First of all open-loop process is much too sensitive. In addition, it is not possible to
correct the control as the process evolves since the control does not explicitly depend
on the current state.

MATHEMATICAL IDENTITY BETWEEN FUZZY CONTROLLER ALGORITHM AND A MULTILEVEL RELAY

Before we introduce the concept of sector bound nonlinearity to the fuzzy controller,
we give a brief mathematical exposition that justifies the identity between fuzzy controller and multilevel relay.

Let us consider a fuzzy control algorithm of the following form: if A_i then B_i
, where fuzzy set A_i defined over error input support set E and the fuzzy set on the
contorller's output support set Y and I = 1, ..., N. N represents the number of rules
employed. In the fuzzy controller the error inputs are measured quantities and hence
nonfuzzy in nature. Such input can be treated as degenerated fuzzy set A' with all
membership values $\mu_{A'}$ (E) equal to zero, except the value at the measured point E_0:
$\mu_{A'}$ (E_0) which is equal to one, the compositional rule of inference reduces to

$$\mu_{A'}(y) = \max_E \min\left[\mu_{A'}(E)\mu_s(y,E)\right]$$
$$= \min\left[\mu_{A'}(E_0), \mu_s(y,E_0)\right]$$
$$= \mu_s(y,E_0).$$

We assume that the control action is taken in accordance with the mean of maximum decision method and is represented as follows:

$$y_d = \sum_{j=1}^{j} y_j / J \qquad (3.71)$$

For which

$$\mu_{B'}(y_j) = \max_y \mu_{B'}(y) = \max_y \mu_s(y, E_0)$$

$$= \max_y \max_i \min\left[\mu_{A_i}(E_0); \mu_{B_i}(y)\right] \quad I = 1, ... N \qquad (3.72)$$

where $\mu_{A_i}(E_0)$ is the membership value of the input at the measured point. Let us also assume that all the fuzzy output sets are normal. Hence, the above mentioned (3.72) can be modified as:

$$\max_y \min\left[\max_i \mu_{A_i}(E_0), \mu_{B_i}(y)\right] \qquad (3.73)$$

where is determined from $\mu_{A_{i_0}}(E_0) = \max \mu_{A_i}(E_0)$.

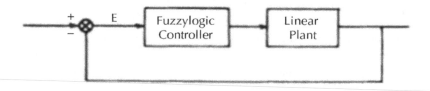

FIGURE 33 Closed loop representation of system associated with fuzzy logic controller.

This latter expression (3.73) indicates that one first decides to which input set A_{i_0} the error input belongs and only works out the corresponding rule (rule number i_0).

By examining the resulting fuzzy output set B_{i_0}, it can be shown that the final computed control action y_d will be the point at which:

$$\mu_{B_{i_0}}(y_d) = \max_y \mu_{B_{i_0}}(y) \qquad (3.74)$$

when one of the following sufficient conditions is satisfied:

- $\mu_{A_{i_0}}(E_0) = 1$
- $\mu_{B_{i_0}}(y)$ is symmetrical around its maximum y_d.

Moreover, when $\max \mu_{A_i}(E_0) = \mu_{A_{i_0}}(E_0)$ for several different the final output y_d will be the mean of the several corresponding maxima y_d.

When a fuzzy output set is not symmetrical (either around zero of its maximum) the algorithm remains a multilevel relay in all other region. Again input lies at a unity membership function is highly improbable in the continuous case and can easily be made impossible in the discrete case.

Fuzzy controller having more than one-input and single-output can be treated in a similar manner and can be shown to be a multidimensional multilevel relay.

FUZZY CONTROLLER AND SECTOR BOUND NONLINEARITY

Let us consider a type of fuzzy logic controller that can be represented by a multilevel relay and that is symmetrical around its maximum value as well as the origin. This type of controller can be represented as shown in Figure 34.

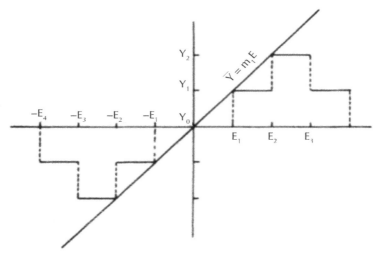

FIGURE 34 Sector Bound fuzzy logic controller that is symmetric around zero and its maximum.

Now, if we draw a line $\bar{y}=m_1E$, then it is apparent from Figure 34 that the entire fuzzy controller is contained in an angle $0\leq m_1E/E \leq Em_1$.

In a similar fashion, we can represent a fuzzy logic controller as shown in Figure32 that is not symmetric around its maximum value, but symmetric around origin.

From Figure32, it is obvious that the entire fuzzy logic controller is contained in an angle. $0\leq m_2E/E \leq m_2$.

Thus, all fuzzy logic controllers which can be represented within the domain of definition of Kickert and Mamdani can be defined as sector bound nonlinearity.

STABILITY ANALYSISWITHSECTOR BOUND NONLINEARITY

To introduce the idea of stability analysis with sector bound nonlinearity of the fuzzy logic controller, we are giving an exposition of the theoretical development of circle criteria for stability analysis of systems with nonlinear feedback.

SISO CASE

Consider a single-input single-output system having transfer-function (TF), g(S) that g(S) that is rational, strictly proper, and asymptotically stable. Let u and y be the system's input and output, respectively, as shown in Figure 35.

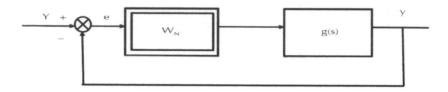

FIGURE 35   The SISO system with nonlinear feedback.

The nonlinear feedback controller of the system satisfies the restriction of the form:

$$K_1 \le (f(E)) \le K_2$$

where K_1 and K_2 are two real numbers that for simplicity we take to be positive.

Definition 3.3 The system is globally and asymptotically stable provided the complete Nyquist locus of g(S) does not enter and encircle in an anticlockwise manner the

closed disc on $(-k_1^{-1}, -k_2^{-1})$ as shown in Figure 36.

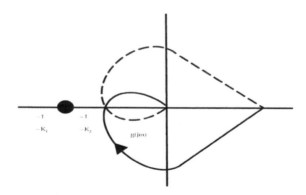

FIGURE 36   Nyquist plot of the nonlinear feedback system.

MIMO CASE

In case multi-input multi-output system, we assume that G(S) is a square m x m, rational, strictly proper transfer-function matrix for an asymptotically stable linear system. Let U and Y be the system's input vector and output vector respectively as shown in Figure 37.

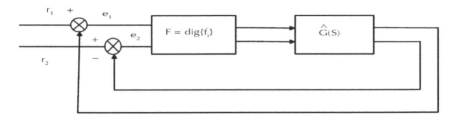

FIGURE 37   The MIMO system with nonlinear feedback.

The nonlinear feedback element of the system F(E, t) is a diagonal matrix, that is:

$$F(E, t) = \text{diag}, \quad f_i \ (E, t), \quad I = 1, 1, \ldots, m$$

where m represents the number of input and output in case of a square system and the functions (E,t) satisfy bounds of the form:

$$k_i \le f_i(E,t) \le k_2, \ldots I = 1, \ 2 \ldots, m$$

Now, we consider the possible generalization of stability criteria for SISO systems to MIMO systems. Here, the MIMO system has been decomposed into a set of SISO subsystems by making the plant diagonally dominant (row dominant or column dominant). It is convenient to work out a MIMO problem in inverse form and hence, the corresponding inverse form of the system's stability criteria (using the inverse Nyquist bands that formally surround the Nyquist plot $\hat{g}_{ii}(jw)$ (inverse of $\hat{g}_{ii}(jw)$) with discs of radius $\hat{r}_i(jw)$, where $\hat{r}_i(jw)$ is represented by (3.75)) can be represented by definition 3.4.

$$\hat{r}_i(jw) = \sum_{\substack{k=1 \\ k \ne 1}}^{m} [|\hat{g}_{ik}(jw)|] , \text{ in case of dominance}$$

$$(3.75)$$

or

$$\hat{r}_i(jw) = \sum_{\substack{k=1 \\ k \ne 1}}^{m} [|\hat{g}_{ki}(jw)|] \text{ in case of dominance.}$$

Definition 3.4 A MIMO system is globally and asymptotically stable provided the Nyquist band of the inverse plant avoids both the origin and the closed disc on

$[-k_1,-k_2]$ as a diameter and encircles (clockwise manner) both same number of times as shown in Figure 38.

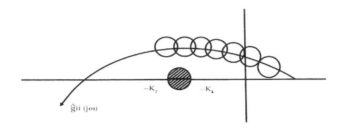

FIGURE 38   Inverse Nyquist Band of nonlinear MIMO feedback system.

STABILITY ANALYSIS WITH SECTOR BOUND FUZZY CONTROLLER

The sector bound nonlinearity of the fuzzy logic controller as discussed in Section 4will degenerate, depending on its slope k_1 that is always zero and , the disc on $[-k_1^{-1},-k_2^{-1}]$ to a straight line passing through k_2^{-1} and parallel to the imaginary axis (in case of a direct plant).

In such case the stability criteria will be modified as follows:

Definition 3.5 A SISO system will be globally and asymptotically stable provided the complete Nyquist locus of g(s) does not enter and encircle in anticlockwise direction the forbidden region left to the line passing through k_2^{-1} as shown in Figure 39.

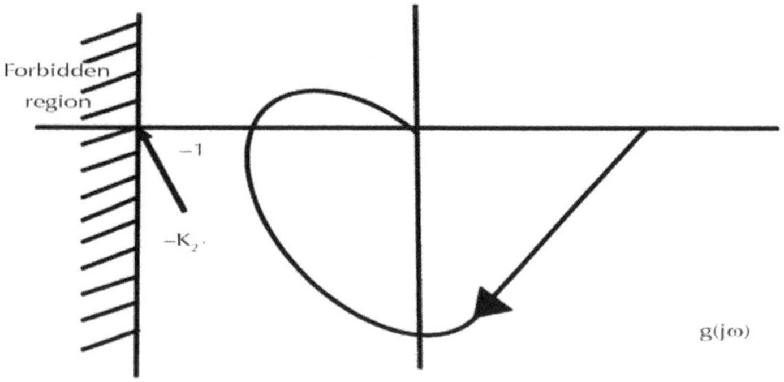

FIGURE 39   Nyquist plot with fuzzy feedback system.

SOFT VERSION OF STABILITY CRITERIA

Definition 3.6 When the disc on $(k_1^{-1},-k_2^{-1})$ degenerated to a straight line parallel to an imaginary axis then for asyumptotical stability the complete Nyquist locus of g(s) will just lie outside the forbidden region.

JUSTIFICATION

In such case, there is no chance for the Nyquist locus of g(s) to encircle the forbidden region without entering into it and once it enters that region the question of encirclement would be meaningless.

EXTENSION TO THE MIMO SYSTEMS

In case of MIMO System, we are considering an inverted system.

The stability criteria will be defined as follows:

Definition 3.7 For asymptotically stability of a MIMO system, the complete inverse Nyquist band avoids both the origin and the closed disc that passes through the

origin with $(-k_1, -k_2)$ as diameter and encircles both the same number of times. Figure40 depicts Definition 3.7.

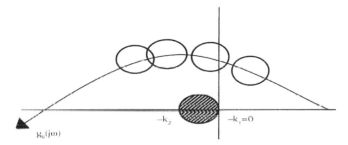

FIGURE 40   Inverse Nyquist band with fuzzy feedback system.

Here, the disc passes through the origin, because one of the slopes,, of the fuzzy logic controller is always zero.

Example 3.10

• A single-input single-output system has been considered.

The transfer-function of the system is given by:

$$G(S) = \frac{1}{(S(S^2 + S + 2))}$$

A set of fuzzy linguistic rules has been generated depending upon the systems open-loop dynamics to control it within the desired limit. Here, the input of the fuzzy logic controller is the error between desired value and measured value and the output

is the system's input change, that is, one-input one-output controller. The slopes k_1

and k_2 of this fuzzy logic controller are 0 and 1.5. The forbidden region and Nyquist locus is shown in Figure41. By definition 5.4 closed-loop system is absolutely stable within the sector (0, 1.5).

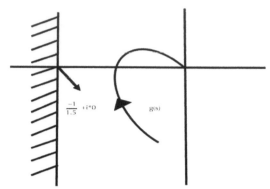

FIGURE 41 Nyquist plot with sector bounded nonlinearity of the fuzzy logic controller.

- Consider a multivariable plant whose transfer-function matrix is given by:

$$G(S) = \begin{bmatrix} \dfrac{1}{(S+1)^3} & \dfrac{1}{2(S+1)^3} \\ \dfrac{1}{(S+2)^3} & \dfrac{3}{2}\dfrac{1}{(S+2)^3} \end{bmatrix}.$$

Inverted version of the plant is given by:

$$\hat{G}(S) = \begin{bmatrix} \dfrac{3}{2}(S+1)^3 & -\dfrac{1}{2}(S+2)^3 \\ -(S+)^3 & (S+2)^3 \end{bmatrix}$$

The open-loop system is column dominant because

$$\frac{3}{2}(\sqrt{w^2}+1)^3 > |-(\sqrt{w^2}+1)^3|$$

and

$$(\sqrt{w^2}+2)^3 > |-\frac{1}{2}(\sqrt{w^2}+2)^3|.$$

Now, our two-input two-output multivariable plant can be treated as a collection of two SISO subsystems.

Table 5 and 6 represent two sets of linguistic tables for the fuzzy controllers of the decoupled subsystems. Here, the inputs of the controllers are error and error sum. The slopes ($(k_1 k_2)$) of the controllers are (0, 1) and (0, 4).

From Figure 42, it is seen that closed-loop system will still remain diagonally dominant and as per definition 3.7 it will be stable.

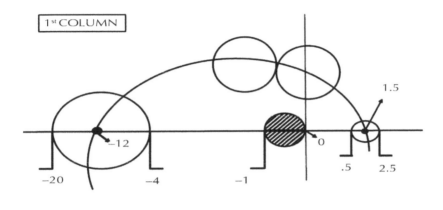

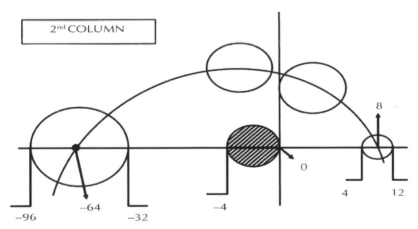

FIGURE 42 Inverse Nyquist band with sector bound nonlinearity of the fuzzy logic controller.

In the case of SISO system, when the frequency domain concept of circle criteria is applied to the sector bound fuzzy logic controller for the stability analysis of a system we do not have to necessarily assume that the system is behaving like a low-pass filter. So from this point of view, our treatment is more generalized than that of Kickert and Mamdani. Kickert and Mamdanihinted that the concept of Popov stability criteria can be applied but they could not extend it to the case of MIMO system. In this section, a more generalized concept, the circle criteria, than Popov concept has been applied to the square MIMO plant having rational and proper transfer-function matrix. Concept of Rosenbrock's diagonal dominance has been applied to the square plant for approximately decoupling it into a set of SISO subsystems. Once the plant is decoupled then the generalization of stability criteria for SISO system has been extended to MIMO problem.

Disadvantages of the present treatment are as follows:
- If the MIMO plant is nonsquare this concept cannot be applied in a straightforward way.
- When the plant is diagonally dominant (DD) (either row or column) it is nice to deal with the plant for stability analysis. But if it isnot DD and it has low dimension, for example, 2 x 2, it can be easily made DD by pre-multiplying the plant with some nonfuzzy gain controller. But if the dimension is 3 or more, inputs/ outputs DD is generally very difficult to achieve and often impossible to obtain without the use of very complicated controllers.
- The condition of DD of inverse plant is only a necessary condition for the application of inverse Nyquist band but certainly not a necessary condition for good system performance or even stability.
- When we compute and plot the DD plant, the entire computation is truncated at some frequency which acts as the end of the frequency list. This is unfortunate because the one possible use for DD would be the reduction of high-frequency interaction. As we truncate at some frequency that is not the true end frequency, uncertainty is introduced there. On the other hand, if we inject high gain at low frequency, required for good steady state accuracy, which will make it non-interactive at that frequency even if the plant is not DD at low frequency.
- A system may have small misalignment angle even though it not DD.

We have explained the above said phenomenon as follows:

$$G(S) = \frac{1}{0.99(S+1)}\begin{bmatrix} 9 & 9 \\ -9 & 99.9 \end{bmatrix}$$

The inverted version of the plant is given by:

$$\hat{G}(S) = \frac{0.99^2(S+1)}{9 \ x \ 108.9}\begin{bmatrix} 99.9 & 8.0 \\ 9 & 9 \end{bmatrix}.$$

Hence, the Gershogorin band based on element $g_{22}(s)$ will go through the origin for both row and column DD.

On the other hand, the eigenvalues of G(S)are:

$$g_1(S) = \frac{10}{S+1}, g_2(S) = \frac{100}{S+1}$$

and the Eigen vectors are:

$$w_1 = \begin{bmatrix} 1 \\ 0.1 \end{bmatrix}, w_2 = \begin{bmatrix} 0.1 \\ 1 \end{bmatrix}$$

leading to the misalignment angles:

$$\theta_i = \cos^{-1} \frac{|(w_i \ e_i)|}{||w_i||} = \cos^{-1} 0.995 = 5.7^o, I = 1,2.$$

The "cybernetic approach" has made available fairly sophisticated methods for analysis, synthesis, and design controller for practical situations. But when confronted with engineering situation in which the control system is to be built and when the controller based on the mathematical model of the system which is to be matched with the situation at hand, the designer must still revert to trial and error methods combined with his own experience and intuition, which is nothing but an effort to find out an approximate reasoning of fuzzy practical situation and which does not follow, all the time the nice mathematical rules. Hence, the fuzzy logic controller that is not based on the mathematical description of the process is gaining importance from application point of view. Moreover, these sorts of controllers are easy to implement in any industrial environment and they are very robust in nature. It is hoped that some additional research work in this direction can extend the concept of the present text to the case where system dynamics are unknown that is, mathematical modeling either in state-space form or in transfer-function form is not variable.

TABLE 5 Linguistic Statements of 1st subsystem

S	E	P S	P M	P B	Z E	N B	N M	N S
P	B	PB	PB	PB	PB	ZE	PS	PM
P	M	PM	PB	PB	PM	NS	NM	PS
P	S	PS	PM	PM	PS	NM	NS	ZE
Z	E	PS	PM	PB	ZE	NB	NM	NS
N	B	NB	NS	PS	NB	NB	NM	NM
N	M	NS	ZE	PS	NM	NB	NB	NB
N	S	ZE	PM	PB	NS	NB	NM	NS

E represents error.
S represents error sum
ZE represents zero.
PS, PM, and PB represent positive small, positive medium, and positive big, respectively.

TABLE 6   Linguistic Statements of 2nd subsystem

S	E	P S	P M	P B	Z E	N B	N M	N S
P	B	PS	PM	PM	PB	ZE	PM	PS
P	M	PM	PM	PM	PS	NS	ZE	PM
P	S	PS	PM	PB	PS	NS	NS	ZE
Z	E	PS	PS	PM	ZE	NB	NM	NS
N	B	NS	NS	ZE	NM	NB	NM	NM
N	M	NS	ZE	PS	NS	NM	NM	NM
N	S	ZE	PS	PS	NS	NB	NM	NS

Optimal Controller Design: The stable controller determines the range for fuzzy controller parameters for which the stability is guaranteed, however, it does not show how to determine specific values of the parameters. On the other hand, optimalcontro llerdetermines the specific values of the fuzzy controller parameters such that certain performance criterion is minimized.

From the stable fuzzy controller (3.70), we define the fuzzy basis functions $b(x) = b(x)..b_N(x))^T$ as:

$$b_1(x) = -\frac{\Pi_{i=1}^{n}\mu_{A_i^{1_i}}(y_i)}{\Sigma_{1_1=1}^{2N+1}...\Sigma_{m^{1}=1}^{2N+1}\left(\Pi_{i=1}^{m}\mu_{A_i^{1_i}}(y_i)\right)} \qquad (3.76)$$

where $1_i = 1,2 . ...,$ $2N_i + 1$, $1 = 1,2$, N and $N = \Pi_{i=1}^{n}(2N_i + 1)$. Define an m × N parameter matrix Θ as

$$\Theta = \begin{bmatrix} -\Theta_1^T \\ ... \\ -\Theta_m^T \end{bmatrix} \qquad (3.77)$$

Where $\Theta_j^t \in R^{1\times N}$ consists of the N parameters $u_j^{-1_1...1_n}$ for $1_j = 1,2, ..., 2 N_i+1$ in the same ordering as $b_i(x)$ for $1 = 1,2, ..., N$. Then the fuzzy controller $u = (u_1, ..., u_m)^T$ can be expressed as

$$u = \Theta b(x) \qquad (3.78)$$

Substituting (3.78) into (3.60), the closed-loop system is obtained as

$$x(t) = Ax(t) + B \; \Theta \; (t) \, b(x(t)) \tag{3.79}$$

where the arameter atrix is assumed to be time-varying. The optimal control problem can then be formulated to minimize the following performance criterion

$$J = \frac{1}{2} x^t (T) \, Sx(T) + \frac{1}{2} \int_0^T \left[x^t Qx + b^t (x) \Theta^t b(x) \right] dt \tag{3.80}$$

Thus, the problem of designing the optimal fuzzy controller becomes the problem of determining the optimal $\Theta(t)$, which can be solved by applying the Pontryagin maximum principle. Specifically, by minimizing the Hamiltonian function

$$H\left(x, p, \Theta = x^t (T) x^t Qx + b^t \; \Theta^t \; R \, \Theta \, b + p^t \left(\Lambda x + B \, \Theta \, b \right) \right) \tag{3.81}$$

The optimal fuzzy controller parameter matrix is obtained as

$$\Theta^* (t) = -\frac{1}{2} R^{-1} B^T p^* b^T \left(x^* \right) \left[b \left(x^* \right) \left(b^T \left(x^* \right) \right) \right]^{-1} \tag{3.82}$$

where x and p are the solution of the Hamiltonian system:

$$x^* = \frac{\partial H\left(x^*, p^*, \Theta^* \right)}{\partial p}, \quad x(0) = x_0 \tag{3.83}$$

$$p^* = \frac{\partial H\left(x^*, p^*, \Theta^* \right)}{\partial x}, \quad p(T) = Sx(T)$$

and thus the optimal fuzzy controller is

$$u^* = \Theta^* (t) b(x) \tag{3.84}$$

We note that the optimal fuzzy controller (3.84) is a state feedback controller with time-varying parameters.

    iii. *Sliding mode controller design:* For a single input and single output continuous nonlinear system with n state variables, the companion form is as follow[190]:

$$\dot{x}^{(n)} (t) = f\left(X(t)\right) + b\left(X(t)\right) u(t) + d(t) \tag{3.85}$$

and

$$y(t) = x(t) \text{ for } t \geq 0 \tag{3.86}$$

where the state vector is:

$X(t) = \left[x(t), \dot{x}(t), \ldots, x^{(n-1)}(t) \right]^T$, $u(t)$ is the control output, $y(t)$ is the system output and $d(t)$ is an external disturbance. If the reference output is $y_r(t)$, the above dynamic equations can be transferred into the above dynamic equations can be transferred into the following state equations with error signal $e_1(t) = y(t) - y_r(t)$ and its derivatives as state variables:

$$\dot{e}_1(t) = e_2(t)$$
$$\dot{e}_2(t) = e_3(t)$$
$$\vdots \qquad\qquad \text{for } t > 0 \tag{3.87}$$
$$\dot{e}_n(t) = f(E(t)) + b(E(t))u(t) + d(t)$$

Let $E(t) = \left[e_1(t), e_2(t), \ldots e_n(t) \right] \in R$ and $\delta \in R$. A linear functional $s: E \rightarrow \delta$ is defined by

$$S(t) = CE(t) \tag{3.88}$$

Where $C = [c_1, c_2, \ldots c_{n-1}, 1]$ (c_i s are all real numbers).
Then, a sliding hyperplane can be represented as $s(t) = 0$ or

$$c_1 e + (t)_1 + c_2 e_2(t) + e_n(t) = 0 \tag{3.89}$$

The scalar $s(t)$ of (3.88) is defined as the distance to the $s(t)$ hyperplane of (3.89).
The motion sliding on the sliding hyperplane is commonly referred to as a sliding mode.
If the following condition is satisfied with the designed control input, the just mentioned requirements on the state trajectories can be fulfilled:

$$s(t)\dot{s}(t) < 0 \tag{3.90}$$

where represents the time derivative of $s(t)$ inequality of (3.90) is called the reaching condition of sliding control for continuous systems under which the state will move toward and reach a sliding surface.

If the control input is so designed that the inequality $s(t)\dot{s}(t) < 0$ is satisfied, together with the properly chosen sliding hyperplane, the state will be driven toward the origin of the state space along the sliding hyperplane from any given initial state. This is the way of SMC that guarantee asymptotic stability of the systems.

The discretization form of (3.85) with first order approximation is as follow:

$$x_1(k+1) = x_1(k) + Tx_2(k)$$

$$x_2(k+1) = x_2(k) + Tx_3(k)$$

$$\cdot$$
$$\cdot$$
$$\cdot$$
$$\cdot$$
$$\cdot$$

$$x_{n-1}(k+1) = x_{n-1}(k) + Tx_n(k)$$

$$x_n(k+1) = x_n(k) + Tf(X(k)) + Tb(X(k))u(k) + Td(t) \quad \text{(3.91) (a)}$$

and

$$y(k) = x_1(k), \text{ for } k = 0, 1T, 2T, \ldots, nT \qquad \text{(3.91) (b)}$$

(T is the sampling rate

Where $X(k) = [x_1(k), x_2(k), \ldots, x_n(k)]^T$

is defined similar to that in continuous time domain

$$s(k) = CX(k). \qquad (3.92)$$

where $C = [c_1, c_2, \ldots, c_{n-1}, 1]$ (c_is are all real numbers), $s(k) = 0$ is the so-called hyperplane which is equivalent to the sliding surface in continuous time. Since, it cannot be ensured that the states remain on the surface for all time because of the discretization, it is also called quasi-sliding mode. Again, C is chosen such that the system is asymptotically stable while being on the hyperplane.

One way to evaluate, C is to use the pole placement method. The system has to be written in its controllability canonical form and the final state can be represented in terms of remaining when saying on the sliding surface S.

In discrete case, discretization form of (3.90) will be:

$$s(k)[s(k+1)-s(k)]<0 \qquad (3.93)$$

This is the necessary reaching condition for the sliding mode control, it only makes the sliding, motion toward the sliding surface.

In order to satisfy the reaching, the following inequality has to be satisfied to meet the requirement of the sufficient reaching condition for the existence of a sliding motion, too.

$$|s(k+1)|<|s(k)| \qquad (3.94)$$

The combination of (3.93) and (3.94) can make sure the sliding motion convergent.

Just as in continuous time, in discrete time, equivalent controlis designed to try to keep the system on sliding surface which is represented as:

$$s(k+1)=s(k) \qquad (3.95)$$

and the switching term, $u_s(k)$ is designed to (satisfy the reaching condition (3.93) and (3.94) overcome the external disturbance and reaching the stable state.

However, the most disadvantage of using SMC is the chattering phenomenon. Because a discontinuous switching control is applied to the plant, chattering always appears as a source to excite the unmodelled high frequency dynamics of the controlled system. One commonly used method to eliminate the chattering is to replace the relay control by a saturating approximation. Another method is to apply fuzzy control to the SMC system such that a smooth and reasonable hitting control can be generated to reduce the chattering.

The purposed fuzzy control is called fuzzy sliding mode control (FSMC) as it is based on the principle of SMC. Here, an FSMC for discrete nonlinear systems is proposed.

For the discrete time system (3.91), assume that the sliding surface is:

$$s(k)=\sum_{i=1}^{n}c_i x_i(k) \qquad (3.96)$$

where $c_i > 0$, $i = 1, 2,....,n$ And we can get:

So from (3.93), the necessary reaching condition is as follow:

$$s(k)s(k+1)-s(k))$$

$$=\sum_{i=1}^{n}c_i x_i(k)\left(\sum_{i=1}^{n}c_i x_i(k+1)-\sum_{i=1}^{n}c_i x_i(k)\right) \qquad (3.97)$$

$$= \sum_{i=1}^{n} c_i x_i(k) \left(\sum_{i=1}^{n} c_i x_i(k) + c_n f(X(k)) + c_n b\big(X(k)\big) u(k) + c_n d(k) \right) T < 0$$

Suppose that c_n is positive and is negative, (3.97) presents that as is positive, increasing $u(k)$ will result in decreasing $s(k)s(k+1) - s(k)$ and that as is negative, decreasing will result in decreasing $s(k)s(k+1) - s(k)$. On the other hand, suppose $c_n b(X)$ is positive, (3.97) denotes that decreasing will cause decreasing $s(k)[s(k+1) - s(k)] < 0$, as $s(k)$ is positive, and increasing $u(k)$ will cause decreasing $s(k)s(k+1) - s(k))$, as $s(k)$ is negative. Therefore, all such statements above can be summarized as a fuzzy rule base used in FLC. The design of a fuzzy sliding mode controller is given below with respect to Inverted Pendulum problem. Here, the mathematical description of the system is little different from the one stated in Example 3.8.

Note that the control law should meet the requirement for the sufficient reaching condition (3.89) too.

Example 3.11 The inverted pendulum is often used as a benchmark for all kinds of controllers, it is a nonlinear unstable system which makes it challenge to control. The system is composed of a rigid pole and a cart on which the pole is hinged to the cart on which the pole is hinged to the cart through a pivot such that it has only one degree of freedom. The goal of the control is to make the pole upright.

The dynamic model equations for the plant are:

$$M\ddot{x} + N = u \tag{3.98}$$

$$N = m\ddot{x} + ml\ddot{\theta} \cos\theta - ml\dot{\theta}^2 \sin\theta \tag{3.99}$$

$$P - mg = -ml\left(\ddot{\theta} \sin\theta + \dot{\theta}^2 \cos\theta\right) \tag{3.100}$$

$$I\ddot{\theta} = Pl \sin\theta \, 0 \, Nl \cos\theta \tag{3.101}$$

where M is the mass of the cart, m is the mass of the of the pendulum, $I = (1/3)ml^2$ is the moment of the inertia of the pendulum, θ is the angular position of the pendulum deviated from the equilibrium position, x is the position of the cart, l is the half length of the pendulum. The system friction is omitted for simplicity.

The dynamic equation of θ can be rewritten as

$$\left[(M+m)\left(ml^2 + I\right) - (ml\cos\theta)^2\right]\ddot{\theta} + \left(ml\,\dot{\theta}\right)^2 \cos\theta \sin\theta - (M+m)ml\sin\theta + ml\cos\theta u = 0 \quad (3.102)$$

If we define $x_1 = \theta$ and $x_2 \theta$, then the first order approximation of the plant plus zero order hold for the sampling representative of (4.5) can be expressed as

$$x_1(k + 1) = x_1(k) + Tx_2(k)$$

$$x_2(k+1) = x_2(k) + T\left[\frac{(M+m)mlg\sin x_1(k)}{M+m)(ml^2+I)-(ml\cos x_1(k))^2} - \frac{(ml(k))^2\cos x_1(k)\sin x_1(k)}{(M+m)(ml^2+I)-(ml\cos x_1(k))^2} - \frac{ml\cos x_1(k)u(k)}{(M+m)(ml^2+I)-(ml\cos x_1(k))^2}\right] \quad (3.103)$$

(T is the sampling rate).

CONTROLLER DESIGN

The expression for the linear functional s(k) is chosen as:

$$S(k) = c_1 x_1(k) + x_2(k) = 0 \quad\quad\quad (3.104)$$

The corresponding sliding hyperplane is represented by:

$$S(k) = c_1 x_1(k) + x_2(k) = 0 \quad\quad\quad (3.105)$$

Review the necessary and sufficient reaching conditions

$$S(k)\left(s(k + 1) - s(k)\right) < 0 \quad\quad\quad (3.106)$$

and

$$\left| s(k + 1) \right| < \left| s(k) \right| \quad\quad\quad (3.107)$$

S, ΔS, $\Delta|S|$, and ΔU are the fuzzy variables of s(k), (s(k + 1) – s(k)), | s(k + 1) – s(k)| and control variable increment Δu, respectively. The membership functions for S, ΔS, $\Delta|S|$, and ΔU are chosen to be in the shape of triangular type.

From (3.103), we know:

$$b = -T\left[\frac{ml\cos x_1(k)}{(M+m)(ml^2+1)-(ml\cos x_1(k))^2}\right] < 0, \text{for} -\frac{\pi}{2} < x_1(k) < \frac{\pi}{2}$$

which is the same as assumption in (3.106).

Then the fuzzy rules described in controller design are further detailed as follow:
- Ifs(k) > 0 and - s(k) < s(k + 1) < s(k), increasing u(k) will strengthen (3.106) and meet the sufficient condition (3.107).
- If s(k) > 0 and s(k + 1) > s(k), greatly increasing u(k) will be helpful to reach the conditions of (3.106) and (3.107).

- $s(k) > 0$ and $s(k + 1) < - s(k)$, reasonably decreasing $u(k)$ will be helpful to meet the sufficient reaching requirement of (3.107).
- If $s(k) < 0$ and $s(k) < s(k + 1) < - s(k)$, decreasing $u(k)$ will strengthen (3.106) and meet the sufficient condition (3.107).
- If $s(k) < 0$ and $- s(k + 1) > - s(k)$, greatly increasing $u(k)$ will be helpful to meet (3.107).
- If $s(k) < 0$ and $s(k + 1) < s(k)$, reasonably decreasing $u(k)$ will be helpful to meet (3.106) and (3.107).

SIMULATION RESULTS

The parameters of the inverted pendulum for simulation are $l = 0.5$m, $M = 2$ kg, and m $= 0.3$ kg. And the coefficient c_1 is chosen as $c_1 = 6$. The initial conditions of the inverted pendulum are supposed to be: (a) $\theta = - 1$ and $\omega = 1$, and (b) $\theta = 0.5$ and $\omega = 1$ at $t = 2.5$ second, an external disturbance with $d(t) = 20$ is added to the pendulum to verify the robustness of the controller [190]. The simulation results with the proposed FSMC are shown on Figure 43 (a) and (b).

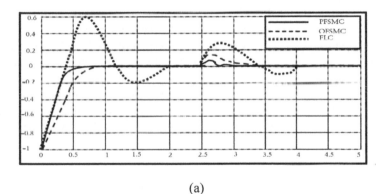

(a)

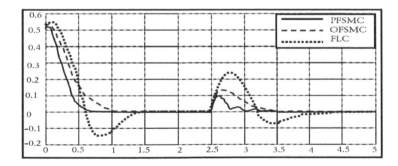

(b)

FIGURE 43   Simulation results of fuzzy sliding mode control.

v. Fuzzy Bang-Bang control: Classical linear feedback control theory is useful for regulation problems with small errors. Therefore, it is usually necessary to design a separate tracking controller for the system to accomplish large movements. Traditional design approach uses a two-stage control. During the first stage, when the actuator is underdoing large accessing motion, (the control algorithm may be designed by using the target position) the controller is switched to a regulation stage and conventional feedback control algorithms may be employed to obtain a high performance closed loop response. These approaches seem feasible theoretically, however, the transition between the accessing stage and regulation stage can be rather rough, and make the system hard to settle[30].

Many techniques have been used in industry to achieve a smooth transition between the control modes. Some people have tried to feed the error signal to the regulation controller before switching in order to minimize the effect of the wrong initial condition. Others insert a third controller, called the "setting controller", to damp out the transitional overshoot. In 1987, Workman et al. proposes the so called "Proximate Time-Optimal Servomechanism (PTOS)". The method utilizes a nonlinear state feedback law with which the feedback gain can be made equal to the regulation control during transition between the accessing and the following modes.

In this section, a new class of nonlinear saturated control methodology is discussed. The method is based on the classical time optimal bang–bang control(Suitable nonlinear control action can be superior to the linear control action). While preserving the original time optimal characteristics of the classical bang–bang control, the new method does not inherit the chattering and steady state offset problem often encountered in the traditional suboptimal switching control approach. A fuzzy approach is used for the controller implementation.

THE STRUCTURE OF FLC

The implementation of the proposed control algorithm used a fuzzy controller for making judgment on whether the state is close to the switching surface.

A fuzzy logic controller comprises five principle components(as shown in Figure 44):

- A fuzzifier, which transforms real numbers into fuzzy set(fuzzy vectors)according to membership function provided by the data base,
- A database, which provides the membership function of fuzzy set to use in fuzzifier and defuzzifier,
- A real base, which provides the control rules to be used in the inference engine,
- An inference engine, which performs the fuzzy reasoning upon the fuzzy vectors provided by the fuzzifier and the rules provided by the rule base, and
- A defuzzifier, which transforms the outcome of the inference engine into real numbers to provide single valued signals. The weighted average method is computational simple and efficient. We will use this method as the defuzzification method in this Section [30].

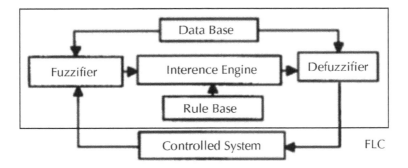

FIGURE 44   The structure of fuzzy control.

*Example 3.12*An example of the time optimal position control of a DC motor is used to illustrate the implementation and to evaluate the performance of the algorithm. The model for the position control of a DC motor is given in Equation3.108

$$\dot{X} = AX + BU \tag{3.108}$$

where where $A = \begin{bmatrix} 0 & 1 \\ 0 & -1 \end{bmatrix}, B = \begin{bmatrix} 0 \\ 1 \end{bmatrix}$ $X = \begin{bmatrix} x_1 \\ x_2 \end{bmatrix}$

If u is bounded, one may assume $|u| \le 1$ without losing generality.

According to the maximum principle of Pontryagain, the switching curve of this system is s=0

$$\text{where } S = x_1 + \frac{1}{a} x_2 - Sgn(x_2) \frac{1}{a} Ln\left(1 + |x_2|\right) \tag{3.109}$$

INPUT VARIABLE

In this system, the time-optimalcontrol to move a state to zero is known to consist of two parts:

(1) From the state to the switching curve and

(2) Along the switching curve to zero.

Let S_1 and S_2 be the trajectory length of (1) and (2) respectively.S_1 and S_2 are assumed to be negative and positive respectively if the state lies above the switching curve, as shown in Figure45.

Thus, given a state, say (y_1, y_2), S_1, and S_2, used as the input variable of the fuzzy controller are:

$$S_1 = -\text{Sgn}(S) \int_0^{\frac{1}{a}} \sqrt{\left(1+a^2\right)\left(y_2 + \frac{1}{a}\right)^2 e^{-2at} - \frac{2}{a}\left(y_2 + \frac{1}{a}\right)e^{-at} + \frac{1}{a^2}} \, dt \quad (3.110)$$

$$S_2 = -\text{Sgn}(S) \int_{Ln}^0 \sqrt{\left(1+\frac{1}{a^2}\right)e^{-2at} - \frac{2}{a^2}e^{-at} + \frac{1}{a^2}} \, dt \quad (3.111)$$

$$\text{where } X_B = \sqrt{\frac{1}{a^2} - \frac{1}{a}\left(y_2 + \frac{1}{a}\right)e^{-a^2 y_1 - ay_2}} \quad (3.112)$$

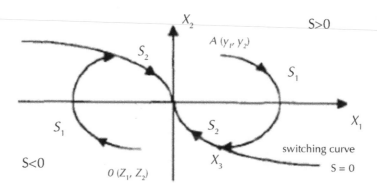

FIGURE 45   Trajectory of S_1 and S_2.

DATA BASE

The membership function of fuzzy sets S_1 and S_2 is depicted in Figure46.Specified on domains of S_1 and S_2 are five fuzzy sets: PL,PS, ZR, NS,andNL, where P,N,ZR,S, and L correspond to positive, negative ,zero small, and large,respectively.Thus, for instance, NL stand for "negative large" and PS stands for "positive small" and so on.In the same manner, we also define five sets on the domain of input u.Figure 47 illustrates the membership function of these fuzzy sets.

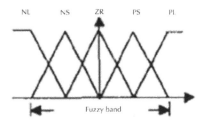

FIGURE 46   Membership function of S_1 and S_2.

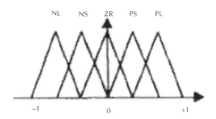

FIGURE 47   Membership function of u.

DETERMINATION OF THE MAXIMUM VALUE OF FUZZY BAND

Given an allowable final target state error $|x_1| \le e_1$ and $|x_2| \le e_2$, then the fuzzy band can be found as follows: The value of S_2(defined as S_2) at the intersection of $x_2 = e_2$ and $S = 0$(point a) is the maximum value of the fuzzy band in MSF of S_1. The area a b c d is half of the fuzzy zone. By symmetry, the whole fuzzy zone is shown in Figure48.

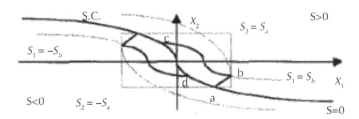

FIGURE 48   The maximum fuzzy band determination.

RULE BASE

The control rules for OPEM are described on human's driving behavior. For example, a typical rule might be:

 IF S_1 is Positive Small AND S_2 is Negative Large
 THEN the effort is Negative Large

Which means, when the state lies near and below the switching curve while still far away from the origin, a large negative effort is applied in order to attain the Bang–Bang type strategy Another typical rule may be:

IF S_1 is Positive Small and S_2 is Negative Small

THEN the effort is Negative Small

Which means, when the state lies near the target and below the switching curve, a small negative effort is used to drive the state to the origin in order to avoid chattering.

Based on the designer's judgment, seventeen control rules are formed. The rule base is shown in Table 7.

TABLE 7   Rule base

S1

	NL	NS	ZR	PS	PL
PL	NL	NL	PL		
PS	NL	PS	PS		
S2 ZR	NL	ZR	ZR	ZR	PL
NS			NS	NS	PL
NL			NL	NL	PL

RESULT AND DISCUSSION

For comparison purposes, the simulation results based on the classical time optimal Bang–Bang control is shown in Figure49.Chattering phenomenon and steady state offset exist near the target position. The effectiveness of the suggested controller over Bang–Bang algorithm is illustrated in Figure50,with the fuzzy band set to 0.001 (Figure50(d)).It is found that the chattering phenomenon can be restrained(Figure50(a) (b)) and the trajectory eventually enters a region around the target and stays there from then on(Figure50(c)).If the fuzzy band is reduced to 0.0005 (Figure51(d)), it is found that the state may run across the boundary of the fuzzy zone (Figure51(c)).That is, chattering occurs(Figure51(a)(b)).This is because too large a sampling period is used. The input effort u is decided only at each sampling instance: the effort u is then preserved at a constant value during that sampling interval. Therefore, the input effort may drive the state out of the fuzzy zone if too long a sampling period is selected.

There are two ways to avoid the phenomenon. The first is to decrease the sampling rate, and the second is to tune Membership functions (MSF) of S1 and S2.

The method of tuning MSF is as follows:

When the state comes into fuzzy zone, the magnitude of the input effort is decreased to a much smaller value. Thus, during the following sampling interval(the control effort is uncontrollable),the state is then be driven more slowly and may stay in the fuzzy zone. This can be obtained by appropriately adjusting membership function such as in (Figure52(d)).The simulation result for the tuned MSF case is illustrated in Figure 52.It is found that the chattering phenomenon disappears (Figure52(a)(b)) and the final states still stay in the fuzzy zone(Figure52(c)).

A new method for nonlinear saturated control is proposed. The method is based on the classical time optimal bang–bang control. While preserving the original time optimal characteristics of the classical bang–bang control,the new method does not encounter the chattering and steady state offset problem. A fuzzy controller is utilized for the controller implementation. The method is inherently robust.

The proposed controller emerges from the concept of successively suppressing dimensions of the state space and finally reducing to the target point. The feedback signal for the fuzzy logic controller is based on the distance from the present state to the switching surface along the optimal trajectory. In order to avoid chattering, the control effort is decreased as the distance approaches zero: however, once the state moves past the switching surface, the feedback signal is measured along a different path and a full power control is again used. This avoids the state to wonder around the switching surface thus eliminating the chattering phenomenon.Numerical simulation of both the proposed controller and the traditional Bang–Bang controller behavior are also presented to demonstrate the advantages of the new approach.

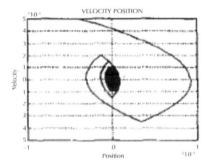

(a). Magnified phase plane near target.

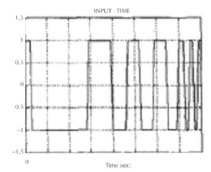

(b). Time history of effort.

FIGURE 49   *(continued)*

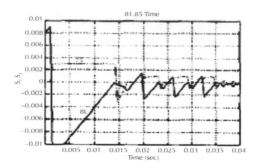

(c) Time history of S₁ and S₂

FIGURE 49   Simulation results based on the Bang–Bang controller.

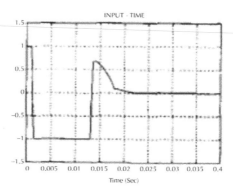

(a). Magnified phase plane near target.

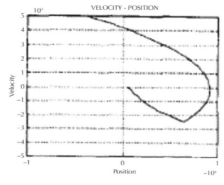

(b). Time history of effort.

FIGURE 50   *(continued)*

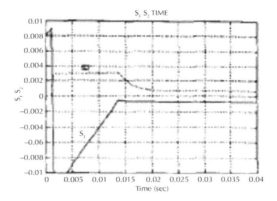

(c). Time history of S_1 and S_2

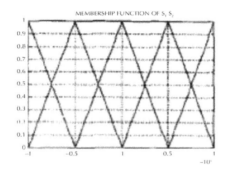

(d). MSF of S_1 and S_2

FIGURE 50   Simulation results based on the suggested controller.

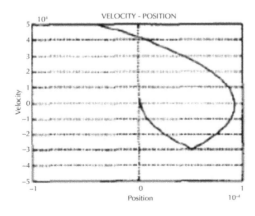

(a). Magnified phase plane near target.

FIGURE 51   *(continued)*

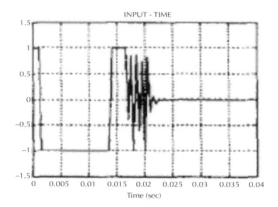

(b). Time history of effort.

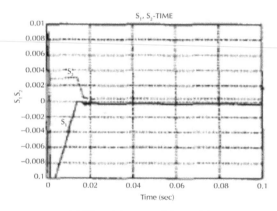

(c)Time history of S_1 and S_2.

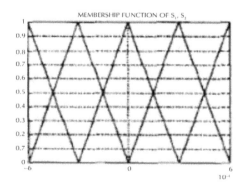

(d) MSF of S_1 and S_2.

FIGURE 51   Simulation results based on OPEM with fuzzy band decreased to 0.005.

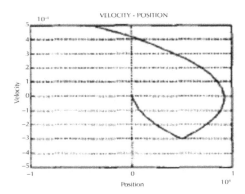

(a). Magnified phase plane near target.

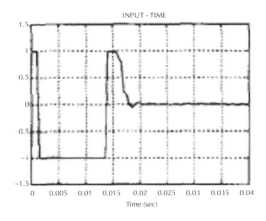

(b). Time history of effort.

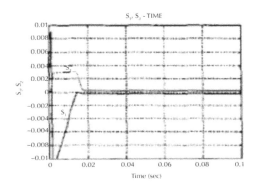

(c). Time history of S_1 and S_2.

FIGURE 52   *(continued)*

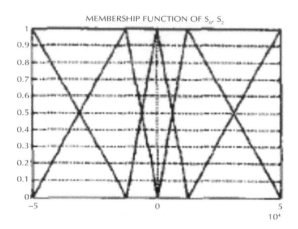

(d). MSF of S_1 and S_2.

FIGURE 52   Simulation results of turn MSF based on OPEM with 0.005 as fuzzy band.

---

vi. Supervisory Controller Design: The fuzzy control systems discussed above are all single-loop (or single-level) controllers. For complex systems, the single-loop control systems may not effectively achieve the control objectives, and multi-level control structure becomes a necessity. The low level controllers perform fast direct control and the higher-level controllers perform low-speed supervision.

There are two types of two-level controls:

a)   Low-level fuzzy control and high-level nonfuzzy supervisory control, and

b)   Low-levelnonfuzzy control and high-level fuzzy supervisory control.(See Figure53).

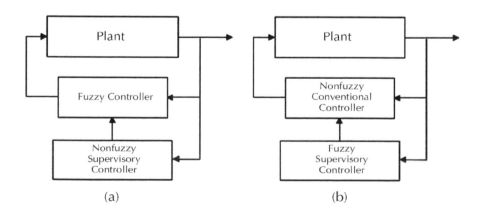

       (a)   (b)

FIGURE 53   Two level fuzzy control systems. (a) Fuzzy-local nonfuzzy-supervisory control, (b) nonfuzzy-local fuzzy supervisory control

In the two-level control system in Figure53(a), the fuzzy controller can be designed without considering stability and the supervisory controller can be designed to ensure the stability and other performance requirements. In this way, there is much freedom in choosing the fuzzy controller parameters and consequently, the design of the fuzzy controller is simplified. Since, the fuzzy controller is to perform the main control action, the supervisory control will play a supplementary action, that is, if the fuzzy controller works well,m the supervisory control will be idle, if the fuzzy control system tends to be unstable, the supervisory controller starts working to enforce stability.

Consider the nonlinear system

$$x^{(n)} = f\left(x, \dot{x}, ..., x^{(n-1)}\right) + g\left(x, \dot{x}, ... x^{(n-1)}u\right) \qquad (3.113)$$

where $x \in R$ is the output, $u \in R$ is the control, $\left(x, \dot{x}, ..., x^{(n-1)}\right)^T$ is the vector, and f and g are unknown nonlinear function with $g > 0$ assumed. This type of system can be linearized with nonlinear feedback and a stable linear controller can be designed.

Suppose, a fuzzy controller is already designed and we want to guarantee the stability of the closer-loop system in the sense that the state x is uniformly bounded, that is $|x(t)| \le M_x, \forall t > 0$, where M_x, is a constant.

This can be achieved by supplementing a supervisory controller to the fuzzy controller:

$$u = u_{fuzz}\left(x\right) + I * u_s\left(x\right) \qquad (3.114)$$

where the indicator function $I^* = 1$ if $|x| \ge M_x$ and $I^* = 0$ if $|x| \le M_x$. The goal is now to design the supervisory controller u_s such that $|x| \le M_x$ for all $t > 0$.

The closed-loop system then becomes:

$$x^{(n)} = f\left(x\right) + g\left(x\right)u_{fuzz}\left(x\right) + g\left(x\right)I * u_s\left(x\right) \qquad (3.115)$$

The feedback linearization controller for the system (3.113) is given by:

$$u_{FL} = \frac{1}{g(x)}\left[-f(x) - k^T(x)\right] \qquad (3.116)$$

Where $\mathbf{k} = \left(k_n, ..., k_1\right)^T \in R^n$ is such that all roots of the polynomial $S^n + k_1 S^{n-1} + ... + k_n$ are in the left-half complex plane.

The system (3.115) is then rewritten as:

$$x^{(n)} = -k^T x + gx \left[u_{fuzz} - u_{FL} + I^* u_s \right] \qquad (3.117)$$

or, in the matrix form,

$$\dot{x} = \wedge x + b \left[u_{fuzz} - u_{FL} + I^* u_s \right] \qquad (3.118)$$

where

$$\wedge = \begin{bmatrix} 0 & 1 & 0 & 0 & \dots & 0 & 0 \\ 0 & 0 & 1 & 0 & \dots & 0 & 0 \\ \dots & \dots & \dots & \dots & \dots & \dots \\ 0 & 0 & 0 & 0 & \dots & 1 & 1 \\ -k_n & \dots & \dots & \dots & -k_1 \end{bmatrix}, b = \begin{bmatrix} 0 \\ \dots \\ 0 \\ g \end{bmatrix} \qquad (3.119)$$

The supervisory controller u_s can be designed to guarantee $|x| \le M_x$ for all $t > 0$ by introducing a Lyapunov function

$$V = \tfrac{1}{2} x^T P_x \qquad (3.120)$$

where P is a symmetric positive definite matrix satisfying the Lyapunov equation

$$\wedge^T P + P \wedge = -Q \qquad (3.121)$$

where Q is specified by the designer. Using (3.119) and (3.121), we have:

$$\dot{V} = -\tfrac{1}{2} x^T Q x + g_L Pb \left[u_{fuzz} - u_{FL} + u_s \right] \le x^T Pb \left[|u_{fuzz}| + |u_{FL}| \right] + x^T Pb \, u_S \qquad (3.122)$$

The supervisory controller u_s can be designed such that $\dot{V} \le 0$ by choosing:

$$u_s = -\text{sign} \left(x^T Pb \left[\frac{1}{g_L} \left(f^u + k^T x | \right) + u_{fuzz} \, \| \right] \right) \qquad (3.123)$$

where f^U and g_L are the upper and lower bounds of f and g, respectively.

Since, the indicator function is a step function it may cause chattering at the boundary $|x| = M_x$, and this can be avoided by defining a continuous function:

$$I^* = \begin{cases} 0 & |x| \le a \\ \dfrac{|x| - a}{M_x - a} & a \le |x| \le M \\ 1 & |x| \ge M \end{cases}, \qquad (3.124)$$

Example 3.13. In this section, we apply a fuzzy controller with the supervisory controller to the inverted pendulum balancing problem. The control goal is to balance the inverted pendulum and at the same time guarantee that the state is bounded within a fixed interval. Let $x_1 = q$ be the angle of the pendulum with respect to the vertical line and $x_2 = \dot{\theta}$, the dynamic equations of the inverted pendulum system are [237]

$$\dot{x}_1 = x_2 \qquad (3.125)$$

$$\dot{x}_2 = \frac{-g \sin x_1 - \dfrac{mlx \dfrac{2}{2} \cos x_1 \sin x_1}{m_c + m}}{1\left(\dfrac{4}{3} - \dfrac{m \cos^2 \times 1}{m_c + m}\right)} + \frac{\dfrac{\cos x_1}{m_c + m}}{1\left(\dfrac{4}{3} - \dfrac{m \cos^2 \times 1}{m_c + m}\right)} u \qquad (3.126)$$

where $g = 9.8$ m/s^2 is the acceleration due to gravity, m_c is the mass of cart, m is the mass of pole, l is the half length of pole and u is the applied force (control). We choose $m_c = 1$kg, m = 0.1 kg, and l=0.5 m in the following simulations.

Assume that the fuzzy controller u_f is constructed from the following four fuzzy IF-THEN rules:

IF x_1 is positive and x_2 is positive:
Then u is negative big   (3.127)
IF x_1 is positive and x_2 is negative:
THEN u is zero   (3.128)
IF x_1 is negative and x_2 is positive:
THEN u is zero   (3.129)
IF x_1 is negative and x_2 is negative:
THEN u is positive big   (3.130)
Where the fuzzy sets "positive," "negative," "negative big," "zero," and"positive big" are characterized by the following membership functions, respectively

$$\mu_{\text{positive}}(x) = \frac{1}{1 + e^{-30x}} \qquad (3.131)$$

$$\mu_{positive}(x) = \frac{1}{1+e^{30x}} \tag{3.132}$$

$$\mu_{negative}(u) = e^{-(u+5)^2} \tag{3.133}$$

$$\mu_{zero}(u) = e^{-u^2} \tag{3.134}$$

$$\mu_{positive\,big}(u) = e^{-(u-5)^2} \tag{3.135}$$

Using center average defuzzifier and product inference, we obtain the fuzzy controller as:

$$u_f(x_1,x_2) = \left(5\frac{1}{1+e^{30x_1}}\frac{1}{1+e^{30x_2}} - 5\frac{1}{1+e^{-30x_1}}\frac{1}{1+e^{-30x_2}}\right) \Big/ \left(\frac{1}{1+e^{30x_1}}\frac{1}{1+e^{30x_2}} + \frac{1}{1+e^{-30x_1}}\frac{1}{1+e^{-30x_2}} + \frac{1}{1+e^{30x_1}}\frac{1}{1+e^{30x_2}} + \frac{1}{1+e^{-30x_1}}\frac{1}{1+e^{-30x_2}}\right). \tag{3.136}$$

To design the supervisory controller, we first need to determine the bounds f^U and gL.

For this system, we have:

$$|f(x_1,x_2)| = \left| \frac{g\sin x_1 - \frac{mlx_2^2\cos x_1 \sin x_1}{m_c+m}}{1\left(\frac{4}{3} - \frac{m\cos^2 x1}{m_c+m}\right)} \right| \le \frac{9.8 + \frac{0.025}{1.1}x_2^2}{\frac{2}{3} - \frac{0.05}{1.1}} = 15.78 + 0.0366x^2 := f^U(x_1,x_2) \tag{3.137}$$

If we require that $|x_i| \le \frac{\pi}{9}$ (we will specify the design parameters such that this requirement is satisfied), then:

$$|g(x_1,x_2)| \ge \frac{\cos \frac{\pi}{9}}{1.1\left(\frac{2}{3} + \frac{0.05}{1.1}\cos^2\frac{\pi}{}\right)} = 1.1 := gL(x_1,x_2) \tag{3.138}$$

Our control objective is to balance the inverted pendulum from arbitrary initial angles $x_1 \in \left[-\dfrac{\pi}{9}, \dfrac{\pi}{9} \right]$ and at the same time guarantee that $\left\| (x_1, x_2) \right\|_2 \leq \dfrac{\pi}{9} \equiv M_x$.

The design parameters are specified as follows:

$a = \dfrac{\pi}{18}, k_1 = 2, k_2 = 1$ (so that $s^2 + k_1 s + k_2$ is stable) and Q=diag(10, 10).

Then, we solve (11) and obtain:

$$P = \begin{bmatrix} 15 & 5 \\ 5 & 5 \end{bmatrix}. \tag{3.139}$$

We simulated three cases:

1) Without the supervisory controller, that is, only use the fuzzy controller (3.136),

2) Use the supervisory controller together with the fuzzy controller, and

3) Same as 2) except that a white Gaussian noise with variance 3 was added to the control which may represent some wind-gusts disturbance. For each case, we simulated the closed-loop system for five initial conditions: $(x_1(0), x_2(0)) = (4°, 0), (8°, 0), (12°, 0), (16°, 0), (20°, 0)$. The simulation results for cases 1), 2), and 3) are shown in Figures54, 55, and 56, respectively, where we show the angle $x_1(t)$ as a function of for the five initial conditions.

We see from these results that:

1) The pure fuzzy controller could balance the inverted pendulum for smaller initial angles4°, 8°,and 12°but the system became unstable for larger initial angles 16° and 20°. and

2) By appending the supervisory controller to the fuzzy controller, we success-fully balanced the inverted pendulum for all the five initial angles and guaranteed that the angle is within [- 20°, 20°]

3) The fuzzy controller was robust to random disturbance.

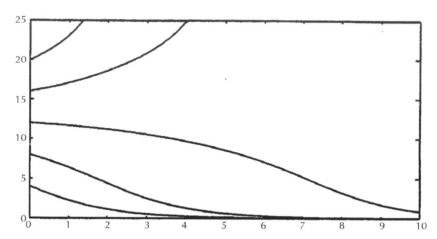

FIGURE 54   The closed loop system state $x_1(t)$ for the five initial conditions using only the fuzzy controller.

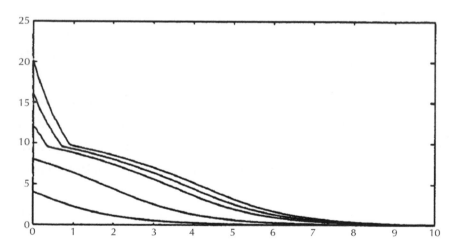

FIGURE 55   The closed-loop system state $x_1(t)$ for the five initial conditions using the fuzzy controller with the supervisory controller.

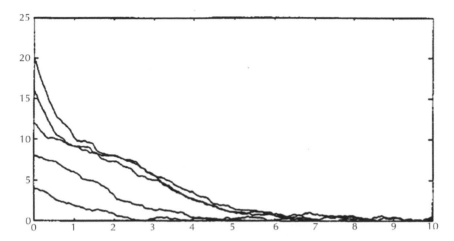

FIGURE 56 The same as Figure 55 except that a white Gaussian noise with variance was added to control u.

Fuzzy controller can be used to tune the gains of conventional propositional-integral-derivative (PID) controller.

The transfer function of a PID controller has the following form:

$$G_c(s) = K_p + K_i/s + K_d s \tag{3.140}$$

where K_p, K_i and K_d are the proportional, integral, and derivative gains, respectively.

Another useful equivalent form of the PID controller is:

$$G_c(s) = K_p(1 + \frac{1}{T_i s} + T_d s) \tag{3.141}$$

where $T_i = K_p/K_i$ and $T_d = \frac{K_d}{K_p} \cdot T_i$ and T_d are known as the integral and derivative time constants, respectively.

The discrete-time equivalent expression for PID control used in this section is given as: $u(k) = K_p e(k) + K_i T_s \sum_{i=1}^{n} e(i) + \frac{K_d}{T_s} \Delta e(k).$

Here, $u(k)$ is the control signal, $e(k)$ is the error between the reference and the process output, T_s is the sampling period for the controller, and $\Delta e(k) \triangleq e(k) - e(k-1)$.

The parameters of the PID controller K_p, K_i and K_d or K_p, T_i and T_d can be manipulated to produce various response curves from a given process. Finding optimum adjustments of a controller for a given process is not trivial. In the following section, an on-line gain scheduling scheme of the PID controller based on fuzzy rues is introduced [273].

The PID gains are usually tuned by experienced experts based on heuristics. This is where fuzzy IF-THEN rules can be used. The PID gains can be tuned by analyzing the responses of the system on-line. The input to the fuzzy system can be e(t) and Δe(t) and outputs of the fuzzy system can be the PID gains.

Figure 57 shows a PID control system with a fuzzy gain scheduler. The approach taken here is to exploit fuzzy rules and reasoning to generate controller parameters.

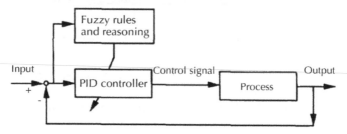

FIGURE 57   PID control system with a fuzzy gain scheduler.

It is assumed that K_p, K_d are in prescribed ranges $[K_{p.\min}, K_{p.\max}]$ and $[K_{p.\min}, K_{p.\max}]$, respectively. The appropriate ranges are determined experimentally and will be given in equation (3.147). For convenience, K_p and K_d are normalized into the range between zero and one by the following linear transformation:

$$K'_p = (K_p - K_{p.\min}) / (K_{p.\max} - K_{p.\min})$$

$$K'_d = (K_d - K_{d.\min}) / (K_{d.\max} - K_{d.\min}) \tag{3.142}$$

In the proposed scheme, The PID parameters are determined based on the current error $e(k)$ and its first difference $\Delta e(k)$.

The time constant is determined with reference to the derivative time constant, that is:

$$T_i = \alpha T_d \tag{3.143}$$

and the integral gain is thus obtained by:

$$K_i = \frac{K_p}{\alpha T_d} = \frac{K_p^2}{\alpha T_d} \qquad (3.144)$$

The parameters K_p', K_d', and are determined by a set of fuzzy rules of the form.

if $e(k)$ is A_i and $\Delta e(k)$ is B_i, then K_p' is C_i, K_d' is D_i, and $\alpha = \alpha_i$

$$i = 1, 2, \ldots, m \qquad (3.145)$$

Here, A_i, B_i, C_i, and D_i are fuzzy sets on the corresponding supporting sets, α_i is a constant. The membership functions (MF) of these fuzzy sets for $e(k)$ and $\Delta e(k)$ are shown in Figure58. In this Figure, N represents negative, P positive, ZO approximately zero, S small, M medium, and B big. Thus, NM stands for negative-medium, PB for positive big, and so on.

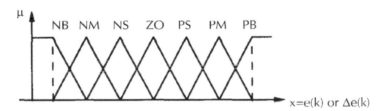

FIGURE 58   Membership functions for $e(k)$ and $\Delta e(k)$.

Once K_p', K_d', and are obtained, as stated below (See Figure 60).

$$K_p' = \Sigma_{i=1}^m \mu_i K_{pi}' \qquad K_d' = \Sigma_{i=1}^m \mu_i K_{di}' \qquad \text{and} \qquad \alpha = \Sigma_{i=1}^m \mu_i \alpha_i$$

The PID controller parameters are calculated from the following equations that are due to (3.142) and (3.144):

$$K_p = \left(K_{p.\max} - K_{p.\min} \right) K_p' + K_{p.\min} \qquad (3.146a)$$

$$K_d = \left(K_{d.\max} - K_{d.\min} \right) K_d' + K_{d.\min} \qquad (3.146b)$$

$$K_i = \frac{K_p^2}{\alpha T_d} . \qquad (3.146c)$$

Based on an extensive simulation study on various processes, a rule of thumb for determining the range of K_p and the range of K_d is given as:

$$K_{p.\min} = 0.32 K_u , \qquad K_{p.\max} = 0.6 K_u$$

$$K_{d.\min} = 0.08 K_u T_u , \qquad K_{d.\max} = 0.15 K_u T_u \qquad (3.147)$$

where K_u and T_u are, respectively, the gain and the period of oscillation at the stability limit under P-control.

Note that there are other forms for the fuzzy tuning rules in (3.145).

Some examples are as follows:

1. If $e(k)$ is A_i and $\Delta e(k)$ is B_i, then Kp' is C_i, K_d' is D_i, and K_i' is E_i

2. If $e(k)$ is A_i and $\Delta e(k)$ is B_i, then K_p' is C_i, T_d' is D_i, and T_i' is E_i

3. If $e(k)$ is A_i and $\Delta e(k)$ is B_i, then $u(k) = K_{p0}^i e(k) + \left(K_{i0}^i T_s\right) \sum_j e(j) + \left(K_{d0}^i / T_s\right) \Delta e(k)$

Example 3.14 The fuzzy gain scheduling scheme has been tested on a variety of processes. Table 4 shows the representative simulation results of the following second-, third-, and fourth- order processes:

$$G_1(s) = \frac{e^{-0.5s}}{(s+1)^2} \qquad\qquad 3.148(a)$$

$$G_2(s) = \frac{4.228}{(s+0.5)(s^2+1.64s+8.456)} \qquad\qquad 3.148(b)$$

$$G_3(s) = \frac{27}{(s+1)(s+3)^3} \qquad\qquad 3.148(c)$$

In the table, represents the percent maximum overshoot, T_s stands for the 5% settling time, and IAE, ISE are the integral of the absolute error and the integral of the squared error, respectively. The time responses are plotted in Figure 59, Figure 60, and Figure61, respectively. The results obtained by using Ziegler–Nichols PID controllers and Kitamori's PID controllers are also presented for comparison. The parameters of Ziegler–Nichols PID controllers are determined as $K_p = 0.6 K_u$, $T_i = 0.5 T_u$, and $T_d = 0.125 T_u$, while those of Kitamori's controllers are obtained by partial model matching method. A brief description of the method is given in the Appendix. Figure

10 shows the PID parameters determined by the fuzzy gain scheduling scheme for controlling the second-order process (3.148(a)). The determination process is as follows. First the error and its first difference are calculated from the sampled process output. Then, the values of K_p' and K_d' for each rule are determined by the fuzzy reasoning process, as shown in Figure62. Finally, the PID parameters are obtained by using (3.146) [273].

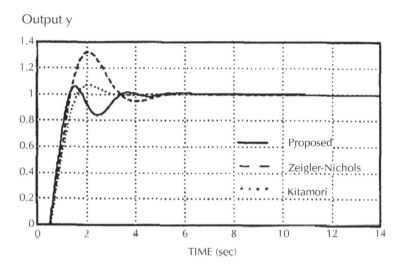

FIGURE 59 Comparison of step responses of the controlled second order process.

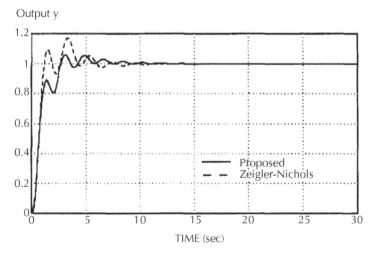

FIGURE 60 Comparison of step responses of the controlled third order process.

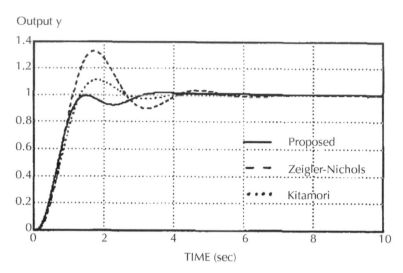

FIGURE 61   Comparison of step responses of the controlled fourth order process.

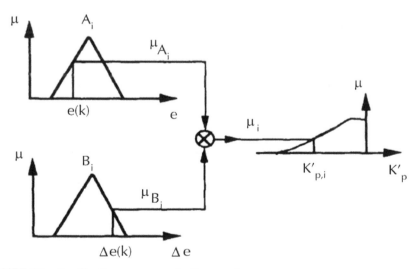

FIGURE 62   Implication process of a fuzzy rule.

The above simulations show that a variety of processes can be satisfactorily controlled by the fuzzy gain scheduling PID controller. It yields better control performance than the Ziegler–Nichols controller does, which is confirmed by comparing
performance indexes such as the percent maximum overshoot, the settling time, IAE,

and ISE. It seems that the derivative time constant T_d for the Ziegler–Nichols controller could be chosen slightly larger in order to obtain a smaller maximum overshoot.

It is also found that the proposed controller is as good as or better than the delicately tuned PID controller of Kitamori's, which needs much more information on the plant.

 vii. Fuzzy System Model-Based Controller Design: The fuzzy control systems discussed above systems under control are represented by ordinary liner or nonlinear dynamic system models. In many practical problems, however, human experts may provide linguistic descriptions about the system that can be combined into a model of the system; this model is called a *fuzzy system model*. There are two types of fuzzy system models, the Takagi–Sugeno–Kang (TSK) fuzzy system model and the fuzzy-autoregressive-moving-average (FARMA) model [181].

In Section 3.4.2, we have already explained the basic concepts of TSK fuzzy system with examples.

The Takagi-Sugeno-Kang Fuzzy System Model: The Takgi–Sugeno–Kang (TSK) fuzzy system was proposed as an alterntive to the usual fuzzy systems. The TSK fuzzy system is made of the following rules:

$$\text{IF } x_1 \text{ is } C_1^l \text{ and } x_n \text{ is } C_n^l, \text{ THEN } y^l = c_0^l + c_1^l x_n + \ldots + c_n^l x_n \quad (3.149)$$

Where C_i^l are fuzzy sets, C_i^l are constants, and $l = 1, 2, \ldots, M$. Thus, the antecedent parts of the rules are the same as in the usual fuzzy IF-THEN rules but the consequent parts are linear combinations of the input variables. Given an input $x(x_1, \ldots, x_n)^T \in U \subset R^n$, the output $f(x) \in V \subset R$ of the TSK fuzzy system is computed as the weighted average of the outputs, that is:

$$f(x) = \frac{\sum_{l=1}^{M} y^l w^l}{\sum_{l=1}^{M} w^l} \quad (3.150)$$

where the weights w^l are computed as:

$$w^l = \prod_{i=1}^{n} \mu_{C_i}(x_i) \quad (3.151)$$

The fuzzy system is a mapping from $\in \subset R^n$ and $V \subset R$, and the output is a piecewise linear function of the input variables, where the change from one piece to another is smooth rather than abrupt. If $C_i^l = 0$ for $l = 1, 2, \ldots, n$ and c_0^l equals the center y^l of the fuzzy set B^l in the usual fuzzy IF-THEN rules, then the TSK fuzzy system is identical to the fuzzy system with product inference, singleton fuzzifier, and center average defuzzifier.

If the output of a TSK fuzzy system appears as one of its inputs, a *dynamic* TSK fuzzy system is obtained:

$$\text{IF } x(k) \text{ is } A_1^p \text{ and } \dots \text{ and } x(k-n+1) \text{ is } A_n^p \text{ and } u(k) \text{ is } B^p \qquad (3.152)$$

$$\text{THEN } x^p(k+1) = \alpha_1^p x(k) + \dots + \alpha_n^p x(k-n+1) + b^p$$

where a_i^p and b^p are fuzzy sets, a_i^p and b^p are constants, $p = 1,2, \dots, N$, $u(k)$ is the input to the system, and $x(k) = (x(k), x(k-1), \dots, x(k-n+1))^T \in R^n$ is the state vector of the system.

The output of the dynamic TSK fuzzy system is computed as:

$$x(k+1) = \frac{\sum_{p=1}^{N} x^p(k+1) v^p}{\sum_{p=1}^{N} v^p} \qquad (3.153)$$

where the weights v^p are computed as:

$$v^p = \Pi_{i=1}^{n} A_{P_i}\left[x(k-i+1)\right] \mu_{B^p}\left[u(k)\right] \qquad (3.154)$$

This dynamic TSK fuzzy system is used to model the plant under control, and the TSK fuzzy control (3.150) is used to control the plant (See Figure 63).

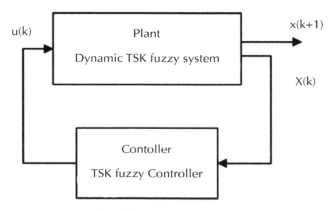

FIGURE 63   Fuzzy control with fuzzy system model.

It remains to determine the stability of the closer-loop fuzzy control system, in other words, the controller parameters, C_i^l and μ_{c1} in (3.149), need to be designed to guarantee the stability of the fuzzy controlled system. Assuming that the parameters of the dynamic TSK fuzzy system model (3.152) are known, the following gives the sufficient condition for stability:

Theorem3.4.The dynamic TSK fuzzy system is globally asymptotically stable if there exists a common positive definite matrix P such that:

$$A_{1p}^T PA_{lp} - P < 0 \tag{3.155}$$

for all $l = 1,2, \dots, M$ and $p = 1,2, \dots, N$, where

$$A_{lp} = \begin{bmatrix} a_1^p + b^p c_1^l & a_2^p + b^p c_2^l & a_{n-1}^p + b^p c_{n-1}^l & a_n^p + b^p c_n^l \\ 1 & 0 & \cdots & 0 & 0 \\ 0 & 1 & \cdots & 0 & 0 \\ 0 & 0 & \cdots & 0 & 0 \end{bmatrix} \tag{3.156}$$

Since, there is no direct way to find the common P satisfying for all possible l and p, trial and error need to be used.

Fuzzy Autoregressive Moving Average Model (FARMA): In general, the output of a system can be described with a function or a mapping of the plant input-output history. For a single-input single-output (SISO) discrete-time system, the mapping can be written in the form of a nonlinear autoregressive moving average (NARMA) as follows:

$$y(k+1) = f(y(k), y(k-1), \dots, u(k), u(k-1), \dots), \tag{3.157}$$

where y(k) and u(k) are respectively the output and input variables at the k-th time step.

The objective of the control problem is to find a control input sequence which will drive the system to an arbitrary reference set point .

Re-arranging (3.157) for control purpose, the value of the input u at the k-th step that is required to yield the reference output y_{ref} can be written as follows:

$$u(k) = g(y_{ref}, y(k), y(k-1), \dots, u(k-1), u(k-2), \dots), \tag{3.158}$$

which is viewed as an inverse mapping of (3.157).

The proposed controller doesnot use rules pre-constructed by experts but forms rules with input and output history at every sampling step. The rules generated at every sampling step are stored in a rule base, and updated as experience is accumulated using a self-organizing procedure.

The system (3.157) yields the last output value y(k+1) when the output and input values, y(k), y(k-1), y(k-2), ..., u(k), u(k-1), u(k-2), ..., are given. This implies that u(k) is the input to be applied when the desired output is as indicated explicitly in (3.158).

Therefore, a FARMA rule with the input and output history is defined as follows:

IF y_{ref} is A_{1i} , y(k) is A_{2i} , y(k-1) is A_{3i} ,..., $y(k-n+1)$ is $A_{(n+1)i}$

AND u(k-1) is B_{1i} , u(k-2) is B_{2i} , ..., u(k-m) is B_{mi}

THEN u(k) is C_i ,   (for the ith rule)   (3.159)

where, n,m: number of output and input variables A_{ij}, B_{ij} : antecedent linguistic values for the ith rule.

The rule (3.159) is generated at (k+1) time step. Therefore, y(k+1) is given value at

(k+1) step. The rule (3.159) explains that "If desired y_{ref} is y(k+1) with given input-output history, y(k), y(k-1), y(k-2), ..., u(k), u(k-1), u(k-2), ..., THEN u(k) is the input to be applied".

In a conventional fuzzy control, an expert usually determines the linguistic values

A_{ij}, B_{ij} , and C_i by partitioning each universe of discourse and the formulation of fuzzy logic control rules is achieved on the basis of the expert's experience and knowledge. However, these linguistic values are determined from the crisp values of the input and output history at every sampling step. Therefore, at the initial stage, the assigned u(k) may not be a good control, but over time, the rule base is updated using the self-organizing procedure, and better controls are applied.

A fuzzification procedure for fuzzy values of (3.159) is developed to determine

$A_{1i}, A_{2i}, ..., A_{(n+1)i}, B_{1i}, B_{2i}, ..., B_{mi}$, and C_i from the crisp y(k+1), y(k), y(k-1), ..., y(k-n+1), u(k-1), u(k-2), ..., u(k-m), and u(k), respectively. The fuzzification is done with its base on a reasonably assumed input or output ranges.

When the assumed input or inoutput range is [1,b], the membership function for crisp x_1 is determined in a triangular shape as follows:

$$\mu_A = \begin{cases} 1 + \dfrac{(x - x_1)}{b - a} & if\ a \leq x < x_1 \\ 1 - \dfrac{(x - x_1)}{b - a} & if\ x_1 \leq x < b \\ 0 & else. \end{cases}$$ (3.160)

A FARMA rule is generated at each sampling step, and stored in a rule base. This means that every experience is regarded initially a fuzzy logic control rule. As the run continues, the experience will be accumulated and the FARMA rule is updated for each domain in the rule space [181].

INFERENCE AND DEFUZZIFICATION

To attain the consequent linguistic value, it is necessary to determine a "truth value" of the input fuzzy set with respect to each rule.

The consequent linguistic value, that is the net linguistic control action, C_n is deduced with the φ-operation as follows:

$$C_n \cap_i (\omega_i \varphi \mu_{Ci}) \tag{3.161}$$

$$\omega_i \varphi \mu_{c_i} = \begin{cases} 1 & \text{if } \omega_i \leq \mu_{c_i} \\ \mu_{c_i} & \text{if } \omega_i > \mu_{c_i} \end{cases} \tag{3.162}$$

where, C_n : net linguistic control action,

w_i : truth value of i-th rule,

μ_{c_i} : membership degree of the consequent linguistic value C_i in the i-th rule.

With the C_n, we take the α-cut of the C_n where $= \max \mu(C_n)$, to find a control range for the highest possibility. As a result of the inference, the *net control range* (NCR) is determined as a subset [p, q] of [a,b] with the constant membership value α.

Defuzzification is a procedure to determine a crisp value from a consequent fuzzy

C_n set In FARMA controller, defuzzification is to determine a crisp value from the net control range (NCR) resulting from the inference. The NCR is modified to compute a crisp value by using the prediction or "trend" of the output response. The series of the last outputs is extrapolated in time domain to estimate y(k+1) by the Newton backward-difference formula.

If the extrapolation order is l, the estimate (k+1) is calculated as follows:

$$\hat{y}(k+1) = \Sigma_{i=0}^{l} (-1) \binom{-1}{1} \nabla^i y(k) \tag{3.163}$$

where

$$\nabla^i y(k) \triangleq \nabla(\nabla^{i-1} y(k) \text{ for } i \geq 2$$

$$\nabla y(k) \triangleq y(k) - y(k-1).$$

Defuzzification is performed by comparing the two values, the estimate $\hat{y}(k+1)$ and the reference output y_{ref} or the temporary target $y_r(k+1)$, generated by:

$$y_r(k+1) - y(k) + \alpha(y_{ref} - y(k)) \qquad (3.164)$$

where is the target ratio constant $(o < \alpha \leq 1)$. The value of describes the rate with which the present output y(k) approaches the reference output value, and thus has a positive value between 0 and 1. The value of α is chosen by the user to obtain a desirable response.

When the estimate exceeds the reference output, the control has to slow down. On the other hand, when the estimate has not reached the reference, the control should speed up. To modify the control range, the sign of $\nabla u(k)(= u(k) - u(k-1))$ is assumed to be the same as the sign of $y_r(k+1) - \hat{y}(k+1)$ without the loss of generality.

Thus, for the case of $y_r(k+1) > \hat{y}(k-1)$, hence, the sign of $\nabla u(k)$ is positive, u(k) has to be increased from the previous input u(k-1). On the other hand, when the sign of $\nabla u(k)$ is negative and u(k) has to be decreased from the previous input u(k-1).

The final crisp control value u(k) is then selected as one of the mid-points of the modified net control ranges as follows:

$$u(k) = \begin{cases} \dfrac{u(k-1)+q}{2} & \text{for } y_r(k+1) > \hat{y}(k+1), \\[2ex] \dfrac{p+u(k-1)}{2} & \text{for } y_r(k+1) < \hat{y}(k+1). \end{cases} \qquad (3.165)$$

where p and q are the respective lower and upper limits of the net control range (NCR) resulting from the inference.

SELF-ORGANIZATION OF THE RULE BASE

The FARMA rule defined in the previous is generated at every sampling time. Each rule can be represented as a point in the (n+m+1)-dimensional rule space, that is

$$\left(x_{1i}, x_{2i}, \ldots, x_{(n+m+1)i} \right)$$

.

To update the rule base, the following performance index is defined:

$$J = \left| y_r(k+1) - y(k+1) \right| \qquad (3.166)$$

where y(k+1) is the real plant output and $y_r(k+1)$ is the reference output. There-fore, at the (k+1)-th step, the performance index J is calculated with the real plant output y(k+1) resulting from the k-th step control [181].

The fuzzy rule space is partitioned into a finite number of domains and only one rule, that is, a point, is stored in each domain. If there are two rules in a given domain, the selection of a rule is based on J.That is, if there is a new rule which has the output closer to the reference output in a given domain, the old rule is replaced by the new one. The self-organization of the rule base, in other words, "learning" of the object system, is performed at each samplingandtime.(See Figure64).In Figure 64 the refer-ence model block represents (3.164).

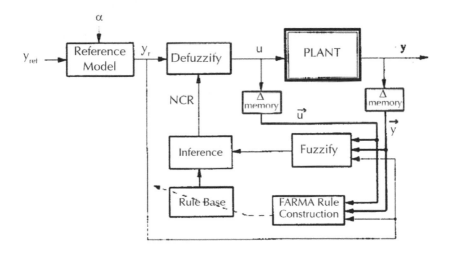

FIGURE 64   The FARMA control system architecture.

Example 3.15The purpose of this example is to demonstrate the self-organizing feature of the self-organizing power system stabilizer (SOPSS) when there is no math-ematical model, either on the generator not on the power system to which the machine is connected. The SOPSS will be learning the system from the input-output data as it stabilizes the unknown system. Consequently, the SOPSS will be adaptive from system to system, from one operating condition to another operating condition. For illustration purpose, the system considered in this example is a synchronous generator connected to an infinite bus through two transmission lines.(See Figure65). During low frequency oscillations, the linearized model can be drawn as Figure66.

TABLE 8   Constants of one-machine, infinite-bus model

Generator	M= 9.26, D=0, T_{do} = 7.76
Constants	X_d = 0.973, X_d = 0.19, X_q = 0.55
Exciter Constants	K_A= 50, T_A= 0.05
Line Constants	R_1=-0.051,X_1 =-1.149,R_2 = -0.102
	X_2 = 2.99, G = 0.249, B = 0.262
Initial Constants	P_{eo} = 1.0,Q_{eo} = 0.015,V_{to} = 1.05

For the calculation of constants $K_1 \sim K_6$, the initial currents, voltages and torque angle of the system in a steady state must be known. These initial values are found from a load flow study. Since the real system is nonlinear, the parameters $K_1 \sim K_6$ are changed with the load and the system conditions. However, for demonstration purpose, we select few operating conditions for the linearized model [181].

Table 8 shows the values of system parameters. The negative R_1 and R_2 stem from deriving the one-machine, infinite bus model for a multi-machine system by equivalencing smaller generators by equivalent impedances with negative resistances. Without supplementary excitation, the system is unstable and has a non-minimum phase zero and a zero at the origin.

The supplementary control u_ε is applied through the T_A, T_{do} and K_2 blocks in Figure66 to obtain the extra damping ∇T_E in Figure66. Since it is a linearized model, a conventional PSS as a phase lead compensation is included by the superposition principle.

If $\nabla \omega$ is the control input, the control including the reset block becomes as follows:

$$u_\varepsilon = \left(\frac{1+0.685s}{1+0.1s} \right) \left(\frac{7.091.3s}{1.3s} \right) \Delta \omega \qquad (3.167)$$

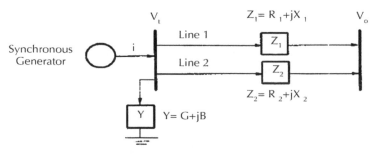

FIGURE 65   A one-machine, infinite-bus power system.

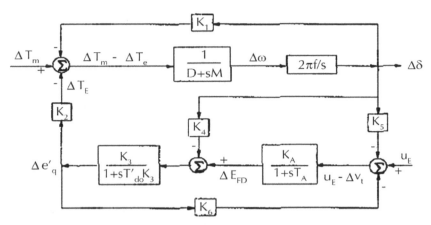

FIGURE 66   A linearized one-machine, infinite bus model.

SELF-ORGANIZING POWER SYSTEM STABILIZER

It is noted the system has a non-minimum phase zero and a zero at the origin. The FARMA fuzzy control can be interpreted as a kind of inverse model trainer by (3.158). However, it is well known that the non-minimum phase zero plant cannot be controlled by pole-zero cancellation because of the internal instability. In other words, the control value u_ε can diverge in order to main the $\Delta\omega$ to zero. Moreover, the system has a zero at the origin, which means u_ε is not unique in the steady state. It is recommended the steady state control value u_ε of PSS be zero since it is a supplementary control. Therefore, a modification of the FARMA fuzzy control is necessary to prevent the divergence and non-zero steady state value of u_ε.

To overcome these problems, we directly limit the control value according to the output error as follows:

$$u'(k) = K\,(y_{ref} - y(k))\,u(k) \tag{3.168}$$

where, u'(k): modified control value,

K: feedback constant,

u(k): control value of FARMA FLC.

In (3.168), y_{ref} is the reference output, that is, zero for speed deviation. Then, the modified control value is decreased with the output error ($y_{ref} - y(k)$). Moreover, in steady state it always becomes zero.

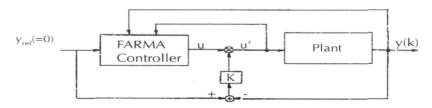

FIGURE 67   The Self-organizing power system stabilizer.

Figure 67 shows the modification of the FARMA FLC for PSS. The plant input u' is u_g and the output y is $\Delta\omega$ as in the conventional method. The plant output and input values, y(k+1), y(k), ..., y(k-3), u'(k), ..., u'(k-3) are used to form the FARMA rule. The target ratio constant and feedback constant K are chosen by off-line. The sampling time is 0.02 sec.The proposed FARMA PSS doesnot assume a plant model, instead it learns the behavior of the plant by input-output history. Therefore, it can cope with unexpected load conditions and faults.

After setting the parameters for the conventional PSS and the SOPSS, we consider four disturbances in simulations. According to each disturbance, the plant parameters are changed. To compare the closed loop characteristics of two systems, it is assumed that small torque angle deviations ($\Delta\delta$) are suddenly applied at 0 sec. for each disturbance.

CASE 1: NORMAL LOAD CONDITION

Figures 68 and 69 show the speed deviations of the conventional PSS and the SOPSS, respectively. It is assumed that initial torque angle deviations ($\Delta\delta$) at 0 sec. are 0.06, 0.08, and 0.1 [radian] for a,b, and c, respectively. The rising times are similar but the speed deviations of the SOPSS show smaller overshoots and settling times than those of the conventional method.

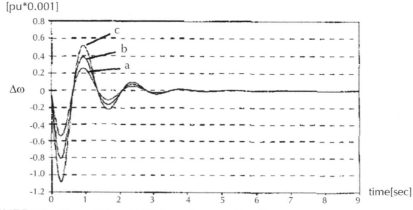

FIGURE 68   Conventional PSS(case 1:normal load).

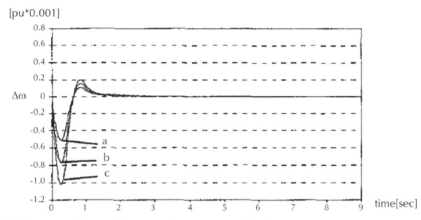

FIGURE 69   Self organizingPSS(case 1:normal load).

CASE 2: HEAVY LOAD CONDITION

In case B, we consider different operating condition, that is the real power P is increased to 1.3 from 1. Figures70 and 71 show the speed deviations of the conventional PSS and the SOPSS, respectively. The initial torque angle deviations ($\Delta\delta$) are 0.06, 0.08, and 0.1 for a, b, and c, respectively. Because the conventional controller is designed for the normal operating condition, the overshoots and the settling times are increased somewhat than those in case A. On the contrary, the undershoots and overshoots, in the case of SOPSS, are improved from case A. This is because the SOPSS doesnot assume any operating condition,instead, it constructs the rule base of the system by on-line adaptation.

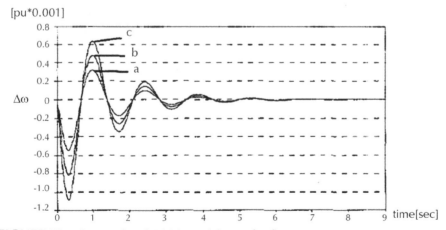

FIGURE 70   Conventional PSS(case 2:heavy load).

[pu*0.001]

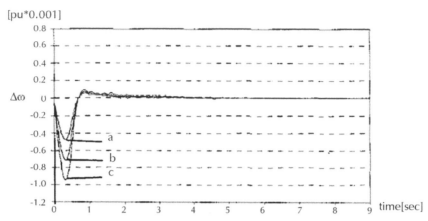

FIGURE 71 Self-organizing PSS(case 2:heavy load).

CASE 3: ISOLATION OF A TRANSMISSION LINE

In this case, transmission line 2 in Figure 65 is isolated with normal load condition. The isolation of line 2 may result from three-phase fault or three-phase to ground fault, and so on. To simulate this case, the Z_2 is removed, and Y is changed in Figure65 accordingly. Figures72 and 73 show the speed deviations of the conventional PSS and the SOPSS, respectively. The initial torque angle deviations are 0.06, 0.08, and 0.1 for a, b, and c, respectively. The settling times of the conventional PSS are increased to almost 7 sec. On the other hand, the SOPSS shows no significant difference from cases A and B.

[pu*0.001]

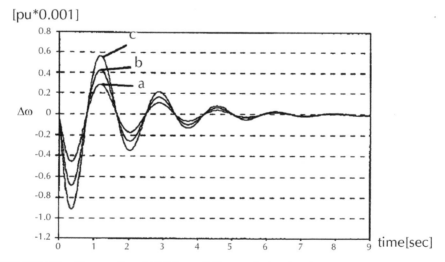

FIGURE 72 Conventional PSS(case 3:Transmission loss).

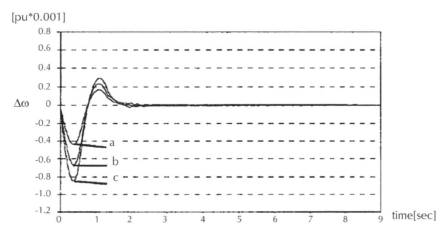

FIGURE 73   Self organizing PSS(case 3:Transmission loss).

CASE 4: DIFFERENT INERTIA CONSTANT

Here, we consider different inertia constant for the synchronous generator with normal load condition. The purpose of this case is to consider the modeling error of the synchronous generator. That is, the real values can be either 7, 9.26, or 12, respectively, while the assumed value is 9.26 in the model. Figures 74 and 75 show the speed deviations of the conventional PSS and the SOPSS, respectively. The INERTIA Constants are 7,9.26, and 12 for a, b, and c, respectively. The initial torque angle deviation ($\Delta\delta$) is 0.1. When the real inertia constant is 12, the settling time of the conventional PSS is increased to 6 sec (c of Figure74). On the other hand, the SOPSS shows no significant difference.

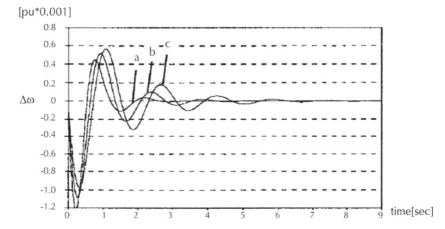

FIGURE 74   Conventional PSS(case 4:Modelling error).

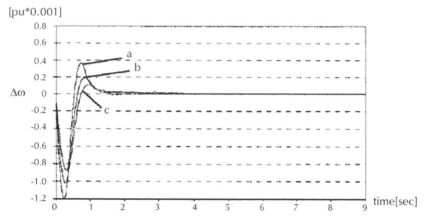

FIGURE 75   Self-organizing PSS(case 4:Modelling error).

3.5   ADAPTIVE FUZZY CONTROLLER DESIGN

The motivation behind the fuzzy control is to handle uncertainties or unknown variations in mnodel parameters and structures. Similarly, the basic objective of adaptive
control is to control systems in the presence of these uncertainties. Therefore, it is
natural to combine the two and design *adaptive fuzzy control*. Figure76 shows the
basic configuration of an adaptive fuzzy control system. The reference model is used
to specify the ideal response that the controlled system should follow. The plant is assumed to contain unknown parameters. The fuzzy controller is constructed from fuzzy
systems whose parameters θ are adjustable. The adaptation law adjusts the parameters
θ online such that the plant output y(t) tracks the reference model output y_m(t).

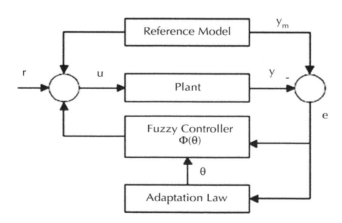

FIGURE 76   Adaptive fuzzy control system.

The main advantages of adaptive fuzzy control systems are:
(i)   Better performance is usually achieved because the adaptive fuzzy controller
      can adjust itself to the changing environment and
(ii) Less information about the plant is required because the adaptation law can
      help to learn the dynamics of the plant during real-time operation.

The main disadvantages, on the other hand, are:
(i)   The resulting control system is more difficult to analyze because it is not only
      nonlinear but also time-varying and
(ii) Implementation is more costly.

Although, adaptive fuzzy control and conventional adaptive control are similar in
principles and mathematical tools, they differ in the sense that:
(i)   The fuzzy controller has a special nonlinear structure that is universal for
      different plants, whereas the structure of a conventional adaptive controller
      changes from plant to plant, and
(ii) Human knowledge about the plant dynamics and control strategies can be in-
      corporated into adaptive fuzzy controllers, while such knowledge is not con-
      sidered in conventional adaptive control systems, which is the main advantage
      of adaptive fuzzy control over conventional adaptive control.

Human knowledge about a control system can be classified into categories:
• Plant knowledge and
• Control knowledge.

Depending upon the human knowledge used and the structure of the fuzzy controller, adaptive fuzzy controller is classified into the following three types:
• *Indirect adaptive fuzzy control*: The fuzzy controller comprises a number of
  fuzzy systems constructed from the plant knowledge.
• *Direct adaptive fuzzy control*: The fuzzy controller is a single fuzzy system constructed from the control knowledge.
• *Combined indirect/direct fuzzy control*: The fuzzy controller is a weighted average of the indirect and direct adaptive fuzzy controllers.

INDIRECT ADAPTIVE FUZZY CONTROLLER

Consider the nonlinear system:

$$x^{(n)} = f\left(x, \dot{x}, ..., x^{(n-1)}\right) + g\left(x, \dot{x}, ..., x^{(n-1)}\right) u \qquad (3.169)$$

where $x \in R$ is the output, y, $u \in R$ is the control, $x = \left(x, \dot{x}, ..., x^{(n-1)}\right)^{T}$ is the state vector,
and f and g are unknown nonlinear functions with $g > 0$ assumed. This type of system
can be linearized with nonlinear feedback and a stable liner controller can be designed.

Since the functions $f(x)$ and $g(x)$ are unknown, the fuzzy system describes their
input-output behavior:

$$\text{IF } x_1 \text{ is } F_1^r \text{ and } x_n \text{ is } F_n^r, \text{ THEN } f(x) \text{ is } C^r \qquad (3.170)$$

$$\text{IF } x_1 \text{ is } G_1^r \text{ and } x_n \text{ is } G_n^r \text{ THEN } g(\mathbf{x}) \text{ is } D^r. \tag{3.171}$$

If the nonlinear functions $f(\mathbf{x})$ and $g(\mathbf{x})$ are known, then the feedback linearization controller for the system (3.169) is given by:

$$u^* = \frac{1}{g(x)}\left[-f(\mathbf{x}) + y_m^{(n)} + \mathbf{k}'e\right] \tag{3.172}$$

where $e = y_m - y, e\left(e, \dot{e}, ..., e^{(n-1)}\right)^T$ and $\mathbf{k} = \left(k_n, ..., k_1\right)^T \in R^n$ is such that all roots of the polynomial $s^n + k_1 s^{(n-1)} + ... + k_n$ are in the left-half complex plane.

The system (3.169) with control (3.172) is then rewritten as:

$$e^{(n)} k_1 s^{(n-1)} + ... + k_n e = 0 \tag{3.173}$$

which, because of the choice of k, implies $e(t) \to 0$ as $t \to \infty$, that is the plant output y converges to the ideal output y_m asymptotocally.

Since $f(x)$ and $g(x)$ are unknown, the ideal controller (64) cannot be implemented. However, the fuzzy IF-THEN rules (3.170)–(3.171) give estimates $\hat{f}(\mathbf{x}) = \hat{f}(\mathbf{x}|\ \theta_f)$ and $\hat{g}(\mathbf{x}) = \hat{g}(\mathbf{x}|\ \theta_g)$, where $\theta_f \in R^{M_i}$ are unknown parameter vector in$(\mathbf{x})$ and$(\mathbf{x})$, respectively.

Thus, the fuzzy controller becomes:

$$u = u_i = \frac{1}{\hat{g}(x|\ \theta_g)}[-\hat{f}(x|\ \theta_f) + y_m^{(n)} + k'e] \tag{3.174}$$

Typically, the unknown parameters are the centers of the output fuzzy sets and in the rules (3.170) and (3.171), respectively. Using the product inference, singleton fuzzifier, and center average defuzzifier, and following the similar procedure leading to 3.70 and 3.76–3.78, the estimates are in the form:

$$\hat{f}(x|\ \theta_f) = \theta\frac{t}{f}\xi_x \tag{3.175}$$

$$\hat{g}(x|\ \theta_g) = \theta_f^T \eta_x \tag{3.176}$$

where $\xi(\mathbf{x})$ and $\eta(\mathbf{x})$ are the fuzzy basis function defined in (3.76) for fuzzy sets F_i^r and G_i^r, respectively, and θ_f and θ_g are vectors of the centers of the output fuzzy sets c^r and D^r in the rules (3.170) and (3.171), respectively.

Next step is to adjust the parameter vectors θ_f - θ_f and θ_g - θg are minimized. The Lyapunov synthesis approach defines the following Lyapunov function:

$$V = \frac{1}{2}e^{\mathrm{T}}Pe + \frac{1}{2\gamma_1}\left(\theta_f - \theta_f^*\right)^{\mathrm{T}}\left(\theta_f - \theta_f^*\right) \qquad (3.177)$$

$$+ \frac{1}{2\gamma_2}\left(\theta_g - g\right)^{\mathrm{T}}\left(\theta_g - \theta_g^*\right)$$

where and are constants and P is a positive matrix satisfying the Lyapunov equation (3.121).

An adaptation law which minimizes the Lyapunov function is given by:

$$\dot{\theta}_f = \gamma_1 e^T P b \xi(x) \qquad (3.178)$$

$$\dot{\theta}_g = \gamma_2 e^T P b \eta(x) u_1. \qquad (3.179)$$

DIRECT ADAPTIVE FUZZY CONTROLLER

Consider the nonlinear system

$$x^{(n)} = f(x, \dot{x}, ..., x^{(n-1)}) + g(x, \dot{x}, ..., x^{(n-1)})u \qquad (3.180)$$

where $x \in R$ is the output, y, $u \in R$ is the control, $\mathbf{x} = (x, , ..., x^{(n-1)})^T$ is the state vector, and f and g are unknown functions as before. For simplicity, assume that g = b, an unknown positive constant. The control objective remains the same as in the indirect adaptive fuzzy control, that is design a feedback controller u = u(x| θ) basedon fuzzy systems and adaptation law for adjusting the parameter vector θ, such that the plant output y follows the ideal output y_m as close as possible. The main difference lies in the assumption about the human knowledge.

Instead of knowing the plant knowledge (3.170) and (3.171), we are provided with some control knowledge, that is the following IF-THEN rules that represent human control actions:

IF x_1 is P_1^r and ... and x_n is P_n^r, THEN u is Q^r \qquad (3.181) where P_i^r and Q^r are fuzzy sets in R, and r = 1,2, ..., L_u .

Using the product inference, singleton fuzzifier, and center average defuzzifier, and following the similar procedure leading to (3.70) and (3.76)–(3.78), the fuzzy controller is in the form:

$$u_D(x \mid \theta_f) = \theta_f^T \xi_x \qquad (3.182)$$

where $\xi(x)$ and $\eta(x)$ are the fuzzy basis function defined in (5.49) for fuzzy sets P_i^r and θ^r is the vector of the centers of the output fuzzy setsin the rule (5.155).

Next step is to adjust the parameter vectors θ^r such that the tracking error e and the parameter $\theta - \theta$ is minimized.

The Lyapunov synthesis approach defines the following Lyapunov function:

$$V = \frac{1}{2} e^T P e + \frac{1}{2\gamma} \left(\theta - \theta^*\right)^T \left(\theta - \theta_f^*\right) \qquad (3.183)$$

where is a positive constant and P is a positive matrix satisfying the Lyapunov equation (3.121).

An adaptation law which minimizes the Lyapunov function is given by:

$$\dot{\theta} = -\gamma e^T p_n \xi(x) \qquad (3.184)$$

where p_n is the last column of P.

COMBINED DIRECT/INDIRECT ADAPTIVE FUZZY CONTROLLER

This adaptive fuzzy controller incorporate both types of linguistic information, plant knowledge and control knowledge. Consider the system (3.180) with b = 1, for simplicity.

Assume that the following information is available:

- Information 1: The plant in (3.180) is represented by an approximate model $\hat{f}$.
- Information 2: The modeling error $\tilde{f} = f - \hat{f}$ is given by the fuzzy IF-THEN rules:

$$\text{IF F } x_1 \text{ is } S_1^r \text{ and ... and } x_n \text{ is } S_n^r \text{, THEN } \hat{f} \text{ is } E^r \qquad (3.185)$$

where S_i^r and E^r are fuzzy sets in R and r = 1,2, ..., L_e .
- Information 3: Control actions are given by the fuzzy IF-THEN rules (3.181). From (3.172), if f(x) is known, then the optimal control is:

$$u^* \ f(x) + y_m^{(n)} + k^t e \qquad (3.186)$$

to guarantee $y(t) \rightarrow y_m(t)$. However, the best estimate of $f(x)$ based on Information 1 and 2 are:

$$\hat{f}(x) + \hat{f}(x \mid \theta_t) \tag{3.187}$$

Thus, the controller based upon Information 1 and 2 is:

$$u_{12} = -\hat{f}(x) - \tilde{f}(x \mid \theta_t) - f(x) + y_m^{(n)} + k^t e \tag{3.188}$$

The fuzzy controller based upon Information 3 is, from (3.181):

$$u_3 = u_D(x \mid \theta_D) \tag{3.189}$$

Therefore, the combined fuzzy controller is:

$$u = \alpha u_{12} + (1 - \alpha)u_3 \tag{3.190}$$

where $\alpha \in [0,1]$ is a weighting factor.

The fuzzy system $\tilde{f}(x \mid \theta_t)$ and $u_D(x \mid \theta_D)$ are respectively designed following the same steps in the indirect and direct fuzzy controller design:

$$\tilde{f}(x \mid \theta_t) = \theta_I^T \xi(x) \tag{3.191}$$

$$u_D(x \mid \theta_D) = \theta_D^T \eta(x) \tag{3.192}$$

Next step is to adjust the parameter vectors θ_I^T and θ_D^T such that the tracking error e and the parameter errors $\theta_I - \theta_I^*$ and $\theta_D - \theta_D^*$ are minimized.

The Lyapunov synthesis approach defines the following Lyapunov function:

$$V = \frac{1}{2}e^T Pe + \frac{\alpha}{2\gamma_1}\left(\theta_1 - \theta_1^*\right)^T \left(\theta_1 - \theta_1^*\right)\left(\theta_1 - \theta_1^*\right)$$
$$+\frac{1-\alpha}{2\gamma_2}\left(\theta_D - \theta_D^*\right)^T \left(\theta_g - \theta_g^*\right)\left(\theta_D - \theta_D^*\right) \tag{3.193}$$

where γ_1 and γ_2 are constants and P is a positive matrix satisfying the Lyapunov equation (3.121).

An adaptation law which minimizes the Lyapunov function is given by

$$\dot{\theta}_1 = \gamma_1 e^T pb\xi(x)$$ (3.194)

$$\dot{\theta}_D = \gamma_2 e^T Pb\eta(x)u_1$$

3.6   SELF-TUNING OF FUZZY CONTROLLER

In this section, we concentrate on fuzzy control as an alternative control strategy to the current proportional-integral-derivative (PID) method used widely in industry. Consider a generic temperature control application shown in Figure 77[79]:

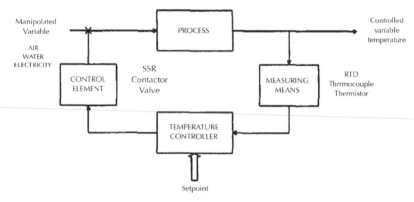

FIGURE 77   A typical industrial temperature control problem

The temperature is measured by a suitable sensor such a Thermocouples, Resistive Thermal Devices (RTD's) Thermistors, and so on,and converted to a signal acceptable to the controller. The controller compares the temperature signal with the desired set point temperature and actuates the control-element. The control element alters the manipulated variable to change the quantity of heat being added to or taken from the process. The objective of the controller is to regulate the temperature as close as possible to the set point.

To test the new fuzzy control algorithms, two temperature regulation processes were used in this research. One uses hot and cold water as manipulated variable and valve as the controller element, the other uses electricity as power source to a heater, actuated by a Solid State Relay (SSR). The new algorithms were tested extensively in both simulation and the hardware tests.

MOTIVATION

Currently, the classical PID (Proportional, Integral, and Derivative) control is widely used with its gains manually turned based on the thermal mass and the temperature setpoint. Equipment with large thermal capacities required different PID gains than equipment with small thermal capacities. In addition, equipment operation over widely ranges of temperatures (140 to 500°), for example, require different gains at the lower and higher end of the temperature range to avoid overshoots and oscillation. This is necessary since even brief temperature overshoots, for example, can initiate nuisance alarms and costly shut downs to the process being controlled. Generally, tuning the Proportional, Integral, and Derivative constants for a large temperature control process is costly and time consuming. The task is further complicated when incorrect PID constants are sometimes entered due to the lack of understanding of the temperature control process.

The difficulty in dealing with such problems is compounded with variable time delays existed in many such systems. Variations in manufacturing, new product development, and physical constraints place, the RTD temperature sensor at different locations, inducing variable time delays (dead time) in the system.

It is also well-known that PID controllers exhibit poor performance when applied to systems containing unknown nonlinearity such as dead zones saturation and hysteresis. It is further understood that many temperature control processes are nonlinear. Equal increments of head input, for example, do not necessarily produce equal increments in temperature rise in many processes, a typical phenomenon of nonlinear systems.

The complexity of these problems and the difficulties in implementing conventional controllers to eliminate variations in PID turning motivate us to consider fuzzy control techniques such as fuzzy logic as a solution to controlling systems in which time delays, nonlinearities, and manual tuning procedures need to be addressed.

THE TIME DELAY PROBLEM AND EXISTING SOLUTIONS

To study the temperature control problem using classical control techniques, a simplified block diagram, in Figure 78, is used, instead of Figure 77, where C(s) represents the controller and $G(s)e^{-s\tau}$ the plant with a pure time delay of τ. It is well known that the time delay makes the temperature loops hard to tune. The time delay problem may be characterized by *large* and *small* delays. A linear time invariant system with finite delay τ can be modeled $G(s)e^{-s\tau}$, where G(s) is a rational transfer function of s. Note that the delay corresponds to a phase shift of $-\omega\tau$, where ω denotes the frequency. Small phase shift of $-\omega\tau$, where ω denotes the frequency. Small phase shifts at frequencies of interest may be viewed as perturbations and incorporated into a delay free design with sufficient phase margin. A large delay is classified as a delay that significantly affects the stability and phase margins to the point that delay free design methods are not sufficient.

A number of time delay compensation and prediction schemes have been developed and/or improved with modifications. The performance of Smith Predictor Control (SPC) was studied experimentally. It shows that the system performs well if the process model is accurate but that performance degrades rapidly with inaccuracy in the process parameters and time delay. Clearly, for an unknown or variable time delay, Smith predictive compensation is no longer a viable technique.

FIGURE 78   A closed loop Temperature control system.

Several control design methods for systems with varying time delays have appeared in recent literature including an estimation and self-tuning method proposed by Brone and Harris, a variable structure controller by Shu and Yan, and a model reference adaptive approach by Liu and Wang, to name a few.

For systems with large time delays, most design approaches use a prediction mechanism as part of the controller to simulate the process for given system parameters and time delay. In the well-known Smith predictor, the controlled output is fed through models of the process with delay, and the process without delay, respectively. The difference of the output signals is added to the actual plant output and then fedback to the controller, thus allowing the controller to act of the prediction of the plant output.

Using this well-known time delay compensation technique on a simple first order plant in an industry standard PIDcontroller such as Bailey's Infi-90 single loop controller is still not an easy task. The predictor parameters including the plant gain, time constant, and time delay, addition to the three PID parameters must be determined. These parameters used in a predictive compensator increase tuningand operational complexity on even the simplest plants. The additional complexity of the Smith predictor is the main reason industry still uses non-predictive PI or PID control for time delay using tuning methods such as Ziegler–Nichol method.

FUZZY CONTROL

Fuzzy control is an appealing alternative to convention control methods when systems follow some general operating characteristics and a detailed process understanding is unknown or traditional system models become over complex. The capability to qualitatively capture the attributes of a control system based on observable phenomenon is a main feature of model-free fuzzy control (See Section 3.3). These aspects of model-free fuzzy control have been demonstrated in various research literature and commercial products from vendor like Reliance Electric and Omron. The ability of fuzzy controller to capture systems dynamics qualitatively, and execute the qualitative idea in a real time situation is an attractive feature for temperature control systems.

Of course, fuzzy control has its own limitations. The analytical study of fuzzy is still trailing in implementation and much work is still ahead, particularly in the area of stability and performance analysis. Furthermore as solutions to practical problems, fuzzy control design is problem dependent and the adaptation of an existing fuzzy controller to a different control problem is no straightforward. The available design tools, such as the Fuzzy Toolbox provided by Math works Inc., generally required further improvements before they become acceptable to control engineers.

In this section, the validity of fuzzy control as an alternative approach to temperature control applications is investigated.

3.6.1 FUZZY CONTROL DESIGN

The fuzzy control considered here is a two-input single-output controller. The two

inputs aretheerror(deviation from setpoint),e(k), and error rate, $\Delta e(k)$. The fuzzy control is implemented in a discrete-time form using a zero-order-hold as shown in Figure 79(a). The operational structure of the Fuzzy controller is shown in Figure 79(b).

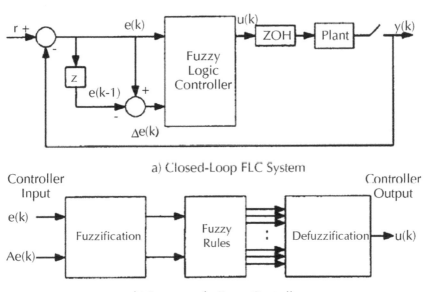

a) Closed-Loop FLC System

b) Structure of a Fuzzy Controller

FIGURE 79 Fuzzy logic control system.

FUZZIFICATION/DEFUZZIFICATION

Fuzzification and defuzzification involve mapping the fuzzy variables of interest to "crisp" numbers used by the control system. Fuzzification translates a numerical value

for the error, e(k), or error rate, $\Delta e(k)$ into a linguistic value suchas positive large with a membership grade. Defuzzfication takes the fuzzy output of the rules and generates a "crisp" numeric value used as the control input to the plant.

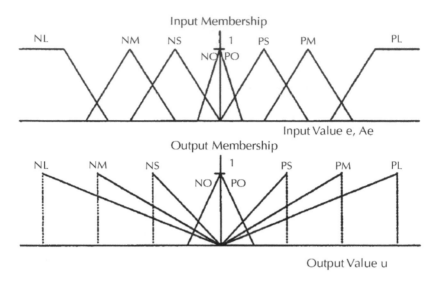

FIGURE 80 Fuzzy membership functions.

The membership functions are defined over the range of input and output variable values and linguistically describes the variable's universe of discourse as shown in Figure 80. The triangular input membership functions for the linguistic labels zero, small, medium, and large, had their membership tuning center values at 0, 0.2, 0.35, and 0.6, respectively. The universe of discourse for both e and Δe is normalized from -1 to 1. The left and right half of the triangle membership functions for each linguistic label was chosen to provide membership overlap with adjacent membership functions. The straight line output membership functions for the labels zero, small, medium, and large are defined as shown in Figure 80 with end points corresponding to 10, 30, 70, and 100% of the maximum output, respectively. Both the input and output variables membership functions are symmetric with respect to the origin.

Selection of the number of membership functions and their initial values is based on process knowledge and intuition. The main idea is to define partitions over the plant operating regions that will adequately represent the process variables.

RULE DEVELOPMENT

Our rule development strategy for systems with time delay is to regulate the overall loop gain to achieve a desired response. The output of the fuzzy control is based on the current input e(k) and $\Delta e(k)$, without any knowledge of the previous input and output data or any form of model predictor. The main idea is that if the fuzzy control is not designed with specific knowledge of mathematical model of the plant (See Section 3.3). The rules developed are able to compensate for varying time delays on-line by tuning the output membership functions of fuzzy control based on system performance.

The fuzzy control rules are developed based on the understanding of how a conventional controller works for a system with fixed time delay. The rules are separated into two layers, the first layer of FLC rules mimics what a simple PID controller does when the time delay is fixed and known and the second layer deals with the problem when the time delay unknown and varying.

In developing the first layer rules, consider the first order plant, $G(S)e^{-s\tau}$, where G(s)=a/(s+a).In the PID design, the following assumptions are made:
- • The time delay π is known

- • The rise time, t_r, or equivalent, the location of the pole is known.
- •The is significantly smaller than τ.
- •The sampling interval is Ts

The conventional PI-type controller in incremental form is given by:

$$u(k) = u(k\text{-}1) + f(e, \Delta e)$$ (3.195)

where + f(e, Δe) is computed by a discrete-time PI algorithm. This control algorithm is applied to a first order plant with delay. Initial tuning of PI parameters is carried out by using the Ziegler–Nichols method. The step response obtained has a 20% overshoot for a fixed time delay.

Next, a fuzzy control law is set up where $F(e,\Delta e)$ the output of the fuzzy control for the kth sampling interval, replace $f(e,\Delta e)$ in the incremental controller described in (3.195). The rules and membership functions are developed using an intuitive understanding of what a PI controller does for a fixed delay on a first order system. They generalized what a PI controller does for each combination of e and Δe 12 rules as shown in Table 9 are generated.

TABLE 9 Fuzzy control rules

NL		Δe						
		NM	NS	NO	PO	PS	PM	PL
	NL	NL						
	NM	NM					PS	
	NS					NM	PS	
e	NO					NO		
	PO					PO		
	PS					NS	PM	
	PM					pm		
	PL	PL						

The output from each rule can be treated as a fuzzy singleton. The fuzzy control action is the combination of the output of each rule using the weighted average defuzzification method and can be viewed as the center of gravity of the fuzzy set of output singletons.

TUNING OF MEMBERSHIP FUNCTIONS IN DESIGN STAGE

Since, there is little established theoretical guidance the tuning of rules and membership functions in the design stage is largely an iterative process based on intuition. The membership functions are tuned based on observations of system performance such as rise time, overshoot, and steady state error.

The number of membership functions can vary to provide the resolution needed. Note that the number of rules can grow exponentially as the number of input membership functions increases. The input membership functions for e and Δe generate 64 combinations which can be grouped into twelve regions corresponding to each rule in Table 9.

The center and slopes of the input membership functions in each region is adjusted so that the corresponding rule provides an appropriate control action. In case when two or more rules are fires at the same time, the dominant rule, that is the rule corresponding to the high membership grade, is tuned first. Modifying the output membership function adjusts the rules contribution relative to the output universe of discourse. Once input membership rule tuning is completed, fine-tuning of the output membership functions is performed to achieve the desired performance.

Although,thefuzzy control is constructed based on the assumption that the time delay is fixed and known, the only element of the controller that is a function of the delay is the universe of discourse for the output. It is shown below that with some adjustment and extra rules, the fuzzy control can be made to adapt to an unknown nature or change in delay.

SELF-TUNING

The fuzzy control structure presented above can be directly modified to compensate for changes in the plant dynamics and variable time delays by adding a second layer of self-tuning rules to the controller. We consider the self-tuning function to the fuzzy control in the presenceof variable time delay.

In the case of varying time delay, the fuzzy control gain must be adjusted to offset the effects of the changes in delay. It is shown that the maximum gain or control action is inversely proportional to the time delay. Therefore, if the delay increases, we should decrease the gain to reduce the control action, and vice versa. Based on this relationship, the system performance can be monitored by a second layer of rules that adapts the output membership functions of the first layer of rules to improve the performance of the fuzzy controller.

Consider an output membership function tuned for a nominal delay. When the true system time delay is larger than the nominal delay, the control action determined by the nominal delay causes the control output to be too large for the true system. This condition effectively increases the controller gain, and as the difference between the true and nominal delay becomes large, system stability problems may arise. Conversely, when the true delay is smaller than the nominal delay, the controller gain is too small and the system becomes sluggish.

The output membership functions (See Figure80) of the controller are defined in terms of the maximum control action. A viable mechanism to compensate for a varying time delay is—adjust the size of the control action under the assumption that the number of control rules remains fixed and the linguistic control strategy is valid for different values of time delay. These conditions are reasonable given the plant parameter are known and that the control strategy developed is based on a plant with delay.

To adjust the FLC on-line for systems with varying time delay, a second layer of six rules is added as an adaptation mechanism to modify the output membership function use by the first layer rules with a scaling factor. This effectively changes the fuzzy control output universe of discourse (that is the maximum control action) based on system performance. These rules adjust the fuzzy control output based on rise time and overshoot. The overshoot is monitored and classified as large(L), medium (M), and small (S). It is observed that changes in overshoot are indicative of a change in time delay. A long delay results in a larger overshoot. Such effects can be alleviated by reducing the output scaling factor appropriately. Rise time performance is classified as Very Slow (VS), Medium Slow (MS), and Slightly Slow (SS), and an increase—in the output scaling factor can help to speed up the response.

The design strategy for the second layer of rules is based on two different aspects of tracking performance, that is, rise time and overshoot calculated from $(e, \Delta e)$ The second layer rules are listed in Table 10. They monitor the plant response and reduce or increase thecontroller output universe of discourse. The fuzzy membership functions are defined using a membership configuration similar to the control strategy.

The adjustment rules perform two actions:
- Reduce the controller gain when the plant is significant overshooting the desired response and
- Increase the gain when rise time performance is slow.

Remark3.1 A unique fuzzy control system is presented in the section. Although, a PI controller is used as a guideline for setting up the fuzzy control, it limits its ability to perform more complicated tasks. Similar approaches can be used to set up a fuzzy control that mimics more complex controller. The emphasis here, however, is to deal with unknown dynamics and variable time delay problems which we have difficulty with using analytical approaches.

TABLE 10 Output adjustment of fuzzy control

Rise Time Rules		Overshoot Rules	
If Tracking is L_1		If Overshoot is 3	
Then Adjust is L_2		Then Adjust is L_4	
L_1	L_2	L_3	L_{14}
SS	PS	L	NL
MS	PM	M	NM
VS	PL	S	NS

SIMULATION

The fuzzy control developed above is simulated for the tank temperature control system shown in Figure 81. The temperature of the tank fluid with constant flow rates in an out is to be controlled by adjusting the temperature of the incoming fluid. The incoming fluid temperature is determined by a mixing valve which controls the ratio if hot and cold fluid in the supply lines the tank. The distance between the mixing valve and the supply line discharge to the tank illustrates the classic material transport delay in pipes. The temperature/pressure of the fluids will also affect the delay [79].

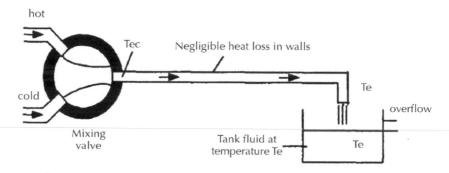

FIGURE 81   Tank temperature control

The transfer function for the tank temperature control problem in Figure 81 is given by:

$$G(S) = \frac{T_e(S)}{T_{ec}(S)} = \frac{e^{-s\tau}}{\frac{s}{a}+1} \tag{3.196}$$

where T_e = tank temperature, T_{ec} = temperature at exit of mixing valve, τ = time delay for material transport in the pipe $a = \dot{m}/M$, $\dot{m}$ = mass flow rate ($= \dot{m}_m = \dot{m}_{out}$) and M=fluid mass contained in the tank.The plant described in equation (3.196) is having value a=1. Assuming the hot and cold supply enters the mixing valve at a constant pressure, the time delay from the material transport will also be constant. Conversely, if the hot and cold supply pressure is varying, the transport delay will also vary. The variable time delay aspects of this system are investigated in the following simulations.

The simulation results are obtained using an 18 rule.The 12 first layer rules in Table 9 provide the control strategy.The six second layer rules in Table 10 adjust the control output membership function universe of discourse based on the system performance. For comparison purposes, simulation plots include a conventional PID controller,theSPC, and the fuzzy algorithm. The PID, SPC, and fuzzy controlare tuned on the plant with a 10 second time delay with the response shown in the top plot of Figure 82. As expected, the SPC has the fastest response in the presence of an accurate plant model and a known time delay but the PID and fuzzy control provide good performance in terms of rise time and overshoot in the absence of a prediction mechanism. The middle and bottom plot of Figure 82 shows how the controllers react as the true system time delay increases from the nominal 10 second delay used to tune the controllers. The fuzzy control algorithm adapts quickly to longer time delays and provides a stable response while the PID controller drives the system unstable and the SPC oscillates around a final value due to the mismatch error generated by the inaccurate time delay parameter used in the plant model.

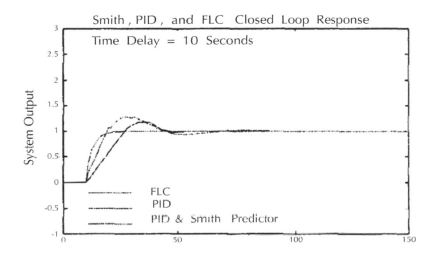

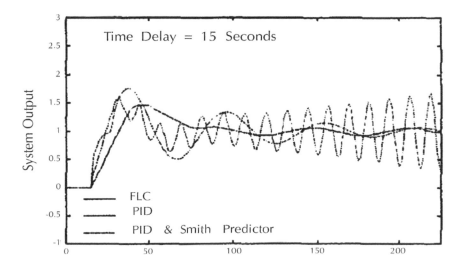

FIGURE 82   *(continued)*

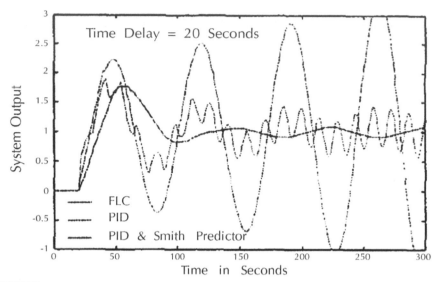

FIGURE 82   The PID,SPC, and FLC Comparison.

From the simulations, clearly the SPC provides the best response with an accurate model of the plant and delay. In the presence of an unknown or possibly varying time delay, the designedfuzzy control shows a significant improvement in maintaining performance and preserving stability over standard SPC and PID methods.

3.7   SINGLE INPUT RULE MODULE (SIRM)

A fuzzy controller for stabilization control of inverted pendulum system is presented based on the Single Input Rule Modules (SIRMs) dynamically connected fuzzy inference model (See Section 1.9 of Chapter 1). The fuzzy controller has four input items, each with a SIRM and dynamic importance degree. The SIRMs and the dynamic importance degrees are designed such that pendulum angular control has priority over cart position control. The fuzzy controller performs the task of control the pendulum angularand the cart position in parallel.Switching between the two controls is realized by automatically tuning the dynamic importance degrees according to control situations. The simulation results show that the proposed fuzzy controller has a high generalization ability to stabilize completely a wide range of the inverted pendulum systems within 9.0s for an initial angle up to 30.0°C.

Inverted pendulum is a nonlinear system and often used as a benchmark for verifying the performance and effectiveness of a new control method. Since the system has strong nonlinearity and inherent instability, the variable structure control system has to linearize the mathematical model of the object near upright position of the pendulum. Recently, a lot of researches on stabilization control of inverted pendulum systems by using fuzzy inference have been done.

To control both the angle of the pendulum and the position of the cart, Kanadadai modified the structure of Berenjito a hierarchical controller and enabled it to generate fuzzy knowledge base automatically. It took more than 12.0 s, however, to asymptotically stabilize an invertedpendulum system with some offset besides its structure complexity. Based on the variable structure systems theory and the trajectory of linearized dynamic equation of an inverted pendulum on phase plane, Kawajiconstructed a fuzzy controller consisting of two simple rule modules. One module is for the magnitude of the manipulated variable, and the other for the sign of the manipulated variable. Since, the control of the cart position can be regarded as a disturbance to the pendulum angle, the information of the cart position is first changed into a virtual target angle, and the virtual target angle is then imbedded into the control of the pendulum angle. Although, this method is rather simple, it is difficult to completely stabilize an inverted pendulum system within a short time interval. Kyung presents a fuzzy controller, whose rule base is derived from three neural networks. Although, the fuzzy controller can stabilize an inverted pendulum system in about 8.0 s, it needs 396 rules even after a smoothing procedure and a logical reduction procedure. Matsuura and Yasunobu both uses the information of the cart to build a set of 49 fuzzy rules for conducting the virtual target angle, and then uses the virtual target angle and the information of the pendulum to construct another set of 49 fuzzy rules for total stabilization. Sakai applied a nonlinear optimization method to train a fuzzy controller for stabilization, however, the controller spends more than 200.0 s on stabilizing an inverted pendulum system [250].

In this section, a new fuzzy controller for the stabilization control of inverted pendulum systems is presented based on the SIRMs dynamically connected fuzzy inference model [250]. The fuzzy controller takes the angle and angular velocity of the pendulum and the position and velocity of the cart as its input items, and the driving force as its output item. Each input item is given with a SIRM and a dynamic importance degree. The SIRMs of the four input items have the same rule setting. The four dynamic importance degrees all select the absolute value of the pendulum angle as the antecedent variable. The dynamic importance degrees are set up such that the angular control of the pendulum takes priority over the position control of the cart when the pendulum is still not balanced upright. By using the SIRMs and the dynamic importance degrees, the fuzzy controller realizes smoothly the angular control of the pendulum and the position control of the cart in parallel with totally only 24 fuzzy rules. Switching between the angular control of the pendulum and the position control of the cart is smoothly realized by automatically adjusting the dynamic importance degrees according to control situations.

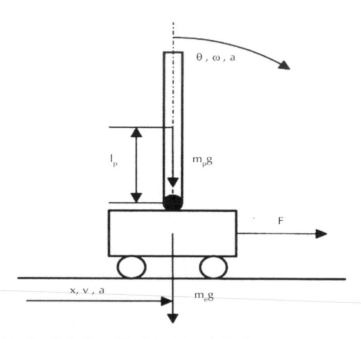

FIGURE 83   Configuration of the inverted pendulum system.

The inverted pendulum system considered here is shown in Figure 83, which consists of a straight-line rail, a cart, a pendulum, and a driving unit. The cart can move left or right on the rail freely. The pendulum is hinged on the center of the top surface of the cart and can rotate around the pivot in the same vertical plane with the rail.

Given that no friction exists in the system, the dynamic equation of the inverted pendulum system can be expressed as:

$$\alpha = \frac{\left(m_c + m_p\right)g \, \sin\theta - \left\{F + m_p l_p w^2 \, \sin\theta\right\}\cos\theta}{\left\{\frac{4}{3}\left(m_c + m_p\right) - m_p\left(\cos\theta\right)^2\right\}l_p} \tag{3.197}$$

$$a = \frac{\frac{4}{3}\left\{F + m_p l_p w^2 \, \sin\theta\right\} - m_p g \, \sin\theta\cos\theta}{\left\{\frac{4}{3}\left(m_c + m_p\right) - m_p\left(\cos\theta\right)^2\right\}} \tag{3.198}$$

Here, the parameters m_c and m_p are, respectively, the mass of the cart and the mass of the pendulum in the unit [kg], and g=9.8 m/s² is the gravity acceleration. The parameter l_p is the length from the center of the pendulum to the pivot in the unit [m] and equals to the half length of the pendulum. The variable F means the driving force in the unit [N] applied horizontally to the cart. The variables θ, ω, α represent, respectively, the angle of the pendulum from upright position, its angular velocity, its angular acceleration, and the clockwise direction is positive. The variables x, v, a denote the position of the cart from the rail origin, its velocity, its acceleration, and right direction is positive.

The variables θ, ω, x, v are the four state variables to describe the dynamic system. In the following simulations, the Euler approximation method is adopted in order to obtain the values of the four state variables.

3.7.1 SIRMS DYNAMICALLYCONNECTEDFUZZY INFERENCE MODEL

We briefly describe the SIRMs dynamically connected fuzzy inference model for systems of n input items and 1 output item. The model can be easily extended for multi-output systems (See Section 1.9 of Chapter 1).

In the conventional fuzzy inference model, we put all the input items into the antecedent part of each fuzzy rule and as a result the total number of possible fuzzy rules increases exponentially with the number of the input items.

To overcome the problems in the SIRMs dynamically connected fuzzy inference model, we first set up a SIRM separately for each input item as:

$$\text{SIRM-i: } \{R_i^j : \quad if \; x_i = A_i^j \quad then \; f_i = C_i^j\}_{j=1}^{m_i} \qquad (3.199)$$

where SIRM-i denotes the SIRM of the ith input item and R_i^j is the jth rule in the SIRM-i. The ith input item x_i is the only variable in the antecedent part, and the consequent variable f_i is an intermediate variable corresponding to the output item $f.A_i^j$ and C_i^j are the membership functions of the x_i and f_i in the jth rule of the SIRM-i. Further, i = 1,2,......,m_i is the index number of the rules in the SIRM-i.

The inference result f_i^0 of the consequent variable f_i can be calculated by using the min-max-gravity method or the product-sum-gravity method or the simplified inference method. Since all the consequent variables of the SIRMs correspond to the output item, the simplest way to obtain the value of the output item is just summing up the inference results of all the SIRMs. But, this does not work well because each input item usually plays an unequal role in system performance. Among the input items, some may contribute significantly while the contribution of the others may be relatively small. Some input items may improve system performance more if their roles are strengthened, while others may not have a positive influence on system performance if emphasized.

To express clearly the different role of each input item on system performance, the SIRMs dynamically connected fuzzy inference model defines a dynamic importance degree w_i^D independently for each input item $x_i (i = 1, 2, \ldots, n)$ as:

$$w_i^D = w_i + B_i \cdot \Delta w_i^0 . \qquad (3.200)$$

On the right side of Equation (3.200), the first term and the second term separate the base value and the dynamic value. The base value guarantees the necessary function of the corresponding input item through a control process. The dynamic value, defined as the product of the breadth and the inference result Δw_i^0 of the dynamic variable Δw_i, plays a role in tuning the degree of the influence of the input item on system performance according to control situation changes. The base value and the breadth are control parameters, and the dynamic variable can be described by fuzzy rules. Because the inference result of the dynamic variable is limited in [0.0, 1.0], the dynamic importance degree varies between $[w_i, w_i + B_i]$.

Suppose that each dynamic importance degree w_i^D and the fuzzy inference result f_1^0 of each SIRM are already calculated. Then, the SIRMs dynamically connected fuzzy inference model obtains the value of the output item f by:

$$f = \sum\nolimits_{i=1}^{n} w_i^D \cdot f_i^0 \qquad (3.201)$$

as the summation of the products of the fuzzy inference result of each SIRM and its dynamic importance degree for all the input items.

As shown in Equation (3.201), the model output is linear to the inference result of each SIRM. If the inference result of each SIRM is identical, then the contribution of one input item to the model output is controlled by its dynamic importance degree. Therefore, the input items with larger importance degrees will contribute more to the model output, while the input items with smaller importance degrees contribute less to the model output.

Since the dynamic importance degrees change with control situations to adjust the model output, Equation (3.200) is in effect an adaptive control law. Moreover, each SIRM has only one antecedent variable, and each dynamic importance degree usually handles only one or two antecedent variable(s). Therefore, the SIRMs dynamically connected fuzzy inference model has a simple structure and is suitable for real applications. Although, the adaptive membership function scheme of Lotfi tunes the parameters of the membership functions based on a generalized neural network, the obtained parameters are fixed through a control process and training patterns are also necessary. For a real control system, collecting training patterns usually is difficult, and the training patterns directly affect the performance of the controller based on such a scheme. On the other hand, the fuzzy model reference learning controller of Moudgal has an ability to modify online the rule base of a fuzzy controller, making the fuzzy controller more flexible. It needs to design a reference model and a fuzzy inverse model for each plant.

TABLE 11 SIRM for each input item

Antecedent variable x_i (i = 1, 2, 3, 4)	Consequent variable f_i (i = 1,2,3,4)
NB	-1.0
ZO	0.0
PB	1.0

3.7.2 STABILIZATIONFUZZY CONTROLLER

In this section, the stabilization control of the inverted pendulum system means to balance upright the pendulum and put the cart back to the origin of the rail in a short time. The desired position of the cart can be set to any reasonable point on the rail, however, the rail origin is selected here as the desired position of the cart without losing generality. Since the desired values of the state variables are all zeros, the control problem can be regarded as a regulator design problem. Here, the fuzzy controller for the stabilization of the inverted pendulum system is constructed based on the SIRMs dynamically connected fuzzy inference model. The four state variables (pendulum angle, pendulum angular velocity, cart position, and cart velocity) after normalization by their scaling factors are chosen in this order as the input items x_i ($i = 1, 2, 3, 4$), and the driving force after normalization by its scaling factor are selected as the output item f [250].

SETTING THE SIRMS

As stated earlier, each input item is given with a SIRM and a dynamic importance degree in the SIRMs dynamically connected fuzzy inference model. The SIRMs of the four input items in the stabilization control of the inverted pendulum system are considered first.

In setting up the SIRMs for the angle and the angular velocity of the pendulum, it is enough to utilize the relation of the input items with the whole control performance from experience and intuition. When the angle and the angular velocity of the pendulum are positive, the driving force should be positive from the sign definition in Figure 83 so that the cart moves toward the right direction. As a result, the pendulum rotates counterclockwise toward the upright position, and the angle and the angular velocity tends to decrease toward zero. In the same way, when the angle and the angular velocity are negative, the driving force should become negative to make the cart move toward the left direction. Consequently, the pendulum turns clockwise toward the upright position, and the angle and the angular velocity increase toward zero.

In the stabilization control, the cart position can be considered as a disturbance to the pendulum angle. In setting up the SIRMs for the position and the velocity of the cart, the position control of the cart can be indirectly realized by intentionally putting the pendulum a little down to the direction opposite to the cart position. If the position and the velocity of the cart are positive, then the driving force of positive value is executed on the cart so that the cart moves further toward the right direction, causing the pendulum down counter clockwise to the negative direction deliberately. If the position and the velocity are negative, then the driving force of negative value is given to drive the cart further toward the left direction, causing the pendulum down clockwise to the positive direction deliberately. Since the pendulum falls down toward the rail origin, the driving force changes to move the cart toward the rail origin if the angular control of the pendulum takes priority over the position control of the cart. As a result, the pendulum is balanced upright and the cart is returned to the rail origin [250].

From the above analysis, the fuzzy rules for each SIRM can all be set up to Table 11. Here, membership functions NB, ZO, and PB of the antecedent variable of each SIRM are defined in Figure 84 as triangles or trapezoids. The consequent variable f_i

is an intermediate variable corresponding to the output item f of the fuzzy controller. Because the simplified reasoning method is adopted here, real numbers are assigned as singleton membership functions to the consequent variable of each SIRM.

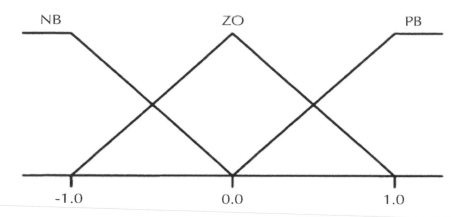

FIGURE 84   Membership functions for each SIRM.

SETTING THE DYNAMIC VARIABLE OF THE DYNAMIC IMPORTANCE DEGREES

From Table 11, each SIRM directly corresponds to the output item. To obtain the value of the output item by Equation (3.201), each input item is given with a dynamic importance degree defined by Equation (3.200). If the position control of the cart takes priority over the angular control of the pendulum, then the angular control of the pendulum should have priority over the position control of the cart when the pendulum does not stand up yet, and the position control of the cart should be done after the pendulum is almost balanced upright. The dynamic importance degree shows the influence strength on system performance and hence can signify the priority orders.

TABLE 12   Fuzzy rules for the two dynamic variables of the pendulum

Antecedent variable	Consequent variable
$\lvert x_1 \rvert$	$\Delta w_i \ (i = 1,2)$
DS	0.0
DM	0.5
DB	1.0

The priority order of the pendulum depends on the two dynamic importance degrees of the angle and angular velocity of the pendulum, and the priority order of the cart depends on the two dynamic importance degrees of the position and velocity of the cart. Because each dynamic importance degree consists of two control parameters and one dynamic variable, the fuzzy rules of the dynamic variables are established here.

First consider the dynamic variables of the angle and the angular velocity of the pendulum. In the case where the absolute value of the pendulum angle is big, the pendulum falls down if it is not controlled to rotate towards the upright position at once. Therefore, in order to balance the pendulum upright in this case, the dynamic importance degrees of the angle and the angular velocity of the pendulum should be set up to rather large values to strengthen their influences on system performance. In the case where the absolute value of the pendulum angle is near zero, meaning that the pendulum already stands almost upright, the almost balanced state is destroyed, if the angular control of the pendulum is emphasized too much. In order to achieve and keep the balanced state in this situation, it is necessary to reduce the importance degrees of the angle and the angular velocity to weaken their influences. Since the dynamic variables bring about changes in the dynamic importance degrees, the fuzzy rules for the dynamic variables of the dynamic importance degrees of the angle and the angular velocity are given in Table 12. Here, the absolute value of the pendulum angle after normalization is selected as the only antecedent variable. Membership functions DS, DM, and DB are defined in Figure85 as trapezoids or triangles.

As stated above, the angular control of the pendulum must be done with priority over the position control of the cart in order to achieve complete stabilization of the whole inverted pendulum system. When the pendulum is not located in the upright position yet, the angular control of the pendulum is first executed so that the pendulum is balanced almost upright. While the balanced state of the pendulum is kept, starting the position control of the cart is allowable. This fact means that in the stabilization control of the inverted pendulum system, the angular control of the cart. Therefore, the angle and the angular velocity of the pendulum should be assigned with larger importance degrees, and the dynamic variables of the position and the velocity of the cart should be determined based on the angle of the pendulum. When the pendulum is far from the upright position, the stabilization control is impossible if the angular control of the pendulum is not done immediately. In this case, the importance degrees of the position and the velocity of the cart should be reduced, and the control focus should be brought into the angular control of the pendulum. When the pendulum is almost balanced upright, the importance degrees of the position and the velocity of the cart can be increased to some extent so that, the angular control of the pendulum is maintained and at the same time the position control of the cart is started. Therefore, the dynamic variables of the dynamic importance degrees of the position and the velocity of the cart can be inferred by using the fuzzy rules of Table 13 which also takes the absolute value of the pendulum angle as the antecedent variable. The membership functions of the antecedent variable are the same as the ones shown in Figure 85.

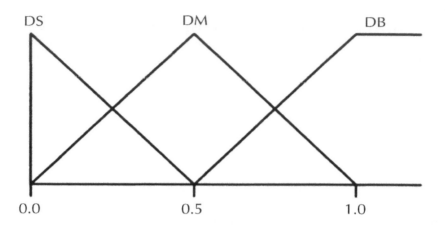

FIGURE 85 Membership functions for each dynamic variable.

SETTING THE CONTROL PARAMETERS

Since, the SIRMs and the dynamic variables of the dynamic importance degrees all have been determined, the structure of the proposed fuzzy controller becomes clear. As stated above, however, each dynamic importance degree also has two control parameters, thatare the base value and the breadth. The rule setting of the dynamic variables only does not guarantee the necessary control priority orders. If the control parameters of the cart are bigger than the control parameters of the pendulum, for example, the cart position control takes priority over the pendulum angular control even though the dynamic variables are settled as given in Tables 12 and 13. Therefore, the control parameters also have to be adequately set up.

To determine the base value and the breadth of the dynamic importance degree of each input item, a typical inverted pendulum system is selected. The mass of the pendulum is pendulum = 0.1 kg, the half length of the pendulum is $l_p = 0.5\,m$, and the mass of the cart is $m_c = 1.0$ kg. The angle of the pendulum is limited to [-30.0°, + 30.0°] and the moving range of the cart is limited to [-2.4 m, +2.4 m]. If the pendulum angle or the cart position gets out of the above range, then the stabilization control is regarded as a failure.

TABLE 13 Fuzzy rules for the two dynamic variables of the cart

Antecedent variable	Consequent variable
$|x_1|$	$\Delta w_i\ (i= 3,4)$
DS	1.0
DM	0.5
DB	0.0

Although, the maximum angular velocity of the pendulum and the maximum velocity of the cart are unknown, in this section, the scaling factors of the four input items to the fuzzy controller are set to $30.0°$, $100.0°/s$, 2.4 m, and 1.0 m/s, respectively. Since the fuzzy controller does not take the mass of the pendulum and the cart into consideration, the scaling factor of the output item should include a factor reflecting the mass of the objects. Control simulations reveal that if the scaling factor of the output item is selected to just 10 times as large as the total mass of the pendulum and the cart, the stabilization control can be performed satisfactorily. Resultantly, the scaling factor of the output item is set up to 10 times the total mass of the pendulum and the cart.

It is understood from the above discussion that the two importance degrees of the pendulum have to be larger than the two importance degrees of the cart in order to stabilize the whole pendulum system. That is, the base values and the breadths of the two importance degrees of the pendulum should be bigger than the base values and the breadths of the two importance degrees of the cart. To cover all the control situations, the importance degree of the pendulum angle when the pendulum angle is big, should almost be the same as the importance degree of the angular velocity when the angular velocity is big. Similarly, the importance degree of the cart position when the positive is big should almost be the same as the importance degree of the cart velocity when the velocity is big. Therefore, the base value and the breadth of the pendulum angle should almost equal to the base value and the breadth of the angular velocity, and the base value and the breadth of the cart position should almost equal the base value and the breadth of the cart velocity.

The final set of the base values and the breadths tuned by trial and error is given in Table 14. Because the control parameters of the pendulum are about 10 times as large as the control parameters of the cart, the two dynamic importance degrees of the pendulum get bigger when the pendulum is not balanced yet. In this way, the priority order of the angular control of the pendulum over the position control of the cart is guaranteed.

The control parameters of Table 14 and the scaling factors of the input items are fixed in the following simulations:

TABLE 14   The base value and breadth of the input items

Input item	Base value	Breadth
Pendulum angle	2.00	2.50
Angular velocity	1.50	1.00
Cart position	0.15	0.20
Cart velocity	0.15	0.20

BLOCKDIAGRAMOFTHEFUZZY CONTROLLER

The block diagram of the fuzzy controller for the stabilization control of the inverted pendulum system is shown in Figure 86. The state variables of the pendulum system is fed back and compared with the desired values. Because the desired values. Because the desired values are all zeros in the stabilization control, the variables are reversely inputted into the Norm block. The Norm block normalizes the state variables by their scaling factors each and creates the input items x_1, x_2, x_3, x_4 from θ, ω, x, v, respectively. Each input item $x_i (i = 1, 2, 3, 4)$ is then guided to the SIRM-I block, where the fuzzy inference of the SIRM corresponding to the input item x_i is done. All the Dynamic Importance Degree (DID) blocks take the absolute value of the input item x_1 as their antecedent variable. The DID-i block calculates the value of the dynamic importance degree of the input item. After the output of each SIRM-i block is multiplied by the output of the DID-i block, summing them for all the input items gives the output value of the output item f of the fuzzy controller. The OSF (Output Scaling Factor) block finally multiplies the output value of the output item of the fuzzy controller by its scaling factor to generate the actual driving force F to the cart. Because each of the SIRM blocks and the DID blocks has only three 1-input 1-output fuzzy rules, the proposed fuzzy controller has a simple structure and is easy to realize in hardware.

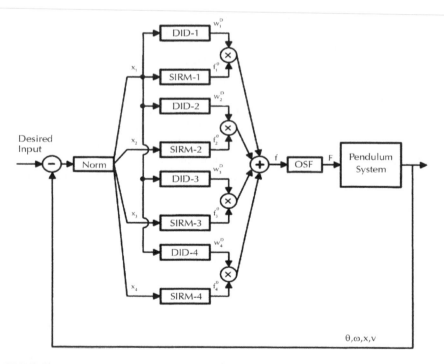

FIGURE 86   Block diagram of the stabilization fuzzy controller.

As shown in Table 11 for the four input items, the consequent variable in the fuzzy rules of each SIRM corresponds to the same output item, and the consequent part of each SIRM has the same setting. According to Equation (3.201), each SIRM with its dynamic importance degree contributes directly to the output item, and the angular control of the pendulum and the position control of the cart are treated in parallel. Because the two SIRMs for the position and the velocity of the cart are built such that the cart position is controlled indirectly by putting down the pendulum intentionally, the information about the position and the velocity of the cart is changed essentially into part of the angle of the pendulum. Although, similar to the virtual target angle method, the proposed fuzzy controller executes completely in parallel the pendulum angular control and the cart position control to directly obtain the driving force without inferring a virtual target angle.

Moreover, it is clear that the setting order of the real number membership functions in the consequent part of Table 13 for the position and the velocity of the cart is just reverse to that of Table 12 for the angle and the angular velocity of the pendulum. By this setting, the inference results of Tables 12 and 13 become complementary with each other. If the absolute value of the pendulum angle is large, the dynamic variables of the angle and the angular velocity of the pendulum take large values, while the dynamic variables of the position and the velocity of the cart can only take small values. Because the control parameters of the pendulum are bigger than the control parameters of the cart, the two dynamic importance degrees of the pendulum become much bigger than the two dynamic importance degrees of the cart. Consequently, the angular control of the pendulum takes priority over the position control of the cart and makes the pendulum rotate toward the upright position. On the contrary, if the pendulum is almost balanced upright, the dynamic variables of the pendulum become small, while the dynamic variables of the cart become large. In this case, the two dynamic importance degrees of the pendulum decrease almost to their base values and the two dynamic importance degrees of the cart increase almost to the sums of their base values and breadths. Although, either of the base values of the pendulum is still larger than the sum of the base value and the breadth of either the dynamic importance degrees of the cart, the inference result of the SIRM corresponding to the pendulum angle becomes almost zero. As a result, the contribution from the cart in Equation (3.201) will exceed the contribution from the pendulum so that the position control of the cart is started while the pendulum is kept balanced. In this way, the pendulum angular control and the cart position control are switched smoothly by adjusting automatically the dynamic importance degrees according to control situations, and then the stabilization control of the inverted pendulum system is realized.

3.7.3 SIMULATION STUDY

To verity the effectiveness of the proposed fuzzy controller, stabilization control simulations are first done for the inverted pendulum system as stated earlier. The Figure 87 shows the control result, where the initial angle of the pendulum is 30.0° and the other initial values are all zeros. The left axis and the right axis indicate, respectively, the pendulum angle and the cart position, and the horizontal axis indicates the control time. The numbers in Plant (0.100, 0.500, 1.000, and 0.010) denote the pendulum mass, the pendulum half length, the cart mass, and the sampling period in this order, respectively. The sampling period is set up to 0.01 s. The numbers in State (30.00,

0.00, 0.00, and 0.00) mean, respectively, the initial values of the pendulum angle, the angular velocity, the cart position, and the cart velocity in order [250].

As can be seen from Figure 87, since the initial pendulum angle is positively big, the cart is first driven from the rail origin to the right side such that the pendulum is put a little down in the negative direction. Then by moving the cart back toward the rail origin, the pendulum is balanced upright and the cart is returned to the rail origin. Apparently from control beginning until complete stabilization, the cart makes only one round trip and the pendulum swings around the upright position only once a time except the initial part. Here, the complete stabilization means that all the state variables converge, respectively, to 0.1°, 0.1/s, 0.01 m, and 0.01 m/s. In this example, the complete stabilization time is 8.24 s, the maximum driving force is about 50.0 N, and the maximum velocity of the cart is about 2.5 m/s.

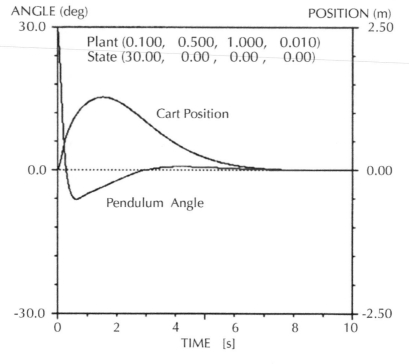

FIGURE 87   Control result of 1.0 m pendulum system for initial angle 30.0°.

The Figure 88 depicts the control result of the same pendulum system, where the initial position of the cart is 2.0 m and the other initial values are all zeros. Since at the control beginning the cart position is big and the pendulum stands up, the fuzzy controller starts the cart position control first. The cart is moved further toward the right direction such that the pendulum is inclined to about -5.0°. After that, the pendulum angular control takes priority over the cart position control, and the fuzzy controller

moves the cart toward the rail origin so that the pendulum is rotated toward the upright position. As a result, the pendulum system is completely stabilized in 7.16 s. The
maximum driving force is only about 3.0 N, and the maximum velocity of the cart is
about 0.7 m/s.

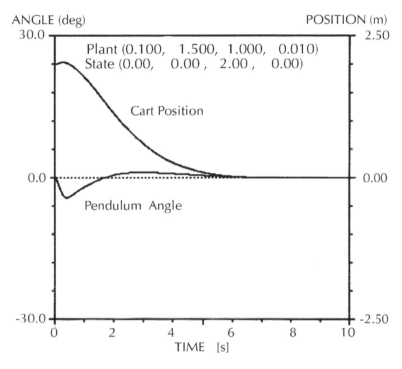

FIGURE 88   Control result of 1.0 m pendulum system for initial position 2.0 m.

To check the generalization ability of the proposed fuzzy controller, the length of
the pendulum is changed, while the other parameters are all fixed. The Figure 89 and
draws the simulation result, where the pendulum is 0.2 m long. Since, the pendulum
is rather short, a small amount of the cart moving can cause the pendulum to rotate
because the pendulum has a high natural frequency. Therefore, even though the cart
moves a little, the pendulum is balanced upright in a short time. The complete stabilization time in this case is 6.65 s. The Figure 90 depicts an example, where the
pendulum has a length of 2.2 m. Since the pendulum is long, the pendulum has a small
natural frequency and a big momentum. To balance the pendulum, then the cart has to
move for a long distance. As a result, the cart moves from the rail origin to almost the
margin of the rail and returns back to the rail origin. At the same time, the pendulum is
rotated to the negative direction and then stood up. The complete stabilization time of
this example is 9.04 s. By the way, the maximum driving forces in these two examples
are both about 50.0 N.

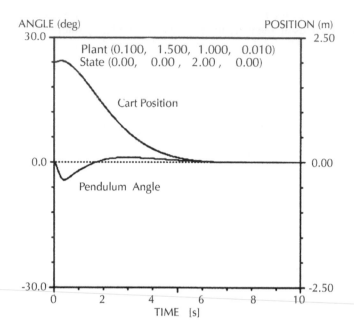

FIGURE 89 Control result of 0.2 m pendulum system for initial angle 30.0°.

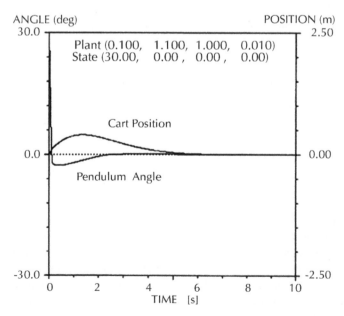

FIGURE 90 Control result of 2.2 m pendulum system for initial angle 30.0°.

From Figures 87–90, it is found that the control result changes largely with the pendulum length. When the pendulum length is short, the pendulum is controlled first to the reverse direction sharply and then balanced smoothly. When the pendulum is long enough, it will be rotated at first to the reverse direction rather smoothly and then stood up with some fluctuation. Moreover, as the pendulum gets longer, the cart is moved further away from the rail origin in order to put the pendulum a little down toward the rail origin.

If the sampling period is bigger than 0.01 s, it may give a bad influence on the stabilization control of a short pendulum system because of the high natural frequency of the pendulum. In fact, if the sampling period is 0.02 s, the fuzzy controller fails to stabilize the pendulum system, when the pendulum is only 0.1 m long. Because a short pendulum responds sharply to the cart moving, a small sampling period I effective to stabilize smoothly a short pendulum system with a quick control action. The Figure 91 illustrates such a control result of the pendulum system used in Figure 89, where the sampling period is changed from 0.01 s to 0.001d s. Although, the moving distance of the cart from the rail origin to the right side increases, the pendulum is smoothly rotated from its initial position to the negative direction and then smoothly balanced upright. In this case, the complete stabilization time is 7.41 s, almost equal to that shown in Figure 89.

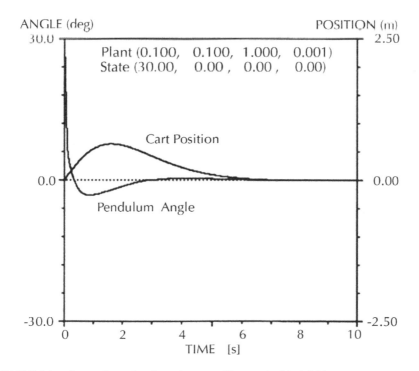

FIGURE 91 Control result when the sampling period is 0.001 s.

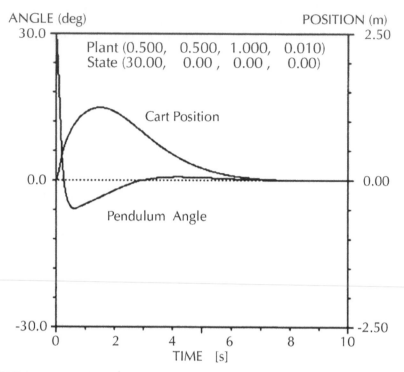

FIGURE 92   Control result when pendulum mass is 0.5 kg.

Because the scaling factor of the output item is set as 10 times the total mass of the pendulum and the cart, the influence of the pendulum mass or the cart mass is basically absorbed by the scaling factor of the output item. The Figure 92 displays a simulation result of the pendulum system used in Figure 87, where only the pendulum mass is changed from 0.1 to 0.5 kg. Compared with Figure 87, the control result is very similar to that of Figure 87, and the complete stabilization time is 8.18 s. The result indicates that the pendulum mass has little influence on the control performance. In fact, if the pendulum length is within [0.2 m, 2.2 ml, the pendulum mass is equal to or larger than 0.001 kg, the cart mass is equal to or larger than 0.002 kg, and the ratio of the pendulum mass to the cart mass is within [0.005, 0.500], then the pendulum system can be stabilized, when the initial angle is within [- 30.0°, + 30.0°] or the initial position is within [- 2.25 m, + 2.25 m]. Note that the upper limits of the pendulum mass and the cart mass are not given here because they relate with the driving force. If there is no limit to the magnitude of the driving force, then the stabilization control is theoretically possible no matter how heavy the pendulum and the cart are. In the control simulations, the inverted pendulum system, where the pendulum mass is 5.0 kg and the cart mass is 10.0 kg, is successfully stabilized. Since, the controllable parameter range covers almost all the inverted pendulum systems reported till now, the proposed fuzzy controller is shown to have a high generalization ability to stabilize a wide range of the inverted pendulum systems.

On the other hand, if the pendulum is shorter than 0.2 m or longer than 2.2 m, the stabilization control may fail, since, the scaling factor of the output item is given as a function of only the pendulum mass and the cart mass without consideration of the pendulum length. If the pendulum is rather short, small driving force is enough. For a short pendulum that has a high natural frequency, a big driving force may cause the pendulum to rotate sharply to fall down. On the other hand, if the pendulum is rather long, a bigger driving force is necessary. For a long pendulum that has a low natural frequency and a big momentum, the stabilization control becomes impossible if the driving force is not big enough. Therefore, it would be ideal for the scaling factor of the output item to be a function of the pendulum length also. For example, the pendulum system, whose pendulum is only 0.04 m long, can be stabilized if the scaling factor of the output item is reduced to half. The stabilization control of the pendulum system, whose pendulum has a length of 3.0 m, is possible if the scaling factor of the output item is enlarged three times.

3.8   CONSTRUCTION OF PID CONTROLLER BY SIMPLIFIED FUZZY REASONING METHOD

The PID controllers are widely used as simple and effective controllers. It is shown that PID controllers can be realized by fuzzy control methods of "product-sum-gravity method" and "simplified fuzzy reasoning method". Therefore, PID controls are shown to be a special case of fuzzy controls. The PID controllers, however, cannot be constructed by min-max-gravity method, which is known as Mamdani's fuzzy reasoning method. Furthermore, extrapolative reasoning can be executed by the product-sum-gravity method and simplified fuzzy reasoning method by extending the range of membership functions of antecedent parts of fuzzy rules from [0, 1] to ($-\infty$, ∞).

3.8.1   PRODUCT-SUM-GRAVITY METHOD AND SIMPLIFIED FUZZY REASONING METHOD

We consider the following multiple fuzzy reasoning forms:

Rule 1: A1 and B1 = > C1
Rule 2: A2 and B2 = > C2

....   (3.202)

Rule n: An and Bn = >Cn
Fact: x and y.

Cons: C'

where Ai is a fuzzy set in X, Bi in Y, and Ci in Z and x $\in$ X, y $\in$ Y.

At first, we explain the case of fuzzy reasoning method called product-sum-gravity method [145] (See Figure93).

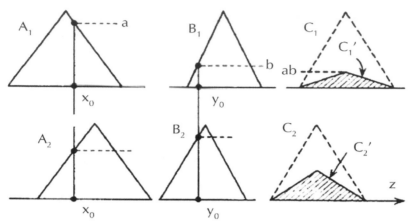

FIGURE 93   Product-sum-gravity method.

The inference result C_i', which is inferred from the fact [x and y] and the fuzzy rule [Ai and Bi = >Ci] is given as:

$$\mu_{c_i},(z)= \mu_{Ai}(x)\cdot\ \mu_{Bi}(y)\cdot\ \mu_{ci}(z) \tag{3.203}$$

The final consequence C' of Equation 3.202 is aggregated by taking the sum (+) of C_1', C_2', ..., C_n' obtained above. Namely:

$$C' =C_1' + C_2' + \ldots + C_n'$$

$$\mu_{C'}\left(z\right)=\mu_{C1'}\left(z\right)+\ldots+\mu_{cn'}\left(z\right) \tag{3.204}$$

where + stands for sum.

The representative point z_0 for the resulting fuzzy set C' is obtained as the center of gravity of C':

$$z_0 = \frac{\Sigma zi\cdot\mu_{C'}\left(zi\right)}{\Sigma\mu_{C'}\left(zi\right)} \tag{3.205}$$

Note that it is possible to define min-max-gravity method known as Mamdani's fuzzy reasoning method by replacing product with min in Equation 3.203 and sum with max in Equation 3.205.

As a special case of product-sum-gravity method, we can give a simplified fuzzy reasoning method for the following fuzzy reasoning form:

Rule 1: A1 and B1 = > z1
Rule 2: A2 and B2 = > z2

....   (3.206)

Rule n: An and Bn = >zn

Fact: x and y

Cons:z_0

where z1, z2, ..., zn, z_0 are not fuzzy sets but real numbers in Z.

The consequence z_0 by the simplified fuzzy reasoning method is obtained as follows (See Figure 94):

The degree of fitness of the fact [x_0 and y_0] to the antecedent part [Ai and Bi] is given as:

$$hi = \mu_{Ai}(x_0) \cdot \mu_{Bi}(y_0) \qquad (3.207)$$

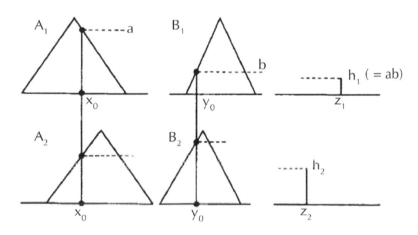

FIGURE 94 Simplified fuzzy reasoning method.

The degree of fitness, hi may be regarded as the degree with which zi is obtained. Therefore, the final consequence z_0 of Equation 3.206 is obtained as the weighted average of zi by the degree hi. Namely:

$$z_0 = \frac{h_1 \cdot z_1 + h_2 \cdot z_2 + ... + h_n \cdot z_n}{h_1 + h_2 + ... + h_n} \qquad (3.208)$$

Note that the simplified reasoning method is regarded as a special case of product-sum-gravity method but not a special case of min-max-gravity method.

3.8.2 REALIZATION OF PID CONTROLLERS BY FUZZY REASONING METHODS

As is well-known, a control action u of PID controller is obtained in the form of the linear combination of the error e, the change in error Δe and the integral, $\int e dt$, namely:

$$u = \alpha\, e + \beta\, \Delta e + \gamma \int edt \qquad\qquad (3.209)$$

where α is the proportional coefficient, β is the derivative coefficient, and γ is the integral coefficient for e.

For simplicity, we shall first consider the case of PD controller:

$$u = \alpha\, e + \beta\, \Delta e \qquad\qquad (3.210)$$

Let e_1 and e_2 be the minimal and maximal values of the possible error e, and let $\Delta e1$ and $\Delta e2$ be the minimal and maximal values of Δe that is:

$$e_1 \le e \le e_2;\Delta e_1 \le e \le \Delta e_2 \qquad\qquad (3.211)$$

then we shall define fuzzy sets e_1 and e_2 for the error e as in Figure 95(a). Similarly, fuzzy sets Δe_1 and Δe_2 for the change in error Δe are given in Figure 95(b).

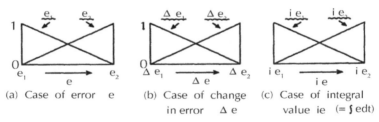

(a) Case of error   e   (b) Case of change   (c) Case of integral
                              in error Δ e   value ie (= $\int$ edt)

FIGURE 95   Fuzzy sets of error , change in error Δe and integral $\int edt$.

Then, we can construct fuzzy control rules for PD controller in the case of a simplified fuzzy reasoning method as follows:

Rule 1: $e1$ and $\Delta e1 => u1$
Rule 2: $e1$ and $\Delta e^2 => u2$
Rule 3: $e2$ and $\Delta e1 => u3$ \qquad (3.212)
Rule 4: $e2$ and $\Delta e2 => u4$
Fact: e and Δe

Cons: u

where u1, u2, u3, and u4 are real numbers such that:

u1 = $\alpha e1 + \beta \Delta e1$
u2 = $\alpha e1 + \beta \Delta e2$ \qquad (3.213)
u3 = $\alpha e2 + \beta \Delta e1$
u4 = $\alpha e2 + \beta \Delta e2$.

Then we can obtain an inference result u of Equation 3.212 from Equation 3.207 and Equation 3.208 in the following (See Figure 96):

$$u = \frac{abu1 + a(1-b)u2 + (1-a)bu3 + (1-a)(1-b)u4}{ab + a(1-b) + (1-a)b + (1-a)(1-b)} \qquad (3.214)$$

$$= abu1 + a(1-b)u2 + (1-a)bu3 + (1-a)(1-b)u4 \qquad (3.214)$$

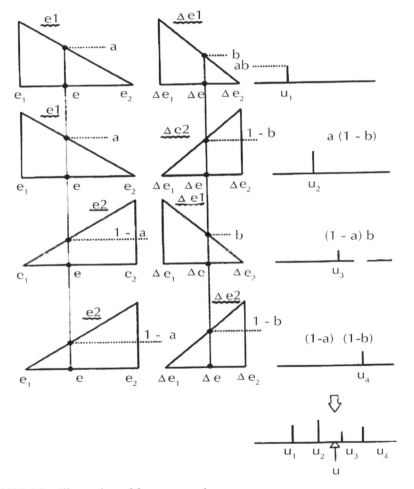

FIGURE 96   Illustration of fuzzy reasoning.

It is noted that the denominator of the above equation is equal to 1. And a and b is given as:

$$a = \mu_{e1}(e) = \frac{e2 - e}{e2 - e1}, \quad b = \mu_{\Delta e1}(\Delta e) = \frac{\Delta e2 - \Delta e}{\Delta e2 - \Delta e1} \qquad (3.215)$$

The consequent parts u1, u2, u3 u4 of (3.213) are the heights at the lattice points (e1, Δe1), (e1, Δe2), (e2, Δe1) and (e2, Δe2), and are on the same plane.

Therefore, the inference result (i.e., control action) u can be derived as follows by inserting (3.213) and (3.215) into (3.214):

u =   (3.214)

$$= \alpha\, e + \beta \Delta e \qquad (3.216)$$

which indicates the construction of PD controller by means of a simplified reasoning method (See Figure 97(a)).

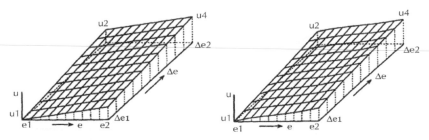

(a). Case of product-sum-gravity method.
(b). Case of min-max-gravity method.
And simplified fuzzy reasoning method
FIGURE 97   Inference result u from e and Δe.

In the same way, we can realize PD controller under the product-sum-gravity method by extending the points u1, u2, u3, and u4 to fuzzy sets, u1 (around u1), u2, u3, and u4 of the same width.

Note that min-max-gravity method cannot realize such PD controller, since it does not generate a plane as shown in Figure 97(b).

We shall next consider the case of PID controllers of Equation 3.209.

Let *ie* be the integral value $\int e\,dt$ of an error e, and its minimum and maximal values be ie_1 and ie_2, respectively. Namely:

$$ie1 \leq ie \leq ie2 \qquad (3.217)$$

Fuzzy sets ie1 and ie2 are given in Figure 95(c).
Then the fuzzy control rules for PID controllers are obtained as:
Rule 1: $e1$ and $\Delta e1$ and $ie1 => $ u1
Rule 2: $e1$ and $\Delta e1$ and $ie2=> $ u2
Rule 3: $e1$ and $\Delta e1$ and $ie1 => $ u3

Rule 1: e1 and Δe1 and ie1 $\geq$ u1

Rule 2: e1 and Δe1 and ie2 $\geq$ u2

Rule 3: e1 and Δe1 and ie1 $\geq$ u3

Rule 4: e1 and Δe1 and ie2 $\geq$ u4

Rule 5: e1 and Δe2 and ie1 $\geq$ u5   (3.218)

Rule 6: e1 and Δe2 and ie2 $\geq$ u6

Rule 7: e1 and Δe2 and ie1 $\geq$ u7

Rule 8: e1 and Δe2 and ie2 $\geq$ u8

Fact : e and Δe   and   ie

Cons :   u

where u1, u2, ..., u8 are real numbers such that

$$u1 = \alpha\ e1 + \beta\ \Delta e1 + \gamma\ ie1$$

$$u2 = \alpha\ e1 + \beta\ \Delta e1 + \gamma\ ie2$$

$$u3 = \alpha\ e1 + \beta\ \Delta e2 + \gamma\ ie1$$

$$u4 = \alpha\ e1 + \beta\ \Delta e2 + \gamma\ ie2 \qquad\qquad 3.219)$$

$$u5 = \alpha\ e2 + \beta\ \Delta e1 + \gamma\ ie1$$

$$u6 = \alpha\ e2 + \beta\ \Delta e1 + \gamma\ ie2$$

$$u7 = \alpha\ e2 + \beta\ \Delta e2 + \gamma\ ie1$$

$$u8 = \alpha\ e2 + \beta\ \Delta e2 + \gamma\ ie2 .$$

The control action u for e, Δe and ie is given as

$$u = \frac{\begin{array}{c} abcu1 + ab(1-c)u2 + a(1-b)cu3 + a(1-b)(1-c)u4 \\ +(1-a)bcu5 + (1-a)b(1-c)u6 + (1-a)(1-b)cu7 + (1-a)(1-b)cu8 \end{array}}{\begin{array}{c} abc + ab(1-c) + a(1-b)c + a(1-b)(1-c) \\ +(1-a)bc + (1-a)b(1-c) + (1-a)(1-b)c + (1-a)(1-b)(1-c) \end{array}}$$

= abcu1+ab(1-c)u2+a(1-b)cu3+a(1-b) (1-c)u4
+(1-a)bcu5+(1-a)b (1-c)u6+(1-a) (1-b)cu7+(1-a) (1-b)cu8

$$= \alpha\ e + \beta\ \Delta e + \lambda\ \int edt \qquad\qquad (3.220)$$

$$c = \mu_{ie1}\ (ie) = \frac{ie2 - ie}{ie2 - ie1} . \qquad\qquad (3.221)$$

Therefore, it is shown that PID controller can be constructed by the simplified reasoning method. The same holds for product-sum-gravity method.

3.8.3 EXTRAPOLATIVE REASONING BY FUZZY REASONING METHODS

In the discussion of the realization of PD controller and PID controller, it is assumed that $e, \Delta e$, and ie are in the intervals between the minimum value and the maximal value as in Equation 3.211 and Equation 3.217, and thus the grades a, b, and c of equation 3.215 and Equation 3.221 of fuzzy sets are in the unit interval [0, 1]. However, in the derivations of Equation3.216 and Equation3.220, we did not use the condition that a, b, and c are in [0, 1]. Thus, fuzzy sets, say, e_1 and e_2 should not necessarily be of triangular type with height 1 but may be characterized by such functions as in Figure 98 with the range $(-\infty, \infty)$ rather than [0, 1].

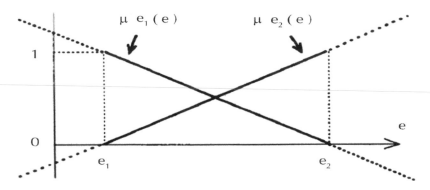

FIGURE 98   Membership functions extended to ($-\infty$ - *gure*).

As a simple example, we shall consider P controller ($u = \alpha e$), which is realized by the following two fuzzy rules:

   Rule 1: $e1 => u1$
   Rule 2: $e2 => u2$ (3.222)
where,
       $-a =$ (3.215).

It is found from Figure 99 that the inference result u is given by dividing externally u1 and u2 in the ratio 1 + a: a. Namely, when e is outside [$e1$, $e2$], u is given as the external division point of u1 and u2, which indicates the possibility of extrapolation. Obviously, when e is in [$e1$, $e2$], u is in the [u1, u2].

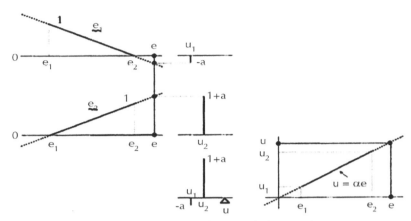

FIGURE 99   Extrapolative reasoning and extrapolation result.

In the same way, we can discuss PD and PID controllers by extending the ranges of membership functions of $e1$, $e2$, $\Delta e1$, $\Delta e2$, $ie1$ and $ie2$ from [0, 1] to $(-\infty, \infty)$.

3.9   FUZZY CONTROL AS A FUZZY DEDUCTION SYSTEM [82, 83, 84]

In control theory, we define a function $\underline{f} : X \rightarrow Y$ with an aim to demonstrate that $\underline{f}$ (x) is the correct answer given the input x. Fuzzy approach to control, as devised in [8, 10, 11, and 12], furnishes an approximation of such a (ideal) function $\underline{f} : X \rightarrow Y$ on the basis of pieces of fuzzy information (fuzzy granules). This approximation is achieved by a system of fuzzy IF–THEN rules like (See Chapter 1),

IF x is A THEN y is B

where A and B are labels for fuzzy subsets. In formalized logic the interpretation of such a rule as a logical implication $A(x) \rightarrow B(y)$ is questionable.

Remark 3.2 Observe that, by generalization rule, $A(x) \rightarrow B(y)$ entails the formula $\forall x \, \forall y (A(x) \rightarrow B(y))$. In turn, by the virtue of two rewriting rules for the reduction of a formula in prenex form such a formula is now equivalent to $\forall x (A(x) \rightarrow \forall y \, B(y))$ and therefore to $(\exists x \, A(x)) \rightarrow \forall y \, B(y)$. Then, we can admit the IF–THEN rule only in the cases that $\exists x \, A(x)$ is false or $\forall y \, B(y)$ is true. This is obviously unsatisfactory.

In fact, the user of an IF–THEN system of rules implicitly assumes a dependence of y from x, while such dependence is not expressed in an IF–THEN rule at all. In other words, they write $A(x) \rightarrow B(x)$ to denote the formula $A(x) \rightarrow B(\underline{f}(x))$, where such a dependence is expressed.

Remark 3.3 In literature there are several interesting attempts to reduce fuzzy control to fuzzy logic in narrow sense.

We propose a different reduction, in which we give a logical meaning to a fuzzy IF–THEN rule by translating it into a first order formula (namely, a clause) like:

$$A(x) \wedge B(y) \rightarrow Good(x, y).$$

The intended meaning of Good(x, y) is that given x the value y gives a correct control.

Remark 3.4 We show that the information carried on by a system of fuzzy IF–THEN rules can be represented by a fuzzy theory in a fuzzy logic.

Remark 3.5 Such a theory is a fuzzy program, that is, a fuzzy set of Horn clauses.

Remark 3.6 We show that the computation of the fuzzy function arising from a fuzzy IF–THEN system is equivalent to the computation of the least fuzzy Herbrand model of a fuzzy program.

This gives an interesting theoretical framework and new tools for fuzzy control. Finally, we explore the possibility of giving a logical meaning to the centroid method of defuzzification.

MATHEMATICAL PRELIMINARIES

Denote by U the real interval $[0, 1]$, and let S be a set. Then a fuzzy subset of S is any map s: $S \rightarrow U$ from S to U and it is also called fuzzy granule of S. Given $\lambda \in U$, we denote by $C(s, \lambda)$ the λ-cut $\{x \in S: s(x) \geq \lambda\}$ of s. The set $Supp(s) = \{x \in S: s(x) \neq 0\}$ is called the support of s. We denote by $\mathcal{P}(S)$ (by $\mathcal{P}_f(S)$) the class of all (finite) subsets of S and by $\mathcal{F}(S)$ the class of all fuzzy subsets of S. Given a family $(s_i)_{i \in I}$ of elements in $\mathcal{F}(S)$, we define the union:

$$U_{i \in I} s_i (x) = \text{Sup } s_i (x),$$
$$i \in I$$
$$\cap_{i \in I} s_i (x) = \text{inf } s_i (x)$$
$$i \in I$$

for any $x \in S$. The complement $\sim s$ of a fuzzy subset s is defined by setting $\sim s(x) = 1 - s(x)$ for any $x \in X$. If $(s_i)_{i \in I}$ is directed, i.e., for any i, j $\in I$, an index h exists such that both s_i and s_j are contained in s_h, then the union $\cup_{i \in I} s_i$ is also denoted by $\lim_{i \in I} s_i$. A fuzzy function f from X to Y is any fuzzy relation, that is, any fuzzy subset f of $X \times Y$. The domain of a fuzzy function f is the fuzzy subset Dom(f) of X defined by setting:

$$Dom(f)(x) = Sup\{f(x, y): y \in Y\}$$

We call fuzzy operator in S any map $J : \mathcal{F}(S) \rightarrow \mathcal{F}(S)$ and we say that J is continuous if:

$$\lim D(s_i) = D(\lim s_i)$$
$$i \in I \qquad\qquad i \in I$$

for every directed family $(s_i)_{i \in I}$ of elements in F(S). Moreover, we say that J is a fuzzy closure operator if

(i) $s \subseteq s' \Rightarrow J(s) \subseteq J(s')$ (order − preserving),

(ii) $s \subseteq J(s)$ (inclusion),

(iii) $J(J(s)) = J(s)$ (idempotence).

A fixed point of J is a fuzzy subset s such that $J(s) = s$. Let H $\mathcal{F}(S) \to \mathcal{F}(S)$ is a continuous operator such that $H(s) \supseteq s$ for any fuzzy subset s and define $\mathcal{D}: \mathcal{F}(S) \to \mathcal{F}(S)$ by setting:

$$\mathcal{D}(s) = \text{Sup}\{H^n(s) \mid n \in N\}$$

Then, it is immediate to prove that $\mathcal{D}$ is a continuous closure operator, we call the closure operator generated by H.

A fuzzy closure system is any class C of fuzzy subsets closed with respect to the finite and infinite intersections. Given a fuzzy closure system C and a fuzzy set s, the intersections of all the elements in C containing s is called the fuzzy subset generated by s.

A continuous T-norm, in brief a norm, is any continuous, associative, commutative operation:

$$\odot: U \times U \to U,$$

non-decreasing with respect to both the variables such that $x \odot 1 - x$. A continuous T-co-norm, in brief a co-norm, is an operation $\oplus$ obtained from a norm $\odot$ by setting $x \oplus y = 1 - (1 - x) \odot (1 - y)$ for any x, y in U. A basic example of norm is the minimum, which we denote by $\sqcap$, and whose associated co-norm is the maximum, denoted by us The Łukasiewicz norm is defined by setting $x \odot y = (x+y-1) \sqcup 0$, the related co-norm is defined by setting $x \odot y = (x + y) \sqcap 1$. Another simple norm is the usual product whose related co-norm is defined by setting $x \odot y = x + y - xy$.

Given two set X and Y and two fuzzy subsets $a: X \to U$ and $b: Y \to U$, the Cartesian product is the fuzzy subset $a \times b: X \times Y \to U$ of $X \times Y$ defined by setting $(a \times b)(x, y) = a(x) \odot b(y)$
for any $x \in X$ and $y \in Y$. Given a finite subset X of S we set

$$\text{Incl}(X, s) = \begin{cases} 1 & \text{if } X = \varphi; \\ s(x_1) \odot, \dots \odot s(x_n) & \text{if } X = \{x_1, \dots x_n\} \end{cases}$$

and we say that Incl (X, s) is the inclusion degree of X in s (with respect to $\odot$).

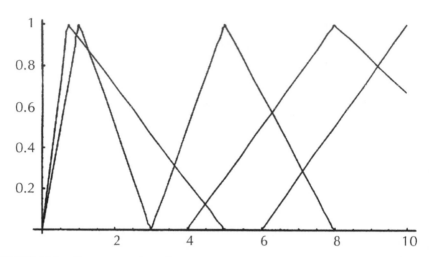

FIGURE 100   Fuzzy granules of X.

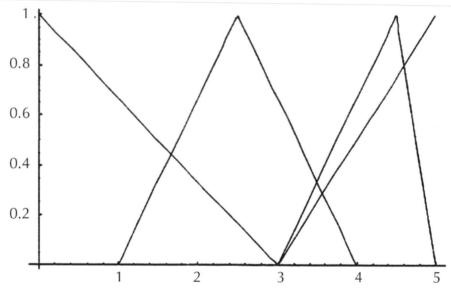

FIGURE 101   Fuzzy granules of Y.

BRIEF REVIEW OF THE STATE OF ART

Let $f : X \rightarrow Y$ is the ideal function, which we approximate. The fuzzy control theory granulates the set X of possible inputs and the set Y of possible outputs by a finite number of fuzzy subsets.

  Example 3.16 Assume that X = [0, 10] is the set of possible temperatures and Y = [0, 5] the set of possible speeds of a ventilator. Then a granulation of X can be furnished by the fuzzy quantities "little", "small", "medium", "big", and "very big" (See

Figure 100), a granulation of Y can be given by the fuzzy quantities "slow", "moderate", "fast", and "very fast" (See Figure 101). As in the classical case, any pair of fuzzy quantities defines a fuzzy point, that is, a two-dimensional fuzzy granule, obtained as the Cartesian product of these granules. For instance, the pair (small, fast) defines the fuzzy point small × fast: $X \times Y \to U$. The set of two-dimensional granules obtained in such a way gives a "granulation" of $X \times Y$. The basic question is to approximate the ideal function $f : X \to Y$ by a finite number of these granules.

This is achieved by a system S of fuzzy IF–THEN rules like:

IF x is Little THEN y is Slow,
IF x is Small THEN y is Fast,
IF x is Medium THEN y is Moderate,
IF x is Big THEN y is Very fast, and
IF x is Very big THEN y is Moderate   (3.223)

where "Little", "Slow", "Small", "Fast", "Medium", "Moderate", "Big", "Very fast", and "Very big", are labels for the fuzzy granules:

Little: $X \to U$, small: $X \to U$,
Medium: $X \to U$, big: $X \to U$,
Very big: $X \to U$, slow: $Y \to U$,
Fast: $Y \to U$, moderate: $Y \to U$, and
Very fast: $Y \to U$.

respectively. In the rules, an expression as "x is Small" is intended as an abbreviation of "x is equal to the fuzzy quantity Small". The whole system of rules says that the ideal function f can be approximated by the following Table 15.

TABLE 15   Approximation of ideal function f

X	y
Little	Slow
Small	Fast
Medium	Moderate
Big	Veryfast
Verybig	Moderate

In fact, Table 15 represents the fuzzy function obtained by the union of the fuzzy points Little× Slow, Small × Fast, Medium × Moderate, Big × Very fast, and Very big × Moderate. This is basically the fuzzy counterpart of the discretization process, in which a function f is partially represented by a Table 16.

TABLE 16   Partial representation of $\underline{f}$

x	y
x_1	y_1
...	...
x_n	y_n

where $x_1, \ldots\ldots, x_n$ are elements of X and $y_1, \ldots.., y_n$ the corresponding elements in Y (See Example 1.2 and Example 1.3of Section 1.2 of Chapter 1).

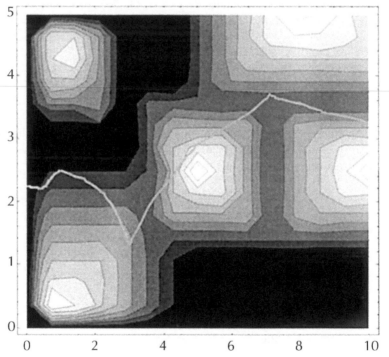

FIGURE 102   The fuzzy function and the result of the defuzzification process.

Remark 3.7 "IF x is Small THEN y is Fast" is not intended as a logical implication but as a reading of the ordered pair (Small, Fast) as stated in Table 15.

Definition 3.8 A system of IF–THEN fuzzy rules is a system of rules like:

$$\text{IF } x \text{ is } A_i \text{ THEN } y \text{ is } B_i$$

Where $i = 1, \ldots., n$ and where the labels A_i and B_i are interpreted by the fuzzy granules $a_i: X \rightarrow U$ and $b_i: Y \rightarrow U$.

Definition 3.9 If a rule is associated with a Cartesian product $a_i \times b_i : X \times Y \to U$, then the whole system with the fuzzy function f defined by:

$$f = \cup_{i=i,\dots,n} a_i \times b_i$$

The defuzzification process enabling us to associate a classical function f' with the fuzzy function f. Usually, the defuzzification process is obtained by the centroid method by setting, for

every $r \in X$:

$$f'(r) = \frac{\int_Y f(r,y)\, y dy}{\int_Y f(r,y) dy}.$$

In Figure 102 both the fuzzy function f and the result f' of the defuzzification process are represented (the used triangular norm is the minimum $\sqcap$).

The final phase is the learning process, in which the rules and the fuzzy granules associated with the labels are changed until we can accept f' as a good approximation of the ideal function f.

3.9.1 FUZZY DEDUCTION SYSTEMS

We denote by a set, whose elements we interpret as sentences of a logical language. We call them formulas. If α is a formula and $\lambda \in U$, the pair (α, λ) is called a signed formula. To denote the signed formula (α, λ) we can also write as $\alpha(\lambda)$.

Any fuzzy set of formulas s: $F \to U$ can be identified with the set $\{(\alpha,\lambda) \in F \times U: s(\alpha)=\lambda\}$ of signed formulas. We define a fuzzy Hilbert system as a pair S = (a, R), where a is a fuzzy subset of F, the fuzzy subset of logical axioms, and R is a set of fuzzy rules of inference. In turn, a fuzzy inference rule is a pair r = (r', r''), where:
- r' is a partial n-ary operation on F, whose domain we denote by Dom(r),
- r'' is an n-ary operation on U preserving the least upper bound in each variable, that is:

$$r''(x_1, \dots, \underset{i \in I}{\mathrm{Sup}}\, y_i, \dots, x_n)$$
$$= \underset{i \in I}{\mathrm{Sup}}\, r''(x_1, \dots, y_i, \dots, x_n) \tag{3.224}$$

In other words, an inference rule r consists of:
- A syntactical component r' that operates on formulas (in fact, it is a rule of inference in the usual sense),

- A valuation component r" that operates on truth-values to calculate how the truth-value of the conclusion depends on the truth-values of the premises [82, 83].

We indicate an application of an inference rule r as:

$$\frac{\alpha_1, \dots \alpha_n}{r'(\alpha_1, \dots \alpha_n)}, \frac{\lambda_1, \dots, \lambda_n}{r''(\lambda_1, \dots, \lambda_n)}$$

whose meaning is that:

IF you know that $\alpha_1, \dots \alpha_n$ are true (at least) to the degree $\lambda_1, \dots, \lambda_n$

THEN $r'(\alpha_1, \dots \alpha_n)$ is true (at least) at level $r''(\lambda_1, \dots, \lambda_n)$.

A proof Π of a formula α is a sequence $(\alpha_1, \dots \alpha_n)$ of formulas such that $\alpha_m = \alpha$, together with the related "justifications". We call length of Π the number m.

This means that, given any formula α_i, we must specify,

Whether

(i) α_i is assumed as a logical axiom, or

(ii) α_i is assumed as an hypothesis, or

(iii) α_i is obtained by a rule (in this case we must also indicate the rule and the formulas from

$$(\alpha_1, \dots \alpha_{i-1} \text{ used to obtain } \alpha_i)$$

Remark 3.8. We have only two proofs of α whose length is equal to 1. The formula α with the justification that α is assumed as a logical axiom and the formula α with the justification that α is assumed as an hypothesis. Moreover, as in the classical case, for any $i \leq m$, the initial segment $\alpha_1, \dots \alpha_i$ is a proof of α_i which we denote by Π (i).

Differently from the crisp case, the justifications are necessary since different justifications of the same formula give rise to different valuations.

Let: F→U be any initial valuation andΠ a proof. Then the valuation Val(Π) ofΠ with respect to v is defined by induction on the length m ofΠ as follows. If the length ofΠ is 1, then we get:

Val(Π, v) = a(α_m)

if α_m is assumed as a logical axiom,

Val(Π, v) =v (α_m)

if α_m is assumed as an hypothesis.

Otherwise, we get:

Val(Π, v)

$$= \begin{cases} a\left(\alpha_m\right) \\ \text{if } \alpha_m \text{is assumed as a logical axiom,} \\ v\left(\alpha_m\right) \\ \text{if } \alpha_m \text{is assumed as an hypothesis,} \\ r"(\text{Val}(v\left(i(1)\right),v), \ \ldots\ldots, \ \text{Val}(\Pi\left(i(n)\right),v)) \\ \text{if } \alpha_m = r"\left(\alpha_{i(1)}, \ \ldots\ldots, \ \alpha_{i(n)}\right), \end{cases}$$

where, $1 \le i(1) \le m, \ldots, 1 \le i(n) < m$.

Remark 3.9 If α is the formula proven byΠ, the meaning we assign to $\text{Val}(\Pi, v)$ is that: Given the information$v$, Π assures that α holds at least at level $\text{Val}(\Pi, v)$.

Definition 3.9 Given a fuzzy Hilbert's system S, we call deduction operator associated with S the operator $\mathcal{D}: \mathcal{F}(F) \to \mathcal{F}(F)$ defined by setting:

$$D\ (v)\ (\alpha) = \text{Sup}\{\text{Val}(\Pi, v){:}\Pi \text{ is a proof of } \alpha\}, \tag{3.225}$$

for every initial valuation and every formula α.

Remark 3.10 The meaning of $D(v)$ (α) is that given the information v, we may prove that α holds at least at level $D(v)$ (α).

Remark 3.11 We also have the statement that $D(v)$ (α) is the best possible valuation we can draw from the information v.

We say that a proof $\Pi = \alpha_1, \ldots\ldots, \alpha_n$ is normalizedif the formulas inΠ are pairwise different and two integers h and k exist such that $1 \le h \le k \le n$ and

- $\alpha_1,\ldots, \alpha_h$ are the formulas assumed as hypothesis,
- $\alpha_{h+1},\ldots, \alpha_k$ the formulas justified as logical axiom,
- $\alpha_{k+1},\ldots, \alpha_n$ are obtained by an inference rule.

Obviously, in computing(v) (α) we can limit ourselves only to normalized proofs.

We are interested in a very simple logic, in which F is the set of formulas of a first-order logic, the characteristic function of the set Tau of all logically true formulas and R contains the two rules:

GENERALIZATION

$$\frac{\alpha \qquad \lambda}{\forall\, x_i(\alpha),\ \lambda}$$

FUZZY MODUS PONENS

$$\frac{\alpha,\, \alpha \to \beta}{\beta} \quad \frac{\lambda,\, \mu}{\lambda \odot \mu}$$

Remark 3.12A fuzzy logic having a continuous triangular norm $\odot$ is called a canonical extension of a first order logic.

We can consider some derived rules.

EXTENDED GENERALIZATION

$$\frac{\alpha}{Q(\alpha)}, \frac{\lambda}{\lambda}$$

where $Q(\alpha)$ is the universe closure of the formula α,

EXTENDED FUZZY MODUS PONENS

$$\frac{\alpha_1,...,\alpha_n,\, \alpha_1 \wedge ... \wedge \alpha_n \to \alpha}{\alpha}, \frac{\lambda_1,...,\lambda_n,\, \lambda}{\lambda_1 \odot ...,\odot \lambda_n \odot \lambda}$$

$$(\alpha_1,...,\alpha_n,\, \alpha_1 \wedge ... \wedge \alpha_n \to \alpha) \to \alpha_1 \to (...(\alpha_n \to \alpha)...)$$

which we can obtain by observing that the formula

$$(\alpha_1,...,\alpha_n,\, \alpha_1 \wedge ... \wedge \alpha_n \to \alpha) \to \alpha_1 \to (...(\alpha_n \to \alpha)...)$$

is logically true.

PARTICULARIZATION RULE

$$\frac{\alpha(x_1,...,x_n)}{\alpha(t_1,...,t_n)}, \frac{\lambda}{\lambda}$$

where $t_1,......, t_n$ are ground terms. Such a rule can be obtained by observing that the formula

$$\alpha(x_1,...,x_n) \to \alpha(t_1,...,t_n) \text{ is logically true.}$$

Theorem 3.5 Let $\mathcal{D}$ be the deduction operator of a canonical extension of a first-order logic. Then,

$$\mathcal{D}(v)\,(\alpha) = \mathrm{Sup}\{\mathrm{Incl}(X,v) \colon X \in \mathcal{P}_f(\mathbb{F}) \text{ and } X \vdash \alpha\} \qquad (3.226)$$

Proposition 3.1 Let $\mathcal{D}$ be the deduction operator of the canonical extension of first-order logic by the minimum $\sqcap$. Then:

$$\mathcal{D}(v)\,(\alpha) = \mathrm{Sup}\{\lambda \in U \colon C(v, \lambda) \vdash \alpha\} \qquad (3.227)$$

Observe that Equation 3.226 is based on a multi-valued interpretation of the meta-logic claim:

"A proof Π of α exists, whose hypotheses are contained in v".

This in accordance with the fact that in a first-order multi-valued logics and in fuzzy logic the existential quantifier is usually interpreted by the operator Sup: $(U) \to U$. Now, this is rather questionable everywhere as for why the logical connective "and" is interpreted by a triangular norm different from the minimum. In fact, the operator used to interpret $\exists$ must extend the interpretation of the binary connective "or", to the infinitary case that is, the co-norm $\oplus$ associated with $\odot$. Obviously, Sup satisfies such a condition only in the case that $\odot$ is the minimum and therefore $\oplus$ is the maximum.

Then a natural candidate for the general case is the operator $\oplus : P(U) \to U$ defined by setting, for any subset X of U,

$$\oplus(X) = \mathrm{Sup}\{x_1 \cdot \oplus, ..., \oplus x_n \colon x_1, .., x_n \subset X\}$$

Remark 3.13 Hence, it is interesting to examine a fuzzy logic, whose deduction operator is defined by:

$$\mathcal{D}(v)\,(\alpha) = \oplus\,(\{\mathrm{Incl}(X,) \colon X \in \mathcal{P}_f(\mathbb{F}) \text{ and } X \vdash \alpha\}) \qquad (3.228)$$

Remark 3.14 It is not clear, whether $\mathcal{D}$ is a closure operator or not.

3.9.2 FUZZY PROGRAMS AND FUZZY HERBRAND MODELS

We recall some basic notions in logic program. Let L be a first-order language with some constants and denote the related set of formulas by F. A ground term of L is a term not containing variables. The set U_L of ground terms of L is called the Herbrand universe for L. If L is function free, then U_L is the set of constants. A ground atom is an atomic formula not containing variables and the set B_L of ground atoms is called the Herbrand base for L. We call any subset M of B_L a Herbrand interpretation. The name is justified by the fact that M defines an interpretation of L, in which [83]:

- The domain is the Herbrand universe U_L,
- Every constant in L is assigned with themselves,
- Any n-ary function symbol f in L is interpreted as the map associating any $t_1, ..., t_n$ in U_L with the element $f(t_1,....,t_n)$ of U_L, and
- Any n-ary predicate symbol r is interpreted by the n-ary relation r' defined by setting:

$$(t_1, ...,t_n) \in r' \Leftrightarrow r(t_1, ..., t_n) \in M.$$

A ground instance of a formula α is a closed formula β, obtained from α by suitable substitutions of the free variables with closed terms. Given a set X of formulas, we set:

$$\text{Ground}(X) = \{\alpha \in \Pi : \beta \in \text{ exists s.t } \alpha \text{ is a ground instance of } \beta\}$$

A *definite program clause* is either an atomic formula or a formula of the form

$\beta_1, \wedge, ... \wedge \beta_n \to \beta$ where $\beta, \beta_1, ... ,\beta_n$ are atomic formulas. We denote by PC the set of program clauses. A *definite program* is a set P of definite program clauses. We associate P with the operator

$J_P : P(B_L) \to P(B_L)$ defined by setting, for any subset X of B_L,,

$$J_P(X) = \{\alpha \in B_L, \alpha_1 \wedge, .., \wedge \alpha_n \to \alpha \in \text{Ground}(P), \alpha_1, ..., \alpha_n \in X\} \cup \{\alpha \in B_L, : \alpha \in \text{Ground}(P)\} \cup X$$

J_P is called the *immediate consequence operator*. We denote by H_P the closure operator generated by J_P, i.e., for any set X of ground atoms

$$H_P(X) = \bigcup_{n \in N} (J_P)^n (X). \tag{3.229}$$

Definition 3.10 We call Herbrand model of P any fixed point of J_P (equivalently, of H_P). Given a set X of ground atoms, we say that H_P is the least Herbrand model for containing X. We denote the model $H_P(\varphi)$ by M_P and we call it the least Herbrand model for P.

Let $\mathcal{D}$ denote the deduction operator of a firstorder calculus and $\vdash$ the associate consequence relation. Then the following theorem shows that the least Herbrand model for P is the set of ground atoms that we can derive from P.

Theorem 3.6 For every program P:

$$M_P(= \{\alpha \in B_L : P \vdash \alpha\}. \tag{3.230}$$

The above definitions can be extended to many-sorted languages.

We observe that, there is no adequate semantics for the proposed fuzzy logic (See also observation (d) at section 3.9.6).

Hence, to extend the above definitions for the proposed fuzzy logic we proceed as follows:

We define a fuzzy Herbrand interpretation of L as the restriction m of a fuzzy theory to B_L. Like the classical case, m defines a multi-valued interpretation of L in the Herbrand universe, in which any n-ary predicate symbol r is interpreted by the fuzzy n-ary relation r' on U_L defined by setting:

$$r'(t_1, ..., t_n) = m(r(t_1, ..., t_n)).$$

We call fuzzy program any fuzzy subset p: PC →U of program clauses. We define the least-fuzzy Herbrand model of p as the fuzzy subset of ground atoms that can be proved from p.

Definition 3.11 Let $\mathcal{D}$ be the deduction operator of a canonical extension of a predicate calculus by a norm and let p be a fuzzy program. Then, the least-fuzzy Herbrand model for p is the fuzzy set m_p: B_L→U defined by setting:

$$m_p(\alpha) = \mathcal{D}(p)(\alpha) \tag{3.231}$$

for any $\alpha \in B_L$

Then, if α is a ground atom, in accordance with Equation 3.226:

$$m_p(\alpha) = Sup\{Incl(P, p): P \in \mathcal{P}_f(Supp(p)) \text{ s.t. } \alpha \in M_p\}. \tag{3.232}$$

Assume that the triangular norm under consideration is the minimum and denote by $P(\lambda)$ the program $C(p, \lambda)$.

Then, in accordance with Proposition 3.1:

$$m_p(\alpha) = Sup\{\lambda \in U: \alpha \in M_{P(\lambda)}\}.$$

In the case that, Supp(p) is finite, in the co-domain of p there are only a finite number of elements $\lambda(1) > \lambda(2) > \ldots > \lambda(n)$ different from zero. As a consequence, to calculate $m_p(\alpha)$ it is sufficient to calculate the least Herbrand models $M_{P(\lambda(1))} \subseteq \cdots \subseteq M_{P(\lambda(n))}$ by a parallel process.

3.9.3 FUZZY CONTROL AND LOGIC PROGRAM [83]

Consider a fuzzy system S of IF–THEN rules like:
IF x is A_1 THEN y is B_1
...   (3.233)
IF x is A_n THEN y is B_n.

To give a logical interpretation of such a system, we consider A_i and B_i as names for fuzzy predicates and not labels for fuzzy granules. In accordance, we interpret "x is A_i" and "y is B_i" as "x satisfies A_i" and "y satisfies B_i", respectively. Moreover, we associate the IF–THEN fuzzy system Equation 3.233 with the set:

$$A_1(x) \wedge B_1(y) \rightarrow Good(x, y) (\lambda_1);$$

$$\ldots$$

$$A_n(x) \wedge B_n(y) \rightarrow Good(x, y) (\lambda_n)$$

of signed clauses, where $\lambda_1 = \bullet \bullet \bullet = \lambda_n = 1$ and Good(x, y) is a new predicate whose intended meaning is "given x, y is a good value for the control variable".

The meaning of the value λ_i is that the i-rule is accepted at level λ_i. In the general case, $\lambda_1 \bullet \bullet \bullet \lambda_n$ can be different from 1 and are the result of a learning process. Also, by assuming that A_i and B_j are interpreted by the fuzzy subsets a_i and b_j, we consider, for $i, j = 1, \ldots\ldots, n, r \in X$ and $t \in Y$, the signed ground atoms:

$A_i(r) (a_i(r))$,

$B_j(t) (b_j(t))$.

In other words, we associate system Equation 3.233 with the fuzzy program p: PC $\rightarrow$U defined by setting:

$$p(\alpha)=\begin{cases} \lambda_i & \text{if } \alpha \text{ is the clause } Ai(x) \wedge Bi(y) \\ & \rightarrow Good(x, y), \\ a_i(r) & \text{if } \alpha \text{ is the ground atom } A_i(r), \\ b_i(t) & \text{if } \alpha \text{ is the ground atom } B_i(t), \\ 0 & \text{otherwise:} \end{cases} \qquad (3.234)$$

Each element in X or in Y is considered as a constant. Therefore, the Herbrand universe of p is $X \cup Y$.

Theorem 3.7 Define the fuzzy relation good: $X \times Y \rightarrow U$, by setting; for any r $\in X$ and t $\in Y$

$$\text{Good(r, t)} = \mathcal{D} \text{ (p) (Good(r, t))}.$$

Then good coincides with the fuzzy function associated with the fuzzy control system Equation 3.233.

Proof: Consider the fuzzy program p associated with system Equation 3.233:

$A_1(x) \wedge B_1(y) \rightarrow$Good(x, y) $[\lambda_1]$

$\bullet \bullet \bullet$

$A_n(x) \wedge B_n(y) \rightarrow$Good(x, y) $[\lambda_n]$

$A_i(r) [a_i(r)]$

$\bullet \bullet \bullet$

$B_j(t) [b_j(t)]$

where $\lambda_1 \bullet \bullet \bullet \lambda_n$ are elements in U; r varies in X and t varies in Y. Then, given the constants r and t, we can try to prove the ground atom Good(r, t). Consider the ground instance of the first rule,

$A_1(r) \wedge B_1(r) \rightarrow$Good(r, t)

and the ground atoms

$A_1(r)$,

$B_1(t)$.

Then, by the extended fuzzy Modus Ponens rule, we can prove Good(r, t) at level $\lambda_1 \odot a_1(r) \odot b_1(t)$.Likewise, from the second fuzzy clause we can prove Good(r, t) at

$\lambda_2 \odot a_2(r) \odot b_2(t)$, and so on. It is immediate that these are the only possible proofs of Good(r, t) and therefore that:

Good(r, t) = $\mathcal{D}$ (p) (Good(r,t)) = Max$\{\lambda_1 \odot a_1(r) \odot r\, b_1(t), \ldots., \lambda_n \odot a_n(r) \odot r\, b_n(t)\}$.

By using the notion of Cartesian product, and assuming that $\lambda_1 = \cdots = \lambda_n = 1$, we can conclude that:

Good = $(a_1 \times b_1) \cup \cdots \cup (a_n \times b_n)$

in accordance with Definition 3.8.

Theorem 3.7 gives a well-based theoretical framework to fuzzy control. It shows that, we can look at the calculus of the fuzzy function associated with a IF–THEN system as at the calculus of the least Herbrand model of a suitable program. More precisely, in account of the fact that "Good" is the only predicate occurring in the head of a rule, we have complete information about all the predicates different from "Good", and the only calculus we have to do is related to ground atoms like "Good(r,t)".In the following we demonstrate that, such a logical approach gives the possibility of expressing the information of an expert in a more complete way.

3.9.4 LOGIC AS A NEW TOOL FOR FUZZY CONTROL

The interpretation of an IF–THEN system of fuzzy rules as a fuzzy system of axioms enables us to define several notions, which may be useful for fuzzy control. In the following, we list some possibilities [83, 84].

DEGREE OF COMPLETENESS

The completeness of a fuzzy system of rules S is represented by the fact that whatever is the situation r a good control t exists.

Alternatively, we can state that the following formula:

$\forall x \exists y$ Good(x, y)

is satisfied. Now, on account of the fact that in a multi-valued logic the quantifiers $\forall$ and $\exists$ are interpreted by the operators Inf and Sup, respectively, we can propose the following definition.

Definition 3.12 The degree of completeness of a fuzzy system of IF–THEN rules S is the number

$Compl(S)$ = Inf Sup good(x, y).
$\qquad\qquad x \in X\; y \in Y$

Equivalently, by denoting by Dom(good) the domain of good:

$Compl(S)$ = Inf Dom(good)(x)
$\qquad\qquad x \in X$

If each predicate b_i is normal, i.e, $b_i(\underline{y}) = 1$ for a suitable $\underline{y} \in Y$, then:

Dom(good) = $a_1 \cup \cdots \cup a_n$.

In fact, for any x $\in$ X:

$a_1(x) \sqcup \cdots \sqcup a_n(x)$

$\geq a_1(x) \odot b_1(y) \sqcup \cdots \sqcup a_n(x) \odot b_n(y)$

and therefore $a_1(x) \sqcup \cdots \sqcup a_n(x) \geq$ good(x, y). Moreover, assume that $a_1(x) \times \cdots \sqcup a_n(x)$ = $a_i(x)$ and that $\underline{y}$ is an element in Y such that $b_i(\underline{y}) = 1$.

Then $a_1(x) \, x \cdots \sqcup a_n(x) = a_i(x) \, xb_i(y) \leq Sup\{a_1(x) \odot b_1(y) \, y \cdots \sqcup a_n(x) \odot b_n(y): y \in Y\}$.

Thus:

$Compl(S) = Inf \, (a_1(x) \vee \ldots \ldots \vee a_n(x))$
$\qquad\qquad x \in X$

and, consequently,

$Compl(S) = 1 \Leftrightarrow$ the set of fuzzy predicates in X is a covering of X:

LINGUISTIC MODIFIERS

Another possibility is to define some linguistic modifiers that are well-known tools in fuzzy logic. As an example, we can define the modifiers "Clearly" and "Vaguely" by associating the functions clearly: $u \rightarrow U$ and vaguely: $U \rightarrow U$ defined by setting clearly$(x) = x^2$ and vaguely$(x) = x^{0.5}$ for any $x \in U$ to these predicates. In accordance, the predicate"Vaguely(Good)"is interpreted by the fuzzy subset:

Vaguelygood(x, y) = vaguely(good(x, y))

= good$(x, y)^{0.5}$.

The predicate Clearly(Good) is interpreted by the fuzzy subset:

Clearlygood(x, y) = clearly(good(x, y))

= good$(x, y)^2$.

The predicates "Clearly(Good)" and "Vaguely (Good)" are represented in Figures 103 and 104, respectively. These linguistic modifiers can be applied to predicates that are also premises in a rule. As an example, we can consider rules as:

Vaguely(Little)$(x) \wedge$Fast$(y) \rightarrow$Good(x, y),

Little$(x) \wedge$Vaguely(Slow)$(y) \rightarrow$Good(x, y).

NEGATIVE INFORMATION FOR A SAFE CONTROL

The use of "negative" information is very delicate in classical logic program. This is obtained by the closed-world rule. It says that, if a ground atom A is not a logical consequence of a program P, and then we are entitled to infer $\sim A$. Such a rule is useful in several cases but rather questionable both from a semantical and computational viewpoint.

We can try to extend it to fuzzy logic program by assuming that the negation $\sim A$ of a ground atom A is true at level $1 - \mathcal{D}(p)(A)$.. As in the classical case, this "rule" originates several difficulties. As an example, if a proof Π gives a lower bound Val(Π, p)

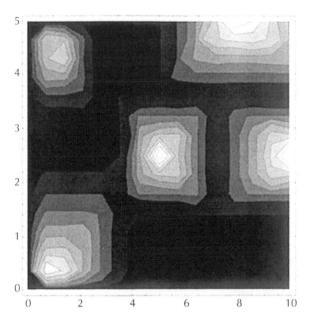

FIGURE 103   The predicate clearly (Good) [82].

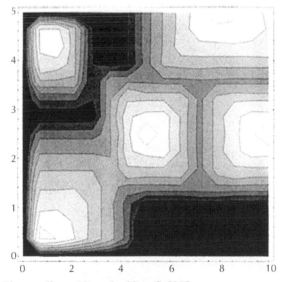

FIGURE 104   The predicate Vaguely (Good) [82].

for the truth value of A, then 1 -Val(Π, p) gives an upper bound for the truth value of ~ A. Unfortunately, the fuzzy logic deduction machinery as proposed in literature is not able to manage these upper bounds. Some suggestions for an approach to fuzzy logic, in which this is possible, can be found in [84].

In the simple fuzzy programs, we associate negation with a fuzzy IF–THEN system. No difficulty arises since we have a complete description of all the predicates different from Good. Consequently, the negation of such predicates is at semantical level, in a sense, and it can be achieved directly by the complement operator.

Example 3.17 Suppose that, we need to take into account that there are some control actions, we have to avoid. For instance, assume that we consider dangerous a "too fast" control y. Then, we can express this by adding the following rule:

Clearly(Veryfast)(y) →Dangerous(y)

In accordance, we can define the predicate "Safe" by adding the rule:

Good(x, y) ∧~(Dangerous(y)) →Safe(x, y),

where dangerous: $Y \rightarrow U$ and safe: $X \times Y \rightarrow U$ are the interpretations of Dangerous and Safe, respectively. Then, given $r \in X$ and $t \in Y$, the first clause enables us to calculate:

dangerous(t) =$\mathcal{D}$(p)(Dangerous(t))

= clearly(veryfast(t)).

By the closed world rule

(p) (~ Dangerous(t)) = 1 - $\mathcal{D}$(p) (Dangerous(t))

=1 – clearly (very fast(t)).

Then, by the second clause

safe(r, t) =$\mathcal{D}$(p)(Safe(r, t))

= (good(r, t)⊙(1 –clearly(veryfast(t)).

Obviously in such a case, we have to refer to the predicate "Safe" and not "Good"in the successive defuzzification process. In Figure 105 such a new predicate is represented.

NEGATIVE INFORMATION FOR A DEFAULT RULE

Another interesting use of the negation is the possibility of defining a "default" rule, that is, to suggest the control we have to choose in the case, in which:

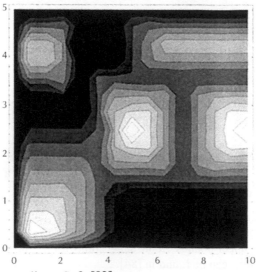

FIGURE 105   The predicate Safe [82].

no condition "Little", "Medium", "Big", "Verybig", and "Small" is satisfied.

Example 3.18 Assume that an expert suggests to choose a slow y. Then, by assuming that Domain(x) is the formula

Little(x) ∧Small(x) ∧Medium(x)

∧Big(x) ∧Verybig(x),

we can add the rule

~Domain(x) ∧Slow(y) →Good(x, y).

In such a case the predicate "Good" is represented by Figure 106 and the degree of completeness of the system increases.

Note that the fuzzy relation safe is contained in the fuzzy relation good,while the default rule increases the fuzzy relation interpreting the predicated Good. This shows that, by adding new information, it is possible:

- To increase the area of the fuzzy upper covering of the ideal function f, in order to obtain completeness, that is, to be sure that the whole set of points of $\underline{f}$ is covered,
- To decrease such an area, in order to obtain a more precise representation of $\underline{f}$.

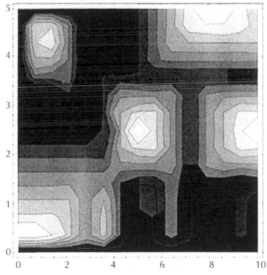

FIGURE 106   Adding the default rule [82].

RECURSION

The power of classical logic program is mainly based on the recursion. This is possible, for example, by setting a predicate name for both in the head and in the body of a rule. Then, we would not be surprised if recursion showed all its potentialities in fuzzy program and, whence, in our logical approach to fuzzy control. However, no investigation is made in this promising direction. Obviously, recursion can originate some computational difficulties. These difficulties can be roughly bypassed by substituting the recursion with stratified definitions of new predicates.

Example 3.19. Instead of a rule like

$$\left(...\wedge \mathrm{Good}\left(x',y'\right)\wedge,...\right)\rightarrow \mathrm{Good}\left(x,y\right)$$

we can consider the new predicates *Good*** and *Good** and the rules

$$\left(...\wedge \mathrm{Good}\left(x'',y''\right)\wedge,...\right)\rightarrow \mathrm{Good}^{*}\left(x',y'\right)$$

$$\left(...\wedge \mathrm{Good}^{*}\left(x',y'\right)\wedge,...\right)\rightarrow \mathrm{Good}^{**}\left(x,y\right)$$

In general, the interpretation of Good** represents a good approximation of the fuzzy predicate Good definite by recursion.

CONTROL BY SIMILARITY AND PROTOTYPES

Recall that a similarity or fuzzy equivalence in a set S is a fuzzy relation near: $S \times S \rightarrow U$ that is a model of the clauses:

Near(x, y) $\wedge$Near(y, z) $\rightarrow$Near(x,z),

Near(x,x),   (3.135)

Near(x, y) $\rightarrow$Near(y, x).

This is equivalent to saying that:

near(x,y)$\odot$ near(y,z)$\leq$near(x, z),

near(x, x) = 1,

near(x,y)$\leq$near(y, x).

Let P be a set of elements of S, which we call prototypes and let near be a similarity in S. Then we define the fuzzy subset of elements that are similar to some prototype by setting:

$$s(x) = \mathrm{Sup}\{\mathrm{near}(x, x'): x' \in P\}.$$

We can use such a notion to propose a system of rules that emphasizes the geometrical nature of fuzzy control. Consider a first-order language with two relation names "Near" and "Sim" to denote a similarity in X and Y, respectively. Assume that the ideal function $\underline{f}$ has been scheduled in the following Table 17:

TABLE 17 Representation of ideal function $\underline{f}$

x	y
x_1	y_1
...	...
x_n	y_n

where x_1, ..., x_n are elements in X and y_1, ..., y_n the related images. Then we can consider the fuzzy program obtained by considering the rules saying that "Near" and "Sim" are similarities and the rules:

$$\text{Near}(x,x_1) \wedge \text{Sim}(y, y_1) \rightarrow \text{Good}(x,y) \qquad (3.236)$$

....

$$\text{Near}(x, x_n) \wedge \text{Sim}(y, y_n) \rightarrow \text{Good}(x, y).$$

This fuzzy program defines the fuzzy relation goodas a union of n fuzzy points centered in (x_1, y_1), ..., (x_n, y_n), respectively. It is immediate that $\text{good}(x_i, y_i)=1$ for any $i \in \{1,.....,n\}$.

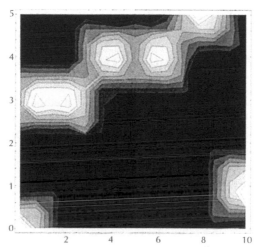

FIGURE 107   Control by similarity [82].

Example 3.20 We can consider the fuzzy program obtained by the rules saying that "Near" and "Sim"are similarities and the rules:

$$\text{Near}(x, 0) \wedge \text{Sim}(y, 0) \rightarrow \text{Good}(x, y),$$
$$\text{Near}(x, 1) \wedge \text{Sim}(y, 3) \rightarrow \text{Good}(x, y),$$
$$\text{Near}(x, 2) \wedge \text{Sim}(y, 3) \rightarrow \text{Good}(x, y),$$
$$\text{Near}(x, 4) \wedge \text{Sim}(y, 4) \rightarrow \text{Good}(x, y),$$
$$\text{Near}(x, 6) \wedge \text{Sim}(y, 4) \rightarrow \text{Good}(x, y),$$
$$\text{Near}(x, 8) \wedge \text{Sim}(y, 5) \rightarrow \text{Good}(x, y),$$
$$\text{Near}(x, 10) \wedge \text{Sim}(y, 1) \rightarrow \text{Good}(x, y).$$

In Figure 107 we represent the resulting fuzzy relation good. Such a relation is an union of 7 fuzzy points centered in (0, 0), (1, 3), (2, 3), (4, 4), (6, 4), (8, 5), and (10, 1), respectively. More precisely, we assume that:

- X and Y are the intervals [0, 10] and [0, 5], respectively,
- The points 1, 2, 4, 5, 6, 8, 9, and 10 are prototypes in X,
- The points 0, 1, 3, 4, and 5 are prototypes in Y, and
- The similarities are defined by setting:

$$\text{Near}(x, x') = \text{Min}\{1 - (|x - x'|=2), 1\},$$

$Sim(y, y') = Min\{1 - |y - y'|, 1\}$.

Remark 3.14 In general, the defuzzification process by the centroid method gives a function f' such that $f'(x_j) \neq y_i$. In fact, the value $f'(x_j)$ depends on all the rules, in which an x_j occurs such that $near(x_i, x_j) \neq 0$. Only in the case that $near(x_i, x_j) = 0$ for any $j \neq i$, and under the rather natural hypothesis that the centroid of $Sim(y_i, y)$ is y_i, we have that $f'(x_i) = y_i$. Instead, the choice of the maximum in the defuzzification process gives always the property $f'(x_i) = x_i$. In the proposed example, in spite of the fact that we start from the point (0, 0), $f'(0) = 1.5833 \neq 0$. Indeed, 0 is near to 1 to a degree different from zero.

Also, we can use the predicates "Near" and "Sim" to improve the predicate "Good" defined in the previous sections. As an example, we can add to the recursive rule:

$Good(x, y') \wedge Sim(y, y') \rightarrow Good(x, y)$

whose meaning is obvious.

3.9.5 LOGIC INTERPRETATION OF DEFUZZIFICATION: AN OPEN QUESTION

It is rather hard to give a logical meaning to centroid method. Indeed, in the logical approach we propose to interpret good(r, y) as a degree of preference on y given $r \in Y$. Then, it should be better to take a value y that maximizes good(r, y). Now, observe that, as a matter of fact, the centroid method does not work well in several cases. The following is an example.

Example 3.21 Assume that a driver looks at a yellow traffic light. Then, the suitable way to adjust the speed depends on the distance from the traffic light and the car speed. On the other hand, sometimes both rapidly increasing the speed and rough braking are good choices (in a sense that the choice between the two different behaviors depends only on the driver's temperament).

In accordance, both the following rules seem to be valid:

$High(x) \wedge Little(y) \wedge Big\ positive(z) \rightarrow Good(x, y, z)$,

$High(x) \wedge Little(y) \wedge Big\ negative(z) \rightarrow Good(x, y, z)$

where x is the speed, y the distance between the car and the traffic light and z the (positive or negative) acceleration. Let x and y be such that high(x)=1 and little(y)=1, then, due to the symmetry of the fuzzy predicates big positive and big negative, the centroid method suggests an acceleration equal to zero. This means that the driver does not modify his speed and this leads to a probable disaster. Then, an important question is how to make explicit (by a suitable set of first-order formulas) the conditions under which the centroid method is correct. In accordance with these considerations we try to formulate the following conjecture.

Conjecture 3.1 [82] The conditions under which the centroid method is correct can be expressed by a fuzzy subset p' of formulas. By adding to the fuzzy program p the information p' a new Herbrand model $m_{p \cup p'}$ is defined. Let good' be the fuzzy predicate defined by setting:

$Good'(r, t) = m_{p \cup p'}(Good(r, t))$.

Then:

i.   Good'(r, y) has a unique maximum (with respect to y) and

ii.   Such a maximum coincides with the centroid of good(r, y).

We are not able to prove this conjecture. We expose only some considerations and results as a hint for further investigations. Now, the considered example suggests that the centroid method can be applied only in the case, in which if two control y'and y''are acceptable then all the intermediate controls are acceptable (we assume that Y is a set of real numbers).

We can express such a property by adding the rule:

Good(x, y') ∧Good(x, y'') ∧(y'≤y≤y'')→Good(x, y).

In order to avoid the recursion, we can also add a new predicate name Good' and the rule:

Good(x, y') ∧Good(x, y'') ∧(y'≤y≤y'')→Good'(x, y).   (3.237)

The corresponding fuzzy relation good' is defined by setting:

Good'(x, y) = Sup{good(x, y')⊙good(x, y'') |y'≤y≤y''}.

Recall that a convex fuzzy subset of the real line is a fuzzy subset s: R →U such that, for every x, x_1, and x_2,

$x_1 ≤ x ≤ x_2 ⇒ s(x) ≥ s(x_1) ⊙ s(x_2)$.

It is immediate to prove that the class of the convex fuzzy subsets is a closure system. The proof of the following proposition is immediate.

Proposition 3.2 Assume that ⊙is the minimum and that r ∈X. Then good'(r, y) is the convex closure of good(r, y).

Unfortunately, this is not sufficient. For example, if good'(r, y) is constant with respect to y (and therefore convex), then good'(r, y)coincides with good(r, y) and such a function has not a unique maximum as required. A better result can be obtained by interpreting the rule (3.237) by the usual product as a triangular norm and by substituting the operator Sup with the Lukasiewicz disjunction, that is, by setting:

good'(r, y) = ⊕ good(x, y'). good(x, y'').
y' ≤ y ≤ y''

In the case that the values assumed by good are sufficiently small, a numerical simulation shows that such a method is sufficiently satisfactory. In fact, the maximum of good'(r, y) is approximately equal to the centroid of good(r, y).

Another attempt to give a logical meaning to the centroid method is suggested by the following proposition.

Proposition 3.3 Assume that Y = [a, b], define far: [a, b] × [a, b] →U by setting far(x, y) = |x − y|/(a − b)² and good': X × Y →U by setting; for any x ∈X and y ∈Y:

$$good'(x, y) = (\int_a^y far(y, y') good(x, y') dy')$$

$$(\int_y^b far(y, y') good(x, y') dy').$$

Then, for every r ∈X, the fuzzy subset good'(r, y) is a fuzzy interval of Y with only a maximum. Moreover, such a maximum is the centroid of good(r, y).

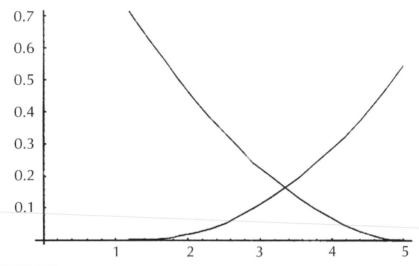

FIGURE 108.

Proof: Set

$$h(y)= \int_a^y far(y,y')good(r,y')dy',$$

$$k(y)= \int_y^b far(y,y')good(r,y')dy'.$$

Then, it is immediate that h: [a, b] →U is a strictly increasing continuous function such that h(a) = 0 and that k: [a, b] →U is a strictly decreasing continuous function such that k(b) = 0 (See Figure 9, where r = 8).

Moreover, the maximum of good*(r, y) is the unique point y_0 such that $h(y_0) = k(y_0)$, that is, satisfying the equation:

$$\int_a^y far(y,y')good(r,y')dy'$$

$$= \int_y^b far(y,y')good(r,y')dy'$$

Now, since:

$$\left(h(y) - k(y)\right)(b - a)^2$$

$$= \int_a^y |y - y'| \, good(r, y') \, dy'$$

$$- \int_y^b |y - y'| \, good(r, y') \, dy'$$

$$= \int_a^y (y - y') good(r, y') \, dy'$$

$$- \int_y^b (y - y') good(r, y') \, dy'$$

$$= y \int_a^b good(r, y') \, dy' - \int_a^b good(r, y') \, dy'$$

the zero of such an equation is the centroid of good(r, y).

We can try to translate Proposition 8.2 in logical terms by noticing that the integral operator $\int$ coincides with the sum operator $\sum$ under finiteness hypothesis for Y. In turn, $\sum$ coincides with the operator $\oplus$ associated with Lukasiewicz disjunction under the hypothesis that the values of good and far are not too big. In such a case, let Good$_1$, Good$_2$, and Good' are two place predicates and add to the fuzzy program defining Good the rules:

(y'≤y) & Far(y', y) & Good(x, y') →Good$_1$(x, y),
(y'≥y) & Far(y', y) & Good(x, y') →Good$_2$(x,y),
Good$_1$(x, y) ∧Good$_2$(x, y) →Good'(x, y).

Moreover, interpret the resulting program in a multi-valued logic, in which ∃ is interpreted by the operator $\oplus$ associated with Lukasiewicz disjunction, and is interpreted by the product and ∧by the minimum ⊓. Then, a simple calculation shows that the resulting interpretation ofGood' coincides with the fuzzy predicate good' defined in Proposition 8.2, that is that has only a maximum and such a maximum is the centroid of good(r, y).

This answer to the conjecture is rather unsatisfactory. In fact, the meaning of the proposed formulas is not clear and the logic we need is rather obscure. Then, the question whether a logical interpretation of the centroid method is possible remains open.

3.9.6 SOME OBSERVATIONS [82, 83, 84]

We provide a list of observation emphasizing the differences with the "granular approach".

(a) The fuzzy relation "good" is not a fuzzy function defined by cases. As a matter of fact, "good" is a fuzzy predicate enabling to say, given r, if a control t is good or not. Indeed, the aim of the fuzzy program p is not to calculate the ideal function $f : X \to Y$ representing the correct answer t = f (r) given the input r but to define vague predicates as "Good", "Stable", and "Dangerous" expressing our graded opinion (degreeof preference, taste) on a possible control t, given an input r. Consequently, it is very natural to admit that two different elements t and t' exist in Y such thatgood(r, t)=good(r, t') (See the example in Section8). If we admit this, then we have to admit the following claim, too.

(b) The set of fuzzy granules in X is not necessarily a partition. By referring to our example, this means that it is not necessary for the class:

$$C = \{little, small, medium, big, very\ big\}$$

of fuzzy predicates defined in X to be a partition. In particular, it is not necessary that these predicates are pairwise disjointed. In the considered example, the predicate "Small" is a synonymous of the predicate "Little" and therefore the related interpretations small and little almost completely overlap. Also, it is not necessary that C is a covering of X. In fact, it is possible that the available information is not complete and therefore that there is an element r such that:

$$little(r) = small(r) = medium(r) = big(r) = verybig(r) = 0$$

(See also the possibility of defining a default rule in Section 6).

(c) The number good(r,t) is not a true value but a constraint. Indeed, good(r, t) is the degree at which Good(r, t) can be proved and not the truth degree of Good(r, t). As a matter of fact, as it is usual in fuzzy logic, good(r, t) represents the information"givenr,we can prove that the control t is good at least at level good(r, t)".

Consequently, the number good(r, t) represents only the value we can derive from the available information. By adding new information, as an example a new clause A(x)∧B(y)→Good(x,y), it is possible that good(r, t) assumes a new value. Only by referring to the least-fuzzy Herbrand model of the program p we can claim that good(r,t) is a truth value.

(d) The elements in U can be interpreted as degrees of preference rather that truth values. Indeed, as a matter of fact, the number good(r,t) can represent the information"given r, t is preferred at least at level good(r, t)".

This leads to the question as for whether the fuzzy logic can be considered as a basis for a logic of the judgment values (subjective in nature), while usually one propose the logics of the truth values (whose purpose is an objective description of the world).

(e) A second-order logical approach to fuzzy control is perhaps reasonable. As an example, we can consider rules like:

"If x is small then the function f is lightly increasing",

"The function f has only a maximum", and

"If x is medium then f is almost constant".

A system of rules of such a kind defines a fuzzy predicate Good(f) in the class Y^X of possible functions from X to Y.

We conclude this section by emphasizing that "the reduction of fuzzy control to logic proposed in this chapter does not coincide with the one proposed here".

We define the predicate MAMD(x, y) by the axiom:

$$\text{MAMD}\left(x, y\right) \leftrightarrow \left(\left(A_1\left(x\right) \wedge B_1\left(y\right)\right) \vee \ldots \vee \left(A_n\left(x\right) \wedge B_n\left(y\right)\right)\right)$$

It is immediate that in a Herbrand model of such an axiom the predicate MAMD is interpreted in the same way as Good, that is, by the fuzzy relation good. So, from an extensional point of view the two approaches look to be equivalent. Nevertheless, they are different in nature. As an example, as we have earlier observed, the number good(r, t) represents only the information (a lower constraint) we can derive from the available information. By adding new information it is possible that good(r, t) assumes a new value. Since, in our approach good(r, t) is only a lowerbound for an exact value, this is not contradictory: We have only more complete information. Instead, we cannot add this new information to Axiom(H), in which one can establish the exact truth value of MAMD(x, y). Because any new information on the predicate MAMD contradicts Axiom(H).

Based on the discussion of Section 3.9 and being motivated by the notion of multi-valued logic viz. Łukasiewicz/fuzzy logic as stated in chapter 3 of volume 1 of this book we hereby propose the future generation of control architecture as given in Figure 108. So far in the discussions on control system design we have never mentioned about the safety/protection of the system, which is under conventional control or fuzzy control. In industry in addition to the dynamic control of the system there is a circuit called interlock protection circuit, which surrounds the systems behavior and trip system if any abnormality is observed. At present in industrial applications such interlocked protection circuits are based on two valued logic and always clip the system if it slides over nonlinear operating zone; that means in terms of protection the interlocked protection circuit essentially restrict the system/plant on linear operating zone over which the dynamics of the system has been normally considered. As a result either system runs smoothly (with rated output) or trips if abnormality occurs. But in reality or practice in many situations, we run the system under below rated condition by manual takeover to overcome this problem. We propose to switch over to a multi-valued concept in interlocked protection circuit. Hence, we propose the following architecture for future generation of control, where controller is basically a non-monotonic deductive database system, which will behave in a non-monotonic manner and which will receive error e(t), derivative of error $\Delta e(t)$ and integral error $\int e(t)$ as input to the non-monotonic deductive database system. Thus, this set of errors is basically the queries to the database system and the output of the database system is basically the reply to the queries of the database system.

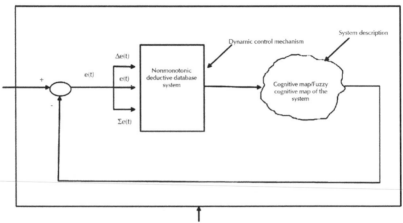

Interlock protection circuit based on either Lukasiewicz logic or Fuzzy logic

FIGURE 109   Future generation of control under multi valued environment.

KEYWORDS

- **Adaptive control**
- **Control theory**
- **Fuzzy Control**
- **Nonlinear system**
- **Stability analysis**

CHAPTER 4

CONCLUDING REMARKS

4.1 REVIEW OF THE APPLICATIONS AND FUTURE SCOPE

The industrial applications of fuzzy logic started in the early 1980s, of which the prime examples are the F. L. Smidth Cement Kiln and the Sendai subway system designed by Hitachi-laid the groundwork for the use of fuzzy logic in the design and production of high Machine Intelligence Quotient (MIQ) consumer products. The first such product—a fuzzy-logic-controlled shower head was announced by Matsushita in 1987. This was followed by the first fuzzy-logic-based washing machine also designed by Matsushita in 1989.

In 1990, high-MIQ consumer products employing fuzzy logic began to grow in number and visibility. Somewhat later, neural network techniques combined with fuzzy logic began to be employed in a wide variety of consumer products, endowing such products with the capability to adapt and learn from experience. Such neuro-fuzzy products are likely to become ubiquitous in the years ahead. The same is likely to happen in the realms of robotics, industrial systems, and process control.

It is from this perspective that the year 1990, may be viewed as a turning point in the evolution of high-MIQ products and systems. Underlying, this evolution was an acceleration in the employment of soft computing (SC) and especially fuzzy logic in the conception and design of intelligent systems that can exploit the tolerance for imprecision and uncertainty, learn from experience, and adapt to changes in the operating conditions.

At this juncture of time (early 1990s) the term "soft computing" was coined by Zadeh. The industrial applications of SC often lead to two questions. First, what is SC? Second, is there something peculiar about industrial processes that require special consideration of the techniques needed to solve the problems that arise from them?

The SC is a concept that its practitioners easily recognize but have trouble articulating. Attempts to define SC often degenerate into a listing either of the special techniques that it uses or of the problems intractable by hard computing but amenable to solution by SC. Actually, the distinguishing feature of SC is straightforward. Hard computing uses an explicit model of the process under consideration, for example, an algorithm that implements solutions to Maxwell's equations to answer questions about the properties of electromagnetic waves. The SC does not do this. Instead, as an indispensable preliminary step, it infers an implicit model from the problem specification and the available data.

We may ask why a technique based on implicit models is necessary. Naively, we might argue that SC is a stopgap that might serve until an explicit model is discovered. This answer is valid sometimes. Often the processes about, which we need to make engineering decisions, are profoundly non-stationary. In other words, the constraints that we presume to be fixed, when we derive an explicit engineering model turn out to be variable, the variation being caused by a meta-level dynamic process. A seemingly ready-made solution to the non-stationarity is presented by artificial intelligence (AI). One of the objectives of AI strategies is to capture the meta-dynamics that entail the dynamics of "intelligent" behavior. The strategy is rooted in the fact that both levels of dynamics affect the relationship between the input and the output of a process. It presupposes that a useful description of both the dynamics of the input–output relationship and the meta-level dynamics entailing low-level dynamics can be found by observing the input and output values and using AI algorithms to estimate the properties of both levels of dynamics from the patterns in the data. This approach has seen some success in industrial problems. However, there is a need for ongoing research, particularly with respect to two classes of problems. The first class is strategic. The AI algorithms were not originally developed for industrial applications and industrial SC requires more flexibility than that afforded by the traditional AI. The second class is tactical, tailoring an algorithm to meet the needs that arise in specific real-world industrial applications. Developments in the computer hardware during the last two decades have made it easier for the AI techniques to grow into more efficient frameworks. It has been proven that several AI techniques may be used as tools in problems, where conventional approaches fail or perform poorly. An excellent example to demonstrate this potential is the field of engineering design due to its specific characteristics and requirements. A survey of the existing literature could easily confirm this fact but it could also reveal the growing interest of the research community on the relatively new field of SC from the existing state of art of engineering point of view. Considering this interest, the author suggests that the engineering design should be further equipped with fuzzy logic, artificial neural network (ANN), genetic algorithm, neuro-fuzzy approach, fuzzy-genetic approach, domain specific heuristics, and other fusion methodologies to handle vagueness, imprecision, uncertainty, and partial truth. The relevant research activity has been directed towards the development of architectures and ontologies to apply AI in design, in order to assist the design activity and to apply automation to the more complex, conceptual and decision-making tasks. It is also a fact that a parallelism between engineering design and AI is noticed in both historical and current trends [56]. However, the AI is still not widely used in CAD/CAM systems, which, nevertheless, incorporate developments from the domain of applied mathematics and information technology.

The reasons for that could be:

(a) The difficulty of deploying several AI techniques in a concurrent or collaborative framework,

(b) The increased demands in computational power, and

(c) The need to address the issues of conceptualization, visualization and detailed representation.

At the advent of SC, which is an evolving collection of AI methodologies aiming to exploit the tolerance for imprecision and uncertainty that is inherent in human thinking and in real life problems, to deliver robust, efficient and optimal solutions, and to further explore and capture the available design knowledge.SC yields rich knowledge representation (symbol and pattern), flexible knowledge acquisition (machine learning), and flexible knowledge processing (inference by interfacing symbolic and pattern knowledge). Additionally, the SC techniques can either be deployed as separate tools or be integrated in unified and hybrid architectures. The fusion of SC techniques causes a paradigm shift (breakthrough) in engineering and science fields including engineering design by solving problems, which could not be solved with the conventional and/or stand-alone computational tools.

Research has been deployed in the direction of applying SC to engineering design in the context of replacing existing analytical models with approximated models or meta-models. Simpson et al. [216] investigated the potential of SC techniques by comparing them to the statistical techniques in meta-modeling and they provided some recommendations about their appropriate use. Besides meta-modeling, the SC techniques may be combined with expert and knowledge-based systems. The common path of expert systems (ES) and SC techniques was surveyed by Liao [131] in a decade (1995–2004) review. In another literature review, Rao et al. [195] change their focus to the new product development (NPD) activities. In their article, they categorize the applications in five discrete areas, in NPD stages and NPD core elements. The penetration of SC in activities that are strongly related with engineering design is also evident in the research work of Hsu et al. [15]. The NPD is also the main research direction of the work but this time in the context of deploying two SC techniques, namely ANN and FL, in an integrated framework. A general neuro-fuzzy model is suggested, while different formulations of neuro-fuzzy networking are discussed.

The acceptance of SC techniques by the scientific community is also based on the potential of fusing SC with conventional hard computing techniques. The advances of successfully applying SC in demanding domains like engineering, design, have also promoted the use of SC techniques to a wide spectrum of industrial applications. Dote et al. [57] review a significant number of such SC-based applications. The consideration that the art of designing still remains a special human activity, which is in most times an entertainment for the designer. Therefore, future advances in engineering design should perhaps be limited to the cognition of this human natural intelligence. Having confirmed the efficiency of SC either in terms of stand-alone techniques or as supportive tools to other conventional design methodologies, many researchers have been investigating the possibility of enhancing the existing design methodologies by simulating the design process through SC techniques using a multi-agent system. These agents mimic the behavior of a design team and a set of design methodologies, which is constructed by using learning techniques. Numerous SC-based methodologies and applications have been reported in the literature in a variety of scientific domains. In the context of the present volume, representative approaches with high relation to the design process are presented [205].

ENGINEERING DESIGN-BASED ON FUZZY LOGIC

Zadeh initially introduced fuzzy logic in the mid 1960s. The transition from the Aristotelian logic (between two competing states one and only one is true) to the fuzzy logic (multiple competing states may be true at the same time, each one at a different degree of truth) was accepted by the scientific community with hesitation. The ability, however, of modeling the uncertainty through fuzzy logic attracted many researchers that contributed to the foundation of various fuzzy logic concepts relative to engineering design. In complex domains with a large set of parameters and in a changing environment, the hierarchical organization of the knowledge is considered as common practice. Torra [224] reviewed the construction of hierarchical fuzzy systems and focused on aspects related to the construction of this hierarchy. Moreover, the advances in object-oriented programming influenced a significant number of researchers in suggesting object models with relations expressed via fuzzy sets.

Considering these fuzzy relations, there are three kinds of relationships inherent to object models:

(a) An instance-of,

(b) A-kind-of, and

(c) A category on the basis of a generalized object model incorporating the perspectives of semantic data modeling, the AI and database systems.

During the last decades, researchers have been using fuzzy logic as a representation framework in design problems characterized by inherent uncertainty during decision-making. Fuzzy logic has also been applied to design activities, where there are needs other than knowledge representation, for example, for cognitive support in reverse engineering and for decision making in demanding domains, such as conceptual design. Design structure matrices (DSM) have also been used as representation and analysis tools that manage the design process under diverse perspectives. Saridakis et al. [205] address the DSM as a communicating design tool among multiple designers by introducing a fuzzy-logical inference mechanism that permits the collaboration among designers on the qualitative definition of the interrelations among the design problem's entities or tasks. Quality function deployment (QFD) has also been used to translate customer needs into technical design requirements, aiming at the increase of customer satisfaction. The co-founder of QFD, Dr. Yoji Akao, has recently published a book that describes QFD, through case studies from big Japanese companies and industries, ranging from manufactured and assembled products, to construction, chemical process, service, and software. The QFD methodologies are based on the house of quality (HOQ), which is a matrix providing a conceptual map for the design process. Temponi et al. [222] implement a fuzzy logic-based methodology to business decision making within the context of the HOQ. In this approach, the communication between different team members is facilitated through fuzzy representation of requirements and identification of conflicting and cooperative interrelationships. Finally, a fuzzy inference scheme is used for the reasoning of the implicit relationships between requirements. Towards the direction of effectively capturing the genuine requirements of customers (voice of customers-VOC), Yan et al. [243] use repeated single-criterion sorting combined with fuzzy evaluation. The definitions of relative rankings of design requirements, customer needs and design concepts have also been a topic for research. Buyukozkan et al. [25] use a general form of the analytic hierarchy process and more specifically of the analytic network process, in order to prioritize the design requirements by taking into account the degree of their interdependence with the customer needs. In this approach, triangular fuzzy numbers are used to improve the quality of the responsiveness to customer needs and design requirements. Jiao et al. [108] introduce a fuzzy ranking methodology for concept evaluation within the framework of configuration design for mass customization. This methodology uses fuzzy numbers and linguistic terms to model combinations of tangible and intangible criteria. Wang [233] utilizes a fuzzy outranking model to determine the non-dominating design concepts. The concepts are compared in pairs and the evaluation is performed by using three types of indices. A significant part of the research activity focuses on fuzzy decision-making in design. The proposed framework expresses the uncertainty of these criteria through fuzzy numbers and solves the design/procurement proposal selection problems through underlying conflicting objectives. Hsiao [107] proposes a fuzzy decision-making methodology on the basis of hierarchical structures of evaluation objectives. In this approach, fuzzy membership functions are used to model the relative contribution of each objective to the overall value of the solution and the degree of approximation of a solution with respect to a given objective. Furthermore, a generalized weighted mean method is utilized in order to calculate the fuzzy probability ascending level by level. Chan et al. [32] propose an enhanced weighted fuzzy reasoning algorithm that is capable of evaluating a decision and is based on the combined effect of individual factors in the antecedent of a rule. The importance of individual factors or the weights assigned to the factors can also be tailored according to individual user preference. However, the fuzzy analysis may result in severe computational cost in complex design problems. Under this consideration, Jensen et al. [109] introduce a methodology based on approximation concepts and fuzzy calculus. In the context of this approach, explicit approximate responses reduce the number of system analyses that are required in the fuzzy weighted algorithm in order to estimate the membership functions for system outputs.

Some other researchers incorporate functions or features in fuzzy design models. For instance, Fenga et al. [70] propose a framework for mapping the component requirements into feature-related functions through a fuzzy relation system.

This mapping is performed in the context of two perspectives:

(a) The importance of requirements/functions and

(b) Their measurement.

In other approaches, functions and functional requirements are modeled through other design entities. In his thesis, Law [127] describes the method of imprecision, a method that models the design problem via design parameters and performance variables. Both design parameters and performance variables may be expressed with fuzzy sets that represent various levels of preferences on specific intervals of values. The proposed reasoning scheme uses mathematics of fuzzy sets, suitably adapted to the domain of engineering design, in order to provide solutions that meet the highest overall preference. Scott [208] used this method of imprecision in his thesis as a basis for the development of a framework capable of accommodating the preferences of multiple designers and for the production of formally optimal solutions according to the criterion of maximum overall preference. Thus, collaboration among multiple designers could be accomplished through different proposed aggregation strategies. Jones et al. [110] augmented the method of imprecision with a fuzzy knowledge base that includes a library of components, parameters of components expressed with fuzzy sets and stored membership functions. The utilization of the aforementioned knowledge base contributed to the reduction of the time required for an exhaustive search of the design space. The research activity on implementing fuzzy logic in design is also reported through a large number of applications in various domains such as the design of comfort systems (heating, cooling, ventilation, and shading) [54], the design of machining activities [35], the preliminary design of re-entry aeroshells [207], the preliminary design of vehicle structure [206], the conceptual design of robot grippers [148], and so on.

ENGINEERING DESIGN-BASED ON GENETIC ALGORITHMS

The genetic algorithms are members of a collection of methodologies known as evolutionary computation (EC). These techniques are based on the selection and evolution processes that are met in nature and imitate these principles in many scientific domains. One of the researchers that worked for the establishment of the genetic algorithms' theory was Holland. A few years later Goldberg, studied several aspects of the implementation of genetic algorithms and examined their potential in the context of optimization and learning for large-scale complex systems. By changing their focus to engineering design, Bullock et al. [24] investigated the advances of the genetic algorithms, while Rosenman [201] performed an even more specific survey on evolutionary models that are applicable to non-routine design problems. Another important review about approaches that apply both evolutionary and adaptive search in engineering design problems was authored by Parmee [179]. Genetic algorithms have also been utilized as creative design tools [89] or as support tools to computer-based systems applied to detailed design [199].

The efficiency of the different architectures of evolutionary algorithms in comparison to other heuristic techniques has been tested in both generic and engineering design problems. Through these tests, the genetic algorithms are identified as robust heuristic tools capable of delivering efficient and robust solutions to diverse design problems. An interesting research topic for the implementation of genetic algorithms is the area of assembly design. The genetic algorithm produces near-optimal assembly plans starting from a randomly initialized population of assembly sequences in the context of minimizing both the orientation changes of the product and the gripper replacements, while grouping technologically similar assembly operations. The quality of the generated assembly sequences is assessed by a space-state search algorithm that adopts a best-first search algorithm and seeks the path that corresponds to a feasible sequence with the lowest total cost. Another approach for the assembly line planning problem is proposed by Chen et al. [33]. In this study, a hybrid genetic algorithm addresses assembly planning with various objectives, including minimizing cycle time, maximizing workload smoothness, minimizing the frequency of tool change, minimizing the number of tools and machines used, and minimizing the complexity of assembly sequences. Moreover, a self-tuning method was developed to enhance the effective schemata of chromosomes during the deployment of the proposed genetic operators. Taura et al. [221] studied the implementation of an adaptive-growth-type 3D representation based on evolutionary algorithms in the configuration design. The evolution of the shapes expressed in the process takes place through the interaction with a defined outside environment and their interaction among the shapes themselves. The underlying framework allows the determination of 3D shapes and their layouts in the same framework and generates a diversity of shapes and configurations that help the designer develop his/her insights and ideas.

Other researchers focus on the product's underlying architecture and develop evolutionary methods to manipulate the design knowledge. Souza et al. [218] examine the trade-off between commonality and individual product performance within a product family and introduce a genetic algorithm-based method in order to find an acceptable balance between commonality in the product family and desired performance of the individual products in the family. In this approach, design of experiments is used to help the screening of unimportant factors and identify factors of interest to the product family, while a multi-objective genetic algorithm optimizes the performance of the products in the resulting family by using a non-dominated sorting strategy. Fan et al. [70] propose an approach for synthesizing system-level designs for multi-domain dynamic systems in an automated manner. This approach uses genetic program as a competent search method for designs, bond graphs as a representation scheme for dynamic systems, while a hierarchical competition model is adopted for preventing the premature convergence often encountered in EC. The result is a design environment that accomplishes open-ended topological search for system-level models of various classes of engineering systems, while providing the designer the option to continue with the next step of embodiment of the conceptual designs or, instead, to gain design insight by analyzing the design candidates.

Although, genetic algorithms are well suited for design problems, where explicit design knowledge is available, they can also be excellent tools for manipulating vague design knowledge. Zechman et al. [271] suggest that the optimal solution in a real optimization problem, in which some decision-making objectives cannot be modeled or quantified, must be tagged with a set of good alternative solutions. In the latter chapter, an evolutionary algorithm is proposed that systematically searches regions of the objective space, close to the optimal solution in order to locate alternative solutions that are maximally different in the decision space. If sets of diverge solutions are introduced to the designer and/or to the design team, an interactive/ collaborative decision-making discourse may take place that preserves the flexibility of the design process. In the context of supporting the designer during the early phases of the design process, there are schemes of free-form shape features and aims to the generation of a system capable of holding and manipulating the shape features after synthesis. The proposed shape feature generating process model takes advantage of developmental biology to devise a computational model of the representation (cell division model) by using a classifier system. Although, this model has a limited capability of representing shapes, it can hold specific features, while showing a variety of alternative shapes after combining already existing shapes. Several researchers have concluded that genetic algorithms may be properly modified in order to be used in engineering design. Rasheed et al. [196] presented a method to improve the efficiency of a genetic algorithm to perform optimization in engineering design by utilizing a sequence of previously explored points to guide further exploration. The proposed methodology recognizes both good and bad solution spaces and is suitable for continuous spaces with expensive evaluation functions, such as those that appear in engineering design. Gero et al. [80] deployed a genetic algorithm that operates in conjunction with the problem solving process in order to automate the knowledge acquisition and reuse in design. The described algorithm relies on the fact that structural features of the genotype influence the fitness or behavior of the resulting designs and, if these features could be isolated, they could be used for the benefit of the design process. These genetic features can also be subjected to genetic engineering operations, such as gene surgery and gene therapy. Since, the genetic features are in the form of genes, they can be replaced by a single "evolved" gene and thus extend the range of symbols used in the genetic representation. This could allow the achievement of a more focused solution search by using knowledge, which was not previously available.

Considering the presence of multiple conflicting objectives in many engineering design problems, Andersson et al. [4] introduce a method that combines the struggle genetic-crowding algorithm with Pareto-based population ranking in order to locate both discontinuous Pareto frontiers and multiple Pareto frontiers in multi-modal search spaces. In the proposed, Pareto multiple-objective struggle-genetic algorithm, the ranking of each individual is based on how many members of the population are preferred in a Pareto-optimal sense, while parents are selected uniformly from the population before crossover and mutation operators are initiated. Each produced child is inserted into the population and replaces the most similar individual to itself only, if it has a better ranking. The similarity between two individuals is measured through a function, which considers the differences in both parameter and attribute space. Parmee [178] describes a dual agent strategy, which concurrently combines ant colony search with evolutionary search to manipulate both discrete and continuous variable parameter sets. The communication between the two search-agents results to a more efficient search across the system design hierarchy when compared to that achieved by a structured genetic algorithm and also to a simplification of the chromosomal representation. This simplification allows further development of the preliminary design hierarchy. Other researchers suggest that the underlying knowledge of the considered design problem may be involved in the genetic operations. Ryoo et al. [191] adopt a genetic algorithm to search a globally compatible solution in a decomposition- based design environment. In this approach, the design problem is decomposed into subproblems, whose solutions are obtained through co-evolution. Mechanisms-based on modification of genetic makeup through experiential inheritance (exposure to another species) and through interspecies' migration are deployed in order to exchange design information among the temporarily decoupled sub-problems. Moreover, different forms of coupling among sub-problems are investigated, ranging from simple coupling through constraints to coupled objective and constraint functions. In their chapter, Wallace et al. [232] suggest a specification-based design evaluation method that emulates the way that specifications are used by product designers in a concurrent design environment. The specifications are mapped to acceptability functions, which are capable of capturing the subjective probability and the different performance levels of the design attributes of each solution. The proposed methodology is augmented by a genetic algorithm that uses a penalty-based fitness function on the basis of a logarithmic acceptability metric. Genetic program may also contribute to the extraction of knowledge about the design problem under consideration. Ishino et al. [111] have developed a methodology for estimation of design intent (MEDI) on the basis of a staged design evaluation model that uses two basic algorithms. The first algorithm includes multiple genetic programs, while the second involves both principal component analysis and multivariate regression. Therefore, MEDI can provide an approximate evaluation of how preferable a specific product model is, while both the structure of target performance functions and the approximate values of their weights can be estimated through multivariate genetic program. A significant common characteristic of several approaches is the evolution of the design problem under consideration through genetic operations. Maher [136] identifies design as a co evolutionary process, with parallel search for both design requirements and design solutions. In this approach, the interaction between requirements and solution redefine the current fitness function that is not necessarily related with convergence in computational evolution. This is explained by the fact that fitness is used to determine, which individuals survive and convergence occurs, when new ideas cannot be found, thus, the termination conditions do not rely on the fitness of individuals. Parmee et al. describe an environment that integrates evolutionary search methodologies and exploration technologies as well as other computational intelligence techniques. The latter research work has been deployed in the perspective of capturing (a) knowledge generated from human-based reasoning and (b) activity by providing interaction between the designer and an iterative evolutionary search procedure. The proposed methodology may be used in the conceptual phase of the design process during, which the design knowledge processing together with the discussion among the members of the design team in an iterative designer/evolutionary search procedure may result to a problem reformulation. This reformulation will provide a more explicit definition and greater reliability in the machine-based representation. Cvetkovic et al. [28] introduce an evolutionary conceptual design system. This system is developed on the basis of a simple architecture based on several software agent classes that perform different tasks, supporting the designer to solve various design issues. In the context of this research work, the proposed agents are designed for a conceptual design environment, where design goals and constraints are still rather vague. The role of the agents in this environment is to provide help to the designer. Liu et al. [132] suggest a framework to dynamically manage cooperative agents in a distributed environment on the basis of a tree-structure-based genetic algorithm and interactive selection. The proposed framework serves as a continuous novelty generator that may stimulate the imagination of designers through the explorative evolution and not as an optimizing tool. Kampis et al. [49] study systems with both incomplete specification and an incomplete environment description and they introduce an agent-based simulation informed from biological evolution. In their approach, they deal with the problem of persistent species evolution in an artificial evolutionary system and argue that a species evolution process can help addressing design problems. The incomplete knowledge is handled without human intervention, through an iterated process with changing function space and changing attribute space. The developments in the research field of genetic program have been utilized in various application domains, such as the optimization of linear elastic structures, the conceptual design of supersonic transport aircraft, the conceptual design of a micro-air vehicle, the domain of fashion design, telecommunication network design, wind force analysis and analysis, design and optimization of steel structures, the design of elastic flywheels, the design rolling element bearing, the design of four bar mechanism, the design of combinational logic circuits, the problem of manufacturing cells formation, and many others.

ENGINEERING DESIGN-BASED ON ARTIFICIAL NEURAL NETWORKS

The ANNs were first introduced by McCulloch et al., who suggested that the biological function of the human brain could be emulated by a simplified computational model. The theory of ANNs remained out of interest for a long time. However, during the last three decades a huge growth in this research field has been reported and several ANN architectures have already proved their efficiency in diverse aspects. A good book for reviewing the fundamentals of ANNs through graphs, algorithms and real-world applications has been authored by Bose et al. [21]. In another book authored by Gallant [78], neural network learning algorithms are discussed from a computational point of view together with an extensive exploration of neural network ES showing how learning via neural networks could automatically generate ES. Potter et al. [189] investigate the applicability of inductive machine learning to the design synthesis in the conceptual design tasks and discusses several issues that must be considered in order to achieve efficient design solutions and qualified underlying design knowledge. Although, some researchers still believe that there are other techniques that perform better than ANNs in specific problems, the increasing approaches and applications that implement ANNs as core or supportive elements dominate and characterize the current research trend. Ivezic et al. [107] introduced a simulation-based decision support system approach in order to support the early stages of collaborative design, where collaborative, distributed design teams refine selected conceptual design solutions under uncertain design specifications.

The proposed system is based on four components:A behavior evaluation model, which is used to structure individual, domain-specific decision models and to organize these models into a collaborative decision model,A probabilistic framework that enables the management of the uncertainty within a constraint satisfaction environment by using simulation-based knowledge,A statistical neural network, which captures the simulation-based knowledge and builds the probabilistic behavior models based on this knowledge, andA Monte Carlo simulation mechanism, which samples the trained neural networks and approximates the likelihoods of design variable values.Hsu et al. [104] proposed a sequential approximation method that utilizes a back-propagation neural network in order to simulate a rough map of the feasible domain formed by the constraints that are modeled as pass/fail functions. The approximate model follows an iterative process in searching for the optimal point in new approximated feasible domains. This approach can be implemented in design optimization problems characterized by the existence of implicit or binary constraints and discrete variables.

Chen et al. [37] proposed an approach that is based on the laddering technique and the radial-basis function neural network. The proposed system facilitates the NPD by eliciting the customer requirements through a three level hierarchical laddering technique and by overcoming the qualitative nature of the imposed requirements through the RBF neural network. This prototype system makes it possible for the similarities and differences between among several respondent groups to be studied both psychologically and computationally.

Ding et al. [55] present a feature recognition method that integrates design by features, the ANN techniques and a heuristic algorithm in order to handle feature interactions. A unified data structure models the underlying feature classes. An input representation that is based on F-adjacent and V-adjacent matrices is implemented in the neural network, which is capable of recognizing the features. Moreover, the proposed heuristic algorithm recognizes the interactions of internal features and classifies them in four types: Parent child, connection, non-connection, and overlap hiding.

Yasuda et al. [244] introduce a design methodology of a fault-tolerant autonomous multi-robot system, which integrates the design of an on-line autonomous behavior acquisition mechanism. This mechanism develops cooperative roles and assigns them to a robot appropriately in a noisy embedded environment, by applying (a) reinforcement learning that adopts the Bayesian discrimination method for segmenting a continuous state space and a continuous action space simultaneously, and (b) a neural network to predict the average of the other robots' postures at the next time step in order to stabilize the reinforcement learning environment.

Barai et al. [11] propose a heuristic approach called the SG (k-NN) ensemble that is utilized for the systematic generation of good-quality and diverse models. In this approach, several neural network models are used in combinations and the results show that even the worst combination performs better that any single model thus proving that careful generation of ensembles can improve good quality models created from good-quality data. However, the effectiveness of the ensemble modeling depends on the accuracy and the diversity of the individual networks. Granitto et al. [96] investigate how to tune the ensemble members in order to have an optimal compromise and perform an extensive evaluation of several algorithms for ensemble construction, including new proposals and comparing them to standard methods used in the literature.

In some approaches, the computational neural network model is augmented with a visualization scheme that is compliant with the designers' perception. Towards this direction, Hsiao et al. [106] introduce an approach that utilizes back-propagation neural networks to establish the relationships between product-form parameters and adjective image words. The connections among the design elements, product images and shape generation rules are stored in a database that is used by a CAD system that helps designers generate 3D models with different images by providing basic design elements and shape generation rules. Wang et al. [234] developed Creative Stimulator (Crea Stim), which is an intelligent interface that enhances creativity in pattern design by helping designers explore innovative pattern designs. Crea Stim relies on the catastrophe theory, which implies that sudden realization in the thinking process of design may lead to creativity and it is based on a neural network-based imagining engine, a data repository, and its learning strategies. The ANN learns the psychological factors and generalizes new patterns with different psychological requirements.

ENGINEERING DESIGN-BASED ON SOFT COMPUTING PARADIGM

Fuzzy logic, genetic algorithms and ANNs are not competing to each other but instead, they may be combined on the basis of integrated frameworks to outperform conventional design approaches. Four books that extensively describe architectures and models of the computational intelligence and their possible fusion have been authored by Kosko [102], Kasabov [113], Koza [117], and Cordon et al. [46]. Keeping in mind the engineering design process, several approaches are described in the following paragraphs, which implement combinations of SC techniques. Vico et al. [230] consider design synthesis as an optimization problem and under this perspective a neural network is utilized to implement a fitness function for a genetic algorithm that searches for the optimal solution. In this framework, the designer supervises the system and each time a new good result is extracted, he/she checks the validity before feeding the neural network, which adapts and fits better the designer's criteria. Sasaki et al. [219] propose a method to solve fuzzy multiple-objective optimal system design problems with hybridized genetic algorithms. This approach enables the design of flexible optimal system by applying fuzzy goals and fuzzy constraints. Moreover, generalized upper bounding is applied in order to structure the representation of the chromosomes in the genetic algorithm. Wang et al. [235] suggest an interactive evolutionary approach to synthesize component-based preliminary design engineering problems by combining agent-based hierarchical design representation, set-based design generation with fuzzy design tradeoff strategy and evolutionary synthesis. The proposed framework facilitates the human-computer interaction to define the fitness function of solutions incorporating both multi-criteria evaluation and constraint satisfaction. Lim et al. [134] automate the formulation of fuzzy rules by means of a genetic algorithm. They suggest that, instead of using the entire solution space, the latter must be systematically partitioned into smaller subspaces, in which the GA could focus for optimal solutions. This process continues iteratively for various subspaces, until finally a compact set of fuzzy rules is derived.Xiong et al. [242] present a synthetic mixed-discrete fuzzy nonlinear programming optimization method that combines the fuzzy formulation with a genetic algorithm and a traditional, gradient-based optimization strategy. This method can find a globally compromise solution for fuzzy optimization problems containing mixed-discrete design variables, even when the objective functions are non-convex and/or non-differentiable. Delgado et al. [53] utilize Takagi-Sugeno fuzzy models on the basis of a co-evolutionary hierarchical collaborative design approach. The proposed framework induces collaboration among individuals of genetically different populations through fitness sharing among individuals of different species. Critical model parameters such as antecedent aggregation operators, number of fuzzy rules, type, location, and shape of membership functions emerge from the underlying co-evolution. Yang et al. [245] suggest three approaches for implementing and constructing fuzzy neural networks: fuzzy neuron based on fuzzy logic operations, fuzzy neural networks based on fuzzy logic blocks and fuzzy neural networks based on fuzzy reasoning computation. Additionally, a genetic algorithm is proposed as neural learning algorithm. Marcelin [135] describes the use of back-propagation neural networks in creating function approximations of computationally intensive finite element calculations in combination with optimization based on genetic algorithms. Su et al. [220] propose a hybrid approach on the basis of integration of a knowledge base, neural networks, genetic algorithm and CAD/CAE/CAM in a single environment, which can be implemented in various stages of the design process. The genetic algorithm is used to conduct optimization tasks in the context of achieving the optimal combination of design parameters, as well as the optimal architecture of the ANNs used in this hybrid system. Yeun et al. [251] have developed a hybrid system of neural networks and genetic program trees for problem domains, where the complete input space can be decomposed into several different subregions, which are represented in the form of an oblique decision tree. The architecture of this system, called federated agents, consists of a facilitator, neural networks, used as local agents that are expert in different subregions, and genetic program trees that serve as boundary agents. A boundary agent is specialized at the borders of sub-regions, where discontinuities or different patterns coexist, while the facilitator is responsible for choosing the boundary agent that is suitable for given input data using the information obtained from oblique decision tree.

Tsai et al. [229] suggest that designers may create a new design in shorter time by modifying previous designs and with this perspective they propose an intelligent design retrieval system that utilizes SC techniques. Fuzzy relation and fuzzy composition are used for features associations, while a fuzzy neural network is responsible for the composition of object association functions allowing designers to control the similarity of retrieved designs. Zha [272] studies the assemblability and the assembly sequence evaluation in the engineering design through a neuro-fuzzy approach. According to this approach, the fuzziness is a property of the degree of difficulty assigned to the operation, which can be represented by a fuzzy number between 0 and 1. The assembly operations have been evaluated based on various criteria, such as time and equipment required, although the analysis focuses on the difficulty of operation. Moreover, a neural network automatically tunes the membership functions of assemblability factors, so as to adjust the assembly difficulty score. Using the neuro-fuzzy approach, the relationships between product definition data, assembly factor, and assemblability can be formulated followed by sensitivity analysis that could predict how a design parameter change will affect the assemblability. Saridakis et al. [204] represent the design problem in terms of qualitative and quantitative design parameters and their associative relationships of different formalisms, with a genetic algorithm to be deployed to find the optimum solution according to a specific optimization criterion. During genetic optimization, the best solutions are recorded and are submitted to a neuro-fuzzy process that limits the number of inputs and outputs and resolves problem's complexity by substituting existing associative relations with a fuzzy rule system.

The fusion of SC techniques has also been reported in a significant number of design applications, such as civil engineering (pre-stressed concrete pile diagnosis, concrete mix design, design of industrial roofs) [202], design of adaptive car-following indicator [133], the purchasing decisions at crude oil market [90], the explosive cutting process of plates by shaped charges [155], the maintenance of road pavements [126], the optimization of clamping forces in a machining operation [98], the hum human-machine workstation design and simulation [274], and so on.

USE OF SOFT COMPUTING TECHNIQUES IN CASE-BASED DESIGN

The use of SC techniques in activities related to machine learning has been noticed in the literature. An important reasoning methodology that resembles the natural human perception is case-based reasoning (CBR), which in the context of engineering design may be referred to as case-based design (CBD). The inclusion of SC techniques gains in popularity, as the proposed hybrid systems seem to outperform the conventional CBR systems in demanding scientific domains such as engineering design. Dubois et al. study the opportunities of implementing fuzzy logic to perform different activities, which are incorporated in CBR cycle.In general, the CBR algorithms rely on domain knowledge and heuristics in order to adapt past designs to new problems. Rosenman utilizes an evolutionary algorithm to perform adaptation tasks in CBR system and evaluates his method in 2D spatial design of houses.

In the context of acquiring knowledge that is used in retrieval and adaptation tasks in CBD systems, researchers have been investigating the impact of specific-to-general and general-to-specific learning on adaptation knowledge [240]. Towards the aforementioned research directions, Craw [49] proposes a GA method that optimizes the decision tree index and applies a "leave-one-out" k-NN method for retrieval. In Soft-CBR [5], in component-based architecture, fuzzy logic concepts are integrated with an evolutionary algorithm that facilitates the optimization and the maintenance of the system. Tsai et al. [72] combine the fuzzy logic theory with the adaptive resonance theory (ART) to introduce model, which helps designers searching for similar design cases on both geometric and technological basis through vague and incomplete two stage queries. Kraslawski et al. [116] use a fuzzy neural network to model the problem of selection heat-exchange equipment in mixing tanks and to generate possible solution cases that are incorporated by a CBR system.Saridakis et al. have developed Case-DeSC, a CBD system that uses:

a.   Fuzzy preferences to model the design objectives,Hybrid genetic algorithms to execute optimization tasks, andA competitive neural network to retrieve similar past design cases.Several different modules exist in the proposed system, providing the designer with the capability to extract design solutions for ill-structured/creative design problems through CBR or to support the optimization procedure with the CBR solutions. Moreover, they have developed a framework, named CopDeSC, which addresses parametric design in the context of collaborative development of fuzzy objectives on design parameters.

SOFT COMPUTING AND ENGINEERING DESIGN: EVALUATION AND RESEARCH OPPORTUNITIES

In the previous sections of this chapter, a significant number of references have been discussed and commented on. A significant research activity has been reported towards addressing the collaboration, communication, and coordination in engineering design but according to the author's beliefs, there are a lot of opportunities in the context of integrating the three aforementioned issues with the support of SC techniques. Although, collaborative discourses may enhance the design approaches in detailed parametric design by communicating the knowledge and reasoning about the individual objectives, the creative and conceptual design problems require a different perspective. This perspective should preserve the rationality and consistency of the design knowledge representation, whereas the designers' intuition and experience should be utilized in a systematic way. Identifying this difference of perspectives on developing approaches for design problems, different development paths should be followed, according to the degree of the encapsulated design knowledge. Although, the SC techniques are applied to both problem types, there is no unified SC-based approach that addresses both conceptual and detailed designs. This remark is also enforced by the fact that there are still difficulties in modeling and solving geometry-based and visualized/conceptualized design problems. In order to have these design issues addressed, there is a need for holistic approaches using information and AI technologies as integrated frameworks capable of accommodating the Soft computing aided design (SCAD) modules as autonomous and independent agents. These integrated frameworks should be deployed through web-based platforms enhancing collaborative and argumentative discourses among designers. Although, the ideal SCAD system should provide the maximum level of automation and/or support to the designer, its underlying architecture should preserve a human-centric character that takes advantage of human intuition, creativity and experience. In the following, we further discuss some specific industrial innovations using SC techniques.

AEROSPACE APPLICATIONS

In the early 1990s, Werbos developed nonlinear optimal neuro control (adaptive critics). It has been applied to aerospace and aircraft control systems. The SC (neuro, fuzzy, and evolutionary computings) is used for aerospace systems because of the high degrees of nonlinearity, uncertainty, and complexity of these problems and because of the involvement of human beings.

COMMUNICATIONS SYSTEMS

Since, communication systems involve in human beings, the SC can be effectively applied to such systems. The SC enables solutions to be obtained for problems that have not been able to be solved satisfactorily by hard computing methods.

CONSUMER APPLIANCES

The field of consumer or home appliances is not a popular research area in the academic community. Almost, all such research activities are related to practical product development. Therefore, most of the sparse literature (mainly conference papers) on SC in consumer appliances has its origins in industry. Due to commercial confidentiality reasons, these conference papers do not usually give detailed descriptions of algorithms and methods used but, rather, tend to be fairly superficial. Such industrial research and development is particularly active in Japan and South Korea, while corresponding industries in Europe and the United States are only just starting to use SC in the control of various consumer appliances. In Japan, even ordinary consumers are aware of the great potential of fuzzy logic, neural networks, and chaos computing, which have already brought machine intelligence into their daily lives. There is clearly a demand in developed countries in Asia for intelligent, human-like, and user-friendly control features. The figurative term "heartware" is sometimes used in respect to such consumer products that support the following general objectives:

- Comfortable way of life,Ease of life to manage time and space, and Health and environment-conscious life.

Although, the field of research on consumer appliances differs greatly from the other application fields reviewed in this chapter, an overview of state-of-the-art appliances should be given in view of the considerable and rapidly growing monetary value of the intelligent home appliance business. Besides, numerous interesting innovations have been made in this field during the past ten years.

ELECTRIC POWER SYSTEMS

Neural networks were applied already in the early 1990s to electric power systems. The first conference on application of ANNs to power systems was held in 1991. In the mid-1990s, fuzzy logic was applied to power system applications such as control, operation, and planning. The SC was applied to power systems in the mid-1990s as reported in [215], which describes in detail the methods for applying SC to various power system problems. Recently, the EC has been used mainly to solve control, operation, and planning problems of power systems, since, power systems are typically large-scale and complex. Data mining technology, which essentially involves searching for stable, meaningful, and easily interpretable patterns in databases using SC, has recently become popular, and this new technology may be used to solve certain power system problems in the near future. Software for data mining in a power generation station, for example, power station performance optimization (reducing energy consumption, identifying measures to reduce operating costs) is now commercially available.

MANUFACTURING AUTOMATION AND ROBOTICS

The term intelligence has been frequently used in this field, since robotic technologies that mimic human thinking and behavior of bio-systems have been developed. Contemporary intelligence is sometimes considered to be interactive information processing among human beings, environment, and artificial objects. Intelligence is defined as human-like information processing and adaptation to environment by leaning, evolution, and prediction in order to survive. The use of structured intelligence by SC for intelligent robots has been considered. However, the interaction with human beings is also important. Recently, emotional robots that interact with human beings have attracted much interest by researchers. KANSEI (emotion, feeling) information processing has become popular in Japan. This technology is needed for the development of human-friendly robots. Other technologies, for example, fuzzy associative memory and chaotic computation have also been used for developing human-friendly robots (intelligent robots, welfare robots). The SC is widely used in this field.

POWER ELECTRONICS AND MOTION CONTROL

It is well known that I/O mapping by an NN can be approximated by FL. However, an NN has advantageous knowledge acquisition capabilities by learning and more accurate mapping properties. On the other hand, the FL can explain the I/O relations and is rich in knowledge representation. Besides, it is suitable for fine-tuning and representation of easily understandable knowledge expressions for human beings with less computation time. Fuzzy neural networks have therefore been applied to power electronics and motion control. In the FL approach, various kinds of clustering methods in the I/O spaces from numerical data are used and fuzzy rules are extracted adaptively.

In this field, systems are often nonlinear and uncertain. It is difficult to obtain rigorous mathematical models. Self-tuning (adaptive) capabilities and automated design methods are needed. The SC has innovatively solved such real-world problems at low cost. For hardware realization of the schemes, fast DSPs are widely available.

PROCESS ENGINEERING

Fuzzy logic was first used in the process industry in Japan in 1987. Since, processes are usually nonlinear, uncertain and complex, highly skilled operators have controlled process plants. Fuzzy control was devised to mimic skilled operator's control. In the U.S., neural networks were applied to the chemical process industry in the late 1980s. Since, the chemical industry has typically a lot of operation data available, neural networks are suitable for nonlinear time series analysis. The SC offers additional adaptation capability to solve nonlinear and uncertain process engineering problems. Since, these processes are large-scale and complex, data mining technology, which has been developed since the late 1980s using heterogeneous methodologies, including SC methods based on pattern recognition technology, has recently been used for interpreting and understanding important associations hidden in large process databases. Due to commercial confidentiality reasons, people working in process industries do not usually publish detailed technical papers, their work is focused on the development of practical products. However, data mining software for process industry is now commercially available. Data mining provides the understanding of process and plant performance and builds a solid basis for remarkable degree of cost savings and profitability.

Data mining technology is being used in the following demanding areas:
- Load forecasting and operation guidance for air conditioning systems, Monitoring of the performance of heating systems, Inner state estimation for stills (soft sensing), Quality modeling and quality improvement operation guidance for dissolution processes, Virtual sensors for the paper industry, Virtual sensors for a furnace, Oil ingredient prediction,Final quality prediction for chemical reactor process, and
- Evaluation of drug effects.

TRANSPORTATION

Transportation is a large field with diverse and challenging problems to solve. Since, the field of transportation mostly serves ordinary people, passengers, human-orientation and safety in various controls, fault diagnosis, and logistics operations are of considerable importance Based on this consideration, it can be concluded that SC forms an important collection of methodologies in transportation research and development. On the other hand, less than 4% of all SC papers are related to transportation. These two proportions have remained fairly constant during the five-year period of 1995–1999. Thus, the use of SC has already a mature position in the field of transportation. Since, the early 1990s SC has attracted intelligent automobile researchers. The SC is widely used in this field, since, ground transportation systems are human related, and also nonlinear and uncertain.

Intelligent vehicle control requires the following functions:
- Recognition of the driving environment,Planning of driving based on the recognized environment, and
- Planning of driving that is easily acceptable for drivers.

FUTURE SCOPE

The successful applications of SC suggest that SC will have increasingly greater impact in the coming years. The SC is already playing an important role both in science and engineering. In many ways, the SC represents a significant paradigm shift (breakthrough) in the aim of computing, a shift that reflects the fact that the human mind, unlike state-of-the-art computers, possesses a remarkable ability to store and process information, which is pervasively imprecise, uncertain, and lacking in categoricity. The SC can be extended to include computing not only from human thinking aspects (mind and brain) but also from bio-informatics aspects. In other words, cognitive and reactive distributed AI will be developed and applied to large-scale and complex industrial systems. In fuzzy systems, computation with words will be investigated increasingly and also EC will be emerging. It is expected that they will be applied to the construction of more advanced intelligent industrial systems. The SC is already a major area of academic research. However, the concept is still evolving, and new methodologies, for example, chaos computing and immune networks are nowadays considered to belong to SC. While this methodological evolution is taking place, the number of successful SC-based products is increasing concurrently. In the majority of such products, the SC is hidden inside systems or subsystems, and the end user does not necessarily know that SC methods are used in control, diagnosis, pattern recognition, signal processing, and so on. This is the case, when SC is mainly used for improving the performance of conventional hard computing algorithms or even replacing them. However, the SC is very effective, when it is applied to real-world problems that are not able to be solved by traditional hard computing. Another class of products uses SC for implementing novel intelligent and user-friendly features. The SC enables industrial systems to be innovative due to the important characteristics of SC: Tractability, high-MIQ, and low cost.

KEYWORDS

- **Design structure matrices**
- **Fuzzy logic**
- **Genetic algorithms**
- **Quality function deployment**
- **Soft computing**

REFERENCES

1. Adams, E. W. and Levine, H. F. On the uncertainties transmitted from premises to conclusions in deductive inferences. Synthese, 30, 429–460 (1975).
2. Albert, P. The algebra of fuzzy logic. Fuzzy Sets Syst., 1. 203–230 (1978).
3. Aliev, R. A., Fazlollahi, B., Aliev, R. R., and Guirimov, B. G. Fuzzy time series prediction method based on fuzzy recurrent neural network. Lecture Notes in Computer Science (LNCS), pp. 860–869 (2006).
4. Andersson, J. and Wallace, D. Pareto optimization using the struggle genetic crowding algorithm. Engineering Optimization, 34, 623–643 (2002).
5. Aggour, K., Pavese, M., Bonissone, P., and Cheetham, W. SOFT-CBR: A self-optimizing fuzzy tool for case-based reasoning. ICCBR, pp. 5–19 (2003).
6. Balasubramaniam, J. Rule reduction for efficient inferencing in similarity-based reasoning. International Journal of Approximate Reasoning, 48(1), 156–173 (April, 2008).
7. Balasubramaniam, J. Rule reduction for efficient inferencing in similarity-based reasoning. International Journal of Approximate Reasoning, 48, 156–173 (2008).
8. Balasubramaniam, J. Yager's new class of implications Jf and some classical tautologies. Inform. Sci., 177, 930 946 (2007).
9. Balbes, R. and Dwinger, P. Distributive Lattices. Univ. of Mossouri Press (1974).
10. Baldwin, J. F. A new approach to approximate reasoning using fuzzy logic. Fuzzy Sets Syst., 2, 309–325 (1979).
11. Barai, S. V. and Reich, Y. Ensemble modeling or selecting the best model: Many could be better than one. Artificial Intelligence for Engineering Design, Analysis, and Manufacturing, 13, 377–386 (1999).
12. Baranyi, P. and Yam, Y. Fuzzy rule base reduction in fuzzy IF-THEN rules. D. Ruan and E. E. Kerre (Eds.), Computational Intelligence: Theory and Applications, pp. 135–160 (2000).
13. Baranyi, P., Yam, Y., Tikk, D., and Patton, R. J. Trade-off between approximation accuracy and complexity: TS controller design via HOSVD based complexity minimization. J. Casillas, O. Cordon, F. Herrera, and L. Magdalena (Eds.), Studies in fuzziness and soft computing, Interpretability Issues in Fuzzy Modeling, Springer-Verlag, 128, 249–277 (2003).
14. Bargiela, A. and Pedrycz, W. Granular Computing. Kluwer Academic Publishers (2002).
15. Běhounek, L., Bodenhover, U., and Cintula, P. Relations in fuzzy class theory: Initial steps. Fuzzy Sets and Systems, 159, 1729–1772 (2008).
16. Běhounek, L. and Daňková, M. Relational compositions in fuzzy class theory. Fuzzy Sets and Systems, 160(8), 1005–1036 (2009).
17. Běhounek, L. and Cintula, P. Fuzzy class theory. Fuzzy Sets and Systems, 154, 34–55 (2005).
18. Bonissone, P. P. Soft Computing: The convergence of emerging reasoning technologies. Soft Computing, 1(1), 6–18 (1997).

19. Biacino, L., Gerla, Giangiacomo, and Ying, Mingsheng. Approximate Reasoning Based on Similarity. Math. Log. Q., 46(1), 77–86 (2000).

20. Bien, Z. and Chun, M. G. An inference network for bidirectional approximate reasoning based on equality measures. IEEE Trans. Fuzzy Syst., 2(2), 177–180 (1994).

21. Bose, N. K. and Liang, P. Neural Network Fundamentals with Graphs, Algorithms, and Applications. McGraw-Hill International Editions (1996).

22. Booth, R. and Richter, E. On revising fuzzy belief bases. Studia Logica, 80, 29–61 (2005).

23. B. Bouchon-Meunier, R. R. Yager, and L. A. Zadeh (Eds.). Uncertainty in Intelligent and Information Systems, Advances in Fuzzy Systems Applications and Theory: Volume 20, World Scientific, Singapore (2000).

24. Bullock, G. N., Denham, M. J., Parmee, I. C., and Wade, G. Developments in the use of the genetic algorithm in engineering design. Journal of Design Studies, 16, 507–524 (1995).

25. Buyukozkan, G., Ertay, T., Kahraman, C., and Ruan, D. Determining the importance weights for the design requirements in the house of quality using the fuzzy analytic network approach. International Journal of Intelligent Systems, 19, 443–461 (2004).

26. Bui, T. X. A Group Decision Support System for Cooperative Multiple criteria Group Decision making. Springer Verlag, Berlin (1987).

27. Bustince, H., Kacprzyk, J., and Mohedano, V. Intuitionistic fuzzy generators: Application to intuitionistic fuzzy complementation. Fuzzy Sets Syst., 114, 485–504 (2000).

28. Cvetkovic, D. and Parmee, I. Agent-based support within an interactive evolutionary design system. Artificial Intelligence for Engineering Design, Analysis, and Manufacturing, 16, 331–342 (2002).

29. Carlsson, C. and Fuller, Robert. Possibility and necessity in weighted aggregation. ′R. R. Yager and J. Kacprzyk (Eds.), The ordered weighted averaging operators: Theory, Methodology, and Applications. Kluwer Academic Publishers, Boston, pp. 18–28 (1997) [ISBN 0-7923-9934-X].

30. Chang, S. Y., Huang, T. L., and Huang, T. Y. Fuzzy bang–bang controller for servo systems via optimal path estimation method. Proceedings of 1995 International Conference on Power Electronics and Drive Systems (1995).

31. Chang, C. C. Algebraic analysis of many valued logic. Trans, Amer. Soc., 87, 1–53 (1958).

32. Chan, C. W. and Lau, P. Representing user preference in engineering design domains using an enhanced weighted fuzzy reasoning algorithm. Artificial Intelligence in Engineering, 13, 1–10 (1999).

33. Chen, R. S., Lu, K. Y., and Yu, S. C. A hybrid genetic algorithm approach on multi-objective of assembly planning problem. Engineering Applications of Artificial Intelligence, 15, 447–457 (2002).

34. Chen, S. M., Yeh, Ming-Shiow, and Hsiao, Pei-Yung. A comparison of similarity measures of fuzzy values. Fuzzy Sets and Systems, 72, 79–89 (1995).

35. Chen, Y., Hui, A., and Du, R. Fuzzy expert system machining operations. Int. Journal Mach. Tools Manufact., 35(12), 1605–1621 (1995).

36. Chun, M. G. A similarity-based bidirectional approximate reasoning method for decision making system. Fuzzy Sets and Systems, 117, 269–278 (2001).

37. Chen, C. H., Khoo, L. P. and Yan, W. Evaluation of multicultural factors from elicited customer requirements for new product development. Research in Engineering Design, 14, 119–130 (2003).

38. Church, A. A formulation of the simple theory of types. J. Symbolic Logic, 5, 56–68 (1940).

39. Cignoli, R. L. O., D'ottaviano, I. M. L., and Mundici, D. Algebraic Foundations of Many-valued Reasoning. Kluwer, Dordrecht (2000).

40. Cignoli, R., Esteva, F., Godo, L. et al. Basic logic is the logic of continuous t-norms and their residua. Soft-computing, 4, 106–112 (2000).
41. Cintula, P. and Hajek, P. Triangular norm based predicate fuzzy logics. Fuzzy sets and systems, 161, 311–346 (2010(a)).
42. Cintula, P., Esteva, F., Gispert, J., Godo, L., and Noguera, C. Distinguished algebraic semantics for t-norm based fuzzy logics: Methods and algebraic equivalencies. Annals of Pure and Applied Logic, 160, 53–81 (2009).
43. Cintula, P. The Ł Π and Ł Π½ propositional and predicate logics. Fuzzy Sets and Systems, 124, 289–302 (2001).
44. Cintula, P. Weakly implicative (fuzzy) logics I: Basic properties, Archive for Mathematical Logic, 45, 673–704 (2006).
45. Cintula, P. From fuzzy logic to fuzzy mathematics. Ph.D. Thesis, Technical University, Prague (2005).
46. Cordon, O., Herrera, F., Hoffman, F., and Magdalena, L. Genetic Fuzzy Systems: Evolutionary Tuning and Learning of Fuzzy Knowledge Bases. World Scientific Co. Ltd (2001).
47. Combs, W. E. and Andrews, J. E. Combinatorial rule explosion eliminated by a fuzzy rule configuration. IEEE Trans. Fuzzy Syst., 6, 1–11 (1998).
48. Cordero, P., Enciso, M., Mora, A., and de-Guzman, I. A complete logic for fuzzy functional dependencies over domains with similarity relations. In proc. of INANN 09 (2009).
49. Craw, S. Introspective Learning to Build Case-based Reasoning (CBR) Knowledge Containers. MLDM, Springer-Verlag, Berlin, Heidelberg, pp. 1–6 (2003).
50. Mundici, D. The C*-algebras of three-valued logic. R. Ferro et al. (Eds.), Logic Colloquium '88, Elsevier-Science Publ., Amsterdam (1989).
51. Hong, D. H. and Hwang, S. Y. On the compositional rule of inference under triangular norms. Fuzzy Sets and Systems, 66, 25–38 (1994).
52. Da, R. A critical study of widely used fuzzy implication operators and their influence rules in fuzzy expert systems. Ph.D. Thesis, State University, Ghent (1990).
53. Delgado, M. R., Zuben, F. V., and Gomid, F. Co-evolutionary genetic fuzzy systems a hierarchical collaborative approach. Fuzzy Sets and Systems, 141, 89–106 (2004).
54. Dounis, A. I., Santamouris, M. J., Lefas, C. C., and Argiriou, A. Design of a fuzzy set environment comfort system. Energy and Buildings, 22, 1–87 (1995).
55. Ding, L. and Yue, Y. Novel ANN-based feature recognition incorporating design by features. Computers in Industry, 55(2), 197–222 (2004).
56. Dias, W. P. S. Reflective practice, artificial intelligence, and engineering design: Common trends and interrelationships. Artificial Intelligence for engineering Design, Analysis, and Manufacturing, 16, 261–271 (2002).
57. Dote, Y. and Osaka, S. J. Industrial applications of soft computing: A review. Proceedings of the IEEE, 89(9), 1243–1265 (2001).
58. Driankov, D., Hellendoorn, H., and Reinfrank, M. An Introduction to Fuzzy Control. Springer-Verlag, Berlin, Heidelberg (1993).
59. Dubois, D. and Prade, H. Fuzzy logics and the generalized modus ponens revisited. Cybernetics and Systems, 15, 293–331 (1984).
60. Dubois, D., Prade, Henri, and Smets, Philippe. Partial truth is not uncertainty-Fuzzy logic versus possibilistic logic. IEEE Expert, 9, 15–19 (1994).
61. D. Dubois and H. Prade (Eds.). Fuzzy information engineering: A guided tour of applications, John Wiley & Sons (1996).
62. Dubois, D. and Prade, H. A class of fuzzy measures based on triangular norm. A General Framework for the Combinations of Uncertain Information (1982).

63. Dubois, D. and Prade, H. Fuzzy Sets and Systems: Theory and Applications. Academic Press, New York (1980).

64. Dubois, D. and Prade, H. Fuzzy sets in approximate reasoning. Part 1: Inference with possibility distributions. Fuzzy Sets Syst., 40(1), 143–202 (1991).

65. Dubois, D. and Prade, H. Non-standard theories of uncertainty in knowledge representation and reasoning, KR, pp. 634–645 (1994).

66. Dubois, D. and Prade, H. On the combination of uncertain or imprecise pieces of information in rule-based systems–A discussion in the framework of possibility theory. Int. J. Approx. Reason, 2, 65–87 (1988).

67. Dubois, D. and Prade, H. Possibility Theory. Plenum Press, New York (1988).

68. Dubois, D. and Prade, H. The generalized modus ponens under sup-min composition: a theoretical study. M. M. Gupta, A. Kandel, W. Bandler, and J. B. Kiszka (Eds.), Approximate Reasoning in Expert Systems, Elsevier, North Holland, pp. 157–166 (1985).

69. Eslami, E. and Buckley J. J. Inverse approximate reasoning. Fuzzy Sets Syst., 87, 155–158 (1997).

70. Fan, Z., Seo, K., Hu, J., Goodman, E. D., and Rosenberg, R. C. A novel evolutionary engineering design approach for mixed-domain systems. Engineering Optimization, 36(2), 127–147 (2004).

71. Filev, D. and Yager, R. R. On the issue of obtaining OWA operator weights. Fuzzy Sets and Systems, 94, 157–169 (1998).

72. Filev, D. and Yager, R. R. Essentials of Fuzzy Modeling and Control. Wiley Interscience (1994).

73. Fuller, R. On fuzzy reasoning schemes. C, Carlsson (Ed.), The State of Art of Information System in 2007, TUCS general publications No. 16, Turku centre for computer science, pp. 85–112 (1999).

74. Fuller, R. and Werners, Brigitte. The compositional rule of inference: Introduction, theoretical considerations, and exact calculation formulas, working paper, RWTH Aachen, instititut fur wirtschaftswissenschaften, NO: 1991/7.

75. Fuller, R. On the generalized method-of-case inference rule. Annales Univ. Sci. Budapest: Section Computatorica, 12, 107–113 (1991).

76. Fuller, R. and Zimmermann, Hans-Jurgen. Computation of the compositional rule of inference under triangular norms. Fuzzy Sets and Systems, 51, 267–275 (1992).

77. Fuller, R. and Zimmermann, Hans-Jurgen. On Zadeh's compositional rule of inference. R. Lower and M. Roubens (Eds.), Fuzzy Logic: State of the art, Theory, and Decision library, Series D, Kluwer Academic publisher, Doldrecht, pp. 193–200 (1993).

78. Gallant, S. I. Neural network learning and expert systems. The MIT Press (1993).

79. Gao, Z. Trautzsch, Thomas A. and Dawson, James G. A Stable Self-Tuning Fuzzy Control System for Industrial Temperature Regulation. Industry Applications Conference, 2, 1232–1240 (2000).

80. Gero, J. S. and Kazakov, V. Machine learning in design using genetic engineering-based genetic algorithms. Workshop on Machine Learning in Design Research, Artificial Intelligence in Design, Worcester, pp. 1–6 (2000).

81. Geering, H. P. Introduction to Fuzzy Control: 3rd Edition. IMRT Press, Institut für Mess- und Regeltechnik, ETH, Zurich (September, 1998).

82. Gerla, G. Fuzzy control as a fuzzy deduction system. Fuzzy Sets and Systems, 121(3), 409–425 (2001).

83. Gerla, G. Fuzzy logic program and fuzzy control. Studia Logica, 79(2), 231–254 (2005).

84. Gerla, G. Fuzzy Logic: Mathematical tools for approximate reasoning. Kluwer Academic Publishers, Dordrecht. Publication Date: April 30, 2001, ISBN-10: 0792369416|ISBN-13: 978-0792369417|Edition: 2001.

85. Gerla G., Sessa, Maria I., and Formato, Ferrante. Similarity-based unification. Fundamenta Informaticae archive, 41(4), 393–414 (March, 2000).

86. Giles, R. Lukasiewicz logic and fuzzy set theory. Internat. J. Man-Machine Studies, 8, 313–327 (1976).

87. Glockuer, I. Fuzzy Quantifiers: A Computational Theory. Springer, Berlin (2006).

88. Godo, G. and Ricardo, O. Rodriguez logical approaches to fuzzy similarity-based reasoning: An overview. Preferences and Similarities, Springer, 504, 75–128 (2008).

89. Goldberg, D. E. The design of innovation. Kluwer Academic Publishers, Massachusetts (2002).

90. Gholamiana, M. R., Fatemi Ghomia, S. M. T., and Ghazanfarib, M. A hybrid systematic designs for multi-objective market problems a case study in crude oil markets. Engineering Applications of Artificial Intelligence, 18, 495–509 (2005).

91. Goguen, J. A. Concept representation in natural and artificial languages: Axioms, extensions, and applications for fuzzy sets. Int. J. Man-Machine Stud. 6, 513–561 (1974).

92. Goguen, J. A. L-fuzzy sets. J. Math. Anal Appl. 18, 145–174 (1967).

93. Goguen, J. A. The logic of inexact concepts. Synthese, 19, 325–373 (1968–1969).

94. Gelenbe, E., Habib, I. W., Palazzo, S., and Douligeris, C. Guest editorial: Intelligent techniques in high speed networks. IEEE J. Select. Areas Commun., 18, 145–149 (February, 2000).

95. Goodman, I. R. and Nguyen, H. T. Uncertainty models for knowledge-based systems. North Holland, Amsterdam (1985).

96. Granitto, P. M., Verdes, P. F., and Ceccatto, H. A. Neural network ensembles: Evaluation of aggregation algorithms. Artificial Intelligence, 163, 139–162 (2005).

97. Hamedi, M. Intelligent fixture design through a hybrid system of artificial neural network and genetic algorithm. Artificial Intelligence Review, 23, 295–311 (2005).

98. Hájek, P. Meta-mathematics of Fuzzy Logic. Trends in Logic, I Kluwer Acad. Publ., Dordrecht, 4 (1998).

99. Hellendoorn, H. Closure properties of the compositional rule of inference. Fuzzy Sets and Systems, 35(2), 163–183 (April 13, 1990).

100. Herceg, M., Kvasnica, Michal, and Fikar, Miroslav. Transformation of Fuzzy Takagi-Sugeno Models into Piecewise Affine Models. Rough Sets and Intelligent Systems Paradigms, Lecture Notes in Computer Science, 4585, 211–220 (2007).

101. K. Hirota and M. Sugeno (Eds.). Industrial applications of fuzzy technology in the world. Advances in Fuzzy Systems Applications and Theory, World Scientific, Singapore, 2, (1995).

102. Höhle, U. Commutative, residuated l-monoids. Non-Classical Logics and Their Application to Fuzzy Subsets, Dordrecht, pp. 53–106 (1995).

103. Honka, A. Total Similarity-based Fuzzy Reasoning: Theory and Application. Master of Science thesis. The Department of Mathematics and Statistics, University of Tampere (2009)

104. Hsu, Y. L., Wang, S. G., and Yu, C. C. A sequential approximation method using neural networks for engineering design optimization problems. Engineering Optimization, 35(5), 489–511 (2003).

105. Hsiao, S. W. Fuzzy logic-based decision model for product design. International Journal of Industrial Ergonomics, 21, 103–116 (1998).

106. Hsiao, S. W., and Huang, H. C. A neural network based approach for product form design. Design Studies, 23, 67–84 (2002).
107. Ivezic, N. and Garrett Jr., J. H. Machine learning for simulation-based support of early collaborative design. Artificial Intelligence for Engineering Design: Analysis and Manufacturing, 12, 123–139 (1998).
108. Jiao, J. and Tseng, M. M. Fuzzy ranking for concept evaluation in configuration design for mass customization. Concurrent Engineering: Research and Application, 6(3), 189–206 (1998).
109. Jensen, H. A. and Sepulveda, A. E. Use of approximation concepts in fuzzy design problems. Advances in Engineering Software, 31, 263–273 (2000).
110. Jones, J. D. and Hua, Y. A fuzzy knowledge base to support routine engineering design. Fuzzy Sets and Systems, 98, 267–278 (1998).
111. Ishino, Y. and Jin, Y. Estimate design intent: A multiple genetic program and multivariate analysis-based approach. Advanced Engineering Informatics, 16, 107–125 (2002).
112. Julian, P. and Rubio-Manzano, C. A similarity-based WAM for bousi~prolog. Bio-Inspired Systems: Computational And Ambient Intelligence. Lecture Notes in Computer Science, 5517, 245–252 (2009).
113. Kasabov, K. N. Foundation of Neural Networks. Fuzzy Systems and Knowledge Engineering, MIT Press (1996).
114. Kaufman, A. and Gupta, M. M. Introduction to fuzzy arithmetic. Van Nostrand Reinhold, New York (1985).
115. Keefe, R. Theories of Vagueness. Cambridge University Press, Cambridge (2000).
116. Kraslawski, A. Pedrycz, W., and Nystrom, L. Fuzzy neural network as instance generator for case-based reasoning system an example of selection of heat exchange equipment in mixing tanks. Neural Computing and Applications, 8, 106–113 (1999).
117. Koza, R. J. On the program of computers by means of natural selection. Genetic Programming, The MIT Press (2000).
118. Kowalski, R, Logic for problem solving. North Holland (1979).
119. Robinson, J. A. Automatic deduction with hyper-resolution. Int. J. Computer Math., 1, 227–234 (1965).
120. Kosko, B. Fuzzy systems as universal approximators. IEEE Trans. Computers, 1994 an early version appears in Proc. 1st IEEE Int. Conf. on Fuzzy Systems, pp. 1153–1162 (March, 1992).
121. Kosko, B. Fuzzy Engineering. Prentice Hall, Upper Saddle River, New Jersey (1997).
122. Kosko, B. and Dickerson, J. A. Function approximation with additive fuzzy systems. Theoretical Aspects of Fuzzy Control, pp. 313–347 [ISBN 0-471-02079-6].
123. Kosko, B. Neural Networks and Fuzzy Systems: A Dynamical Systems Approach to Machine Intelligence. Prentice-Hall, Englewood Cliffs (1992).
124. Kovacs Szilveszter, Interpolation-based fuzzy reasoning as an application oriented approach. Acta Polytechnica Hungarica, 2(1), 2005.
125. Kukkurainen, P. and Turunen, Esko. Many-valued similarity reasoning an axiomatic approach. Multiple-valued logic: An International Journal, 8(5–6), 751–760(10) (January 1, 2002).
126. Loia, V., Sessa, S., Staiano, U. A., and Tagliaferri, R. Merging fuzzy logic, neural networks, and genetic computation in the design of a decision-support system. International Journal of Intelligent Systems, 15, 575–594 (2000).
127. Law, S. Evaluating Imprecision in Engineering Design. PhD thesis, California Institute of Technology, Pasadena, California (1996).

128. J. Lawry, J. G. Shanahan, and A. L. Ralescu (Eds.). Modeling with Words: Learning, Fusion, and Reasoning within a Formal Linguistic Representation Framework. Springer (2003).
129. Lee, C. C. Fuzzy logic in control systems: Fuzzy logic controller–Part 1. IEEE Trans Syst. Man and Cybern., SMC-20(2), 404–418 (1990).
130. Lee, R. C. T. and Chang, C. L. Some properties of fuzzy logic. Inform and Control, 19, 417–431 (1971).
131. Liao, S. H. Expert system methodologies and applications–A decade review from 1995 to 2004. Expert systems with Applications, 28, 93–103 (2005).
132. Liu, H. and Tang, M. Evolutionary design in a multi-agent design environment. Applied Soft Computing, 6(2), 207–220 (2006).
133. Lu, P. C. The application of fuzzy neural network techniques in constructing an adaptive car-following indicator. Artificial Intelligence for Engineering Design, Analysis, and Manufacturing, 12, 231–242 (1998).
134. Lim, M. H. and Ng, W. Iterative genetic algorithm for learning efficient fuzzy rule set. Artificial Intelligence for Engineering Design, Analysis, and Manufacturing, 17, 335–347 (2003).
135. Marcelin, J. L. Evolutionary optimization of mechanical structures towards an integrated optimization. Engineering with Computers, 15, 326–333 (1999).
136. Maher, M. L. A model of co-evolutionary design. Engineering with Computers, 16, 195–208 (2000).
137. McCarthy, J. Programs with common sense. Proceedings of the Teddington Conference on Mechanization of Thought Processes, Her Majesty's Stationery Office, London, pp. 75–91 (1959).
138. Mencattini, A., Salmeri, M., and Logacono, Roberto. Type-2 fuzzy sets for modeling uncertainty in Measurement. International workshop on advanced Methods for uncertainty Estimation in Measurement, Sardangna, Trento, Italy, pp. 20–21, (April, 2006).
139. Mehran, K. Takagi-Sugeno Fuzzy Modeling for Process Control. (EEE8005): Industrial Automation, Robotics, and Artificial Intelligence (2008).
140. Mendel, J. Uncertain Rule-Based Fuzzy Logic Systems: Introduction and New Directions. Prentice Hall, Upper Saddle River, New Jersey (2001).
141. Michels, K., Klawonn, F., Kruse, R., and Nurnberger, A. Fuzzy Control: Fundamentals, Stability, and Design of Fuzzy Controllers. Springer, Berlin (2006).
142. Mizumoto, M. Fuzzy controls under various fuzzy reasoning methods. Inform. Sci., 45, 129–151 (1988).
143. Mizumoto, M. Fuzzy reasoning under new compositional rule of inference. IEEE Trans. Systems Man Cybernet., 14, 272–278 (1983).
144. Mizumoto, M. and Zimmermann, H. J. Comparison of fuzzy reasoning methods. Fuzzy Sets Syst., 8, 253–283 (1982).
145. Mizumoto, M. Realization of pid controls by fuzzy control methods. Fuzzy Sets and Systems, 70(2–3), 171–182 (March 20, 1995).
146. Mizumoto, M. Fuzzy controls under various fuzzy reasoning methods. Information Sciences, 45, 129–151 (1988).
147. Moisil, G. C. Lectures on the logic of fuzzy reasoning. Scientific Editions, Bucharest (1975).
148. Moulianitis, V. C., Aspragathos, N. A., and Dentsoras, A. J. A model for concept evaluation in design: An application to mechatronics design of robot grippers. Mechatronics, 14, 599–622 (2004).

149. Morsi, N. N. and Fahmy, A. A. On generalized modus ponens with multiple rules and a resituated implication. Fuzzy Sets Syst., 129(2), 267–274 (2002).

150. Moses, D., Degani, O., Teodorescu. H. N., Friedman, M., and Kandel, A. Linguistic coordinate transformations for complex fuzzy sets. Proc. of the IEEE Int. Conf. on Fuzzy Systems, Seoul, Korea, pp. 1340–1345 (August 22–25, 1999).

151. Mostowski, A. On a generalization of quantifiers. Fundamenta Mathcmaticae, 44, 12–36 (1957).

152. Mukaidono, M., Shen, Z., and Ding, L. Fundamentals of fuzzy prolog. International Journal of Approximate Reasoning, 3(2), 179–193 (1989).

153. H. T. Nguyen, M. Sugeno, R. Tong, and R. Yager (Eds.). Theoretical aspects of fuzzy control, J. Wiley, New York (1995).

154. Nguyen, H. T., Kreinovich, V., and Tolbert, D. A measure of average sensitivity for fuzzy logics. International Journal on Uncertainty, Fuzziness, and Knowledge-Based Systems, 2(4), 361–375 (1994).

155. Nariman–Zadeh, N., Darvizeh, A., and Dadfarmai, M. H. Adaptive neuro fuzzy inference systems networks design using hybrid genetic and singular value decomposition methods for modeling and prediction of the explosive cutting process. Artificial Intelligence for Engineering Design, Analysis, and Manufacturing, 17, 313–324 (2003).

156. Niittymäki, J. and Turunen E. Traffic signal control on similarity logic reasoning. Fuzzy Sets and Systems, 133(1), 109–131 (2003).

157. Novák, V. Fuzzy type theory. Fuzzy Sets Syst., 149, 235–273 (2004).

158. Novák, V. A comprehensive theory of trichotomous evaluative linguistic expressions. Fuzzy Sets and Systems, 159(22), 2939–2969 (2008).

159. Novák, V. A formal theory of intermediate quantifiers. Fuzzy Sets and Systems, 159(10), 1229–1246 (2008).

160. Novák, V. and Dvořák, A. Fuzzy logic: A powerful tool for modeling of vagueness. Research report No. 125, Institute for Research and Applications of Fuzzy Modeling University of Ostrava (2008).

161. Novák, V. Are fuzzy sets a reasonable tool for modeling vague phenomena? Fuzzy Sets and Systems, 156, 341–348 (2005).

162. Novák, V. and de-Baets, B. EQ-algebras. Fuzzy Sets and Systems, 160, 2956–2978 (2009).

163. Novák, V. EQ-algebra-based fuzzy type theory and its extensions. Logic Journal of the IGPL (2010) doi: 10.1093/jigpal/jzp087.

164. Novak, V. First-order fuzzy logic. Studia Logica, pp. 87–109 (1984).

165. Novák, V. Fuzzy logic deduction with words applied to ancient sea level estimation. R. Demicco and G. Klir (Eds.), Fuzzy Logic in Geology. Academic Press, Amsterdam, pp. 301–336 (2003).

166. Novák, V. Fuzzy logic with countable evaluated syntax revisited. Fuzzy Sets and Systems, 158, 929–936 (2007).

167. Novák, V. Fuzzy sets as a special mathematical model of vagueness phenomenon. B. Reusch (Ed.), Computational Intelligence: Theory and Applications, Springer, Heidelberg, pp. 683–690 (2006).

168. Novák, V. and Perfilieva, I. On the semantics of perception-based fuzzy logic deduction. International Journal of Intelligent Systems, 19, 1007–1031 (2004).

169. Novák, V. and Kovář, J. Linguistic IF-THEN rules in large scale application of fuzzy control. R. Da and E. Kerre (Eds.), Fuzzy if-then rules in computational intelligence: Theory and applications, Kluwer Academic Publishers, Boston, pp. 223–241 (2000).

170. Novák, V. Mathematical fuzzy logic in modeling of natural language semantics. P. Wang, D. Ruan, and E. Kerre (Eds.), Fuzzy Logic: A Spectrum of Theoretical and Practical Issues, Elsevier, Berlin, pp. 145–182 (2007).

171. Novák, V. On the syntactico-semantical completeness of first-order fuzzy logic: I; II, Kybernetika, 26, 47–66; 134–154 (1990).

172. Novak, V. Perception-based logical deduction. B. Reusch (Ed.), Computational Intelligence: Theory, and Applications, Springer, Berlin, pp. 237–250 (2005).

173. Novak, V., Perfilieva, I., and Mockor, J. Mathematical Principles of Fuzzy Logic. Kluwer, Boston, Dordrecht (1999).

174. Novák, V., Perfilieva, I., and Jarushkina, N. G. A general methodology for managerial decision making using intelligent techniques. E. Rakus-Anderson, R. Yager, N. Ichalkaranje, and L. Jain (Eds.), Recent Advances in Decision Making, Springer, Heidelberg, pp. 103–120 (2009).

175. Novák, V. and Lehmke, S. Logical structure of fuzzy IF-THEN rules. Fuzzy Sets and Systems, 157, 2003–2029 (2006).

176. Novák, V., Ste'pnic'ka, M., Perfilieva, I., and Pavliska, V. Analysis of periodical time series using soft computing methods. D. Ruan, J. Monicro, J. Lu, L. Martinez, P. D'hondt, and E. Kerre (Eds.), Computational Intelligence in Decision and Control, World Scientific, New Jersey, pp. 55–60 (2008).

177. Novák, V., Štěpnička, M. U., Dvořák, A., Perfilieva, I., Pavliska, V., and Vavříčková, L. Analysis of seasonal time series using fuzzy approach. International Journal of General Systems, 39, 305–328 (2010).

178. Parmee, I. C. Evolutionary and adaptive strategies for efficient search across whole system engineering design hierarchies. Artificial Intelligence for Engineering Design, Analysis, and Manufacturing, 12, 431–445 (1998).

179. Parmee, I. C. A review of evolutionary and adaptive search in engineering design. Evolutionary Optimization: An International Journal, 1(1), 13–39 (1999).

180. Pappis, N. and Karaopilidis, J. A comparative assessment of measures of similarity of fuzzy values. Fuzzy sets and Systems, 56, 171–174 (1993).

181. Park, Y. M., Moon, Un-Chul, and Lee, Kwang Y. A self-Organizing Power System Stabilizer using Fuzzy Auto-Regressive Moving Average (FARMA) Model. IEEE Transactions on Energy Conversion, 11(2) (June, 1996).

182. Pedrycz, W. and Gomide, F. Fuzzy Systems Engineering: Toward Human-Centric Computing. Wiley-IEEE Press (2007).

183. Pedrycz, W. Neuro computations in relational systems. IEEE Trans. Pattern Anal. Machine Intell., 13(3), 289–297 (1991).

184. Perfilieva, I. Fuzzy logic normal forms for control law representation. H. Verbruggen, H. J. Zimmermann, and R. Babuška (Eds.), Fuzzy Algorithms for Control, Kluwer, Boston, pp. 111–125 (1999).

185. Perfilieva, I. Fuzzy transforms: a challenge to conventional transforms. P. W. Hawkes (Ed.), Advances in images and election physics: Volume 147, Elsevier Academic Press, San Diego, pp. 137–196 (2007).

186. Perfilieva, I. Logical approximation. Soft Computing, 7(2), 73–78 (2002).

187. Perfilieva, I. Logical foundations of rule-based systems. Fuzzy Sets and Systems, 157, 615–621 (2006).

188. Pionka, L. and Mrozek, A. Rule-based stabilization of the inverted pendulum. Computational Intelligence: An International Journal, 11, 348–356 (1995).

189. Potter, S., Darlington, M. J., Culley, S. J. and Chawdhry, P. K. Design synthesis knowledge and inductive machine learning. Artificial Intelligence for Engineering Design, Analysis, and Manufacturing, 15, 233–249 (2001).

190. Qiao, F., Zhu, Q. M., Winfield, A., and Melhuish, C. Fuzzy sliding mode control for discrete non-linear systems. Transactions of China Automation Society, 22(2) (Sum No. 86), (June, 2003).

191. Ryoo, J. and Hajela, P. Decomposition-based design optimization method using genetic co-evolution. Engineering Optimization, 36(3), 361–378 (2004).

192. Ray, K. S. and Chatterjee, Piyali. Approximate reasoning on a DNA-chip. International Journal of Intelligent Computing and Cybernetics, 3(3), 514–553.

193. Raha, S. Similarity-based approximate reasoning. Ph.D. Thesis, under supervision of Prof K. S. Ray, Indian statistical Institute Kolkata-700108 (1999).

194. Ray K. S. and Mondal, Mandrita. Similarity-based fuzzy reasoning by DNA Computing. International Journal of Bio-Inspired Computation, 3(2), 112–122 (2011)

195. Rao, S. S., Nahm, A., Shi, Z., Deng, X., and Syamil, A. Artificial intelligence and expert systems applications in new product development a survey. Journal of Intelligent Manufacturing, 10, 231–244 (1999).

196. Rasheed, K. and Hirsh, H. Learning to be selective in genetic-algorithm-based design optimization. Artificial Intelligence for Engineering Design, Analysis, and Manufacturing, 13, 157–169 (1999).

197. Ray, K. S. Soft Computing Approach to Pattern Classification and Object Recognition: A Unified Engineering Concept. Springer, New York (2012).

198. Ray, K. S. Bottom-up Inferences using fuzzy reasoning. BUSEFAL, 42, 81–90 (1990).

199. Renner, G. and Ekart, A. Genetic algorithms in computer-aided design. Computer-Aided Design, 35, 709–726 (2003).

200. Ross, T. J. Fuzzy Logic with Engineering Applications: Second Edition. Wiley & Sons (2004).

201. Rosenman, M. A. An exploration into evolutionary models for non-routine design. Artificial Intelligence in Engineering, 11, 287–293 (1997).

202. Rajasekaran, S., Febin, M. F., and Ramasamy, J. V. Artificial fuzzy neural networks in civil engineering. Computers and Structures, 61 (2), 291–302 (1996).

203. Sanchez, E. Resolution of composite fuzzy relation equations. Inform and Control, 30, 38–48 (1976).

204. Saridakis, K. M. and Dentsoras, A. J. Evolutionary neuro-fuzzy modeling in parametric design. First I*PROMS Virtual International Conference on Intelligent Production Machines and Systems, IPROMS 2005 (2005).

205. Saridakis, K. M. and Dentsoras, A. J. Soft Computing in Engineering Design: A review. Advance Engineering Informatics, 22, 202–221 (2008).

206. Scott, M. J. and Antonsson, E. K. Preliminary vehicle structure design: An industrial application of imprecision in engineering design. Proceedings of DETC'98 ASME Design Engineering Technical Conferences, Atlanta, Georgia (September 13–16, 1998).

207. Scott, M. J., Kaiser, R. W., Dilligan, M., Claser, R. J., and Antonsson, Erik K. Managing uncertainty in aero shell design analysis. Proceedings of DETC'97 ASME Design Engineering Technical Conferences, Sacramento, California (September 14–17, 1997).

208. Scott, M. J. Formalizing Negotiation in Engineering Design. PhD thesis, California Institute of Technology, Pasadena, California (1999).

209. Seising, R. Proposals for future developments in fuzzy set technology. IEEE International Conference on Fuzzy Systems, pp. 1655–1662 (2006).

210. Seki, H., Ishii, H., and Mizumoto, M. On the property of single input rule modules connected type fuzzy reasoning method. FUZZ-IEEE 2007, IEEE International Fuzzy Systems Conference (2007).

211. Sessa, M. I. Approximate reasoning by similarity-based SLD resolution. Theoretical Computer Science, 275, 389–426 (2002).

212. Setnes, M., Lacrose, V., and Titli, A. Complexity reduction methods for fuzzy systems. H. Verbruggen, H. J. Zimmermann, and R. Babuska (Eds.), Fuzzy Algorithms for Control. Kluwer Academic Publishers, Boston, pp. 185–218 (1999).

213. Setnes, M. and Babuska, R. Rule-base reduction: Some comments on the use of orthogonal transforms. IEEE Trans. Syst. Man Cybernetics: Part C, 31(2), 199–206 (2001).

214. Sgall, P., Hajičová, E., and Panevová, J. The Meaning of the Sentence in its Syntactic and Pragmatic Aspects. D. Reidel, Dordrecht (1986).

215. Sharkawi, M. A. Role of soft computing in power systems. Proc. IEEE Int. Workshop Soft Computing in Industry, Muroan, Japan, pp. 9–14 (1996).

216. Simpson, T. W., Peplinski, J. D., Koch, P. N., and Allen, J. N. Meta-models for computer-based engineering design: Survey and recommendations. Engineering with Computers, 17, 129–150 (2001).

217. De Soto, A. R. and Trillas, E. On antonym and negate in fuzzy logic. Int. J. Intell. Syst., 14, 295–303.

218. Souza, B. and Simpson, T. W. A genetic algorithm-based method for product family design optimization. Engineering Optimization, 35(1), 1–18 (2003).

219. Sasaki, M. and Gen, M. Fuzzy multiple objective optimal system design by hybrid genetic algorithm. Applied Soft Computing, 2(3), 189–196 (2003).

220. Su, D. and Wakelam, M. Evolutionary optimization within an intelligent hybrid system for design integration. Artificial Intelligence for Engineering Design, Analysis, and Manufacturing, 13, 351–363 (1999).

221. Taura, T. and Nagasaka, I. Adaptive-growth-type 3D representation for configuration design. Artificial Intelligence for Engineering Design, Analysis, and Manufacturing, 13, 171–184 (1999).

222. Temponi, J., Yen, W., and Tiao, A. House of quality: A fuzzy logic-based requirement analysis. European Journal of Operational Research, 117, 340–354 (1999).

223. Thongchai, Sisripun, and Sethakul, Panarit. Fuzzy sliding mode controller design. The Journal of KMITNB, 14(1) (January–March, 2004).

224. Torra, V. A review of the construction of hierarchical fuzzy systems. International Journal of Intelligent Systems, 17, 531–543 (2002).

225. Tsukamoto, Y. An approach to fuzzy reasoning method. M. M. Gupta, R. K. Regade, and R. R. Yager (Eds.), Advances in fuzzy set theory and applications, North Holland, Amsterdam, pp. 137–149 (1979)

226. Turksen, I. B. Fuzzy normal forms. Fuzzy Sets Syst., 69, 319–346 (1995).

227. Türksen, I. B. Meta-linguistic axioms as a foundation for computing with words. Information Sciences, 177(2), 332–359 (2007).

228. Türksen, I. B. Ontological and epistemological perspective of fuzzy set theory. Elsevier Science and Technology Books (2005).

229. Tsai, C. Y. and C. A. Chang, Fuzzy neural networks for intelligent design retrieval using associative manufacturing features. Journal of Intelligent Manufacturing, 14, 183–195 (2003).

230. Vico, F. J., Veredas, F. J., Bravo, J. M., and Almaraz, J. Automatic design synthesis with artificial with artificial intelligence techniques. Artificial Intelligence in Engineering, 13, 251–256 (1999).

231. Varzi, A. C. Supervaluationism and Paraconsistency. D. Batens, C. Mortensen, G. West, and J. P. A. Van Bendegem (Eds.), Frontiers in Paraconsistent Logic, Baldock, pp. 279–297 (2000).

232. Wallace, D. R., Jakiela, M. J., and Flowers, W. C. Design search under probabilistic specifications using genetic algorithms. Computer-Aided Design, 28(5), 405–421 (1996).

233. Wang, J. R. Ranking engineering design concepts using a fuzzy outranking preference model. Fuzzy Sets and Systems, 119, 161–170 (2001).

234. Wang, X., Tang, M. X., and Frazer, J. Creative stimulator: An interface to enhance creativity in pattern design. Artificial Intelligence for Engineering Design, Analysis, and Manufacturing, 15, 433–440 (2001).

235. Wang, J. and Terpenny, J. Interactive evolutionary solution synthesis in fuzzy set-based preliminary engineering design. Journal of Intelligent Manufacturing, 14, 153–167 (2003).

236. Wang, W. J. New similarity measures on fuzzy sets and on elements. Fuzzy Sets and Systems, 85, 305–309 (1997).

237. Wang, Li-Xin and Mendel, J. M. Generating fuzzy rules by learning from examples. Proceedings of the IEEE International Symposium on Intelligent Control, Arlington, Virginia, pp. 263–268 (1991).

238. Wang, X. Z., Bzets, B. D., and Kerre, E. A comparative study of similarity measures. Fuzzy Sets and Systems, 73, 259–268 (1995).

239. Wang, Z. and Klir, G. J. Fuzzy Measure Theory. Springer (1992).

240. Wiratunga, N., Craw, S., and Rowe, R. Learning to Adapt for Case-based Design. ECCBR, Springer-Verlag, Berlin, Heidelberg, pp. 421–435 (2002).

241. Woolery, L. K. and Grzymala-Bus.se, J. Machine learning for an expert system to predict preterm birth risk. Journal of the American Medical Informatics Association, 1, 439–446 (1994).

242. Xiong, Y. and Rao, S. S. Fuzzy nonlinear programming for mixed discrete design optimization through hybrid genetic algorithm. Fuzzy Sets and Systems, 146, 167–186 (2004).

243. Yan, W., Chen, C. H., and Khoo, L. P. An integrated approach to the elicitation of customer requirements for engineering design using picture sorts and fuzzy evaluation. Artificial Intelligence for Engineering Design, Analysis, and Manufacturing, 16, 59–71 (2002).

244. Yasuda, T., Ohkura, K., and Ueda, K. A homogeneous mobile robot team that is fault-tolerant. Advanced Engineering Informatics, 20, 301–311 (2006).

245. Yang, Y., Xu, X., and Zhang, W. Design neural networks based fuzzy logic. Fuzzy Sets and Systems, 114, 325–328 (2000).

246. Yamakawa, T. Stabilization of an inverted pendulum by a high-speed fuzzy logic controller hardware system. Fuzzy Sets and Systems, 32(2), 161–180 (1989).

247. J. Yen, R. Langari, and L. Zadeh (Eds.). Industrial applications of fuzzy logic and intelligent systems. IEEE Press, New York (1995).

248. Yen, J. and Wang, Liang. Simplifying fuzzy rule-based models using orthogonal transformation methods. IEEE Trans. Syst. Man Cybernetics, Part B, 29(1), 13–24 (1999).

249. Yeung, D. S. and Tsang, E. C. C. A comparative study on similarity-based fuzzy reasoning methods. IEEE Trans. Syst. Man Cybernetics, 27, 216–227 (1997).

250. Yi, J. and Yubazaki, N. Stabilization fuzzy control of inverted pendulum systems. Artificial Intelligence in Engineering, 14, 153–163 (2000).

251. Yeun, Y. S., Lee, K. H., and Yang, Y. S. Function approximations by coupling neural networks and genetic program trees with oblique decision trees. Artificial Intelligence in Engineering, 13, 223–239 (1999).

252. Zadeh, L. A. The concept of a linguistic variable and its application to approximate reasoning: Part III. Information Sciences, 9, 43–80 (1975).

253. Zadeh, L. A. A computational approach to fuzzy quantifiers in natural languages. Computers and Mathematics, 9, 149–184 (1983).
254. Zadeh, L. A. A fuzzy-algorithmic approach to the definition of complex or imprecise concepts. International Journal of Man Machine Studies, 8, 249–291 (1976).
255. Zadeh, L. A. A fuzzy-set-theoretic interpretation of linguistic hedges. Journal of Cybernetics, 2, 4–34 (1972).
256. Zadeh, L. A. A New Direction in AI: Toward a Computational Theory of Perceptions. AI Magazine, 22(1), 73–84 (2001).
257. Zadeh, L. A. A rationale for fuzzy control. Journal of Dynamic Systems, Measurement, and Control, 94, Series G, 3–4 (1972).
258. Zadeh, L. A. A theory of approximate reasoning. J. Hayes, D. Michie, and L. I. Mikulich (Eds.), Machine Intelligence, Halstead Press, New York, 9, 149–194 (1979).
259. Zadeh, L. A. Calculus of fuzzy restrictions. L. A. Zadeh, K. S. Fu, K. Tanaka, and M. Shimura (Eds.), Fuzzy Sets and Their Applications to Cognitive and Decision Processes, Academic Press, New York, pp. 1–39 (1975).
260. Zadeh, L. A. From Computing with Numbers to Computing with Words: From Manipulation of Measurements to Manipulation of Perceptions. IEEE Transactions on Circuits and Systems, 45, 105–119 (1999).
261. Zadeh, L. A. From imprecise to granular probabilities. Fuzzy Sets and Systems, 154, 370–374 (2005).
262. Zadeh, L. A. From search engines to question answering systems: The problems of world knowledge relevance deduction and precisiation. Elie Sanchez (Ed.), Fuzzy Logic and the Semantic Web, Elsevier, pp. 163–210 (Chapter 9) (2006).
263. Zadeh, L. A. Fuzzy logic and approximate reasoning. Synthese, 30, 407–428 (1975).
264. Zadeh, L. A. Fuzzy logic and the calculi of fuzzy rules and fuzzy graphs. Multiple-Valued Logic, 1, 1–38 (1996).
265. Zadeh, L. A. Fuzzy sets and information granularity. M. Gupta, R. Ragade, and R. Yager (Eds.), Advances in Fuzzy Set Theory and Applications, North-Holland Publishing Co., Amsterdam, pp. 3–18 (1979).
266. Zadeh, L. A. Fuzzy sets as a basis for a theory of possibility. Fuzzy Sets and Systems, 1, 3–28 (1978).
267. Zadeh, L. A. Possibility theory and soft data analysis. L. Cobb and R. M. Thrall (Eds.), Mathematical Frontiers of the Social and Policy Sciences. Westview Press, CO, Boulder, pp. 69–129 (1981).
268. Zadeh, L. A. Precisiated natural language (PNL). AI Magazine, 25(3), 74–91 (2004).
269. Zadeh, L. A. Precisiation of meaning via translation into PRUF. L. Vaina and J. Hintikka (Eds.), Cognitive Constraints on Communication, Reidel, Dordrecht, pp. 373–402 (1984).
270. Zadeh, L. A. PRUF-a meaning representation language for natural languages. International Journal of Man-Machine Studies, 10, 395–460 (1978).
271. Zechman, E. M. and Ranjithan, S. R. An evolutionary algorithm to generate alternatives (EAGA) for engineering optimization problems. Engineering Optimization, 36(5), 539–553 (2004).
272. Zha, X. F. Neuro-fuzzy comprehensive assemblability and assembly sequence evaluation. Artificial Intelligence for Engineering Design, Analysis, and Manufacturing, 15, 367–384 (2001).
273. Zhao Zhen-Yu, Masayoshi Tomizuka, Satoru Isaka Fuzzy Gain Scheduling of PID Controllers. IEEE transactions on system man and cybernetics, 23(5) (September/October, 1993).

274. Zha, X. F. Soft computing framework for intelligent human-machine system design, simulation, and optimization. Soft Computing, 7, 184–198 (2003).
275. Zimmermann, H. J. Fuzzy program and linear program with several objective functions. Fuzzy Sets and Systems, 1, 45–55 (1978).
276. Zwick, R., Carlstein, E., and Budescu, D. V. Measures of similarity among fuzzy concepts: A comparative analysis. Int. J. Approx. Reason, 1, 221–242 (1987).

INDEX

A

Adaptive resonance theory (ART), 428
Agent-based simulation, 424
Aggregation in fuzzy system modeling, 45
multiple fuzzy reasoning, 46–54
Aggregation operator, 144
Algorithm to construct fuzzy if-then inference systems, 193–195
features, 195–198
Approximate Analogical Reasoning Scheme (AARS), 141–142
Approximate reasoning, 1
and method interpolation, 2
model, 2–15
model, 2–15
relational matrix, 3–4
results according to λ, 211
uses, 2–3
Artificial neural network (ANN), 416

B

Basic property, 21

C

Case-based design (CBD), 428
system, 428
Case-based reasoning (CBR), 428
algorithms, 428
cycle, 428
system, 428
Centre of gravity, 241. *See also* Defuzzification
Centre of sums, 242. *See also* Defuzzification
Compatibility Modification Inference (CMI), 141–142
Compositional rule of inferences (CRIs), 82–87, 141

computation, under T-norms, 87–92
Conditional relation, 177
Conjunction forest, 7
projection of, 8
Conjunction principle, 110. *See also* Generalized disjunctive syllogism
Consequent Dilation Rule (CDR), 142
Coriolis parameter, 37–38
Cylindrical forest corresponding to "medium," 7

D

Deduction of consequence using Larsen's implication operator, 57
Defuzzification, 3, 408
future generation of control, 414
logic interpretation of, 408
methods of, 240
centre of gravity, 241
centre of sums, 242
max-membership, 241
mean-max membership, 242
weighted average, 241
Discrete causal link between "salary and loan," 58
Disjunctive syllogism, 112. *See also* Generalized disjunctive syllogism

E

Engineering design-based on
artificial neural networks, 424
fuzzy logic, 418
fuzzy relations, kinds of, 417
genetic algorithms, 420
soft computing paradigm, 426
Entailment principle, 111. *See also* Generalized disjunctive syllogism
e-Resolvent, 227

e-SLDrefutation, 228
Euclidean distance, 166–167
Expert systems (ES), 417
Extended fuzzy reasoning, 25–28
    mathematical formulation of problem,
    29–33

F

FARMA control system architecture, 339.
    See also Fuzzy control
Firing strength based and similarity based
    reasoning, 184
Four-rule fuzzy model, 275. *See also* Fuzzy
    control
Fuzzifiers
    gaussian, 237
    singleton, 237
    trapezoidal or triangular, 237
Fuzzy constraints, 426
Fuzzy control
    action corresponding to fuzzy output, 289
    bang-bang controller, 316
    birth of control theory, 233
    conventional control law, 235
    crisp boundaries, 279
    defuzzification method
        methods of..., 244
        types of..., 240
    design, 355
    discrete-time control law, 233
    dog chasing, 255, 256
    FARMA control system architecture, 339
    FLC, structure of, 310
    four-rule fuzzy model, 275
    fuzzification/defuzzification, 355
    fuzzification process, 237
    fuzzifiers
        types of ..., 237
    fuzzy associative memory, 253, 254
    fuzzy controller, 234, 253, 256, 289, 293
        algorithm, 291
        sector bound fuzzy logic, 293
    fuzzy deduction system, 387
    fuzzy feedback control, 285
    fuzzy feedback controller, 233
    fuzzy gain scheduler, 328
    fuzzy inference system, 261
    fuzzy logic controller, 298

fuzzy mathematics for modeling, 266
fuzzy model, 264
fuzzy partition space, 272
fuzzy rule, implication process of, 332
generalized predictive control (GPC), 276
illustration on basic approaches, 247
infinite-bus power system, 340
Mamdani fuzzy system, 264, 265
maximum fuzzy band determination, 313
membership function, 248, 283, 313, 329
    fuzzy, 356
    linear, 278
    triangular, 287
MIMO, 294, 295, 296, 297, 300
mulitlevel relay analogy, 289, 291
nonlinear feedback system, 294
Nyquist plot, 294, 296, 298
output adjustment of, 359
regions corresponding to fuzzy error input
set, 289
rule base, 313, 314, 338
rules, 235, 260
sector bound nonlinearity, 266, 293, 299
self-organizing power system stabilizer
    (*See* Self-organizing power system stabi-
    lizer)
simulation, 261, 318, 360
    of fuzzy sliding mode control, 309
SIRM, 362, 366
SISO, 293, 294
stability
    analysis, 296
    criteria, 296
structure of, 311
system, types of, 237
Takagi-Sugeno fuzzy system, 265, 333
    modeling, 270, 272
    transformation of, 276
transformation procedure, 278
    shift, 282
tuning of, 358
Fuzzy controller, 234
    block diagram of, 372
    closed loop temperature control system,
    354
    combined direct/indirect adaptive, 350
    direct adaptive, 349
    indirect adaptive, 347

industrial temperature control problem, 352
self-tuning of, 352
stabilization, 367
time delay problem, 353
Fuzzy controller design, 256
adaptive, 346
ball beam system, 259
theoretical approach, 263
fuzzy bang-bang control, 285, 310
fuzzy system model-based controller, 285
input-output stability study, 285, 288
optimal controller, 285, 302
sliding mode controller, 285
stable controller, 285
supervisory controller, 285, 320
trial-and-error approach, 257
Fuzzy control system, 237
centroid defuzzification method, 246, 247
defuzzificationinterface, 237
effectivity of, 245
fuzzification interface, 237
fuzzy inference machine, 237
fuzzy rule-base, 237
gaussian membership function, 245
singleton fuzzifier, 245, 246
symmetric triangular membership function, 246
Fuzzy deduction system, 387
defuzzification process, 392
fuzzy deduction systems, 393
fuzzy granules, 390
fuzzy Herbrand model, 398
fuzzy modus ponens, 396
extended, 396
generalization, 395
extended, 396
linguistic modifier, 402
logic program, 399
mathematical preliminaries, 388
safe control, 403
tool for fuzzy control, 401
Fuzzy design models, 419
Fuzzy goals, 426
Fuzzy Herbrand model, 398

Fuzzy reasoning method
SBR inference for SISO fuzzy rule base, 143–144
similarity (compatibility) measure, 142–143
similarity measures and computational rule of inference, 165–168
Fuzzy relations, 418
basis of, 418
instance of, 418
kind of, 418
Fuzzy resolution based on similarity based unification
and clouds
compactness of systems, 219–220
e-unifiers of systems, 222–225
similarity relations, 216–218
extended resolution, 227–229
extending unification through, 220–222
similarity in deductive data base, 230
unifiers, 225–227
Fuzzy sets, 176, 420
Fuzzy similarity-based reasoning
logical approaches, 212–215
Fuzzy singleton, 51

G

Gaines Reschers operator, 140
Generalized disjunctive syllogism, 109
mathematical formulation, 112–120
mathematical preliminaries
conjunction principle, 110
disjunctive syllogism, 112
entailment principle, 111
formulas in fuzzy logic, 111–112
projection principle, 110–111
Generalized form of fuzzy reason, 33–34
Generalized method-of-case inference rule, 107–109
Generalized modus ponens (GMP), 141
with Larsen's implication operator, 24–25
with Mamdani's implication operator, 23
Generalized predictive control (GPC), 276. See also Fuzzy control
Genetic algorithm, 416, 422, 427
Gödel implication, 25
Gödels operator, 140

H

Human reasoning, 1
HUTSIM traffic simulator, 198

I

Induced relation, 177
Inference
    with Gödel implication operator, 52
    with Mamdani's implication operator, 52,
    64
Inferred fuzzy set B, 178
Input/output function derived from fuzzy
    rules, 60
Integrated frameworks, 426
Interpolative fuzzy reasoning, 96–107
Inverse approximate reasoning
    statement of problem and, 92–96

K

Kleene's implication operator, 140

L

Larsen's implication operator, 24–25
Layout and three phases of T-junction, 196
Lukasiewiczs operator, 140

M

Machine-oriented measures of similarity, 164
Mamdani's implication operator, 23
Mamdani's min-rule, 171
Mamdani-style fuzzy controller, 198
Maximum fuzzy band determination, 313.
    See also Fuzzy control
Max-membership, 241. *See also* Defuzzifica-
    tion
Max-min composition operator, 8
Mean-max membership, 242. *See also* De-
    fuzzification
Medium representation, 6
Membership functions for "small" and "big,"
    58
Method of interpolation, 9–10
Min operator, 5
Multidimensional fuzzy reasoning based
    on multidimensional fuzzy implication,
    126–137
Multi-input-multi-output fuzzy system, 61

Multi input single output (MISO) fuzzy, 144
Multiple fuzzy reasoning, 61–70

N

Neuro-fuzzy, 416
Nonlinear feedback system, 294. *See also*
    Fuzzy control

O

Ordered weighted aggregation (OWA) opera-
    tor. *See also* Similarity
    and similarity measure, 199–205

P

PID controller by simplified fuzzy reasoning
    method, 379
    extrapolative reasoning, 386
    fuzzy reasoning., 383
    fuzzy sets of error, 383
    product-sum-gravity, 379, 380
    realization of, 381
    simplified fuzzy reasoning, 379, 381
Projection principle, 110–111. *See also* Gen-
    eralized disjunctive syllogism
Proposed method, 168–169
    algorithm SAR, 170
    schema, 170
    scheme C1, 170–172
    scheme C2, 172–179
Proposed similarity measure, 150
    verification of
        P3, 151–152
        P4, 152–154
        P5, 154–164

R

Radiation fog, prediction, 40
    fuzzy reasoning, application of, 34
        algorithm, 43–44
        Coriolis parameter, 37–38
        dewpoint, 41
        effectiveness, 44–45
        fuzzy rule based approach, 39
        geostropic wind, 38
        governing equations for, 35–37
        modification of, 39–40
        number of rules generated, 42–43

potential temperature, 37
sky condition, 42
visibility, 37
wind speed, 41–42
parameters
algorithm, 43–44
dew point, 41
sky condition, 42–43
wind speed, 41–42
Ray's bottom-up inferences
bottom up inference with fuzzy reasoning, 121–126
fuzzy logic and formulas, 120–121
RBF neural network, 425
Reasoning, 1
based on total fuzzy similarity, 188
mathematical preliminaries, 189–193
Relational forest, 6
Relation matrices, 13
Reschers operator, 140
Richardson number, 36–37
Rule-based models, 180–185
Rule reduction technique, 145–150

S

Self-organizing power system stabilizer
conventional, 343
heavy load condition, 343
inertia constant, 345
isolation, 344
normal load condition, 342
self organizing, 343
Separated rule-base, 54
Settling velocity, 37
Similarity. *See also* Fuzzy resolution
based on similarity based unification
examples of, 140–141
fuzzy reasoning using, 141–142
index, 164
measures, categories, 139
Similarity
theoretic similarity, 139–140
Similarity-based bidirectional approximate reasoning, 198–199
and decision making systems, 205–212
Similarity based fuzzy reasoning (SBR)
inference
rule reduction technique, 145–150

schemes, 145
for SISO fuzzy rule base, 143–144
schemes, 142
Simplified fuzzy reasoning, 54–60
SIRMS reasoning method and, 72–82
Simulation, 360
inverted pendulum system, 364
tank temperature control, 360
Single input rule module (SIRM), 362
control parameters, 370
dynamic variable, 368, 370
simulation study, 373
Single input rule modules (SIRMS) connected fuzzy reasoning method, 70–72
SISO fuzzy, 143–144. *See also* Fuzzy reasoning method
Soft computing and engineering design
evaluation and research opportunities
aerospace applications, 429
communications systems, 429
consumer appliances, 429
electric power systems, 430
manufacturing automation, 430
power electronics, 431
process engineering, 431
robotics, 430
transportation, 432
Soft computing techniques, 415, 428
State-transition rule base, 106
Statistical neural network, 424
Superset property, 22

T

Takagi-Sugeno (TS) fuzzy system, 265, 277. *See also* Fuzzy control
T-norm operator, 179
Total indeterminance, 21
Turbulent kinetic diffusion coefficients, 36

U

Unifiers, 225–227. *See also* Fuzzy resolution based on similarity based unification

V

von Karman constant, 36–37

W

Weighted average, 241. *See also*
    Defuzzification

Y

Yager's t-norm, 92

Z

Zadeh's fuzzy reasoning, basic approach,
    15–25
Zadehs operator, 140